Wilfried Loth
Building Europe

Wilfried Loth
Building Europe

A History of European Unification

DE GRUYTER
OLDENBOURG

Translated by Robert F. Hogg

ISBN 978-3-11-057725-9
e-ISBN (PDF) 978-3-11-042481-2
e-ISBN (EPUB) 978-3-11-042488-1

Library of Congress Cataloging-in-Publication Data
A CIP catalog record for this book has been applied for at the Library of Congress.

Bibliographic information published by the Deutsche Nationalbibliothek
The Deutsche Nationalbibliothek lists this publication in the Deutsche Nationalbibliografie; detailed bibliographic data are available in the Internet at http://dnb.dnb.de.

© 2015 Walter de Gruyter GmbH, Berlin/Boston
This volume is text- and page-identical with the hardback published in 2015.
Cover image rights: ©UE/Christian Lambiotte
Typesetting: Michael Peschke, Berlin
Printing: CPI books GmbH, Leck
♾ Printed on acid free paper
Printed in Germany

www.degruyter.com

Table of Contents

Abbreviations —— vii

Prologue: Churchill's Congress —— 1
    Four Driving Forces —— 1
    The Struggle for the Congress —— 8
    Negotiations and Decisions —— 13
    A Milestone —— 18

1 Foundation Years, 1948–1957 —— 20
    The Struggle over the Council of Europe —— 20
    The Emergence of the Coal and Steel Community —— 28
    The Drama of the EDC —— 36
    The Difficult "*Relance*" —— 53
    The Negotiations on Euratom and the European Economic Community —— 62

2 Formative Years, 1958–1963 —— 75
    The European Commission —— 75
    The Struggle over the Free-Trade Area —— 83
    The Construction of the Common Market —— 90
    Fouchet Plans and British Membership Application —— 101
    Accession Negotiations and Franco-German Treaty —— 108
    The Success of the Economic Community —— 117

3 Crises of the Community of the Six, 1963–1969 —— 123
    Erhard's Relaunch —— 123
    Hallstein's Offensive —— 132
    The Crisis of the "Empty Chair" —— 138
    The Time of the Arrangements —— 147
    The Return of the British Question —— 155
    France on the Way to Turning —— 162

4 Expansion and New Perspectives, 1969–1975 —— 170
    Turning Point: The Summit in The Hague —— 170
    The Completion of the Common Market —— 177
    The First Enlargement —— 183
    The Project of Monetary Union —— 195
    Political Cooperation —— 204
    Crisis and New Beginning —— 213

5 Consolidation, 1976–1984 —— 222
    The Path to Direct Elections —— 222
    The European Monetary System —— 229

    Expansion to the South —— 242
    The Defense of Détente —— 251
    Thatcher, Genscher, and Colombo —— 261
6 **The Era of Development, 1984–1992** —— 271
    The Single European Act —— 271
    The Internal-Market Project —— 281
    The Project for an Economic and Monetary Union —— 289
    European Security and German Unity —— 300
    The Path to Maastricht —— 310
7 **From Maastricht to Nice, 1992–2001** —— 323
    Implementing the Monetary Union —— 323
    The Northern Expansion —— 336
    The Way to Amsterdam —— 342
    Security and Eastern Policy —— 356
    The Nice Complex —— 367
8 **Constitutional Struggle and Euro Crisis, 2001–2012** —— 372
    The Eastward Enlargement —— 372
    The Constitutional Treaty —— 384
    From Prodi to Barroso —— 393
    The Constitutional Crisis —— 404
    The Euro Crisis —— 417
Conclusion: The Future of the Union —— 433

Afterword —— 441

The European Parliament 1979–2014: Party memberships —— 444

The European Parliament 1979–2014: Presidents —— 445

The Presidents of the High Authority and the Commissions —— 446

Sources —— 447

Bibliography —— 452

Index —— 474

Abbreviations

AKP	Adalet ve Kalkınma Partisi
BRRM	Bank Recovery and Resolution Mechanism
CAP	Common Agricultural Policy
CDE	Conference on Disarmament in Europe
CDU	Christian Democratic Union
CFSP	Common Foreign and Security Policy
CIA	Central Intelligence Agency
COMECON	Council of Mutual Economic Assistance
COPA	Committee of Agricultural Organizations in the European Community
COREPER	Committee of Permanent Representatives
CSCE	Conference on Security and Cooperation in Europe
CSDP	Common Security and Defense Policy
CSU	Christian Social Union
DM	Deutsche Mark
EAC	European Advisory Commission
EC	European Communities
ECA	European Cooperation Administration
ECB	European Central Bank
ECJ	European Court of Justice
ECOFIN	Economic and Financial Affairs Council
ECSC	European Coal and Steel Community
ECU	European Currency Unit
EDC	European Defense Community
EEA	European Economic Area
EEC	European Economic Community
EFSF	European Financial Stability Facility
EFSM	European Financial Stabilization Mechanism
EFTA	European Free Trade Association
EKD	Evangelische Kirche in Deutschland
EMS	European Monetary System
EMA	European Monetary Agreement
EMU	Economic and Monetary Union
EPC	European Political Community
EPC	European Political Cooperation
EPP	European People's Party
EPU	European Parliamentary Union
EPU	European Payments Union
ESM	European Stability Mechanism
EU	European Union
EURATOM	European Atomic Energy Community
EUSE	Comité international pour les États-Unis socialistes d'Europe
FDP	Freie Demokratische Partei
GATT	General Agreement on Tariffs and Trade
GDP	Gross domestic product

GDR	German Democratic Republic
GNP	Gross national product
ILEC	Independent League of European Co-operation
IMF	International Monetary Fund
JDP	Justice and Development Party of Turkey
MBFR	Mutual and Balanced Force Reduction
MLF	Multilateral Force
MSEUE	Socialist Movement for the United States of Europe
NATO	North Atlantic Treaty Organization
NEI	Nouvelles Équipes Internationales
OECD	Organization of Economic Cooperation and Development
OEEC	Organization of European Economic Cooperation
OPEC	Organization of Petroleum Exporting Countries
PASOK	Panellinio Sosialistikó Kinima
PES	Party of European Socialists
PHARE	Poland and Hungary Aid for Restructuring of the Economies
PKK	Partiya Karkerên Kurdistan
SAA	Stability and Association Agreement
SALT	Strategic Arms Limitation Talks
SDI	Strategic Defense Initiative
SEA	Single European Act
SFIO	Section Française de l'Internationale Ouvrière
SPD	Sozialdemokratische Partei Deutschlands
SSM	Single Supervisory Mechanism
TEU	Treaty on European Union
UDF	Union pour la Démocratie Française
UEF	Union Européenne des Fédéralistes
UEM	United Europe Movement
UMP	Union pour un Mouvement Populaire
UNO	United Nations Organization
USA	United States of America
WEU	Western European Union
WTO	World Trade Organization

Prologue: Churchill's Congress

From 7 to 10 May 1948, 722 representative figures from twenty-eight European countries met in The Hague to discuss paths and possibilities for a unification of Europe. Six former prime ministers of European countries took part in the gathering along with fourteen active and forty-five former ministers. In addition, West German governors, leading members of parliaments, business leaders, key representatives from organized labor, academics, artists and religious officials were present. Winston Churchill, Britain's celebrated prime minister during the war years and now leader of the opposition in the House of Commons gave the opening address. Outside the official halls, public interest was evident. Around forty thousand people attended a public declaration during the third day of negotiations. The congress led to the formation of the European Movement and indirectly to the founding of the Council of Europe.[1]

Four Driving Forces

The Hague Congress set off crucial negotiations for the creation of European institutions. These negotiations—otherwise than the talks around the proposal for "a kind of federative association" among the peoples of Europe that had been proposed by French Foreign Minister Aristide Briand in September 1929 to the assembly of the League of Nations—would prove successful and lead to the foundation of a European community that today has great influence over the lives of Europeans. This community concentrated movements that aimed to overcome the functional deficits of nation states and of the nation-state-dominated European political system and that had developed as early as the First World War. They were driven by four varying yet closely linked agendas.[2]

The first objective was to deal with the problem of anarchy among states which had been the spark for all "classical" plans to secure the peace, ranging

---

[1] On the pre-history and course of The Hague Congress, cf. Frank Niess, *Die europäische Idee aus dem Geist des Widerstands*, Frankfurt am Main: Suhrkamp, 2001, pp. 158–173 and 181–220; Wilfried Loth, "Vor 60 Jahren: Der Haager Europa-Kongress," in: *Integration* 31 (2008), pp. 179–190; Jean-Michel Guieu and Christophe Le Dréau (eds.), *Le "Congrès de l'Europe" à la Haye (1948–2008)*, Brussels: Peter Lang, 2009.

[2] This systematization was presented for the first time in Wilfried Loth, "Der Prozess der europäischen Integration. Antriebskräfte, Entscheidungen und Perspektiven," in: *Jahrbuch für Europäische Geschichte* 1 (2000), pp. 17–30. For a complete presentation developing these motivations, cf. Wilfried Loth: *Der Weg nach Europa. Geschichte der europäischen Integration 1939–1957*, Göttingen: Vandenhoeck & Ruprecht, 1990, 3rd edition, 1996.

from Dante to Kant. The urgency of finding a better institutional solution to deal with its prospects was ever more pressing with the development of modern military technology and the resulting death of millions of victims followed by economic damage of a magnitude unimagined in the era of cabinet warfare. Hence, the experience of the First World War had led to multiple European peace initiatives, of which the "Pan-Europe" campaign by Count Richard Coudenhove-Kalergi and Aristide Briand's Europe Plan were the most notable. With the peace order established at Versailles incrementally breaking down from 1938 onward, this movement received further impetus. For example, Léon Blum, the French Socialist leader and prime minister of the People's Front governments of 1936 to 1938, wrote in the spring of 1941: "In one point, my convictions are profound and unshakable, whatever the world may say. If this war does not at last give rise to fundamentally stable international institutions, to a really effective international power, then it will not be the last war."[3]

A special challenge to secure the peace involved the German question: How to allow the strongest nation in the center of the European continent to develop while at the same time avoiding the consolidation of German hegemony? Or conversely: How to put a check on the Germans without provoking renewed desires for revenge via one-sided discrimination against them? Blum captured the view of many authors from the Resistance against the German occupation and the National Socialist regime as he wrote "there is only a single way to resolve the contradiction, to make Germany harmless in a peaceful and stable Europe, and that is the incorporation of the German nation in an international community."[4] This would include not merely the supervision of the Ruhr District but also a common steering of all European heavy industry, not only a reduction of German military sovereignty, but a common command over all European armed forces. After the failure of the peace order established at Versailles and the rise of National Socialism, the value of these measures could not be ignored.

A third functional deficit of the nation-state system stemmed from the development of productive forces in the industrial age. Over the course of time, it became more and more clear that national markets in Europe were too narrow for rational production methods. Mutual walling-off only made sense temporarily and for some sectors—over the long term, however, it resulted in a loss of productivity. This had an economic as well as a power-political aspect; both had been present since the 1920s, above all in the form of American competition. Thus,

---

[3] Léon Blum, *For All Mankind*, London and New York: Gollancz, 1946, pp. 116f. (French original written in 1941). Cf. Wilfried Loth, *Sozialismus und Internationalismus. Die französischen Sozialisten und die Nachkriegsordnung Europas 1940–1950*, Stuttgart: Deutsche Verlags-Anstalt, 1977.
[4] Blum, p. 121.

unification initiatives in the economic sphere were correspondingly numerous, and here too the experience of the Second World War provided an additional motivational push: Whereas the Europeans largely exhausted their resources in that conflict, the US more than doubled its production for being the most important supplier of materiel to the Allied coalition in addition to being favored by the absence of European countries from the world market.

The fourth reason for European unification initiatives has thus already been touched upon: The effort of European nations to assert themselves *vis-à-vis* the new world powers. The concern over American economic and political supremacy as well as the fear of an expansion of the Bolshevik Revolution had already provided motives for European unification plans in the 1920s. Both were strengthened by the power-political results of the Second World War. With the US as the leading world power and the Soviet Union as the strongest military power on the European continent, earlier divergences in interests among the European nation-states lost meaning to the benefit of the common interest in autonomy and in avoiding a conflict between the two main victors of the war.

British Labour Party leader Clement Attlee, who was to serve as prime minister from 1945 to 1951 captured this dynamic best in 1939: "Europe must federate or perish."[5] This became a plausible slogan in several respects in the aftermath of the First World War already, when the insufficiency of the peace order established at Versailles was criticized. The plausibility increased when the Munich Agreement made it clear that the established order was no longer sustainable; and increasingly from 1943 onwards when Allied victory was in the offing. This watchword evoked fascination in the most divergent political camps. It also created links extending across national borders and—as must be emphasized given the later fixation on the East-West conflict and the resultant ahistorical attitude toward the countries that belonged to the Soviet Bloc until 1990—it was by no means only a Western-European phenomenon. The European organizations had branches in Prague and Budapest, just as they did in Paris and Brussels.[6]

The numerous unification plans developed in the resistance all over Europe did not immediately coalesce at the end of the conflict into a concrete unification policy. Joseph Stalin blocked any kind of federation in Eastern Europe (so sys-

---

[5] Speech before the Labour MPs on 8 Nov. 1939, in: Clement R. Attlee, *Labour's Peace Aims*, London: Peace Book Co., 1940, pp. 12ff.
[6] Cf. Walter Lipgens, *A History of European Integration 1945–1947. The Formation of the European Unity Movement*, Oxford: Clarendon Press, 1982; idem. (ed.), *Documents on the History of European Integration*, vol. 1: *Continental Plans for European Union, 1939–1945*, Berlin and New York: De Gruyter, 1985; vol. 2: *Plans for European Union in Great Britain and in Exile, 1939–1945*, Berlin and New York: De Gruyter, 1986; Michel Dumoulin (ed.), *Plans des temps de guerre pour l'Europe d'après-guerre 1940–1947*, Brussels: Émile Bruylant, 1995.

tematically that such plans passed out of memory there); at the same time, every step toward unification in Western Europe threatened to deepen the division of the continent between East and West. This made it questionable whether the peace could be secured through unification initiatives. Many shrank back from making substantive decisions, including the British government under Winston Churchill—and that was decisive given the power relations among Hitler's opponents in Europe. Furthermore, France under the leadership of Charles de Gaulle enmeshed itself in demands for separating the territories on the left bank of the Rhine along with the Ruhr District from the German federation, something for which his British allies had little enthusiasm.

Churchill was however the first European politician of rank to put the theme of European unification back on the agenda of international politics after the war. In July of 1945, just after his hard-won victory over Hitler, Churchill had been sent into the opposition following elections in Britain. In the winter of 1945–46, he then began to worry about an expansion of the Soviet domain beyond the "Iron Curtain." In a spectacular speech in the town of Fulton, Missouri, on 5 March 1946, he warned for the first time publicly about the "expansive and proselytizing tendencies" of the Soviet Union and international communism.[7] In order to avert the danger of such expansion, he thought it was now necessary to embark upon the unification of those European countries that had remained outside the Soviet sphere. He regarded the federation of such countries as the prerequisite not only for the economic recovery of Europe but also for the stabilization of democracy. In another speech, this time before students in Zurich on 19 October 1946, he therefore asserted that "we must build a kind of United States of Europe" based on "a partnership between France and Germany." He saw Great Britain among "the friends and sponsors of the new Europe" rather than among its members. For Churchill, the island nation was to play a highly-active role in Europe's creation.[8]

In order to mobilize public opinion, Churchill commissioned his son-in-law and close political ally Duncan Sandys to organize a non-partisan group of representative figures who were to promote European unification ideas in Britain. Sandys' efforts soon bore fruit: On 16 January 1947, he was able to present a provisional "British United Europe Committee," that included among its members not only conservative MPs (including Robert Boothby) but also Labour politicians

---

[7] Speech of 5 March 1946 in: Robert Rhodes James (ed.), *Winston S. Churchill. His Complete Speeches, 1897–1963*, vol. VII: 1943–1949, London: Chelsea House, 1974, pp. 7285–7293.

[8] Speech of 19 Sept. 1946 in: Walter Lipgens and Wilfried Loth (eds.), *Documents on the History of European Integration*, vol. III: *The Struggle for European Union by Political Parties and Pressure Groups in Western European Countries, 1945–1950*, Berlin and New York: De Gruyter, 1988, pp. 662–666.

and trade union representatives (Gordon Land, George Gibson, Victor Gollancz), representatives of the Liberal Party, church officials and even scholars such as Bertrand Russell and British federalists such as Frances L. Josephy. It was the case however that the executive committee of the ruling Labour Party spoke out against the endeavor as it neither wanted to promote Churchill's idea of creating a Western bloc nor give the opposition leader a platform for domestic political successes. Therefore, the activities of the group, which constituted itself definitively on 14 May 1947 as the "United Europe Movement" (UEM), developed predominantly in the conservative and liberal milieu.[9]

Parallel to the UEM, an "Independent League of European Co-Operation" (ILEC) was organized by Paul van Zeeland, a former Belgian prime minster, and Józef Retinger, a long-time colleague of Polish Prime Minister in exile Władysław Sikorski; this organization, working in Belgium, Luxembourg, Great Britain, and France, sought to build on the European customs union committees of the 1920s and 1930s. On 7 March 1947, they were able to announce the formation of a provisional central committee on the international level. The group brought together influential economists, bankers, and managers who were worried about the hindrances to the rebuilding of Europe posed by national economic boundaries. By no means did they all share Churchill's fear of Soviet expansion. Yet, given that they pushed for a rapid start to economic integration without taking Soviet reservations into account and that they were just as little decided as to the particular method of integration as was the British opposition leader, they were predestined for cooperation with Sandys' group. Many politicians such as former director of the International Labour Office Harold Butler and later British Prime Minister Harold Macmillan were active in both organizations simultaneously.[10]

In the wake of the Churchill speech, Coudenhove-Kalergi, the founder of the Pan-European Movement, once again became active in European politics. Initially, he suggested to Churchill that the Pan-European Union be revived "under our joint leadership." After the Briton had responded with reluctance, Coudenhove organized a poll in November of 1946 among Western European members of parliament. Over four thousand deputies were asked to decide, either positively or negatively, on the question of whether they supported "a European federation within the framework of the United Nations." This was intended to show the general attitude towards unification in the countries of Western Europe and to put pressure on the governments to begin initiatives for creating a Western Europe at last. Those deputies in agreement were called upon to set up non-par-

---

[9] Cf. Lipgens, *History*, pp. 317–334; Niess, *Europäische Idee*, pp. 131–144.
[10] Lipgens, *History*, pp. 334–341.

tisan committees in the parliaments that were to gather for a European Congress in Geneva in June of 1947.[11]

This action clearly demonstrated that the idea of a federation that excluded Eastern Europe from the beginning and hence that deepened the already-emerging division of Europe was not yet particularly popular in the winter of 1946–47. Only a few deputies were willing to identify themselves with such a conception. By the end of April of 1947, Coudenhove had received 660 answers of which 646 were positive—but that was hardly more than an eighth of those who had been asked. The ambitious plans for a congress had to be postponed for the time being. Similarly, the efforts of René Courtin, co-publisher of *Le Monde*, to establish a committee in France parallel to the UEM remained without success. In most cases, French adherents of Europe baulked at the risk of being associated with Churchill's West-bloc conception.[12] The voices advocating a unification even without Soviet approval did gradually become more numerous, but overall, the negative reactions to Churchill's initiative predominated by a wide margin.[13]

Most Europeans saw a unified Europe as a "Third Force," which under the leadership of a Britain ruled by the Labour Party would mediate between the US and the Soviet Union, thus avoiding a division of Europe. The adherents of the organized federalist movement, who in December of 1946 constituted themselves as the "Union Européenne des Fédéralistes" (UEF), were hoping for a Europe structured ultimately along social-democratic lines, one that could maintain its autonomy *vis-à-vis* the US as well as the Soviet Union. According to their program declaration passed on 15 April 1947 in Amsterdam, "We do not want a moribund Europe, marked out as a victim for ambitions of every kind, and governed either by pseudo-liberal capitalism that subordinates human values to the money power, or by some totalitarian system seeking, by fair means or foul, to exalt its idea of justice over the rights of man and communities. What we want is a Europe which shall be an open society, friendly to both East and West, prepared to co-operate with all."[14]

This changed only after the Soviet rejection of the Marshall Plan on 2 July 1947. The many adherents of a Europe that constituted a "Third Force" now came to the conclusion that European unification could only realistically begin in the West. In general, the conviction grew that in view of European reconstruction and the integration of the western parts of Germany—both of which were to be promoted

---

11 *Ibid.*, pp. 435–441.
12 *Ibid.* pp. 623ff.; Niess, *Europäische Idee*, pp. 145–147.
13 Cf. the collection of different reactions in Lipgens, *History*, pp. 341–345 and 432–435.
14 Quoted from Lipgens, *History*, p. 382; on the constituting of the UEF, *ibid.*, pp. 107–153, 274–278, 296–316, and 346–385.

by the Marshall Plan—there was not much time to lose. On 16 July 1947, Courtin was able to announce the founding of a "Conseil français pour l'Europe unie," which understood itself as the French counterpart of Churchill's UEM. Leading representatives of the French Socialists declared themselves willing to join in—figures such as Robert Lacoste, Francis Leenhardt, André LeTrocquer, and Prime Minister Paul Ramadier. Among those representing the Christian Democrats were Paul Coste-Floret, François de Menthon, and Pierre-Henri Teitgen; left liberals were represented by Paul Bastid and René Mayer, Independent Republicans by Paul Reynaud, the social-liberal UDSR by Édouard Bonnefous, chairman of the Foreign-Affairs Committee of the National Assembly. Among others belonging to the council were Michel Debré as representative of the Gaullists, Emmanuel Monick as governor of the Bank of France, trade union leaders, representatives of the churches, as well as prominent journalists and scholars (Raymond Aron, Paul Claudel, André Siegfried, and Edmond Vermeil among others). The honorary chairmanship was assumed by Édouard Herriot, the long-time prime minister of the Third Republic.[15]

Coudenhove's poll now had much greater resonance. After he had in April of 1947 once again reminded the deputies who had not replied, the number of positive responses reached 1,735 by the end of September. Altogether, some forty-three percent of the deputies asked had thus spoken out in principle in favor of a "European federation," among them sixty-four percent of Italian deputies, fifty-three percent of Dutch deputies as well as fifty percent of both French and Belgian deputies. However, only twenty-six percent of British MPs responded positively along with a mere twelve percent of Scandinavian deputies.[16] After federalist parliamentarians had begun to organize themselves in France, Belgium, Italy, and Greece, Coudenhove-Kalergi was able to hold what was not a "pre-parliament" but nevertheless a gathering of 114 active deputies from ten countries at his residence in Gstaad. This group founded a "European Parliamentary Union" (EPU) and decided to work toward calling a European Constituent Assembly.[17]

For Duncan Sandys, it was now a matter of not only strengthening the unification movement in the various countries but also of keeping it under control. He was convinced that the movement could be successful only if it initially concentrated on the functional cooperation among the governments. Only then could

---

15 Ibid., pp. 622–625.
16 Ibid., pp. 437–441.
17 Ibid., pp. 601–614; Heribert Gisch, "The European Parliamentary Union," in: Walter Lipgens and Wilfried Loth (eds.), *Documents on the History of European Integration*, vol. IV: *Transnational Organizations of Political Parties and Pressure Groups in the Struggle for European Union, 1945–1950*, Berlin and New York: De Gruyter, 1990, pp. 112–185.

British participation be ensured. He feared that without the UK, France would not dare to enter into a European Community alongside a strong West Germany. Consequently, British participation in the work of unification was for Sandys much more indispensable than it was for his father-in-law.[18] Therefore, in the run-up to the establishment of the "Conseil français," he invited the other Europe groups to form a "liaison committee" of the European movements. This took place on 20 July 1947 in Paris over the course of a luncheon on the Champs Élysées. Along with the UEM, the French Council, the ILEC, and the EPU, the European federalists around the Dutchman Hendrik Brugmans and the Frenchman Alexandre Marc were represented.[19]

The Struggle for the Congress

The federalists were convinced that the time was ripe for a federalist reorganization of the peoples of Europe. Hence, they envisioned the summoning of an "estates general of Europe" that against national governments and parliaments was to develop into the constituent assembly of a United Europe. Based on a comprehensive mobilization campaign, the various societal groups were to be represented: "One might for instance envisage eight basic categories or 'estates': (a) employers, (b) workers, (c) farmers, (d) middle class, executives and professionals, (e) intellectual and religious groups, (f) consumer's organizations (co-operatives), (g) political and parliamentary bodies, the judiciary etc., (h) youth movements." This "sensational assembly" was not only to "impress public opinion" but also to create "standing committees" for working out the pending legal, social, economic, and cultural questions, among others; and "the heads of these committees would form the nucleus of a future European government."[20] Versailles was envisioned as the meeting place of this revolutionary manifestation.

To Sandys, these plans for a corporative federalism were dangerous pipe dreams that would discredit the European unification movement and ruin the chances of British participation. Even before the UEF leaders could begin organizing their initiative, he therefore came to an agreement with the leadership of the ILEC in late September of 1947 for the preparation of a very different type of congress: a "conference of between 500 and 800 prominent Europeans" that would meet "during the first weekend after Easter" in order to pressure and encourage the European governments to take the first steps toward the unification of Europe.

---

[18] Cf. Lipgens, *History*, pp. 666–669.
[19] *Ibid.*, pp. 659–666.
[20] Note by Hendrik Brugmans, 24 Sept. 1947, in: Lipgens and Loth (eds.), *Documents* IV, pp. 41ff.

Pieter Kerstens, a Dutch senator and former economy minister who was working to establish a branch of the ILEC in his country, agreed to provide the funds necessary for such a congress. Accordingly, The Hague was chosen as the site of the meeting. The federalists were invited to participate as co-sponsors of the congress and for that purpose also to join the liaison committee.[21]

This invitation presented dangers for the federalists: On the one hand, there was the danger of accepting it and entering into an alliance with high-ranking conservative politicians and economic leaders: "...[T]o go to the Hague under the auspices of a union vaguely outlined by Churchill instead of calling the Estates-General–did this not involve running the risk of losing not only the benefit of numbers but also the creative and revolutionary dynamism which the federalist doctrine brought with it?" Yet, if they persisted in their own plans for a congress, they would not only split the European movement but also run the "risk of courting rapid destruction or of becoming a sect."[22] What proved decisive in the end was the greater realism of the British project: It would definitely be implemented and would have significant resonance; on the other hand, it was unclear how the "Estates-General" could be financed and whether it would have the sought-after effect given the competing project undertaken by establishment forces. It was especially Brugmans who for this reason advocated acceptance of the invitation. Marc and the Italian federalists around Altiero Spinelli were in principle against it but kept a low profile. On 15 November 1947 the central committee of the UEF decided to participate in the congress in The Hague and to agree to the expansion of the liaison committee into a "coordinating committee."[23]

In the vague hope of perhaps still being able to "transform" The Hague Congress into an "Estates-General of Europe,"[24] the federalists accepted a situation in which they were a minority in the coordinating committee, possessing a quarter of the votes; the UEM and the French Council and the ILEC, all of whom were in agreement programmatically, each had the same number of votes. The federalists had to concede the chairmanship to Sandys and a secretary's post to Retinger.[25] Perforce, they also accepted the provisions for the organization of the congress

---

21 Protocol of a meeting of Sandys, van Zeeland, Retinger, and Kerstens, 28 Sept. 1947 in Brussels, quoted in Lipgens, *History*, p. 673.
22 The characterization of the dilemma after the fact by Denis de Rougement, "The Campaign of the European Congresses," in: *Government and Opposition*, vol. 2, no. 3, April–July 1967, pp. 329–349. here p. 338.
23 Lipgens, *History*, pp. 676–679.
24 According to Alexandre Marc writing to Marceau Pivert, 10 Dec. 1947, quoted in Lipgens, *History*, p. 679.
25 *Ibid.*, pp. 674–676; Text of the agreement of 11 Nov. 1947 in Lipgens and Loth (eds.), *Documents* IV, pp. 325–328.

that Sandys presented at a further meeting of the committee on 13 and 14 December 1947. It was "to demonstrate in striking fashion the powerful and widespread support which already exists for the European idea; to produce material for discussion, propaganda and technical studies." It should therefore be put together in as representative a way as possible; the decision about the invitations was to be reserved for the coordinating committee, however. It was decided that the event would be called "Congress of Europe"; the presidency of the congress was offered to Churchill.[26]

In practice, the decision on invitation policy meant that Sandys and Retinger collected suggested names, decided who would actually receive an invitation, and then also registered the acceptances. Regarding the number of delegates per country, Sandys prevailed with a formula that would be moderately representative: fifteen delegates per country plus two more for each million residents. This meant a total of 104 delegates for France, 118 for Great Britain, 33 each for Belgium and the Netherlands, and so forth. Countries whose governments denied entry to representatives of the coordinating committee and which did not authorize the necessary visas for their citizens to participate in the congress were only to be represented by small observer groups.[27] This meant that Western Europe would gather as comprehensively as possible. At the same time the self-exclusion of the Soviet Union and the countries dominated by it would be reinforced once again.

As to organizational implementation, the coordinating committee had a large Dutch bank set up a representational office. Kerstens collected so much in donations that the over seven hundred participants could be offered not only a free stay in The Hague but also payment of all their travel costs as well. Given the still-precarious conditions in war-torn Europe, this was a noteworthy achievement that was very decisive for the success of the endeavor. When a gap in the financing of the Congress did nonetheless appear, Sandys had Prince Bernhard of the Netherlands introduce him to the board of directors of Phillips, which then helped out with a very generous donation. In late January of 1948, the date of the congress was definitively set for 7 to 10 May of that year; Retinger as secretary could then send out the official invitations.[28]

Sandys, Retinger, and Brugmans too sought out prominent persons in the various countries to convince them to participate. In most cases, they were successful: "We've done really great work," as Retinger was able to report to former

---

[26] Draft by Sandys, 11 Dec. 1947 in Lipgens and Loth (eds.), *Documents* IV, pp. 328–339; exerpts from the protocol of the session in Lipgens, *History*, pp. 682ff.
[27] Appendix A of the draft by Sandys, 11 Dec. 1947. As "Appendix B," Sandys immediately attached a list intended to provide examples of possible members of the British delegation.
[28] Niess, *Europäische Idee*, pp. 181ff.

Romanian Foreign Minister Gregor Gafencu as early as the end of 1947: "Of the great statesmen (but this is still confidential) the following have given us their support: Mister Churchill and Sir Stafford Cripps from Great Britain, Monsieurs Herriot and L. Blum from France, Messrs. van Zeeland and Spaak from Belgium, as well as Sforza from Italy. The Dutch government with its prime minister at the head will receive us where our sessions will take place: in the historic Riddarzaal."[29]

Paul Ramadier and Italian Prime Minister Alcide De Gasperi also agreed to participate. In the western German occupation zones, the organizers managed to gain the acceptance of the governor of North Rhine-Westphalia, Karl Arnold, and the mayors of Hamburg and Bremen, Max Brauer and Wilhelm Kaisen; likewise Konrad Adenauer, who was chairman of the CDU in the British Occupation Zone; Martin Niemöller of the council of the Protestant Church in Germany (EKD); Gustav Heinemann as justice minister of North Rhine-Westphalia; as well as Thomas Dehler, Heinrich von Brentano, and Walter Hallstein as chairman of the South German Rectors Conference.[30]

Likewise, there was success in gaining the participation of the Christian-Democratic "Nouvelles Équipes Internationales" (NEI); from February of 1948, it was another of the invited organizations on the coordinating committee.[31] Conversely, all the efforts of the federalists failed to bring aboard the "Comité international pour les États-Unis socialistes d'Europe" (EUSE). After a visit to London, Henri Frenay of the French branch of the committee lamented that British members of the EUSE "fell into a kind of trance as soon as one mentioned the name of Churchill, and that was an end of any possibility of rational discussion." With a vote of nine to seven, the executive of the committee decided against participation in The Hague Congress.[32] For his part, Coudenhove-Kalergi refused to ratify the agreement of July 1947 on forming the liaison committee and then repeatedly issued new conditions for his participation, ones that in principle amounted to having him take over the leadership of the project and control its programmatic

---

29 Retinger to Gafencu, 27. Dec. 1947, quoted in *ibid.*, p. 173.
30 Cf. Christoph Stillemunkes, "The Discussion on European Union in the German Occupation Zones," in: Lipgens and Loth (eds.), *Documents* III, pp. 441–565, here p. 454.
31 Lipgens, *History*, p. 679; cf. Heribert Gisch, "The 'Nouvelles Équipes Internationales' (NEI)," in: Lipgens and Loth (eds.), *Documents* IV, pp. 477–540; Michael Gehler and Wolfram Kaiser (eds.), *Transnationale Parteienkooperation der europäischen Christdemokraten. Dokumente 1945–1965*, Munich: De Gruyter Saur, 2004; Wolfram Kaiser, *Christian Democracy and the Origins of European Union*, Cambridge and New York: Cambridge University Press, 2007, pp. 191–205.
32 Henri Frenay to Marcel Hytte, 15 Dec. 1947, quoted in Lipgens, *History*, p. 679; cf. Loth, *Sozialismus*, pp. 199–201; Wilfried Loth, "Le Mouvement pour les États-Unis d'Europe (MSEUE)," in: Lipgens and Loth (eds.), *Documents* IV, pp. 277–318.

direction. Only in early April of 1948 did he become willing to participate in the congress without preconditions, that is, after most of the substantive decisions had already been made. His contribution to the direction of the congress was correspondingly marginal.[33]

More serious than the refusal of the socialist committee or the long hesitancy of Coudenhove and his parliamentary union was the opposition of the executive committee of the British Labour Party. Leaders such as Morgan Phillips, Hugh Dalton, and Denis Healey were decided opponents of British participation in a supranational Europe. Hence, they saw in the congress a very dangerous project that additionally constrained the freedom of action of Foreign Secretary Ernest Bevin and, furthermore, gave impetus to the Conservative opposition. At a conference of Socialist parties of all the countries participating in the Marshall Plan, held in London on 21 and 22 March 1948, the decision was made not to accept the invitation of the coordinating committee; forty Labour MPs who had already decided to take part in The Hague Congress were called upon to withdraw. In order to preserve the solidarity of international Socialism, the party executive committees of the French SFIO and the German SPD also banned their office-holders from participating.[34]

Not all Socialist or Social-Democratic European politicians were influenced by the bans. Some twenty-three of the forty Labour MPs held fast to their acceptance of the invitation, among them Ronald W.G. Mackay, the initiator of the "All-Party Group for European Unity" in the House of Commons, who in the meantime was also playing a leading role in the European Parliamentary Union as Coudenhove's deputy. Léon Blum, Paul Henri Spaak, Carlo Schmid, and Max Brauer stayed away from the congress; conversely, Paul Ramadier and Wilhelm Kaisen took part—in open revolt against the decisions of their party leadership. Yet, they could not prevent the gathering from taking on a liberal-conservative flavor. The Hague Congress ended up not being as representative as Sandys—with good reason—had striven for it to be.[35]

---

33 Lipgens, *History*, pp. 679–681; Martin Posselt, "Richard Coudenhove-Kalergi und die Europäische Parlamentarier-Union," Diss. Graz, 1987, pp. 234–237, 275–284; Heribert Gisch, "The European Parliamentary Union (EPU)," in: Lipgens and Loth (eds.), *Documents* IV, pp. 112–185.
34 Loth, *Sozialismus*, pp. 204–209; Clemens A. Wurm, "Great Britain: Political Parties and Pressure Groups in the Discussion on European Union," in: Lipgens and Loth (eds.), *Documents* III, pp. 628–762; Wilfried Loth, "The Socialist International," in: Lipgens and Loth (eds.), *Documents* IV, pp. 436–475.
35 Cf. his argumentation in the strategy paper of 11 Dec. 1947, *ibid.*, p. 330.

Negotiations and Decisions

Nevertheless, the gathering—which opened on the afternoon of 7 May 1948 in the presence of Princess Juliane and Prince Bernhard of the Netherlands—had great political weight. In the end, some 722 delegates had accepted the invitation; there were additionally about two hundred fifty guests and observers from the press. France sent the largest delegation, with 185 members; along with Ramadier, the contingent included Édouard Bonnefous, Édouard Daladier, Edgar Faure, André François-Poncet, Edmond Giscard d'Estaing, Pierre-Olivier Lapie, François de Menthon, François Mitterrand, and Paul Reynaud. Some 147 delegates came from Britain, among them Anthony Eden and Harold Macmillan. Italy was not so prominently represented, however: Due to the formation of a government after the elections of 18 and 19 April, De Gasperi and other leading politicians had needed to bow out. The representatives of Portugal, for whom twenty places were planned, stayed home after António Salazar had expressed his displeasure. Poland, Czechoslovakia, Hungary, Romania, Bulgaria, and Yugoslavia were only represented by exile politicians. Spain had to content itself with the role of an observer; this was exercised by four delegates led by the philosopher and former minister Salvador de Madariaga. One delegate each came from Iceland and Turkey.[36]

In accordance with the political goals that Churchill had specified, the Germans were invited as delegates with full status. Given that discussions about that had once again come up in the coordinating committee, their invitations were delayed. For many of those who were invited, there was thus no longer sufficient time to arrange the required exit permits from the occupation authorities or come up with foreign currency; in the end, the German delegation thus numbered only fifty-one. The Germans were pleased that in his opening address, Churchill explicitly greeted them as necessary partners in the construction of Europe and when for the first time since the end of the war they were able to appear on the international stage on a par with others once again. In the discussions of the congress, however, they were mostly restrained due to their awareness of continued dependence on the decisions of the occupying powers. Instead, the Germans used the opportunity to make contact with prospective partners. For example, after the opening ceremony, Adenauer met with Churchill for the first time and found himself "treated with conciliatory kindness by him."[37] Within the German

---

36 Niess, *Europäische Idee*, pp. 183ff. and 190–192.
37 Konrad Adenauer, *Erinnerungen 1945–1953*, Stuttgart: Deutsche Verlags-Anstalt, 1965, p. 210.

delegation, Adenauer got to know Walter Hallstein, who would later become his closest colleague in the area of European politics.[38]

Churchill's opening address was followed by speeches by Ramadier, Coudenhove-Kalergi, Brugmans,[39] and van Zeeland. Right after Churchill spoke, there was an attempt by the federalists to pull the event more strongly in the direction of an "Estates-General" by reading a "preamble" that aimed for the creation of a "European Assembly where the live forces of all our nations shall be represented." The efforts were rejected. Denis de Rougement, who had made the proclamation of such a target for the congress a condition for his participation in the preparations, was able to read the text as edited by him only as a "Message to the Europeans" after statements by Sandys, de Madariaga, and Ramadier. After some thirty participants objected to the demand for a common defense, the signing of the message by all delegates—which had initially been conceded to the federalists—did not occur.[40]

On the other hand, the administration of the congress ensured that Churchill was by no means able to dominate the gathering. The members of the coordinating committee had arrived five days before the opening of the congress and had agreed in detail about the course of events.[41] The reports on political, economic, and cultural questions, which the committee members had been working on since the beginning of the year in groups of differing composition, were not simply put up for a vote. Instead, they were discussed intensively in the corresponding committees of the congress during the whole second day of talks and then once again on the evening of the third day, while undergoing substantial change once again. Immediately after his return from The Hague, Eugen Kogon, who had been recruited as a German participant by the UEF, recorded in his *Frankfurter Hefte*: "The participating Socialists, Christian Socials, Syndicalists, and Progressives were successful in decisively preventing Churchill—whose significance for the unification of Europe was by the way acknowledged by everyone—and his mostly

---

38 Walter Hallstein, *United Europe. Challenge and Opportunity*, Cambridge, Mass.: Cambridge University Press, 1962, p. 8. Further eyewitness reports on the German delegation in Niess, *Europäische Idee*, pp. 193–197.
39 Text in Lipgens and Loth (eds.), *Documents* IV, pp. 51–55.
40 De Rougement, "Campaign," pp. 339–345; speeches and resolutions in: "Europe Unites. The story of the campaign for European Unity, including a full report of the Congress of Europe, held at The Hague," London 1949; verbatim report of the congress (hectographed) in the Archives of the European Movement. Deposit in the Historical Archives of the European Union, Fonds ME, Florence; online in: Council of Europe. Documents and Archives.
41 De Rougement, "Campaign," p. 342.

wealthy and arch-conservative followers from being able to give the congress their imprint."[42]

The negotiations of the Political Committee were characterized by disputes regarding the aims, methods, and tempo of European unification. Indirectly, the question of British participation was thereby present too, although many were not at all aware of it. In a framework draft for the Political Resolution of the congress that he had drawn up in late 1947 and had circulated among the committee members, Sandys had called for the congress to speak out for "the ultimate goal of European unity" but in so doing the congress was only to "explain in extremely general terms the various forms which this unity might be expected to flow from it." As the institution for promoting the unification process, he wanted to call for a "European Council" that would consist of "a system of regular conferences between European Ministers (...) with the object of developing as far as possible a common European point of view, and a permanent international secretariat" that would study current European problems and present proposals to the council.[43]

In the report submitted to the delegates after the vote in the coordinating committee, the supranational dimension of the "Political Union" to be created was more clearly addressed, being undertaken at the prompting of the federalists: "Sooner or later," incremental political integration "must involve the renunciation or, to be more accurate, the point exercise of certain sovereign powers." The report cited "the creation of a complete federation with an elected European Parliament" as the final goal of the development. The European Council was now termed an "Emergency Council" that was to be "responsible for directing joint action to secure not only economic recovery and military defence but also to preserve democratic freedom." Beyond that, the Council was to "plan the further stages of the political and economic integration of Europe." Added to this was the call for creation of a "European Deliberative Assembly" that was "to give valuable support and advice to the European Council." Its members would initially be sent by the national parliaments; "later, a system of popular election should be instituted."[44]

Under the influence of Mackay, the idea of a European Assembly came to be the centerpiece of the catalogue of demands during negotiations within the committee. This entity was "to advise upon immediate practical measures designed progressively to bring about the necessary economic and political union of

---

[42] Eugen Kogon, "Der Haager Europäische Kongreß," in: *Frankfurter Hefte*, vol. 3, no. 6, June 1948, pp. 481–483, here pp. 481ff.
[43] Duncan Sandys, "Suggested Outline of the Political Report for the Hague Congress," 21 Dec. 1947, in: Lipgens and Loth (eds.), *Documents* IV, pp. 330–332.
[44] *Ibid.*, pp. 333–338.

Europe" and to develop plans "to examine the juridical and constitutional implications arising out of the creation of such a union or federation..." The call for setting up a European Council was dropped. Instead, it was declared "that the time has come when the European nations must transfer and merge some portion of their sovereign rights."[45] The demand by the Italian federalists for the immediate transformation of the European Assembly into a constituent assembly was rejected by a large majority. Also, only a few delegates were enthusiastic about a motion by Reynaud to call for the direct election of the assembly right from the beginning. Mackay correctly warned against provoking the British as well as the French government with such a proposal: It would only reduce the chances of actually being accorded an assembly charged with working out a draft constitution capable of winning a majority. The resolution was finally passed on the night of 9 to 10 May. Of over three hundred delegates that had worked together on the Political Committee, fewer than a dozen voted against it.[46]

On the Economic and Social Committee, the liberal integration conceptions of the ILEC, which had been in charge during the preparations,[47] ran into criticism from the Socialists and the trade union representatives. Hence, the goal of the sought-after "economic union" perforce remained somewhat vague. It was nevertheless stated that in regard to European reconstruction, "there is no hope of recovery if each country simply strives to rebuild its national economy by the old methods," but that "progress in this direction will only be achieved if it is accompanied at every step by a parallel policy of even closer political union." The measures called for were incremental elimination of trade and tariff barriers; a common, if not lower, external tariff; budget stabilization; convergence of prices and wages; free convertibility of currencies and in the end, a currency union; likewise, common planning for the development of agriculture and basic industries as well as coordination of budget and credit policy along with social legislation.[48]

By endorsing the principles of the social-welfare state, the majority of the commission accommodated criticism from the left. Hence, the professional, economic, and social organizations of the individual countries were called upon "to study together ways and means of increasing production still further and rationalizing distribution while improving social conditions and ensuring a fair distribution of the product of economic activity." The promotion of the free movement

---

[45] Political resolution of The Hague Congress, *ibid.*, pp. 345–347. The oft-reprinted translation in *Europa-Archiv* 3 (1948), pp. 1443ff., is of the penultimate draft, not the version that was passed.
[46] Excerpts from the contributions to the debates in Lipgens and Loth (eds.), *Documents* IV, pp. 339–345. Cf. also Henri Brugmans, *L'idée européenne 1920–1970*, Bruges, 1970, p. 133.
[47] Text of the submitted report in Lipgens and Loth (eds.), *Documents* IV, pp. 208–212.
[48] Economic and social resolution in Lipgens and Loth (eds.), *Documents* IV, pp. 347–350.

of labor was to be linked with securing "the standards of wages, social security, living conditions of employment"; the economic policies of the individual countries were to be coordinated "so as to secure full employment."[49] The majority of the delegates did not want to commit themselves to concrete measures such as supranational control over the movement of capital or an Europeanization of Ruhr industry. Nor was there a majority for promoting the participation by workers and their organizations in the European entities. The protest by union representatives against this rebuff could only be contained—after prolonged negotiations that dragged into the wee hours of 10 May—by having the committee establish a "post-Congress Economic Committee" that was to "work out a compromise policy for Europe incorporating the best features from Capitalism and Socialism."[50]

The Cultural Committee was presented with a report that Denis de Rougement had developed in contact with authors such as Étienne Gilson, Ignazio Silone, and Salvador de Madariaga. He spoke of a "common heritage of Christian and other spiritual and cultural values and our common loyalty to the fundamental rights of man" that were to be valid for the members of a "European Union." Passages that were all too federalist were removed from the proposal at the last minute after intervention by Retinger. In concrete terms, there was a call for the establishment of a "European Cultural Centre" that would "promote an awareness of European unity" independently of any governmental supervision and that would "provide a meeting-place for leaders of thought." Further, there was a call to create a "European Institute for Childhood and Youth Questions" that would "encourage exchanges between the young people of all classes in Europe." Lastly, the draft included the creation of a "Supreme Court with supra-state jurisdiction to which citizens and groups can appeal, and which is capable of assuring the implementation of the Charter."[51]

The debate on the cultural report "unfolded in the usual confusion," as de Rougement sarcastically commented. Whereas the writer Charles Morgan wanted to leave cultural affairs wholly in the hands of the national governments, others called for the immediate creation of an entity to carry the work of the Congress forward. A Captain Cheshire from the Movement for Moral Re-Armament wanted to have the return to God anchored in the document and attacked the draft as

---

49 Ibid.
50 "Europe Unites," p. 48. Cf. the contributions to the discussion in *ibid.*, pp. 46–65 as well as the presentation in Loth, *Sozialismus*, p. 210.
51 Resolution of the Culture Committee, German translation in *Europa-Archiv* 3 (1948), pp. 1445ff.; on the origins, de Rougement, "Campaign," pp. 339–341. Unfortunately, de Rougement does not indicate what exactly the corrections were that he had to make after a meeting on 26 April 1948 in London.

"anti-Christian." Lastly, Bertrand Russell spoke emphatically for the proposed cultural center: It would help the people of different countries maintain close contact and learn to understand the viewpoints of others. His authority contributed to the unanimous passage of all the substantive proposals of the report.[52]

A Milestone

Some committed federalists were so disappointed at the direction the Congress was taking that they wanted to depart under protest shortly before it ended. Sandys had to bring in van Zeeland as a mediator to avoid such an open break. It is possible that the reading of the "Message to the Europeans" was the price he had to pay for it—he himself had initially wanted to strike it completely after objections had been raised to an endorsement of European defense.[53] Marc then succeeded in pushing through a press declaration of the UEF in which the Congress was criticized for being insufficiently representative and for "half-measures" in its decision-making.[54] At the second annual conference of the UEF from 7 to 11 November 1948 in Rome, Brugmans had to accept severe criticism for his willingness to cooperate with the UEM.[55]

The disappointment of the radical federalists over the lack of a breakthrough to a European constituent assembly should not take away from the fact that the initiators of the Congress in The Hague had actually succeeded in putting European unification on the agenda of Western European politics. Agreement among more or less representative delegations from nearly all the countries of Europe on a common program allowed Sandys to bring together the various European organizations in a common "European Movement" that was officially constituted on 25 October 1948—with Léon Blum, Winston Churchill, Alcide De Gasperi, and Paul-Henri Spaak as prestigious honorary presidents. At the same time, the high-ranking politicians who had been among the participants in the Congress now approached their respective heads of government in order to make it clear that concrete initiatives for summoning the European Assembly were expected

---

52 *Ibid.*, p. 342.
53 De Rougement is not very precise here either: He reports on a crisis session in which van Zeeland proposed a compromise of reading the Message without the objectionable passage (*ibid.*, p. 344) but does not mention the threat to leave. Sandys informed Frank Niess of that in a conversation on 25 Nov. 1966; see Niess, *Europäische Idee*, p. 210.
54 Declaration of 20 May 1948 in Lipgens and Loth (eds.), *Documents* IV, p. 56.
55 *Ibid.*, pp. 57–78.

of them.⁵⁶ Given the resonance that the Congress enjoyed in large segments of the European public, the governments could not off-handedly deny this request.

A few weeks after the Congress in The Hague, Winston Churchill expressed his confidence in its success: "This Europe Conference will be acknowledged by historians as a milestone in the development of our continent toward unity."⁵⁷ It was in fact in The Hague that the transnational societal consensus on which the later European Communities would rest had become palpable for the first time. In light of the convoluted paths to "more Europe" that would be embarked upon in subsequent decades, it is noteworthy that this initiative had been primarily organized by British politicians and that it aimed for a much greater Europe than the "Europe of the Six" that subsequently came into being. This consensus was unavoidably imprecise as regards the institutional configuration of a united Europe. Very clearly, however, it included acceptance of the partial amalgamation of national sovereign rights, the social-welfare configuration of the Community, and the stabilization of the democratic order in the participating countries.⁵⁸ After The Hague Congress, this consensus did not simply vanish. Instead, it developed in critical analysis of the experience of concrete European politics, which in turn came to be influenced by it.

---

56 Niess, *Europäische Idee*, pp. 223–227.
57 Recorded by Sandys in a memorandum for the coordinating committee, quoted in Niess, *ibid.*, p. 219.
58 The characterization of Sandys and the committee majority as "unionists," which stems from the radical federalists, is misleading.

1 Foundation Years, 1948–1957

The momentum that the European Movement had developed by the spring of 1948 was especially welcome to the French government. The conviction that a Western European federation was indispensable for reconstruction and for resolution of the German problem had in the meantime gained significant ground there. Jean Monnet, as the head of the French planning commission, wrote from Washington on 18 April 1948 to Prime Minister Robert Schuman, "All my thoughts and all my observations have now led me to a conclusion that has become a deep conviction: The efforts of the countries of Western Europe to rise to the circumstances, to the danger that threatens us, and to the American drive must become a genuinely European effort, which only a *federation* of the West could accomplish. I understand all the difficulties that stem from such a perspective, but I am convinced that we can save ourselves only by such an endeavor."[1] The creation of a federation seemed all the more urgent when the founding of a West German state was decided on by the Six-Power Conference in London on 7 June 1948, which put France under pressure: If Western European unification did not quickly achieve a supranational quality, the Germans threatened to take up their traditional great-power policy once again. Perhaps they would even ally themselves with the Soviet Union, which held the key to German unity. There was still an opportunity to incorporate the Germans into Europe, as Jean Laloy, political advisor to the French occupation commander in Germany, noted on 30 August 1948, but "One must grasp it quickly; in a year, it will already be too late."[2]

The Struggle over the Council of Europe

At the urging of Paul Ramadier and other members of the French government, Foreign Minister Georges Bidault decided to advance the unification project along the lines sketched out by the Hague Congress. At the second session of the Consultative Council of the Brussels Pact on 19 July 1948, he called for summoning a "European Parliamentary Assembly" for an "exchange of views" on the problems of European federation and for the preparation of an economic and monetary union of the Five. This assembly was initially to have a consultative character,

---

[1] FJME, AME 22/1; quoted in part in Jean Monnet, *Mémoires*, Paris: Fayard, 1976, p. 323.
[2] Jean Laloy, note of 30 Aug. 1948, quoted from Raymond Poidevin, "Le facteur Europe dans la politique allemande de Robert Schuman (été 1948 – printemps 1949)," in: *idem.* (ed.), *Histoire des débuts de la construction européenne (mars 1948 – printemps 1950)*, Brussels: Émile Bruylant, 1986, pp. 311–326, here p. 318.

as was explained in an instruction from the Quai d'Orsay to the French ambassador in London; after an understanding had been reached on the Europe Project, however, it was soon to receive its own decision-making authority and thereby "constitute the core of a federative organization of Europe."[3] Bidault himself did not really believe that such an ambitious project could be realized; nevertheless, in consideration of the criticism of the London agreements on Germany that had been voiced by his colleagues in the Christian-democratic MRP, he felt it advisable to place himself at the head of the European movement.[4]

British Foreign Minister Ernest Bevin, who initially had not taken Bidault's announcements seriously, was anything but enthusiastic about the French foray: Unlike his colleagues at the head of the Labour Party, this former leader of the British Transport and General Workers' Union did envision the creation of a "close association between" the United Kingdom and the countries of the "Mediterranean and Atlantic fringes of Europe," one that would serve the economic reconstruction of all participants as well as their security.[5] With this perspective, he had promoted the formation of the Brussels Pact with France, Belgium, the Netherlands, and Luxembourg, which was signed on 17 March 1948 and which contained an automatic commitment of support in the event of an attack by a third power in Europe. In his view, however, the expansion of this pact into a "European Union" ought to remain in the hands of the Consultative Council of the pact members, which had been set up for that purpose. As he said of the idea of a parliamentary assembly, "I don't like it. When you open that Pandora's box, you will find it full of Trojan horses."[6] It threatened to produce demagogic demands for unification that could not win the acceptance of the British government and would thereby endanger the incorporation of the Western Europeans into an order led by Britain. Beyond that, it naturally offered Winston Churchill an excellent forum from which he could increase his attacks on the inaction of the Labour government in the area of Europe policy. Angry at the extent of irresponsibility displayed by Bidault, Bevin demanded, to begin with, more specific

---

3 Quoted from René Massigli, *Une comédie des erreurs 1943–1956*, Paris: Plon, 1978, p. 157.
4 On this and the following, Loth, *Sozialismus*, pp. 211–214 and 221–223; Marie-Thérèse Bitsch, "Le rôle de la France dans la naissance du Conseil de l'Europe," in: Poidevin, *Débuts*, pp. 165–198; Geoffrey Warner, "Die britische Labour-Party und die Einheit Westeuropas 1949–1952", in: *Vierteljahrshefte für Zeitgeschichte* 28 (1980) pp. 310–330; Young, *Britain*, pp. 110–117; Antonio Varsori, *Il Patto di Bruxelles (1948): tra integrazione europea e alleanza atlantica*, Rome: Bonacci, 1988, pp. 185–211 and 244–269.
5 Stated in this way in a discussion of principles with the diplomats of the Foreign Office on 13 Aug. 1945, quoted from Greenwood, "Ernest Bevin, France and 'Western Union': August 1945 – February 1946," in *European History Quarterly* 14 (1984), pp. 319–338, here pp. 322ff.
6 Quoted from William Strang, *Home and Abroad*, London: André Deutsch, 1956, p. 290.

proposals before he agreed to a discussion of the project. Given that Bidault was poorly prepared, Belgian Foreign Minister Paul-Henri Spaak agreed to the call for adjournment: Only in this way was a failure of the unification project due to British opposition prevented right then.

If Bevin thought that with the adjournment the project was dead, he was soon to be disabused of that notion. As early as 29 July, Spaak declared in the Belgian parliament his willingness to advance the proposal among the allied governments if the Coordinating Committee of the European organizations presented more precise suggestions about its composition and tasks. A few days later, Ramadier signaled to committee leaders Duncan Sandys and Józef Retinger that the new French government—to which he himself belonged as minister of state, along with Léon Blum and Pierre-Henri Teitgen as deputy prime ministers, and Paul Reynaud as finance minister—would likewise be ready for such a step. As chairman of the Institutional Committee, which the Coordinating Committee had set up on 29 May, he worked out a proposal together with Sandys and others that envisioned in short order the summoning of a preparatory conference made up of seventy-five representatives sent by the parliaments of the five Brussels Pact countries. On 19 August, the Executive Committee passed this proposal on to all OEEC governments; on 2 September, the French and Belgian governments together called for it to be studied in detail in the Permanent Commission of the Brussels Pact so that a determination could be made at the next session of the Consultative Council.

Bevin initially sought to parry this foray too with delaying tactics. He had a questionnaire presented to the Permanent Commission that demanded exact information as to the competencies of the European Assembly as well as its relationship to the national governments and other international organizations and overseas territories. After the French side had offered more precise details to the effect that the assembly should at first only develop proposals on which the governments would then decide, Bevin presented to Schuman (who had replaced Bidault as foreign minister on 24 July) a counterproposal on 2 October: the idea of a "Council of Europe" that would gather once a year to bring home to the public the intensity of Western European cooperation. Given that there was no further convergence of standpoints, the Consultative Council was only able to decide on a very superficial compromise on 25 October: An eighteen-member Study Committee was created to confer on both proposals until the next session of the Council.

This Study Committee took up its work on 26 November, and the opposing standpoints once again collided. Whereas the French—in order to save at least something of the idea of the representative preparatory conference—sent high-ranking European politicians (Édouard Herriot, Paul Reynaud, François de Menthon, and Léon Blum, who then became ill and was replaced by SFIO General

Secretary Guy Mollet), the British put the firm Europe opponent Hugh Dalton at the head of their delegation and other than him sent only civil servants. By 16 December, a subcommittee had finally developed a compromise proposal that was approved in principle by all delegations. A "Council of Europe" consisting of ministers and deciding unanimously, as proposed by the British delegation, was to be combined with a Consultative Assembly, which in accordance with French conceptions was to be sent from the national parliaments and in two fortnight-long sessions per year develop proposals for the governments. The contents of the Assembly's discussions were to be decided by a two-thirds vote of the Council; further-reaching proposals of the Assembly could be banned with the same Council majority. A permanent secretariat was to support the work of both bodies.

After this preliminary result, Bevin came to the view that a parliamentary assembly was indeed unavoidable if he did not want to risk severely endangering the stabilization of Western Europe. He insisted however that the members of this assembly by appointed by the governments and that they vote *en bloc* in national delegations. This was significantly too little for his Continental negotiation partners, and so after furious accusations against the British side, the Study Committee dispersed on 20 January without having come to agreement on a common report. Only at the session of the Consultative Council on 27 and 28 January 1949 did Bevin realize that he could no longer lag too far behind the compromise formula that had been found in December. After Schuman had conceded to him that each country could decide for itself on the process for choosing the delegates, he accepted that they would be free in their voting and could also participate in setting the agenda. On this basis, the creation of the new organization was in principle decided. At the same time, there was agreement that Italy, the Scandinavian states, and Ireland should immediately be invited to participate in the project.

There were further negotiations on the details in the Permanent Commission of the Brussels Pact, and beginning on 28 March, representatives of the additional founding members that had been invited also took part. The delegates accepted the British suggestion that the assembly be based in Strasbourg—which to an extent certainly accommodated the ambitions of the French but was also meant to dampen the possible resonance of the new organ from the beginning. In regard to the meeting place of the Council of Ministers, the French sought in vain to have Paris chosen, whereas Bevin insisted on London. Likewise, all of Schuman's efforts to have the new organization dubbed "European Union" remained fruitless; the name remained open right up to the last moment. At the next meeting of the Consultative Council on 5 May, which definitively decided on the statutes of the new organization, Bevin succeeded in his efforts to have the designation

"Council of Europe" now serving for the ensemble of organs. He hoped that over the long term this new organization—even though he had not wanted it—would serve to ensure economic cooperation after the end of assistance from the Marshall Plan and to integrate Germany into the Western community.[7]

The modest and belated results of the negotiations, as measured against initial hopes, made for a certain disappointment among the Continental Europeans. That could not however keep them from now concentrating all their energy on the rapid development of the new institution. It was especially the Continental Socialists, for whom Britain's participation in the work of unification was especially close to the heart, who importuned their visibly-hesitant political counterparts across the Channel not to keep their minds closed to the necessity of a supranational "Third Power." The Socialist Europe Movement (MSEUE), which was now significantly gaining in popularity, joined the European Movement in November of 1948, thereby correcting the tactical error of its decision against the Hague Congress. Leading Socialists participated on an equal footing in the second congress of the European Movement from 25 to 28 February 1949 in Brussels. Decisions on European economic planning and the creation of common institutions for European heavy industry served to push the programmatic statements of the movement significantly to the left and thereby signaled to Labour politicians that there would certainly be a place in the future Europe for their socio-political beliefs. At an international socialist conference in the Dutch city of Baarn in May of 1949, Labour representatives agreed that all Socialist deputies in the future Consultative Assembly would meet with each other.[8]

Parallel to this, Jean Monnet and his colleagues made efforts in detailed talks to win over British planning experts for an Anglo-French economic union, which was to constitute the centerpiece of the future European community. Given that the British were still interested in developing cooperation with France, Chancellor of Exchequer Stafford Cripps agreed to informal preliminary conversations on the project between Monnet and Sir Edwin Plowden, chairman of the British Economic Planning Board. In talks that took place in late April of 1949 in Monnet's home, it was the case however that there was hardly any convergence of views; yet, given that Plowden had much sympathy for practical proposals such as exchanging British coal for French agricultural products, the French negotiators came away with the impression that with further exploration of common

---

[7] Cf. his remarks in a conversation with Dalton on 17 Nov. 1948, reported in Young, *Britain*, p. 113.
[8] Cf. Loth, *Sozialismus*, pp. 225–229; Lipgens and Loth, *Documents* IV, pp. 298–300, 379–399, 462–469.

and reciprocal interests, the British could be won over for common solutions in the end.⁹

When the first term of the Consultative Assembly of the Council of Europe began on 10 August 1949 in Strasbourg, it could indeed seem that the breakthrough to a supranational Europe was not far off. The national parliaments had sent top-level politicians of their factions, often those who had already been participating in the European Parliamentary Union or the European Movement. Even the British government, which was the only one to make use of the opportunity to appoint delegates itself, decided to send a delegation in which Churchill could play a prominent role. The assembly elected Spaak, who had just left the Belgian government, as its president and then showed sufficient self-confidence to expand its competencies to the greatest extent possible within the provisions of the statute of the Council of Europe. It created a Standing Committee (likewise under the chairmanship of Spaak), which ensured the presence and continuity of the Assembly between its brief terms and which could serve as negotiation leader *vis-à-vis* the Council of Ministers. It then endowed the six other committees (among them a general "Political Committee") with the right to meet outside the designated terms. Lastly, it called for the Council of Ministers to refrain from exercising influence over the agenda and to create the office of a deputy general secretary who was to be responsible only to the Assembly.

In terms of content, the assembly cautiously moved toward supra-nationality. Given that Sandys, the EPU, and the MSEUE were working zealously behind the scenes, Churchill made use of the opportunity to inflict upon the Labour deputies a series of defeats in votes taken. They soon withdrew in exasperation, and hence the federalists succeeded in having a goodly portion of their own ideas approved. At the close of their talks on 5 September, the Assembly passed with the required two-thirds majority a declaration from Mackay specifying that "the purpose and goal of the Council of Europe is the creation of a European political authority with limited functions but genuine authority." The Standing Committee was given the task of dealing in greater detail with the issue of political authority and of bringing about a special session of the Assembly at the beginning of 1950 that was to confer on the results of the Standing Committee's work. The Political Committee was also to draft a "European Pact" that was to define "the guiding principles of the Council of Europe in political, economic, social, and cultural areas" and was to be "binding for all members and associate members"; the assembly was

---

9 Cf. the reports of Etienne Hirsch (in: Erling Bjøl, *La France devant l'Europe. La politique européenne de la IV*ᵉ *République*, Copenhagen: Munksgaard, 1966, p. 67), Pierre Uri (*ibid.*, p. 381) and Monnet (*Mémoires*, pp. 329–332); Éric Roussel, *Jean Monnet 1888–1979*, Paris: Fayard, 1996, pp. 504–508.

to decide on this draft during the next regular term. The Council of Ministers was called upon to make the membership of the new West German Federal Republic possible before the next term and to provide for the strengthening of the European consciousness. Beyond that, the deputies developed the draft of a European human rights convention; they charged the Economic Committee with the task of grappling with the Ruhr question and coordinating the coal and steel industries; and they also called for dealing with the issue of a European university during the next term.[10]

With these decisions and these demands, the assembly certainly went beyond Bevin's worst fears. He was anyway in the process of correcting his European policy preferences and now saw himself confirmed in the suspicion that the independent Europe that he envisioned was not to be realized with the hot-headed and irresponsible politicians of the Continent. He had already given up the customs union project in September of 1948—in part because he had grown tired of the continuing opposition of the Chancellor of the Exchequer, the Treasury, and the Commonwealth representatives and in part because the political instability and, as he thought, immaturity of France made an irrevocable linkage between Britain and the Continent seem less and less advisable. More important to him than the creation of a unified European economic area, which would obviously be difficult to harmonize with the interests of the Commonwealth, was the political stabilization of the Western European region, which he saw as being threatened by a combination of internal weaknesses and the pressure of Soviet expansion. It was first of all important that a stable Western German state needed to be created and that European reconstruction be protected by an American security guarantee (which engaged him to the greatest extent up to the time of the Washington agreements on the North Atlantic Pact and the occupation statute for the Federal Republic of Germany, completed on 4 and 8 April 1949, respectively). Great Britain needed to support European integration, but it must not engage itself to the extent that it would not alone remain viable in the event of a collapse of Europe, as he and Cripps wrote in a cabinet presentation in late January of 1949.[11]

Assessing Bevin's attitude towards the Council of Europe the American planners around George Kennan came to the conclusion that the British would

---

10 Text of the resolutions in: *Europa-Archiv* 4 (1949), pp. 2557–2560 and 2579–2584; on the course of negotiations, Édouard Bonnefous, *L'idée européenne et sa réalisation*, Paris: Éditions du Grand siècle, 1950, pp. 125–149 and 301–333; Charles Melchior de Molènes, *L'Europe de Strasbourg. Une première expérience de parlementarisme européen*, Paris: Édition Roudil, 1971, pp. 181–197; Loth, *Sozialismus*, pp. 244–247.

11 Report of 26 Jan. 1949, reported in Young, *Britain*, p. 122; cf. *ibid.*, pp. 118–123; on Bevin's fear of France, also David Dilks, "Britain and Europe, 1948–1950: The Prime Minister, the Foreign Secretary and the Cabinet," in: Poidevin, *Débuts*, pp. 391–418, here p. 407.

never accept the level of integration regarded as indispensable for integrating the Germans. For Kennan, one consequence of this assessment was that in accordance with their economic interests, Great Britain and the Commonwealth should be drawn closer to the US and Canada. On the other hand, France should be called upon to take on the leadership of a closer Continental unification; and as part of that, French fears of German superiority were to be allayed by the military presence of the US in Europe. This conception ran into opposition from experts at the State Department such as Charles Bohlen, who feared that France would be unwilling to enter into an association with the new Germany without Britain, and who therefore called for greater pressure on the British. Kennan found support however from the Anglophile Secretary of State Dean Acheson, and he was therefore able to communicate it to the British side in formal conversations in London during the second half of August 1949. In early September, Washington then accommodated the British in trilateral financial talks (with the inclusion of Canada): Under the influence of Acheson, the British were accorded easier importation, special rights for the sterling zone, and a special American-British-Canadian financial organization in return for the devaluation of the British pound. All this strengthened the British resolve "not to be drawn further into Europe."[12] Bevin now completely gave up the idea of a European "Third Power"; he was satisfied that the American guarantee at least ensured British independence, and was all the more concerned for independence *vis-à-vis* the Continental Europeans in light of his estimate that it would still take at least ten years before they would be in a position to resist a Soviet attack.[13]

Full of gratitude for the special role that the American course correction gave the British, the Labour government organized the devaluation of the pound without any consideration for its partners in the OEEC, the Brussels Pact, or the Council of Europe. Fundamentally, though, it was in their interest too: The alarmingly-increasing dollar deficit served everywhere in Europe as a barrier to economic integration and dimmed the prospects of a lasting recovery of the European economies. Given that it had to entail adjustments in other currencies, the partners hoped for concerted action in which the timing and the extent of the devaluations would be coordinated. It was a clarion call for the Continent when

---

[12] According to the formulation of Foreign Office official Eric Berthoud in an analysis of the trilateral conversations of 13 Sept. 1949, quoted from Hogan, *Marshall Plan*, p. 265; cf. *ibid.*, pp. 238–278; Alan Milward, *The Reconstruction of Western Europe, 1954–51*, London: Routledge, 1984, pp. 287–295; on the conceptional shift, also Klaus Schwabe, "Der Marshall-Plan und Europa," in: Poidevin, *Débuts*, pp. 47–69, here pp. 61–67.

[13] Cf. Milward, *Reconstruction*, pp. 308ff.; Young, *Britain*, p. 127; Dilks, *Britain and Europe*, pp. 411–414.

the British, after having long rejected calls for devaluation, now unilaterally announced a thirty percent devaluation of the pound on 18 September without any consultation and did so after a separate agreement with the US. Léon Blum characterized this unilateral action by the British a "scandal" that was happening "exactly at the moment in which one was creating Europe."[14]

Still greater was the disappointment when at the Council of Ministers meeting of the Council of Europe from 3 to 5 November, Bevin objected to nearly all the demands of the Consultative Committee, doing so with American assurances of support. Only the call for allowing the Federal Republic to become an associate member gained his support (full membership not being possible as long as the new state did not possess sovereignty in foreign policy). All recommendations on economic issues were referred to the OEEC. Because the Council could only decide unanimously, those proposals that amounted to an expansion of the Council of Europe (among them the call for a special session of the assembly) were rejected after Bevin's veto.[15] This meant that the path of the Council of Europe toward becoming a European constituent assembly was blocked even before it had really been embarked upon in the work of the Commissions of the Consultative Assembly. The federalists who had sought to persuade the British in Strasbourg felt themselves rebuffed; with dismay the French government saw the task of integrating the Germans falling to it alone.

The Emergence of the Coal and Steel Community

There was no quick way out of the blind alley in which the European unification movement found itself after the British veto of the decisions of the Consultative Assembly. It was indeed the case that conservative politicians such as de Gaulle and Coudenhove-Kalergi, who had always regarded the possibility of British participation with skepticism, now energetically advocated for a Continental federation.[16] The Union of European Federalists (UEF), in which the constitutional wing around Altiero Spinelli had in the meantime come to the fore, pushed for the conclusion of a federal pact that was to come into force "as soon as it is ratified by states with a total population of at least one hundred million"; the British and the Scandinavians, who would certainly not participate, were offered the prospect of "especially amicable organic connections" to the members of the pact in the

---

14 Pierre-Olivier Lapie, *De Léon Blum à de Gaulle. Le caractère et le pouvoir*, Paris: Fayard, 1971, p. 214.
15 Text of the resolutions in: *Europa-Archiv* 4 (1949), pp. 2697 and 2609–2612.
16 Cf. Lipgens and Loth, *Documents* III, pp. 110–113; Posselt, *Coudenhove-Kalergi*, pp. 374ff.

vague hope that those countries would later revise their views.[17] The majority of the Continental forces favoring unification shrank back from a break with the British, however: The Benelux states once again saw French dominance in store for them; for their part, the French feared the dominance of the Germans; and the various adherents of the "Third Power" saw their final hopes for a socialist Europe dwindling. French Socialist Francis Leenhardt was expressing a widespread sentiment when in the National Assembly he said that a Europe without Great Britain would mean "the industrial dominance of Germany, France as a vegetable garden; it would be the realization of Hitler's dream despite his defeat; it would be a German Europe."[18]

Under these circumstances, it proved impossible to expand a planned Franco-Italian customs union to the Benelux states. From May of 1949, talks with Belgium were carried on and with the Netherlands from October onward. It emerged that France and Italy were only willing to accept an incremental reduction in import restrictions and insisted on setting up coordinating organs, whereas the Benelux countries pushed for the quickest possible liberalization and wanted the Federal Republic incorporated into the union as quickly as possible. The experts of the Five reached agreement in principle on 9 December on the creation of a "Fritalux" or "Finebel" group; the participation of the Federal Republic remained an open question, and the antagonisms solidified over the following weeks at the governmental level. The British, who did not want to be excluded from a closer Continental market, reinforced the Dutch in their opposition to a customs union without the Federal Republic and at the same time warned the French so forcefully against burdening Anglo-French cooperation that the Bidault government—in the face of the generally pro-British opinion of the French public—no longer dared to continue pursuing the project against multiple group interests. When in late February of 1950 the British government announced a plan for a European customs union that meant the end of the Finebel negotiations. The treaty on a bilateral customs union between France and Italy, which had already been signed, remained in parliamentary committees and was finally laid to rest in July of 1951.[19]

---

17 Quotes from "Die Resolution der außerordentlichen Generalversammlung der UEF 29.–31.10.1949 in Paris," Lipgens and Loth, *Documents* IV, pp. 84–91, on the strategy of the UEF, Sergio Pistone, *The Union of European Federalists*, Milan: Giuffrè, 2008, pp. 50–57.
18 Journal Officiel de la République française, Assemblée nationale, Débats parlementaires 2511.1949, pp. 6214–6218. Cf. Wilfried Loth, "Der Abschied vom Europarat. Europapolitische Entscheidungen im Kontext des Schuman-Plans," in: Klaus Schwabe (ed.), *Die Anfänge des Schuman-Plans 1950/51*, Baden-Baden: Nomos, 1988, pp. 183–195.
19 Milward, *Reconstruction*, pp. 306–316; Richard T. Griffith and Frances M. B. Lynch, "L'échec de la 'Petite Europe': les négociations Fritalux/Finebel, 1949–1950," in: *Revue historique* 109

Although in a "personal message" of 30 November Acheson had called upon Schuman to take over leadership in integrating West Germany into a supranational Europe,[20] the French government remained inactive for a long while. It neither wanted to relieve Great Britain of responsibility for the European community nor could it allow a break with the British given French public opinion and the attitude of its Socialist coalition partners. There were no responses to the public advances by which Konrad Adenauer as chancellor of the new West German republic sought to set in motion the move from one-sided occupation restrictions to Western integration on an equal footing: On 25 August 1949, there was Bonn's proposal to internationalize the *Thyssen* steelworks as a first step toward mutualizing heavy industry, then on 8 March 1950, the grandiose idea of a comprehensive union between France and Germany, and on 21 March the proposal for a progressive economic union of the two countries.[21] Instead of responding, the Bidault government enmeshed itself in unedifying controversies over dismantling policy in the Federal Republic, the Ruhr statute, and the future status of the Saarland—controversies that burdened Franco-German relations as well as relations with the Allies without at the same time bringing any greater security against a German resurgence.

Nevertheless, Schuman and many others in authority in Paris knew that time was against them. The longer they waited with concrete offers of integration, the less the likelihood that the Germans, who in principle could demand equality in the Western alliance, would accept. The chance offered them by Adenauer's fundamental Western orientation could not last indefinitely. To this was added the concern that after the end of Marshall aid, the prospects of a lasting economic recovery were anything but rosy. Furthermore, many experienced their own powerlessness on the world stage as increasingly depressing after the detonation of a Soviet atomic bomb in late August of 1949 and the resultant militarization of American containment policy. The pressure that was then weighing on the French government to make a decision became all the greater when, according to a report of the Economic Commission for Europe of late 1949, a crisis of overproduction was threatening to develop in the European steel industry, which would allow the Germans—who alone possessed the necessary coal reserves—to gain dominance

---

(1985), pp. 159–193; Pierre Guillen, "Le projet d'union économique entre la France, l'Italie et le Benelux," in: Poidevin, *Débuts*, pp. 143–157.

20 FRUS 1949, III, pp. 624ff.

21 Cf. Hans-Peter Schwarz, *Adenauer. Der Aufstieg: 1876–1952*, Stuttgart: DVA, 1986, pp. 684 and 701ff.; on Adenauer's conception of Europe, Wilfried Loth, "Konrad Adenauer und die europäische Einigung," in: Mareike König and Matthias Schulz (eds.), *Die Bundesrepublik Deutschland und die europäische Einigung 1949–2000*, Stuttgart: Franz Steiner, 2004, pp. 81–105.

in heavy industry again. Moreover, with the end of the American monopoly on nuclear weapons, a German contribution to defense became ever more unavoidable. It was obvious that the Germans would make use of this strategic chance to push through their sovereignty.

Only in late April of 1950 did Schuman decide to act when it became known that Acheson and Bevin would at the upcoming foreign ministers conference of the three Western allies (set for 11 to 13 May) call for lifting the limit of 11.1 million metric tons per year that had been imposed on West German steel production. A weakening of the occupation statute was also on the agenda, and after Churchill on 16 March had in the House of Commons proposed the creation of a West German troop contingent within the framework of a European army, the possibility could no longer be excluded that there would need to be negotiations over corresponding demands by the American and British general staffs.[22] In this situation, Monnet presented—with a sure sense for the appropriate moment—the project for a European authority for coal and steel on 28 April. Unlike Prime Minister Bidault, who hardly took notice of it, Schuman resolved after a weekend in his homeland of Lorraine to dare a breakthrough on supra-nationality without Great Britain: "It'll be on my head," as he said to his assistant Bernard Clappier as he arrived in the Gare de l'Est on Monday.[23]

He benefitted from the fact that the Socialist ministers had left the government in February due to differences over social policy. In order to circumvent further opposition, he ensured that his decision was initially known only to a few confidants; he informed the Council of Ministers only superficially too. On 8 May, he obtained Adenauer's approval; and on the morning of 9 May, he brought about a positive decision by French government—against the opposition of Bidault but with energetic support from René Mayer and René Pleven. On the evening of the same day, just before the opening of the foreign ministers conference, he announced the project in a press conference: subordination of the "totality of Franco-German coal and steel production to a common Highest Supervi-

---

22 Cf. Norbert Wiggershaus, "Zur Frage einer militärischen Integration Westdeutschlands (bis Mai 1950)," in: Poidevin, *Débuts*, pp. 343–366.
23 Quoted from Pierre Gerbet, "La naissance du Plan Schuman," in: Andreas Wilkens (ed.), *Le Plan Schuman dans l'Histoire. Intérêts nationaux et projet européen*, Brussels: Émile Bruylant, 2004, pp. 13–51. On the prehistory of the Schuman Plan, cf. also Milward, *Reconstruction*, pp. 358–401; Raymond Poidevin, *Robert Schuman – homme d'Etat 1886–1963*, Paris: Imprimerie nationale, 1986, pp. 244–263; Ulrich Lappenküper, "Der Schuman-Plan. Mühsamer Durchbruch zur deutsch-französischen Verständigung," in: *Vierteljahrshefte für Zeitgeschichte* 42 (1994), pp. 403–445, here pp. 405–413; Roussel, *Monnet*, pp. 519–529; William I. Hitchcock, *France Restored. Cold War Diplomacy and the Quest for Leadership in Europe, 1944–1954*, Chapel Hill and London: University of North Carolina Press, 1998, pp. 116–129.

sory Authority [...] which stands open for entry by other European countries and whose decisions will be binding."[24]

There were several reasons why Monnet and Schuman took up the project of a coal and steel union as a way to escape from the blind alley in European politics.[25] Firstly, it was the given means by which the feared steel crisis could be dealt with and by which the necessary Ruhr coal could be secured over the long term for the expansion of the French steel industry. It thereby simultaneously rescued France's modernization plan, which without that expansion would have failed and which had already come under fire in domestic politics anyway. Given that it exposed French steel industrialists to West German competition it even exercised a modernizing pressure, which the planners around Monnet had up to that point sorely missed. Above all, however, it offered a promising alternative to the vain struggle against a new German dominance, one that at the same time served to strengthen European self-assertion: "German resources and energies," as Schuman formulated it in a personal note, "to confine ourselves to containing them and retarding them by means of prohibitions and hostile coalitions or to enhance them and make them bear fruit for the common benefit of the whole of unified Europe."[26] At the same time, the project of a High Authority for Coal and Steel was less ambitious than the customs union and less spectacular than a political federation; consequently, there were better prospects of success with those who advocated a Europe with Great Britain, a group whose parliamentary support was still necessary.

In fact, the Labour government, completely surprised by Schuman's initiative, attempted to bring the Continental Socialists on board so as to take the supranational vanguard away from the Schuman Plan. On the one hand, the British definitely had an interest in integrating the Federal Republic through France; on the other, the prospect of Continental autonomy and possibly a Continental steel cartel caused them significant unease. In order to escape from the dilemma, they decided on British participation in the endeavor, though under the provision that it, like the Council of Europe, would be trimmed down to a "realistic" level that would not hinder Britain's freedom of action. However, Monnet put a stop to that in conversations in London, in which he made the acceptance

---

[24] Text of the declaration in: *Europa-Archiv* 5 (1950), pp. 3091ff.
[25] Enlightening for the motive is Monnet's exposé of 3 May 1950, published in *Le Monde* on 9 May 1970. Cf. also Monnet, *Mémoires*, pp. 341–353.
[26] Undated note in Schuman's papers, investigated by Gilbert Trausch, "Der Schuman-Plan zwischen Mythos und Realität. Der Stellenwert des Schuman-Plans," in: Rainer Hudemann, Hartmut Kaelble, and Klaus Schwabe (eds.), *Europa im Blick der Historiker*, Munich: Oldenbourg, 1995, pp. 105–128, here pp. 113ff.

of the supranational principle a prerequisite for the beginning of negotiations. For some days, Schuman thought about whether the British should be accorded a special status in the negotiations and in the future organization. However, when Monnet had shown him that such a course would stimulate the covetousness of the other partners for special rights, he demanded of the British on 1 June that they decide by the evening of the next day whether they wanted to participate in talks on a supranational authority or not. The answer was negative: Bevin, for whom such an engagement went too far, proposed instead an Anglo-French meeting at the ministerial level. This was in turn rejected by Schuman, and so on 3 June, the governments of France, the Netherlands, Belgium, Luxembourg, Italy, and the Federal Republic issued a joint communiqué announcing negotiations on a coal and steel union along the lines of the Schuman Plan.[27]

In the talks that began on 20 June in Paris, Monnet had to accept some modifications of his concept. Originally, he had hoped that the right of decision-making in the coal and steel sectors could be transferred more or less wholesale to a High Authority and that the treaty could over the course of the summer of 1950 be made ready for signing. However, the negotiation partners, particularly the Benelux governments, insisted on specifying the competencies of the new organization in detail and on precisely determining the relationship between the supranational realm and national decision-making areas. In the process, differing conceptions as to the scope of the supranational competency as well as differing economic interests manifested themselves. The talks thus dragged out and several times also wound up in dangerous waters. It was not until the middle of December that a draft treaty was ready, and then the resolution of contentious individual issues took so much time that the foreign ministers of the Six where only able to sign the treaty on the "European Coal and Steel Community" (ECSC) on 18 April 1951.[28]

Whereas Monnet had spoken only vaguely of the "possibility of appeals" regarding decisions of the High Authority, its competence would now be limited by no fewer than three organs: A Council of Ministers (which the Benelux representatives originally even wanted to place above the High Authority) was

---

27 The decision-making process is documented in: *Documents on British Policy Overseas*, Series II, Vol. I: *The Schuman Plan, the Council of Europe and Western European Integration, May 1950 – December 1952*, London, 1986. Cf. Monnet, *Mémoires*, pp. 360–372; Massigli, *Comédie*, pp. 185–209, 236ff.; Young, *Britain*, pp. 150–157; Roger Bullen, "The British Government and the Schuman Plan, May 1950 – March 1951," in: Schwabe, *Anfänge*, pp. 199–210; Roussel, *Monnet*, pp. 535–537 and 540–550; David Gowland, Arthur Turner, and Alex Wright, *Britain and European Integration since 1945. On the Sidelines*, London and New York: Routledge, 2010, pp. 28–35.
28 Treaty text in: *Europa. Dokumente*, vol. 2, pp. 702ff. On the negotiations, the contributions in Schwabe, *Anfänge*; Lappenküper, *Schuman-Plan*, pp. 418–438; Roussel, *Monnet*, pp. 553–566 and 602–604.

able to issue instructions in precisely-defined crisis situations and had to give its approval for measures of the Authority likely to have an influence over other economic areas; depending on the sensitivity of the subject matter, it was specified that there be either a simple majority or a qualified majority or unanimity. True, the Parliamentary Assembly (which the West German delegation would have gladly had as the first chamber of a legislature) possessed only the right to demand reports and to topple the High Authority (with a two-thirds majority); *de facto* however it could be brought into play by the High Authority against the interests of individual governments or the Council of Ministers. There was also a court functioning as constitutional court, administrative court, and arbitration authority, to which there could be appeals not only by all organs and member states but also by all natural and juridical persons of the Community.

In regard to the harmonization of wages and prices (which was finally to bring the presumed locational advantage of the Lorraine steel industry[29] to the fore), the French side had to cut back significantly: Only targeted wage dumping and discriminatory pricing were forbidden; beyond that, the High Authority could only have a steering effect by determining highest and (in crisis situations) lowest prices. Nevertheless, the Council of Ministers and the High Authority could in crisis situations set production quotas and allocate resources: This secured access to Ruhr coal for France and made it possible to dispense with the International Authority for the Ruhr after the common coal market had come into effect. The French, with American support, also succeeded in breaking the opposition of the Federal Republic and Belgium to a far-reaching ban on mergers. Monnet was able to push through a provision requiring approval of all future mergers and stakes and specifying that no group could have more than a twenty-percent share of the market in coal or steel. Together with the break-up terms for the Ruhr industry, which Adenauer had to concede after extremely-crucial negotiations in Mid-March of 1951, these regulations offered effective measures against the renewed dominance of German heavy industry.

The French government had thus pushed through the core of its integration conception literally at the last minute. With the unified French and American threat of otherwise providing for harsher deconcentration regulations, it was possible to hinder the Federal Republic—which had grown quiet self-confident due to the Korean War—from insisting on a thoroughgoing restitution of its heavy industrial structure and thus bringing about the failure of the coal and steel union. In comparison to this success, it was of only secondary importance that Belgian Foreign Minister Paul van Zeeland had in the last negotiation round

---

29 In fact, that was the case only for the pure production costs but was not operative for most consumers, who additionally had to take transport costs into account.

secured a practically unlimited transition period during which Belgium could subsidize its ailing coal industry with "compensatory payments." And it was a mere blemish that the foreign ministers could not agree on the seat of the new organization. This issue had still not been resolved after the conclusion of the ratification process, and Luxembourg's Foreign Minister Joseph Bech—at the end of an exhausting night session of the six foreign ministers on the morning of 24 July 1952—suggested that one could provisionally begin in Luxembourg and then see. The High Authority with Monnet as first president was thereupon able to take up its work in the capital of the smallest member state on 10 August 1952.[30]

The European Payments Union (EPU) came into existence more quickly than the ECSC. After the liberalization of foreign trade in the OEEC had initially been gotten underway only extremely cautiously, the American threat not to pay the third and fourth annual tranches of Marshall aid led to an acceleration in late 1949: It was first of all decided that fifty percent of the foreign trade of the OEEC states would be liberalized; and then the Executive Committee of the OEEC agreed on 18 June 1950 to the establishment of a multilateral payment system. From 1 July 1950, the OEEC states settled their interstate trade via a common clearing house; accordingly, countries with debts received a loan of as much as nine percent of the previous year's payments, whereas a growing portion of debts had to be settled immediately in gold or dollars. After the official founding of the EPU on 19 September, the OEEC countries extended the liberalization ratio to sixty percent and agreed on a further increase to seventy-five percent for the coming February. In July of 1951, the OEEC Council approved an expansion-oriented list of goods for which foreign trade would be completely liberalized.[31]

Yet, there was no rapid progress to be seen on unification via the level of economic integration that had been reached up to that point. This became clear when in late June of 1950 Dutch Foreign Minister Dirk Stikker presented the OEEC Council with a plan that combined the liberalization of individual economic sectors with the establishment of a European modernization fund. This "sectoral integration" was to encompass all economic areas that three quarters of the OEEC members wanted to mutualize and then would be in force for those countries only. The British government saw in this the dangerous beginning of a supranational economic organization extending beyond the coal and steel realms and therefore made use of a request by the Economic Cooperation Administration for

---

30 Cf. Gilbert Trausch, "Robert Schuman, le Luxembourg et l'Europe," in: *Robert Schuman. Les racines et l'œuvre d'un grand Européen*, exhibit catalogue, Luxembourg, 1986, pp. 24–83, here p. 67–73.
31 Cf. Milward, *Reconstruction*, pp. 320–334 and 421–434; Hogan, *Marshall-Plan*, pp. 292, 295–303, 320–325, 355–364.

some specifications in order to push through the setting up of a special committee to review the plan more closely, together with proposals of Italian Finance Minister Giuseppe Pella for a staggered reduction of internal tariffs and the plan of French Finance Minister Maurice Petsch for founding a European Investment Bank. In this way, any momentum on the path to a common market was stopped for the time being.[32]

Further steps toward integration that would be confined to the area of the six ECSC members could not be so quickly accomplished either. There was an unsuccessful attempt by federalists from the UEF, MSEUE, and parts of the NEI to force the Consultative Assembly of the Council of Europe to embrace the project of a European federation pact by mobilizing public opinion. Neither signature campaigns nor local public opinion polls or the formation of a "Council of Vigilance" that attempted to have a direct effect on the deputies in Strasbourg during the term of 18 to 24 November 1950 could alter the fact that the majority of those forces on the Continent favorably disposed toward unification shrank back from deepening integration without having the British onboard.[33] Despite the hopes of such figures as Italian Prime Minister Alcide De Gasperi and despite what Monnet had suggested, there was no direct route from the ECSC to the political federation of Europe.

The Drama of the EDC

The danger that Monnet and others in authority in France saw looming in the spring of 1950 materialized more quickly than expected: Owing to the change in European public sentiment in favor of a German contribution to defense—a change sparked by the North Korean attack on South Korea on 25 June 1950—the Truman administration decided over the course of August to combine the strengthening of its military engagement in Europe with the creation of West German troops. On 12 September, Acheson confronted his British and French colleagues at a gathering in New York with the demand for the establishment of a West German army under the auspices of a NATO "European Defense Force." In return, he offered American participation in this integrated NATO force, which included an increase in the number of US divisions stationed in Europe from two to six and the assumption of command of this force by an American general.[34] The

---

32 Cf. Milward, *Reconstruction*, pp. 446–451; Hogan, *Marshall-Plan*, pp. 350–353.
33 Cf. Loth, *Sozialismus*, pp. 274ff.
34 Cf. Norbert Wiggershaus, "Die Entscheidung für einen westdeutschen Verteidigungsbeitrag 1950," in: *Anfänge westdeutscher Sicherheitspolitik 1945–1956*, vol. 1: *Von der Kapitulation bis*

Federal Republic was thereby offered possibilities for advancement even without supranational integration. With a linkage of interests between the US and West Germany, France was threatened with isolation; and in the long term there was also the threat of either complete American dominance over the European continent or the rise of Germany to the status of great power once again.

French authorities registered with great concern how the West German position in the negotiations over the Schuman Plan stiffened and how Adenauer's domestic political freedom of action was noticeably reduced. In this situation, nothing was left to them except forcing the development of a political Europe with a military dimension if they did not want to risk having their policy on Germany and Europe turned into a heap of ashes. As Monnet reported, "The circumstances compelled us to cut corners: The European federation was becoming a near-term goal." He importuned Schuman to save the Schuman Plan by expanding it: "The army, weapons, and basic production would be placed under a common sovereignty at the same time. We could not wait, as we had envisioned, for a political Europe to crown a growing construction, because a common defense could only be conceived of under a common sovereignty right from the beginning."[35]

However, it was difficult to prevail with this realization even in the French Council of Ministers. The Socialists, who in the meantime were in the government once again, still shrank back from forcing the unification process without Great Britain; Defense Minister Jules Moch, whose son had been brutally killed by the Germans, and President Vincent Auriol were bitter opponents of any form of German rearmament. In accordance with Monnet's elucidations, Schuman suggested "seeking a European solution to German rearmament" but was initially called off by the Council of Ministers. He was given a binding instruction to play for time at a second negotiation round in late September in New York. While Schuman was there, Monnet was able to convince Prime Minister René Pleven that agreement to West German rearmament could not be dragged out any further if an increase in American engagement in Europe was desired and that the government's fall could only be avoided if West German forces were integrated into a European defense community in addition to NATO. After an abundance of further conversations as well as planning drafts from the Monnet group and sounding-out of the Americans, the government agreed on 19 October to the pro-

---

zum Pleven-Plan, Munich: Oldenbourg, 1982, pp. 325–402; Rolf Steininger, *Wiederbewaffnung. Die Entscheidung für einen westdeutschen Verteidigungsbeitrag: Adenauer und die Westmächte 1950*, Erlangen, Bonn, and Vienna: Straube, 1989.
35 Monnet, *Mémoires*, pp. 401.

posal to counter the Allied demand for the creation of West German forces with the project of a European army.[36]

In all this, however, there was not much left of the idea of expanding the coal and steel union into a political federation. In his government declaration of 24 October (formulated point by point by Monnet), Pleven spoke only very vaguely of having this army "linked with the political institutions of a united Europe." A "European defense minister" was proposed as the political steering organ of the integrated European army, an official who was to "fulfill" the "existing international commitments" (that is, the provisions of NATO) "on the basis of directives that he would receive from the Council of Ministers." There were no exact statements as to the relationship between NATO structures and the European Army or statements as to the decision-making mechanisms of the Council of Ministers or the competencies of the Parliamentary Assembly that was likewise named as a control organ. Instead, it was explained that member states already in possession of an army would only submit their forces incrementally to the common command and would do so only insofar as those forces did not have "other needs to meet than those of common defense." Also, integration of the national contingents was to occur "on the basis of the smallest possible unit."[37] This amounted to two-fold discrimination against the Federal Republic: It was to be the only participant that neither was a member of the Atlantic Alliance nor had forces outside the European Army, and that did not have its own general staff or its own defense minister; in the anticipated integration at the level of the battalion or in any event at the level of the regiment, access to higher headquarters was also more or less barred. Beyond that, the proposal had aspects that would clearly have a retarding effect: Pleven specified that the creation of the European Army, which itself would take time, would occur only after the signing of the ECSC treaty.

The discriminatory and dilatory aspects of the proposal did indeed secure it a majority in the French National Assembly (349 to 235 votes on 25 November) and thereby saved Pleven's government. Among the Allies, however, it unleashed a nearly-unanimous outcry. British Defense Minister Emanuel Shinwell privately termed it nothing less than "disgusting: military folly and political madness."[38] Most politicians, with Acheson at the forefront, saw the proposal only as an attempt to sabotage the planned creation of a NATO armed force. Only the Belgian and Luxembourg governments, for which the creation of West German troops also caused major concern, could find any positive elements in the proposal. The most that the Allies were willing to do at the end of November was to concede a confer-

---

36 *Ibid.*, pp. 425–440; Roussel, *Monnet*, pp. 578–589; Hitchcock, *France Restored*, pp. 139–144.
37 Text of the declaration in: *Europa. Dokumente*, vol. 2, pp. 813–815.
38 Quoted from Steininger, *Wiederbewaffnung*, pp. 267.

ence on the Pleven Plan, for which France was to extend invitations. Regardless of the result of that gathering, the French government was to agree to the creation of West German "battle troops" (halfway between battalions and divisions). On 6 December, the French Council of Ministers accepted this deal, after dramatic arguments within the SFIO party leadership.[39]

The prospects for creating the European Army had not been increased with this minimal compromise—which was nonetheless approved by the Atlantic Council in Brussels on 19 December. Adenauer was now seeking direct membership in NATO for the Federal Republic. After the Brussels decision, he no longer regarded the detour via the European Army as necessary and considering the mood of the West German public, no longer supportable either. Yet, he did participate in the talks on the Pleven Plan, which began in Paris on 15 February 1951; but he demanded military equality for the Federal Republic from the beginning and also concentrated on the conversations about the creation of West German troops that he had to have with the three High Commissioners. Beyond the Federal Republic, only Belgium, Luxembourg, and Italy accepted the French invitation; the Netherlands and Britain along with the other NATO partners were represented only by observers. Given that the French were not prepared to give up the discriminatory elements of their draft, the negotiations dragged out endlessly without a convergence of viewpoints.[40]

A breakthrough in the project for a European Army began to emerge only in early June of 1951 when Monnet was able to persuade General Dwight Eisenhower, who had been named supreme commander of NATO forces in Europe, that the contradiction between the French need for security and German demands for equality could at base only be overcome with a European Army. In response, the general made it clear to Monnet that a European Army could not be had without an improvement in the status of the Germans; both men then worked to push through these viewpoints in their respective governments. In early July, Acheson made up his mind to approve the European Army in principle; Adenauer was then informed that the American government was now seeking this solution. Then, in the Paris negotiations, Schuman accepted the incorporation into the European Army of all units earmarked for the defense of Europe as well as the recruiting of

---

39 Cf. Loth, *Sozialismus*, pp. 287–289.
40 On the negotiations up to the conclusion of the EDC Treaty in May of 1952, Klaus A. Maier, "Die internationalen Auseinandersetzungen um die Westintegration der Bundesrepublik Deutschland und um ihre Bewaffnung im Rahmen der Europäischen Verteidigungsgemeinschaft," in: *Anfänge westeuropäischer Sicherheitspolitik 1945–1956*, vol. 2: *Die EVG-Phase*, Munich: Oldenbourg, 1990, pp. 1–234, here pp. 29–124; Wilhelm Meier-Dörnberg, "Die Planung des Verteidigungsbeitrags der Bundesrepublik Deutschland im Rahmen der EVG," *ibid.*, pp. 605–756, here pp. 630–670.

German soldiers by West German authorities. Also, he no longer insisted on a veto over a West German defense ministry. Lastly, at a foreign ministers conference of the three Occupying Powers from 10 to 14 September in Washington, he also gave up his resistance to integration at the division level. In return, Acheson dispensed with the demand that West German troops be mustered before the European Defense Community (EDC) had come into existence. Adenauer, who wanted both sovereignty and West German troops before the conclusion of the necessarily-complex EDC negotiations, had to come to terms with the fact that the removal of the occupation statute was bound up with West German entry into the EDC.[41]

With this late success of the Pleven Plan, the problem of the political federation of Europe posed itself once again with great stridency: If the European Defense Ministry was to function, a European political authority had to be created to which it would be subordinated. In any event, that was the conclusion to which Italian Prime Minister Alcide De Gasperi came over the course of the summer of 1951. Not only did a purely military community seem impracticable to him but also problematic given the low enthusiasm for defense matters among the Italian people. Furthermore, he feared a Franco-German hegemony within the defense community; and that was a sufficient reason itself for pursuing a supranational orientation. At the first foreign ministers conference of the six EDC negotiation partners on 11 December 1951 in Strasbourg, he thus argued for the beginning of talks on the creation of a political community.

Meanwhile, Churchill's victory in parliamentary elections on 25 October had kindled new hopes of British participation in the unification project. As a consequence, the Dutch and Belgian governments rejected any thought of political expansion of the defense community; and Schuman too held back with an eye toward fluctuating majorities in France. Adenauer, for whom equal status and quick integration into the West were more important than the further development of the Political Community, mediated a dilatory compromise: The Parliamentary Assembly of the future defense community was given the task of "concerning itself with the creation of a European organization of a federal or confederal character." At the next gathering of the six ministers from 27 to 30 December, it was specified that the assembly should present proposals for preparing such an organization within six months after meeting; these proposals were then to be reviewed by a government conference. With this agreement, which was then incorporated as Article 38 of the EDC Treaty, the project of a Political Community

---

41 Cf. the conference protocols in FRUS 1951, III, Part 1, pp. 1228ff.; the Allied memorandum for Adenauer, *ibid.*, Part 2, pp. 1528ff.

was definitively linked to the EDC, although the decision on its coming into existence was postponed for the time being.[42]

In further negotiations, the Benelux representatives prevailed with extensive cuts in the supranational character of the treaty construction. In place of a European defense minister, there was to be a nine-member commission whose independent activities were limited to carrying out the current operations of armament and supply. Almost all essential decisions, from the issuing of regulations to the drafting of a budget, were made dependent on unanimous votes of the Council of Ministers. In regard to operations, the troop commands were subordinated to the NATO headquarters for Europe; the supreme Allied commander was accorded wide-ranging inspection rights and in the event of a crisis was also to be entrusted with supreme command of EDC troops by the Council of Ministers. Due to French resistance, Adenauer was unable to push through the Federal Republic's direct membership in NATO, which would have been consistent with the close linkage of these two organizations; the other treaty partners and the US too did continue to seek it, however. For the transition period, the Federal Republic was accorded the right to demand joint sessions of the NATO Council and the EDC Council of Ministers if its security were threatened. In this form, which had been in the offing since the EDC foreign ministers meeting of 26 and 27 January 1952 in Paris, the Treaty on the European Defense Community was signed in the French capital on 27 May 1952.[43]

The absence of any supranational integration attached to this construction drove the French to demand from the British and the Americans additional guarantees against German high-handedness. They succeeded in that the British government extended the pledges of assistance that it had made in the Brussels Pact to include the Federal Republic and Italy, and that the British and Americans agreed to a Three-Power Declaration in which the Allies put forth their intention to maintain troops on the European continent and to regard any violation to the integrity of the EDC as a threat to their own security.[44] Beyond this, full

---

[42] Protocols of the conference of 11 Dec. 1951 in Walter Lipgens, "EVG und politische Föderation. Protokolle der Konferenz der Außenminister der an den Verhandlungen über eine europäische Verteidigungsgemeinschaft beteiligten Länder am 11. Dezember 1951," in: *Vierteljahrshefte für Zeitgeschichte* 32 (1984), pp. 637–688; the communiqué of 30 Dec. 1951 in: *Europa. Dokumente*, vol. 2, pp. 829ff. On Gasperi's initiative, cf. Ralf Magagnoli, *Italien und die Europäische Verteidigungsgemeinschaft. Zwischen europäischem Credo und nationaler Machtpolitik*, Frankfurt am Main: Peter Lang, 1999, pp. 91–122; Daniela Preda, *Alcide De Gasperi federalista europeo*, Bologna: Il Mulino, 2004, pp. 613–639.

[43] Text in: *Europa. Dokumente*, vol. 2, pp. 836–886; on military structure, also Meier-Dörnberg, "Planung," pp. 698–714.

[44] Text in: FRUS 1952–54, V, Part 1, pp. 686ff.

sovereignty was denied the Federal Republic: In the "general treaty" replacing the occupation statute, which was signed in Bonn a day before the EDC Treaty, the Allies reserved the right to proclaim a state of emergency, the right to station troops, as well as all rights regarding "Germany as a whole."[45] Likewise, according to the terms of the EDC Treaty, the Federal Republic was forbidden to produce ABC weapons, long-range missiles, military aircraft, and warships. With these terms and above all with the guarantee declaration, it was at base NATO that was the actual control organ of West German armament. For the time being, the EDC ministers could only demonstrate European independence by unanimously contradicting the deployment orders of the American supreme commander.

British and American declarations of intent clearly did not suffice to eliminate French worries. Hence, the Pinay government procrastinated until the last moment in signing the treaty at all. Immediately after the signing, voices demanded supplements—either expansion to a Political Community or a British presence guarantee, perhaps British entry too. Many even wanted both at the same time, and many sought an escape from the unpleasant situation in which they found themselves (thanks to the decision for a Western military alliance), by once again looking at the possibilities for an arrangement with the Soviet Union. The Socialists began to split over the issue of agreeing to the treaty, and the Gaullists, who had advocated a political confederation with national contingents, announced their opposition. After that, a parliamentary majority for ratification of the treaty was not to be expected. The government, which was itself divided over the question of signing, consoled itself with the thought that it had at least succeeded in linking the creation of West German troops and the release of the Federal Republic from the occupation statute to the ratification of the EDC Treaty: That gave French authorities breathing room in which they could seek an exit from this unpleasant situation. They therefore decided to await the result of the ratification debate in the West German Bundestag and the outcome of the American presidential election in November before having parliament grapple with the treaty.[46]

In order to force an exit in the direction of Europe, De Gasperi now suggested that the Parliamentary Assembly of the ECSC—which according to the terms of the

---

[45] Text in: *Die Vertragswerke von Bonn und Paris. Dokumente und Berichte des Europa-Archivs*, vol. 10, Frankfurt am Main, 1952, pp. 1ff.

[46] Raymond Poidevin, "Frankreich und das Problem der EVG: Nationale und internationale Einflüsse (Sommer 1951 bis Sommer 1953)," in: Hans-Erich Volkmann and Walter Schwengler (eds.), *Die Europäische Verteidigungsgemeinschaft. Stand und Probleme der Forschung*, Boppard: Boldt, 1985, pp. 101–124, here pp. 114–118; Wilfried Loth, "Die EVG und das Projekt der Europäischen Politischen Gemeinschaft," in: Hudemann, Kaelble, and Schwabe (eds.), *Europa im Blick der Historiker*, pp. 191–201, here pp. 194–196.

EDC Treaty was in the future also to function as the EDC Assembly with the incorporation of nine new deputies from among the three largest member countries—should right then be given the task of working out a draft treaty for the founding of a Political Community as envisioned in Article 38. Schuman agreed and was then able to convince his fellow ministers of the usefulness of this attempt to take the wind out of the sails of the critics of the treaty. At the Paris meeting of the six foreign ministers from 23 to 25 July, Gasperi and Schuman together made a motion for early implementation of the process provided for in Article 38. They did not initially prevail in this because there had in the meantime been parliamentary elections in the Netherlands, and Stikker did not want to forestall the future government on this issue. At the constituent session of the ECSC Council of Ministers on 10 September in Luxembourg, the Benelux representatives then also agreed. After more than two years of vain efforts to push through the Stikker Plan within the framework of the OEEC, the Dutch government was now ready to concentrate its customs union project on the community of the Six. This contributed to the fact that the British-oriented Stikker lost his office and that with the appointment of his successor, Johan Willem Beyen, there was now someone in the post who saw in the planned EDC expansion a chance for advancing economic integration in the area of the Six. Beyen therefore parried the Franco-Italian initiative with a demand to investigate the possibilities for economic integration as well. There were no fundamental objections to that, and so the ministers gave the assembly an expanded assignment along those lines.[47]

After the nine additional deputies were brought onboard, the ECSC Parliament on 13 September declared itself an "*ad hoc* Assembly" and created an "*ad hoc* Commission," which was to work out a draft of the "statue of the European Community." This commission followed the draft of a hastily-established Study Commission of the European Movement (featuring the decisive participation of Spinelli) to the extent that it advocated the establishment of an Executive Council to be checked by a bicameral parliament made up of a directly-elected popular chamber and a senate elected by the national parliaments. Differing from the recommendation of the Study Commission, the *ad hoc* Commission reduced the competencies of the Executive Council in essence to the sum of the competencies of the ECSC and the EDC Commission. The scope and the financing of the budget of the Community were to remain dependent on unanimous votes of the Council

---

[47] Richard T. Griffith and Alan S. Milward, "The Beyen Plan and the European Political Community," in: Werner Maihofer (ed.), *Noi si mura*, Florence: European University Institute, 1986, pp. 596–621; Magagnoli, *Italien*, pp. 135–148; Preda, *De Gasperi*, pp. 671–684; Anjo G. Harryvan, "In Pursuit of Influence. Aspects of the Netherlands' European Policy during the Formative Years of the European Economic Community," 1952–1973, Diss. EUI Florence, 2007, pp. 23–54.

of Ministers, likewise any expansion of its competencies into the realms of foreign or economic policy. At the initiative of the Dutch deputies, for whom the indicated path to an economic community was much too indefinite, a provision was added to the effect that one year after the treaty came into force, the Council of Ministers was to take measures to create a Common Market; and from the seventh year onward, decision-making was to be by majority rule. In this form, the draft was passed by the *ad hoc* assembly with fifty votes in favor and five abstentions on 10 March 1953.[48]

The fact that some thirty-one delegates were absent when the vote was taken—half of them known to be opponents of the draft—indicated however that the statute draft of the *ad hoc* Commission would not necessarily win a consensus. Beyen called an additional foreign ministers conference that took place on 24 and 25 February 1953. There, the Dutchman in fact made it clear that without a binding arrangement on economic integration—he was thinking especially of the creation of a customs union within a period of ten years—the EPC did not have a chance with either the Dutch government or the Dutch parliament. For its part, however, the French side wanted nothing to do with such a stipulation: There had been price increases following upon the boom stemming from the general military buildup. The price increases had in turn led to a dramatic worsening of the French balance of payments, and the French government had been forced to impose import restrictions in February of 1952; after that, it was more strongly convinced than ever that it could involve itself only in a controlled market integration. It regarded the French economy as too weak for a further advance, if only one leading into economic supranationality.[49] Bidault, who had replaced Schuman as foreign minister after the latter had come under fire due to the EDC Treaty,[50] thus insisted to Beyen that the arrangement of economic integration be reserved for a special treaty. Hence, the path to adopting the statute draft was blocked for the time being.

Moreover, it was the case that the engagement of the new French government on behalf of the Political Community diminished over time. The Gaullists,

---

[48] Text in: Lipgens, *45 Jahre*, pp. 335–360; on this and the following, cf. Magagnoli, *Italien*, pp. 175–205 and 221–236; Richard Griffith, *Europe's First Constitution. The European Political Community (1952–1954)*, London: Federal Trust, 2000; Seung-Ryeol Kim, *Der Fehlschlag des ersten Versuchs zu einer politischen Integration Westeuropas von 1951 bis 1954*, Frankfurt am Main: Peter Lang, 2000.

[49] Cf. Gérard Bossuat, "La vraie nature de la politique européenne de la France (1950–1957)," in: Gilbert Trausch (ed.), *Die Europäische Integration vom Schuman-Plan bis zu den Verträgen von Rom. Pläne und Initiativen, Enttäuschungen und Mißerfolge*, Baden-Baden: Nomos, 1993, pp. 191–230.

[50] Poidevin, *Schuman*, pp. 363–365.

on whom the government of René Mayer depended, regarded the competencies given to the EPC in the draft of the *ad hoc* assembly as insufficient; and thus they tended more and more toward a complete rejection of the EDC Treaty. In a press conference of 25 February, Charles de Gaulle concentrated his attacks on the loss of sovereignty that the EDC threatened to usher in. In light of this change of course, it seemed to make little sense to many members of the government to continue insisting on the Political Community.[51] Furthermore, with the death of Stalin on 5 March and the campaign of tension-reduction being pursued by his successors, hopes grew for an arrangement with the Soviet Union. There was no longer any question of ratifying the EDC Treaty in the eyes of a majority of deputies or the government before the chances of a settlement for all of Germany had been tested at a new summit called for by Churchill on 11 May. In this situation, Bidault thought it for the best that the EPC project be shelved for the time being. At the Paris meeting of the foreign ministers on 12 and 13 May, he agreed to the Belgian and Dutch demand for establishing an expert commission to examine the possibility of expanding the treaty into the economic realm. In light of the Franco-Dutch disagreement on the issue of the Economic Community, Adenauer—who had been pushing for limiting things to the sectors already agreed upon—was left with nothing.

After the fall of the Mayer government on 21 May, the French position hardened still further. The disputes about the EDC made it more difficult to form a government, but one was put together after fourteen days with Gaullist participation (and with the conservative Joseph Laniel as prime minister). The Gaullist ministers insisted that there not be an amalgamation of the High Authority and the EDC Commission into a new executive. The French representatives then declared at the expert conference, which convened in Rome on 22 September after a long delay, that a new executive without new areas of responsibility was undesirable. At the same time, they were adamant in rejecting any form of automatic integration in the economic realm. Because the Dutch representatives for their part were not willing to give up on the package deal of the customs union and the Political Community, the fate of the EPC was sealed: The experts could not reach agreement on the main issues and therefore gave the negotiation package back to the foreign ministers after fourteen days. At their meeting of 26 to 28 November in The Hague, the foreign ministers only appointed a new study commission that was to produce an audit report by 15 April 1954. Shortly before this deadline, the foreign ministers passed a resolution at the initiative of Bidault to the effect that further

---

51 Against a widespread cliché that depicts the Gaullists as strict opponents of political supranationality, it must be explicitly stated that this change of course occurred only after the passage of the *ad hoc* draft.

handling of the EPC complex be postponed until after the ratification of the EDC. On 4 May 1954, they then announced that the High Authority of the ECSC and EDC Commission were to be subject to the oversight of an elected parliament; this was a minimal consensus.[52]

Somewhat more successful than the efforts on behalf of the Political Community was Mayer's attempt to wrestle from the Allies "supplemental protocols" to the EDC Treaty that would again expand the national share of control over the armed forces. In the protocols signed on 24 March 1953, the treaty partners conceded that France could withdraw forces from the European Army if they were needed to deal with a crisis situation overseas. Furthermore, the production, export, and import of war material for use overseas was not to be subject to any limitations from the EDC Commission; and the officer corps made up of national and European contingents was to continue to constitute a unified whole. Yet, neither the complete control over the armed forces nor the autonomy in arms production that the French proposals had been aiming for was achieved. The path to building a national nuclear force remained barred, and there was no lever available for indefinitely extending the transition period in which the French veto in the Council of Ministers could block the construction of a supranational armed force. The chiefs of the general staff characterized the concessions as insufficient and then made their resistance to the EDC construction clear in public.[53]

Mayer's efforts to achieve a "satisfactory" settlement of the Saar issue remained completely unsuccessful; this was the third precondition made by the Gaullists for their agreement to the EDC Treaty, after the Political Community and the supplementary protocol. Indeed, Adenauer was fundamentally willing to see an Europeanization of the Saar and with it to sacrifice the demand that the region be incorporated into the Federal Republic. Under pressure from nationalist opposition in his own ranks, however, he had to insist on quick and fundamental change in the conditions regarding the Saar, especially on permitting parties that would fight the Franco-Saarland economic union. Given that the Gaullists understood a satisfactory settlement of the Saar issue to be a codification of the economic union, there was no room for negotiation here; Mayer sought in vain to move Adenauer to take up negotiations with the Saar government. He had just as little success in his attempt to gain US support for French policy on the Saar: John Foster Dulles, who became secretary of state after Eisenhower's election victory

---

[52] Cf. *Europa. Dokumente*, vol. 1, pp. 604.
[53] Pierre Guillen, "Die französische Generalität, die Aufrüstung der Bundesrepublik und die EVG 1950–1954," in: Hans-Erich Volkmann and Walter Schwengler (eds.), *Die Europäische Verteidigungsgemeinschaft. Stand und Probleme der Forschung*, Boppard: Boldt, 1985, pp. 125–157, here pp. 155ff.; Poidevin, "*Frankreich*", pp. 119–124.

in November of 1952, believed—in a striking misjudgment of the French psyche—that he could move the French to ratify the treaty through pressure rather than through accommodation.⁵⁴

Nor was there any success in efforts to move the British and American allies to make more hard-and-fast guarantees. Churchill and Eden did indeed pledge the close military cooperation of British European units with the EDC and also consultations before the withdrawal of British troops from the European continent. They were not however willing to make binding statements on the strength of British contingents or even allow the EDC a veto over withdrawals, as Bidault was demanding. Eisenhower and Dulles rejected an increase of the term of the Atlantic Alliance from the agreed-upon twenty years to the fifty of the EDC and neither could a substantial increase in American financial assistance for French defense be won from them. It was not only the British vote against supra-nationality and the well-known restrictive attitude of the American Congress but also financial bottlenecks that stood in the way of increased British and American engagement. Eden was greatly worried over whether British engagement on the Continent could be maintained in its existing scope; Eisenhower was even firmly resolved to cut the American presence in Europe drastically if the EDC and along with it a German contribution to defense were realized.⁵⁵

Instead of making approval of the EDC easier, the "New Look" in the American conception of defense, which was being discussed more and more openly in the autumn of 1953, increased aversion to the Europeanization of the French defense contribution in a double way: Firstly, the apparent inclination of the US to reduce its presence in Europe made Paris shrink back from having the creation of the European Army give impetus to that feared disengagement. Secondly and above all, the increased American recourse to nuclear weapons awakened the need for France itself to become a nuclear power: That promised not only to compensate for the distressing inadequacy of its armaments (which could not be eliminated due to constraints on financial resources) but also under closer consideration was the sole means of avoiding complete dependence on the US in terms of security policy. Given that no one could seriously imagine sharing responsibility for nuclear weapons with the Germans, these reflections inevita-

---

54 Cf. Wilfried Loth, "Die Saarfrage und die deutsch-französische Verständigung. Versuch einer Bilanz," in: *Zeitschrift für die Geschichte der Saargegend* 34/35 (1986–87), pp. 276–291, here pp. 286–288; Martin Kerkhoff, *Großbritannien, die Vereinigten Staaten und die Saarfrage 1945 bis 1954*, Stuttgart: Franz Steiner: 1996, pp. 188–202.
55 Cf. Maier, *Internationale Auseinandersetzungen*, pp. 125–190; Stephen F. Ambrose, "Die Eisenhower-Administration und die europäische Sicherheit 1953–1956," in: Bruno Thoss and Hans-Erich Volkmann (eds.), *Zwischen Kaltem Krieg und Entspannung. Sicherheits- und Deutschlandpolitik der Bundesrepublik im Mächtesystem der Jahre 1953–1956*, Boppard: Boldt, 1988, pp. 25–34.

bly led to the desire for a national nuclear force. From this perspective, the EDC seemed to be nothing less than an instrument of American hegemony.[56]

The stubbornness with which Dulles demanded the ratification of the EDC Treaty—most spectacularly with the threat of an "agonizing reappraisal" of the totality of America's European policy in the event that the EDC failed, a threat made during a press conference in Paris on 13 December 1953—served to strengthen this suspicion further and frequently also allowed it to arise where there was not yet any awareness of the strategic contexts. Together with the robust Cold War rhetoric of the Eisenhower administration and its refusal to support France militarily in the Indochina war or to help bring about negotiations, it produced an instinctive resistance to American impertinence, which often rose to the level of an intense anti-Americanism and which regarded the battle against the EDC as its most pressing goal. Specifically, it was the proponents of a "Third Power," who had long hesitated after the British rejection and the decision for West German rearmament, who now developed into the most determined opponents of an EDC during the winter of 1953-54. They saw in it an instrument of an aggressive American power politics that all in all threatened to bring about exactly the opposite of what had been fought for: Independence, détente, and incorporation of the Germans.

Resistance to ratification of the treaty therefore did not diminish after the Berlin foreign ministers conference of the four victorious powers from 25 January to 18 February 1954 had demonstrated the vanity of hopes for a Four-Power settlement of the German question. The realization grew that the arming of the Federal Republic within the framework of the Western security system was unavoidable, even if the Germans could negotiate an extensive removal of occupation restrictions in return. At the same time, there was less willingness to give up one's own freedom of action to a community that neither offered sufficient protection against the German danger nor was particularly plausible as an instrument of European self-assertion. A growing minority of the political public now, like the military, was coming to regard direct integration of the Federal Republic into NATO as the lesser evil. It seemed all the more acceptable when the prospect of a say in nuclear matters within the leadership ranks of the Western Alliance promised to guarantee a security advantage over the Federal Republic that had been vainly hoped for from the EDC.

---

56 Cf. Bidault's anxious statements at the Bermuda Conference of 4 to 8 Dec. 1953, FRUS 1952-54, V, Part 2, pp. 1799ff.; Guillen, «Französische Generalität,» pp. 155ff.; Aline Coutrot, "La politique atomique sous le gouvernement de Mendès France," in: François Bédarida and Jean-Pierre Rioux (eds.), *Pierre Mendès France et le Mendésisme*, Paris: Fayard, 1985, pp. 309-316.

Decisive for the failure of the EDC after the long deadlock was the spectacular defeat of French troops at Dien Bien Phu on 7 May 1954. France's American allies had refused to provide massive air support to help the French forces besieged by the Vietnamese. This drove the animus against the US to its zenith and at the same time made autonomous national armed forces, which apparently could alone be relied upon, seen more necessary than ever. The military weakness of France, which had now become clear in such a humiliating fashion, accentuated fears of the dynamism of the Germans. In French public opinion polls, the ranks of those opposing the treaty grew faster than those of its supporters (from twenty-one percent in May of 1953 to thirty-one percent in July of 1954, versus thirty and thirty-six percent for the supporters, with thirty-three percent undecided).[57] The foreign affairs committee of the National Assembly, to which the treaty had finally been presented, gave a negative recommendation by a vote of twenty-four to eighteen on 9 June. In the defense committee, voting on 18 June, the negative majority was even greater: twenty-nine to thirteen.

Pierre Mendès France, prime minister since that same 18 June (Laniel and Bidault had been toppled due to their hesitancy to pull French troops out of Indochina), nevertheless undertook a last effort to save the EDC. As he explained to Spaak and Dulles, in order to win over "sixty to eighty deputies" for the EDC from among the advocates of arming the Federal Republic at the national level,[58] he presented the EDC partners on 14 August with an "implementation protocol" approved by the Council of Ministers that amounted to a significant thinning of the EDC. According to this proposal, the principle of unanimity was to apply for the first eight years in the Council of Ministers as well as the Commission; NATO decisions affecting Europe were always to be made in joint sessions with the EDC Council of Ministers; the terms for which NATO and the EDC were in effect were to be harmonized; and the consequences of Article 38 were to fall by the wayside. Additionally, integration was to be limited to West German armed forces and Allied forces stationed in the Federal Republic, including British and American units. Also, the production of nuclear fuel for areas outside the "strategic exposed zone" would no longer be subject to required approval by the Commission.[59]

---

[57] Quoted in Jean-Pierre Rioux, "Französische öffentliche Meinung und EVG: Parteienstreit oder Schlacht der Erinnerungen?" in: Volkmann and Schwengler (eds.), *Europäische Verteidigungsgemeinschaft*, pp. 159–176, here pp. 168ff.
[58] Quoted from Maier, *Internationale Auseinandersetzungen*, pp. 190. On the decision-making process of the summer of 1954, *ibid.*, pp. 190–230; Georges-Henri Soutou, "La France, l'Allemagne et les accords de Paris," in: *Relations internationales*, No. 52, 1987, pp. 451–470.
[59] Text in: *Europa-Archiv* 9 (1954), pp. 6869ff.

These amendment proposals went too far for many EDC advocates, however. They correctly argued that the European finality of the treaty would thereby be totally lost. In order to prevent that, Schuman, Mollet, and others encouraged Adenauer to oppose the French proposals more or less openly; West German Special Minister Franz Josef Strauss even brought news back from Paris that a parliamentary majority could still be counted on for the EDC in its original form. More important for Adenauer than these assurances was the impression, factually incorrect, that Mendès France was aiming for an arrangement with the Soviet Union. In order to forestall that, the chancellor was only too glad to help work for the fall of the new prime minister. He could not completely exclude the danger of a failure of the treaty despite the confident reports from Paris, but the goal seemed worth the effort. Moreover, he knew that the US was on his side to such an extent that he trusted he would not fall any too hard if the French National Assembly rejected the treaty. The other treaty partners were just as unwilling to make concessions: The Dutch government wanted to remain open to the chances for an economic community via Article 38, and Spaak had once again assumed leadership of foreign affairs in the Belgian government. At the Brussels meeting of the foreign ministers from 19 to 22 August, Mendès France thus found himself faced with an almost solid front rejecting his proposals. The conference was broken off with the Six having established nothing beyond their lack of agreement.

After this rebuff, Mendès France urgently wanted to ensure that with a failure of the EDC, France would not, as Dulles had threatened, be excluded from an "Atlantic" regulation of West German rearmament. He thus called for a conference of three with the British and Americans. Immediately after the Brussels conference, he sought out Churchill in order to win the Briton for an association of the UK with the six EDC countries in a "modified structure within the framework of NATO." Churchill once again urged that the EDC be ratified and in other respects played things more or less close to the vest; Mendès France took from his statements the idea that the British were not to be had for a solution without France. Reassured in this way, he now believed he could risk the failure of the EDC. Nevertheless, he did support the motion of the EDC advocates to postpone the ratification debate in the National Assembly so as to be able to negotiate at a conference with the British and Americans once again over the French amendment proposals. However, he offered no further resistance when, against this last attempt to save the project, EDC opponents brought a motion to remove the treaty completely from the agenda. That motion was then adopted on 30 August by a vote of 319 to 264.

This ignominious burial demonstrated that Mendès France had correctly read the majority situation within parliament. Many EDC opponents had voted against the removal motion only in order to be able to present their reasons for rejecting it. Consequently, the oppositional majority was even larger than the vote had indicated; and an engaged advocacy of the treaty, as Schuman and Adenauer had wanted, would no longer have saved the Defense Community. Overall, however, it was by no means the case that the maneuvering room of the political class was limited by the pressure of entrenched public opinion: Only in the very week of the parliamentary vote were there more French people voicing opposition to the treaty than support for it (thirty-six versus thirty-one percent); there had clearly been influence from the mobilization of national resentment on the part of EDC opponents. A week later, the percentage of supporters was once again larger (thirty-four to thirty-three percent)—just as it had been during the whole period of public dispute over the treaty! The fundamental majority for a united Europe, which had amounted to some seventy percent in May of 1953, still oscillated between fifty-five and sixty-four percent in the spring of 1955.[60]

To that extent, it is correct that the flight forward into security-policy supra-nationality had failed not least of all because of the lack of consistency and decisiveness on the part of the actors involved.[61] It must also be added that the project was doubly impeded: firstly, by emotional barriers that stood in the way of rearming the Germans and, secondly, by the development of the bipolar deterrence system, which no longer admitted of an autonomous European defense. Given this combination of hindrances, it is not at all surprising that the interest in European autonomy lost out. Rather, what gives one pause is that a large portion of the political forces in France too clung so long to the project of a European defense community: This indicates that the willingness to work on the Europe of the Six had in the meantime grown—even if it did not meet with the ideal conceptions of many who envisioned a united Europe.

For this reason, the damage that the failure of the EDC had caused was not as severe as distraught EDC advocates such as the very embittered Adenauer thought in their initial consternation. To be sure, the military protection of the Germans would now certainly be definitively assumed by NATO. The bundling of Western European security-policy interests became even more difficult than it already had been. And it was not only in France that the tendency grew to strive for national ways of securing independence. Yet, the feeling for the unsatisfactory nature of such solutions remained rather vivid, likewise the mutual understanding among

---

60 Rioux, *Französische öffentliche Meinung*, pp. 168–170. Rioux's thesis that the EDC "was conceived without taking the popular mood into account" and had to fail because it revived German trauma (pp. 175ff.) is not supported at all by the adduced data!
61 According to Walter Lipgens, "Die Bedeutung des EVG-Projekts für die politische Einigungsbewegung," in: Volkmann and Schwengler (eds.), *Europäische Verteidigungsgemeinschaft*, pp. 9–30.

the European partners, which had grown on all sides over the course of the protracted EDC negotiations. Above all, however, the consolidation of the Western alliance that stemmed from the overcoming of the EDC crisis would provide a solid foundation on which the project of European unification could be continued.

With the danger of a collapse of the Western security community confronting them, all the negotiation partners now found themselves willing to make concessions that they had always previously avoided. Mendès France accepted the direct entry of the Federal Republic into NATO and the elimination of the Allies' reserved rights regarding a state of emergency in a revised general treaty. Adenauer conceded Mendès France a Saar statute stipulating monetary and economic ties to France until definitive settlement in a peace treaty, thereby linking an Europeanization of the Saar to progress on the economic integration of Europe. Eden granted the right to the Brussels Pact—now expanded into the Western European Union (WEU) with the entry of the Federal Republic and Italy—to determine the scope of the British troop presence on the European continent via majority vote. And Dulles, who in the event of a failure of the supranational defense organization had already been looking to return to a "peripheral" defense conception, made up his mind to transfer to the WEU the guarantee of the presence of American troops that had been made to the EDC. All these concessions came about after dramatic disputes,[62] but given that all participants understood that they were condemned to success, they succeeded in agreeing on a compromise package in relatively short order. The "Treaties of Paris" were thus signed on 23 October 1954.[63]

After some delay, attributable not least of all to the demand by Mendès France that a supranational armaments agency of the WEU remain an open issue, the French National Assembly ratified this compromise on 30 December 1954 by the relative majority of 287 to 260, with seventy abstentions. On 27 February 1955, the Bundestag also agreed to it—likewise after intense disputes among the West German public that once again endangered the compromise. Yet, exactly because success had been so difficult to achieve, it was the case that after the ratification processes, no one dared call into question the structure of internal Western relations established by the Treaties of Paris.

---

[62] Cf. Paul Noack, *Das Scheitern der Europäischen Verteidigungsgemeinschaft. Entscheidungsprozesse vor und nach dem 30. August 1954*, Düsseldorf: Droste, 1977, pp. 93–138 and 151–163; and Rolf Steininger, "Das Scheitern der EVG und der Beitritt der Bundesrepublik zur NATO," in: *Aus Politik und Zeitgeschichte* B 17, 1985, pp. 3–18.
[63] Texts in: *Europa. Dokumente*, vol. 1, pp. 354ff.; vol. 2, pp. 988ff.

The Difficult "*Relance*"

With the failure of the EDC in August of 1954, the project of a political Europe receded into the distance for the time being. Essential security functions were now to be carried out by NATO. In an upsurge of emotion, a group decisive for making a majority in France had turned against the supranational principle; and in the remaining countries of the Community of the Six, the French rejection had had a demoralizing effect. Yet, the problem clearly still remained of the independence of the Europeans *vis-à-vis* the US as the leading power, though under the changed circumstances of inclusion in the nuclear security community. Also, the problem of incorporating the Germans, which was ever more clearly a problem of incorporating German economic strength, had not yet been satisfactorily resolved. The problem of economic unification became more urgent, not only because the sectoral integration of coal and steel was oriented toward expansion but also because there was a growing number of firms and branches urging the elimination of hindrances to trade. In this situation, what mattered more than ever was skillful crisis management: Only if the remaining interests in unification were successfully bundled was there a prospect of overcoming the hurdles stemming from the consolidation of nation-state structures that had in the meantime been achieved.

In the search for unification projects that could be implemented without major resistance and were therefore suitable for overcoming the paralysis of the integration process resulting from the EDC shock, the High Authority of the ECSC firstly aimed for the extension of the union to other energy branches and to transport policy. This seemed logical because coal was in many ways linked to other promising sources of energy and because the pricing of coal and steel was to a great extent dependent on arrangements involving transport costs. The German vice president of the High Authority, Franz Etzel, who had floated the idea of extension, therefore hoped that it would not be any too difficult to find the necessary majorities for it in the parliaments of the Six. On 2 December 1954, the Parliamentary Assembly of the ECSC voiced its approval for an extension of ECSC competencies into the realms of gas, electricity, nuclear energy, and transport.[64]

Jean Monnet placed his hopes especially on the integration of nuclear energy. It seemed urgent to him for no fewer than three reasons: firstly, to meet the growing energy demand of France and the other European countries cheaply and at the same make them independent of oil imports that gobbled up foreign

---

[64] Cf. Pierre Gerbet, "La 'relance' européenne jusqu'à la conférence de Messine," in: Enrico Serra (ed.), *Il rilancio dell'Europa e i Trattati di Roma*, Milan: Émile Bruylant, 1989, pp. 61–91; also on the following.

currency; secondly, in order to develop nuclear weapons independent of the US; and thirdly, to keep the civilian use of nuclear energy by the Federal Republic under supervision (after the elimination of the occupation statute, such use was no longer forbidden). Given that there were not yet any established national nuclear industries and the lobbyists of the French nuclear energy commission realized that they could not accomplish their ambitious plans unilaterally there was no appreciable opposition in sight. Instead, concentration on this energy sector promised to unleash new enthusiasm for Europe; it was quite clear that the future belonged to this sector and that this new initiative could bring it a significant step forward after so few successful efforts aimed at securing independence up to that point. After Louis Armand of the French atomic energy commission convinced him that the creation of a European atomic energy pool was indispensable if France and the other Europeans wanted to keep pace in the third industrial revolution, Monnet decided to seek the creation of Europe's own atomic authority alongside and before the expansion of the ECSC.

Unlike in 1950, Monnet could not mobilize the French government to get this project underway. After the fall of Robert Schuman in late 1952, Monnet no longer had direct access to the leaders responsible for French foreign policy. Pierre Mendès France, French prime minister in the crisis year 1954, even sought to have him replaced as head of the High Authority at the end of his first term. In order to forestall such a loss of confidence, Monnet declared on 9 November 1954 that he would not be available for a second term so as to be able to devote himself wholly to the struggle for the development of the Community without being bound by government directives. He offered the new unification initiative to Spaak, who agreed to it—though in fact only after Mendès France had fallen from power and after the Council of the Republic (as the second house of parliament) had confirmed the vote of the National Assembly for the Treaties of Paris. On 2 April 1955, he sent identically-worded letters to Konrad Adenauer, Italian Foreign Minister Gaetano Martino, and Antoine Pinay, who had assumed the post of foreign minister in the French government of Edgar Faure that had been formed in February. In this communication, Spaak proposed that a delegate conference of the Six be summoned to discuss the expansion of economic integration. As goals, he cited the expansion of ECSC responsibilities over the other energy sectors as well as transport, along with the establishment of a special organization of the ECSC for the peaceful use of nuclear energy.

The reaction to this initiative was not particularly encouraging. Dutch Foreign Minister Jan Willem Beyen saw in the expansion of sectoral integration new hindrances to the Common Market that the Dutch government was seeking; therefore, he immediately developed a counterproposal. In a memorandum submitted to Spaak on 4 April, the Dutchman condemned sectoral integration as an integration hostile to consumers at the cost of non-integrated economic sectors, which would more likely lead to new cartels than to increases in overall economic productivity. Instead, he wanted to suggest to the foreign ministers of the Six the establishment of a "supranational community" that "via the path of a customs union was to progress to the realization of an economic union." More clearly than during the talks on the European Political Community in 1952–53, Beyen was now aware that a supranational orientation of the Economic Community was necessary from the beginning, not only in order to cushion economic modernization but also to develop a feeling of responsibility for the Europeans' common future. Given that in the meantime the engagement of the Dutch public for European unification had intensified, he was largely able to prevail with this position in the cabinet *vis-à-vis* the still-reserved Prime Minister Willem Drees.[65]

Conversely, French opposition to the Common Market had increased even further: Added to the fear of the sell-off of economic sectors that were not yet competitive there was now also the widespread aversion to supra-nationality. With the danger of another parliamentary rejection in mind, the Faure government was wary of embracing a project that threatened to draw the unanimous protest of all trade and workers' organizations. The sole portion that the government did endorse, after some hesitation, was the plan for a community for civilian use of nuclear energy, which was promoted by both the planning commission and the nuclear energy commission. The stipulation that nuclear weapons were to remain the responsibility of individual countries was retained; an isotope separation facility to be erected jointly would only secure the supply of enriched uranium necessary for nuclear arms.[66] Faure only spoke vaguely about the collectivization of the other energy sectors and transportation.

The West German government was not enthusiastic about either the Common Market or the Atomic Community. Economy Minister Ludwig Erhard saw in the customs union of the Six only a statist impediment to a worldwide system of free trade that suited the export interests of the West German economy. Special Minister Franz Josef Strauss (who was entrusted with responsibility for nuclear issues in October of 1955) preferred cooperation with the far more technically-advanced British and Americans to an atomic community that clearly would be of primary benefit to France. Chancellor Adenauer, who viewed the integration of the Federal Republic into the West as still much too uncertain, was keenly in favor of continuing political integration so as to secure West German integration over

---

[65] Anjo G. Harryvan and Albert E. Kersten, "The Netherlands, Benelux and the relance européenne 1954–1955," *ibid.*, pp. 125–157.
[66] Pierre Guillen, "La France et la négociation du Traité d´Euratom," in: *Relations internationales* 44, 1985, pp. 391–412.

the long term. However, he feared that economic integration would not be of any help in reaching that goal: In light of divergent economic interests, efforts toward convergence in this area threatened to strengthen resistance to integration in both France and the Federal Republic.[67] He prevailed with his ECSC partners in postponing the foreign ministers conference (which was to discuss the Belgian initiative) until the Treaties of Paris had come into force; and he let Spaak and Monnet know that he considered their initiative "premature."[68]

Given the multifarious opposition, Monnet once again decided to take the bull by the horns. A conversation with Carl Friedrich Ophüls, leader of the Europe division of the Foreign Office in Bonn, had made clear to him that the consent of the West German government to an economic community would indeed be easier to achieve than to an atomic community. Monnet then sought to win over Spaak and Beyen for combining the proposals for expanding the sectoral integration and the plans for a Common Market. The prospect of a Common Market was to move the Dutch and the Germans to participate in sectoral integration as well; at the same time, realization of the Atomic Community was intended to ease French opposition to the Economic Community. In a draft of a common declaration of the Six that his assistant Pierre Uri revised for him on 13 April, he specified that the delegate conference proposed by Spaak for expanding the tasks of the Community should work out treaty texts "in the areas of transport, energy, and nuclear energy" and "in a second step the program and the terms for a general integration of the economy" should be determined. With an eye to French resistance, he hastened to add that there of course must be transition regulations regarding the Economic Community, and that there must be a social fund along with an investment fund in order to shape the unification in a socially-bearable way. He recommended himself for the chairmanship of the conference; he also offered to

---

[67] In his memoirs, he gives as the reason for his reluctance only the fear that economic integration could distract from political integration: Konrad Adenauer, *Erinnerungen 1955–1959*, Stuttgart: Deutsche Verlags-Anstalt, 1967, p. 27. That he had in mind opposition in France and the Federal Republic is seen in his behavior during the EPC negotiations.

[68] Cf. Hanns Jürgen Küsters, "Adenauers Europapolitik in der Gründungsphase der Europäischen Wirtschaftsgemeinschaft," in: *Vierteljahrshefte für Zeitgeschichte* 31 (1983), pp. 646–673; Wilfried Loth, "Deutsche Europa-Konzeptionen in der Gründungsphase der EWG," in: Serra (ed.), *Rilancio*, pp. 585–602; Wilfried Loth, "Deutsche und französische Interessen auf dem Weg zu EWG und Euratom," in: Andreas Wilkens (ed.), *Deutsch-französische Wirtschaftsbeziehungen 1945–1960*, Sigmaringen: Jan Thorbecke, 1997, pp. 171–187; Mathieu L. L. Segers, *Deutschlands Ringen mit der Relance. Die Europapolitik der BRD während der Beratungen und Verhandlungen über die Römischen Verträge*, Frankfurt am Main: Peter Lang, 2008, pp. 96–99 and 113–116.

remain in office as president of the High Authority if the governments embraced this *"relance."*[69]

In terms of his own person, he had gone too far here. Beyen, who discussed the draft on 23 April together with Spaak, struck the name Monnet from the submission out of consideration for the French government; the French then decided to nominate René Mayer for the office of president. Beyen also insisted on striking the reference to the ECSC and the mention of an adaptation fund. In principle, however, he accepted the compromise suggested by Spaak and then won over his cabinet. It was then possible to communicate the revised Uri memorandum to the other ECSC partners on 18 May as a joint proposal of the Benelux governments. Parallel to this, Faure signaled that his government could also support the compromise: On the fringes of the Atlantic Council meeting of 9 to 11 May, he assured his ECSC colleagues that the Common Market would not fail because of France. After the Benelux proposal was already on the table, the West German government fundamentally accepted the idea of a Common Market: In its answer of 27 May, it spoke in favor of a progressive liberalization of trade and capital movement among the Six, linked with the free movement of labor, the establishment of rules for competition, and the creation of an investment fund.[70]

Yet, that was not sufficient for the success of the undertaking. Bonn's memorandum said nothing about the institutions that were to regulate sectoral or horizontal integration; in concrete terms, it only proposed the establishment of a consultative organ within the ECSC that was to present the Council of Ministers with proposals for the configuration of "economic cooperation." The French government did not present a memorandum at all and thus left more open as to the framework and the time frame in which it would accept the continuation of economic integration. In order to avoid the danger of a failure of the initiative, Beyen helped push a proposal to hold an expert conference first, which, independent of government instructions, would review all the possibilities for economic integration; the report of this commission would then serve as the basis for the treaty negotiations. Spaak added to this proposal by suggesting that an established "political personality" function as general secretary of the expert group so

---

69 Text excerpts in Gerbet, *La "relance,"* pp. 79ff. Cf. also the report by Pierre Uri in Serra (ed.), *Rilancio*, pp. 166ff.
70 Text of the Benelux Memorandum as well as the Italian and West German replies in *L´Année politique 1955*, pp. 714–718, on the French reaction, Edgar Faure, *Mémoires II*, Paris: Plon, 1984, p. 211; on the origins of the West German memorandum, Hanns Jürgen Küsters, *Die Gründung der Europäischen Wirtschaftsgemeinschaft*, Baden-Baden: Nomos, 1982, pp. 112–119; Segers, *Deutschlands Ringen*, pp. 117–127.

that it did not end up suffering the same unfruitful confrontation of irreconcilable viewpoints that had been the case with the EPC expert rounds.[71]

In fact, at the Conference of Messina where the six foreign ministers met from 1 to 3 June 1955, agreement was reached only on this minimal step. After Pinay had rejected a binding commitment to the Common Market and after Walter Hallstein, who had to represent Adenauer, had rejected the creation of new institutions, the accompanying officials were compelled to declare on the evening of the second day of negotiations that there had been no agreement at all. In great haste, in a night session following dinner and a ballet, a declaration was passed that listed the integration goals of the Benelux memorandum and of the West German memorandum as subjects for study and commissioned a group of experts under the leadership of a "political personality" to examine them. As Beyen had suggested, the British government was to be invited to participate in the conversations of the experts; representatives of existing European institutions would also be brought in as needed.[72] That did not seem to be much. When the ministers left the session at four in the morning, officials and journalists present had "the impression that they were interested in the sunrise over Mount Etna rather than full of admiration for their work."[73] In any event, the decisions put the governments under a certain pressure to act, pressure that they could not so easily avoid if the committee were once to reach common viewpoints.

The pressure coming from the decision at Messina became all the greater when as a follow-up to the conference, the governments reached agreement by diplomatic means that Spaak should be appointed chairman of the committee of experts. The man himself had not sought this position because he saw difficulties in reconciling it with the office of Belgian foreign minister. After the job had become his, however, his firm and independent leadership of the talks ensured that the delegates, some of whom he knew from the ECSC work, grew to become a genuine expert group. Right at the beginning of the talks in early July in Brussels, he got approval for having the representatives of the High Authority continuously participate with an advisory voice in the work of the steering committee, while the representatives of the OEEC, the Council of Europe, and the European Conference of Transport Ministers would be brought in only as needed.

---

71 On this and the following, Harryvan and Kersten, *The Netherlands*, pp. 153–156; Segers, *Deutschlands Ringen*, pp. 127–135.

72 Text of the declaration in: *Europa. Dokumente*, vol. 3, pp. 1240–1242; on the course of the conference, also the reports of Jean-Charles Snoy et d'Oppuers, Max Kohnstamm, and Christian Calmes in Serra (ed.), *Rilancio*, pp. 168ff. and 175–178, as well as Brigitta Thomas, *Die Europa-Politik Italiens. Der Beitrag Italiens zur europäischen Einigung zwischen EVG und EG*, Baden-Baden: Nomos, 2005, pp. 71–81.

73 According to the report by Christian Calmes, *Rilancio*, p. 178.

After the four technical committees and four subcommittees had left a whole series of substantial questions open at the planned deadline, Spaak concentrated his work from November onward with the national delegation leaders. Also, with Pierre Uri and Hans von der Groeben, he brought in two more conceptually-gifted experts.[74] He indicated to the leader of the British delegation, which had up to that time participated as observers, that in future conversations only the unambiguous supporters of a customs union could take part. The British cabinet then made the decision on 11 November not to participate in the planned Common Market.[75]

In the smaller circle, there soon emerged a recommendation for a Common Market with external tariffs, rules of competition, and promotion of modernization; it was to be realized in three steps of four years each. This Common Market was to be directed by a Council of Ministers initially making decisions unanimously and by a Commission appointed by the Council of Ministers; the Commission was autonomously to oversee adherence to agreed-upon regulations. Both a mere free-trade zone and an expansion of the ECSC were rejected as unachievable and to an extent undesirable too. For its part, the French delegation under the leadership of Félix Gaillard opposed setting a binding timetable. Instead, the French sought flexible responses to developing economic conditions, harmonization of social costs, and a common investment fund to make it easier for underdeveloped branches of the economy and regions to catch up. Even when the representatives of the Federal Republic agreed in principle to the idea of promoting modernization, the French stuck by their opposition to a binding commitment to the integration program. Conversely, the Germans under the leadership of State Secretary Walter Hallstein showed little inclination to warm to the Atomic Community, which was being vigorously promoted by Gaillard. In late November, the negotiations thus ended in an impasse for which no quick solution was to be found. After Faure's government fell on 29 November, Spaak interrupted the work and then made efforts to move the British government to alter its decision; he

---

[74] On the conception of von der Groeben, having an instutitionally-regulated internal market in mind, see Jürgen Elvert, "Weichenstellungen für die Römischen Verträge – Akteure und Überlegungen der Bundesregierung 1955," in: *Integration* 30 (2007), pp. 301–312.

[75] Cf. the negotiation reports (though incomplete) in Küsters, *Gründung*, pp. 135–218, 232–251, and Michel Dumoulin, "Les travaux du Comité Spaak (juillet 1955 – avril 1956)," in: Serra (ed.), *Rilancio*, pp. 195–210; also the reports of Hans von der Groeben and Baron Snoy, *ibid.*, pp. 294–300; on the British stance, also Roger Bullen, "Britain and 'Europe' 1950–1957," *ibid.*, pp. 315–338, here p. 333–337.

believed that only in this way could French opposition to the Common Market be broken in the end.[76]

Clearly, Spaak's emphatic warnings that the Western Alliance would fall apart after Adenauer were only successful in making the Eden government refrain from attacking a customs union of the Six. A breakthrough in the negotiations of the Spaak Committee only came after Adenauer—with reference to his guideline competence as chancellor—had instructed his ministers on 19 January 1956 not to allow the talks to fail and after French President René Coty had on 31 January appointed in Guy Mollet as Faure's successor a figure who was likewise urgently interested in the success of the Messina project.[77] At a hastily-called foreign ministers conference of the Six on 11 and 12 February in Brussels, Spaak was now able to convince West German Foreign Minister Heinrich von Brentano to agree to the preparation of a recommendation for the Atomic Community. At the same time, the Belgian was able to win from French Foreign Minister Christian Pineau the concession that a recommendation for the Common Market would be prepared as well. Hence, the path was now clear for the vote on the fundamentals of both projects, and things progressed to such an extent by 9 March that Spaak was able to give Uri and von der Groeben the task of editing a summary report based on the prepared working papers. The result, which was ready four weeks later,[78] did run into opposition on both the German and the French sides once again; but the national delegation leaders then adopted the report on 20 March without major changes.[79]

Along with the basic principles of a Common Market, the proposal for an atomic community was thus now on the table, though the French delegates did have to accept some deletions to their conception. Euratom, as the new organization was to be named at the suggestion of Armand, was only to have control over the trade monopoly for nuclear fuel; the call for ownership rights to be transferred to the Community was not incorporated into the report. Research was only

---

[76] On this action, Paul-Henri Spaak, *Memoiren eines Europäers*, Hamburg: Hoffmann und Campe, 1969, pp. 309–314.

[77] On Adenauer, cf. his *Erinnerungen 1955–1959*, pp. 253–255; the letter to the ministers in Konrad Adenauer, *Briefe 1955–1957*, Berlin: Siedler, 1998, pp. 139–141; on Guy Mollet, the report of his Foreign Minister Christian Pineau in Serra (ed.), *Rilancio*, pp. 281–286; as well as François Lafon, *Guy Mollet. Itinéraire d'un socialiste controversé (1905–1975)*, Paris: Fayard, 2006, pp. 491–497.

[78] Uri and von der Groeben worked (while being shielded) at Cape Ferrat on the French Mediterranean coast, supported by Spaak's colleague Albert Hupperts and the committee secretariat official Giulio Guazzugli; cf. the report of Pierre Uri in Serra (ed.), *Rilancio*, pp. 305–307.

[79] The report was published in all the languages of the Community on 21 April 1956 by the secretariat of the Spaak Committee; a brief except from the German version is in Lipgens, *45 Jahre*, pp. 390–395.

to a lesser extent to be organized by the Community itself. Also, in the industrial application of the results of research, enterprises owned by the Community were only to play a subordinate role; instead of an atomic fund directing the buildup of industrial capacities, there would only be support for public and private enterprises via resources from the general investment fund of the Common Market.[80] In all its sections, the Spaak Report thus bore signs of the compromise between differing conceptions of economic policy and integration policy. One could see how difficult it had been to bring it about at all.[81]

The production of the Spaak Report did not however mean that the two new integration projects had turned the corner. Guy Mollet was indeed resolved to push through not only the Atomic Community but also the Economic Community so as to bind the Federal Republic to the West over the long term and help provide the Europeans with more autonomy from the leading power the US. He was the head of only a minority government, however, which also included Jacques Chaban-Delmas, a representative of the Gaullists; Mollet could not be any more certain of a parliamentary majority for the Common Market than his predecessor. Together with Foreign Minister Christian Pineau and Maurice Faure (general secretary of the Radical Party who had been appointed state secretary for European questions), Mollet thus sought to win over partner governments for passing the Euratom Treaty first and then, based on this success, hope to be able to bring about a change in public opinion in France to the benefit of the Common Market. "We had to create a kind of smokescreen," as Pineau later explained. "For us, Euratom was the smokescreen behind which the Common Market had hidden itself."[82]

The negotiation partners evinced little understanding for the mobilization strategy of the Mollet government. The West German government in particu-

---

80 On this negotiation thread, Peter Weilemann, *Die Anfänge der Europäischen Atomgemeinschaft. Zur Gründungsgeschichte von Euratom 1955–1957*, Baden-Baden: Nomos, 1983, pp. 31–47, 76–86.
81 Due to the many contradictions and open questions, one should certainly not characterize it as an "intrinsically closed concept for economic and atomic integration," in the words of Küsters, *Gründung*, p. 239.
82 Report at the colloquium in Rome, 25 to 28 March 1987, in: Serra (ed.), *Rilancio*, pp. 281–286, the quote pp. 282ff. Cf. also the account of Maurice Faure, esp. pp. 286–290; Pierre Guillen, "L' Europe remède à l'impuissance française? Le gouvernement Guy Mollet et la Négociation des traités de Rome (1955–1957)," in: *Revue d'histoire diplomatique* 102 (1988), pp. 319–335; idem., "La France et la négociation des traités de Rome: L' Euratom," in: Serra (ed.), *Rilancio*, pp. 513–524; Wilfried Loth, "Guy Mollet und die Entstehung der Römischen Verträge 1956–57," in: *Integration* 30 (2007), pp. 313–319; Maria Grazia Melchionni/Roberto Ducci, *La Genèse des traités de Rome*, Paris: Economica 2007 ; on Maurice Faure, also Bruno Riondel, "Itinéraire d'un fédéraliste: Maurice Faure," in: *Journal of European Integration History* 2 (1997), pp. 69–82.

lar was only willing to agree to the Atomic Community if the Common Market were realized at the same time. Faced with Erhard's opposition to the Economic Community and Strauss's opposition to the Atomic Community, Adenauer had already presented a package deal on the two entities in the cabinet meeting of 10 February; and he now was holding firm to it. He was too unfamiliar with his new French colleagues and was also too irritated by support for the demand for a package deal by West German industry to be able to push through the requisite flexibility in carrying out negotiations from the beginning. He feared that once the French had gotten the Atomic Community, they would reject the Economic Community once and for all; even greater opposition to the Messina initiative was then to be expected than was already visible.[83]

The Negotiations on Euratom and the European Economic Community

At the foreign ministers conference of the Six in Venice on 29 and 30 May, Pineau—with a heavy heart and without prior backup from his Council of Ministers—agreed to the beginning of talks on not only the Atomic Community but also the Economic Community, doing so because of Bonn's package deal.[84] Yet, he continued to seek to bring the Atomic Community to fruition before the Economic Community and specified three conditions that his government wanted for the passage of a treaty on the Common Market: Firstly, overseas territories were to be incorporated into the Common Market as a way of sharing the cost of their modernization rather than accelerating their break with the motherland by the erection of a tariff wall; this condition had especially been pushed by Socialist Oversees Minister Gaston Defferre. Secondly—and what Mollet's Socialist Party put the most emphasis on overall—social benefits and taxes in the Community were to be largely harmonized by the end of the first integration phase in order to avoid distortions of competition and prevent the undermining of social-welfare achievements by a market focused on promoting competition. Thirdly, the transition from the first phase to the second was not to occur automatically; instead, the governments were to determine the regulations for further phases only after

---

[83] *Die Kabinettsprotokolle der Bundesregierung* 1956, vol. 9, Munich: Oldenbourg, 1998, p. 191. Cf. Segers. *Deutschlands Ringen*, pp. 180–183; on the domestic political opposition, Loth, "Deutsche Europa-Konzeptionen," pp. 591–595.

[84] Cf. Segers, *Deutschlands Ringen*, pp. 208–211. "We had the impression, Maurice Faure and I, of letting ourselves in for a competition," according to Pineau in Serra (ed.), *Rilancio*, pp. 283. "What we had to avoid at all events was [another] non-ratification of a treaty."

the conclusion of the first phase. Over against the liberal integration concept of the free-market economists that would naturally be of benefit primarily to the Federal Republic, which was then experiencing a full-fledged boom, the French side thereby once more put up a political concept of steering that was to diminish the risks entailed by the opening of markets.[85]

In order to generate the necessary support in parliament for the project, the Mollet government organized a parliamentary debate on the Atomic Community in early July. It specified that France expressly held open the possibility of developing its own nuclear weapons; opponents of nuclear weapons and the West Germans, who did not want to promote the special position of the French any further with their resources, were only offered a (rather theoretical) moratorium of four or five years in which there were to be no French nuclear tests. Beyond that, the French insisted that their country would represent itself to the International Atomic Energy Agency (and not by the Atomic Community). Also, different from what was provided for in the Spaak Report, there were not to be any joint organs of the Atomic Community and the ECSC. With these concessions to the champions of a "national" policy of independence and with a markedly-technical presentation of the project, the government secured a broad majority (332 to 181) for continuing the negotiations on the Atomic Community. With this success under its belt, the Mollet government then pushed for a rapid conclusion of both treaties while taking into account the French conditions; talks had begun on 26 June in the Chateau de Val Duchesse near Brussels and were once again under the chairmanship of Spaak.[86]

However, the partners had no intentions to cater to the French demands. German advocates of the free market regarded the call for harmonizing social benefits as downright absurd and also showed little inclination to concede France a special role as a nuclear military power or colonial power. Erhard focused his hopes on a free-trade zone among the OEEC countries, which OEEC General Secretary René Sergent presented to the OEEC Council of Ministers meeting of 17 to 19

---

[85] The details of the French conceptions were contained in a memorandum that the government delivered to the five negotiation partners. Excerpts from it are in Robert Marjolin, *Le travail d´une vie. Mémoires 1911–1986*, Paris: Robert Laffont, 1986, pp. 283–286. As Pineau's cabinet chief, Marjolin had a major role in working out the French negotiating position.

[86] Cf. Küsters, *Gründung*, pp. 294–298, und Weilemann, *Anfänge*, pp. 103–109. The corresponding intervention by Maurice Faure in the session of 26 July 1956 (*ibid.*, p. 109) shows that the Mollet government actually did not wait until the Suez Crisis before accepting a simultaneous signing of both treaties and thereby confirms the criticism of Pineau and Emile Noël (*Rilancio*, pp. 525–527) of the presentation by Guillen (*ibid.*, p. 519). In any event, it still regarded the postponement of the treaty on the Economic Community as a way out if the partners did not agree on its terms.

July in Paris after discussions on the issue with the British government.[87] Erhard accordingly encouraged the West German delegation in Brussels in its reticence. Consequently, nothing more than an exchange of differing viewpoints could be achieved; and so on 24 July, the delegation leaders decided to take a summer break.

After the resumption of talks on 6 September, the French government modified its position a bit: It no longer insisted on leaving the continuation of market integration open after the end of the first phase but now maintained that the transition to the second phase would occur only if the governments had agreed that the goals of the first phase had been achieved. In return, however, the French demanded that it be possible to retain the system of export assistance and import duties until the French trade deficit had been eliminated and in the event of renewed balance-of-payment difficulties to be able to return to such protective measures. Furthermore, the French wanted to retain the right to postpone the coming into effect of the treaty on the Common Market if the Algerian War continued to generate the exorbitant costs that was the case at that time.[88] This was indeed acceptable to the others. On the questions of social benefits and of incorporating overseas territories, however, the differences continued to be unbridgeable. Mollet therefore once again aimed for a chronological separation of the two treaties; and Jean Monnet, who anyway promised himself a much greater mobilization push for the Atomic Community, urged Adenauer to bring forward the completion of the Euratom Treaty. The chancellor initially agreed but then, after having been persuaded otherwise by Etzel and Hallstein, held fast to the package deal.[89]

In October, the treaty negotiations thus came to a dead end, like those of the Spaak Committee hardly a year before. At a new foreign ministers meeting, called for 20 and 21 October in Paris, there was convergence on the question of transition regulations. The partners in principle granted France the possibility of taking special protective measures during difficulties over balance of payments; in return, Pineau conceded—after consultation with Mollet—that after six years, a

---

[87] On the origins of the proposal, cf. Wolfram Kaiser, *Großbritannien und die Europäische Wirtschaftsgemeinschaft 1955–1961. Von Messina nach Canossa*, Berlin: Akademie, 1996, pp. 71–84; Alan S. Milward, *The United Kingdom and the European Community*, Vol. 1: *The Rise and Fall of a National Strategy 1945–1963*, London: Whitehall History: Frank Cass cop. 2002, pp. 236–247; Dieter Krüger, *Sicherheit durch Integration? Die wirtschaftliche und politische Zusammenarbeit Westeuropas 1947 bis 1957/58*, Munich: Oldenbourg, 2003, pp. 417ff.

[88] The position was determined at an inter-ministerial session on 4 Sept.; cf. Guillen, *L'Europe remède*, pp. 330, and Marjolin, *Le travail*, pp. 301ff.

[89] Küsters, *Gründung*, pp. 310ff. Etzel had been mobilized by von der Groeben who feared for the passage of economic "total integration."

qualified majority would suffice for deciding on the transition to the second integration phase. Yet, when the West German delegation, to which both Erhard and Strauss belonged, categorically refused to agree to reducing the workweek from forty-eight to forty hours over the course of the first treaty phase, Pineau retracted his concession on the transition issue; after a further round of talks had brought no results, he declared the conference a failure.[90]

This setback was all the more dangerous to the project as on 3 October the British government officially embraced the proposal for a free-trade zone, though with the exclusion of agricultural products (for which the Commonwealth system of preferences was to continue). Erhard, who with his demonstratively-propounded liberal credo had contributed not a little to the failure of the Paris conference, then immediately urged that the negotiations in Brussels be broken off and instead that there be talks with the British on what he regarded as the "most decisive political and economic initiative for the integration of Europe in years." It was in this way that he hoped to eliminate once and for all the danger of a protectionist and *dirigiste* customs union of the Six and at the same time take a significant step toward a general liberalization of trade. In this, he knew that he had on his side the West German industrial organizations and chambers of commerce along with broad circles of exporting chemical and processing industries, which likewise placed great hope in the British initiative.[91] In light of all this, Paul-Henri Spaak and many other advocates of the Messina project believed that its failure was almost certain.

Adenauer clearly did not allow himself to be impressed by Erhard's economic argumentation. As much as he had treated the project of the Economic Community standoffishly at the beginning because he saw no significant chance that it could win approval in France,[92] he was also resolved that it not be allowed to fail now owing to differences between the Federal Republic and France. After the Radford Plan for reducing the American troop presence in Europe had presented

---

90 On this and the following, *ibid.*, pp. 313–320; Segers, *Deutschlands Ringen*, pp. 257–262; as well as the account of Karl Carstens, "Das Eingreifen Adenauers in den Europa-Verhandlungen im November 1956"; in: Dieter Blumenwitz, *et al.* (eds.), *Konrad Adenauer und seine Zeit. Politik und Persönlichkeit des ersten Bundeskanzlers. Beiträge von Weg- und Zeitgenossen*, Stuttgart: Deutsche Verlags-Anstalt, 1976, pp. 591–602. Carstens led the inter-ministerial working group that had been created for coordinating the German departmental standpoints in the negotiations.
91 Cf. Loth, "Europa-Konzeptionen," p. 595; the quote from Erhard's declaration to the OEEC Council of Ministers on 12 Feb. 1957, *Europa-Archiv* 12 (1957), p. 9651.
92 Not because the resolution of the Saar question and the arming of the Federal Republic had been more important to him than European integration, according to the exaggerated thesis of Segers, *Deutschlands Ringen*, p. 315.

to him in the summer of 1956 the danger of a Soviet-US understanding at the cost of the Europeans, his interest in Western European security-policy cooperation had even grown. Initial arrangements for activating the Western European Union, which he had agreed on with Mollet during his visit to Bonn on 29 September "owing to concern over developments in America"[93] were not to be called into question once again by the failure of the Brussels negotiations.

On 3 November, Adenauer thus agreed to the proposal made by representatives of the Foreign Office to seek an escape from the negotiation crisis via bilateral Franco-German conversations and announced that he himself would go to Paris in order to talk to Mollet. He held fast to his travel plans even when two days later the Mollet government came under heavy fire due to the military attack on Egypt that it was then undertaking alongside the British so as to force a reversal of the nationalization of the Suez Canal by Gamal Abdel Nasser.

It was not completely without significance for overcoming the negotiation crisis—which was causing Spaak and many others to fear that the Messina project would fail—that the Franco-German talks on the future of the Saar were successfully completed at just this time. On 23 October 1955, the statute worked out in the Treaties of Paris, contrary to expectations, had been rejected by the population of the Saar by a large majority; the Faure government had then taken up negotiations with Bonn with the goal of winning some economic compensation in the now clearly-inevitable incorporation of the Saarland into the Federal Republic. Ever since the meeting between Adenauer and Mollet on 4 and 5 June 1956 in Luxembourg, a compromise had been in the offing. This amounted to having Bonn honor a shortening of the transition period to at most three years, with partial financing of the canalization of the Mosel and further exploitation of a portion of Saar coal deposits from French soil. After a series of difficult questions over details had been resolved, it was possible to sign the Treaties of Luxembourg on 27 October, allowing the entry of the Saarland into the Federal Republic on 1 January 1957.[94] Naturally, the fact that this compromise succeeded contributed to an improvement in the basic sentiment between France and the Federal Republic and above all brought negotiation partners such as Faure and Hallstein as well as Pineau and von Brentano closer to each another.[95]

---

[93] *Ibid.*, pp. 244–249; the quote from the negotiation transcript from Karl Carstens, PAAA.
[94] Cf. Ulrich Lappenküper, *Die deutsch-französischen Beziehungen 1949–1963. Von der "Erbfeindschaft" zur "entente élémentaire,"* vol. 2: *1958–1963*, Munich: Oldenbourg, 2001, pp. 1094–1138; Segers, *Deutschlands Ringen*, pp. 212–215.
[95] Faure reports having become a friend of Hallstein through the negotiations on the Saar: *Rilancio*, pp. 287ff.

In any event, what was more important was that the unified pressure of the US and the Soviet Union—which together had forced the governments of Mollet and Eden to break off their Suez undertaking in the night of 6 to 7 November—lastingly increased the feeling in France for the necessity of European unification. Mollet immediately made use of this improvement in the climate to accelerate the treaty negotiations via greater willingness to make concessions. As early as Adenauer's visit on 6 November, he instructed his officials at all events to find a compromise on the contentious issue of harmonization. A group of experts, led on the French side by Robert Marjolin and on the West German side by Karl Carstens, then negotiated a compromise formula that transformed a commitment to upward harmonization of social benefits into a vague declaration of intent: National legislation and the effects of the Common Market itself would by the end of the first phase make possible a harmonization of the workweek along French lines; if that was not achieved, then the Commission of the Community would be entitled to add protective clauses to the benefit of disadvantaged industries. On the basis of this agreement, the group once again confirmed the compromises on the issue of compensatory payments and the modalities of transition to the second phase, which had already been discussed at the foreign ministers meeting. When the compromise package was presented to both heads of government, Mollet had just learned in a telephone conversation with Eden that the British government had already agreed to the American demand for an immediate armistice in the Suez. Adenauer acknowledged the news with the injunction "And now we must create Europe!" Both leaders then agreed to the results of the negotiations without further discussion and thereby cleared the path for the talks to continue at an accelerated pace.[96]

Mollet prevailed in the cabinet—which was very impressed by the solidarity shown by Adenauer during the Suez Crisis—with a resolution to have the treaty on the Economic Community completed as quickly as possible and for this purpose to be content with laying down "rather general principles" on other disputed issues too, which were then to be fleshed out by the "supranational authority" of the Community.[97] At the same time, he began to prepare the parliament as well as the public systematically as to the necessity of both treaties by presenting them

---

96 Cf. Carstens, "Eingreifen," pp. 599ff.; Küsters, *Gründung*, pp. 327–330; Guillen, *L' Europe remède*, pp. 331; Krüger, *Sicherheit*, pp. 440–442; Segers, *Deutschlands Ringen*, pp. 280ff. The quote from the report by Pineau in Christian Pineau and Christiane Rimbaud, *Le Grand Pari. L'ouverture du traité de Rome*, Paris: Fayard, 1991, p. 223.

97 According to the communication by Marjolin in a session of the inter-ministerial committee for preparing the Common Market, quoted from Guillen, *L'Europe remède*, p. 332. Guillen's presentation does not however disinguish clearly enough between Mollet's views and the campaign of persuasion.

as means through which such humiliations for France could be avoided in the future—humiliations as Nasser's expropriation maneuver and the superpowers' intervention in the Suez Crisis. In light of the distressing dependency on Arab oil and the clear distancing of Adenauer from the leading power the US, Europe seemed to be the stronghold of independence for the first time since the intensification of the EDC crisis: This impression was increased by Mollet's propaganda offensive and so prepared the soil for a weakening of the protectionist opposition to the Common Market.

With the background of the success on the Saar issue, the solidarity in the Suez Crisis, and the growing maneuvering room in talks shown by the French delegation, nothing less than a cordial negotiating climate developed in Brussels, one that made it possible for remaining differences to be moved out of the way step by step, with much appreciation of the domestic political difficulties of the partners and with some creativity too. Pierre Uri once again played a role in this; he had been brought into the negotiations by Spaak as a personal advisor and was now leading the talks out of bottlenecks by means of compromise formulations that he drafted on an *ad hoc* basis. Spaak himself repeatedly gave Hans von der Groeben, whom he had named as chairman of the committee for the Common Market, sufficient backup to defend the line on economic integration found in the Spaak Report against divergent forays from national bureaucracies.[98]

In the process, it proved possible to come to grips with as a delicate a problem as the incorporation of agriculture into the Common Market. Negotiations on this had been going on since September of 1950 when then French Agriculture Minister Pierre Pflimlin presented a plan for the sectoral integration of European agriculture; the various rounds of talks had always failed however due to unbridgeable opposing interests. The experience that an agreement within the framework of the OEEC was not possible owing to the great a diversity of interests as well as a systematic export offensive by American grain producers since the middle of 1950 led the French to attempt to use the Common Market as an export market for its agricultural products, which offered protection from the competition of the global market via price subsidies and external tariffs.[99] With this, they admittedly ran into opposition from West German agricultural representatives, who

---

[98] Cf. the accounts by Faure und Uri, in: Serra (ed.), *Rilancio*, pp. 288ff. and 307ff. as well as the account by von der Groeben in Küsters, *Gründung*, p. 335. On the negotiations, Segers, *Deutschlands Ringen*, pp. 286–290, 300–305, 307–309.

[99] Cf. Gilbert Noel, *Du Pool vert à la politique agricole commune. Les tentatives de Communauté agricole européenne entre 1945 et 1955*, Paris, 1989; Ulrich Kluge, "Du Pool noir au Pool vert," in: Serra (ed.), *Rilancio*, pp. 239–280; Guido Thiemeyer, *Vom "Pool Vert" zur Europäischen Wirtschaftsgemeinschaft. Europäische Integration, Kalter Krieg und die Anfänge der Gemeinsamen Europäischen Agrarpolitik 1950–1957*, Munich: Oldenbourg, 1999, pp. 243–260.

feared intra-European competition, and from the Dutch too, for whom the proposed subsidies were conversely much too high.

The result of this tug-of-war was the decision to seek a European market for agriculture but to leave the task of working it out to a government conference to meet immediately after the treaty had come into effect. The French representatives were not given any guarantee that the future protection of agriculture would not be less than the existing protection via national markets; German negotiators had to give up special regulations for the reduction of intra-Community tariffs; and the Dutch had to accept that the governments would retain the right to set minimum prices for certain products. Furthermore, the dismantling of discrimination was made dependent on incremental convergence on subsidized domestic prices; and the Community was saddled with subsidizing raw materials whose processed products were destined for export to third countries.[100] This meant that a European agricultural protectionism of a middling sort was in the offing, linked with a promotion of modernization that was curbed by regional considerations. Clearly, there would still need to be negotiations over the methods of subsidy; here, the agreements hid many sources of conflict.

Regarding the Atomic Community, Adenauer conceded in principle to Mollet during the November meeting that Euratom would not exercise any kind of control functions in the military realm. In return, the Frenchman accepted that the community's supply monopoly could be broken if it could not deliver fissionable material in sufficient quantities or did so only under "improper" conditions. With special regulations that guaranteed priority supply to reactors already completed and to isotope separation facilities to be established over the next seven years, both sides moved further from the idea of operator functions for the community itself. In the question of ownership of fissionable material, the French side was able to gain a victory at the last moment: Monnet, who was now involved only indirectly in negotiations via an expert committee of "Three Wise Men," was able to make it clear to Adenauer that only in this way was it possible to gain the support of the US for the development of European nuclear energy. Yet, the community's right of ownership was limited to "especially fissionable materials," and the users could utilize the community's property without constraint as long as they adhered to safety regulations. In contrast, French efforts for the construction of a common European isotope separation facility remained wholly without success: Here, the disinclination of the partners was reinforced by pressure from the US, which under all circumstances wanted to prevent the development of an independent French nuclear weapons force. The project thereby lost much

---

[100] Details from the negotiation papers in Küsters, *Gründung*, pp. 347–359.

meaning in both military and civilian regards, and in France too it now retreated into the background compared to the Common Market.[101]

On the issue of institutions, there was a collision of differing conceptions leading to a compromise that was both complicated and capable of being developed in different directions. The French government advocated a strong position for the Council of Ministers, which was as a rule to decide by majority, but opposed substantial participation by the European Parliament due to the anti-European mood in French public opinion. The Dutch government, whose conceptions here were substantially influenced by Sicco Mansholt, envisioned a strong Commission that, as a non-partisan body of experts, as it were, would pursue "objective politics." It was to have the sole right to make proposals to the Council of Ministers, which was to decide on them by majority rule. Participation by a parliament was not provided for in this construction. With this and with the binding commitment of the Council of Ministers to the proposals of the Commission, the expansion of the Community beyond the creation of a Common Market was to be prevented. Over against this, the Italian and West German governments insisted on a strong position for the European Parliament, which was to decide on the Community budget and participate in legislative acts of the Commission and the Council of Ministers. Yet, Adenauer impressed upon his country's delegation the need to show a willingness to compromise when in doubt so that the project as a whole would not fail due to institutional questions.[102]

A compromise on these divergent conceptions was found only at the last minute at the conference of the foreign ministers of the Six from 26 to 28 January 1957. It essentially amounted to this: The competencies of the Council and of the Commission would be limited *because* the rights of the European Parliament remained limited. Regarding the budget, Parliament received only the right to make amendment proposals to the Council, which was to decide on them by qualified majority. Other than that, Parliament could force the Commission to resign by a two-thirds majority but was given no influence over the composition of a new Commission. Direct election of Parliament was made dependent on a future

---

[101] The presentation in Weilemann, *Anfänge*, pp. 122–143 and 171–179, is rather unclear. Important additions in Richard T. Griffith and Wendy Asbeek Brusse, "The Dutch Cabinet and the Rome Treaties," in Serra (ed.), *Rilancio*, pp. 461–493, here pp. 482–491, und Guillen, *La France*, ibid., pp. 523ff.

[102] Cf. Guido Thiemeyer, "Die Ursachen des 'Demokratiedefizits' der Europäischen Union aus geschichtswissenschaftlicher Perspektive," in: Wilfried Loth (ed.), *Das europäische Projekt zu Beginn des 21. Jahrhunderts*, Opladen: Leske und Budrich, 2001, pp. 27–47; Jean-Marie Palayret, "Les décideurs français et allemands face aux questions institutionnelles dans la négociation des traités de Rome," in: Marie-Thérèse Bitsch (ed.), *Le couple France-Allemagne et les institutions européennes*, Brussels: Émile Bruylant, 2001, pp. 105–150.

unanimous vote of the Council. In return, the Council was established as the sole lawmaker of the Community. However, decisions in the Council could initially be made by qualified majority only in a few areas (whereby a recommendation along those lines by the Commission was adopted as a requirement in order to prevent small member states from being outvoted). Central issues such as the naming of Commission members, the shaping of common agricultural policy, and the development of common social policy were to remain dependent on unanimous votes even after the expiration of the transition period.[103]

After this, greater difficulties were once again caused by the French demand that overseas territories be included. As deputy delegation leader Marjolin specified on 19 November, the French government understood by this the incremental opening of overseas markets to the Community countries, the commitment to accept overseas products, and the financing of a comprehensive investment fund by the Community. This was supported by the Belgian government, which saw the same problems in the Congo, but was treated with great distance by the West German government—it was indeed agreeable to the opening of markets on the basis of reciprocity, but on the issue of financing, it initially agreed to nothing more than a nonbinding declaration of intent. In contrast to the situation with social burdens, Paris was not satisfied with that: On the one hand, the government was fascinated by the vision of a "Eurafrica" that would be independent in world politics; and on the other, this vision played a central role in mobilizing the French public, which was then primarily occupied with the drama in Algeria. Once the National Assembly had approved the continuation of negotiations on 22 January 1957 with the proviso that the association of overseas territories would be regulated "on the basis of the principles proposed by the government," Adenauer could not avoid giving in at the closing meeting of the heads of government on 19 and 20 February in Paris. After a private conversation between him and his French counterpart, the creation of an investment fund in the amount of 581 million US dollars for the first five years was agreed upon; its continuation beyond that period was made dependent on a unanimous vote of the Council of Ministers. This was less than half the sum originally regarded as necessary by the French side, and it completely left out the demand for sales guarantees. Nevertheless, it naturally served as a signal for ratification in the eyes of the French public.[104]

---

[103] Cf. the overview of the EEC procedural regulations in Hans R. Krämer, *Die Europäische Wirtschaftsgemeinschaft*, Frankfurt am Main and Berlin: Metzner, 1965, pp. 26–40.
[104] Küsters, *Gründung*, pp. 333ff. and 379–392; René Girault, "La France entre l'Europe et l'Afrique," in: Serra (ed.), *Rilancio*, pp. 351–378; on the debate in the French National Assembly, also Gerhard Kiersch, "Parlament und Parlamentarier in der Außenpolitik der IV. Republik," Diss. Berlin, 1971, pp. 287–315.

The treaties on the creation of the European Atomic Energy Community (Euratom) and the European Economic Community (EEC) were signed on 25 March 1957 in Rome by two representatives of each of the six founding states, mostly the heads of government and their foreign ministers. The ceremony took place in the Hall of the Horatii and Curiatii in the Palazzo dei Conservatori on the Capitoline Hill; the rain that continually fell on that raw Monday in Rome marred the festive mood a bit.[105] This fit with the course of the ratification debates in the coming weeks and months: Nowhere did the Treaties of Rome spark great enthusiasm, but after the careful preparation neither did they meet with stubborn resistance.

In contrast to the situation with the EDC, Mollet immediately presented the treaties to the National Assembly so as not to permit the formation of an oppositional movement. Jean Monnet, who after leaving the presidency of the ECSC had assembled an "Action Committee for the United States of Europe" consisting of about a hundred political personalities,[106] then made efforts to have the Bundestag ratify the treaties quickly so as to bring hesitant French deputies to agreement too. In the process, he had some difficulties with the Social Democratic Party (SPD), which did not necessarily want to grant Adenauer another foreign-policy success in light of the parliamentary elections set for the coming autumn. After a conversation with Erich Ollenhauer and Herbert Wehner, Monnet was able to prevail, however. It was due to his influence and the efforts of Maurice Faure that progress continued on preparing for ratification in France despite the fall of the Mollet government on 21 May.[107] On 6 July, the Bundestag approved the treaties with the votes of the SPD, which for the first time had thereby backed away from its fundamental opposition to integration into the West. Only a minority of seventeen SPD deputies, among them Helmut Schmidt, voted against the treaties, doing so because of the absence of Great Britain and the Scandinavian countries. Likewise, the opposition parties FDP and BHE voted against the treaties, though they had earlier, as part of the government, supported Adenauer's course on integration into the West.[108] Three days later, the French National Assembly also

---

105 Cf. Franz Knipping, *Rom, 25. März 1957. Die Einigung Europas*, Munich: Deutscher Taschenbuch-Verlag, 2004, pp. 9–13. The treaty texts in: *Europa. Dokumente*, vol. 3, pp. 1153–1219 (Euratom) and 1248–1327 (EEC).
106 Cf. Antonio Varsori, "Jean Monnet e il Comitato d'Azione per gli Stati Uniti d'Europa fra MEC ed Euratom (1955–1957)," in: Sergio Pistone (ed.), *I movimenti per l'unità europea 1954–1969*, Pavia: Giuffrè, 1996, pp. 349–371.
107 Cf. Monnet, *Mémoires*, pp. 480–499; Roussel, *Monnet*, pp. 715ff.; Martial Libera, "Jean Monnet et les personnalités allemandes du Comité d'action pour les États-Unis d'Europe (1995–1975)," in: *Une dynamique européenne. Le Comité d'action pour les États-Unis d'Europe*, Paris: Economica, 2011, pp. 37–56.
108 Cf. Loth, "Europa-Konzeptionen," pp. 592–594 and 597ff.

approved the treaties—with the surprising majority of 342 to 239. Mollet's mobilization strategy had now paid off, likewise the concessions and gestures that Adenauer had been willing to make in the interest of stabilizing the Franco-German core of the Community.

After the breakthrough in the French National Assembly, the ratification of the treaties was no longer in danger in the remaining parliaments. On 30 July, the Italian parliament approved them; on 4 October the Second Chamber of the Dutch States-General followed suit; the Belgian Chamber of Representatives and the Luxembourg parliament did likewise on 19 and 26 November, respectively. Both treaties then came into effect on 1 January 1958.[109]

The appointments to the top offices of the new institutions were decided only at the last minute in bilateral contacts at the turn of the year 1957–58. Jean Monnet pulled a few strings to secure the presidency of the Euratom authority for Louis Armand; he wanted the office of the president of the EEC Commission to go to Sicco Mansholt, the spry agriculture minister of the Netherlands who was disappointed at not having become foreign minister in the most recent government in The Hague. For Adenauer, however, it was unacceptable to have two Socialists in the new top offices; and so agreement was reached that Armand would receive the Euratom post and that Jean Rey, the liberal economy minister of Belgium, would become president of the EEC Commission. As to the latter, Adenauer would only consent if the Belgian capital were not at the same time the seat of the Commission. When Brussels refused to give up on that, he then insisted that the presidency of the EEC Commission be held by a German and presented State Secretary Walter Hallstein as his choice. Hallstein's candidacy was met with rapid agreement in the other capitals, not least because people had learned to value him as a competent and engaging West German delegation head in the talks on the ECSC as well as those on the Treaties of Rome.[110]

The approval of the Treaties of Rome demonstrated that the European unification movement was indeed stronger than it might have appeared at the time of the failure of the EDC. The success in creating an organizational core for "Europe"— which even with all the modesty of its functions was nevertheless capable of being developed—made possible a continuation of this movement. Problematic was only the fact that there had been very little in the way of an understanding on the political finality of this Community, nor was this arrangement concen-

---

[109] On the ratification processes, see Küsters, *Gründung*, pp. 441–483.
[110] Michel Dumoulin, "The Interim Committee (April 1957 to January 1958)," in: *The European Commission, 1958–72. History and Memories*, Luxembourg: Office for Official Publications of the European Communities, 2007, pp. 37–49; on Hallstein as a person, Wilfried Loth, "Walter Hallstein, a committed European," *ibid.*, pp. 79–90.

trated on executive and bureaucratic elites well suited to making up for that in the near future—and this in a Community that, despite its economic functions, was still more strongly motivated by politics than by economics. Thus, in terms of the further course of integration history, an ambivalent result had been achieved with the Treaties of Rome: They could serve as the basis for further development, which however would again and again require unambiguously-convergent interests and an unambiguous political creative will. At the same time, they also embodied within them the risk of lapsing into mere administration of the crisis of Community development. The European Communities thus offered a challenge that could prove the creativity and courage of the Europeans.

2 Formative Years, 1958–1963

The European Commission

Representatives of the governments of the six member states met in Paris to name the members of the first Commission of the European Economic Community on 5 and 6 January 1958. As agreed, the president of the Commission was to be the German Walter Hallstein. Vice presidents were to be the Frenchman Robert Marjolin, the Italian Piero Malvestiti, and the Dutchman Sicco Mansholt. Other members of the Commission were the Belgian Jean Rey, the Luxembourger Michel Rasquin, the German Hans von der Groeben, the Frenchman Robert Lemaignen, and the Italian Guiseppe Petrilli. The three Benelux states would thus be represented by one member each on the Commission, while the larger states would have two each.

It was initially unclear what role this Commission would play. According to the treaty, the Commission was to "ensure that the provisions of this Treaty and the measures taken by the institutions pursuant thereto are applied" and "exercise the powers conferred by the Council for the implementation of the rules laid down by the latter."[1] The Commission also held the sole right of initiative over the budget of the Community and over key politico-economic areas such as the realization of the customs union, the rules of competition, the standardization of law, trade policy, and the design of the agricultural system: In these areas, the Council of Ministers could make regulations only on the basis of a proposal from the Commission. The Council could alter such proposals only by unanimous vote. In those cases in which a majority decision of the Council was specified, it could only adopt the Commission's proposal unaltered or reject it in its entirety.

Beyond this, there were some areas in which the governments had retained the sole authority to make decisions: Changes in the common tariff rates, proposals for the design of a common agricultural policy, common transport policy, the granting of government aid, the passage of trade agreements with third parties during the first two phases of the Economic Community, the transfer of responsibilities in the area of social security to the Commission, new tasks of the European Social Fund, decisions about the continuation of association agreements with overseas territories, the naming of members of the Commission and of the Economic and Social Committee, as well as the acceptance of new members and the association of new states. In all these cases, agreement among all member states was necessary, but the Council was not bound by proposals of the Commis-

---

1 Article 155 EEC Treaty.

sion. The Council could solicit the position of the Commission on an issue, and for its part, the Commission could make recommendations and take positions at any time, although the Council was not bound by them.

Lastly, the Commission could in some cases make decisions in the form of decrees, rulings, and guidelines independent of the Council. These included the dismantling of tariffs, the granting of tariff quotas, import quotas, common agricultural policy, the free movement of labor, rules of competition, government aid, cooperation in the realm of trade policy, as well as the right to file a case in the European Court against the Council or the European Investment Bank.

Decisions within the Commission were to be made by a majority of the nine members. In the Council of Ministers, majority voting was specified in only a few cases—for example, in the standardization of tariff rates or the conclusion of trade treaties with third parties. At the beginning of the second phase of the Common Market (after four years or six at the most), quantitative limitations as well as measures for implementing freedom of establishment and free trade in services were to be decided with a qualified majority. In the third phase (planned to begin after eight years), a majority would decide in a large number of additional areas, from tariff reductions and common agricultural policy to common trade policy with third parties. After the end of the transition period (lasting from twelve years to fifteen at the most), decisions on courses of action in international organizations would be made by qualified majority. Unanimity would then be required for only a few central issues such as the naming of Commission members, the transfer of new responsibilities to the Commission, the acceptance of additional members, and the conclusion of association agreements.

The qualified-majority provision in the Council meant that member states would be accorded different numbers of votes roughly proportional to population and that for a majority, close to two thirds of the total votes would be necessary. France, the Federal Republic, and Italy were each given four votes, while Belgium and the Netherlands were given two and Luxembourg one. This made seventeen votes altogether, and twelve were required for a majority decision. If the decision stemmed from a recommendation of the Commission, then the votes of the three large states would suffice for a majority. If the Council was addressing an issue outside the realm in which the Commission had initiative, then a majority of four states was required. This eliminated the possibility that the three large states could simply outvote the Benelux countries.

Initially, the Community did not have any income of its own but was instead financed by contributions from the member states. Based on a proposal from the Commission, the Council decided on the annual budget by qualified majority. The Parliamentary Assembly could propose changes in the draft budget, but the Council was not bound to heed them. Members of the Commission served four-year terms and the president a two-year term. Unanimity was required for appointments. Members were allowed to serve more than one term. They were not dependent on instructions from their governments and were only responsible to the Parliamentary Assembly. In the event of a vote of no confidence by the Assembly, the Commission members were required to resign as a group; the Assembly did not however have any influence over the composition of a new Commission.

The Commission thus oscillated between serving as an institution carrying out the will of the Council of Ministers and one constituting the executive of the Community. It had to share the executive function with the Council and remained dependent on the vote of the Council in all substantive questions. In the event of conflict with a national government, the Commission would have no support from a parliamentary majority; it could only resort to the more difficult task of finding allies among the national governments and the public. On the other hand, its sole right of initiative gave it an excellent means by which to shape the policy of the Community. From a combination of the right of initiative and the system of majority decision-making by the Council, there emerged the prospect of strengthening executive competencies and expanding supranational government. This was also the case with the broadening of the Parliamentary Assembly's right of participation, even though that body's powers were very limited at first, and also for the transition to a system of income specifically intended for the Community, an issue closely linked to the rights of Parliament. In principle, both were possible according to the terms of the treaty but remained dependent on unanimous decisions of the Council of Ministers. Initially, the members of the Parliamentary Assembly were to be sent from the national parliaments. Representation in the body was weighted in a manner similar to that of the majority votes on the Council (thirty-six seats each for France, the Federal Republic, and Italy; fourteen each for Belgium and the Netherlands; six for Luxembourg).

The ambivalent character of the Commission corresponded to the relative open-endedness of the substantive provisions of the treaty. What was clearly agreed upon however was the gradual elimination of hindrances to trade in all industrial products and services, the establishment of the free movement of labor and of capital, as well as the creation of common tariff rates and a common trade policy for the Community. Likewise, it was agreed that there should be common rules of competition. Regarding the design of a common agricultural policy, however, the treaty contained only discretionary provisions. The content of common transport policy remained undetermined. A European social fund for improving employment opportunities was to exist only during the transition period. Likewise open was the retention of an investment fund for overseas territories after a period of five years; there was only very vague talk about "coordination" of economic and currency policy thereafter. The nature of "cooperation in social questions" also remained unspecified: The Council could transfer responsibilities to the Commission but was not required to do so.

The treaty thus had the character of a framework agreement. The customs union was to be realized gradually, and it remained an open question as to the extent that harmonization of economic policy was to go beyond the creation of that customs union. There certainly were no arrangements regarding the transition from an economic community to the integration of further policy areas. The fathers of the treaty had indeed declared their intention of "creating the bases for an ever closer union of the European peoples" by means of an economic community,[2] but they refrained from offering a more detailed description of the path to such a union.

Walter Hallstein regarded it as his task to promote the potential for development contained within the treaty to the greatest extent possible. As a close associate of Konrad Adenauer, he saw the creation of a European Union primarily as a political necessity. In order to secure the peace among its members and to combine their forces, it must have a compulsory character. Given that the integration of democratically-constituted states was only acceptable on the basis of equality, supranational structures had to be created that would bind all member states to the same degree. Hallstein was thus determined to interpret the competencies of the Commission as broadly as possible and with its help promote the "Community in the making" as much as possible. For him, the Commission was not only the guardian of the treaty and the embodiment of "pure Community interests."[3] Its task was also to initiate Community policy and to promote the process of European unification. It was therefore incumbent upon the Commission to expand its area of influence continually and to strengthen its responsibilities at the expense of the national governments and of the Council of Ministers.[4]

The members of the first Commission shared this view of their tasks more or less explicitly. Sicco Mansholt, who had previously served as agriculture minister in the Netherlands, had in the treaty negotiations fought for a Commission that would be as strong and independent as possible from the Council of Ministers. Jean Rey, previously Belgian economy minister, belonged to the ranks of dedicated European federalists. Robert Marjolin, a colleague of Jean Monnet, had served from 1947 to 1953 as general secretary of the Organization for European Economic Co-Operation (OEEC) and thereafter as professor of political economy

---

2 Preamble of the EEC Treaty.
3 Walter Hallstein, *Der unvollendete Bundesstaat. Europäische Erfahrungen und Erkenntnisse*, Düsseldorf and Vienna: Econ, 1969, p. 56.
4 On this and the following see Wilfried Loth/Marie-Thérèse Bitsch, "The Hallstein Commission 1958–67," in: *The European Commission 1958–72*, pp. 51–78.

at the University of Nancy; he regarded the potential of the Commission much more skeptically, not least of all in light of the views of Charles de Gaulle, who came to power in Paris in June of 1958. Fundamentally, however, the direction in which Hallstein sought to move was in sync with Marjolin's own views: "I leaned, to a certain extent instinctively, toward the idea of a European federation but felt no less instinctively that it did not as yet exist."[5] This was also more or less the case with Hans von der Groeben, the second German member of the Commission; he had previously been head of the European department within the West German economy ministry and had played a major role in the development of the Spaak Report.[6] For the moment, however, all commissioners were in agreement with Hallstein that "what was most important was allowing the Treaties of Rome become a reality."[7]

Standing in the way of that process were not only minimalist interpretations of the treaty but also the difficulties stemming from competition with national institutions. When the Commission began its work, no decision had yet been made as to its seat. Until May of 1958, meetings of the Commission alternated among Luxembourg (where it could be supported by the administration of the High Authority of the European Coal and Steel Community), Strasbourg (at the Maison de l'Europe), and Brussels (where the secretariat of the "Interim Committee" for preparation of the EEC and Euratom had been located). The administrative office of the Commission was provisionally headquartered in Brussels. Office space provided by the Belgian government in the rue Belliard and the château Val Duchesse quickly proved much too small. As early as May of 1958, the Commission rented an additional office complex in the city center on rue de Marais. In July of that year, the members of the Commission and their staffs moved into a building on avenue la Joyeuse Entrée. In December, this headquarters was enlarged by the addition of the Dépendence "Cortenberg." In April of 1959, two directorates-general—that for competition and that for agriculture—were moved into a new building on avenue de Brocqueville. This spatial separation was not exactly beneficial for the integration of the rapidly expanding administration.

Although the Commission had thereby *de facto* installed itself in Brussels, the governments of France and Luxembourg in July of 1958 rejected a Belgian proposal to designate the city as the sole seat of the Communities. Only in February of the following year did the foreign ministers of the six member states determine that Brussels would be the provisional seat of the Economic Community—and only for the subsequent three years; before the end of that period, a definitive

---

5 Robert Marjolin, *Le travail d'une vie. Mémoires 1911–1986*, Paris: Robert Laffont, 1986, p. 312.
6 Interview with Hans von der Groeben, 16 December 2003.
7 Marjolin, p. 312.

decision was to be made. That did not occur, however, and in February of 1962, Brussels was again declared the provisional seat. As a result, the Commission was not in a position to purchase its own real estate; and the Belgian government remained hesitant to invest in construction for the future seat of the Community.

Likewise, the various national financial authorities dragged their feet when it came to financing the Community. In order to begin its work at all, the Commission had to resort to a monetary advance from the High Authority of the ECSC. Repeated urgent calls to individual finance ministers were necessary in order to ensure that salaries could be paid at the last moment.[8] Moreover, in doing the work assigned it by the treaty, the Commission regularly ran into resistance from national bureaucracies that were not in agreement with it. Even in the recruiting of personnel for the new administration, national authorities proved anything but helpful—there were serious disputes about the filling of individual positions.

The Commission sought to overcome these difficulties with spirit and vigor. It made use of the general disinterest in European issues in the crisis-filled final months of the Fourth French Republic as well as the difficulties in the administrative structuring of the Council of Ministers in order to establish its own authority as the first effectively functioning institution of the new Community. Right at the beginning of the Commission's work, the issue of division of labor among the commissioners was taken up and was definitively resolved after ten weeks. Three weeks later, the Commission's first organizational chart was adopted. With clear directives from the president, the commissioners immediately chose their directors-general, who in turn—still during the spring of 1958—picked their department heads. By the autumn, most of the higher-level administrative officials and the vast majority of the lower-level personnel had been recruited. When the Budget Committee of the Council of Ministers took up its work, most hiring had already been done and the personnel ranks were practically full. The Commission had approximately one thousand people on its staff by the end of 1958. The national governments saw themselves confronted with a *fait accompli*.

In light of the large number of responsibilities potentially accruing to the Commission according to a literal interpretation of the treaty, Hallstein's aim from the beginning was to create a "grand administration" whose character would extend far beyond that of the High Authority of the ECSC. As a precaution, an administrative structure was created for those areas in which the governments had not as yet settled on a concrete program. Altogether, eight administrative units were established, so-called "Directorates-General," at whose head sat a "Director-General": External Relations, Economic and Financial Affairs, Internal Market (customs,

---

[8] Robert Lemaignen, *L'Europe au Berceau. Souvenirs d'un technocrate*, Paris: Plon, 1964, pp. 36ff.; Interview with Karl-Heinz Narjes, 24 May 2004.

quotas, services), Competition and Standardization of Law, Social Affairs, Agriculture, Transport, as well as Overseas Countries and Territories.

Adhering to the principle of collegiality, the High Authority organized the Commission into work groups: For each of the eight areas, three to five commissioners constituted a work group that would prepare the decisions to be reached in the plenum of the Commission. The chairman of the work group also bore responsibility for the directorate-general of the area in question. He thereby functioned *de facto* as a minister, and the areas, which had been structured along the lines of West German administration, perforce developed separately from one another. Following the practice in Latin countries, each commissioner had a few private staff—a *cabinet*. Along with this cabinet, the president had a secretariat, but this body had no authority over the administrative structure. Hallstein, who had administrative experience in the formation of the West German Rector's Conference and the Foreign Office of the Federal Republic, did not want to permit the rise of any strong administrative heads independent of the political leadership of the Commission.[9]

The division of responsibilities was decided by collegial agreement. It was clear from the outset that Mansholt would take agriculture; he immediately plunged into that work with extraordinary energy. Marjolin, who was the second political heavyweight alongside Mansholt, initially claimed foreign affairs for himself. Hallstein did not however want to give it to him, presumably because he himself wanted to take on the representation of the Community to the outside world. Marjolin was compensated with comprehensive authority over economics and finance.[10] By means of his tactical restraint, von der Groeben gained for himself what was especially important to him as the father of competition policy: Responsibility for cartels and monopolies, subsidies, as well as the standardization of law and of taxes.[11] External relations were entrusted to Jean Rey, a skilful negotiator who was to become one of the heavyweights of the Commission following the negotiations of the General Agreement on Tariffs and Trade (GATT).[12] Piero Malvestiti was given charge of the internal market. Overseas areas, in whose integration France took an especially strong interest, were assigned to the second French commissioner, Robert Lemaignen. The initially less important realm of social policy was given to the second Italian commissioner, Guiseppe Petrilli. Transportation policy, which was likewise of lower priority at the time, became

---

9 Interview with Fernand Braun, 8 December 2003.
10 Interview with Karl-Heinz Narjes, 24 May 2004.
11 Interview with Hans von der Groeben, 16 December 2003.
12 Interview with Fernand Braun, 8 December 2003.

the responsibility of the commissioner from the smallest member state, Michel Rasquin.

Care was taken to ensure that the directors-general were not of the same nationality as the commissioners who oversaw them. In late March of 1958, Emile Noël was appointed secretary of the Commission with the title "executive secretary" so as to set the position apart; he had been a longtime associate of the former French Prime Minister Guy Mollet and had played an important role as early as the passage of the Treaties of Rome. Party-political considerations did not come into consideration in the appointments at all; Hallstein strongly believed that national governments should have no influence over the filling of positions in the administrative structure. For him, the primary issue was the qualifications of the applicant; this often led him to advocate for younger applicants who combined outstanding expertise with an ability to learn. To a certain extent in conflict with that approach were his efforts to seek out officials who had already attained positions of great authority within national bureaucracies and who had a correspondingly-persuasive presence. In the filling of higher positions, there was a certain concern, though a flexible one, to achieve a balance of nationalities: A quarter of the officials were to come from each of the three larger member states and the remaining quarter from the Benelux countries. This last group was thereby somewhat overrepresented, but at the same time, any kind of hegemony by a particular member state was avoided.

Hallstein directed the formation and the work of the Commission with an authority stemming from a masterful command of the dossier, combined with extraordinary analytical intelligence and straightforward humanitarianism. He allowed the commissioners great latitude in the shaping of their work, respecting their areas of authority but also demanding much of them. He took personal charge of strategically important concerns such as the choice of leading officials, key conversations with national governments, and the matter of representing the Commission in public. In preparing his public appearances, he had only a small staff of competent colleagues upon whom to rely. He entrusted Noël with the issue of communication among the departments. Owing to Noël's rare combination of absolute loyalty and precise expertise, he proved an indispensable guarantor of quick information-flow through the hierarchy as well as flexible responses.

It was not only through the quality of its work that Hallstein sought to convince the governments and the public of the Commission's necessity. He also put much value in the formal and symbolic demonstration of its autonomy. When the governments went beyond the provisions of the treaty by establishing a Committee of Permanent Representatives (COREPER) at the headquarters of the Commission, he refused to send commissioners to attend the meetings of the new entity. The task of preparatory exchanges with the standing representatives was instead normally undertaken by the directors-general, who were accorded a status equivalent to ambassadors in COREPER. The commissioners themselves were normally to have ministers as their interlocutors, not only in workaday contacts in Brussels but also during visits to the capitals of the member states. Efforts were made to ensure that in visits to non-member states, commissioners were received by the appropriate ministers. The Commission president was to meet officially with heads of state and of government.

In dealings with non-member states, the Community's claim to sovereignty as a whole was to be demonstrated. Hallstein thus introduced the practice of officially receiving the credentials of ambassadors of countries outside the Community in a formal ceremony. Further opportunities to highlight the sovereignty of the Community and the authority of its executive organ were the reception of "state guests" and the Commission's annual New Year's reception. All these occasions were characterized by strict adherence to diplomatic protocol. Hallstein made certain to stand on a red carpet during such events. Television cameras provided images for the public and ensured that the claims of the Commission were perceived in member states as well as in many countries outside the Community. As Commission president, Hallstein consciously paid frequent visits to the US, where he quickly became known as "Mr. Europe."

The Struggle over the Free-Trade Area

Hallstein and his colleagues expended such energy in quickly building up a powerful Commission not least of all because implementation of the treaty terms was being called into question in numerous respects. Since October of 1957, representatives of the seventeen OEEC states had been negotiating on a European free trade area in a committee led by the British special minister Reginald Maudling. It was especially the British government that was pushing for such negotiations after having decided on 11 November 1955 not to participate in a European Economic Community, just as had been the case with the European Coal and Steel Community. In July of 1956, the general secretary of the OEEC had proposed the creation of a free trade area, and the British government had officially adopted the idea on 3 October.[13]

In economic terms, the British decision against participation in an economic community was by no means compelling: Although in the mid-1950s approxi-

---

[13] Jim Burgess and Geoffrey Edwards, "The Six plus One: British Policy Making and the Question of European Economic Integration, 1955," in *International Affairs* 64 (1988), pp. 393–413; Milward, *The Rise and Fall*, pp. 190–216, 229–276.

mately fifty percent of British foreign trade was still with the Commonwealth and a customs union with lower external tariffs threatened greater competition from American and West German industrial products, there was on the other hand the attraction of increased rationalization through a common market; it was also foreseeable that trade with Western Europe would greatly expand in the coming years. Commonwealth countries such as Australia and Canada were keenly interested in building up their own industries and diversifying their foreign trade. Decisive for the British rejection of the EEC was the insistence on a special role vis-à-vis the Continent, one rooted in a belief in the superiority of British civilization and greatly strengthened by the experience of the Second World War. The British establishment stubbornly clung to the illusion of a special role even though the economic and geopolitical bases for it were rapidly being lost.[14]

In creating a free trade area that would gradually eliminate industrial tariffs among the OEEC states but not affect tariff barriers with non-member states, the government of Harold Macmillan demonstrated that it was prepared to alter the very protectionist trade policy that the UK had been pursuing for the previous twenty-five years. At the same time, Britain was hoping to be able to prevent the formation of an economic community of the six ECSC states. Lastly, the project of a common market was opposed on many sides—on the one hand because it implied too much protectionism and on the other because it offered too little protection from foreign competition. It was especially Ludwig Erhard, the popular father of the West German "economic miracle," who demonstratively pushed for the British initiative. He hoped it would be a significant step toward a general liberalization of trade, which was in the interest of strongly export-oriented West German industry. In 1956, some twenty-one percent of imports into the Federal Republic came from EEC countries and some twenty-eight percent of exports went to them. If the eleven OEEC states were added, the import tally was forty-three percent and the export tally no less than fifty-nine percent.[15] When a crisis developed in the negotiations on the Treaties of Rome in October of 1956, Erhard spoke within the West German government in favor of breaking off talks for an economic community and instead advocated an accord with the British, as

---

[14] Cf. Wolfram Kaiser, "Not present at the creation. Großbritannien und die Gründung der EWG," in Michael Gehler (ed.), *Vom gemeinsamen Markt zur europäischen Unionsbildung. 50 Jahre Römische Verträge 1957–2007*, Vienna: Böhlau, 2009, pp. 225–242.
[15] Note for Erhard 29 October 1957, provided by Gabriele Brenke, "Europakonzeptionen im Widerstreit. Die Freihandelszonen-Verhandlungen 1956–1958," in *Vierteljahrshefte für Zeitgeschichte* 42 (1994), pp. 595–633, here p. 602.

he said, on "what has for years been the decisive political and economic initiative for the integration of Europe."[16]

After the crisis in negotiations among the Six had been overcome, Macmillan's government concentrated its efforts to use a free trade area including the EEC to hinder and if possible thwart the construction of the Common Market in accordance with the treaty terms. In any event, access to the markets of the Six was to be secured and the political self-isolation of Britain avoided. The prime minister also hoped that British engagement in the free trade area would prevent the Federal Republic, at the time growing noticeably stronger economically, from dominating the Community of the Six; his motive was concern over what he regarded as an ominous German tendency toward authoritarian power politics. Instead of Germany, it would be Britain that would maintain or regain its leading role in Europe.

Realization of the British plans for a free trade area would have meant that the UK and the smaller states could gain for their industrial products all the advantages of the Common Market without at the same time having to accept the obligations to which members of the Economic Community had agreed: the creation of a common foreign tariff, the development of a common trade and agricultural policy, as well as the standardization of certain aspects of social, economic, and monetary policy. It was very doubtful that member states such as the Federal Republic or Belgium would adhere to those obligations if the Common Market for industrial products, which was what interested them the most, could be had without the other terms from which Britain and its partners would be freed. Thus, those portions of the Community treaty might well remain a dead letter.

Aside from that, a free trade area of all OEEC countries threatened to make the common foreign tariffs of the Six obsolete. Countries with lower foreign tariffs than the common rate could import goods from other countries more cheaply and then sell them in the countries of the Community, whether or not those goods had been further processed. It was especially the case that Britain, which was also a member of the Commonwealth preference area, could hope for unilateral advantages: Inexpensive raw materials and foodstuffs imported from the Commonwealth would give British industry cost advantages and would draw American investment into the country. Here too it was doubtful as to how long competitive industry in the Community of Six would participate under such circumstances; their governments would be subject to pressure to adjust their tariffs to British levels.

Economic mechanisms and political pressure thus threatened to collaborate in sooner or later bringing about the dissolution of the EEC "like a lump of sugar

---

16 Wilfried Loth, *Der Weg nach Europa. Geschichte der europäischen Integration 1939–1957*, Göttingen: Vandenhoeck & Ruprecht, 1990, p. 125; the quote from Erhard's declaration before the OEEC Council of Ministers on 12 February 1957 is in *Europa-Archiv* 12 (1957), p. 9651.

in a cup of English tea," as opponents of the British initiative remarked with a note of bitterness.[17] For those hostile to EEC protectionism, such as Erhard and the free-trader circles of German industry, that was a welcome prospect and one that paradoxically also helped overcome initial opposition to conclusion and ratification of the Treaties of Rome: If an expansive free trade area followed in their wake, then they could do little harm. For the adherents of a socially acceptable modernization (especially in France and Italy) as well as for those seeking a political Europe, the British initiative constituted a tremendous challenge, however. Hard-won unity on an approach to modernization featuring social solidarity would be threatened with collapse; the prospect of attaining a Political Community via common economic development would vanish entirely.

Further questions were raised when Charles de Gaulle came to power in France on 1 June 1958. Gaullist deputies had rejected both the ECSC and the European Defense Community (EDC) and then had gone on to vote against the Treaties of Rome. De Gaulle himself had told the press that the treaties meant for a "mutilated Europe" in which France was threatened with the status of "servant" to a dynamic Germany.[18] He was supposed to have said to his like-minded colleague Michel Debré, "What are these treaties good for? When we come to power, we'll tear all of them up."[19] The fathers of the Treaties of Rome and the members of the European Commission had to reckon with the likelihood that the new French prime minister and future president of the Fifth Republic would carry out those intentions. There was thus a real danger that the rug would be pulled out from under the Commission before its work had really gotten going.

It was the case however that de Gaulle's criticism had always been aimed at the alleged mediocrity of the politicians of the Fourth Republic—people who needed to be gotten rid of—and not at the principle of European unity itself. Establishing a Europe that was a power-political collective enabling Europeans to play an autonomous role between the superpowers of the Cold War and "could open a career for the capacities of the German people without endangering its neighbors"[20]—all this was also an important goal for de Gaulle. He had always emphasized that such a Europe would only be possible if the participating states

---

17 Pierre Gerbet, *La construction de l'Europe*, 4th edition, Paris: Armand Colin, 2007, p. 166.
18 *Paris-Presse-l'Intransigeant*, 13 February 1957, quoted in William B. Cohen, "De Gaulle et l'Europe d'avant 1958," in *De Gaulle en son siècle*, vol. V: *L'Europe*, Paris: Plon, 1992, pp. 53–65, here p. 62.
19 Quoted in Edmond Jouve, *Le Général de Gaulle et la construction de l'Europe (1940–1966)*, Paris: Librairie Générale de Droit et de Jurisprudence, 1967, p. 253.
20 As formulated in a communication to the founder of the Pan-European Movement, Richard Graf Coudenhove-Kalergi, 30 December 1948, Charles de Gaulle, *Lettres, Notes et Carnets, Mai 1945 – Juin 1950*, Paris: Plon, 1984, pp. 330ff.

would "cede sovereignty in the spheres of economics and defense."[21] He had thus been criticizing not an excess of supranational elements in the concrete European treaties but rather a scarcity of them.

It was therefore by no means only opportunism that led de Gaulle to assure the worried Guy Mollet during conversations on the formation of his government: "The Common Market is an excellent thing, but I find it, shall we say, a bit narrow."[22] On 10 June 1958 in his first foreign policy meeting after taking office, he expressed himself somewhat more clearly: "The main issue is the Common Market—which in and of itself is not a bad thing—and above all the political and cultural organization of Europe."[23] De Gaulle was enough of a realist not to try to begin from scratch with European integration; he instead accepted the existing organizations as starting points for his farther-reaching plans. The worth of the Common Market itself for the modernization of France and for the power-political self-assertion of Europe became clearer to him in the following weeks via Jacques Rueff. Since late September, this finance specialist had headed a council of experts working on a plan to bolster the French currency. If France wanted to keep its place in Europe and in the world, it needed to become economically competitive once again; and that was only possible via a politically regulated modernization in agreement with its European partners.[24]

Thus, the change of government in France did not mean any change in the French view of the project for a free trade area. Paris saw to it that the EEC Commission as well as the High Authority of the ECSC participated in the negotiations of the Maudling Committee, and then in February of 1958, it presented a free trade plan that amounted to the creation of an economic union among the seventeen OEEC states. The liberalization of intra-European trade was to be negotiated separately for each economic category; agriculture was to be included, and every step toward liberalization was to be linked to progress in the harmonization of conditions of production, trade in goods, and social policy. In order to secure the advantages that the EEC treaty offered France, it was also to be the case that rules at the OEEC level would take effect "only some years" after the consolidation of

---

21 Statement of 17 July 1950, Charles de Gaulle, *Discours et messages*, vol. 2, Paris: Plon, 1970, pp. 379–383, here p. 381. On this and the following, Wilfried Loth, "De Gaulle und Europa. Eine Revision," in *Historische Zeitschrift* 253 (1991), pp. 629–660.
22 Quoted in Jean Lacouture, *De Gaulle*, vol. II: *Le politique*, Paris: Éditions du Seuil, 1985, p. 491.
23 Notes of Foreign Minister Couve de Murville, quoted in Gérard Bossuat, "Face à l'histoire? Les décideurs politiques français et la naissance des traités de Rome," in Michael Gehler (ed.), *Vom gemeinsamen Markt zur europäischen Unionsbildung*, pp. 147–168, here p. 167.
24 Cf. Laurent Warlouzet, *Le choix de la CEE par la France. L'Europe économique en débat de Mendès-France à de Gaulle (1955–1969)*, Paris: Comité pour l'Histoire économique et financière, 2011, pp. 172–185.

the EEC. The dismantling of tariffs would then follow the terms of the EEC treaty, but three years later in each case.[25]

De Gaulle was essentially committed to the free trade area but also had the French negotiators insist on some fundamentals that were unacceptable to the British government: Compensatory taxes for products whose raw materials had been imported at tariff rates more than three or four percent below those of the EEC; autonomous decisions by the member states regarding implementation of protective clauses; unanimity in the decision to move to each new phase; and a three-year period between the EEC's tariff reduction and the launching of the free trade area. After the EEC Commission had striven to convince the governments of the member states not to allow themselves to be drawn away from Community agreements by British proposals, de Gaulle worked hand in hand with the Commission: Hallstein's deputy Marjolin went to Paris almost every weekend to consult with Foreign Minister Couve de Murville.[26]

Adenauer was much relieved when in his first meeting with de Gaulle on 14 September in Colombey-les-deux-Églises, the Frenchman assured him that he would continue supporting the Treaties of Rome and moreover was seeking "organized" cooperation in Europe.[27] At the same time, the West German leader was subject to strong pressure regarding the free trade area. The French conditions were opposed not only by his economy ministry, which was charged with leading the negotiations. The business wing of the CDU and the FDP opposition as well as large segments of export-oriented industry declared their enduring opposition to the implementation of EEC regulations if the free trade area did not come into existence. On 2 October, the Bundestag passed a resolution calling upon the government to do everything possible to expand upon the EEC via a free trade area. Beyond that, Macmillan was threatening consequences if negotiations failed: difficulties in talks on the compatibility of EEC provisions with the GATT Treaty, the withdrawal of British troops from the Continent, and potentially even Britain's departure from NATO.[28]

Consequently, Bonn sought to mediate between the French and British positions in the negotiations of the Maudling Committee. In the process, Adenauer made certain that the priority of the Common Market was maintained. At a meeting of the EEC Council of Ministers in Brussels on 18 September, Couve de Murville did succeed in getting his partners to commit themselves to autonomous

---

25 Memorandum of 24 February 1956, *Archiv der Gegenwart* 24 February 1956, A 6911.
26 Interview with Karl-Heinz Narjes, 24 May 2004.
27 Notes on the conversation of 14 September 1958, quoted in Hans-Peter Schwarz, *Adenauer: Der Staatsmann 1952–1967*, Stuttgart: Deutsche Verlags-Anstalt, 1991, p. 456.
28 Cf. Brenke, "Europakonzeptionen," pp. 625–627.

protective measures, unanimity in the organs, and a three-year buffer between EEC and OEEC tariff reductions. The only item left unresolved was the stance on the French demand for compensatory taxes, which amounted to retention of internal tariffs. At the next gathering of the committee, from 23 to 30 October, it seemed that the participants were on a path to abandoning negotiations. Only with difficulty did Erhard's state secretary, Alfred Müller-Armack, succeed in bringing the parties back to the negotiation table by means of bilateral discussions. On the issue of provisions against distortions of competitiveness due to differing external tariff rates, the negotiators agreed to follow an EEC Commission proposal calling for the various economic sectors to be discussed separately.

At this juncture, Erhard appealed to Adenauer to convince the French to make greater concessions. In order to leave nothing untried in preventing the collapse of negotiations, Erhard sought to participate personally in the next gathering of the Maudling Committee on 13 and 14 November in Paris. For his part, Adenauer thought that the risk of damaging Franco-German relations was too great. He summarily made use of his guideline competence as chancellor to declare that the negotiations on the free trade area had priority. Erhard had to remain in Bonn. After French Minister of Information Jacques Soustelle told the press on the evening of the second day of negotiations that France rejected a free trade area constituted along the lines proposed by Britain, the West German chancellor acknowledged in a second meeting with de Gaulle on 26 November in Bad Kreuznach that the Maudling Committee should meet again only after the six EEC states had agreed upon a unified position. Compromise formulations written into the draft of the official communiqué of this meeting were deleted by de Gaulle himself, and Adenauer gave his consent.[29]

In agreeing on the priority of a unified position among the Six, Adenauer had *de facto* opted for termination of negotiations. The British government sought once again to mobilize a majority of OEEC members in the OEEC Council of Ministers on 15 December, ultimately demanding that the remaining OEEC members guarantee the same tariff reductions, not just in general but in every respect, as those agreed to among the EEC partners for 1 January 1959. Five of the six EEC states regarded that as by no means unreasonable, and Adenauer himself offered to mediate. De Gaulle however remained adamant, and the other five no longer dared outvote him.[30]

---

[29] Daniel Koerfer, *Kampf ums Kanzleramt. Erhard und Adenauer*, Stuttgart: Deutsche Verlags-Anstalt, 1987, pp. 213–215; Frances Lynch, "De Gaulle's First Veto. Fance, the Rueff Plan and the Free Trade Area," in *Contemporary European History* 9 (2000), pp. 111–135; DDF 1958 II, p. 370.
[30] De Gaulle to Adenauer, 22 December 1958, in Poidevin, "De Gaulle et l'Europe," p. 87.

Britain's final weapon was to force the plan to revert to the convertibility of the British pound. Macmillan was convinced that the French—with their overvalued currency—could not follow suit; and thus the realization of the first phase of the Common Market would need to be postponed. De Gaulle met this British move with a major feat: On 27 December, the French franc was devalued by 17.5 percent and simultaneously declared convertible. Further, strict measures for improving the budget situation were adopted in accordance with recommendations from the Rueff Commission; and limits on trade with OEEC states, which France had adopted during its financial crisis, were reduced by ninety percent.[31] In this way, the effort by Macmillan to maintain a leadership role in Europe was defeated. British threats had in the end functioned counterproductively, serving to strengthen the solidarity of the Six. After all the EEC members and seven additional OEEC states had been able to follow the British move by making their currencies convertible, the European Payments Union was dissolved on 29 December and the European Monetary Agreement (EMA) was put into effect. The first phase of the Common Market could begin punctually on 1 January 1959. De Gaulle now had a clear path for implementing the modernization of France within the framework of the EEC.

The Construction of the Common Market

After de Gaulle had committed himself to a rapid realization of the Common Market and after this decision had been rewarded by noticeable economic growth, the timetable for the creation of the customs union—which the negotiators had written into the treaty with an eye toward French reservations—proved too slow. The ten percent reduction in tariffs on 1 January 1959 and the simultaneous dismantling of limitations on trade through the expansion of import quotas by twenty percent led to an approximately twenty-percent increase of trade among the six states of the Community within one year. In response, the Commission proposed in February of 1960 that the tempo of tariff reductions be accelerated. France supported this but at the same time wanted more rapid imposition of the common external tariff, which was supposed to come into force only after the completion of the first phase of the Common Market. That demand was opposed by the Federal Republic and Benelux states: They wanted not only to delay the transition to higher tariff rates as long as possible but also to prevent the forma-

---

[31] Sylvie M. Schwaag, "Currency Convertibility and European Integration: France, Germany and Britain," in Anne Deighton and Alan S. Milward (eds.), *Widening, Deepening and Acceleration: The European Economic Community 1957–1963*, Baden-Baden: Nomos, 1999, pp. 89–106.

tion of a preference area within the OEEC or GATT. On 12 May 1960, the Council of Ministers agreed to reduce internal tariffs on 1 January 1961 by thirty percent of the initial level (instead of twenty percent on 1 July 1960) and on 1 January 1962 by forty percent (instead of thirty). Quantitative limits on imports were to be abolished completely at that time. Likewise, the first phase in adjusting to a common external tariff was brought forward by one year: The reduction of the difference between national tariff levels and the anticipated common external tariff by thirty percent was to occur on 1 January 1961. In order to take into account the reservations of the low-tariff states, a deduction of twenty percent was to be taken from the mean of the four tariff regions, that is, France, the Federal Republic, Italy, and the Benelux states.[32]

After the completion of the first phase, that is, three years after the first tariff reduction, a doubling of trade within the Community had occurred. The Council therefore decided not only on a punctual transition to the second phase, but on 15 May 1962, it agreed to a further acceleration of tariff reductions: The next drop of ten percent stipulated in the treaty was moved up by one year to 1 July 1962. A halving of the tariff rates within the Community had thereby been attained some two and a half years earlier than the date set forth in the treaty (1 January 1965). Likewise, the next phase in the adjustment of the common external tariff, reducing the difference with national tariff rates by a further thirty percent, was also brought forward by two and a half years, from 1 January 1966 to 1 July 1963.[33] Given that individual states also carried out unilateral tariff reductions—France in 1961, Italy in 1962, and the Federal Republic in 1964—the actual tariff level within the Community sank even more quickly. At the beginning of the third phase of the construction of the Community on 1 January 1966, official tariffs for internal trade were at twenty percent of their initial levels; in most cases, that meant a burden of less than five percent. On 1 July 1968, internal tariffs were completely eliminated. That was eighteen months earlier than specified in the treaty, and when including potential extensions of the first and second phases that could have been implemented, it was some three and a half years shorter than the maximum allowable transition deadline.

What the Commission did not succeed in doing however was abolishing the non-tariff limitations on trade by 1 January 1970, the specified end of the transition period. In order to achieve full free traffic of goods within the tariff union and to ensure free competition, there needed to be a standardization of national legal provisions, technical norms, state monopolies or regulations and practices

---

[32] Hans von der Groeben, *Aufbaujahre der Europäischen Gemeinschaft. Das Ringen um den Gemeinsamen Markt und die Politische Union (1958–1966)*, Baden-Baden: Nomos, 1982, pp. 143ff.
[33] *Ibid.*, p. 211.

in public procurement to the extent that they no longer constituted actual trade barriers or instances of discrimination. At the beginning of 1965, the Directorates-General for the Internal Market and for Competition presented a comprehensive program of measures aimed at eliminating these hindrances but also made the observation that given the amount of necessary changes in national provisions and practices, it would not be possible to meet the deadline with the resources available.[34] The standardization of national regulations did in fact prove to be a difficult task. Opposition from affected interest groups hardened in inverse proportion to the step-by-step elimination of tariffs and import quotas that had served as protective measures.

In the same way, the efforts to implement free movement of labor and free trade in services ran headlong into national regulations for certain medical, technical, and legal professions, for banking, and for certain professions such as pharmacy. Under these conditions, no common European capital market came into being either. It was only the case that capital flows of a personal character were completely liberalized: direct investment, business with on-board securities, real estate investments, and trade credits (Directives of 11 May 1960 and 18 December 1962). Free movement of labor was realized in two steps: Obligatory preferential treatment of workers from one's own country in hiring was abolished in April of 1964. Largely equal treatment of workers from other member states then came into force. In July of 1968, workers from all member states were given full equal rights; work permits for citizens of member states were abolished.

In light of the opposition to eliminating non-tariff limits on trade, it was all the more important for the success of the Economic Community that the commissioner responsible for the rules of competition, Hans von der Groeben, understood the mandate embodied in the ban on anti-commercial agreements and cartels (Articles 85 and 86 of the EEC Treaty) broadly and that he knew how to implement his interpretation. Von der Groeben, who as leader of the European department of the West German economy ministry had already participated in the development of the Treaties of Rome, was an adherent of the German ordo-liberal "Freiburg School" of economics, for which the guarantee of absolutely free competition was key not only to increasing productivity and prosperity but also protection of the consumer. Supported by a relatively young cohort of officials with missionary zeal as well as much scholarly and practical expertise, von der Groeben fought for the application of the provisions of the ban, which were not

---

[34] Eric Bussière, "Not quite a common market yet," in *The European Commission 1958–72*, pp. 289–301, here p. 295.

clearly specified in the treaty, as well as for their extension into a comprehensive code of competition.³⁵

In the draft of regulations for complying with the terms on competition, which were to be met no later than three years after implementation of the treaty, von der Groeben and his colleagues included a general obligation that cartels and other combinations of firms be registered with the Commission, which would then determine if such entities were compatible with the requirements of free competition. Beyond this, the Commission was to have authority on its own or on the basis of complaints from third parties to initiate proceedings against firms and also the power to conduct investigations when cartel formation or misuse of a dominant position in the market was suspected. This draft, presented to the Council on 31 October 1960, generated a storm of protest from representatives of industry in France, Belgium, and the Federal Republic; the proposed powers of the Commission went much too far for the French government as well. Von der Groeben was however able to achieve much in persuading representatives of government, parliamentary deputies, and administration experts. Supported by a positive report from the Committee on Internal Market of the European Parliament as well as a parliamentary vote, he succeeded in getting the draft through the Council. With minor modifications, it was approved on 5 February 1962 as "Directive No. 17."³⁶

The bans and regulations issued by the Commission after it had received this authority were often challenged in the European Court. The rulings almost always upheld the decisions of the Commission—for the first time, in the case of a market-partitioning deal between the West German firm *Grundig* and the French firm *Consten* in September of 1964. A European code of competition was thereby created step by step, one that applied the fundamental principles of German ordo-liberalism. Its application also gained approval because the Commission's decisions took into account the interest in competitiveness on the world market, especially with the US, and also acknowledged the needs of small and medium-sized firms to cooperate in the face of large competitors.

---

35 Katja Seidel, "DG IV and the origins of a supranational competition policy. Establishing an economic constitution for Europe," in Wolfram Kaiser, Brigitte Leucht, and Morten Rasmussen (eds.), *The History of the European Union. Origins of a Trans- and Supranational Polity 1950–72*, New York and London: Routledge, 2009, pp. 129–147.
36 Sibylle Hambloch, "Die Entstehung der Verordnung 17 von 1962 im Rahmen der EWG-Wettbewerbsordnung," in *Europarecht* 17/6 (2002), pp. 877–897; Laurent Warlouzet, "La France et la mise en place de la politique de la concurrence communautaire (1957–64)," in Éric Bussiere, Michel Dumoulin, Sylvain Schirmann (eds.), *Europe organisée, Europe du libre-échange. Fin XIXᵉ siècle – Années 1960*, Brussels: Peter Lang, 2006, pp. 175–201.

Von der Groeben and his colleagues were very successful in eliminating or modifying state aid that infringed upon or distorted competition within the Community. Opposition from governments and interest groups was very strong in this area too. Nevertheless, by 1965, some thirteen of the approximately 450 subsidies had been eliminated as impermissible and another sixty had been altered. Where subsidies were permissible as support for suffering regions or branches of industry or were in the common European interest, the Commission made efforts toward standardizing the various national regulations and toward limiting the duration of the aid.

On the issue of standardizing taxes, the Commission ran headlong into stubborn resistance from France, which sought to protect its sovereignty in that area and also retain the existing system of compensatory levies at the borders. For his part, von der Groeben argued that the exact level of tax actually paid in the various systems of multiple taxation in the individual states was difficult to determine and that compensatory levies or rebates in the change-over from one tax system to another strongly invited manipulation and thus distortions of competition. He therefore advocated the elimination of sales tax systems in favor of uniform value-added taxes imposed in the land of origin of the product or service. He also urged the elimination of tax boundaries and, lastly, an extensive standardization of tax rates so as to banish the threat of a ruinous tax war.

Although von der Groeben's program enjoyed support from the West German government, he was initially only able to obtain a moratorium from the finance ministers in June of 1960 by which they committed themselves to alter compensatory levies at the borders for only purely technical reasons. This would serve as a means of preventing attempts to compensate for sinking tariff levels through higher tax protectionism. A draft directive of November 1962 envisioning the introduction of value-added taxes in connection with the elimination of tax boundaries was rejected by the French government. Only on 9 February 1967 did the Council agree on the introduction of a common system of value-added taxes at the end of the transition period, that is, on 1 January 1970. This did not however include any agreement on a uniform level for the value-added tax. It also lacked any degree of standardization for consumption taxes (on products such as alcohol, tobacco, and gasoline), business taxes, or capital gains taxes. In a program for standardizing direct taxes that the Commission presented in September of 1967, it was correctly argued that these adjustments too were necessary in order to create an internal European market.[37]

---

37 "Programm zur Harmonisierung der direkten Steuern," *Bulletin der EWG*, September–October 1967; cf. overall Éric Bussière, "Competition," in *The European Commission 1958–72*, pp. 303–316.

The interest of the low-tariff states in sinking common tariff levels was supported by the GATT regulations, which allowed the creation of customs unions but only if the joint tariff were lower than the previous tariffs of the member states. Given that some sixty percent of the imports entering the Community went to the low-tariff states (the Federal Republic, Belgium, the Netherlands, and Luxembourg), the overall tariff level was strictly speaking not the arithmetic mean among the four tariff zones.[38] In order to prevent possible action by GATT against the customs union of the Six, the Council of Ministers had, at the suggestion of the Commission, granted the other OEEC states the same ten percent tariff reduction and twenty percent increase in import quotas that were in effect for EEC states. What was not granted was the increase in quotas applied to every single product category down to at least three percent of national production; that was the point de Gaulle in the end did not concede. In negotiations carried on by Jean Rey as commissioner for external trade from September of 1960 to May of 1961 in the GATT Committee, compensatory payments were agreed upon for individual states in response to the increase in import duties of the Federal Republic and the Benelux countries. Beyond this, the EEC was willing to make small reductions in the common tariff levels for some two hundred products and also expressed a willingness to negotiate on further tariff reductions.

In the so-called "Dillon Round" of the GATT negotiations (named after the American delegation leader Douglas Dillon, who had pushed for the round) that began on 29 May 1961 in Geneva and extended until 16 July 1962, the EEC and the US, its most important trading partner, agreed on mutual tariff reductions of twenty percent on 560 respectively 575 commercial products. Britain and other willing states joined in. Altogether, however, this meant for a reduction of the common external tariff of the Community by only about seven percent, the average level sinking from 12.5 to 11.7 percent. This was by no means the great breakthrough on all-round trade liberalization that the Commission had been seeking.[39]

That was not to come very quickly. The American government quickly sought another round of negotiations under the auspices of the Trade Expansion Act of January 1962, which authorized President Kennedy to eliminate tariffs completely in product areas in which the US and the European Community together accounted for eighty percent or more of trade; tariffs on all other products could be halved. Such far-reaching liberalization, which was also to include agricultural

---

[38] Ruggero Ranieri, "The Origins and Achievements of the EEC Customs Union (1958–1968)," in Antonio Varsori (ed.), *Inside the European Community. Actors and Policies in the European Integration 1957–1962*, Baden-Baden: Nomos, 2006, pp. 257–281, here p. 266.
[39] *Ibid.*, pp. 268ff.

products, was not acceptable to France, however. De Gaulle therefore argued that new negotiations only take place after completion of the Common Market. Erhard and the representatives of the Benelux states sought in vain to take up the offer Kennedy had made.[40]

De Gaulle viewed the American offensive all the more critically because it was exactly in the realm of agricultural production that France did not want to dispense with tariff protection through the European Community. For France, the transfer of existing national subsidy systems and external tariffs for agriculture onto the European level presented an opportune means of eliminating the structural crisis in which French farmers found themselves: Through the opening of a larger market but one still protected from world competition, agricultural production could be increased; at the same time, the cost of subsidies would be shared among more parties. It would in this way be easier to tolerate agricultural subsidies that actually did not fit the strategy of accelerated modernization of France but that were indispensable for political reasons. In the treaty negotiations, French representatives thus insisted that beyond inclusion of agriculture in the Common Market, a "common agricultural policy" be developed by the end of the transition period.[41]

France's efforts to create a system of regulation for European agriculture were supported especially by the Netherlands, for which the transfer of agricultural protectionism from the national to the European level was also among the essential goals of European unification policy. The Dutch case was however more strongly driven by economics than politics, and the pressure was correspondingly greater: Whereas France would first become a net exporter of agricultural products in 1968, the share of Dutch exports made up of agricultural products was no less than forty percent in the later 1940s. Additionally, Mansholt, who had become an important political figure in his homeland by designing Dutch agricultural policy, put much more emphasis on modernizing the sector rather than on subsidizing it. Whereas subsidies threatened to perpetuate the structural crisis of agriculture at the cost of consumers and taxpayers, modernization offered the opportunity for lasting improvement of the situation. Specialized products for larger markets were intended to make agricultural concerns competitive, and the resulting profits would facilitate further modernization.[42]

---

[40] Lucia Coppolaro, "The European Economic Commission in the GATT Negotiations of the Kennedy Round (1961–1967): Global and Regional Trade," in Varsori (ed.), *Inside*, pp. 347–366, here, pp. 351–358.

[41] Thiemeyer, *"Pool Vert."*

[42] Guido Thiemeyer, "Sicco Mansholt and European Supranationalism," in Wilfried Loth (ed.), *La gouvernance supranationale dans la construction européenne*, Brussels: Émile Bruylant, 2005,

Mansholt's transfer to Brussels signaled how important this approach was for the Netherlands. As commissioner for agriculture, he sought to implement it as comprehensively as possible. He worked in a way similar to von der Groeben by incorporating representatives of national governments, experts, and lobbyists. In the process, he also sought to transfer as much authority as possible to the supranational level. He was convinced that only in this way could a coherent European agricultural policy be relatively safe from the pressures of particularistic interests or blockades by strategically well-positioned lobbyists. He quickly let agricultural interest groups know that he preferred to deal with entities at the European level rather than with national groups. This soon led to the formation of transnational coalitions and in September of 1958, to the creation of a permanent Committee of Profession Agricultural Organizations (COPA, Comité des organisations professionelles agricoles de la Communauté européenne).[43] In this way, the necessary compromise of interests among agriculturalists would be promoted at the interest group level; the Commission simultaneously gained influence as a supranational actor in common agricultural policy.

The treaty specified that as soon as it went into effect, a conference was to be called in order to compare national agricultural policies and make an assessment of demand. In planning for this event, Mansholt decided to invite not only agricultural ministers as spokesmen of the governments but also the standing representatives of the member states to the Commission, the top officials of agriculture ministries, as well as representatives of agricultural producers, processers, and trade in agricultural products. He thereby activated an international milieu of agricultural experts and representatives of interests that had already participated in the tedious and unsuccessful negotiations on the creation of a "Green Pool" within the framework of the OEEC; and he drew this milieu into the planning for the common agricultural policy.[44] In Stresa, where the agriculture conference of 3 to 12 July 1958 took place, the different concepts and interests naturally emerged in sharp relief. However, with a speech intended as an answer to the presentations of the agriculture ministers, Mansholt succeed in creating a kind of spirit of optimism that resulted in a vague consensus on goal-setting in agricultural policy. The conference issued a resolution calling for the dismantling

---

pp. 39–53.
43 Jan van der Harst, "The common agricultural policy: a leading field of action," in *The European Commission 1958–72*, pp. 317–337, here pp. 321ff.
44 Ann-Christina L. Knudsen, "Politische Unternehmer in transnationalen Politiknetzwerken. Die Ursprünge der Gemeinsamen Agrarpolitik," in Michael Gehler, Wolfram Kaiser, and Brigitte Leucht (eds.), *Netzwerke im europäischen Mehrebenensystem. Von 1945 bis zur Gegenwart*, Vienna: Böhlau, 2009, pp. 105–120.

of trade limits to go hand in hand with the standardization of law and the determination of uniform prices. This was not to be allowed to lead to overproduction, however, and measures to protect against "distortions of competition from outside" were not to be allowed to burden relations with third parties. Additionally, joint "efforts for increasing productivity" were to be undertaken, especially measures to "improve the structure of agriculture."[45]

In developing the Commission proposal for the common agricultural policy—a process occurring in informal agreement with the agriculture ministers and the representatives of COPA—Mansholt also had to give greater consideration to the French interest in subsidies and protection. Commissioner Marjolin and Director-General Louis Rabot made him aware that he could not succeed in the Council of Ministers in any other way. The proposal submitted by the Commission on 7 November 1959 stipulated that uniform benchmark prices would be determined for almost ninety percent of agricultural products. If prices fell below the level of the somewhat lower fixed-intervention prices, the Community would buy products at those lower prices. There would also be export assistance for products that could no longer command the stipulated price levels on the world market, and importers would pay levies compensating for the difference between the lower world prices and Community prices. This proposal included structural reform only to the extent that one third of the money from import levies would be devoted to measures aimed at improving competitiveness. The other two thirds of those funds were to be used for intervention purchases of Community products and for export assistance. The only measure aimed at warding off the danger of overproduction—which could potentially arise under this system—was the decision that authority for setting prices should lie with the Commission. The national governments, which were more vulnerable to pressure from the agricultural lobby, would only establish general criteria for price setting.

Criticism of this proposal focused on the near total absence of anything about the transition from the existing agricultural system to the proposed common system. The Commission made efforts to address this concern and on 30 June 1960 presented a significantly more comprehensive draft proposal. The orientation was unchanged, but the instrument of the import levies was now seen as balancing out the price differentials within the Community during the transition phase. Introduction of minimum prices and compensatory levies, as envisioned

---

[45] Michael Tracy, "The Spirit of Stresa," in *European Review of Agricultural Economics* 21 (1994) pp. 357–374; van der Harst, "Common agricultural policy, pp. 321–327; Ann-Christina L. Knudsen, *Farmers on Welfare. The Making of Europe's Common Agricultural Policy*," Ithaca: Cornell University, 2009, pp. 96–98; Kiran Klaus Patel, *Europäisierung wider Willen. Die Bundesrepublik in der Agrarintegration der EWG 1955–1973*, Munich: Oldenbourg, 2009, pp. 101–109.

in the treaty, were not taken up nor was the conclusion of long-term agreements. The transition period was to be shortened by two and a half years, ending on 30 June 1967. The route to the common agricultural market was thereby becoming clearer; pressure to implement it was at the same time also growing more intense.[46]

In this form, the Commission proposal contradicted West German ideas in a double sense: It contained too much protectionism in the eyes of the economy ministry and a large segment of the West German public, and the German Farmers Association (Deutscher Bauernverband) balked at the accelerated dismantling of special protection from European competition and at the anticipated drop in grain prices, which were markedly higher in the Federal Republic than in any other member state. With an eye to the importance of farmers at the ballot box, Adenauer decided that the agricultural market project would need to be tabled until the next Bundestag election, that is, until the autumn of 1961. At the next meeting of the Council of Ministers on 19 and 20 July 1960, Agriculture Minister Werner Schwarz, himself a representative of the interests of the Farmers' Association, made it unmistakably clear that the Federal Republic could not accept a shortening of the transition period and that his country's grain prices could not be lowered.[47]

In light of the West German chancellor's position, the French and Dutch governments agreed to delay regulation of price levels. Conversely, at the Council of Ministers meeting on 19 and 20 December 1960, they were able to push through an accelerated reduction in agricultural tariffs by five percent for 1 January 1961 against the wishes of the West German delegation, which had not proven very persuasive. Likewise, the system of internal import levies was introduced for at least a third of the agricultural products (among them grain and pork).[48] These measures meant that a significant step toward the planned market had been achieved even though it remained an open question as to when further steps would follow, if ever.

German obstruction continued after the Free Democratic Party (FDP) was able to lure away votes from the CDU with populist agrarian slogans in the Bundestag election of 17 September 1961. De Gaulle's patience had reached an end, however. Under additional pressure from French farmers suffering from an acute profit crisis, he issued an ultimatum demanding agreement on the fundamentals and regulations of the common agricultural policy, including acceleration by two

---

46 Von der Groeben, *Aufbaujahre*, pp. 105–110; van der Harst, "Common agricultural policy," pp.327ff.; Knudsen, *Farmers*, pp. 148–185.
47 Patel, *Europäisierung*, pp. 113–136.
48 Knudsen, *Farmers*, pp. 185–195; Patel, *Europäisierung*, pp. 166–175.

and a half years as proposed by the Commission. He instructed Foreign Minister Couve de Murville to declare in a session of the Council of Ministers meeting on 19 and 20 December 1961 that without an agreement on agriculture, France would not support the transition to the second phase of the Common Market on 1 January 1962.

This threat had an effect. It led to that memorable marathon session of the Council, which was to become the archetype of crisis management in the collective memory of Europeans. Under French pressure, Adenauer and Erhard now decided that a solution had to be found somehow. The government representatives negotiated over the Christmas holiday and into January of 1962. When no agreement had been reached on 31 December, the clocks were officially stopped—in the end, all the participants still aspired to reach the transition to the second phase in accordance with the treaty. As Hallstein summed it up (not without sarcasm), there were altogether "forty-five separate meetings, 7 of them at night; a total of 137 hours of discussion, with 214 hours in subcommittee; 582,000 pages of documents; 3 heart attacks."[49] The final hurdles were cleared on the night of 13 January 1962 after many compromise proposals from Mansholt, who was able to make full use of his professional competence as well as his political skill.

In the end, it was agreed that the originally envisioned transition period through 31 December 1969 would be adhered to; after that, however, the system of benchmark prices and import levies would be in effect, as the Commission had proposed. Into 1965, agricultural expenditures were to be financed primarily out of member contributions in accordance with the budget ratios (which would be much less expensive for the Federal Republic than financing via the levies); by 30 June 1965, a settlement was to be found for the remainder of the transition period. During the transition period, member states would still be allowed to impose import quotas should it be necessary; these could however be lifted by the Commission and by the Council of Ministers. Regarding the price level for grain, there was agreement on an upper and lower price for one year; these corresponded to the German and French prices respectively. There would need to be new negotiations on an arrangement beyond that.

In essence, the West Germans had accepted a settlement that was financially unfavorable to them and that additionally pruned away some support for their farmers. The price they paid for accelerating the movement toward the internal market and for the politically-desirable deepening of integration had been reduced only to the extent that this settlement would come into complete effect

---

[49] Walter Hallstein, *United Europe. Challenge and Opportunity*, Cambridge, Mass.: Cambridge University Press, 1962, p. 55. On this and on the following, cf. Knudsen, *Farmers*, pp. 195–206; Patel, *Europäisierung*, pp. 196–212.

after the planned end of the transition period. In the process, it was not merely Mansholt's envisioned structural reform that had fallen by the wayside; the danger of overproduction had also been increased because the Commission had had to leave authority to set detailed price levels to the Council of Ministers.

Fouchet Plans and British Membership Application

According to de Gaulle, the Common Market that had emerged here was to constitute the starting point for a more comprehensive "political, economic, and cultural reality."[50] Such a Europe had in the meantime come to seem even more urgent in his eyes, given that he viewed the existing dependence of the European allies on American nuclear deterrence as dishonorable and to an increasing extent also insecure: dishonorable in regard to the autonomy of the European nations, which as a consequence were permanently under threat of American coercion and which had no alternative in the case of military conflict; and highly uncertain given that the production of long-range Soviet bombers capable of reaching American territory with nuclear weapons had made the US guarantee extremely questionable. De Gaulle did not doubt that this guarantee would lose further value as the Soviet arsenal was perfected and that the transition to the strategy of "flexible response" only exposed Europe to the risk of a privileged destruction.[51]

According to his understanding, the core of political Europe was autonomy in defense policy; this presupposed that the European partners had agreed on the goal of real independence from the leading Western power—that is, they would certainly remain allies of the US but sovereign in the decision on the use of own their weapons. As he wrote in July of 1961, "There can be no European unity if Europe does not constitute a political entity distinct from other entities. A personality. But there can be no European personality if Europe does not have control over the defense of its personality. Defense is always the basis of politics." That "Europe must have its personality in its own defense," was for him "all the more advisable as Europe becomes a strategic whole. It constitutes a marshalling area for one single and simultaneous battle. America can lose Europe in the battle without disappearing. Europe cannot."[52]

---

50 Notes of his diplomatic advisor Jean-Marc Bœgner, 13 July 1958; Charles de Gaulle, *Lettres, Notes et Carnets, Juin 1958 – Décembre 1960*, Paris: Plon, 1985, p. 73.
51 Loth, "De Gaulle und Europa," pp. 649–651.
52 Note of 17 July 1961; Charles de Gaulle, *Lettres, Notes et Carnets, Janvier 1961 – Décembre 1963*, Paris: Plon, 1986, pp. 107ff. Cf. Wilfried Loth, "Franco-German Relations and European Security,

According to de Gaulle, the path to such a "European Europe, independent, mighty, and influential within the framework of the free world,"[53] was to be found in regular consultations of the interested governments. As he suggested as early as August of 1958, these consultations should "in a certain sense take on an organic character to the extent that they develop."[54] In the long term, this ought to lead to the creation of a "confederation" in which majority rule should certainly be in effect: "We must begin with unanimity, and then we shall see."[55] In the short term, however, de Gaulle also sought to have the existing European organs subordinated to the authority of the council of governments. The tendency of the Commission to develop into a European government, which had its roots in the treaty itself, was a thorn in his side: "There is nothing above the nations, if their states do not jointly decide! The aspirations of the Brussels commissioners to give orders to the governments are risible! Risible!"[56]

A first effort toward realizing this institutionalized cooperation especially in the realms of foreign and defense policy was undertaken by de Gaulle in June of 1959, when he suggested to Italian Prime Minister Amintore Fanfani that there be regular meetings of the foreign ministers of France, the Federal Republic, and Italy, gatherings to be prepared by a small joint secretariat. Fanfani agreed to this proposal, though with the condition that the governments of Belgium, the Netherlands, and Luxembourg also participate. This highlighted the impediments to de Gaulle's plans: Whereas Adenauer strongly agreed with French efforts toward European autonomy and also hoped to make use of de Gaulle's ambitions to achieve equality for the Federal Republic within the Atlantic alliance, the Belgian government and even more so the Dutch government were concerned about preventing French hegemony or a Franco-German condominium within the European Community. Dutch Foreign Minister Joseph Luns and his Belgian counterpart Pierre Wigny therefore proposed that Britain participate in this foreign ministers' conference and that the EEC Commission also be brought in. Neither was acceptable to de Gaulle, and so negotiations on his initiative led only to a modest result: On 23 November 1959, the foreign ministers of the Six resolved to gather thrice yearly in the future. Their talks were not however to "harm consulta-

---

1957–1963," in Deighton and Milward (eds.), *Widening, Deepening and Acceleration*, pp. 41–53.
53 Quoted in Jean Lacouture, *De Gaulle*. Vol. 3: *Le souverain 1959–1970*, Paris: Éditions du Seuil, 1986, p. 313.
54 Note by Bœgner 13 August 1958.
55 Comment in a conversation with Alain Peyrefitte on 24 April 1963; Alain Peyrefitte, *C'était de Gaulle*. vol.1, Paris: Gallimard, 1994, p. 430.
56 Comment to Alain Peyrefitte on 13 July 1960, *ibid.*, pp. 66–69. The widespread characterization of de Gaulle as a stubborn opponent of European integration stems from equating his short-term view with his long-term perspective.

tion in NATO and WEU," and if they were to extend to the field of the Community treaties, it should be possible to bring in the appropriate commissioners. A standing secretariat, as de Gaulle had proposed, was not envisioned.[57]

When the failure of the planned Paris summit among Eisenhower, Macmillan, de Gaulle, and Khrushchev (set for May of 1960) made the problem of European self-assertion more urgent, the French president took up a proposal from Jean Monnet that would help overcome the resistance of the Benelux governments: At a meeting with Adenauer at the château de Rambouillet on 29 and 30 July 1960, de Gaulle proposed the creation of a kind of Franco-German confederation with joint citizenship as a strategic step toward creating political Europe. "Three departments, foreign policy, defense, and finance would be shared by the two countries"; this far-reaching fusion was to be legitimized by a referendum in both countries. "No one in the Community of the Six," according to de Gaulle, "would be able to resist the pull of the new political formation, if Germany and France led the way."[58] In order to make the necessary break with NATO integration palatable to Adenauer, he even alluded to the possibility of participating in a European nuclear weapons program: "Later, when we are really unified, there will perforce be changes, a certain division. And you too will without a doubt one day have nuclear weapons, above all in the event our two countries—and perhaps others as well—can unite on a European level."[59]

For his part, Adenauer wanted nothing to do with a plan that meant France and the Federal Republic would go it alone.[60] After criticism to that effect from his colleagues, he withdrew his consent to the reform of NATO and of the Treaties of Rome. After the Supreme Allied Commander Europe, General Lauris Norstad, held out the prospect of a NATO multilateral nuclear force for Europe and after President Eisenhower had on 6 October threatened the withdrawal of all American forces in the event NATO integration were abolished, Adenauer voiced a clear rejection of any special military force of the Six. For the time being, he wanted political cooperation to be limited to the consultations of the foreign ministers;

---

[57] Gerbet, *Construction*, pp. 195ff.
[58] As witnessed by Adenauer's advisor Franz Josef Bach, quoted in Schwarz, *Adenauer*, Stuttgart: Deutsche Verlags-Anstalt, 1991, pp. 567ff. On Monnet's authorship, see Wilfried Loth, "Jean Monnet, Charles de Gaulle und das Projekt der Politischen Union (1958–1963)," in Andreas Wilkens (ed.), *Interessen verbinden. Jean Monnet und die europäische Integration der Bundesrepublik Deutschland*, Bonn: Bouvier, 1999, pp. 253–267.
[59] As witnessed by de Gaulle's colleague Pierre Maillard, in *De Gaulle en son siècle*, vol. 5: *L'Europe*, Paris: Plon, 1992, p. 417.
[60] He even had the corresponding passages removed from the draft protocol of the conversations at the château de Rambouillet.

he also made an appeal to have Britain brought into Europe.⁶¹ De Gaulle sought in vain to mobilize public opinion for his project by advocating at a press conference on 5 September "a regularly organized concert of the governments involved."⁶²

Two circumstances ensured that this second attempt at initiating a political union did not end up stalled like the first: On the one hand, Monnet made Adenauer and the members of his Action Committee in the various member states forcefully aware of the potential for promoting European unity that was embodied in de Gaulle's proposals.⁶³ On the other hand, de Gaulle declared that for a first time he was willing to do without any discussion of defense issues in the new council of the heads of government. Furthermore, in using the term "organized cooperation," he avoided any hint of an attack on the existing Community organs. On 9 February 1961, Adenauer and de Gaulle were able to agree on this formula; and at a summit of the Six on 10 and 11 February, the representatives of Italy, Belgium, and Luxembourg consented as well. Dutch Foreign Minister Luns blocked a resolution on it, however. He would involve himself in organized political cooperation only if Britain participated too. The meeting ended with the establishment of a "study Commission" that was to work out concrete proposals for organized political cooperation by the time of the next summit in May.⁶⁴

In the Commission, chaired by French delegation leader Christian Fouchet, a report was worked out by 24 April that envisioned regular meetings of heads of state and of government (every three to four months) without limitations on the content of discussion, meaning that there was a possibility that issues of defense and economic integration could be raised. As soon as topics in the area of authority of existing European organizations were treated, representatives of these organizations were to be brought in. Additional proposals included a fusion of the executives of the ECSC, EEC, and EURATOM; the transition to direct elections of the European Parliament; and the founding of a European university in Florence.⁶⁵ Yet, the Dutch delegates did not support the possible inclusion of themes touching on NATO or the EEC, and so the meeting of heads of state and of government was deferred for the time being.

---

61 In a communication to de Gaulle of 8 October 1960, provided in Schwarz, *Adenauer*, pp. 587. On this and the following, cf. Georges-Henri Soutou, *L'alliance incertaine. Les rapports politico-stratégiques franco-allemands, 1954–1996*, Paris: Fayard, 1996, pp. 149–188.
62 Charles de Gaulle, *Discours et messages*, vol. 3, Paris: Plon, 1970, pp. 244–246.
63 Loth, "Jean Monnet," pp. 260–262.
64 Esther Kramer, *Europäisches oder atlantisches Europa? Kontinuität und Wandel in den Verhandlungen über eine politische Union 1958–1970*, Baden-Baden: Nomos, 2003, pp. 67–69.
65 Draft report in Heinrich Siegler (ed.), *Europäische politische Einigung. Dokumentation von Vorschlägen und Stellungnahmen 1949–1968*, Bonn, Vienna, and Zurich: Siegler, 1968, pp. 107–109.

Only after Adenauer and de Gaulle had come to an agreement to negotiate if necessary without Dutch participation did the six governments reach a compromise, one mediated by Spaak and Fanfani at a summit in Bonn on 18 July 1961: Luns accepted regular meetings of heads of state and of government with the goal of "common policy," whereas de Gaulle accepted the formulation that "political cooperation" was also to lead to "strengthening of the Atlantic Alliance" and "carrying forward the work begun with the European Communities." The president also approved reform of the existing Communities "in the interest of greater effectiveness" as well as an expansion of the areas to be dealt with by the European Parliament. Only the issues of direct elections and of the European university had been taken off the table.[66] The study Commission was then charged with preparing a suitable draft treaty.

The consensus reached in Bonn was soon called into question when Harold Macmillan, alarmed not least of all by the danger of an autonomous foreign and defense policy organization of the Six, announced in the House of Commons on 31 July that he would seek to negotiate Britain's entry into the EEC. After the failure of its offensive for a free trade area, the British government had, without any great enthusiasm, contemplated the creation of a "small" free trade area with other OEEC states. Six had already been prepared to join in for various reasons: Sweden, Norway, Denmark, Switzerland, Austria, and, after negotiations had already begun, Portugal, which was ruled by a dictatorship at the time. In accordance with the Stockholm Convention of 4 January 1960, they constituted a European Free Trade Association (EFTA), whose members would abolish tariffs on commercial goods imported from other members. In a treaty of 27 March 1961, Finland was added as an associate member.[67]

EFTA did not however resolve the problems for Britain that had been caused by the founding of the EEC. British trade with the EEC states was not only much more significant than that with the EFTA states, but it was also increasing much more quickly. At the same time, trade with Commonwealth states was falling rapidly, American investors preferred the EEC states, and British industry was losing competitiveness *vis-à-vis* firms operating within the larger Common Market. When the

---

66 Heinrich Siegler (ed.), *Dokumentation der europäischen Integration*, vol. 2: 1961–1963, Bonn, Vienna, and Zurich: Siegler, 1964, pp. 10ff.
67 Mikael af Malmborg and Johnny Laursen, "The Creation of EFTA," in Torsten B. Olesen (ed.), *Interdependence versus Integration. Denmark, Scandinavia and Western Europe, 1945–1960*, Odense: University Press of Southern Denmark, 1995, pp. 197–212; Mikael af Malmborg, *Den ståndaktiga nationalstaten. Sverige och den västeruopeiska integrationen 1945–1959*, Lund: Lund University, 1994, pp. 342–386; Wolfram Kaiser, "Challenge to the Community: The Creation, Crisis and Consolidation of the European Free Trade Association, 1958–72," in *Journal of European Integration History* 3 (1997), pp. 7–33.

US government dashed all hopes of support for a bilateral agreement between the EEC and EFTA, opinion in British industry, in the population, and among experts increasingly came to back the UK's rapid entry into the EEC or at least a status close to full entry. Macmillan opted for full membership because only in this way would there be a possibility "of controlling and dominating Europe, economically and politically." For him, Britain's entry was also a matter of preserving the country's leading role, doubly threatened at the time by the economic success and possible political autonomy of the Six. The political goal of entry was "to balance de Gaulle now and Germany later," he explained in a cabinet meeting on 20 April 1961. The resultant strengthening of the British economy would also benefit the UK's political position.[68]

After the British government had actually submitted its application for membership on 9 August, Luns once again wanted to push through Britain's participation in the political union. In this demand he was supported—in contrast to his previous attempt—by his Belgian colleague Paul-Henri Spaak. The Italians, Luxembourgers, and West Germans as well pushed in the Commission for a more strongly supranational orientation of the new organization than had been promised in Bonn. For France, Christian Fouchet presented a draft treaty (the so-called "Fouchet Plan I") on 19 October that stated the goals of "common foreign policy" and "common defense policy" for the "European Union" that was to be founded. The Union Council was to make decisions unanimously; a European Political Commission (with its seat in Paris) was to be subordinate to it; and the European Parliament was to have only an advisory function. Decisions of the Council were to be binding only for those states taking part in the voting. Three years after the treaty came into effect, it was to be revised with the goal of a step-by-step harmonization of foreign and defense policy as well as a centralization of the existing Communities.[69]

The French foreign ministry felt it could accede to the demands of its partners to the extent that a revised version (approved on 15 January 1962 by Couve de Murville) incorporated the Bonn formulation whereby common foreign and defense policy was to serve the strengthening of the Atlantic Alliance. On the issue of revision after three years, a commitment was made that the European Parliament would be "more strongly incorporated" into the development and implementation of common policies. Beyond that, the envisioned reform of the existing institutions was to occur "with regard for the structures" defined in the

---

[68] Milward, *Rise and Fall*, p. 310–351, the quotes from p. 330 (Cabinet Secretary Bishop) and p. 344; Wolfram Kaiser, *Großbritannien und die Europäische Wirtschaftsgemeinschaft 1955–1961*, Berlin: Akademie-Verlag, 1996, pp. 104–177.
[69] Siegler, *Einigung*, pp. 114–117.

treaties of Paris and of Rome.⁷⁰ De Gaulle persisted in his view however, that avowals of strengthening the alliance and the existing treaties be left out and that the economy be explicitly included among the areas of cooperation, which had not been the case before. Presented on 18 January 1962, the second French draft ("Fouchet Plan II") thus contained to a greater extent than the previous version the danger of curtailing the possibilities for supranational development of the existing Communities.⁷¹

Faced with general opposition to unity on this basis, de Gaulle was willing to make greater concessions: At a meeting with Italian Foreign Minister Antonio Segni on 4 April 1962 in Turin, he once again accepted the declaration of strengthening the alliance and stated more precisely that the realm of economics should be dealt with "by implementing the Treaties of Paris and Rome." A new Article 3 even contained an explicit guarantee of the treaties.⁷² At a meeting of foreign ministers in Paris on 17 April, Couve also made the revision clause more precise by returning to the second French draft.

These concessions were insufficient, however. In negotiations on 17 April on the revision, Segni, Luns, and Spaak called for specifying the transition to direct election of the European Parliament and the strengthening of its authority as well as the gradual transition to majority decision-making in the Council. When Couve did not go along with this, Spaak declared that Belgium would sign the treaty on the creation of the European Union only after Britain's entry into the EEC had been signed. Luns supported him in this view. Thus, the second attempt to develop an autonomous European foreign and defense policy had failed. The foreign ministers parted without setting a date for a new meeting or giving the Commission anything further to clarify.⁷³

Afterwards, Adenauer primarily blamed Luns for the failure of the project. Two years later he was still complaining about the "tall guy," characterizing him as "stubborn like only a Dutchman can be." In the spring of 1962, the chancellor

---

70 Text of the draft in Kramer, *Europäisches oder atlantisches Europa*, pp. 293–297.
71 Text of the draft in *Europa-Archiv* 19 (1964), pp. D 467–485.
72 Protocol of the conversation in *Documents Diplomatiques Français 1962–1*, Paris, 1998, pp. 381–389.
73 On the course of the conference, see the report of Couve de Murville, *ibid.*, pp. 433–436. On this overall, cf. Soutou, *L'alliance incertaine*, pp. 188–201; *idem.*, "Le général de Gaulle et le plan Fouchet," in *De Gaulle en son siècle*, vol. 5: *L'Europe*, Paris, 1992, pp. 126–143; Maurice Vaïsse, "De Gaulle, l'Italie et le projet d'union politique européenne 1958–1963," in *Revue d'histoire moderne et contemporaine 1995*, pp. 658–669; Yves Stelandre, "Les Pays du Benelux, l'Europe politique et les négociations Fouchet," in Deighton and Milward (eds.), *Widening, Deepening and Acceleration*, pp. 73–88.

fumed that "I could wring his neck."[74] In fact, however, it was primarily Spaak who had brought de Gaulle's plans to a stop. The French president could have broken the resistance of *one* of the smaller member states: As it had been demonstrated in the summer of 1961 Luns was convinced the Netherlands could not maintain an isolated position against a political union of the other five members. Two states and certainly three could however resist the pressure emanating from Paris and Bonn. If the Federal Republic and France were in agreement, the Netherlands and Belgium had no need to follow along as automatically as de Gaulle had assumed. The difficulties in implementing the Bonn Resolutions of July 1961 consequently stemmed from a course change by Spaak, one that was aided by the British application for membership. Spaak had perceived that Macmillan's dramatic step had put the Belgians in a position to secure better protection from French or Franco-German hegemony, either through Britain's membership or through a supranational orientation of foreign and defense policy. "If you want more integration," he told Couve de Murville at the Paris foreign ministers conference, "we are in agreement that the English aren't included. But if you don't want an integrated Europe, then you must accept England."[75]

However, de Gaulle would not accept a supranational orientation in foreign and defense policy if he could not be sure that his partners shared his understanding of self-assertion within the Atlantic Alliance. "In three years, we will see what we can do to strengthen our ties," he emphasized repeatedly. "In any case, we will have accustomed ourselves to living and acting together."[76] He did not understand that he needed to be bolder here in order to achieve success.

Accession Negotiations and Franco-German Treaty

Macmillan's announcement of 31 July 1961 about accession negotiations was followed by other candidacies. Ireland submitted its formal application on the very same day as Britain. Given that over seventy percent of Irish exports went

---

[74] Conversation with the Swiss historian Jean Rudolf von Salis on 5 August 1964, quoted in Schwarz, *Adenauer*, p. 737.

[75] Paul-Henri Spaak, *Combats inachevés*, vol. 2: *De l'espoir à la déception*, Paris: Fayard, 1969, pp. 262ff.; his explanation was similar at a press conference of 20 April 1962, Siegler, *Integration*, pp. 91–93. Spaak's statements in the winter of 1961–62 do not support the assumption that an earlier presentation of the concessions made by de Gaulle in April of 1962 would have sufficed to gain his agreement. To that extent, the significance given by French diplomats (and following them, by Soutou as well) to de Gaulle's corrections in the draft treaty of 15 January 1962 seem exaggerated.

[76] Press conference of 15 May 1962, de Gaulle, *Discours*, vol. 3, pp. 401–416, here p. 406.

to the UK, the Irish were practically compelled to take this step, even though it was hardly reconcilable with their position of making a political front against the British or the neutrality stemming from that stance. "It would be economic disaster for us to be outside the Community if Britain is in it," declared Secretary of Finance Kenneth Whitaker to his superiors.[77] Denmark followed on 10 August, one day after the official application of the British. In this case, however, the Continental market was of more concern than the British export market: Denmark was desperately dependent on the continued export of agricultural products to the Federal Republic. The Danish government thus wanted to be quickly brought into the ongoing talks on regulation of the Community's agricultural market. Lastly, the government of Norway also submitted an application, though not until 30 April 1962. Economic interests were very compelling in this case too: Britain was the largest market for Norwegian goods, and an EEC that included Britain, Ireland, and Denmark would be receiving approximately seventy percent of total Norwegian exports. Yet, Norwegian insistence on what was still a young national sovereignty was very strong; anti-German and anti-Western emotions manifested themselves too. For those reasons, it was significantly more difficult for Oslo to come to a decision on the application.[78] There were also applications for association from Austria, Switzerland, and Sweden (all made on 15 December 1961) as well as Portugal (on 18 May 1962). All in all, there was thus the prospect of a substantial expansion of the economic community.

Britain's application for membership came with reservations. In order to take the concerns of the conservative establishment into account, the cabinet had resolved to make the final decision on entry only after membership negotiations had been completed. The British were especially concerned to secure the unhindered import of foodstuffs from Commonwealth countries, along with special regulations for British agriculture and "satisfactory arrangements" with the remaining EFTA states. These conditions were explicitly included in the 3 August resolution of the House of Commons that backed Macmillan's initiative; it was also stated that "no agreement affecting these special interests or involving

---

77 Note of 5 January 1962, quoted in Dermot Keogh, "Irish Neutrality and the First Application for Membership of the EEC, 1961–1963," in Deighton and Milward (eds.), *Widening, Deepening and Acceleration*, pp. 287–298, here p. 293. See also Michael J. Geary, *An Inconveniant Wait. Ireland's Quest for Membership of the EEC 1957–73*, Dublin: Institute of Public Administration, 2009, pp. 9–25.
78 Johnny Laursen, "Next in line: Denmark and the EEC Challenge," in Richard Griffith and Stuart Ward (eds.), *Courting the Common Market: The First Attempt to Enlarge the European Community 1961–1963*, London: Lothian Foundation Press, 1996, p. 211–227; Mikael af Malmborg, "Divergent Scandinavian Responses to the Proposed First Enlargement of the EEC," in Deighton / Milward, *Widening*, pp. 299–315.

British sovereignty will be entered into until it has been approved by this House after full consultation with other Commonwealth countries."[79]

Hence the British negotiating delegation led by Special Minister Edward Heath brought with it a program consisting of maximal exceptional regulations: The transition period for full application of the common tariffs should last twelve to fifteen years; even after that, Commonwealth countries were to be given tariff-free sales at the same level that had been allowed in the British market up to that point; there were to be guaranteed prices for pork, eggs, and dairy products; British farmers were to receive compensatory payments from the structure fund; financing of the Community and of the common agricultural market was to be related to the relative level of national income. Essentially nothing from this list was accepted: The French government was not willing to negotiate with the British on issues of agricultural market regulation as long as the fundamentals had not been decided on. After that had been achieved on 14 January 1962, the French, supported by the Commission, diligently guarded the *"acquis communautaire"*—the sum of already agreed-upon Community regulations—from being called into question by the British. Thus, the transition phase was to end on 1 January 1970 for Britain too; Commonwealth countries were only to be allowed certain kinds of relief during the transition period; prices for agricultural products and the income of agriculturalists were to be "reviewed" at regular intervals, as was the practice in the British system of subsidies.[80]

No more concessions were to be had. Macmillan then attempted to obtain a deal from de Gaulle by means of personal diplomacy: greater concessions especially on the Commonwealth connections in exchange for British support for the development of the French nuclear force. During a state visit with de Gaulle in June of 1962, the Briton outlined a vision for European nuclear defense: "There might be a European organisation allied to the United States. There would be a plan for the defence of Europe. The nuclear power of the European countries would be held as part of this European defence."[81] He presented this to the deputy French ambassador "in terms which suggested that he was thinking mainly of joint manufacture of nuclear weapons."[82] Aside from the fact that Kennedy would not permit Macmillan to share information on the production of

---

[79] Hansard Parliamentary Debates, House of Commons 645, Sp. 1481; cf. Milward, *Rise and Fall*, pp. 346 and 350.

[80] N. Piers Ludlow, *Dealing with Britain. The Six and the First UK Application to the EEC*, Cambridge: Cambridge University Press, 1997, pp. 74–199; Milward, *Rise and Fall*, pp. 352–483.

[81] British Protocol of 2 and 3 June 1962, quoted in Ludlow, *Dealing with Britain*, p. 121.

[82] Conversation of 18 May 1962, quoted in Milward, *Rise and Fall*, p. 468. Also on this, Wolfram Kaiser, "The Bomb and Europe. Britain, France, and the EEC Entry Negotiations, 1961-63," in *Journal of European Integration History* 1 (1995), pp. 65–85.

nuclear weapons with France and that the British Ministry of Defence as well as the general staff were opposed to such a project, this proposal was by no means capable of charming de Gaulle: The French president was sure that American support for the development of a French nuclear force could only be had, if at all, at the price of subordination to American command. That was exactly what he wanted to prevent. In de Gaulle's eyes, Macmillan's more or less clear offers thus seemed to be so many attempts to foil his efforts for European independence.

After negotiations had been stalled since August of 1962, the British government began discussing the question of the issue on which they should be allowed to fail. The inter-ministerial committee charged with the negotiations resolved to postpone agreement on the common foreign tariff until satisfactory regulations had been reached on the import of butter and lamb from New Zealand. Regarding the financing of the agricultural market system by means of import levies (which threatened to be relatively expensive for Britain given its high level of food imports), there was agreement to form a committee to collect data to serve as the basis for acceptable regulations during the transition period.

Macmillan once again attempted to do business with de Gaulle. During another visit to France on 15 and 16 December, he spoke more clearly than before of a "really autonomous instrument of deterrence" as the goal of nuclear cooperation between the two countries. Concretely, he proposed an agreement on the use of nuclear weapons in the event of war, especially regarding targets.[83] Independence in the decision to use nuclear weapons, which was what the issue came down to for de Gaulle, was not yet assured, however. Aside from that, the French president continued to doubt that such independence would be possible if the missiles to carry the nuclear warheads were to be acquired from the Americans, as Macmillan declared was unavoidable. Thus, de Gaulle still saw no reason to agree to Macmillan's offer. Moreover, it certainly could not convince him to be more accommodating in the negotiations on British accession.

Shortly after Macmillan's visit, de Gaulle instead resolved to cancel the negotiations. On 19 December, he told Minister of Information Alain Peyrefitte that he intended to announce this at his next regular press conference.[84] He clearly feared that despite all Macmillan's concessions and avowals, British membership would block his path to an independent Europe. It is possible that he was also plagued by concerns that as a member, Britain would force a reduction in the external tariffs of the customs union to an extent that would not be compatible

---

[83] Vaïsse, *Grandeur*, pp. 205ff. and 215; on de Gaulle's attitude in general, *ibid.*, pp. 191–224.
[84] Peyrefitte, *C'était de Gaulle*, p. 335.

with optimal growth of the French economy.[85] At the same time, the long duration of the talks and the stubborn insistence of the British on exceptional regulation gave him a prospect of success in convincing his partners that Great Britain was not yet ready to play the European game.

Why de Gaulle did not simply wait until negotiations fizzled out, as Couve advised him to do,[86] must remain an open question. Perhaps he feared that the British would in the end make more concessions that would undermine any justification for breaking things off in the eyes of his partners; perhaps he was also simply weary of the endless process and wanted to use the opportunity to educate the European public. Macmillan made an agreement in principle, though very much a non-binding one, on a multilateral nuclear strike force with the American president on 21 December in Nassau in exchange for the urgently needed delivery of Polaris missiles for British nuclear submarines. De Gaulle took this as an occasion to highlight British unreliability: In a press conference of 14 January 1963, he justified his refusal of further negotiations with the UK by citing the agreements in Nassau and went on to warn of a "giant Atlantic Community, dependent on and led by the Americans" that would be a consequence of British entry.[87]

What the British decision on accession ultimately would have been—if de Gaulle had not taken it away from them—also remains an open question. The only certainty is that such a decision would have taken some time. Internal discussions of December 1962 give the impression that Macmillan's government had little power to break things off, in contrast to the firm resolve it had earlier shown in applying for membership. Macmillan had not reduced his goals to a realistic level at an early enough point and had not fought hard enough in the cabinet or in public so as to be able to make an offer de Gaulle could not refuse. To that extent, Macmillan could attribute a good portion of the failure to himself.

The advocates of British entry of course sought to find a way to prevent the termination of negotiations unilaterally declared by de Gaulle. Mansholt's agricultural committee agreed in all haste during the night of 14 January on the planned report as to the effects of British entry on individual products. Although not yet complete, the document was immediately praised by Spaak and Heath as the basis for agreement on regulations during the transition period. Representatives

---

[85] Milward's argument that the negotiations ultimately failed due to the opposition between the British world market strategy and de Gaulle's European preference system (*Rise and Fall*, p. 483), neglects however to take into account the many concessions regarding the customs union and Community policy that the British had made during the negotiations.

[86] Attested by Couve de Murville, *De Gaulle en son siècle*, vol. 4, p. 224.

[87] Charles de Gaulle, *Discours et messages*, vol. 4: Août 1962 – Décembre 1965, Paris: Plon, 1970, p. 69. Most contemporaries believed his reason, and many authors have followed them in doing so.

of the five members pressed for the preparation of a provisional report refuting de Gaulle's assessment of the state of negotiations and also threatened retaliatory measures in the implementation of the agricultural policy, for example. Given that Adenauer did not add his voice to those making threats, all these initiatives failed. When Spaak sought to take Couve de Murville to task at the next gathering of the Six on 28 and 29 January in Brussels, the Frenchman curtly observed that his government regarded the negotiations with Britain as "broken off." After two days of mutual recriminations, the meeting ended without setting a date for continuing negotiations with the British delegation.[88]

The termination of negotiations, which for Macmillan meant "the end of a chapter but certainly not of the volume,"[89] also meant the end of talks with the other applicants. Negotiations with Denmark had made much progress by July of 1962, but even for that country, membership without Britain was not an option. When de Gaulle sought to encourage Danish Prime Minister Jens Otto Krag on 26 January to seek admission on his own, the latter cordially declined, citing his country's links through EFTA.[90] Talks had not even begun with Ireland or Norway; in neither Dublin nor Oslo were they regarded as necessary any longer.

In contrast, the alliance between de Gaulle and Adenauer, which had been decisive for the success of the French maneuver, was strengthened still further in the days thereafter. The chancellor had in the meantime made up his mind to support the president's project even if the other EEC partners did not join in at first. In light of Kennedy's pressure on the Federal Republic to stop holding up a relaxation of international tensions by persisting in its policy of not recognizing the German Democratic Republic, this course seemed to Adenauer a strategic necessity that now had to be pursued regardless of the less-than-clear prospects of success. "Depending on circumstances, we must be prepared," he declared to his colleagues, "to live in tension with the Americans for a few years. We have to put more on the Franco-German and the European horse."[91]

When during Adenauer's extended state visit to France in early July of 1962 de Gaulle posed the question of whether the Federal Republic would be willing "to create a political union with France, which *de facto* and perforce is limited to two members," Adenauer answered "unequivocally with 'yes': We would be willing

---

[88] Ludlow, *Dealing with Britain*, p. 213–226; Edgard Pisani, *Le Général indivis*, Paris: Albin Michel, 1974, pp. 110–113.
[89] According to Italian Foreign Minister Attilio Piccioni 14 March 1963, *ibid.*, p. 226.
[90] Laursen, "Next in line," p. 224.
[91] During a vacation stay in Cadenabbia, 30 April 1962, reported by Horst Osterheld, *"Ich gehe nicht leichten Herzens ...". Adenauers letzte Kanzlerjahre – ein dokumentarischer Bericht*, Mainz: M. Grünewald, 1986, p. 111.

to accept this limited union, in which a place for the other members would of course have to remain available."[92] The two men supported Fanfani's initiative for a new summit of the Six but simultaneously made preparations for a dual confederation in the event that the meeting failed to come off. After de Gaulle had already demonstratively celebrated Franco-German reconciliation during Adenauer's visit, his return visit to the Federal Republic from 4 to 9 September featured aggressive wooing of "the great German people" (as he phrased it in carefully accentuated German in a speech in Bonn's Marktplatz). Before an audience of military officers at the Leadership Academy of the *Bundeswehr* in Hamburg, he stated openly that "the organic cooperation of our armies on a joint defense is of decisive importance for the union of our two countries."[93]

In order to avoid resistance in his own ranks to overly close ties to France, Adenauer wanted the alliance initially to take the form of a convention that would not be made public. Quickly after returning to Paris, de Gaulle had sent him a draft that called for regular consultations and close cooperation in the areas of foreign policy, defense, education, and youth work. After the Italian initiative for a summit of the Six had failed (as expected), Couve de Murville and his West German counterpart Gerhard Schröder agreed on 16 December on a summit of their leaders, who would sign the Franco-German agreement. When Adenauer traveled to Paris on 20 January 1963, he opted for a full-fledged treaty after all, which would need to be ratified by both nations' parliaments. As his assistants had explained to him, opponents of the project were threatening to file a complaint against the signing of the convention in the West German Constitutional Court, and they stood a good chance of success.[94]

De Gaulle was naturally supportive of this upgraded status for the union plan. He even proposed that the treaty be put to a referendum in both countries, which Adenauer had to reject due to the constitutional problems such a procedure would present in the Federal Republic. Given that a full-fledged treaty had not been envisioned, the protocol officials hastily had to acquire the customary parchment paper and Morocco-leather covers in a Paris specialty shop. The "Franco-German Treaty" or "Élysée Treaty" of 22 January 1963 could then be signed at the official residence of the French president. It stipulated regular meetings of the French president and West German chancellor, at least twice annually, along with at least four annual meetings of the countries' foreign and defense

---

92 Conversation of 5 July 1962, French protocol, quoted in Vaïsse, *Grandeur*, p. 251.
93 Speeches in De Gaulle, *Discours et messages 1962–1965*, pp. 4–18.
94 Hans-Peter Schwarz, "Präsident de Gaulle, Bundeskanzler Adenauer und die Entstehung des Elysée-Vertrages," in Wilfried Loth and Robert Picht (eds.), *De Gaulle, Deutschland und Europa*, Opladen: Leske und Budrich, 1991, pp. 169–179.

ministers as well as monthly meetings of top officials in the foreign ministries. The general staffs and those in charge of education and youth affairs would also meet regularly; a joint fund would be established to promote youth exchanges. The governments pledged "to consult one another before every decision on all important foreign policy issues" and in the realm of defense "to bring their basic approaches closer together in order to arrive at joint doctrines."[95]

The agreement between the two symbolic figures of Franco-German reconciliation was by no means complete. De Gaulle was still promising nothing more than the use of French nuclear weapons for the security of the Federal Republic. For his part, Adenauer did not hesitate to signal to the French president that he found the American offer of a multilateral NATO nuclear force very attractive and had therefore assured Kennedy he would participate.[96] Nevertheless, alarm bells sounded in Washington when the treaty was signed. Kennedy did not want to exclude the possibility that de Gaulle was, as a CIA report claimed, negotiating with Moscow on the neutralization of Germany and the withdrawal of the Americans from Europe. In any event, Kennedy was determined to prevent an independent European nuclear force by any means necessary. In the run-up to the signing of the treaty, he had offered Adenauer equal participation in an "executive mechanism" for NATO, which the West German chancellor had declined. The president now threatened a US withdrawal from Europe if the Federal Republic did not choose Atlantic unity over France. General Lucius Clay, who had been sent by Kennedy to Berlin as special ambassador after the construction of the Berlin Wall, let the Bonn government know that ratifying the Élysée Treaty would mean "the end of Berlin."[97]

The US National Security Council met on 5 February and agreed on the form of distancing that would be demanded of Bonn: The treaty should be ratified but with the addition of a resolution strengthening the commitment to membership in NATO and to British membership in the EEC. State Secretary Karl Carstens, whom Foreign Minister Schröder had sent to Washington to work on smoothing things out, quickly agreed. In the following days and weeks, Jean Monnet made his influence felt with his German friends in order to bring about such a solution. On the basis of information from French diplomats who did not concur with de Gaulle's course, Monnet's starting point was the possibility that the French pres-

---

[95] Treaty text in *Europa-Archiv* 27 (1963), D 84–86.
[96] Conversations of 21 and 22 January 1963, provided by Vaïsse, *La grandeur*, pp. 255–257.
[97] Unterredung Knappstein – Clay 28.1.1963, *Akten zur Auswärtigen Politik der Bundesrepublik Deutschland 1963*, Doc. 58; on this and the following, cf. Benedikt Schoenborn, *La mésentente apprivoisée. De Gaulle et les Allemands, 1963–1969*, Paris: Presses Universitaires de France, 2007, pp. 31–34, 41–49.

ident was in the process of leading Western Europe down the path of neutralization, which would benefit only the Soviet Union. A declaration of support for the Atlantic partnership by the Bundestag would prevent that.[98]

The parallel efforts of American diplomacy and Monnet's network met with success. At the end of March, the chairman of the CDU/CSU Bundestag caucus, Heinrich von Brentano, having returned from a visit to the US, suggested to his fellow party members that the ratification be accompanied by commentary that would interpret the Franco-German Treaty "authentically." Adenauer, who did not take Kennedy's threats seriously, was compelled to agree—without such a declaration, the treaty threatened to go down to total defeat in parliament. During a visit by coalition representatives to his vacation home in Cadenabbia on Lake Como on 4 April, he also agreed that the declaration would be made in the form of a preamble to the ratification bill; he did so in order to avoid endangering his coalition with the FDP. The commitment to a policy of Atlantic integration was thus to become legally binding on the West German government.[99]

On 16 May, the Bundestag adopted a resolution along the proposed lines almost unanimously; there were only five votes against and ten abstentions. The ratification of the Franco-German Treaty was passed with a preamble in which the document was interpreted as an instrument for promoting the "great goals" of West German foreign policy, among them a close partnership between Europe and the US, a joint "defense within the framework of the North Atlantic alliance and the integration of the armed forces of the states brought together by that alliance" as well as continued European integration "with inclusion of Great Britain and other states willing to join and the further strengthening of these Communities."[100]

The victory of the "Atlanticists" over the "Gaullists" in the internal West German struggle became all the more clear when Ludwig Erhard, who had initially not wanted to ratify the treaty at all, won the contest to be Adenauer's successor. Against the sitting chancellor's express will, a majority of the CDU/CSU caucus on 23 April nominated Erhard as their candidate for the next election, which was to take place after the agreed-upon resignation of Adenauer the following October. Heeding Monnet's advice, Kennedy made a state visit to the Federal Republic two months later during which he celebrated the Atlantic partnership. His effusive

---

[98] Loth, "Monnet," pp. 265–267.
[99] Cf. Matthias Schulz, "Die politische Freundschaft Jean Monnet – Kurt Birrenbach, die Einheit des Westens und die 'Präambel' zum Elysée-Vertrag von 1963," in Wilkens (ed.), *Interessen verbinden*, pp. 299–327; Tim Geiger, *Atlantiker gegen Gaullisten. Außenpolitischer Konflikt und innerparteilicher Machtkampf in der CDU/CSU 1958–1969*, Munich: Oldenbourg, 2008, pp. 210–217.
[100] *Europa-Archiv* 27 (1963), D 84.

praise of the Germans' desire for liberty ("Today, in the world of freedom, the proudest boast is 'Ich bin ein Berliner'") made his listeners forget the flattery with which de Gaulle had charmed them nine months earlier.[101]

The French president watched the Federal Republic turn away from the vision of an autonomous Europe with impotent anger. As he complained on 24 April in the French Council of Ministers, "The Americans are seeking to rob our treaty of its content. They want to make it an empty shell. And why all this? Because German politicians are afraid of not being subservient enough to the Anglo-Saxons. They're behaving like swine! It would serve them right if we canceled the treaty and reverse the alliances by reaching an understanding with the Russians!" He told Alain Peyrefitte on the same day that "Perhaps we'll actually need to wait fifty years before we have a real political Community." He expressed skepticism to French deputies on 3 July, one day before his next visit to Bonn: "Ah, treaties are like young girls and roses. They last as long as they last. If the Franco-German Treaty doesn't actually come into force, it wouldn't be for the first time in history."[102]

With the preamble to the Franco-German Treaty and with the departure of Adenauer, the third attempt at establishing European political self-assertion as de Gaulle saw it had failed. Bitterness reigned on all sides. Viewpoints were farther apart than ever as to how the European Community should take political action, which states should belong to it at all, and what form the alliance with the Americans should take.

The Success of the Economic Community

It was all the more important that the Community had in the meantime become an economic reality, not only in institutional terms but in practice as well. Since the decisions on accelerating the dismantling of tariff barriers, economic activity had oriented itself more and more on the Common Market of the Six. Lobbyists of every description had set up shop in Brussels. Entrepreneurs and investors were directing their money into the facilitation of inter-European trade and giving the already-strong economic growth of the member states additional impetus. From

---

[101] Pascaline Winand, *Eisenhower, Kennedy and the United States of Europe*, New York: Palgrave Macmillan, 1993, p. 336; Eckart Conze, *Die gaullistische Herausforderung. Die deutsch-französischen Beziehungen in der amerikanischen Europapolitik 1958–1963*, Munich: Oldenbourg, 1995, pp. 280–282.

[102] Peyrefitte, *C'était de Gaulle*, vol. 2, Paris: Fayard, 1997, p. 228 ; *ibid.*, vol. 1, p. 430 ; Lacouture, *De Gaulle*, p. 308.

1958 to 1972, inter-Community trade as a share of the total foreign trade of the Six rose from thirty to fifty-two percent. The gross national product of the Community increased by seventy percent from 1958 to 1970; purchasing power jumped by an average of four to five percent per year. At the same time, the disparity between the Federal Republic and the other member states diminished; France and Italy were both able to achieve decisive productivity increases. Altogether, the industry of the Six witnessed a productivity increase of sixty-six percent from 1961 to 1971. Agriculture saw even better results, with a leap of eighty-eight percent; inter-Community trade in agricultural products grew sevenfold.[103]

The increase in affluence and quality of life resulting from all this was strongly associated with the European Economic Community by the majority of the population. Whoever wanted political success had to embrace the continuation and further expansion of Europe. Step by step, vacation trips as well as the exchanges sponsored by the Franco-German Youth Organization contributed to making "Europe" a lived reality. Reconciliation with the Germans achieved palpable success. A fundamental European consensus established itself piece by piece among the Six, a consensus that survived impassioned political disputes.

At the same time, the EEC took on a constitutional character. When a Dutch firm (*Van Gend en Loos*) importing chemical products from West Germany filed a complaint based on Article 12 of the EEC Treaty (banning new tariffs and levies) against an increase in transport tariffs, the Dutch court sought the opinion of the European Court as to whether the provisions of the EEC Treaty were to be applied directly, that is, without any further legislation on implementation being passed by member states or whether Dutch law, which allowed such a tariff increase, contravened European law. Up to that point, prevailing jurisprudence regarded the EEC Treaty as an international treaty, which thus had no direct effect on natural and legal persons in the member states. The governments of the Netherlands, Belgium, and the Federal Republic supported that interpretation. In a meeting of 31 October 1962, however, the Commission voted in favor of Community law having a direct effect. The European Court adhered to this view. In its legal opinion of February 1963, it found "that the Community represents a new legal order [...] whose legal subjects are not only the member states but also individuals."[104] Citizens of member states were thereby allowed to go before national courts with claims made on the basis of Community law. The court also asserted that it had authority to rule on matters that dealt with European law only implicitly.

---

[103] Gerbet, *La construction*, pp. 181–183.
[104] Court of Justice of the European Union, Case 26/62. NV Algemene Transporten Expeditie Onderneming van Gend en Loos v Netherlands Inland Revenue Administration [1963] ECR-1.

This provided a clarification with far-reaching consequences for the application of Community regulations and for the position of the citizen in the Community. It was made possible by a change in the composition of the European Court, which had led to the introduction of majority decision-making. In May of 1962, the French government nominated Robert Lecourt for a seat on the court. He was a prominent Christian Democratic politician who had been chairman of the Nouvelles Équipes Internationales (NEI) and who was also a member of Monnet's Action Committee. Together with another recently appointed justice, Alberto Trabucchi, Lecourt provided a close four-to-three majority for the supranational interpretation of the treaty.[105]

The issue of the priority of Community law over national law was decided a year later by the European Court when an Italian citizen refused to pay an electric bill to a power company that had recently been nationalized. The court did find that the nationalization was not a violation of European law and that the citizen therefore did not have any right to refuse payment. Whereas the Constitutional Court of Italy had justified its ruling as to the legality of the nationalization on the principle of the priority of newer law over older ("*lex posterior derogat priori*"), the European Court in its ruling of 14 July 1964 in the case of Costa vs. ENEL also determined that subsequent national legislation could not nullify European regulations. This meant "that law created by the treaty could not be overridden by any internal state legal provisions, regardless of their nature." The grounds for this precedence of Community law were that the EEC Treaty had "effected a definitive limitation of their sovereign rights" that "cannot be reversed by subsequent unilateral measures."[106] With this decision, the European Court laid the cornerstone for a new European legal order that bound national legal systems and gave permanence to decisions made on the European level.

Conversely, it was less significant that the European Atomic Energy Community (Euratom) did not really get going and that the European Coal and Steel Community was diminishing in importance. In contrast to his attitude toward the Economic Community, de Gaulle was not particularly interested in the development of Euratom. More important to him than any synergy from a joint nuclear program was the preservation of absolute independence from the American nuclear industry. Thus, the nation that had most strongly advocated the nuclear community for political reasons and that had developed its own nuclear industry to the greatest extent could not serve as a motor for the development of the organization.

---

[105] Morten Rasmussen, "The Origins of a Legal Revolution – The Early History of the European Court of Justice," in *Journal of European Integration History* 14 (2008), pp. 77–98, here pp. 94ff.
[106] Court of Justice of the European Union, Case 6/64, Flaminio Costa v. ENEL [1964] ECR 585, p. 1251.

The skepticism of the other member states was strengthened, and they sought to use the provisions of the Euratom Treaty to develop their own national nuclear industries. Despite these circumstances, the Euratom Commission was able to complete a treaty with the American Atomic Energy Commission in November of 1958 that envisioned the construction of five to eight nuclear power plants fueled by enriched uranium. France did not participate in this program however and instead continued to build plants that did not make use of the advanced enrichment technology, in which the US enjoyed a monopoly. The development of a common reactor type functioning with natural uranium (ORGEL) proved to be an economic failure: No one wanted to operate such cost-intensive reactors. Further efforts to organize a Common Market for reactors were thwarted by the national governments.

Joint organization of nuclear research, one of the main tasks of the Atomic Community according to the treaty, did not advance very far either. In 1960, the Joint Research Center (JRC) was established, with four locations: Ispra (Italy), Petten (the Netherlands), Mol (Belgium), and Karlsruhe (West Germany). These facilities could only play a secondary role *vis-à-vis* the national research centers that continued to exist. Research programs were neither integrated nor even coordinated. The Joint Research Center had to satisfy itself with lower-priority and especially risky research projects; altogether, there was much duplication and unnecessary overlap.

The Euratom Commission, led by Étienne Hirsch after the resignation of Louis Armand due to health reasons in 1959, sought to limit this waste of resources and to position itself as the strategic center of European nuclear research. This only served to kindle de Gaulle's wrath. When the renewal of the commission appointments was pending in December of 1961, the French president refused to allow Hirsch a second term. Given that the other governments had no significant interest in a strong commission and that Bonn was advocating the greatest possible freedom for private initiatives, the Six came to agreement on a new head for the organization, Pierre Chatenet, who was serving as de Gaulle's interior minister. Also, Euratom's budget would no longer be decided at the level of the Community; the commission would have to content itself with the sum of the funding coming from various research projects around which different combinations of interested member states found themselves willing to coalesce.[107]

The European Coal and Steel Community was at least spared such limits on its freedom of action. Its High Authority was not however able to act as a crisis manager when strong demand for coal and steel gave way to oversupply in the

---

[107] Gerbet, *Construction*, pp. 190–192; Laurence Hubert, "La politique nucléaire de la Communauté européenne (1956–1968)," in: *Journal of European Integration History* 6 (2000), pp. 129–153.

autumn of 1958. There were two structural crises in the coal industry: As an energy source, coal was increasingly being supplanted by oil, which was less expensive and easier to utilize; at the same time, high-quality but less expensive American coal was coming onto the European market thanks to the introduction of larger colliers and falling shipping rates. The High Authority, under the chairmanship of the Belgian trade union leader Paul Finet, sought to introduce a system of production quotas on the basis of Article 58 of the ECSC Treaty that addressed instances of "clear crisis" stemming from overproduction. There were to be regulations as to the amount of coal produced at every single mine within a given timeframe. Not only was this opposed by the French government—which cited efforts toward modernization already undertaken there, in contrast to the situation in Belgium, for example. It also met with disapproval in Bonn: The West German government was hostile to *"dirigiste"* measures from the ECSC and instead wanted decisions on production and import limits to be made on the national level, as far as possible in agreement with the gentlemen of industry in the Ruhr. In the Council of Ministers meeting of 14 May 1959, only the representatives of the Benelux governments voiced support for giving the High Authority power to impose production quotas. The ECSC thus had to content itself with stabilizing the Belgian coal market in isolation and using Community funds to subsidize the sale of coal. Measures to assist unemployed miners and to promote modernization remained in the hands of national governments.[108]

A crisis of steel overproduction began to loom in 1963. This was the result of production increases in Britain, the US, Japan, and the Soviet Union, parallel to the expansion of capacity in the Community. The High Authority initially responded by proposing a freeze on imports from East Bloc countries and was able to win approval for the measure in June of 1963. In October of that year, it appealed for a hike in import tariffs on steel products by an average of fourteen percent. After surveying the attitudes in the capitals of the Community, the proposal was modified to the effect that the tariffs in all states would be gradually increased to the level of those in Italy (nine percent). This measure too was pushed through by the energetic new president of the High Authority, Italian Christian Democrat Dino Del Bo—not however as a decision of the Council (stemming from the fact that the governments could not agree among themselves) but rather in the form of a binding recommendation in accordance with Article 74 of the treaty.

The High Authority was not able to win further tariff increases or production quotas so as to overcome the steel crisis. Out of justified fears of renewed

---

108 Dirk Spierenburg and Raymond Poidevin, *Histoire de la Haute Autorité de la Communauté Européenne du Charbon et de l'Acier. Une expérience supranationale*, Brussels: Émile Bruylant, 1993, pp. 529–559, 651–679, 783–816.

deadlock, it did not even dare send proposals along those lines to the Council of Ministers.[109]

In contrast to what the advocates of sector integration hoped, neither the European Coal and Steel Community nor the European Atomic Energy Community served as the driving force of economic and political integration. The ECSC remained limited to the organization of the markets for coal and steel, the rationalization of their production, and the promotion of social balance in these industries; at most, the Atomic Community functioned as a place holder for a missing common energy and technology policy. Hence, the impressive successes in realizing the Economic Community became all the more important for the advancement of the European project.

---

[109] *Ibid.*, pp. 702–707, 783–796.

3 Crises of the Community of the Six, 1963–1969

Erhard's Relaunch

The transition of the West German chancellorship from Adenauer to Erhard in October of 1963 confirmed what had already been seen in the replacement of the Fourth French Republic by de Gaulle's regime in May of 1958: European institutions imposed constraints on the participating governments that could not be evaded. In the beginning, Ludwig Erhard was highly skeptical of the Treaties of Rome as well as the European Coal and Steel Community and the project for a defense community. In his view, it was all a "bureaucratically manipulated Europe" that could not work.[1] What he envisioned instead was a "functional integration" of the economies of all the democratic states of Europe and, beyond that, of the entire Western world, based on confidence-building cooperation among governments.[2] Upon taking the office of chancellor, however, his first official statement included support for the construction of a "European political entity with parliamentary, democratic accountability." As he stated, "Economic integration alone, without political ties" would fail to do justice to "the practical life and the political circumstances of the participating countries."[3] Behind this lay both a realization as to the unsatisfactory nature of his earlier conception as well as efforts to take into account the intra-party and domestic political pressure to which he was exposed.

In fact, despite all prior difficulties, Erhard quickly undertook efforts to bring the Political Union of the Six into existence. On the issue of the Common Agricultural Market, the Federal Republic had recently stepped on the brakes once again: After the disappointment caused by the French veto of British entry into the EEC in April of 1963, Foreign Minister Gerhard Schröder had introduced an "Action Program" for European policy. This fundamentally called into question

---

[1] Erhard to Etzel, 16 Nov. 1956, in BDFD II, pp. 833–836, here p. 835.
[2] Erhard's speech to the club Les Echos in Paris, 7 Dec. 1954, in Ludwig Erhard, *Deutsche Wirtschaftspolitik. Der Weg der Sozialen Marktwirtschaft*, Düsseldorf: Econ, 1962, pp. 253–259, here p. 253. Cf. Horst Wünsche, "Wirtschaftliche Interessen und Prioritäten. Die Europavorstellungen von Ludwig Erhard," in Rudolf Hrbek and Volker Schwarz (eds.), *40 Jahre Römische Verträge: Der deutsche Beitrag*, Baden-Baden: Nomos, 1998, pp. 36–49.
[3] Erhard's government statement, 18 Oct. 1963, in *Verhandlungen des Deutschen Bundestages, Stenographische Berichte*, vol. 53, pp. 4192–4208, here p. 4197. Cf. Ulrich Lappenküper, "'Ich bin wirklich ein guter Europäer.' Ludwig Erhards Europapolitik 1949–1966," in *Francia* 18/3 (1991), pp. 85–121; idem., "'Europa aus der Lethargie herausreißen': Ludwig Erhards Europapolitik 1949–1966," in Mareike König and Matthias Schulz (eds.), *Die Bundesrepublik Deutschland und die europäische Einigung 1949–2000*, Stuttgart: Franz Steiner, 2004, pp. 106–127.

the system of market regulations and levies decided on in 1962. It also proposed that further steps on agricultural integration be made dependent on progress in political integration along with trade liberalization within the framework of GATT. The decision on the next step toward a common price level for grain had to be tabled due to West German obstruction. This was also the case with the decision on the market regulations for milk, other dairy products, beef, and rice.

At a session of the Council of Ministers from 9 to 23 December, Erhard—who was rather annoyed by the economically counterproductive "agricultural nonsense"[4]—succeeded in establishing at least the three markets for milk, beef, and rice. This was accomplished only after clear threats by the French that they would cancel the transition to the second stage of the Common Market if the Germans did not stick to the commitments regarding the plan for achieving the agricultural market. Some eighty-six percent of the agricultural production of the EEC was now subject to the market system. A way back from this, as Schröder had envisioned, was no longer possible. Only on the issue of common grain prices did Erhard advocate a further postponement. During his initial visit to de Gaulle on 21 November, he had asked for understanding because it had not been possible to organize the parliamentary majority necessary for a change of course within a few weeks. He left no doubt however as to his willingness to find a compromise that would be acceptable to France. De Gaulle therefore had to accept that the decision on grain prices would be postponed until 1 April 1964.

This arrangement was made easier by French signals that they would not seek to block a significant reduction in external tariffs at the upcoming round of GATT, the so-called "Kennedy Round." The French delegation acceded to the West German demand for providing the Commission with directives for this round. The Council of Ministers agreed to orient itself fundamentally on the American demand for halving tariff rates, both in the manufacturing and agricultural sectors. The only thing to be excluded was the Kennedy administration's demand for complete elimination of tariffs on goods traded at a level of more than eighty percent between the US and the EEC. Although many potential conflicts remained in the details, it was clear that the principle of "synchronization" between the realization of the agricultural market and general trade liberalization was acknowledged by the French.[5]

On the basis of these understandings, Erhard saw himself in a good position to restart negotiations on a Political Union. In a speech before the Bundestag

---

[4] Note of State Secretary Rudolf Hüttebräuker, quoted in Patel, *Europäisierung*, pp. 180ff.
[5] *Ibid.*, pp. 251–265; Knudsen, *Farmers*, pp. 251–261; Carine Germond, "Partenaires de raison? Le couple France-Allemagne et l'unification de l'Europe (1963–1969)," Thèse Strasbourg, 2009, pp. 383–389.

on 9 January 1964, he emphasized his belief in the necessity of a democratically-legitimated Political Authority of the European Community and the urgency of a new initiative for its realization. Discreetly encouraged by de Gaulle, he then began sounding out his partners as to the chances for such an initiative. The West German Foreign Office began internal work on a "Multi-Stage Plan for European Unity." This plan envisioned the completion of the agricultural market and trade liberalization for 1964–65 along with the merger of the executives of the three European Communities and a strengthening of the rights of the European Parliament. In 1966, there were to be negotiations on the creation of a Political Union in the areas of foreign policy, defense, and culture as well as the possible extension of this to the countries of EFTA. The transition to direct election of the European Parliament was to go hand in hand with the realization of the Political Union in the period 1967–69. The existing treaties would then be replaced by one on European federation in 1974.[6]

De Gaulle drew the conclusion from Erhard's efforts toward a re-launch of the Political Union that prospects for an independent Europe were perhaps not as dismal as he had feared after the Bundestag had supported the preamble to the Franco-German Treaty containing a disavowal. In any event, his resolve grew throughout the spring of 1964 for attempting a foray in this direction once again. The next Franco-German summit on 3 and 4 July would provide an opportunity. To maximize his chances of success, he mobilized the West German "Gaullists" in April. The most politically influential of these, Franz-Josef Strauss, was informed by representatives of the French secret service that the general would "for the final time pose the question as to whether the Germans were prepared to work together with the French, including on nuclear cooperation." In order to underscore the urgent need for support, the emissaries added that "Franco-German friendship and cooperation" were "at stake." If Bonn were to refuse, the general would "make a fundamental course change and go beyond Germany to seek contacts with the East, above all with Poland."[7]

Given the prospect of strengthening the Franco-German alliance, de Gaulle was not any too concerned when Bonn once again postponed a decision on grain prices due to fears over domestic political consequences. In the very next session of the Council of Ministers after the agreement of 23 December, Agriculture Minister Werner Schwarz asserted that the April deadline applied only to prices for the year 1964–65; on 14 April, he declared that he would at present be unable to support a harmonization of prices without further intermediate steps, as the European Commission had proposed. In the face of renewed West German

---

[6] Multi-Stage Plan 23 Jan. 1964, AAPD 1964 I, pp. 118–120.
[7] Franz-Josef Strauss, *Die Erinnerungen*, Berlin: Siedler, 1989, p. 432.

obstruction, the Commission was in sheer desperation. As Hallstein's colleague Klaus Meyer reported in a note to his superior, "A political duty to cooperate in the construction of Europe no longer exists for most of the gentlemen in the cabinet as a guiding principle for their political actions."[8] For their part, however, de Gaulle and Couve de Murville reacted with marked understanding for the difficulties of their West German partners. Given that the American government had delayed the presentation of its proposals for agricultural trade in the GATT round until the autumn, they themselves now found it better to wait until that time to determine what tradeoffs there should be. In early June, it was decided that the issue of common grain prices would be resolved by 15 December.

When news reached de Gaulle of Erhard's visit to US President Lyndon B. Johnson on 12 June, the Frenchman once again had severe doubts. With little concern for the content of a common European foreign and security policy, the chancellor had agreed with Johnson to strive for a treaty on a nuclear-armed Multilateral Force (MLF) by the end of the year. Beyond that, Erhard had promised political and financial support for American engagement in the Vietnam War, which de Gaulle had recently criticized sharply. Erhard had also pledged that he would under no circumstances follow de Gaulle's example of extending diplomatic recognition to the People's Republic of China. All this was done without consulting Paris beforehand. As de Gaulle complained to Peyrefitte, the West Germans had made the Élysée Treaty into "a bad joke."[9]

Disappointment over Erhard's lack of principles led the French president to confront him during the summit of 3 and 4 July. First off, he demonstratively let Erhard wait while he had an extended conversation with Adenauer. Then, de Gaulle explained to Erhard that the Federal Republic must decide whether it wanted to pursue "a policy of subordination to the USA" or "a European policy that is independent of the USA." Now that France had its own nuclear weapons, the time had come for an equal partnership between the US and Europe. In de Gaulle's view, the Franco-German Treaty had to "become the core, the foundation, and the ferment of European unity, in economic as well as in political and military matters." If that did not succeed, then the document was "empty and senseless."[10]

De Gaulle expressed himself only vaguely regarding the path to political and military unity. When asked by Erhard in a private conversation whether France

---

[8] Meyer to Hallstein, 21 May 1964, quoted in Patel, *Europäisierung*, p. 269. Cf. *ibid.*, pp. 265–268 and Germond, "Partenaires," pp. 398–404.
[9] Meeting of 23 June 1964, Peyrefitte, *De Gaulle II*, pp. 257–263.
[10] Meeting of 3 July 1964, French protocol, quoted in Schoenborn, *Mésentente*, p. 70. On this and the following, cf. Germond, "Partenaires," pp. 275–291 and Geiger, *Atlantiker*, pp. 292–300.

was prepared to give the Federal Republic a right of control over French nuclear weapons, the president stressed only the priority of political unity: "Up to the point at which Europe can defend itself, and up to the point at which its political organization has thrived to the extent that a genuine European government would be possible, up to that time there will be the separate nuclear weapons of Great Britain and France."[11] Only in a conversation with Foreign Office State Secretary Karl Carstens did he hint at participatory rights in the less-distant future. When the West German official defended participation in the MLF with the argument that Bonn hoped by that means to be able to exercise a certain influence over nuclear planning and the decision to use nuclear weapons, de Gaulle suggested the possibility of West German influence over French planning: "Why not come along with us? We too have the Bomb. With us, you can have a much larger share (or can participate much more)."[12]

The categorical call to reach an understanding with France on a common foreign and security policy only served to elicit defensive reactions from Erhard. As he told de Gaulle in their second meeting, it was simply the case that the Federal Republic was dependent on American protection; neither Franco-German cooperation nor the future Europe could replace that. The chancellor did not pose any questions as to the French president's vision of the path to common defense. When Carstens reported to Erhard two days later on the content of his conversation with the general, it did not lead to any further sounding out. In the closing session of the two delegations, de Gaulle wrapped his disappointment over the lack of results from his initiative in a warm-hearted appeal to develop a "common policy." Erhard remained silent. He saw no need to repeat what he had already said to his guest during bilateral meetings.[13]

Erhard's behavior embittered the West German "Gaullists" around Adenauer and Strauss, leading them to make severe accusations.[14] In a speech at the state party congress of the CSU on 12 July, Erhard, for his part, emphasized that as long he was chancellor, foreign policy would be based on a close alliance with the US. In turn, during a press conference on 23 July, de Gaulle replied that Bonn had up to that point done nothing to realize a common policy and thus the Community of

---

11 Meeting of 4 July 1964, AAPD 1964 II, pp. 768–777, here p. 775.
12 Note of 6 July 1964, AAPD 1964 II, pp. 766–768. There was no interpreter present at the meeting on the morning of 4 July 1964, conducted in French; the only source is a note prepared two days later by Carstens. Which of the two variants of the offer contained there comes closer to the actual words of de Gaulle is thus not known.
13 AAPD 1964 II, pp. 777–787.
14 Cf. Geiger, *Atlantiker*, pp. 300–331. The enduring controversy over the substance of de Gaulle's offer that has stemmed from this is resolved if one takes into account the factor of communication difficulties between the protagonists.

the Six threatened to crumble. Privately, he referred to the chancellor as a "political nitwit": With him, "nothing could be done."[15]

In light of this public estrangement, the chances sank dramatically for Erhard's attempt to revive the Fouchet Plans. It was not only the case that he had to leave the development of the proposal to Foreign Minister Gerhard Schröder, who fundamentally did not want to allow a new approach to French conceptions of Europe to harm his efforts to strengthen the alliance with the US. Erhard himself strengthened his option for the MLF and made it clear that he absolutely did not want a European nuclear deterrent based on the French *force de frappe*. At a press conference in early October, he declared that if necessary, he would be prepared to go it alone in signing the MLF Treaty with the US if other NATO countries continued to oppose it. When after long delay by the West German Foreign Office the Europe Plan was presented to the EEC partners on 4 November, it contained a statement of support for "strengthening the Atlantic alliance" and a proposal to reach "fundamental agreement that other European states [beyond the Six] participate in a European political union."[16]

The German draft also adopted a proposal that Paul-Henri Spaak had initially made in Bonn in July and had then presented to the WEU Council of Ministers on 9 September—distinguishing between a preparatory and a definitive phase of the Political Union. Initially, agreement was to be reached on regular consultations and a date set for a definitive state treaty. If that date could not be met, then consultations would continue. An advisory commission was to be established alongside the governments to work on proposals for the final treaty and participate in the meetings of the Council of Ministers. Other provisions of the plan contained proposals for strengthening the existing Communities: developing a common currency policy, coordinating national budgets, merging treaties, as well as incrementally strengthening the position of the European Parliament to the point at which it would have full legislative and budgetary responsibility. There were also measures for approaching the EFTA countries and for the worldwide dismantling of trade barriers. The proposal contained no chronology. What remained of the original incremental plan was only the vague statement that the Political Union and the existing Communities would be united in a federative Europe at a "later stage."[17]

---

15 Council of Ministers, 7 July 1964, Peyrefitte, *De Gaulle II*, p. 263.
16 Siegler, *Europäische politische Einigung 1949–1968*, pp. 280–287.
17 On the Spaak Plan, Carine Germond, "Les projets d'Union politique de l'année 1964," in Wilfried Loth (ed.), *Crises and Compromises. The European Project 1963–1969*, Baden-Baden: Nomos, 2001, pp. 109–130, here pp. 114–116; in general, Gabriele Clemens, "'Zwischen allen Stühlen.' Ludwig Erhards Europa-Initiative vom November 1964," in Gabriele Clemens (ed.), *Nation und Europa. Studien zum internationalen Staatensystem im 19. und 20. Jahrhundert*, Stuttgart: Franz Steiner, 2001, pp. 171–193; Germond, "Partenaires," pp. 323–336.

With the nonbinding combination of intergovernmental and supranational as well as European and Atlantic perspectives, the West German government's Europe Plan offered the partners an invitation to take up negotiations on Political Union once again despite the well-known divergences among the parties. At the same time, it reflected the alienation between Paris and Bonn. Couve de Murville quickly made it known to Carstens that there was no sense to the initiative if one were not prepared to reach agreement on common goals independent of the US. In order to avoid the danger of an exclusive agreement between Bonn and Washington, he then declared that the MLF was irreconcilable with the Franco-German Treaty.[18]

Additionally, de Gaulle made use of the initiative as another means of pressing for agreement on common agricultural prices at last. In fact, Erhard had in the meantime been forced to state that the December deadline could not be kept either; sheer terror of losing their seats drove numerous Bundestag deputies within the government coalition to set themselves against a reduction of grain prices. De Gaulle was no longer willing to take that into account—not only because the negotiations in GATT had now become unavoidable, but also because he no longer believed he could do business with Erhard. Moreover, growing criticism from French farmers and consumers made it seem a good idea to have responsibility for agricultural policy shoved off to "Brussels" as soon as possible. He thus had Peyrefitte threaten on 21 October that France would "no longer participate in the European Economic Community if the common agricultural market were not to come into existence as had been agreed upon." Couve communicated to his German interlocutors that the agricultural market must be completed before there could be talk of anything further."[19]

This double threat had an effect. In short order, Hallstein made two trips to Bonn and sought to persuade the chancellor that now—in contrast to the previous crises of the Community—it was a question of all or nothing: "This time, it's a matter of deciding on the continued existence of the Community."[20] In light of this and also the danger of the failure of the GATT negotiations, Erhard finally came to the point where he would accept the domestic political risk stemming from a breakthrough in talks on agriculture. In order to get around continuing opposition in the governing coalition and the Agriculture Ministry, he took up direct negotiations with the President of the German Farmers Association. By the

---

[18] Meeting between Couve de Murville and Carstens, 25 Oct. 1964, AAPD 1964 II, pp. 1187–1193. Cf. Soutou, *L'alliance incertaine*, pp. 277–280.
[19] Germond, "Partenaires," pp. 332 and 407; Peyrefitte's declaration in *L'Année politique en Europe 1965*, p. 104.
[20] State Secretary Neef to Minister Schmücker, 2 Nov. 1964, BA, WH 1114/1. Cf. Hallstein's report to the Commission, AHCE, PV 293 Commission CEE, 9 and 13 Nov. 1964; *ibid.*, 294, 18 Nov. 1964.

end of November, he had succeeded in reaching a deal with the group's leader, Edmund Rehwinkel: The government would agree to the setting of common grain prices by 15 December. These would come into effect only on 1 July 1967, however. Starting then and running from the end of the transition phase to the completion of the Common Market on 1 January 1970, West German farmers would receive compensatory payments from both the Community and from the government. A future grain price of DM 440 per metric ton was agreed upon as a goal in negotiations, some DM 15 more than the Commission had proposed but DM 35 less than farmers were then seeking.

Agreement between the chancellor and the president of the association did not however mean that the agricultural crisis was over. When negotiations began in the Council of Ministers on 12 December, France and the Netherlands (both low-price countries) did per force accept the postponement to 1 July 1967 but rejected a price hike proposed by the Commission, which anyway lay above the average of national prices up to that point. Neither did these countries want anything to do with increased financing of compensatory payments by the Community. In the late evening of 14 December, Mansholt and his colleagues worked out a compromise proposal whereby the postponement of the deadline was combined with the original price and the stipulation that the farmers of the high-price countries would receive only the level of compensatory payments proposed by the Commission. As another high-price country, Italy was conceded the introduction of a market for fruit and vegetables. Under the threat that this was the final proposal the Commission would make, the exhausted ministers finally agreed to it in the early morning hours of 15 December.[21]

The German Farmers Association was not satisfied with the result, of course. Yet, given that there was still a possibility of winning higher compensatory payments in the national budget, they did not make any strong protests. There was general relief that the "long grain night" had not ended in a breakup. Erhard now believed that de Gaulle owed him something in regard to both the GATT negotiations and the initiative for a Political Union. Furthermore, he hoped that the sacrifice the West German government had made for the common agricultural policy would dissuade the French president from continuing to oppose the Federal Republic's participation in the MLF.

Any basis for Erhard's hopes regarding MLF was taken away only two days after the Brussels agreement had been reached. After the elections of 15 October in Britain, the Labour Party took over the government and spoke out decidedly against an MLF with West German participation. In light of this additional oppo-

---

21 Germond, "Partenaires," pp. 409–413; Patel, *Europäisierung*, pp. 270–279; van der Harst, "The common agricultural policy," pp. 329–331.

sition and in order not to endanger the realization of a treaty with the Soviet Union on nuclear nonproliferation, President Johnson stipulated on 17 December that representatives of the US government and of the military exercise restraint in negotiations over nuclear forces. This course change was not immediately communicated to US allies, and so Erhard initially did not want to give up his hopes for a common nuclear force. Owing to the clear hesitancy of the American representative at the NATO Council meeting in the middle of December, the chancellor conceded to the "Gaullists" in his party leadership on 5 January 1965 that negotiations on MLF would resume only after the parliamentary elections that coming autumn.[22]

Without knowing it, Erhard had thereby improved the chances of success for his Europe initiative. At the next Franco-German summit, held at Château Rambouillet on 19 and 20 January 1965, de Gaulle characterized the plan as generally "sensible." The only portion he did not want to accept was the proposal for an Advisory Commission, which in his eyes threatened to behave like an international actor. He was all the more willing to lend his support *vis-à-vis* the other partners when Erhard explicitly confirmed that government negotiations would address not only foreign policy but also military issues. De Gaulle agreed that in May or June of 1965, the foreign ministers of the Six should hold talks on the shape of the Political Union. The heads of state and of government would then come together in July to approve the results of negotiations and to discuss fundamental problems.[23]

Inspired by the "spirit of Rambouillet," the moderate-left Italian government under Christian Democrat Aldo Moro took charge of giving concrete form to the new chance for further developing the Community. At base, the Italian government was interested in avoiding Franco-German hegemony, and its left wing made itself into an advocate of strengthening the European Parliament. After responding in late November to the West German initiative with its own Europe Plan—yet more clearly atlanticist and federalist in orientation—the Italian government sent Foreign Ministry General Secretary Attilio Cattani in mid-February to the European capitals to sound out the matter of how the conferences on the Political Union should be prepared. On 15 March, Foreign Minister Amintore Fanfani invited his counterparts to an informal pre-conference in Venice set for the middle of May.[24]

---

22 Geiger, *Atlantiker*, pp. 331–338.
23 AAPD 1965 I, pp. 101–120 and 140–151.
24 Kramer, *Europäisches oder atlantisches Europa*, pp. 174–176, 187ff.; Germond, "Partenaires," pp. 344–346; Antonio Varsori, "Italy and the 'Empty Chair' Crisis (1965–66)," in Loth (ed.), *Crises*, pp. 215–255.

Hallstein's Offensive

A few days after the Italian government's invitation, Commission President Walter Hallstein surprised European public opinion in a speech he gave to the European Parliament on 24 March 1965: He made a proposal that the transition to the Economic Community's having its own income—as was to follow after the decision of January 1962 with the implementation of common tariffs for agricultural products—be linked to strengthening the rights of the European Parliament.[25] On 15 December 1964, the Council of Ministers had given the Commission the task of coming up with proposals not only for financing the agricultural market during the remaining transition period from 1 July 1965 to 1 January 1970 but also, in accordance with Article 201 of the EEC Treaty, to examine under what conditions the financial contributions of member states could be replaced by revenue under the Community's own control. With his self-understanding as a leader of the integration process, Hallstein made use of the instructions given by the Council in order to press for accelerating completion of the Economic Community once again and to generate pressure for strengthening supranational institutions at the same time.[26]

The proposals that the Commission officially gave to the Council of Ministers on 31 March 1965 initially envisioned that, with the establishment of common grain prices on 1 July 1967, guarantee prices for milk, rice, beef, and sugar would be introduced and that responsibility for all agricultural expenditures would be transferred to the Community. With this, the early completion of the agricultural market—which the Commission had sought in vain in 1960—would be *de facto* achieved. Likewise, the completion of the customs union would be brought forward to this date, which suggested itself in light of the tariff reductions that had in the meantime been accomplished. The Community was to receive not only the levies from the import of agricultural products but also the proceeds of external tariffs, the former immediately with the introduction of guaranteed prices and the latter in six stages up to 1 January 1972.

With the transition to independent sources of income, Article 203 of the EEC Treaty would be amended to the effect that the Council of Ministers could only

---

[25] Text of the speech in *Die internationale Politik 1965*, pp. D 300ff.
[26] Cf. Wilfried Loth, "The 'empty chair' crisis," in *The European Commission 1958–72*, pp. 91–108. On the following, also Jean-Marie Palayret, Hellen Wallace, Pascaline Winand (eds.), *Visions, Votes and Vetoes. The Empty Chair Crisis and Luxembourg Compromise Forty Years On*, Brussels: Peter Lang, 2006; N. Piers Ludlow, *The European Community and the Crises of the 1960s. Negotiating the Gaullist Challenge*, London and New York: Routledge, 2006, pp. 65–124; Philip Bajon, *Europapolitik "am Abgrund". Die Krise des "leeren Stuhls" 1965–66*, Stuttgart: Franz Steiner, 2012.

reject changes in the Parliament's proposed budget if it adopted the vote of the Commission with a simple, non-weighted majority. The Council could only prevail with its own position, independent of change proposals of Parliament and of the vote of the Commission, if at least five of the six member states agreed. Additionally, further proposals for receiving independent income would be adopted if they gained a two-thirds majority in Parliament and a qualified majority in the Council. As soon as the direct election of members was introduced (no date was specified), the decision about independent income would be wholly given over to the Community. In concrete terms, that meant the Commission would be able to push through any proposal that had won either a simple majority in the Council of Ministers or a majority in Parliament and two member states. Parliament would be able to pass any measure for which two member states offered support.[27]

For Hallstein, the synchronization of economic integration and the efforts to link it with a strengthening of the rights of Parliament and the Commission constituted a question of logic as well political opportunity. The proposal would make it possible to avoid distortions of completion during the transition period, would reduce the complexity of the Economic Community, and would be in accord with the principle of parliamentary control, which was specified in the EEC Treaty and which fit with Europeans' democratic self-understanding. The Commission would "cut a good figure" with the proposal, as Hallstein explained in the Commission session of 3 March; and this would ensure victory.[28] Anyone who remained unconvinced would need to yield to the package deal. This was especially the case with the transition to independent sources of income: The governing majority in the Dutch parliament had already indicated that it would only allow that if the powers of the European Parliament were simultaneously strengthened, and the same was to be expected from the parliaments in Bonn and Rome. This offered the Commission an opportunity to strengthen Parliament and thereby also spark public discussion of European issues, an opportunity that would not soon come again.

The proposals would of course meet with opposition, and Hallstein himself was aware of this. No government would be eager to part with tariff income anytime soon or lose influence over the shaping of the budget. De Gaulle would be the least eager of all; his opposition to strengthening Parliament and the Commission was sufficiently well known. Yet, *first of all*, the impositions in the package were consciously limited in nature: The loss of tariff income would come in stages; this guaranteed that the Community would not suddenly find itself with more money than it could spend. In the complicated process of determining

---

[27] Proposals of the Commission to the Council, 31 March 1965, COM (65) 150.
[28] Protocol note by Emile Noël, 3 March 1965, HAEU, EN 780.

the budget, Parliament would by no means have the final say, and direct election of members was not part of the proposals. When the members of the European Parliament made demands on that very issue on 12 May, Hallstein declined to support them given the poor prospects for success. *Secondly*, the Commission president regarded the French interest in economic integration and the Common Agricultural Market as so strong that de Gaulle would simply be forced to pay the price demanded for them. As Karl-Heinz Narjes explained in an *aide-memoire* to his superior, measures to derail them would "even today be seen by the broad mass of French public opinion as being against the interest of France such that de Gaulle would not be able to take steps of that sort in an election year."[29] The Commission definitely had in mind the fact that before the end of the year, the French president would need to face the voters.

It seems that it was above all Mansholt who pushed for appealing to public opinion on strengthening Parliament. When the deputies in Strasbourg reported their agreement on grain prices, he announced that the entire agricultural market system should be introduced at a faster pace and that it should be combined with a strengthening of Parliament. After the Commission had approved the packet of proposals on 22 March, the contents immediately began seeping into the press; Hallstein presented the basics of the deal two days later in a speech before Parliament. De Gaulle and Couve de Murville were enraged by this, not completely without cause given that the Commission was supposed to present its proposals formally to the body that had given them the charge, that is, the Council of Ministers. By revealing the proposals to the public, the Commission was consciously putting the Council of Ministers under pressure. Privately, Hallstein repeatedly made clear to the president and the foreign minister "that the French would not avoid having to make a concession on this issue [parliamentary control of independent sources of income]."[30]

Initially, De Gaulle reacted to Hallstein's challenge by seeking to isolate the Commission. On 27 March, Couve de Murville had to explain to his Italian counterpart that the Venice Conference would have to be postponed because the role of the Commission had not yet been clarified. Four days later, Peyrefitte announced the result of a meeting of the French Council of Ministers: France would agree to a summit meeting of the heads of state and of government only if an agreement were reached by 30 June (as scheduled) about the financing of the

---

29 Narjes to Hallstein, 19 May 1965, BA, WH 1119/1.
30 Report by Hallstein, 21 Oct. 1965, BA WH 1029. It may be the case that Mansholt helped Hallstein along a bit with putting out the news about the Commission decision. In any event, the Commission was not as innocent of the publication as portrayed in the subsequent explanation made to the French government.

Common Agricultural Market during the transition period.[31] If the Germans and Italians were so eager for a new summit, they should then refrain from supporting the demands of the Commission. On 27 April, de Gaulle held a televised speech in which he once again highlighted his vision of an independent Europe that "rejects any foreign intrusion in the domestic affairs of a state." He made it clear to the adherents of a "so-called integrated Europe" that limitations on national sovereignty would perforce lead to the submission of Europe to the hegemony of the United States.[32]

This peremptory stance led in fact to the isolation of France. In a session of the Council of Ministers on 13 and 14 May, the representatives of the Netherlands and of the Federal Republic declared that financing during the transition period was linked to the principle of the transition to independent sources of income in the final phase of the agricultural market, and a decision therefore had to be made regarding the strengthening of control by the European Parliament. The Dutch government went so far as to criticize the Commission's proposals as insufficient and called for complete legislative responsibility for Parliament as well as direct elections and the right to appoint the members of the executive organs. The Italian government praised the Commission's proposal as logical and within the meaning of the Community. The Belgian government declared that it was in agreement "with almost all points." Even the government of Luxembourg, which stated that it would be satisfied with a settlement regarding the transition period, did not raise any objections on principle to the proposals as a whole.[33]

De Gaulle then concentrated on his West German partners. He suggested to the chancellor that the date of the next Franco-German summit be moved forward so that the two could synchronize their positions on the issues at hand before 30 June. Erhard, who regarded the rejection of the Venice Conference as a broken promise on the general's part, agreed to this despite his disappointment. It was the case that he too was unwilling at this juncture to give up hope for a breakthrough leading to Political Union. When the two delegations met on 11 and 12 June in Bonn, it turned out that Erhard's dependence on his party in parliament was greater than his ambition to achieve an agreement with de Gaulle on the issue of Political Union. After the French negotiators had made only vague intimations about strengthening the right of the European Parliament to participate in decision-making on budgetary matters, Foreign Minister Gerhard Schröder spoke with Erhard and succeeded in getting him to agree to accept a provisional regulation of agricultural financing for a year at most. This was much less than

---

31 Germond, "Partenaires," pp. 346–348.
32 Charles de Gaulle, *Discours et messages*, vol. IV, pp. 354–358.
33 AHCE SEC (65) 1541, 13 May 1965.

the chancellor had indicated in conversations with de Gaulle beforehand, and so the summit ended in a state of full confusion.[34]

Very angry that Schröder had tossed a wrench into the works,[35] de Gaulle now found himself willing to dispense with a stepped-up completion of the Common Market and thus also the transfer of levies to the Community on 1 July 1967. For the moment, the question of control over independent sources of income by the European Parliament did not come up in that way; however, France as a net exporter of agricultural products could not yet stop its participation in the financing of export subsidies. De Gaulle was prepared to accept any domestic political difficulties that might arise from that. He was now concerned only that the financing for the whole transition period be agreed upon, given the transition to majority decision-making in the Council of Ministers beginning on 1 January 1966. Couve de Murville presented the new French position at the Council of Ministers meeting in Brussels on 15 June.

As had been agreed in Bonn, West German Foreign Office State Secretary Rolf Lahr and French Foreign Ministry Director Oliver Wormser, who was responsible for economic affairs, met on 22 June in Paris in order to take up the matter of coordinating their countries' positions once again. A compromise presented itself: Bonn would agree to the postponement of the transition to independent sources of income if France would hold to the completion of the customs union on 1 July 1967. Furthermore, as had been discussed among the ministries in Bonn, Lahr went on to assure his counterpart that the West German government would now advocate a settlement for the whole transition period. In regard to the future budgetary rights of Parliament, Lahr emphasized that the Council of Ministers would still have the final word during at least an initial stage.

As can be seen when comparing the reports made by Lahr and by Wormser to their respective superiors,[36] the two remained unclear as to how far French concessions in the Parliament question should go and whether a definitive settlement for the transition period should actually be found by 30 June. Wormser gave the impression that the West German government had fully accepted the positions Couve had presented in the Council of Ministers session of 15 June. There was no mention of Bonn having persisted in its position that there should be two further stages regarding participation by Parliament. The French foreign minister was all the more surprised when in the Council of Ministers on 30 June, Lahr—acting on instructions from Erhard—maintained the position that for the time being, there

---

34 Germond, "Partenaires," pp. 430–434; Bajon, *Europapolitik*, pp. 97ff., 120–126.
35 Peyrefitte, *De Gaulle II*, p. 287.
36 Report by Lahr, 22 June 1965, BA, B136 2591 and report by Wormser, 23 June 1965, MAE, CE-DE, 1111, respectively.

could be negotiations only on provisional financing for the next few months. That same evening, Schröder presented a resolution of the Bundestag (approved that day) calling for the West German government to advocate a strengthening of the rights of Parliament in accordance with the vote taken by that body on 12 May. At this, Couve had reached the point where he thought negotiations should be broken off.[37]

Previously, Fanfani had categorically maintained that only short-term financing could be the subject of negotiations. As long as a market for fruit, vegetables, and olive oil had not been agreed upon, it was the poorest member states that were threatened with having to make hefty net payments. In accordance with a Dutch parliamentary resolution, Luns had stuck to the position that the Commission's package could not be divided into its components. It was thus still the case that the financing of the agricultural market during the transition phase 1965–1970 could not be had if the rights of the European Parliament were not strengthened at the same time. De Gaulle was not prepared to agree to that, however. While the Quai d'Orsay saw the necessity of "doing something more substantial regarding the parliamentary assembly,"[38] the French head of state would rather accept a crisis in the EEC than agree to a strengthening of its institutions. As he had said in the Council of Ministers in April, France would still be able to enjoy a fine existence "if the Treaty of Rome were sent into hibernation."[39]

There is no way to determine the extent to which that was meant in earnest. It was in any event the case that de Gaulle was not prepared to pay the price demanded by Hallstein for the transfer of the system of subsidies for agriculture to the Community. With the strengthening of the Commission that would result from that, along with the transition to majority voting in the Council of Ministers, there was the threat that control over the development of the EEC would be taken from de Gaulle. He thus resorted to a measure that Couve de Murville had been encouraging as early as the end of May in the event that pressure on Erhard did not succeed: "the establishment of a kind of general boycott by France until things arrange themselves."[40]

Couve thus rejected Hallstein's offer to present in short order a new package of proposals that would take the various negotiating positions more fully into account.

---

37 Germond, "Partenaires," pp. 434–438; Bajon, *Europapolitik*, pp. 99–106, 126–128.
38 MAE, CE-DE, 1111, *Règlement financier. Situation au 24 juin 1965*, without date, p. 2.
39 Council of Ministers session of 14 April 1965, Peyrefitte, *De Gaulle II*, p. 282.
40 According to the testimony of Couve de Murville during a hearing at the Institut Charles de Gaulle, 16 Dec. 1988, quoted in Maurice Vaïsse, "La politique européenne de la France en 1965: pourquoi 'la chaise vide'?" in Loth, *Crises*, pp. 193–214. However, Couve suppresses the fact that before the crisis began, there had still been efforts to reach an understanding with Erhard.

He wanted nothing to do with the suggestion from the German delegation that the clocks simply be stopped and that talks continue, as had been done in January of 1962. Instead, he asserted that it was "obvious" that "some of our partners" lack the "will" to reach an agreement. Couve then used his position as chairman, which he held only through that very day, to adjourn the session. With the observation that there was "neither an agreement nor the possibility of an agreement," he broke off the negotiations just before two o'clock in the morning.[41]

The next day, after a meeting of the French Council of Ministers Peyrefitte announced that the French government had drawn conclusions from the fact that the partners had not fulfilled their financial commitments: France would not participate in sessions of the EEC Council of Ministers in July. On 6 July, the Permanent Representative of France in the Commission was withdrawn. The French did no longer take part in sessions of the Permanent Representatives or the work groups that met under the chairmanship of the Commission. "Our chair will remain empty, and the meetings will be worthless," commented de Gaulle in a conversation with Peyrefitte.[42]

It was clear that a certain portion of the blame for the outbreak of this crisis lay with Ludwig Erhard—in that he had suddenly yielded to political pressure from his smaller coalition partner, the FDP, by insisting that only provisional financing could be negotiated on 30 June. This had given Couve and de Gaulle the impression that the government of the FRG was among those that did not keep its word either. Decisive however was de Gaulle's realization that the Parliament issue could not be taken off the table even with the offer of postponing Community financing of the agricultural market. The supposed failure to keep commitments regarding financing was only a pretext with which the blockade of Community institutions could be justified, an "unhoped-for pretext," as de Gaulle said to Peyrefitte.[43]

The Crisis of the "Empty Chair"

With this blockade of Community institutions—something not foreseen in the treaty—de Gaulle wanted to bring about the emergence of differences among the

---

[41] Protocol of Emile Noël, 1 July 1965, FJME, ARM G (65) 329.
[42] Peyrefitte, *De Gaulle II*, p. 291. Cf. Vaïsse, "Politique européenne," pp. 209–213; on de Gaulle's motives, also Wilfried Loth, "Français et Allemands dans la crise de la chaise vide," in Marie-Thèrese Bitsch (ed.), *Le couple France-Allemagne et les institutions européennes*, Brussels: Émile Bruylant, 2001, pp. 229–243.
[43] Peyrefitte, *De Gaulle II*, p. 288.

partners so as to break the common front against the financing of agriculture without strengthening the European Parliament at the same time. It was especially the West German government that in his view was vulnerable to further pressure. "Because in the final instance the Germans cannot bear a situation in which there is no longer a Common Market," as he said optimistically in mid-September, "in the end they'll give in. [...] The new chancellor will come to Paris soon after the election [on 19 September] in order to arrange things." He did not even shy away from intensifying his Eastern policy so as to increase the pressure on the Germans. "They see," as he stated after a visit by Polish Prime Minister Jósef Cyrankiewicz on 11 September in Paris, "that the East is coming closer to us. They're encircled."[44]

In order for the pressure to work, however, it had to continue for a long time. The partners were to be left in the dark as to French goals and were to fear that the Common Market would break apart. "If they aren't afraid, we won't achieve our goal," as de Gaulle said on 13 July.[45] Therefore, the French representatives could not simply be absent for four weeks as Peyrefitte had already announced, and so the president made clear during the Council of Ministers session on 7 July that he was not of a mind to begin any negotiations at all before the end of the year.

It was not only the definitive financing of the Common Agricultural Market without any strengthening of the European Parliament that he was envisioning as the goal of negotiations. He also wanted to change the personnel of a Commission that had caused him so much trouble. He "never again wanted to have anything to do" with Hallstein, Marjolin, or Mansholt, as he said to Peyrefitte after the Council of Ministers meeting on 1 July.[46] Furthermore, he was seeking to stop the transition to majority voting, which—as he now saw more clearly than before—threatened to call into question French successes in agricultural policy once again. "This crisis," as he explained in the Council of Ministers on 7 July, "must be used to put an end to ulterior political motives. It can't be the case that from 1 January 1966 our economy will be subjected to a settlement on majority voting by which our partners force us to accept their will. This opportunity must be used to revise the false concepts by which we have been subjected to the dictates of others. End this nonsense!"[47] In order to prevent the transition to majority voting, he demanded a revision of the EEC Treaty or at least a supplemental protocol "that would restore the veto on fundamental issues."[48] Lastly, he also

---

44 *Ibid.*, p. 300.
45 *Ibid.*, p. 292.
46 *Ibid.*, pp. 290ff.
47 *Ibid.*, p. 292.
48 Thus on 15 Sept. 1965, *ibid.*, p. 299.

considered a revision of the price system for the agricultural market that would banish the threat of overproduction as well as a slowdown in the dismantling of tariffs for the sake of French industry, but this was not essential to him.[49]

Initially, De Gaulle's war of nerves did not have any effect. Hallstein remained convinced that France needed the EEC too, and that the president was therefore merely seeking to knock it into shape so that it did not limit his freedom of action. Hallstein let it be known that no one was "either to give in or to dramatize" the situation.[50] Regarding the concessions that France would be expected to make for the completion of the agricultural market, he argued that the five partner governments ought to agree on a common line and not to give in on the aspiration for democratic control of the Community budget. Hallstein was supported in this view by Schröder; both saw the conflict as a test of power with a man who aspired to French hegemony over Europe. Even if he was not as decisively supranational in outlook regarding objectives as was the Commission president, Schröder thought it was important to adhere to agreements already made, which he saw as the best protection against such hegemony. Given that the Franco-German dialogue had been broken off for the time being and Erhard's initiative for a Political Union was obviously no longer on the agenda, Schröder could now have a more significant influence on West German European policy than before.[51]

In bilateral conversations with his partners, Schröder made sure that the formulation of a new proposal for financing agriculture would be left to the Commission. It focused on the compromise offer that the French government had made on 15 June: Postponing the transition to independent sources of income and thereby also putting off the Parliament issue. The Agricultural Market and the Customs Union were to be completed by 1 July 1967, as the Commission had proposed in March. The financing of the Agricultural Market was however to be accomplished by member contributions until the end of the transition period, and tariff revenues were to be returned to the member states during this period. The funding of agricultural expenses was to occur in diminishing portions according to the general financial ratio of distribution and in a growing percentage according to the level of imports from third countries. If the market for fruit, vegetables, milk, and other commodities could not be passed by 1 July 1967, financing from levies was to be extended so that full financing from the agricultural account would begin only in 1970.

---

49 Conversation with Hervé Alphand, 9 Nov. 1965, quoted in Bajon, *Europapolitik*, pp. 196ff.
50 Horst Osterheld, *Außenpolitik unter Ludwig Erhard 1963–1966. Ein dokumentarischer Bericht*, Düsseldorf: Droste, 1992, p. 210.
51 Bajon, *Europapolitik*, pp. 149–153, 260–267.

Controversially, the Commission discussed the question of the package deal together with that of parliamentary control. Mansholt initially protested this by stating that the Commission was carelessly dropping an essential portion of its proposals. Marjolin still wanted to hold explicitly to the principle of parliamentary control of independent revenues, combined with the recommendation that the role of the body in budget talks be strengthened "even now," while Hallstein finally succeeded with a formulation to the effect that the Commission could not once again take a position in light of the fact that the Council of Ministers had not yet finished discussing the matter: "It does not believe that all possibilities for agreement have been exhausted." In this way, he sought to avoid the possibility that the Commission could be attacked from any angle and yet at the same time preserve the chances of influencing the necessary compromise among the governments at any given moment along the lines of his own views.[52]

The memorandum of the Commission was formally passed on 22 July[53] and was presented to the Council of Ministers on 26 and 27 July. In doing so, however, the foreign ministers in attendance did not go into detail; and there was most certainly no vote taken. The governments of the Five were not sure that they could make any decisions at all without French participation. Beyond this, they wanted to ease the French return to the table without any loss of face. It was rather clear even without a formal vote that the Five were willing to come to an agreement with France on the basis of the Commission memorandum. The French accusation of broken promises was thereby countered, and Paris was forced to show its hand.

There was nothing left for de Gaulle to do but go public with the demand for a revision of the treaty, which he had not yet presented. In a press conference of 9 September, he declared that negotiations in Brussels had been broken off not only because of the "permanent resistance of most of our partners to bringing agriculture into the Common Market" but also because of "certain errors in principle and ambiguities in the treaties on the Economic Community of the Six." After he had denounced the "supranational ambitions" of the Commission and had conjured up the horrific image of the dominance of a "technocratic, unpatriotic, and unaccountable areopagus" over French democracy, he made the abandonment of such "pretentions" a precondition for France's return to the negotiating table.[54]

---

52 *Ibid.* pp. 159–169; Commission memorandum of 22 July 1965, COM (65) 320 final.
53 Along with Rochereau, Marjolin voted against it; he specified in the protocols that he was opposed to leaving the Parliament question open. Amazingly, however, he completely concealed this view in his memoirs. See Marjolin, *Le travail d'une vie*, p. 348.
54 De Gaulle, *Discours IV*, pp. 377–381.

The partners' shock at this demand was actually quite limited. They had long since perceived that the blockade of Community institutions by France was highly selective: French representatives continued to participate in numerous committee meetings and even in gatherings of the Council. On 21 September, the deputy of the permanent representative of the French government, Maurice Ulrich—who had remained in Brussels—bluntly informed his German colleague Eberhard Bömke "that very large portions of the French administration do not approve of the general's policy toward the European Communities, even sharply reject" it and that no preparatory work was being undertaken in Paris on emendations to the EEC Treaty. Not only did Bömke inform his superiors in Bonn of this, he also told Hallstein.[55] One could only conclude from all this that France did not actually want to leave the Community and especially that the intensification of the crisis was wholly the personal work of the general.

This meant too that de Gaulle was not in a position to push through any kind of treaty amendments. It was not only that the French administrative apparatus was hoping that its partners would maintain their hardline stance against the president: De Gaulle increasingly came under domestic pressure due to the worsening of the crisis. After the session of the EEC Council of Ministers in late July, the agricultural associations asked why the government had not accepted the offers of the Commission; and then the employers' organization voiced its criticism too. In order to arrest the growing opposition in the run-up to the presidential election, representatives of the government as well as the Gaullist party newspaper *La Nation* felt themselves compelled to deny that the president had any intention of tearing up the EEC Treaty.[56]

The Five could thus increase their pressure on de Gaulle without any worries. When in the third week of September Belgian Foreign Minister Paul-Henri Spaak proposed that France be invited to an extraordinary session of the Council of Ministers without participation of the Commission, there was quick agreement that there must not be any decision regarding agricultural financing on that occasion. The return of France to the negotiating table was not to be purchased at the price of weakening the position of the Commission. In the Council session of 25 and 26 October, the five foreign ministers came to agreement that France was to be invited to such a special session in order to clear up institutional questions. At the same time, they emphasized in a declaration "that the solution to the problems facing the Communities must be found within the framework of the treaties and existing organs." Among themselves, they were determined that they would

---

55 Bömke to Hallstein, 21 Sept. 1965, BA, WH 1187/2.
56 Bajon, *Europapolitik*, pp. 214–218.

permit neither a treaty revision nor an interpretation of the treaty that limited the responsibilities of the Commission or the principle of the qualified majority.[57]

The position of those who pushed for the president to yield due to economic concerns was strengthened when the Five expressed concern about the problems that de Gaulle had addressed in his press conference and also simultaneously demonstrated their resolve not to allow the supranational dimension of the treaty to be affected. Beyond this, the five foreign ministers composed a resolution on agriculture financing that made it clear that if France still wanted to have influence over the shaping of the Agricultural Market, it would do well to return to the table as soon as possible: Though in July the Commission had sought the postponement of the linked issues of independent sources of income and parliamentary control until 1970, the ministers now made reference to the original proposal from the Commission and observed regarding it "that this issue [must] be reviewed with the participation of all members of the Council."[58]

Schröder, who had played the key role in attaining the agreement of the Five,[59] also let Couve de Murville know what the proposed clearing up of institutional questions would amount to: agreement over how cooperation between governments and the Commission could possibly be "further improved" and how "on issues of objectively clear life-and-death interests [an outvoting by the majority could] be avoided." Formal arrangements were not necessary for this, however—tact and good will should suffice.[60] Such a gentlemen's agreement was actually a concession to de Gaulle's conceptions and thus also a disappointment to all those who were eager for a rapid expansion of the supranational nature of the EEC. Yet, this was much less than de Gaulle had demanded; it corresponded to what was achievable under the circumstances. Not only was Schröder's formulation approved by most of the other governments, with the exception of the Netherlands, but Hallstein too found it "encouraging" that there was to be discussion of "a reasonable application of the majority principle."[61]

---

[57] Schröder to Erhard, 27 Oct. 1965, PAAA, B150, vol. 62, pp. 8383ff.
[58] AHCE, SEC (65) 3145, 26 Oct. 1965.
[59] Cf. Henning Türk, "'To Face de Gaulle as a Community': The Role of the Federal Republic of Germany during the Empty Chair Crisis," in Palayret, Wallace, Winand (eds.), *Visions*, pp. 113–127; Bajon, *Europapolitik*, pp. 274–286.
[60] Circular decree from Schröder, 27 Sept. 1965, AAPD 1965, Doc. 369, pp. 1518–1522; Klaiber to AA, 12 Oct. 1965, AAPD 1965, Doc. 388, p. 1608.
[61] Sigrist to Noel, 8 Oct. 1965, HAEU, EN 1588. The usual picture of an understanding of the governments with de Gaulle at the cost of the Commission (for example, in Ludlow, *European Community*, pp. 87ff.) springs from an exaggeration of Hallstein's ambitions, which de Gaulle had successfully propagated.

Naturally, the president was not immediately prepared to accept Schröder's offer. First, he wanted to test whether the unity of the Five—which he had not at all anticipated—could last or whether by persisting in his demands there was the possibility of achieving more. Secondly and above all, giving up on the blockade without a supplementary agreement on institutional questions would now amount to a defeat; this was to be avoided if at all possible, as long as his re-election was assured. Couve de Murville then quickly let Council President Emilio Colombo know that he was not prepared to take part in a meeting of the Council in Brussels. At the same time, he demanded abolition of the majority principle, the "return" of the Commission "to its rights and duties according to the treaty" and a "review" of its composition.[62] He followed up by making efforts to break the unity of the Five by means of bilateral conversations.

After this had proven unsuccessful, the French Council of Ministers decided on 17 November that it would in principle accept an invitation to an extraordinary meeting of the foreign ministers. This concession was not to be revealed to the wider world yet, however. In order to prevent the Five from increasing the pressure on de Gaulle still further, it was merely the case that the Belgian foreign minister, who was still seeking to negotiate, was told on 22 November that Paris was prepared to accept the recent compromise proposal: a meeting in early January of 1966 in Luxembourg.[63]

After de Gaulle had surprisingly failed by a significant margin to gain an absolute majority in the first round of the presidential elections on 5 December and thus had to contend with François Mitterrand in a runoff, the willingness to compromise was signaled still more clearly: In an encounter with Colombo on 8 December in Rome (on the occasion of the concluding festivities of the Second Vatican Council), Couve proposed leaving the issue open as to whether the meeting in Luxembourg would be a gathering of the Council or a summit. The Frenchman was also less rigid regarding a treaty stipulation on the desired turn away from the majority principle. After this encounter, Couve let it be known that "the main hindrances to resumption of European talks have been eliminated."[64]

Immediately after the re-election of de Gaulle on 19 December, the French government approved a meeting of the six foreign ministers on 17 and 18 January 1966 in Luxembourg. Despite recommendations to the contrary, however, de Gaulle was not willing to agree to the 1966 budget for the EEC or EURATOM; both

---

62 Lahr's notes, 10 Nov. 1965, AAPD 1965, Doc. 412, pp. 1689–1692. Couve gave his answer only orally (to the Italian ambassador) because his government disputed the legality of the Council session of 25 and 26 Oct. 1965.
63 Germond, "Partenaires," pp. 452ff.; Bajon, *Europapolitik*, p. 210ff.
64 Klaiber to AA, 15 Dec. 1965, PAAA, B20 1326, FS 1808.

communities thus had to operate with emergency budgets for the time being. The reduction of tariffs within the Community by ten percent as of 1 January 1966, which had been moved up by agreement, was put into effect; but tariff reduction within the framework of the Dillon round of GATT was postponed.

When the extraordinary Council—which was in French eyes only a summit of the foreign ministers—gathered on 17 January 1966 in Luxembourg, Couve in fact no longer called for an official revision of the Treaties of Rome. Instead, he presented a list of demands that amounted to a circumvention of critical treaty stipulations. In this "Decalogue," there was a call for the Commission to present its proposals initially to the member governments before they were submitted to the Council of Ministers. Also, the Commission was no longer to make any public declarations without prior consultation with the Council of Ministers. The representation of the Community to the outside world was to be left to the Council of Ministers. Majority voting in the Council was to be *de facto* eliminated via agreement on an advance veto: "If a member state declares that a decision touches upon one of its vital interests, the Council cannot vote on this issue until the consent of the affected state has been given."[65]

When it came to appointing a new Commission (whose mandate had expired on 9 January 1966), Couve no longer demanded a completely new slate of members. He did however want the introduction of a rotating presidency; every two years, a Commission member from a different country was to take over the position. After this, a second renewal of Hallstein's mandate was no longer possible. The new regulations would come into force in conjunction with the merger of the executives of ECSC, EEC, and EURATOM—a move that had been decided upon by the Six in March of 1965 before the outbreak of the crisis.[66] Couve demanded that the Merger Treaty of 8 April 1965 be ratified without delay so that the new Commission could take up its work at once.

The partners showed a certain measure of willingness to take the "Decalogue" as the starting point for a dialogue between the Commission and the Council. Schröder and Luns were not however prepared to put any kind of voting-system modification in writing, not even in the significantly weakened forms proposed by Spaak and Columbo as a compromise. Likewise, they did not want to ratify the

---

[65] Note of 8 Jan. 1966, quoted from Gérard Bossuat, "Emile Noël dans la tourmente de la crise communautaire de 1965," in Wilfried Loth (ed.), *La gouvernance supranationale dans la construction européenne*, Brussels: Émile Bruylant, 2005, pp. 89–113, here p. 105.
[66] Marie-Thérèse Bitsch, "La création de la Commission unique : réforme technique ou affirmation d'une identité européenne?" in Marie-Thérèse Bitsch, Wilfried Loth, Raymond Poidevin (eds.), *Institutions européennes et identités européennes*, Brussels: Émile Bruylant, 1998, pp. 327–347.

treaty on the merger of the executives of the three Communities until an understanding had been reached on the reappointment of Hallstein. An altercation almost broke out when on the second day of the meeting the French delegation put forward a timeline which did call for agreement on agricultural financing by the end of March but remained silent on the development of common positions in the Kennedy Round. After Couve had declared that a mandate for that round could only be decided after the settlement of the agricultural financing issue, Schröder and Luns rejected the French proposals lock, stock, and barrel. Luxembourg head of government and Foreign Minister Pierre Werner, serving as Council president, had no recourse but to adjourn the session.[67]

Before the next gathering of the six foreign ministers on 28 January, the Permanent Representatives, with the discreet cooperation of the Commission, worked out a milder version of the "Decalogue," now in seven points; the Commission then "invited" the Council to work on harmonization. The document expressed the desire that the Commission consult the Council before passing "important" proposals. Furthermore, proposals were to be submitted to the Council before being made public. The letters of accreditation of ambassadors to the Communities were to be accepted jointly by the president of the Commission and the president of the Council of Ministers. The Commission and the Council were to share information on their contacts with third states, should consult on the nature of their representation in international organizations, should "cooperate" in the realm of information, and coordinate with each other as to the control of Communities' expenditures. In this form, the rules of conduct — no longer containing any restrictions on the authority of the Commission or criticism of its prior actions — were now accepted by all foreign ministers.[68]

Regarding majority voting, Schröder made a concession to the French with a proposal for a declaration of intent that envisioned striving for a consensual solution "where very important interests of one or more partners are at stake." The partners still opposed the French demand that in such a case "the discussion must be continued until unanimous agreement is reached." Given the danger of another conference failure, Couve was prepared—at 0:45 a.m. on 30 January—to end the blockade without having succeeded in this demand. In a joint declaration, the partners stated "that there is a divergence of views on what should be done in the event of a failure to reach complete agreement."[69]

---

[67] Ludlow, *European Community*, pp. 97–100; Germond, "Partenaires," pp. 454–458; Bajon, *Europapolitik*, pp. 163–165.

[68] Cf. the comparison of the "Decalogue" und the "Heptalogue" in Palayret, *Visions*, pp. 246–249.

[69] Palayret, Wallace, Winand (eds.), *Visions*, pp. 325ff.

Earlier, when establishing a written work program for the coming weeks and months, Couve had had to concede that parallel to a quick resolution to agricultural financing, the working out of common tariffs and a common position for GATT negotiations had to be dealt with as well. The issue of replacing Hallstein was postponed: Couve had to accept that the Five declared an understanding on the composition of the new Commission would be a prerequisite for the merger treaty to take effect.[70]

With his seven-month absence from the Council of Ministers and the meetings of the Permanent Representatives, de Gaulle had achieved nothing more than sowing uncertainty among his partners as to how France would react to the next difference of opinion that would be declared "vital"—whether the French government would then comply with a majority vote or would unleash another crisis. That might well protect one from being outvoted, but it was not a guarantee that the Community would develop in the direction desired by de Gaulle.[71] That the president gave up his opposition at this juncture can only be explained in that he had come to the conclusion that he had played out his hand. In fact, the president of the Permanent Representatives, Albert Borschette, had on 7 January warned the French in the name of the Five that Luxembourg was their "last chance." The Permanent Representatives had agreed upon a Council session for 31 January or 1 February at which the passage of the regular budget for 1966 would be on the agenda.[72] De Gaulle could no longer exclude the possibility that the integration of the Community would continue in a completely normal manner and that France would later have to submit to decisions that had been made without its input.

The Time of the Arrangements

De Gaulle sought to mask his defeat by immediately developing a new initiative for Political Union. After Couve returned from Luxembourg, he stated soothingly in the Council of Ministers on 2 February that they had after all achieved "that which we wanted to a significant degree," and the president insisted that the supranational trap could only be evaded "if we achieve political cooperation among the

---

70 Ludlow, *European Community*, pp. 100–103; Germond, "Partenaires," pp. 460–463; Bajon, *Europapolitik*, pp. 169–175.
71 There is no evidence for the oft-repeated claim that the Luxembourg "compromise" had led to dispensing with majority voting. See Jonathan Golub, "Did the Luxembourg Compromise Have Any Consequences?" in Palayret, Wallace, Winand (eds.), *Visions*, pp. 279–299.
72 Bajon, *Europapolitik*, p. 230ff.

Six."[73] After the session, he let it be known that "organizing European political cooperation would greatly ease the development of economic cooperation."[74] At the next Franco-German summit in Paris on 7 and 8 February, he came to agreement with Erhard on an appeal for political Europe, to which the chancellor was to respond with new efforts to bring about a meeting of the foreign ministers. At a press conference on 21 February, de Gaulle characterized the organizing of political consultations among the Six as "more urgent than ever before" and once again conjured up the vision of a "mighty and independent" European Union that would ultimately also play a decisive role in overcoming the two blocs.[75]

Erhard hesitated to make the case for the Political Union once again, however. After the brutal extortion attempt by de Gaulle, the chancellor had become more than skeptical that it would still be possible to reach a workable arrangement with him. Erhard therefore maintained the position at the Paris negotiations that he would become active again only after de Gaulle had publicly spoken in favor of a new initiative. When the agreed-upon press conference took place, he saw his skepticism confirmed: De Gaulle announced at the same time that France would withdraw from the integrated defense structure of NATO at an unspecified time before the expiration of the Atlantic pact on 4 April 1969. That was not anything fundamentally new—de Gaulle had informed the US government of his intentions in this regard as early as the end of November 1964 and had told Erhard of it in the Franco-German summit, which had been brought forward to June of 1965. Yet, the unilateral declaration without prior consultations served to make clear that de Gaulle was determined to force his conception of European security on his partners. This was not conducive to an understanding on the Political Union.

In the announcement of unilateral withdrawal from NATO, Erhard correctly regarded de Gaulle's Europe appeal as "completely void."[76] The West German Foreign Office did obligatorily sound out the partners as to the chances for a new foreign ministers' conference. After Luns had urgently counseled Bonn not to pursue a new initiative if it wanted to avoid endangering relations with the Netherlands, the chancellor made a public appeal only for the resumption of regular consultations of the foreign ministers; he did not issue an invitation to a new meeting. At the national party congress of the CDU from 21 to 23 March

---

73 Peyrefitte, *De Gaulle III*, pp. 183ff.
74 Press statement of 2 Feb. 1966, quoted in Germond, "Partenaires," pp. 352ff. On the following, *ibid.*, pp. 352–355; Kramer, *Europäisches oder atlantisches Europa*, pp. 213–218.
75 De Gaulle, *Discours et messages*, vol. V, Paris: Plon, 1970, pp. 5–23.
76 Osterheld, *Außenpolitik*, p. 295.

1966 in Bonn, Schröder—the professed "Atlanticist" and victorious adversary of de Gaulle—received tremendous ovations.[77]

For his part, de Gaulle decided to carry through with the withdrawal from NATO integration in short order. Without prior consultation with the responsible staff of the foreign ministry, the defense ministry, or the government, he sent a handwritten announcement to President Johnson on 7 March indicating that France was pulling out of NATO's integrated command and that it would be withdrawing its troops from integrated military units. At the same time, he called for the removal of the integrated general staffs and allied forces from French territory. Two days later, letters to this effect were sent to Erhard as well as British Prime Minister Harold Wilson and Italian Prime Minister Giuseppe Saragat. In a memorandum of 29 March, he specified that the withdrawal of NATO forces and institutions was to take place within one year, that is, by 1 April 1967.[78]

With de Gaulle's decision to withdraw unilaterally from NATO military integration, a politically-independent Europe slid definitively beyond reach. This action, widely perceived as exhibiting a lack of solidarity, did finally spur an overdue discussion of reforming NATO. Contrary to the French president's wishes, this did not however lead to an autonomous European pillar within the alliance but instead strengthened American leadership. On 25 September 1966, the fourteen remaining NATO members reached agreement on the creation of a nuclear planning group and the development of a joint strategy. The negotiations stemming from this led in December of 1967 to official adoption of the strategy of "flexible response" (which de Gaulle had fought as lacking in credibility) and to the issuing of the Harmel Report, named for Belgian Foreign Minister Pierre Harmel, which established defense and détente as tasks of equal priority for NATO. This meant for a strong impulse within the Western alliance to coordinate efforts toward détente with the Soviet Bloc and not, as de Gaulle had envisioned it, emancipation from American leadership.[79]

Erhard was just able to prevent Schröder from pushing through a withdrawal of French forces (heretofore under NATO's supreme command for Europe) from the Federal Republic. Bonn initially declared itself "provisionally" in agreement with having the troops remain and then got negotiations going between the chief of staff of the French land forces, General Charles Ailleret, and NATO

---

77 Geiger, *Atlantiker*, p. 404.
78 Vaïsse, Maurice, *La grandeur. Politique étrangère du général de Gaulle 1958–1969*, Paris: Fayard, 1998, pp. 385ff.; the letters in De Gaulle, *Lettres 1964–1966*, pp. 261–267.
79 Helga Haftendorn, "The Adaption of the NATO Alliance to a Period of Détente: The 1967 Harmel Report," in Loth (ed.), *Crises*, pp. 285–322; Vincent Dujardin, *Pierre Harmel*, Brussels: Éditions Le Cri, 2004, pp. 627–657.

Supreme Commander for Europe Lyman Lemnitzer on the issue of command over the French forces in wartime. In an official exchange of correspondence on the matter with Paris on 21 December 1966, Bonn held firm in its position that French forces would remain as long as the West German government desired them to. Lastly, in an exchange of correspondence on 22 August 1967, it was agreed that in the event of war, French troops would fall under the command of Allied Forces Central Europe; the French government did however reserve the right to determine whether they would participate militarily at all.

Erhard saw no occasion or opportunity for further steps toward Franco-German cooperation in the defense realm, as de Gaulle had offered in his explanation of the withdrawal from NATO integration. Instead, the chancellor let it be known during a trip to Norway and Sweden in early September of 1966 that the economic integration of the EEC and EFTA had once again taken priority in his eyes.[80] For his part, de Gaulle responded to the lack of any agreement on a common strategy among the Europeans with a demonstration of the claim to complete *national* independence: In December of 1967, just before the Harmel Report was issued, the French president had General Ailleret publish an essay with a call for France to be in a position "to intervene everywhere" and to defend itself "in all directions."[81]

In Luxembourg, the negotiations on issues that remained open thus took place in an atmosphere of growing alienation between France and its partners in regard to defense policy. For exactly that reason, however, there was pressure for talks on economic issues to succeed: No one involved believed that it would be possible to withstand another crisis calling into question the existence and further development of the Common Market. France did persist in its position that regulation of agriculture financing in the transition period had priority. In the end, however, the French government had to accept the Federal Republic's insistence that agreements made here would only take effect if accord were reached on establishing additional markets as well as the completion of the Customs Union and common positions for GATT negotiations.

In a series of Council sessions from late February to late July 1966, agreement was first of all reached that the transition to free traffic in agricultural products, which the Commission had envisioned for 1 July 1967, would instead be stretched out over a period of twelve months, that is, to 1 July 1968. The Customs Union for industrial products would also be completed by 1 July 1968 in two stages. As to the financing of the agricultural funds, agreement was essentially reached

---

80 Geiger, *Atlantiker*, pp. 411–424; Kramer, *Europäisches oder atlantisches Europa*, pp. 220ff.; Germond, "Partenaires," pp. 549–563; Vaïsse, *La grandeur*, pp. 392–394, 580–582.
81 *Ibid.*, p. 394.

on a compromise proposal made by the Commission for the transition period: financing from member contributions and levies. The West German government was able to push through a provision specifying that its portion of the financing in the second half of the transition period, that is, from 1 July 1967, would be .8 percent lower than that of the French (31.2 percent versus 32 percent) and that agricultural exports into the GDR would no longer be treated as exports into third countries. The percentage of the agricultural budget available for improving the agricultural infrastructure was limited to a set amount.

After energetic preparatory work by the Commission, the Council agreed on 14 June 1966 on a negotiating position for the Kennedy Round of GATT. True, it did contain some concessions to France regarding the tariff levels to be put forth; but altogether it included the overwhelming portion of the foreign trade of the Community in worldwide tariff reductions, as both the Federal Republic and the Netherlands had especially desired. This agreement was made easier by the fact that in the meantime, French business was likewise becoming increasingly interested in a reduction of industrial tariffs. Lastly, there followed on 27 July 1966 an agreement on the agricultural portion of the negotiating position for the Kennedy Round; the Commission had done preparatory work on this too. Simultaneously, after long and to an extent very difficult negotiations, markets for sugar and fat were passed as well as important additions to those for fruit and vegetables and common prices for milk, beef, sugar, oil seeds, olive oil, and rice. The demands made on the Common Market by Italian and German producers were thus largely acceded to, which was disadvantageous for the budgets of not only those who up to that point had been net payers.[82]

After the Commission had received a comprehensive mandate for negotiations, the Kennedy Round of GATT could finally enter its decisive phase. This led to the signing of a comprehensive agreement on 15 June 1967. The terms on reducing tariffs in agriculture were modest: Instead of dropping them by as much as fifty percent as the US had demanded, the reduction was twenty-two percent on average; this resulted not least of all from the fact that the US government refused to include export subsidies in the calculation. The high level of agricultural protectionism among the industrial nations thus remained essentially intact, which worked against the chances for modernization in the so-called developing nations. Conversely, there was a genuine breakthrough in the realm of industrial goods: For more than two thirds of the products involved in negotiations, tariff reductions of fifty percent were agreed upon. The average reduction on all products was thirty-five percent, to be introduced in stages over a period of five years

---

82 Ludlow, *European Community*, pp. 103–109; Patel, *Europäisierung*, pp. 312–319, 336–340; Germond, "Partenaires," pp. 463–468.

up to 1 January 1972. Thanks to its unified stance, the EEC was able to develop great negotiating strength. This enabled the Europeans to convince the Americans to accept the mutual opening of industrial markets while denying the unilateral opening of the agricultural market, as American farmers were forcefully demanding.[83]

Regarding the merger of the executives and the appointment of a new common Commission, Schröder continued his adamant resistance to French pressure. For him, sticking with Hallstein was an integral component of the as-yet unfinished test of strength with de Gaulle. For reasons having to do with party politics, Erhard could not tolerate a rejection of Hallstein, and in his resentment over the lack of solidarity from the French president, he saw no reason to risk his own position on account of French demands. In the Council of Ministers session of 5 April 1966, the West German delegation did accede to the French call for introducing a two-year rotating presidency of the common Commission. Yet, they also persisted in their position that would allow mandates to be extended for an additional two years and also proposed that the common Commission be entrusted to Hallstein for the first two years.[84]

A Belgian compromise proposal limiting Hallstein's mandate to one year was rejected by Schröder, as was de Gaulle's concession that after the merger Hallstein could remain in office for "several months," as the president had said at the Franco-German summit of 21 July 1966.[85] Instead, Schröder proposed that the current Commission, which had been so helpful in decision-making on the Common Agricultural Market and on GATT negotiations be allowed to remain in office until the Customs Union took effect on 1 July 1968. The merger of the executives was to be postponed until that time. The Federal Republic kept Hallstein *de facto* in office by refusing to agree to a date for filing ratification documents.

A resolution to the mutual blockade came only after the fall of Erhard in November of 1966 and after a grand coalition of the CDU and SPD had taken the reins in Bonn on 1 December. The new chancellor, Kurt-Georg Kiesinger, was a CDU politician who regarded *rapprochement* with France as a high priority. Kiesinger himself was a South German member of the *Bildungsbürgertum* who valued France, its language, and its culture very highly. As longtime chairman of the Foreign Policy Committee of the Bundestag (before he had taken over as prime

---

[83] Coppolaro, *The European Economic Community in the GATT Negotiations*, pp. 360–366; Patel, *Europäisierung*, pp. 348–357; Henning Türk, *Die Europapolitik der Großen Koalition*, Munich: Oldenbourg, 2006, pp. 45–57.

[84] Notes by Lahr, 6 April 1966, AAPD 1966, pp. 446–448. On this and the following, cf. Türk, *Europapolitik*, pp. 35–46; Germond, "Partenaires," pp. 677–688; Bajon, *Europapolitik*, pp. 317–323.

[85] AAPD 1966, pp. 966–973, here p. 971.

minister of Baden-Württemberg in late 1958), he had developed a conception of Europe that was significantly closer to de Gaulle's than to those of Schröder or Hallstein. Without emphasizing a front against the US as strongly as the French president did, Kiesinger placed his hopes on a European core that was capable of taking action, one that possessed real weight *vis-à-vis* the US. With skeptical pragmatism, he assumed that the nation-states would remain the central actors in the European unification process for the foreseeable future.[86]

The new foreign minister, SPD chairman Willy Brandt, was also committed to a united Europe's increased capacity to act. Moreover, he was under pressure from his party colleague Karl Schiller, who as economy minister was pushing for a rapid merger of the executives. Only if this were no longer blocked could a common energy policy be developed, a move the Federal Republic was seeking in light of the crisis in the coal mining industry. In order to overcome the blockade without doing damage to Hallstein, Brandt had State Secretary Lahr propose during a foreign ministers' conference of the Six on 22 December that the Merger Treaty take effect on 1 July 1967 and that, as Schröder had suggested, Hallstein serve as president of the common Commission until completion of the Customs Union on 1 July 1968.

De Gaulle greeted this initiative with the demand that the proposal not be discussed in the Council of Ministers of the Six but rather at the next Franco-German summit on 12 and 13 January 1967 in Bonn. At that meeting, Kiesinger showed himself to be "somewhat more modest"[87] than his foreign minister: He would be satisfied if Hallstein could remain as Commission president "for a period of time" after the merger was carried out. When de Gaulle replied that this period should expire before the end of the year, an agreement was reached that at the summit conference of the Six planned for June, the West German government would support the immediate merger and Hallstein would then be called upon to serve as president of the common Commission for half a year. Fanfani had issued the invitations to that summit, officially in order to celebrate the tenth anniversary of the signing of the Treaties of Rome, but actually in order to take up work on political cooperation once again.

With pressure coming from the ranks of the CDU/CSU and opposition from his Foreign Office, Kiesinger then called this arrangement into question: He now wanted an earlier merger and also an extension of Hallstein's term to 31 December 1967. De Gaulle was unwilling to accept that. After the chancellor had already

---

86 Cf. Philipp Gassert, "'Wir müssen bewahren, was wir geschaffen haben, auch über eine kritische Zeit hinweg' – Kurt Georg Kiesinger, Frankreich und das europäische Projekt," in König and Schulz (eds.), *Bundesrepublik*, pp. 147–166.
87 Conversation notes, 13 Jan. 1967, AAPD 1967, Doc. 17, pp. 94–102, the quote on p. 100.

committed himself to the merger in the coming months, the French president saw no reason to make further concessions. On the contrary, in light of the West German demands to change the arrangement, the French government made clear that along with the appointment of Hallstein, it also wanted to determine right then who would follow him in the post. That threatened to diminish Hallstein's influence over the shaping of the common Commission further.

Thus, the test of strength over Hallstein continued. In the end, there was nothing left for Bonn to do but give in if it did not want to endanger the recent beginnings of an understanding regarding the political Community, which Fanfani had initiated with his invitation to a summit in Rome. As the date for the gathering approached, Brandt sought to have Couve de Murville agree to extend Hallstein's term to 31 March 1968. The West German foreign minister made this request at a dinner on the occasion of the Franco-German foreign ministers conference on 27 and 28 April, however; the meal ended with reconfirmation of the French positions on all essential points: The merger should take place on 1 July; Hallstein's term should end on 31 December 1967; along with his appointment, decisions were to be made as to his successor and the future composition of the Commission. Couve conceded only that Hallstein could remain a member of the Commission, perhaps in the post of vice president.

This was a solution no longer acceptable to Hallstein. He had acceded to the shortening of his term as president of the common Commission to a half year under the condition that all the governments accepted it (and in the hope that at least the Dutch would call for a longer term). Given that his successor was now to be appointed right at the beginning, he no longer saw any sense in further engagement. Hallstein correctly viewed that having him continue in the office of vice president would weaken the political weight of the Commission. He wrote to the chancellor on 3 May requesting that he not be re-nominated. In explaining his request, he argued not only that the proposed term would not be sufficient to move him to offer his experience for integrating the three executives but also asserted that an agreement between the governments and the candidate on limiting the term would endanger the independence of the Commission.[88]

With Hallstein concerning himself so much with damage control, it seemed all the clearer that Kiesinger was the loser in this test of strength. The chancellor's actions became the subject of much criticism not only in the West German press but also among the governments of the member states. In fact, however, de Gaulle's victory was not nearly as great as it seemed: Firstly, it had taken him almost two years to get rid of Hallstein. Secondly, the general had to accept Jean Rey as the next president of the Commission; and Rey had an understanding of

---

88 Hallstein to Kiesinger, 3 May 1966, BA, WH 1126.

the office that was no less political than Hallstein's; moreover, as leader of GATT negotiations, Rey had already gained great prestige. Mansholt, whom de Gaulle had also been targeting, remained vice president. It proved possible to replace only Marjolin, who was succeeded by the economics professor Raymond Barre. Thus, de Gaulle had not succeeded in completely changing the composition of the Commission, as he had initially demanded, nor had he been able to weaken it. For their part, Kiesinger and Brandt could say that they had opened a path for further development of the Community. From that perspective, Schröder's blockade strategy was unrewarding over the long term.

With the implementation of the Merger Treaty on 1 July 1967, the number of Commission members grew temporarily from nine to fourteen. The Committee of the Permanent Representatives, which had not even been envisioned in the Treaties of Rome, was now institutionalized. Luxembourg, having now lost the High Authority of the ECSC, was compensated with a group of new agencies, notably the European Investment Bank, the Office of Official Publications of the European Communities, and the Statistical Office. Beyond this, it was decided that the Council would hold its sessions in Luxembourg for three months per year. The country also remained the seat of the Court of Justice of the European Communities and of the Secretariat of the Parliamentary Assembly. Yet, to a more significant extent than previously, the center of gravity of Community institutions now lay in Brussels. This was expressed symbolically with the completion of the new headquarters of the Commission, the Berlaymont Building, in late 1969. After all the moves from Luxembourg had taken place during the summer of 1968, there were now some five thousand officials of the various directorates of the Commission working in Brussels.[89]

The Return of the British Question

The option of further developing the Community seemed all the more attractive because in the meantime the question of the entry of Great Britain and the neighboring EFTA states was once again on the agenda. In Britain, de Gaulle's harsh rejection had initially given new impetus to the opponents of entry. The parliamentary elections of October 1964 had been won by the Labour Party, which had earlier spoken out against Macmillan's application for membership. In Harold Wilson, Britain now had a prime minister from the left wing of the party, one who regarded EEC membership as incompatible with a socialist planned economy

---

89 Yves Conrad, "Évolution de l'organisation administrative de la Commission et de la question du siège. Un long chemin vers la fusion des exécutifs (1960–1967)," in Varsori, *Inside*, pp. 79–94.

and who sought an independent role for Britain in world politics, supported by a reformed Commonwealth.

The failure of an ambitious national economic plan along with an increasing independence of mind among Commonwealth countries, especially the painfully-felt exodus of Rhodesia in November of 1965, gradually led Wilson to rethink matters, however. In January of 1966, he had a cabinet committee secretly examine the economic implications of British accession to the EEC; in August, he appointed George Brown as foreign secretary, who along with Roy Jenkins and Michael Stewart was among the few dedicated Labourite supporters of EEC membership. On 22 October, Wilson convinced an overwhelmingly-skeptical and to an extent even hostile cabinet to agree to "exploration" with the governments of the Six as to whether British entry was possible and, if so, under what conditions. On 10 November, he announced this intention in the House of Commons, with a statement that while lacking binding force did signal resolve: "I want this House to know that the Government are approaching discussions with the clear intention and determination to enter the EEC if essential British and Commonwealth interests are safeguarded."[90]

In fact, Wilson was now more or less convinced that there was no longer any alternative to British membership. True, it would initially lead to a rise in food prices and thus household expenses; but ultimately new industrial growth would only be possible via free access to the Common Market and participation in its modernization programs. Wilson advocated a "new technological Community" to counter the American challenge and lay the foundations for a strong position for Europe in the world. It is possible that he also hoped this would usher in a leadership role for Britain in Europe and that the Continent could serve as a new basis for British greatness, in place of the declining Commonwealth; it was at least the case that Brown repeatedly expressed these sorts of sentiments.[91] One way or another, Wilson had Europeanized his dreams of modernization. Given that this wholly corresponded with the evolution of French thinking, he saw realistic chances of winning de Gaulle's support—after some defensive reactions—for expansion of the Community.

---

[90] House of Commons Debates, 1966–67, 10 Nov. 1966, col. 1540. See Hugo Young, *This Blessed Plot. Britain and Europe from Churchill to Blair*, London: Macmillan, 1998, pp. 181–198; Anne Deighton, "The Second British Application for Membership of the EEC," in Loth (ed.), *Crises*, pp. 391–405; Oliver Daddow (ed.), *Harold Wilson and European Integration: Britain's Second Application to Join the EEC*, London: Institute of Contemporary British History, 2003; Helen Parr, *Harold Wilson and Britain's World Role: British Policy towards the European Community, 1964–1967*, London: Routledge, 2005.

[91] George Brown, *In My Way. The Political Memoirs of Lord George-Brown*, London: Gollancz, 1971, pp. 209–211.

As his subsequent course of action made clear, Wilson pinned his hopes above all on the Federal Republic. With the SPD's entry into the government, he saw a strengthening of pro-British elements in Bonn. In the common interest of the Socialists, Foreign Minister Brandt was to put pressure on the French government: "Willy, you must get us in, so that we can take the lead," said Brown to his counterpart at a meeting of the Socialist International on 5 January 1967 in Rome.[92] During a visit to Paris on 25 and 26 January, Wilson and Brown were not exactly welcomed with open arms. Yet, De Gaulle did exhibit a certain satisfaction that Britain "now really wished to moor itself alongside the continent," but then went on to emphasize the problems that would face the Community if the country were to join. He suggested his guests consider alternatives to membership: association with the Community or "something entirely new."[93] Brown responded by pressing Brandt to support full membership for Britain during meetings between France and the Federal Republic. In the Briton's view, if everyone were to form a strong front against de Gaulle, the general would ultimately acquiesce

Brandt was little affected by the informal methods that Brown employed. As much as he favored British membership—for political reasons as well as in the interest of German exports—a break with France, which Brown was suggesting as an alternative, was something that he could not and would not risk. Kiesinger did not want to put any special emphasis at all on engagement for British entry. He had great doubts as to whether the British were actually prepared to participate in building a political Europe; at a summit meeting with de Gaulle on 13 January, he therefore raised for the first time the idea of a separation between an expanded economic Community and a closer political Community of the Six. During a visit by the two Britons to sound things out on 15 and 16 February, the chancellor opposed the strong push by Wilson to put pressure on de Gaulle. The West German ambassador in London, Herbert Blankenhorn, who supported British entry, wrote in his diary: "The most negative thing was the extremely reserved coolness, even the almost fearful attitude of the government, which always kept an ear to the ground to determine if negative voices from Paris were becoming perceptible."[94]

---

92 Willy Brandt, *Erinnerungen*, Zurich: Ullstein, 1989, p. 453.
93 Harold Wilson, *The Labour Government, 1964–70: A Personal Record*, London: Weidenfeld und Nicolson, 1971, p. 341; Brown to Brandt, 27 Jan. 1967, quoted in Türk, *Europapolitik*, pp. 64ff. Cf. *ibid.*, pp. 57–70 and Hartmut Philippe, "'The Germans hold the key': Britain's Second Application to the European Economic Community and the Hope for German Help, 1966–67," in Christian Haase (ed.), *Debating Foreign Affairs. The Public and British Foreign Policy since 1867*, Berlin and Vienna: Philo Fine Arts, 2003, pp. 153–182.
94 Diary entry, 15–16 Feb. 1967, quoted in Türk, *Europapolitik*, p. 69.

Wilson did not allow the cool reception in Bonn to dissuade him from pushing for British accession. As Brown noted, "gradually, our line got firmer and firmer" during the tour, and "by the time we finished we had virtually decided to make our application."[95] Wilson reported to his cabinet that he had achieved much during his visits to the capitals of the Six. This gave many ministers the impression that it was now necessary to consider an attempt to join under acceptable conditions. On 2 May, Wilson informed the House of Commons that his government wanted to submit a new application. After a large majority of all three major parties had agreed to the idea on 10 May, the application was filed in Brussels the next day. Applications from the Irish and Danish governments went in the same day. For Ireland, economic necessity provided the motive for joining the British initiative. For Denmark it was a long-awaited opportunity. Danish Prime Minister Jens Otto Krag—like Brandt a Social Democrat—had done everything in his power to support the British application. An application from Norway followed a little later, on 24 July. As in 1961, Prime Minister Per Borten had needed more time to rally reluctant forces in the governing coalition for the initiative.[96]

De Gaulle hastened to make known, publicly too, that he continued to oppose British accession. In a press conference on 16 May, he warned that such a development would divert the Community, steering it into becoming an Atlantic-oriented free-trade zone. He offered the British the alternative of either being content with association or waiting "until this great people has itself completed the far-reaching economic and political transformation it is seeking."[97] In contrast, the governments of the Five wanted to make use of this new chance to expand the Community. In their view, this was all the more attractive because Wilson and Brown had given assurances that they were now willing to accept the regulations of the Common Market without modifications and had voiced their commitment to a political Europe at the same time. Unlike in 1961, the Commission now engaged itself by supporting the applications. On the other hand, the governments of the Five were also concerned to avoid another Community crisis like the one they had

---

[95] Brown, *In My Way*, p. 206.

[96] Geary, *Inconvenient Wait*, pp. 95–114; Johnny Laursen, "Denmark, Scandinavia and the Second Attempt to Enlarge the EEC, 1966–67," in Loth (ed.), *Crises*, pp. 407–436; Hans-Otto Frøland, "The Second Norwegian EEC-Application, 1967: Was There a Policy at All?" *ibid.*, pp. 437–458; Dag Axel Kristoffersen, "Norway's Policy towards the EEC. The European Dilemma of the Centre Right Coalition (1965–1971)," in Katrin Rücker and Laurent Warlouzet (eds.), *Quelle(s) Europe(s)? Nouvelles approches en histoire de l'intégration européenne*, Brussels: Peter Lang, 2006, pp. 209–224.

[97] De Gaulle, *Discours*, vol. V, pp. 168–174. On de Gaulle's view, also Gérard Bossuat, "De Gaulle et la seconde candidature britannique aux Communautés européennes (1966–1969)," in Loth (ed.), *Crises*, pp. 511–538.

just experienced. The result of the conflicting impulses was a call for the Commission to produce a report on the applications, a move that was decided in a session of the Council of Ministers on 26 June. Until the report had been completed, it was the West Germans especially who were to work to dispel de Gaulle's doubts.

Initially, however, Kiesinger did not try to convince de Gaulle of the seriousness of the British change. Himself filled with concerns about watering down the Community, the chancellor instead sought to delay the clearly unavoidable accession of Britain as long as possible, until the political Union had assumed concrete form. So he only made the case with the French president "to buy time with the process [now] begun." Public opinion in the Federal Republic would not forgive de Gaulle for the shock of a second harsh rejection.[98] When on 29 September the Brussels Commission, as expected, made the recommendation to begin negotiations with the candidates for entry, Kiesinger proposed that first of all, the difficulties cited in the report be examined more closely.[99]

De Gaulle was not at all willing to engage in that form of foot-dragging. As he explained to a close circle of his ministers on 16 October, the Community "has some things to do: Merger of the Communities, review of the financial order, and God knows what other problems we'll have. As long as those issues haven't been resolved, the Community can't negotiate. It'll take time for England to be capable of joining and until the Community is in a position for it. One can say that we'll take another look at all that in 1970."[100] De Gaulle was aware that his refusal to begin negotiations on entry now would unleash another crisis in the Community; he was confident however that this crisis would also be of a limited nature because all the partners had a vital interest in a functioning Community.

On 18 November, Wilson's government responded to the demand to eliminate its budget deficit by implementing a spectacular devaluation of the British pound by 13.4 percent. The general countered with another press conference on 27 November in which he characterized the reorganization of the British economy as a mammoth task that would excessively burden the Community and lead to its breakup. More clearly than on 16 May, he rejected negotiations at that point as a rash determination to "destroy the European edifice."[101] The only thing he conceded to Kiesinger was a willingness to leave the applications on the agenda

---

98 Conversation between Kiesinger and de Gaulle at the Franco-German summit of 13 July 1967, AAPD 1967, Doc. 263, pp. 1052–1062, here p. 1058.
99 Türk, *Europapolitik*, p. 118; cf. *ibid.*, pp. 111–130; Ludlow, *European Community*, pp. 137–145.
100 Protocol of Conseil restraint, 16 Oct. 1967, quoted from Gerhard Wille, "'Which Europe? Quelle Europe? Welches Europa?' British, French and German Conceptions of Europe and Britain's Second Attempt to Join the EEC," in Rücker and Warlouzet (eds.), *Quelle(s) Europe(s)*, pp. 225–237, here p. 235.
101 De Gaulle, *Discours*, vol. V, pp. 241–245.

of the Council. In the session of that body on 18 and 19 December, the foreign ministers of the Five, having agreed among themselves beforehand, urged that entry negotiations be started. Couve opposed it, and given that no one called for a vote, the question remained open.

In the following months, the Five sought repeatedly to convince the clearly obstinate general to give in. First off, on 19 January 1968, the governments of the Benelux states called for the establishment of a consultative process between the Community and the applicants as well as agreement on common actions by interested states in areas that had not yet been taken up by the Community, such as arms production and technological development. Bonn agreed to this idea for a linking organization but proposed in place of cooperation among interested states (possibly without France) the creation of a trade policy preference zone including applicants with the prospect of entry. In late September, after de Gaulle had found himself in serious trouble due to the crisis of May 1968, Brandt presented an "action program" that expanded upon the concept of a trade arrangement by adding the idea of a work group of member states and applicants, a body that would concern itself with issues of cooperation and entry. As soon as there was sufficient agreement within the work group, the foreign ministers of the Six and of the applicants would gather at a conference.

Kiesinger was especially unwilling to support the sort of pressure that the Benelux representatives and the Italian government had in mind. West German attempts to convince the French only led to growing frustration between the two states. De Gaulle stuck with his "no" to any proposal that implied a transition to entry negotiations. Michel Debré, serving as de Gaulle's foreign minister since the government shakeup in the wake of the May crisis, responded to Brandt's "action program" not only with a new warning about the profound transformations the Community would experience if it were expanded. In a conversation with journalists, he also dramatized the situation by speaking of a "last chance" for Bonn to embrace the French viewpoint. Otherwise—so his threat went—there could well be a "freezing up of the Common Market."[102]

The crisis resulting from the French refusal to negotiate on the British application took on a more dramatic intensity when first the Dutch government and then the governments of Belgium and Italy refused to agree to further development of the Community in various fields if the issue of British entry were not decided simultaneously. The Dutch boycotted an initiative to revive plans for a

---

[102] Von Braun to Auswärtiges Amt, 2 Oct. 1968, quoted from Germond, "Partenaires," p. 624. Cf. *ibid.*, pp. 607–638; Türk, *Europapolitik*, pp. 130–144, 163–175.

Political Union that Kiesinger, acting on a final impulse from Adenauer,[103] had made during the anniversary summit on 29 and 30 May 1967 in Rome. The Italians supported it in their package deal when the West German government sought to initiate the merger of the three Communities in the interest of a common energy policy. In early 1968, the two governments blocked the issuing of a report on technological cooperation with the stipulation that the Council of Ministers must first decide on incorporating the applicants into the negotiations. In a memorandum of 23 February 1968, the Italian government demanded that nothing be undertaken in the realms of common policy on agricultural, trade, competitiveness, taxes, energy, or industry that would amount to increasing the difficulty of the entry of the four candidates.[104]

The West German government embraced the package deal of the Four by including in its "action program" of 27 September a list of measures for the internal development of the Community, which involved not only those projects already under discussion but also closer coordination of economic and currency policy; moreover, emphasis was placed on "evaluating [the proposals] as a whole."[105] This was not only an attempt to hold together the centrifugal forces in the Community but also signaled to the French government that the development of the Community, which Paris also desired in many regards, would ultimately be possible only if it finally agreed to expansion.

Given the failure of Bonn's attempt at mediation, Belgian Foreign Minister Harmel forced the idea of acting without France: In a speech to the Organization of European Journalists on 3 October, he proposed examining the possibility of close cooperation with Britain in the realms of foreign policy, defense, technology, and currency. This was to occur within the framework of the WEU, whose members were to commit themselves to regular consultations on these areas. If a member were not prepared to cooperate in one area or another, that would not be allowed "to function as permanent brake. If one always waited until all the travelers were ready to leave, no train would ever depart."[106]

For his part, de Gaulle knew how to demolish this bridge being constructed to EEC membership for Britain. When at the next Council of Ministers meeting of the WEU on 21 October in Rome the representatives of the Benelux states made a

---

103 Adenauer to Kiesinger, 22 March 1967, quoted in Kramer, "Europäisches oder atlantisches Europa," pp. 224.
104 *Europa-Archiv 23* (1968), pp. D 137–140. Cf. Türk, *Europapolitik*, pp. 89–92, 99–111; Germond, "Partenaires," pp. 689–708; Ludlow, *European Community*, pp. 155.
105 *Europa-Archiv 23* (1968) pp. D 604–609.
106 *Ibid.*, pp. D 609–612. Cf. Dujardin, *Harmel*, pp. 469–513; Türk, *Europapolitik*, pp. 163–188; Germond, "Partenaires," pp. 639–642, 652–656.

motion to create a study group on the Harmel proposals, Debré's state secretary, Jean de Lipkowski, vetoed it. Renewed negotiations on Harmel's concept at the WEU Council meeting of 6 and 7 February 1969 resulted in "a terrible shambles once again," as Brandt had predicted in a letter to Kiesinger.[107] In order to force the establishment of regular foreign policy consultations, the British government, which happened to hold the WEU Council chairmanship at the time, invited the other states on short notice to a special session to discuss Middle East policy. While the governments of the Four and of the Federal Republic too accepted the invitation, France stayed away from this gathering, which was held on 14 February. Five days later, the French government announced that it would participate in WEU Council sessions only if the partners returned to the rule of unanimity in calling meetings.

Meanwhile, public pressure on the French government was increasing. Demonstratively, Jean Monnet brought not only Wilson into his Action Committee but also Edward Heath, who had led negotiations during the first British application and who was now leader of the Conservative opposition in the House of Commons. Interest groups and parliaments called for accession negotiations to begin soon; Commission President Rey warned publicly of a crisis threatening the achievements of the Community. A European Parliamentary Congress met on 8 and 9 November 1968 in The Hague, demanding rapid development of the Community, including its expansion, as an answer to the crisis of political leadership revealed by May 1968 and the Europeans' shock over the suppression of the Prague Spring.[108]

France on the Way to Turning

Two things were decisive for the end of the crisis that had developed over the second British application for entry into the Community: Firstly, Wilson did not let de Gaulle's negative stance dissuade him from further efforts. Not only did he forbid any discussion of the French refusal in his cabinet, he also intensified his commitment to the Economic Community in its current form and to the development toward a political Community. The necessity of a stronger role for Europe in world affairs, supported by the ability to compete in technological terms with the US, became the centerpiece of his argumentation. He thereby reduced lingering doubts among the Five as to Britain's suitability for participation in Europe and strengthened their engagement for British accession. He developed lively

---

107 Brandt to Kiesinger, 4 Feb. 1969, quoted in Türk, *Europapolitik*, p. 185.
108 *Europa-Archiv 23* (1968), pp. D616ff.

exchanges with Joseph Luns and his Italian colleague Pietro Nenni, the two most engaged proponents of British entry among the Five. He simultaneously promoted a large number of bilateral projects between Britain and continental countries, efforts that promised to get the technological Community underway: for example, the Concorde, Airbus, and the construction of a gas centrifuge for uranium enrichment in partnership with the Federal Republic and the Netherlands.

Behind Wilson's push for quickly gaining full membership was the conviction that Britain's weight within the Community would continually dwindle the longer entry was dragged out. A memorandum from the Foreign Office, received by the cabinet on 23 February 1968, expressed this clearly:

> If we can join them while we still have a substantial lead in various aspects of modern life and industry we should be able to play a major part in shaping the future of Europe and of European relations with the United States. But we have to acknowledge that time is not on our side. Our position in the world league is steadily slipping. The EEC is enormously much more powerful than we are and even the individual countries of the Six, e.g. Germany and France, are in some respects stronger than we are. In some aspects of the race Japan has already passed us. We must therefore bend every effort to join the European Communities at the earliest possible moment.[109]

Efforts to gain a leading role in the Community did not diminish Wilson's willingness to accept everything in the way of supranational elements that the continental partners saw as necessary for effectively constructing the Community. In early 1969, he accepted the view of Foreign Secretary Michael Stewart that foreign policy and conventional defence would in the end need to be subordinated to "some sort of majority vote."[110] In a joint declaration of the British and Italian governments on 28 April 1969, both committed themselves to support the direct election of the European Parliament as well as a common foreign policy that included a common "European identity," along with further integration in areas such as currency cooperation, technological cooperation, the peaceful use of nuclear energy, and cultural cooperation.

Secondly, in light of the continuing refusal of the Four to allow development of the Community without British accession, there grew within the French govern-

---

[109] Quoted in Melissa Pine, "Perseverance in the Face of Rejection: Towards British Membership of the European Communities, November 1967 – June 1970," in Franz Knipping and Matthias Schönwald (eds.), *Aufbruch zum Europa der zweiten Generation. Die europäische Einigung 1969–1984*, Trier: Wissenschaftlicher Verlag Trier, 2004, pp. 287–305, here p. 302. Cf. too Melissa Pine, *Harold Wilson and Europe: Pursuing Britain's Membership of the European Community*, London: I. B. Tauris, 2008, pp. 26–105.

[110] Maitland to Palliser, 1 Feb. 1969, quoted from Pine, "Perseverance," p. 295.

ment the realization that entry was ultimately also in the French interest or, more exactly, that British membership and hence the giving up of French ambitions to lead the Community constituted the price that had to be paid for strengthening Europe *vis-à-vis* the US. It seems that Michel Debré had made this realization after Brandt linked development and expansion in his mediation proposal of 27 September. In any event, the counterproposals that the Frenchman gave his West German colleague on 24 October revealed a certain willingness to compromise: Paris was now proposing a trade arrangement to which all interested European states would have access, not only the candidates for entry to the Community. Debré simultaneously declared that he was very interested in the resumption of negotiations on technological cooperation and offered to speak about such cooperation with non-member states as well. Moreover, at a meeting of the Council of Ministers on 4 and 5 November, he urged rapid measures to develop the Economic Community further.[111]

Debré's willingness to change course was intensified after having experienced West German toughness during the currency crisis that struck France in November of 1968. The social unrest of the previous May and the economic problems that followed upon it had unleashed a capital flight from France to the Federal Republic; the French budget deficit grew rapidly, and the value of the franc fell. In order to prevent the economic weight of the Federal Republic from growing disproportionately, not only the French government but also the British and American governments demanded that the D-mark be allowed to appreciate. For its part, Bonn was not prepared to engage in such an act of solidarity. Economy Minister Karl Schiller and Finance Minister Franz-Josef Strauss agreed to only temporary import relief and export duties (at a level of four percent); investing in the Federal Republic and taking out loans in foreign countries were made subject to approval. At a hastily called currency conference from 20 to 22 November in Bonn, the two held firm against the pressure from their partners. The discussion therefore shifted toward the idea of devaluing the franc by around ten percent. To the surprise of all, this did not occur. Due to fears of more social unrest and more inflation, de Gaulle opted to limit himself to foreign-exchange controls, budget cuts, and a hike in consumption taxes on 23 November.[112]

For Debré, who had spoken out in favour of devaluing the franc, the West German stance was the expression of a new self-confidence—one that without hesitation sought to transform the economic muscle of the Federal Republic into

---

[111] Türk, *Europapolitik*, p. 171; Ludlow, *European Community*, pp. 152ff.; Germond, "Partenaires," pp. 625–628.
[112] Schoenborn, *Mésentente*, pp. 129–138; Türk, *Europapolitik*, pp. 194–196; Germond, "Partenaires," pp. 658–663.

political strength. British accession therefore seemed to be not only a necessary prerequisite for the sought-after development of the Community but also was needed to take steps to prevent German dominance of the Community. Thus, Debré developed a plan to begin private bilateral talks with the British government so as to determine the possibilities for an entry that would take French interests sufficiently into account. "I thought this over and shared my thoughts with the general," as he described the genesis of the plan in his memoirs. "I had no doubt that France would be subject to extortion: either accept the entry of Great Britain or a settlement regarding the agricultural market would be denied."[113] In fact, the expiration of the transition period at the end of 1969 did offer the Four a new lever, and in the West German government a sentiment grew against opposing its use. Debré also summoned the French ambassadors in the partner states to a consultation. All but the ambassador in Rome confirmed to him that a change of course on the British question was advisable.[114]

It took several weeks for de Gaulle to become convinced of the necessity of an approach to Britain. He accepted it only after Richard Graf Coudenhove-Kalergi, the founder of the Pan-European movement, who was still active, had showed him a way in which the goal of an independent Europe could perhaps still be maintained despite the now clearly unavoidable entry of Britain. Coudenhove-Kalergi, a close associate of State Secretary Jean de Lipkowski, had a conversation with the general in which he advocated a new initiative for creating the Political Union, this time however in the form of a political Community of the four "big ones": Britain, France, the Federal Republic, and Italy. If the British government could be won over for that, thought de Gaulle, then the potential political damage of expanding the EEC could be contained.[115]

In the second week of January, de Gaulle therefore accepted the request of the new British ambassador, Christopher Soames, for a private conversation. As a Conservative politician, the son-in-law of Winston Churchill, and someone who was intimately familiar with the pro-European milieu on the Continent, Soames wanted to sound out the possibilities for a political understanding with the general; he did so at the behest of Wilson. In the conversation, which had to be delayed until 4 February due to the ambassador's earlier indisposition, the president began by raising his well-known complaint that the accession of the

---
113 Michel Debré, *Mémoires, Vol. IV: Gouverner autrement 1962–1970*, Paris: Éditions Albin Michel, 1993, p. 266.
114 Vaïsse, *Grandeur*, p. 607.
115 Coudenhove-Kalergi reported for the first time about this conversation in a letter to Franz-Josef Strauss of 13 Feb. 1969, that is, before the contents of the subsequent conversation between de Gaulle and the British ambassador became known. Cf. Schoenborn, *Mésentente*, pp. 239ff.

four applicants would profoundly change the character of the EEC. He then called for the British government to express itself privately on the idea of a reformulation of the European Community: "It would *de facto* be a matter of both governments giving their views as to what a European economic entente could be if the Common Market would disappear in the future to give way to a new regime." On the relationship between economic and political integration, he observed: "There should be a large European economic association, but with a small inner council of a European political association consisting of France and Britain, Germany and Italy." Regarding the political Community, he emphasized—here too latching onto well-known conceptions—that it must be independent of the US. This was to include nuclear cooperation between France and Britain, and would, as he underscored, render the current NATO structure obsolete.[116]

De Gaulle's offer was substantiated in a conversation that de Lipkowski—who had immediately been informed by Soames of the content of his talk with the president—had on the same day on the fringes of the WEU Council of Ministers meeting in Luxembourg with the British Foreign Office State Secretary Lord Chalfont. De Lipkowski explained that it was his conviction that de Gaulle was now willing to accept a trade arrangement "as a form of pre-entry," albeit under the condition that the British government carry out serious negotiations with France, especially regarding the political structure of Europe and defense. He then emphasized that the time was ripe for nuclear cooperation between France and Britain and encouraged an exchange of technical knowledge as well as the formation of a mixed nuclear planning group. In conclusion, de Lipkowski stressed once again that the general was in the process of fundamentally rethinking his foreign policy and also hinted that he—de Lipkowski—had great influence over him. Four days later, Soames was invited to a have a conversation with Debré during which the request for a private exchange of ideas about the economic and political structure of Europe was repeated. The French foreign minister explained that de Gaulle wanted to speak directly with Wilson or at least with Foreign Secretary Stewart.[117]

Once again, de Gaulle was too cautious to be successful. He did not offer the British entry into the EEC or even negotiations on entry as a concession for the commitment to the independent Europe that he was seeking; he declared that he was only agreeable in principle to the "economic entente" that in his mind would replace the Common Market in the event the Community were expanded. Soames

---

116 Neither an interpreter nor a minute-taker took part in the conversation before lunch with the two wives. There thus exist only the two differing sets of notes made afterward, a shorter set by de Gaulle and a much longer one by Soames. The first quote is taken from de Gaulle's version, the second from Soames' version. Cf. Schoenborn, *Mésentente*, pp. 236–238.
117 *Ibid.*, pp. 240ff.; Pine, *Harold Wilson*, pp. 110ff., 113.

however understood him as *wanting* the transformation of the EEC "into a looser form of free trade association with arrangements by each country to exchange agricultural produce"[118] and that the British government was to take a position on this. For Stewart, this was anything but an attractive offer; as a result, he saw the invitation to private conversations as only a maneuver by which Britain was to be isolated from the Five. A 7 February analysis by the Foreign Office reinforced this impression in his mind: John Robinson and Patrick Hancock of the Integration Department wrote that the Five would not permit a reconstruction of Europe outside the Treaties of Rome and that talks on the issue would take many years. If the government were to negotiate privately on it, the British application for entry would be completely discredited. Instead, the analysts recommended informing the governments of the Five about de Gaulle's initiative.[119]

Wilson followed this advice. At a long-planned state visit to Bonn on 12 February, he told Kiesinger that de Gaulle was likely seeking "to achieve the dissolution of NATO as soon as possible," to establish "a loose organization along the lines of a free trade zone" in place of the EEC, and to have "the political and economic fate of Europe" determined "by a leadership group consisting of France, Germany, Italy, and Great Britain." Wilson distanced himself from all that and thereby achieved a strengthening of West German support for British entry, which was embodied in a joint declaration. The governments of the other EEC members and of the US were informed in a similar manner. Soames had to tell the French that Britain regarded it as appropriate to inform the partners of de Gaulle's proposals and that "one rejects the French conceptions of the future of NATO and that it continued to be the wish of the British to join the Common Market."[120]

If de Gaulle had up to this point achieved exactly the opposite of what he intended, the public revelation of his initiative led to an outright poisoning of Franco-British relations. After the Foreign Office had on 14 February informed the ambassadors in most Commonwealth nations as well as NATO and EFTA states about the course of events, there appeared on 18 February a lead article in the French business newspaper *Les Échos* in which it was claimed that de Gaulle wanted to replace the Common Market with a larger free-trade zone to be led by a quadruple "directorate." Three days later, *Le Figaro* accused the British government of having spread a "sensational version misrepresenting Mr. Soames' audience"; an official announcement from the French government declared that the president had said nothing new in his conversation with Soames. In order to

---

118 Notes by Soames, *ibid.*, p. 107.
119 Memorandum of 7 Feb. 1969, PRO FCO 30/416, quoted in Schoenborn, *Mésentente*, p. 242.
120 German protocol, 16 Feb. 1969, AAPD 1969 I, Doc. 56, pp. 186–193, quotes, p. 187; cf. Pine, *Harold Wilson*, pp. 112–118.

counter the accusations, the British government then released the complete notes by Soames. They appeared in *The Times* on 22 February, not without the comment that the text had been approved by the French. That was in turn immediately denied by the Quai d'Orsay.[121]

The "Soames Affair" had thus developed out of a misunderstanding of de Gaulle's message by his British addressee: Paris and London were now accusing one another of having lied. It must in fact remain an open question as to how substantial the desire for change was that Debré described to Soames on 8 February and to what extent the published version incorporated these desires for change. It is possible that it was merely a misunderstanding at this point too.[122] This did not however prevent de Gaulle from drawing the conclusion from the spreading of statements that distorted his intentions that Britain had purposely sought to torpedo the development of an independent Europe and that he had been poorly advised to approach the British. As he noted in his diary, "Perhaps it is indeed better that all uncertainty one may have had regarding the actual intentions of the British has been eliminated in this way." He told Kiesinger during the chancellor's next visit to Paris, on 13 and 14 March, "It is not possible to work seriously with Great Britain."[123] When on 11 April Stewart sought to initiate a conversation with Debré once again, the French foreign minister reacted with indignation: "You have regarded a serious offer as a maneuver and acted accordingly"; now, "the bonds are broken" and one must let time pass before dialogue can be resumed."[124] For the time being, he saw no more possibilities of convincing de Gaulle to approach Britain.

It was advantageous for de Gaulle's disposition that Kiesinger during his visit seemed more "Gaullist" than ever regarding the general's visions of the future. The chancellor assured the French president "that he himself had never seen Europe's salvation in a European Commission" and that "the whole policy could only succeed when one day NATO had become superfluous." He did not share de Gaulle's doubts about expansion regarding Britain but did so in regard to the applications of Ireland, Denmark, and Norway as well as further possible applications from Sweden, Spain, and Portugal. In the following weeks, he did develop a plan for a closer Community that would also be political, one that would be surrounded by a larger Community integrated solely in terms of economics. At the conclusion of the meeting, de Gaulle was more relaxed than he almost ever was,

---

[121] *Ibid.*, pp. 72ff.; Schoenborn, *Mésentente*, pp. 244–246.
[122] Cf. Vaïsse, *Grandeur*, pp. 609.
[123] Notes of 26 Feb. 1969, de Gaulle, *Lettres*, vol. 11, pp. 297ff.; meeting between de Gaulle and Kiesinger, 13 March 1969, AN, 5 AG 1–164.
[124] French protocol of 11 April 1969, quoted in Schoenborn, *Mésentente*, p. 249.

and he was full of praise for his German guest: "The reflections on the current situation by the chancellor and his far-reaching vision had affected him very deeply."[125]

The French president intentionally ignored the fact that the British application for entry was still on the agenda. After the failure of a referendum on the reform of the Senate and of the regions, de Gaulle resigned from office. From that point on, he only engaged in Europe policy in the world of visions, no longer in that of actual politics. In that realm, de Gaulle's failed attempt to turn had only delayed the resolution of the British issue. After his departure from the political stage, it became more pressing than ever.

---

[125] Meeting between de Gaulle and Kiesinger, 13 March 1969, AAPD 1969 I, Doc. 99, pp. 367–377, quotes, pp. 372ff.; file memorandum by Braun, 14 March 1969, quoted in Türk, *Europapolitik*, p. 202; cf. *ibid.*, pp. 199–204, 209–212.

4 Expansion and New Perspectives, 1969–1975

Turning Point: The Summit in The Hague

For Georges Pompidou, who won the election of 15 June 1969 to the French presidency by a large majority, the entry of Great Britain into the European Communities was a strategic necessity. Having served as prime minister (from 1962 to 1968) and worked as a banker, he was more keenly aware than his mentor Charles de Gaulle that France needed the EEC for its economic modernization and that the Communities needed to be developed further. The harmonization of tax and currency policy, technological cooperation, the development of a common industrial policy, and, lastly, the completion of the common industrial market—all this was necessary in his view if France were once again to compete successfully with dynamic industrial nations. After the European partners had rejected all initiatives to develop the Community as long as the accession of Great Britain and the other three applicants had not been approved and after definitive financing of the Common Agricultural Market had become uncertain with the expiration of the temporary settlement of 31 December 1969, Pompidou saw it as necessary to concede on the issue of entry. That the prospect of a French leadership role threatened to vanish with British entry concerned him less than it had his predecessor. At the same time, Pompidou—an advocate of the free market—at base welcomed the prospect of expanding the Common Market.[1]

Along with strategic considerations, there were tactical necessities. In order to ensure that he would not lose the presidential election to the pro-European candidate of the bourgeois middle, Senate President Alain Poher, Pompidou allied himself with independent republicans around Valéry Giscard d'Estaing and a faction of the center around Jacques Duhamel. These forces made their support conditional on a course change on the issue of entry, and so as early as the campaign itself, Pompidou characterized Britain's speedy accession as highly "desirable."[2] Giscard d'Estaing—who had shortly before joined Monnet's Action Committee—was able to secure the Finance Ministry once again in the government of Prime Minister Jacques Chaban-Delmas. The new foreign minister was Maurice Schumann, a representative of the Christian Democrats who had quit Pompidou's government in May of 1962 in protest over de Gaulle's attack on the "integrated Volapük" of unpatriotic EEC Europeans.

---

[1] Cf. Claudia Hiepel, *Willy Brandt und Georges Pompidou: Deutsch-französische Europapolitik zwischen Aufbruch und Krise*, Munich: Oldenbourg, 2012, pp. 25–36.
[2] Speech of 2 May 1969, *Le Monde*, 3 May 1969.

In Pompidou's first meeting with Willy Brandt, who had made efforts to enter into contact with him as soon as possible, the new president let it be known that he was serious about fulfilling his campaign promises. During Brandt's visit on 4 July 1969, Pompidou explained that de Gaulle's offer to the British government had been misunderstood and also assured his guest that France did not have a "fundamentally hostile view" of the entry issue. He wanted only "that the Community reach its definitive stage" and that the Six come to agreement as to "how affairs should be handled." As the forum for such an understanding, he proposed a new summit of the heads of state of and of government.[3]

However, Pompidou was also plagued by worries that Britain could destroy the Community from within. With an eye to Gaullist traditionalists, he also had to avoid giving the impression that he was making an abrupt *volte-face* on Europe policy. No one could guarantee that de Gaulle would continue the self-imposed silence he had maintained since his resignation. Hence Pompidou's proposal for a summit—whose results were by no means assured in advance—and hence too his insistence on a clear sequence of items for negotiation: First, agreement on the completion of the Common Market and especially the definitive financing of the Common Agricultural Policy, then agreement on further integration measures that were in his view urgent. Only thereafter could accord be reached on a concept and roadmap for entry negotiations. When Maurice Schumann officially presented the summit proposal to the Council of Ministers in Brussels on 22 July, he summed it up in the three steps of "deepening" and "widening" and "completion."[4]

The governments of the Netherlands and Italy insisted on binding commitments regarding expansion before they would consent to the definitive financing of the Agricultural Market and further agreements regarding integration and cooperation. In early June, Joseph Luns proposed that a declaration of intent be made by the Six on the issue of expansion; after failing to gain approval for this, he wanted at least a concrete date for the beginning of entry negotiations. His Italian colleague Aldo Moro joined him in this call and also reminded his counterparts that the transition to revenue under Community control was not to be

---
3 Discussion of 4 July 1969, AN 5AG2, 1010; AAPD 1969, Doc. 221, pp. 774–480.
4 On this and the following, Marie-Thérèse Bitsch, "Le sommet de la Haye. La mise en route de la relance de 1969," in: Loth, *Crises*, pp. 539–565; idem., "Le sommet de la Haye. L'initiative française, ses finalités et ses limites," in: *Journal of European Integration History* 9/2 (2003), pp. 83–99; Claudia Hiepel, "In Search of the Greatest Common Denominator. Germany and the Hague Summit Conference 1969," ibid., pp. 63–68; Ludlow, *European Community*, pp.174–191; Andreas Wilkens, "In der 'Logik der Geschichte.' Willy Brandt und die europäische Zäsur 1969/1970," in: idem. (ed.), *Wir sind auf dem richtigen Weg. Willy Brandt und die europäische Einigung*, Bonn: Dietz, 2010, pp. 241–275; Hiepel, *Brandt und Pompidou*, pp. 44–63.

had without increasing the responsibilities of the European Parliament. Belgian Foreign Minister Pierre Harmel urged everyone to remember that the summit must not weaken the existing institutions of the Community and therefore, in contrast to the way Pompidou had made it sound, such gatherings should not become a permanent establishment.

Willy Brandt once again sought to play the intermediary but during a meeting of the EEC Council of Ministers on 15 September could achieve nothing more than a resolution *that* a summit should take place, that it should be in The Hague in mid-November, and that it should focus on deepening, widening, and completion. It was explicitly stated that this summit was not to constitute a precedent for further meetings and that the president of the Commission should be invited, although only for the second day of negotiations. Exactly *what* was to be decided at The Hague regarding expansion was left open, however; it also remained highly doubtful as to whether it would be possible to reach agreement on a definitive settlement for the Agricultural Market by the end of the year. The West German government sought to contain overproduction, which had grown costly, while the Italian government once again insisted on a fundamental course correction to eliminate the structural disadvantages of a country that exported wine and fruit but was also highly dependent on grain imports.

First of all, the attitude of the Commission was helpful in this situation. Having been asked by the Council of Ministers to update the position it had taken on the applications in September of 1967, the Commission presented a report on 1 October 1969 strongly recommending the opening of negotiations on entry but also more clearly than before noting the economic and monetary difficulties that would be associated with any expansion. Consequently, it called for agreement among the Six on a precise mandate for negotiations. Beyond this, the applicant countries should not only wholly accept the level of integration that had already been achieved but also declare themselves in agreement with the principle of strengthening the Community.[5] Jean Rey personally explained these fundamentals to the Council of Ministers once again on 17 October. This went a long way toward alleviating Pompidou's worries about a weakening of the Community, and it also strengthened his position on the development of a common negotiating position.

At the same time, Pompidou understood that his declaration of intent regarding expansion ought not to remain completely non-binding if he wanted to avoid calling into question the completion of the Common Market. As he explained to his staff on 21 October: "If we persist in our systematic rejection, it would amount

---

5 *Europa-Archiv* 24 (1969), pp. D508–526.

to a kind of death for the Common Market."⁶ He thus set aside his call for deepening the Community as a prerequisite for the opening of entry negotiations and sought to make his partners understand that the rejection of a date for the beginning of talks was only meant to ensure that there would actually be a common negotiating position. "We are condemned to success," as he said to the newly named coordinator for Franco-German relations, Carlo Schmid, when the official was making his initial visit on 9 November. "The German government urgently desires that the possibility emerge for the beginning of negotiations with Great Britain. First of all, let me say that we won't put any roadblocks in the way. If we get what we want, we won't cause any new difficulties. You can tell the chancellor: 'We'll be open and cooperative, but we want the completion of the Common Market and the financial settlement.'"⁷

The person to whom this assurance was directed was first of all Willy Brandt, who had been elected chancellor of the social-liberal coalition on 21 October and who was now making the success of the summit in The Hague his chief concern. With the establishment of the office of a Parliamentary State Secretary for European Affairs and the appointment of the European federalist Katharina Focke to the office, he signaled that he would be playing a more active role in European politics in the future.⁸ Very soon after the decision for the formation of the Brandt-Scheel cabinet, Pompidou sent word that he was interested in a direct private exchange regarding the preparations for the summit. Two days after this initiative to Brandt, Maurice Schumann confirmed French assurances on expansion during a conversation with his new West German colleague Walter Scheel. Moreover, he announced that France would be prepared to cut back on agricultural overproduction.⁹

Pompidou's concessions and assurances led to the emergence of a mutual understanding at the next preparatory meeting of the foreign ministers (on 10 November) that the completion of the Common Market should be decided at the summit. Changes would be possible during accession talks, but only if all members were in accord.¹⁰ Brandt and Scheel strengthened this tentative decision by committing their government to accepting mere declarations of intent on expansion and agricultural reform in return for agreement on definitive agricul-

---

6 AN 5AG2, 52.
7 AN 5AG2, 104.
8 Cf. Wilfried Loth, "Abschied vom Nationalstaat? Willy Brandt und die europäische Einigung," in: Bernd Rother (ed.), *Willy Brandt. Neue Fragen, neue Erkenntnisse*, Bonn: Dietz, 2011, pp. 114–134.
9 AAPD 1969 II, pp. 1103–1106 and 1237–1246.
10 AAPD 1969 II, pp. 1258–1260.

tural financing. Moro, who had originally wanted the decision on agricultural financing to be reached only after the conclusion of accession talks, had great difficulties gaining acceptance from the Italian government for this reversal of order and had to request that the summit be postponed until 1 and 2 December. By the original date for the meeting (17 and 18 November), the Italian government had been brought into alignment with the West German position.[11]

In order to be very sure that unity on that position would be reached at the summit, Brandt had the member governments informed of Bonn's negotiation position by diplomatic means. He spoke once again with Luns on 25 November, and two days later, he wrote a first private letter to Pompidou, in which he pointed out the urgency of agreement on the beginning of entry talks and the necessity of reforming agricultural policy. He also signaled that his government was prepared to accept the establishment of a European Reserve Fund that was to protect the Common Market from destabilization due to currency turbulence; here, Brandt was taking up a proposal from Jean Monnet.[12] A clear listing of what Bonn thought essential, along with an additional concession on the issue of deepening the Community, was intended to help elicit from Pompidou the most concrete commitments possible on the issues of expansion and agricultural reform.

Altogether, Brandt had thus answered the request for confidence that was embedded in Pompidou's initiatives and had also forced the resulting negotiating position on the smaller partners because it promised the only escape from the continuing crisis of the Community. At the beginning of talks in The Hague—after Pompidou had touched on the issue of expansion only in very general terms and with pointed reluctance—Brandt increased the pressure on his French partner: He called attention to the fact that the Bundestag would not ratify the system of agricultural financing unless assurances regarding expansion and agricultural reform were fulfilled. Moreover, he openly addressed the unease over the increasing economic strength of the Federal Republic, which actually caused Pompidou himself much less concern than it did many of his compatriots; Brandt suggested that this issue constituted an additional argument for expansion.[13] That sufficed to elicit from Pompidou a commitment to having talks on expansion begin "over the course of the next year," which he announced at a dinner on the first day

---

[11] Cf. Maria Eleonora Guasconi, "Italy and the Hague Conference of December 1969," in: *Journal of European Integration History* 9/2 (2003), pp. 101–116, here p. 109.

[12] Hiepel, "In Search," p. 67; on the role of Jean Monnet, also Gérard Bossuat, "Drei Wege nach dem Gipfel von Den Haag. Monnet, Brandt, Pompidou und das Europa der 70er Jahre," in: Wilkens (ed.), *Interessen verbinden*, pp. 353–386.

[13] Bulletin des Presse- und Informationsamtes der Bundesregierung, No. 146, 2 Dec. 1969, pp. 1241–1243; on the course of the summit in The Hague, especially Bitsch, "Le Sommet," pp. 558–62, und Hiepel, *Brandt und Pompidou*, pp. 63–72.

of the conference. Given the need to take the views of traditional Gaullists into account, this was not to be made public, however. So, on the beginning of the second day of negotiations, the partners contented themselves with a statement from Brandt that they gave credence to Pompidou's declaration on the desirability of entry negotiations and to his notion of the time necessary for their preparation. The Dutch prime minister, as host of the meeting, was given authority to state in a closing declaration that all governments were of the opinion that preparations for entry negotiations could be completed "during the first half of 1970"; Schumann confirmed this once again on behalf of the French government.

Brandt thereby became the actual father of the summit's success. In light of the now-binding assurance from Pompidou, the partners agreed that the transition to definitive financing of the Common Agricultural Policy could be completed on 1 January 1970, and as part of this, that the financial contributions of member states be incrementally replaced by revenue under the Community's own control, as the Commission had proposed. In regard to the expansion process, Pompidou likewise obtained satisfaction: In the closing communiqué, it was stipulated that the candidates had to accept the Community's entire *acquis communautaire* and that negotiations would proceed on the basis of a position previously agreed upon by the Six. It would be possible to make adjustments to the agricultural regulations in the course of entry negotiations but only with the concurrence of all member governments and in such a way that the fundamentals of the regulations were not distorted.[14]

After this breakthrough on the issue of expansion, it was possible to begin moving on numerous deepening projects as well, ones that had previously been blocked by the smaller partners in the face of France's veto. Especially notable was that the heads of state and of government drafted a resolution to develop "during the year 1970 an incremental plan for the establishment of an economic and currency union." This was to include a "review" of Brandt's proposal for a European Reserve Fund; the West German foreign minister was also able to include in the communiqué a call for "the development of cooperation in currency issues that [should] be based on the harmonization of economic policy." Further declarations of intent covered the development of Community programs to foster industrial research and development, the revival of the Euratom research program, a reform of the Social Fund "within the framework of a far-reaching coordination of social policy," and the creation of a "European university." The West German desire for agricultural reform was essentially taken into account, if only with the general call for the Council "to continue its efforts toward better mastery of the

---

14 *Europa-Archiv* 25 (1970), pp. D42–D44.

market by means of an agricultural production policy that permits a containment of the budgetary burden."

Conversely, little was achieved on the goal of a Political Union. During his last months as chancellor, Kurt Georg Kiesinger had intended to make use of the perceptible flexibility of the new French president in order to achieve progress in this area. For Pompidou, however, the development of common foreign and security policy was not a short-term goal at all—firstly, because he was convinced that economic stabilization and development of the Community took precedence and, secondly, because he saw with complete realism that the smaller partners would be the most difficult to win over for the Political Union.[15] Therefore, Brandt's requisite appeal to work toward the creation of a Europe that would play an autonomous role in international politics led merely to a vague assignment for the foreign ministers to examine by the end of July 1970 "how, from the perspective of expansion, progress in the area of political unity could best be achieved."

The summit in The Hague also brought little progress in regard to strengthening European institutions, as the Commission was especially urging.[16] The Five did win the concession from Pompidou that with the transition to revenue under Community control, "the budgetary authority of the European Parliament was to be strengthened" as well. It remained unclear however what exactly that meant; and not a single word of the communiqué was devoted to the idea of simultaneously strengthening the position of the Commission. The issue of transitioning to direct election of the European Parliament was likewise deferred. The concluding communiqué was also silent on correcting the practice—in accordance with the Luxembourg "compromise"—of seeking consensus in the Council of Ministers for cases in which the EEC Treaty had provided for majority voting. Disappointment was evident among the various spokesmen of the European movement, who in the immediate run-up to the summit had once again sought a strong mobilization of public opinion.[17]

Yet, it was generally acknowledged that the heads of state and of government had succeeded at The Hague in helping the European project achieve a new dynamic. The mutual blockade in questions of expansion and deepening had

---

15 Cf. his argumentation in a conversation with Kiesinger, 8 Sept. 1969, AAPD 1969 II, pp. 962–973, here pp. 964ff.; Türk, *Europapolitik*, pp. 209–222.
16 Cf. along with the position paper of 1 Oct. 1969 also a comprehensive *aide-mémoire* of 19 Nov. 1969, *Europa-Archiv* 25 (1970), pp. D.32–D34.
17 Bitsch, "Le sommet," pp. 552–556 and 562–564; on the discussion in the press, also Jan-Henrik Meyer, "Transnational Communication in the European Public Sphere. The Summit of the Hague 1969," in: Wolfram Kaiser, Brigitte Leucht, and Morten Rasmussen (eds.), *The History of the European Union. Origins of a Trans- and Supranational Polity 1950–72*, New York and London: Routledge, 2009, pp. 110–128.

been overcome, and the way was now clear for an expeditious pursuit of both. It was clear to all that there would be collisions among the divergent interests that remained and that there would be tough struggles over them. In the final instance, however, doubts as to the partners' desire for full implementation of the Treaties of Rome and for further pursuit of the European project had vanished. A "spirit of The Hague" was palpable at the ministers meeting held in connection with the summit—a new willingness to take the partners' wishes seriously and to work constructively together.[18] Not least of all, the mutual experience of not having been deceived served to provide the foundation for a trusting relationship between Brandt and Pompidou, which—although it admittedly remained far from a personal friendship—could be used to lead the Community in shaping the new breakthrough.

The Completion of the Common Market

It did prove difficult however to implement the decisions made at The Hague regarding the completion of the Common Market. On the one hand, the financial interests of France and the Netherlands in maintaining the existing agricultural subsidies and the interests of the Federal Republic and Italy on the other in reducing the resulting burdens were too different to allow quick unanimity on the modalities of the transition to financing the entire agricultural policy from revenue under Community control. Also, French concessions were too vague on increasing the rights of the European Parliament, an issue that was linked to the revenue transition; still more vague were the concessions regarding reform of agricultural policy. As a precaution, the heads of state and of government therefore made the decision on the fringes of the summit to "stop" the clocks on 31 December once again if no unity had been achieved on the details of agricultural financing. The stipulations of the treaty regarding completion of the Common Market would at least become valid thereafter.

In fact, however, the foreign, finance, and agricultural ministers of the Six succeeded in gaining a fundamental agreement on the financing of common agricultural policy within the specified timeframe; it had required marathon negotiations beginning on 15 December and, after a break from the 16th to the 19th, ending in the early morning hours of 22 December. This agreement envisioned that for the year 1970, agricultural expenses would once again be financed from contributions from member states as before, though with a slightly altered apportionment. From 1971

---

18 That was the impression of the German delegation at the Council meeting of 5 to 7 Feb. 1970, quoted in Hiepel, "In Search," p. 80.

onward, levies on agricultural imports whose prices lay below Community price levels would flow to the Community budget; from 1971 to 1974, tariff income from the borders of the Community would do so incrementally as well. Whatever financing that would be needed above those levels during this "interim phase" would continue to come from member state contributions. In 1975, such contributions would be eliminated completely. Given that in the medium term it was to be expected that revenue from levies and tariffs would sink (due to sought-after reliance on domestic supply and further tariff reductions under the auspices of the GATT negotiations), it was also decided that a maximum of one percent of the income from value-added taxes would be directed to the Community; beyond this, it was agreed that the level of value-added taxes be harmonized at eleven percent. Up to the end of 1977, there would also be a "corrective" included that would ease Italy's transition from dependence on disproportionately-high levels of revenue from levies and also facilitate the transition of the Netherlands and the Federal Republic from dependence on disproportionately-high revenues from tariffs.

Regarding the budget process to be implemented with the complete transition to revenue under Community control, a draft decision from the Commission was adopted specifying that the Council of Ministers would initially decide on the budget draft of the Commission via qualified majority. Parliament was to be able to make changes in the Council's decision by means of a simple majority. For cases in which such changes were not acceptable to the Council or were modified by it, Parliament would have a second reading and then decide by a three-fifths vote whether and to what extent the Council's changes were to be taken into account.[19] Hence, the Commission's influence over shaping the budget was not to be increased to the extent envisioned in Hallstein's Commission proposal of March 1965. On the other hand, the status of Parliament was enhanced even further than in the 1965 proposal: It was now actually to have the final word on shaping the budget.

Maurice Schumann agreed to this strengthening of Parliament only with the stipulation that there once again be separate talks on the "modalities by which the European Parliament should determine the level of revenues."[20] And when the Brussels decisions were being discussed in Paris on 14 January 1970, Michel Debré, now defense minister, voiced opposition to the idea of Parliament's having

---

[19] Draft of 11 Dec. 1969, COM (69) 1020 final 2; "Kommuniqué über den zweiten Teil der 95. Ratstagung 19.–22.12.1969," in: *Europa-Archiv* 25 (1970), pp. D.50–D52; on the production of the Commission draft, Ann-Christina L. Knudsen, "Delegation as a Political Process. The Case of the Inter-Institutional Debate over the Budget Treaty," in: Kaiser, Leucht, and Rasmussen (eds.), *History*, pp. 167–188, here p. 177–181; on the negotiations, Hiepel, *Brandt und Pompidou*, pp. 73–85.
[20] "Kommuniqué," p. D52.

the authority to increase expenditures.[21] Pompidou concurred, clearly with the conviction that he could not win a struggle with the guardians of Gaullist tradition on the issue at that time. He presumably also feared irresponsible actions by members of the European Parliament, like those he had witnessed in the Fourth Republic. In any event, he claimed in conversation with Brandt on 31 January that the prospect of a legislature's possessing power to initiate expenditures filled him "with horror."[22] This meant that the agreement of 22 December was fundamentally called into question once again.

Brandt showed understanding for Pompidou's concerns. In answering the French president, he had to confess that this discussion was "not to his taste" because it was "an issue that would become current no sooner than 1975, and before that, we have to implement the actual program of The Hague."[23] When in doubt, he regarded the expansion and construction of the Communities as more important than the strengthening of parliamentary rights. He did not want this obviously-continuing difference of opinion on a question of secondary importance to put at risk the great achievements of the summit in The Hague.

Brandt's retreat on the question of parliamentary rights led, after long negotiations, to a compromise that amounted to a defeat for Parliament and the Commission. In the early morning hours of 7 February 1970, the foreign ministers of the Six reached agreement on a settlement that, while it did leave the principle of Parliament's responsibility for the budget untouched, gave the decision on actual expenditures in large measure to the national governments: The right of Parliament to have the final say on changes made by the Council would now only be in effect for expenditures that did not "arise perforce from the Treaty or legal acts passed on the basis of the Treaty." For all other expenditures—and with the agricultural market, this was by far the overwhelming portion of the budget, amounting to some 96.5 percent at the time—proposals for changes would require approval by a qualified majority of the Council. Additionally, the Council of Ministers established narrow boundaries on Parliament's right of initiative regarding non-obligatory expenditures: Potential increases were not to exceed an upper limit calculated from the development of the gross national product, the budget plans, and the cost of living—unless the Council agreed to an increase over and above that, likewise with a qualified-majority vote.[24]

Talks took a bit longer on the introduction of a market for tobacco and wine, which Italy had made a precondition for agreeing to the entire definitive

---

21 Gerbet, *Construction*, p. 259.
22 AN 5AG2, 104, quoted from Hiepel, *Brandt und Pompidou*, p. 81.
23 *Ibid.*, p. 105.
24 Article 203 of the EEC Treaty, version of 22 April 1970.

arrangement on agricultural financing. France feared competition from inexpensive Italian table wine; West German vintners foresaw that the potential profits from their less sun-blessed products would vanish. The result was a wine market that on the one hand was characterized by high guaranteed prices but that also allowed for the possibility of improving West German wines with added sugar. Foreign Minister Scheel observed sarcastically to the leaders of his party that he had made certain that wines he himself would not want to drink could still be produced in Germany.[25] After agreement was in principle reached during the third week of April, the whole system for completing the Agricultural Market was passed on the 22nd of the month.

There was little left of the fundamental reform of agriculture about which Brandt had reminded his interlocutors at the summit in The Hague. The West German and Italian demand for determining a general upper limit on agricultural expenditures ran headlong into stiff opposition from the French, as did the Dutch proposal for a multiyear financial preview. The only decision actually made was to retain a ceiling on the structural funds for agriculture. The plan for restructuring European agriculture that had been proposed by Agriculture Commissioner Mansholt in December of 1968 was thereby essentially blocked. Linking up with Mansholt's earlier reform conceptions, this plan had foreseen investment assistance in place of further increases in price guarantees. It also included removing agricultural land from cultivation (in the range of five million out of a total of seventy million hectares), reducing dairy herds, as well as providing subsidies for agriculturalists chossing to retire early or change their profession. In this way, costly as well as economically-nonsensical agricultural overproduction, which moreover hampered the development of agricultural countries, was to be curbed. By means of the reorientation from price supports to structural assistance, the number of people employed in the agricultural sector was to drop within a decade from approximately ten to five million and the total amount of subsidies was to drop from two billion to 750 million units of account.[26]

Mansholt's ambitious reform plan met with loud opposition from small and part-time farmers, who were faced with the prospect of losing future subsidies in the form of price guarantees. Agricultural interest groups carried out polemical

---

[25] Reported in Patel, *Europäisierung*, p. 424.
[26] On this and the following, van der Harst, "Common agricultural policy," pp. 333–336; Guido Thiemeyer, "The Mansholt Plan, the Definite Financing of the Common Agricultural Policy and the Enlargement of the Community, 1969–1973," in: Jan van der Harst (ed.), *Beyond the Customs Union: The European Community's Quest for Deepening, Widening and Completion, 1969–1975*, Brussels: Émile Bruylant, 2007, pp. 197–222; Patel, *Europäisierung*, pp. 427–452; Katja Seidel, "Taking Farmers off Welfare. The EEC Commission's Memorandum 'Agriculture 1980' of 1968," in: *Journal of European Integration History* 16/2 (2010), pp. 83–101.

campaigns against what was alleged to be a looming forced collectivization along Soviet lines. The governments did acknowledge the need for reform in principle but shrank back from decisive measures in the face of the protests. Under these circumstances, the West German and Italian interest in containing agricultural expenditures led to the elimination of the financial basis of the reform to a significant extent. The Commission reacted with a more modest concretization of its draft: In a package of guidelines and regulations for implementing the plan presented on 29 April 1970, price decreases were no longer included; the criteria for "viable enterprises," which would be the only ones to receive structural assistance going forward, were also more loosely formulated.

Wearisome negotiations on this "Mini-Mansholt Plan" led to a modest success: On 14 March 1971, the Council of Ministers passed guidelines for investment assistance as well as regulations for early retirement and retraining, along with advising affected farmers. The financial resources already available to implement these measures were not increased, however. The criteria for enterprises worthy of support were formulated extremely vaguely and left much latitude to the member states. Proposed guidelines for taking agricultural land out of production and premiums for slaughtering animals were completely rejected. The growing mountains of butter, pyramids of sugar, and oceans of wine could not be dealt with by such half measures.

After the Council of Ministers had increased the rights of the European Parliament by the smallest of doses and after the heads of state and of government had taken on ambitious projects going beyond the Treaties of Rome, the Commission saw the danger of its position within the structure of the Community being weakened. Jean Rey and his successor Franco Maria Malfatti both sought to counter this development by positioning themselves as programmatic pace-setters and by claiming the Commission's right as a full participant in the new areas of activity. Rey's term ended after the Merger Treaty on 1 July 1970. The fourteen-member transition Commission was replaced by one that once again totaled nine and whose head, according to the principle of rotation, was now an Italian. Mansholt remained in office, whereas Rey had to leave the Commission altogether due to the Belgian government's preference for his colleague Alfred Coppé, who had come from the ECSC. Malfatti, a close confidant of Foreign Minister Aldo Moro and at age forty-three probably the most brilliant up-and-coming politician to emerge from Democrazia Cristiana, was surrounded by additional political heavyweights: The liberal intellectual Ralf Dahrendorf, who had significantly contributed to giving the FDP a new left-liberal profile, replaced Hans von der Groeben. The second Italian representative was the European federalist Altiero Spinelli, who after many years of fruitless efforts to persuade the citizens of the Community to support the summoning of a constituent assembly now hoped the leading role on the Commission. General Secretary Émile Noël, who had worked closely with Hallstein and Rey, was able to expand his influence; he would provide continuity in the leadership of the Commission until 1987.

The efforts of Rey and Malfatti to serve as pace-setters for the Commission ran into continued opposition from France, however. Rey was thus unable to gain for the Commission the leadership role in negotiations on expansion this time either. The Council president serving at the time became the negotiation leader; the Commission had to content itself with issuing position statements and developing proposals for solutions at the request of the Council. Malfatti fought in vain for unrestricted participation by the Commission in nascent European Political Cooperation (EPC). In actuality, it would only be allowed to participate if and insofar as issues within the Communities' area of responsibility were being discussed. Proposals for a more efficient and more democratic form of decision-making for the Communities, presented by the Commission at the urging of Noël in May of 1972, were not taken up by the heads of state and of government.

Nevertheless, the Commission succeeded in promoting to a great degree the convergence of differing positions and the development of a common political line; it achieved this by means of task-oriented work and intensive exchanges with the governments. This was the case not only regarding the negotiations on expansion, in which it successfully defended the *acquis communautaire*, but also in the talks on a currency union and the joint preparation for the Conference on Security and Cooperation in Europe (CSCE). When protectionist tendencies began to be noticeable in American politics during the winter of 1970–71, Malfatti convinced the governments of the Six to bind themselves to a common position that served to counteract a deepening of the differences and also established in Washington a high-ranking diplomatic representative of the Commission.[27]

These successes by the Commission were somewhat overshadowed by the fact that after the conclusion of entry negotiations with Great Britain, Ireland, Denmark, and Norway in January of 1972, Malfatti chose to resign from the post of Commission president in order resume his national political career, participating in early elections to the Italian parliament. His successor was long-term Vice President Sicco Mansholt, who took office on 22 March 1972. After de Gaulle had sought in vain to be rid of this man during the crisis of the "empty chair," it was none other than Pompidou who advocated Mansolt's appointment now: Clearly, Paris was of the opinion that in the few months before the creation of a new Com-

---

[27] Yves Conrad, "Jean Rey, moderate optimist and instinctive European," in: *The European Commission 1958–72*, pp. 109–123; Marie-Thérèse Bitsch, "The development of the Single Commission (1967–72)," *ibid.*, pp. 125–151; Antonio Varsori, "Franco Maria Malfatti: a presidency cut short," *ibid.*, pp. 153–163.

mission—with the participation of the new member states—Mansholt would offer no new challenges for French policy and thereafter would no longer be able to serve due to his age. In fact, Mansholt used the office of president to put his new issue on the agenda of international politics: the proclamation of sustainability and environmental protection, with which he had been engaged as a member of the Club of Rome. In the Commission itself, however, he was not able to prevail; it was especially Economic Commissioner Raymond Barre who emphasized the need for further economic growth over against Mansholt's views.[28]

At the summit of the heads of state and of government in Paris on 19 and 20 October 1972, Mansholt called for the "next step": Formation of a genuine European government that would be responsible to a directly-elected Parliament. Over and above the extension of social- and economic-policy cooperation, he encouraged the removal of border controls, the granting of European citizenship rights, and cooperation in the realm of education.[29] That was more than could be obtained given the governments' then-current areas of interest. Yet, by his actions at the Paris summit, Mansholt was able to ensure that the agenda of the breakthrough reached in The Hague was fleshed out and expanded.

That was all the more important given that his successor, François-Xavier Ortoli, demonstrated little ambition to force the institutional extension of the Community. As someone who had personally worked with Pompidou for a long time and who had served as minister of economic development in the cabinets of Jacques Chaban-Delmas and Pierre Messmer, he was primarily concerned with the success of the project for a currency union. Spinelli sought unsuccessfully to be responsible for institutional issues in the new Commission. His proposal to support the call for a European government by appealing for a process to create a constitution was rejected as inappropriate by Ortoli, who was, according to his own admission, "no theologian of Europe."[30]

The First Enlargement

During the preparations for entry negotiations, the well-known antagonisms manifested themselves again: On the one hand, there were French worries over a softening of the *acquis communautaire* that had so recently been won with so much effort; on the other hand, the Five feared that if the Community took too

---

28 Jan van der Harst, "Sicco Mansholt: courage and conviction," *ibid.*, pp. 165–180.
29 Bitsch, "Single Commission," pp. 149f.
30 Altiero Spinelli, *Diario europeo 1970–1976*, Bologna: Il Mulino, 1991, p. 490; Ortoli in a conversation with Brandt, 29 March 1973, AAPD 1973 I, p. 448.

rigid a stance, then failure would be preprogrammed into negotiations. Pompidou's conviction regarding the inevitability of British entry was as great as his mistrust of actual British motives, along with the ulterior motives of his partners. Also, he consciously wanted to seem "hard" so as to avoid giving the impression of having made an abrupt course change away from the stance of his predecessor. Thus, he insisted that the British be required to adopt all the principles of the Common Agricultural Policy, even if this would mean great financial burdens for the country given the high percentage of food it imported. For him, the willingness of the British to accept those burdens was more or less a litmus test to determine the seriousness of their desire to enter.[31]

With commensurate tenacity, Pompidou largely succeeded in pushing through the French positions when the mandate for negotiations was being determined at a Council session on 8 and 9 June 1970. It was thus decided that candidates for entry were fundamentally to accept the preference of the Community, uniformity of prices, and solidarity in financing the agricultural market. Their problems in adjusting were to be addressed solely by exceptional regulations during a transition period, and this was to be kept as brief as possible. The leadership role in negotiations was to be given to the Council, and that meant in practice that the fundamental conflicts of interest between the French and British governments would need to be worked out in those negotiations. The Commission was given the task of supporting the French government in operative detail and at the same time watching that British opportunities would not be overplayed.

For the British government, all this amounted to a poor starting place. Harold Wilson had initially hoped to be able to have a say in the definitive determination of the Common Agricultural Market. After those hopes had been dashed, there was nothing left to do but accept the principles of the Common Agricultural Policy and then, pointing out the unreasonableness of the looming burdens when applied to Britain, negotiate for the longest possible transition period. While the foreign ministers in Brussels were setting the negotiation position of the Six, the British Official Committee on the Approach to Europe determined to call for a transition period of five or six years and then a further period of seven years during which the increase in the British burden would not be allowed to rise above a predetermined percentage. After these twelve or thirteen years, the entire system of

---

[31] Hiepel, *Brandt und Pompidou*, pp. 118ff.; on the negotiations with Great Britain, *ibid.*, pp. 159–177 as well as the report of the British delegation leader Con O'Neill, *Britain's Entry into the European Community*, London: Routledge, 2000, pp. 99–167, and Michael J. Geary, "Enlargement and the European Commission: An Assessment of the British and Irish Applications for Membership in the EEC, 1958–73," Diss. EUI Florence: European University Institute, 2009, pp. 275–315.

revenue under Community control was to be reviewed.[32] In direct conversations with French politicians and diplomats, the British emphasized a shared interest in containing the Federal Republic, which was now causing worries not only with its economic success but also with advances in its "New Eastern Policy."[33] The British approach was intended to help soften Pompidou's noticeably hard position.

The surprising victory of the Conservatives in parliamentary elections on 18 June 1970 changed nothing in regard to strategy. New Prime Minister Edward Heath, who had led the negotiations of 1961–63 as representative of the Macmillan government, now went into the new talks with all the materials that had been prepared by Wilson's government and also pursued the same goals. At the opening of entry negotiations on 30 June, Europe Minister Anthony Barber made it clear right away that his government would need to insist on substantially longer transition periods than the Community had envisioned. No British government could accept responsibility for the burdens that an abrupt transition to the Community system would cause.[34]

After an initial sounding out and after initial talks, the Heath government in early December reduced its demanded transition period to five years; the following "corrective phase" was now only to last three years. British contributions—to be made up of levies, tariffs, and direct payments or tax components—were to be only 2.6 to three percent of the Community budget, however, as new Europe Minister Geoffrey Rippon specified on 17 December; by the end of the transition period, the British share was to rise to thirteen to fifteen percent. A period of six years was envisioned before the complete adoption of the levy system and three years for the complete incorporation into the commercial system of the Community. It was believed that only by this means would it be possible to ensure that the anticipated impetus to British industry would not be negated by drastic increases in food costs. Additionally, London persisted in calling for exceptional regulations for the importation of Caribbean sugar and New Zealand butter: There were long-term agreements on these imports that were essential for the Commonwealth countries involved.

For Pompidou, those were simply risible concessions. Given that the British would from the beginning profit from the advantages of the Common Market, he

---

[32] Negotiating Brief on Community Finance, 8 June 1970, quoted in Alan S. Milward, "The Hague Conference of 1969 and the United Kingdom's Accession to the European Economic Community," in: *Journal of European Integration History* 9/2 (2003), pp. 117–126, here pp. 125ff.
[33] Gabriele Clemens, "Der Beitritt Großbritanniens zu den Europäischen Gemeinschaften," in: Knipping and Schönwald (eds.), *Aufbruch*, pp. 306–328.
[34] *Europa-Archiv* 25 (1970), pp. D358–D361.

regarded an initial proportion of twenty-two percent for the financing of the Agricultural Market as appropriate.³⁵ In his view, attempts to delay the full burden raised the danger that in five or seven years the British would once again seek to topple the entire system of financing. "One gladly concedes to the British three qualities," he said of the offer during a press conference on 21 January 1971, "humor, tenacity, and realism. The thought occurs to me that we still find ourselves a bit in the humor stage. I have no doubt that tenacity will follow. I hope too that realism will come and will triumph."³⁶

What clearly came next was tenacity—on both sides. Whereas the Five wanted to accommodate the British, France persisted in its position and was supported by the Commission. In mid-March, Paris added the demand that Britain give up the pound's status as a second international reserve currency after the dollar; this had been urged by Economy Commissioner Barre. High foreign credits in sterling and the British guarantee of the Commonwealth countries' currency reserves made the pound highly vulnerable to fluctuations in value that were not compatible with the Common Market and certainly not with the sought-after currency union. In light of the country's chronic balance of payments deficit, the British were to commit themselves to a firm stability policy that would promote the desired uniformity among the currencies.

For a time, Heath considered the possibility of making Pompidou more willing to compromise by accommodating him on the issue of a joint nuclear force. No later than 1965, the Briton had become convinced of the necessity of an autonomous European defense; improvements in Soviet anti-missile capabilities, which were now making the development of new missile systems necessary, served to strengthen his conviction. Heath therefore wanted a "radical initiative" both to solve British security problems and to secure entry into the European Community. In February of 1971, interministerial committees recommended that a proposal be made for the creation of an "Organisation for the Co-ordination of European Defence" and for the joint development of a new generation of sea-based missiles. However, Foreign Minister Alec Douglas Home got the impression in mid-April that such an initiative would weigh down the entry negotiations rather than accelerate them; and so the idea was deferred.³⁷

In fact, signs began to multiply in the middle of April that, even without British accommodation on the issue of an autonomous European nuclear force,

---

35 From a conversation with Brandt, 25 Jan. 1971, AAPD 1971/I, 149–162.
36 Quoted from Pierre-Bernard Cousté and François Visine, *Pompidou et l'Europe*, Paris: Libraries techniques, 1974, p. 117.
37 Helen Parr, "Anglo-French Nuclear Collaboration and Britain's Policy towards Europe, 1970–1973," in: van der Harst (ed.), *Beyond the Customs Union*, pp. 35–59.

Pompidou would soften his rigid stance. Via Brandt, Heath had let the French president know at the beginning of the month that he needed a demonstrable success by the summer; otherwise, British opinion threatened to change drastically.[38] This made it clear to Pompidou that it was necessary to yield. If he did not, there would be fears of the failure of the expansion project and also the relapse of the partners into the old lethargy. Commissioner of Foreign Trade Jean-François Deniau, who had been given the leadership of the Commission's negotiating delegation, told Pompidou that "It would be easier for England to block the Community if it stays out rather than if it is in. Its absence gives every member that doesn't want to negotiate a constant excuse."[39]

Michel Jobert, the general secretary of the French president, and British Ambassador Christopher Soames had been holding off-the-record conversations since February. In the second half of April, the two reached agreement on the outline of a compromise: The initial level and the increase in British contributions were to be based on objective criteria; the restriction of Caribbean sugar imports was to be postponed until the end of the transition period; the issue of New Zealand butter imports would be dealt with later. As to resolution of the currency problematic, a British declaration of intent would suffice. Additionally, a timetable for the detailed resolution of contentious issues would be agreed upon: first of all, a sign of willingness to compromise at the next meeting of the Council of Ministers, then an agreement on basic issues during a visit by Heath to Paris, and, finally, the determination of details at the Council of Ministers meetings in June.[40]

In fact, at the Council of Ministers meeting of 11 and 12 May 1971, the British delegation surprised most participants by agreeing to a new regulation of sugar imports after the expiration of the Commonwealth Sugar Agreement (CSA) at the end of 1974. In response, the French delegation accepted the principle of an incremental increase in British contributions. The French also conceded in essence the possibility of extending the transition period beyond five years and presented a mathematical model for calculating the rate of increase.[41] During comprehensive talks between the French president and the British prime minister in Paris lasting altogether some twelve hours on 20 and 21 May, Heath let it be known that he was prepared to take the necessary measures to stabilize the British pound.

---

38 Cf. Rippon to Heath, 1 April 1971, NA, PREM 15–370; Brandt to Pompidou, 6 April 1971, AN, 5AG2, 103.
39 Jean-François Deniau, *Mémoire de 7 vies*. Vol. II: *Croire et oser*, Paris: Omnibus, 1997, p. 278.
40 Pompidou's advisor Jean-René Bernard informed Brandt's State Secretary Katharina Focke on 3 May 1971 about this agreement; see Hiepel, *Brandt und Pompidou*, pp. 131ff.
41 O'Neill, *British Entry*, pp. 95–98.

He likewise made it clear that this would include giving up the pound's link to the US dollar, which had been in place up to that point. Pompidou then assured his visitor that he would be accommodating on the issue of New Zealand butter: After incremental reductions of imports during the transition period, the issue was to be revisited in five years' time in light of world market regulations that would have been determined by that point. Pompidou then declared that over the course of negotiations, the initial level of British contributions to the budget could "come in at something less than ten percent."[42]

The whole thing was less a negotiation than a backup measure to overcome Pompidou's mistrust. Heath willingly gave all the assurances that the French president sought: He would send bureaucrats to Brussels who would be in a position to work in French; he would not demand any reduction of support for Francophone countries in Africa; and, yes, he was in "complete agreement" that when it came to a country's vital interests, unanimity must reign. A protocol of these results prepared at Pompidou's behest but not published held to the Luxembourg Agreement of 1966 "that community decision must in practice be reached by unanimous agreement on issues where the vital national interests of one or more partners are at stake."[43]

Heath did not accept Pompidou's concession on the issue of the initial contribution level. He granted only that the final step at the end of the transition period could not be too high; he also assured his host once again that Britain was serious about the complete adoption of the Community system: His government had no intention of "fudging in one way or another."[44] The personal aides Jean-René Bernard and Peter Thornton were given the task of continuing the talks on that point.

In fact, an initial contribution of "something under ten percent" was still an imposition on the UK. This would mean that the British would experience a higher cost of living immediately upon joining the Community, whereas the fruits of entry—increased exports and productivity—would fail to materialize for the time being. Those in London now had to tell themselves that not much more could be achieved than the reduction to eight percent that the other EEC partners thought appropriate. During another marathon session in Luxembourg from 21 to

---

[42] Protocol in AN, 5AG2, 108; different excerpts in Éric Roussel, *Georges Pompidou 1911–1974*, expanded edition, Paris: Fayard, 2004, pp. 438–446, and Kathrin Rücker, "Le triangle Paris-Bonn-Londres et le processus d'adhésion britannique au marché commun 1969-1973," Diss. Paris, 2009, pp. 453–470.
[43] PREM 15/373, quoted in Jens Kreutzfeldt, *"Point of return". Großbritannien und die Politische Union Europas 1969–1975*, Stuttgart: Franz Steiner, 2010, p. 239.
[44] Second discussion of 20 May 1970.

23 June, the British delegation in the end agreed to an initial level of 8.64 percent that would rise in the fifth and final year of the transition period to 18.92 percent. Additionally, caps were agreed upon for the first two years of full contributions, that is, 1978 and 1979. In the case of "unacceptable situations," there were promises of "equitable solutions." Regarding New Zealand butter, the settlement that Pompidou had offered was defined more precisely. The British declaration of intent to reduce sterling-denominated assets and to take measures for adapting to the planned economic and currency union had already become known at the Council of Ministers meeting of 7 and 8 June—much to the consternation of Barre, who had additionally wanted to negotiate a pledge to stabilize the pound.[45]

The other candidates for entry found these conditions with a five-year transition period unproblematic. Because agricultural self-sufficiency was significantly greater in Ireland, Denmark, and Norway than in Britain, there was no issue of an initial increase in the cost of living in these countries. It was even the case that in the second year of the transition period, Denmark was able to achieve the net gain that was to be expected only upon full membership. The smaller candidates nevertheless defended themselves against any attempt to set transition terms for them that were less advantageous than those granted to Britain. When in December of 1970 the Commission was contemplating exactly that, sharp protests came especially from the Danish government led by Prime Minister Hilmar Baunsgaard. Finally, at a meeting of the Council of Ministers with representatives of the candidates on 11 and 12 July, it was agreed that the terms accorded Britain would apply to the other candidates as well. They thereby received essentially the same terms that the Danish government itself had already proposed in October of 1970.[46]

Denmark had a different problem: Freedom of establishment for enterprises of the member states, which was linked with entry into the Common Market. This threatened to lead to a sell-off of agricultural enterprises and coastal resorts in North Schleswig to Germans with deep pockets. Because opponents of Danish entry made this into a strong argument for their cause, the government called for retention of the ban on freedom of establishment until the end of the transition period. In late November of 1971, the Council of Ministers agreed this.[47]

---

[45] O'Neill, *Britain's Entry*, pp. 136ff. and 177ff.; Runderlass Poensgen, 23 June 1971, AAPD 1971/II, pp. 1004ff.

[46] Morten Rasmussen, "The Hesitant European—History of Denmark's Accession to the European Communities 1970–73," in: *Journal of European Integration History* 11/2 (2005), pp. 47–74, here pp. 56–58; *idem.*, "Joining the European Communities. Denmark's Road to EC-Membership, 1961–1973," Diss. EUI Florence: EUI Working Papers, 2006, pp. 366–498.

[47] Rasmussen, "Hesitant European," p. 61.

For Ireland and Norway, the largest problem was the Common Fisheries Policy (CFP) that the Council of Ministers, after wearisome negotiations, had just completed before the opening of entry talks in June of 1970. Like the agricultural policy, this envisioned the use of Community funds to finance price-stabilizing measures and structural modernization; in exchange, it also called for the opening of territorial waters to the fishing fleets of all member countries. During a transition period of five years, exceptions were to be made for coastal areas whose populations were heavily dependent on fishing. This was a problem for Ireland and Norway in that no later than the end of the transition period, the substantially better-equipped fishing fleets of the large members threatened to exhaust the supply of fish in their waters. The Norwegian government saw as a consequence the depopulation of already thinly-settled coastal regions in the northern half of the country.[48]

Both governments therefore demanded nothing less than retention of the twelve-mile zone of exclusive national fishing rights that had been guaranteed by the London Fisheries Convention of 1964. That was unacceptable to the Commission, as was the proposed requirement that foreign fishermen reside in Norway, which had been presented by the principally more Europe-friendly government of Social Democrat Trygve Bratteli in June of 1971. After tough negotiations beginning in October, the governments of Ireland, Britain, and Denmark accepted a compromise proposal from the Commission on 12 December: The transition regulations for certain coastal regions and for the entire twelve-mile zone would be extended for ten years, and a review of fishing policy was announced for the end of the transition period. The Norwegian government continued to seek guarantees of special treatment for an unlimited period. On 15 January, it had to content itself with an expansion of the Norwegian special zone significantly to the south (as far as Egersund) and with a special protocol that made mention of the possibility of an "extension of the existing system" after the end of the transition period, if the "special demographic and social structure of the country" would make it needful.[49]

The talks with Norway became all the more difficult when the Norwegian government began seeking unlimited exceptional regulations for its entire agri-

---

[48] On this and the following, cf. Geary, *An Inconvenient Wait*, pp. 173–183; Robin M. Allers, *Besondere Beziehungen. Deutschland, Norwegen und Europa in der Ära Brandt (1966–1974)*, Bonn: Dietz, 2009, pp. 274–329; idem., "Attacking the Sacred Cow. The Norwegian Challenge to the EC's Acquis Communautaire in the Enlargement Negotiations of 1970–72," in: *Journal of European Integration History* 16/2 (2010), pp. 59–82.

[49] Summary of the results of the entry negotiations, 19 Jan. 1972, *Europa-Archiv* 27 (1972), pp. D115–D122, here p. D121.

culture sector as well. Given the difficult climatic and topographic circumstances of the country—with mountains and fjords and some third of its territory lying above the arctic circle—Norwegian farmers would be faced with more than a fifty percent drop in income if markets were opened, price levels reduced, and national support measures eliminated. From a technical standpoint, it was hardly possible to create larger units so as to increase productivity. The fear that entire areas of the country would be depopulated was thus not without justification. The Bratelli government proposed that farmers continue to be supported with exceptional regulations for individual products, especially price supports for milk and transport assistance; this was to be financed from the European Agricultural Guidance and Guarantee Fund (EAGGF),

The Commission and Council of Ministers gradually converged on this proposal, not least of all because Brandt made the case for understanding the problems of his "second homeland." They did not however completely embrace it. On 12 December 1971, a special protocol on Norwegian agriculture was finally passed that, although not explicitly mentioning permanent exceptional regulations, did acknowledge the necessity of "specific provisions" even after the end of the five-year transition period.[50] Among these were to be measures for guaranteeing milk production and transport assistance. The Commission was to examine the extent to which the Community could participate in providing the funds needed for this. This was too little for the Norwegian agricultural interest groups; for its part, however, the government thought that it had succeeded in gaining the core of its demands. After the terms of Norwegian entry into the Common Fisheries Policy had also been settled on 15 January, the way was clear for the signing of the common entry treaty for all candidates on 22 January 1972.[51]

In light of the many problems that had delayed the conclusion of negotiations, the atmosphere in Brussels at the signing of the treaty was anything but enthusiastic. In fact, it would soon be seen that there was no majority in Norway for entry. Fishing Minister Knut Hoem resigned in protest even before the Norwegian government had definitively acceded to the Fishing Protocol, due to what he regarded as an unsatisfactory result of negotiations. Bratelli and the other supporters of accession in the government, who were convinced of the need to join the prospering European Community, could not contain the negative trend in public opinion in the northern parts of the country and along its coasts. Together with the anti-Europeanism of the radical left and the conservatism of neo-liberal intellectuals, a majority of 53.3 percent spoke out against entry in a consultative referendum on 24 and 25 September 1972. As it had pledged to do, the Bratelli

---

50 *Ibid.*
51 Treaty text, *ibid.*, pp. D123–D125.

government responded by resigning immediately. The new minority center-right government under Lars Korvald was under much time pressure to negotiate a free-trade agreement with the Community, as Sweden and the other remaining EFTA countries had in the meantime already done.[52]

In Britain, the accession treaty received the necessary majorities. After an intensive campaign in support of it and six days of debate in the House of Commons, a majority of 356 to 244 voted on 28 October 1971 in favor of entry under the terms that the government had negotiated. A law for entry was then passed on 13 July 1972 with a majority of seventeen votes. It was the case however that Heath presented the results of his negotiations in an extremely defensive manner out of fear of the opponents of entry. The political ambitions and economic visions that underlay the application were not mentioned at all; in a white paper of 7 July 1971, the government even asserted that there was "no question of any erosion of essential national sovereignty."[53] Additionally, after Labour's unexpected defeat at the polls, a tendency prevailed in the party to mobilize the diverse cross currents for a quick return to power; Wilson only knew how to unify his party and above all retain his leadership position by taking to the field with the slogan "No entry on Tory terms." In the election campaign over the winter of 1973–74, he vowed to renegotiate those terms and to submit the results of that process to a referendum.[54]

British opponents of entry gained additional momentum when the economic condition of the country, which had long been problematic, became dramatically worse during the first year of membership. A major miners' strike in January of 1973 drove unemployment numbers over one million. Both inflation and the trade deficit increased; the quadrupling of oil prices in October of 1973 led to further burdens. Under these circumstances, Wilson's spectacular and questionable change of course brought results: Elections in February of 1974 gave Labour more seats than the Conservatives. Wilson formed a minority government on 4 March that was then able to win a small majority in new elections in October of 1974.

In office once again, Wilson now had to make good on his promise of new talks. This did not however turn into the "fundamental re-negotiation" that Labour had announced.[55] James Callaghan, Wilson's new foreign secretary and a spokesman of those rejecting the accession treaty, did indeed come off as tough in Brussels at first. He soon had to realize however that nothing could be

---

[52] Hillary Allen, *Norway and Europe in the 1970s*, Oslo: Universitetsforlaget, 1979, pp. 128–159.
[53] Quoted from Young, *Britain and European Unity*, p. 113.
[54] *Ibid.*, pp. 114–117; Young, *Blessed Plot*, pp. 270–278; Kreutzfeldt, *Point of return*, pp. 423–428.
[55] The election manifesto of 11 Jan. 1974: "Let Us Work Together– Labour's Way Out of the Crisis," London, 1974, p. 5.

achieved that way. In the eyes of the partners, the demand for new negotiations was nothing less than a threatened breach of the treaty, confirming the views of all who had warned against British entry. Those who continued to be interested in having the country participate could only shrug their shoulders in acknowledgment that British politics might well be on the verge of squandering the results that had been so tenaciously striven for.

In the end, it was Helmut Schmidt, Brandt's successor as chancellor since 16 May 1974, who helped Callaghan and Wilson save face. More skeptical than Brandt and Scheel as to the chances of a currency union and Political Union, Schmidt—a self-confident native of the Free and Hanseatic City of Hamburg—at the same time had a special interest in seeing that the pragmatic tradition of British politics gained an influence in the Community. This led him to put a high priority on preventing British withdrawal. In a speech at the Labour Party congress in late November, he advocated that Britain remain in the Community, doing so in excellent English, which won him respect, and in a tone tailored to the mindset of British party comrades. This did not actually bring a majority of delegates to the point of changing their minds, but it did strengthen the position of the Europe advocates in the party. Above all, it gave Wilson and Callaghan courage to commit themselves to working for confirmation of the entry decision.

Schmidt then worked to persuade new French President Valéry Giscard d'Estaing to make concessions to the British on some lower-priority issues. While conferring after the speech with Wilson at Chequers, the country retreat of the British prime minister, Schmidt arranged a meeting between the British and French leaders. Wilson then assured Giscard on 3 December that, as Schmidt had requested, he would publicly work for Britain to remain in the Community if the partners would accede to the introduction of a "self-correcting mechanism" for avoiding excessive budget contributions. Four days later, Wilson spoke publicly to this effect. At the meeting of heads of state and of government in Paris on 9 and 10 December, Giscard then made a concession along those lines. Beyond this, Schmidt agreed to provide sufficient financing for a European Regional Fund that would be of benefit to Italy as well as Britain and Ireland. At the summit in Dublin on 10 and 11 March 1975—the "summit of the pocket calculators"—it was decided that the self-correcting mechanism would take effect if the gross national product of a member state fell below eighty-five percent of the average, a level that Britain would continually be able to avoid. It was also decided that the end of favored importation of New Zealand butter could be extended from 1977 to 1980.

Together with the vague announcement of a "review" of the Common Agricultural Policy and the signing of the Lomé Convention, which extended the favored status of former colonial areas to the Commonwealth countries,[56] there were enough concessions to gain majority support in the British cabinet for remaining in the Community. In the House of Commons and at a special party conference, a majority of Labour politicians stuck by their opposition, however. In a referendum, which Wilson scheduled for 5 June 1975 and of whose outcome he was confident, some sixty-seven percent of the voters agreed "that the United Kingdom should stay in the European Community." The unity of the party was saved by this, and Wilson had succeeded after all in what he regarded as necessary for the interests of Great Britain.[57]

Yet, the referendum—which was an absolute innovation in British politics—did not constitute a conscious decision for participation in the European project, as Wilson and in a similar way Heath too had originally envisioned it. Moreover, the Labour prime minister displayed too little public engagement on behalf of European politics. Decisive for the positive vote—which had been advocated very strongly by the business community and the press as well as the Anglican Church—was merely the fear that a withdrawal would threaten to cause still greater economic problems for Britain. As one pro-European Labour deputy summarized this kind of support that stemmed from resignation: "You cannot unscramble the egg."[58]

Looking at the big picture, it was the case that French approval for British entry had come too late to make an active and engaged member of the European Community out of the United Kingdom. If accession had been completed before the end of the postwar boom had struck Britain so very hard, another outcome of this first round of Community expansion could certainly have been imagined. It must remain an open question as to whether Wilson would have been in a position to keep the Europe issue out of intra-party and domestic political power struggles. What is certain is that due to his own interest in securing his leadership role, he contributed over the long term to damaging the Community's potential for development.

This proved all the more fatal when the leaders of the Danish Social Democrats (who since October of 1971 had once again held the office of prime minis-

---

[56] Lili Reyels, *Die Entstehung des ersten Vertrags von Lomé im deutsch-französischen Spannungsfeld 1973–1975*, Baden-Baden: Nomos, 2008.

[57] Young, *Britain and European Unity*, pp. 119–129; Thomas Birkner, *Comrades for Europe? Die "Europarede" Helmut Schmidts 1974*, Bremen: Edition Temmen, 2005; Kreutzfeldt, *Point of return*, pp. 452–457, 465–470, 472–494.

[58] David Ennals at the party conference of 25 April 1975, quoted from Birkner, *Comrades*, p. 116. On the referendum campaign, David Butler and Uwe Kitzinger (eds.), *The 1975 Referendum*, London: Macmillan, 1976; Young, *Blessed Plot*, pp. 286–299; Mark Baimbridge (ed.), *The 1975 Referendum on Europe*, 2 vols., Exeter: Macmillan, 2006–2007.

ter) in their referendum campaign during the summer of 1972 concentrated solely on the economic advantages of membership and emphasized their rejection of supranational solutions in the realms of currency and foreign policy. They did so out of fear of losing the Euro-skeptic segment of their supporters to more radical groups; this strategy was rewarded with a positive vote of 63.3 percent in the referendum of 2 October 1972. The decision to gain approval for entry by means of a referendum also led to an institutional solidification of the opponents of Europe, a development that would place narrow limits on the freedom of action of future Danish governments.[59] Conversely, the transitory danger of a British withdrawal had at least served to make the Irish Republic into a highly active member of the European Community.[60]

The Project of Monetary Union

Parallel to the first expansion, the governments of the Six took up the project of an economic and currency union. It had long been on the agenda of the Community and indeed was a necessary counterpart to the completion of the Common Market. The policies of the Customs Union, the Common Market, and the Community could not succeed over the long term if the currencies of the member states were to develop in divergent ways and if the member states sought to steer divergent let alone contrary courses in economic policy. The EEC Treaty itself had thus foreseen coordination in economic policy with the goal of currency stability and convertibility, bound up with "mutual assistance" in cases of difficulties with balances of payment.[61] In its action program of October 1962 for the second stage of the Common Market, the Hallstein Commission (with the advice of Belgian-American economist Robert Triffin) proposed strengthening monetary cooperation among the Six and creating a European Reserve Fund. No later than the end of the transition period, these two initiatives were to lead to a currency union.[62]

---

59 Rasmussen, "Hesitant European," pp. 65–74.
60 Brian Girvin, "The Treaty of Rome and Ireland's Developmental Dilemma," in: Gehler, *Vom gemeinsamen Markt*, pp. 573–595, here pp. 591–595.
61 Articles 105 to 107 of the EEC Treaty.
62 On this and the following, Régine Perron, "Le discret projet de l'intégration monétaire européenne (1963–1969)," in: Loth (ed.), *Crises*, pp. 345–367; Guido Thiemeyer, "From Convertibility to the Werner-Plan. European Monetary Integration 1958–1959," in: Régine Perron (ed.), *The Stability of Europe. The Common Market: Towards European Integration of Industrial and Financial Markets? (1958–1969)*, Paris: Presses de l'Université Paris Sorbonne, 2004, pp. 161–178; Éric Bussière, "Moves towards an economic and monetary policy," in: *The European Commission 1958–72*, pp. 391–410.

Initially, the proposal for coordination led to only modest results—firstly, because the governments feared the loss of decision-making on currency and economic policy, and secondly, because the Commission's measures included medium-term economic planning of a Keynesian cast, which did not suit the neo-liberal forces in the governments. In May of 1964, the tasks of the Currency Committee of the Council of Ministers were expanded; at the same time, Committees for Budgetary Policy and Medium-Term Economic Policy as well as a Committee of Governors of the Central Banks were put in place.

The currency turbulence of 1968, which had been unleashed by the lax financial policy of the US and the resulting decrease of confidence in the dollar as the leading international currency, spurred the reactivation of the project of an economic and currency union. Without greater convergence in these areas, there was not only the danger of perpetual hindrances to Community policies but also that of the disintegration of the Common Market itself, with devastating economic consequences. In February of 1968, the Commission, now under the leadership of Raymond Barre, therefore presented a new plan for creating a reserve fund and for introducing firm and definitive exchange rates. This did not initially spark any response, however. In the autumn of 1968, Bonn refused the partners' demand that the mark be allowed to appreciate; and de Gaulle defiantly rejected a devaluation of the franc, something that in reality was unavoidable.[63]

The Commission responded with an initiative that was somewhat less ambitious. Its next proposal, ready in December of 1968 and officially presented on 12 February 1969 (the so-called "Barre Plan"), initially envisioned only mutual agreement on every change in exchange rates as well as short-term monetary support actions on the basis of decisions by central banks and medium-term assistance by decision of the Council. At the same time, coordination of economic and business-cycle policy was to be intensified by adding the goal of achieving price stability.[64] Giscard d'Estaing, who had long been urging a European solution to the problem of currency turbulence, was able to convince Pompidou to go in this direction; the Council of Ministers of the European Communities was thus able to approve the fundamentals of the Barre Plan on 17 July 1969. Brandt let himself be convinced by Monnet in November to aim for the creation of a European Reserve Fund as well. When the summit in The Hague decided to produce

---

[63] Cf. Andreas Wilkens, "L'Europe et sa première crise monétaire. Bonn et Paris en novembre 1968," in: *Journal of European Integration History* 18/2 (2012), pp. 221–243.
[64] *Europa-Archiv* 24 (1969), pp. D163–D174.

an incremental plan for establishing an economic and currency union over the course of 1970, Triffin was on hand in the role of an advisor to the chancellor.[65]

In developing the plan, however, different priorities manifested themselves. Whereas for the more economically weak member states the primary concern was support for their endangered currencies, the *Bundesbank* and Economy Minister Karl Schiller insisted on budgetary discipline and bringing about macroeconomic convergence as the perquisite for the introduction of a common currency. In connection with this, a Belgian proposal envisioned in the first phase of the multistage plan a reduction of the range of fluctuation of European currencies against the dollar. The West German draft called for only short-term support measures in this first phase and additionally emphasized the necessity of harmonizing economic policy. On 6 and 7 March 1970, the Council of Ministers established an *ad hoc* committee chaired by Prime Minister and Finance Minister Pierre Werner of Luxembourg. This body ended up in a negotiation crisis due to the differences, and the deadlock was only resolved through discreet intervention by Brandt on behalf of rapid currency integration. The report approved by the committee on 8 October 1970 (the so-called "Werner Plan") proposed beginning in the first phase with efforts to reduce the range of fluctuation on a trial basis and "potentially" establishing a Currency Equalization Fund. The common currency was to be introduced after a decade of dismantling existing imbalances, that is, in the year 1980. Responsibility for the common currency was to be in the hands of a common central bank; economic policy was to be steered by a "European Economic Policy Decision Center" responsible to the European Parliament.[66]

The emphasis on the necessity of binding decisions, which Bonn had negotiated as a *quid pro quo* for its expressions of support, seemed in Pompidou's eyes an attack on his authority over promoting dynamism in the French economy. Additionally, he was motivated by Debré's intense attacks on the results of negotiations[67] in the Council of Ministers, raging at any interference in his budget policy. Schumann and Giscard were directed not to support any transfer of further authority to the Community level. After the president had calmed down somewhat, he admitted to Brandt at the Franco-German summit of 25 and 26 January 1971 that the monetary measures planned for the first phase should only continue to be in effect if, before their expiration, an agreement had been reached on the

---

65 Gérard Bossuat, "Le président Georges Pompidou et les tentatives d'Union économique et monétaire," in: Association Georges Pompidou (ed.), *Georges Pompidou et l'Europe. Colloque 25 et 26 novembre 1993*, Brussels, 1995, pp. 405–447; Andreas Wilkens, "Der Werner-Plan. Währung, Politik und Europa 1968–1971," in: Knipping and Schönwald (eds.), *Aufbruch*, pp. 217–244.
66 *Ibid.*, pp. 226–235; Hiepel, *Brandt und Pompidou*, pp. 93–104.
67 Of which the West German embassy in Paris learned, *ibid.*, p. 142.

further course of currency integration. The West Germans were satisfied that in regard to the final phase, there was only a general reference to a common central banking system and that the issues of its area of authority and its independence were left open. Likewise, Bonn accepted the formulation that the necessary economic policy decisions should be made at the Community level by the organs of the Community.

The Federal Republic had thus received assurance that measures on currency and economic policy would go hand in hand and that in the end, authority would reside on the European level. The actual nature of the currency- and economic-policy decision-making process in the future Union was consciously left open, however. In this form, the plan for creating an economic and currency union was passed by the Council of Ministers on 9 February 1971.[68] A further resolution of the Council of Ministers 22 March specified that the initial phase should last from 1 July 1971 to 31 December 1973. As an initial measure, a minor reduction in the range of fluctuation among the European currencies was passed: from the existing .75 percent upward or downward to .6 percent, altogether from 1.5 percent to 1.2 percent.

The compromise underlying the decisions of March 1971 did not hold up very long, however. Several weeks later, the Federal Republic became the object of speculative dollar influxes that disturbed the external economic balance and conjured up the danger of imported inflation. Schiller reacted with a demand for completely freeing up the DM exchange rate (so-called *floating*) and succeeded in pushing it through, for at least a limited period, at a meeting of the EEC finance ministers on 8 and 9 May 1971. In his view, the other member states simply needed to join in with this so as to save the project of a common currency area. In actuality, a common float threatened to reduce the competitiveness of the weaker economies and to elevate the mark to the status of leading European currency; for that reason, it was out of the question for Pompidou. In isolation, a West German float would disrupt the functioning of the European Agricultural Market and render obsolete the decision to engage in narrowing the range of fluctuation.

Pompidou's disappointment over the swerve by the Federal Republic was all the greater given that the more substantial alternative—a devaluation of the dollar—did not come into question at all. Instead of joining together with its European partners in demanding that the US government make such a move, Bonn helped Washington continue solving its budget problems at the cost of its European allies. A common European response to the American challenge did not materialize, not even when President Nixon eliminated the convertibility of

---

[68] *Europa-Archiv* 26 (1971), pp. D139–D144. Cf. Wilkens, "Werner-Plan," pp. 238–243; Hiepel, *Brandt und Pompidou*, pp. 108–118.

the dollar into gold and thereby definitively undermined the Bretton Woods currency system on 15 August. While Schiller continued to plead for a common float, and the Dutch as well as the Belgians and Luxembourgers *de facto* freed up their currencies to rise, the French decided to split their currency market: For financial transactions, the exchange rate was freed; for trade movements, the existing parities were maintained by means of interventions and capital controls.

Another intervention by Brandt was needed in order to bring the Federal Republic back on course with the Community. The chancellor was in his own estimation a layman regarding currency policy and had initially yielded to his economy minister, not least of all because the policy of defending the mark was very popular. However, when the chancellor perceived that divergence on the issue of how to respond to the flood of dollars was leading toward a point where the project of a currency union would be fundamentally endangered, he sent Ludwig Poullain, the head of the West German *Landesbank*—who was a critic of Schiller—to the French presidential advisor Jean-René Bernard in order to negotiate a compromise that would balance the interests of the two countries: a return to firm exchange rates with a rise in the mark, devaluation of the dollar, and retention of the parity of the franc. At a bilateral meeting with Nixon in the Azores on 14 December, Pompidou reached an agreement on the exact level of the dollar devaluation: 7.9 percent. On 18 December, the subsequent Smithsonian Agreement (named after the Smithsonian Institute in Washington, the location of the G-10 finance ministers meeting) called for the mark to rise by 4.6 percent, a little less than Pompidou had sought. With these preconditions, the European partners accepted an expansion of the range of the fluctuation of their currencies against the dollar from plus/minus .75 to 2.25 percent (altogether from 1.5 to 4.5 percent) and overall reverted to intervention in cases of deviation from the resulting averages.[69]

In order to advance the project of a currency union again, it was also necessary to reduce the range of fluctuation among the European currencies. Schiller bristled against a proposal to this effect made by the Commission. Brandt overrode this, and so on 21 March 1972 the Council of Ministers issued a call for the member states' central banks to reduce the fluctuation margins among their currencies to plus/minus 2.25 percent. Within the "tunnel" of 4.5 percent *vis-à-vis* the dollar, there thus emerged a "snake" with a range of 2.25 percent. Whereas dollars would still be used for interventions against dollar fluctuations, interventions within the snake would for the first time be carried out in currencies of the

---

[69] *Ibid.*, pp. 177–205; Roussel, *Pompidou*, pp. 461–489; on the end of the Bretton Woods system and the Smithsonian Agreement, also Harold James, *Rambouillet, 15. November 1975. Die Globalisierung der Wirtschaft*, Munich: Deutscher Taschenbuch-Verlag, 1997, pp. 131–160.

Community. This meant that the dependence of the weaker European currencies on the mark was lessened and that a core of European solidarity on intervention emerged. On 10 April, the heads of the central banks of the Six met in Basel and signed an agreement that would take effect a fortnight later. The candidates for entry joined in, initially only for the short term, however.

The renewed Franco-German consensus that underlay the establishment of the European currency snake also withstood the next round of attacks on the European currencies. As American dollars once again began flowing increasingly into Europe in June, the British government opted to abandon the snake and allow the pound to float. Schiller wanted to do the same and once again recommended a community float of the European currencies. Conversely, Brandt won over the cabinet on 29 June for initiating capital controls as the French and Italians were doing. This caused Schiller to resign from his ministerial posts. His successor was Helmut Schmidt, an all-round politician who concentrated on what was politically possible rather than on economic theories, which had been Schiller's main focus.

Inspired by this stabilization of Franco-German solidarity, Pompidou now demanded that the planned currency balance fund be introduced soon and that it be given wide-ranging authority as well. Brandt concurred, though with an eye to the goal of stability for the economy of the Federal Republic, he included the restriction that there should be a cap on the credit facilities and monies available each year. With preparations made jointly by Giscard and Schmidt, the economy and finance ministers of the Community met on 11 and 12 September and were able to decide on the establishment of a European Monetary Cooperation Fund in the first phase of a currency union. The fund was initially to serve for the compensation of the central banks in the currency snake and make balance equalization multilateral; for this purpose, a European unit of account was to be introduced. For later phases, an "incremental communitization of reserves" was announced. The Paris summit in October set the launch of this cooperation fund for April of 1973 and confirmed once again the already-determined course to a currency union.[70]

It was admittedly the case that neither the capital controls nor the expansion of currency cooperation offered a guarantee of a return to stable exchange rates. When in late January of 1973 a new torrent of dollars swept into the European currency markets and the US government allowed the dollar to float freely in March, Schmidt—who was serving in the second Brandt cabinet as finance minister with

---

[70] "Erklärungen der Konferenz der Wirtschafts- und Finanzminister der erweiterten Gemeinschaft in Rom 11./12.9.1972," in *Europa-Archiv* 27 (1972), pp. D470ff.; on the negotiations during 1972, Hiepel, *Brandt und Pompidou*, pp. 197–207 and 209ff.

expanded responsibilities—could advocate nothing besides a common float of European currencies as a means of helping out. This time, Pompidou agreed, despite the dangers for French competitiveness that were still bound up with such a move; he consented only with the precondition that the mark be allowed to appreciate once again, this time by three percent, and that the decision only be made after the end of voting for the French National Assembly on 11 March (a delay that cost the *Bundesbank* a large amount of currency reserves). He feared that if France did not participate, then Bonn would go it alone and would be followed by the other countries with hard currencies. On 12 March, the decision was thus made for a common float of the countries of the currency snake. The "tunnel" of pledges to make supportive purchases for maintaining the fluctuation range *vis-à-vis* the dollar now vanished.

The move to initiate bloc floating did not constitute a genuine step on the road to European currency union, however. The currency bloc that had been created was not large enough or strong enough for that. Britain and Italy remained outside, although Brandt had made both governments generous pledges of assistance that ran counter to West German policy oriented on stability. According to Brandt, the "ifs-and-buts of the experts"[71] on both sides ensured that the great gamble envisioned by the chancellor and also energetically advocated by Jean Monnet since the Paris summit had fallen by the wayside in talks among the economic and finance ministers. Along with France, the Federal Republic, and the Benelux states, only Denmark participated.[72]

With the Heath and Andreotti governments shrinking back from involvement in the currency snake, Bonn lost its willingness to promote currency solidarity via steps to curtail its orientation on stability. Schmidt was visibly disappointed that Italy especially—a founding member of the Community—showed little disposition to practice budgetary discipline; he was also simultaneously faced with the growing danger of inflation due to the continuing flow of dollars and so henceforth supported strictly-parallel inflation-fighting and monetary support. Brandt followed him in this, not least of all due to the impression that there had been a change in West German public opinion, which was increasingly critical of the alleged profligacy of the partner countries. As the launch of the currency cooperation fund (set for 1 June 1973) was being prepared, Schmidt insisted on binding

---

71 Willy Brandt, *Begegnungen und Einsichten. Die Jahre 1960 bis 1975*, Hamburg: Hoffmann & Campe, 1976, pp. 329.
72 Gérard Bossuat, "Jean Monnet et l'identité monétaire européenne," in: Gérard Bossuat and Andreas Wilkens (eds.), *Jean Monnet, l'Europe et les chemins de la Paix*, Paris: Publications de la Sorbonne, 1999, pp. 369–398; Kreutzfeldt, *Point of return*, pp. 341–352; Hiepel, *Brandt und Pompidou*, pp. 217–230.

pledges regarding budgetary discipline. When this was rejected, he balked at making a substantial transfer of currency reserves to the Community fund, as Monnet and the European Commission were demanding.

In order to overcome the stagnation in currency integration that had resulted from all this, Monnet once again pushed for taking the bull by the horns. In August, he sent another plan conceived by Triffin to Pompidou, this one calling for the rapid collectivization of all currency reserves, linked with the strengthening of Community authority on currency issues. The Currency Fund was to receive a directorate with decision-making power, and the budgetary rights of the European Parliament were also to be increased. It was clearly Monnet's calculation that the creation of opportunities for the Community to intervene in matters of national budget policy would banish Bonn's fear of a Community plagued by inflation. Pompidou was clearly not ready, or not yet ready, to pay the price of a further loss of national sovereignty that was being demanded here. On the report about Monnet's request that had been prepared by Bernard, he wrote "dangerous or theoretical."[73]

On 3 and 4 December, it nevertheless proved possible for the economy and finance ministers of the Community to reach agreement on a package for the transition to the second phase of currency union. They agreed on stability guidelines and on converging economy policy, a decision that had some credibility even in Bonn's eyes. Schmidt rejected the pooling of reserves, but as a return gesture, he did accept an increase of short-term currency assistance. The package was not passed by the Council of Ministers, however. In the Council session of 17 and 18 December 1973, the British and Italian governments insisted that decisions on economic and currency union could not be taken without the establishment of the European Regional Fund, which they were advocating for the benefit of their structurally-weak regions. For their part, the West Germans were not willing to accept that demand, given their conviction that they could not afford more transfer payments; the transition to the second phase thus remained without new instruments. This second phase was intended to serve as a consolidation of what had been achieved up to that point. However, the qualitative leap into currency integration had been *de facto* put off for an indefinite period.

As massive amounts of dollars flowed into Europe and particularly into the Federal Republic in the wake of the rise in oil prices, the possibility of such a leap became more remote. Pompidou felt that he needed to dip deeply into French currency reserves if he wanted to follow the renewed rise of the mark and thereby the snake overall, but in light of growing domestic criticism of his alleged inaction in the economic crisis, he did not want to risk it. Bonn offered short-term assis-

---

73 Bernard's notes, 14 Aug. 1973, AN 5AG2, 1065; cf. Hiepel, *Brandt und Pompidou*, p. 250.

tance of some three billion dollars, which Pompidou rejected, presumably due to fears of a further loss of prestige in the eyes of traditional Gaullists. Instead, he had Giscard declare on 19 January 1974 that France would temporarily leave the currency snake.[74]

For Brandt, this was a moment of deep skepticism regarding the future of the European Community. As he noted during a conversation in the chancellery in early April, the economic- and currency-policy philosophies of the French and of the Germans were too different, and it was "clearly not possible to make up for the economic crumbling of the Community with political initiatives."[75] Only a few days later, however, he was developing plans once again for unlimited support measures that would ease France's return to the currency snake. According to the vision of the West German government, it would be possible even before 1980 to begin with the construction of a European government on the basis of these plans, one that would even be controlled on the European level by Parliament.[76] Indeed, Brandt had many European policy initiatives in mind at the time he decided to resign from the chancellorship due to the espionage affair involving Günter Guillaume.

Brandt's return to optimism had not been without justification. Giscard d'Estaing had been elected president of France on 19 May after Pompidou's death on 2 April from the blood disease that had afflicted him for many years. The new French leader took measures at once to combat inflation, measures that were to enable the country's quick return to the currency snake. During his first Franco-German summit as president, Giscard announced his intention to seek a "type of stability" comparable to that of the Federal Republic and a "genuine convergence" of the policy of both countries.[77] He was in fact able to bring the franc back into the currency snake in May of 1975, although with serious opposition from his finance minister. From 10 July 1975 onward, the franc was once again an official part of the European currency association, at the same exchange rate against the mark as in the spring of 1973.

It is therefore not appropriate to speak of a failure of the project for an economic and currency union. In actuality, it was only that it had been taken up too late to be put into effect rapidly and consistently. The understandable nervousness with which European societies reacted to the end of the period of continual

---

74 Ibid., pp. 276, 280, 284f.
75 Klaus Happrecht, *Im Kanzleramt. Tagebuch der Jahre mit Willy Brandt*, Reinbek: Rowohlt, 2001, p. 532.
76 Per Fischer's notes, 23 April 1974, provided by Hiepel, *Brandt und Pompidou*, pp. 316f.
77 Protocol of the discussion, 9 July 1974, quoted from Hartmut Soell, *Helmut Schmidt. Macht und Verantwortung*, Munich: Deutsche Verlags-Anstalt, 2008, p. 364.

economic growth served to reduce the freedom for making efforts motivated by solidarity and also prevented the heads of state and of government from carrying through with the collectivization of the currencies as quickly as would have been necessary in order to deal with the currency crisis that had stemmed from the US. On the other hand, additional motives for holding fast to the European project sprang from the crisis and the resulting breakdown of the world currency system. Even though the European currency snake and the common float did not suffice for dealing with currency speculation, they greatly reduced the consequences of such speculation for trade within the Community. At the same time, the awareness of the need for common policy grew as well.

Political Cooperation

As one would expect, differing views came up as well in discussing the issue of "progress in the area of political unity." The most ambitious plan came from the Italian government, having been prepared under the leadership of Foreign Minister Aldo Moro. His memorandum of 25 February 1970 envisioned nothing less than the incremental construction of a Political Community following the model of the Economic Community. It was explicitly to include the areas of defense and justice, which was new for the Italian position. In a first phase, there were to be at least quarterly meetings of the relevant expert ministers and the establishment of a secretariat; during a second phase beginning in 1975, there was to be an incremental combining of responsibilities. In a third phase after 1980, the existing Communities were to fuse into a kind of federal state, with the common Commission of the Political Community and the Economic Community as a federal government and the Council of Ministers exercising the presidential function.[78]

Belgian Foreign Minister Pierre Harmel and his government appealed likewise for the inclusion of defense policy and justice, possibly also education and strong common structures. Harmel also proposed that the agreement to be worked out by July of 1970 immediately be presented to the candidate countries so that they could adhere to it as well. On 21 January, a memorandum from Bonn warned against "burdening the entry negotiations at the beginning with the contentious issue of whether the final phase would have a supranational or a federalist character." In concrete terms, this document only proposed for the time being annual meetings of the heads of state and of government as well as annual

---

[78] Provided by Kramer, *Europäisches oder atlantisches Europa*, p. 260; on Moro's advocacy of increased political cooperation, also Antonio Varsori, *La Cenerentola d'Europa? L'Italia e l'integrazione europea dal 1947 al oggi*, Soveria Mannelli: Rubbettino, 2010, pp. 235–241.

meetings of the foreign ministers (on a different time schedule). The Commission and the Parliament were to be brought into the consultations. Although the paper did emphasize the necessity of common positions reflecting solidarity in foreign policy, the area of defense was not mentioned at all.

At a gathering on 6 March in Brussels, the foreign ministers ordered their Political Directors to sound out the possibilities of finding a common denominator on the issue of political unification. Chairman of the committee was the Belgian Étienne Davignon, who had previously worked out the passage on political unity in the communiqué of The Hague summit along with Brandt's state secretary, Egon Bahr. When the committee came together on 14 April, the French side finally presented a paper that was significantly more reserved than the West German one. Instead of political Community, it only discussed cooperation on foreign policy, and there was explicit emphasis that the realm of defense should remain outside. The decision-making freedom of the participating governments was not to be diminished, and cooperation with the institutions of the Community was to be kept to a minimum. Pompidou was evidently not eager to take up the old debate about the Europeans' relationship to the US. "I don't believe in Political Europe," he explained to his foreign office state secretary, "at least not at the present time. Perhaps there'll come a day, 1980 or later. But I doubt that very much too."[79]

The compromise on which first the Political Directors and then the foreign ministers agreed in several stages up to 20 July followed more or less the line set forth by Bonn. The pledge made by the governments was initially limited to efforts to seek harmonization in "all important issues of foreign policy." This was to be achieved through meetings of the foreign ministers every six months and of the "Political Committee" four times a year, and more often at the request of the chairman. The chairmanship was to be held by the rotating Council chairman. The Commission "will be invited to make known its view," though only if the work of the Ministers should "affect the activities of the European Communities." The European Parliament was to participate as well, though only in the form of a "colloquium" with the members of its Foreign Affairs Committee, which was to take place twice a year. The issue of creating a secretariat remained open because France rejected the link with the Commission that the others wanted. At the same time, however, it was decided to produce in not more than two years another report that would contain proposals for the further development of political cooperation.[80]

---

79 Jean de Lipkowksi's notes, 6 Jan. 1970, AN 5AG2, 1035.
80 *Europa-Archiv* 25 (1970), pp. D520–D524.

Regarding the level and area of activity of this "European Political Cooperation" (EPC), all of this was less than what had been capable of gaining a consensus during the negotiations on the Fouchet Plans. Yet, it was also the beginning of genuine cooperation on foreign policy. The report was officially adopted on 27 October 1970 after approval by the heads of state and of government. This beginning was open-ended. The advocates of greater integration were betting that progress would be possible right away on both the political realms included and on decision-making mechanisms. Joseph Luns commented that, given the meager result of all the hard work put into this initiative, "we need to get to work now."[81]

Right away, in fact, Harmel attempted to make a common security and defense policy appetizing to his French colleague Schumann by citing the strengthening of the international position of the Federal Republic after the conclusion of the Treaty of Moscow on 12 August 1970. He also called attention to tendencies toward an understanding between the US and USSR on arms limitation as well as demands from the American public to reduce the American troop presence in Europe.[82] The Federal Republic held the Council presidency in the second half of 1970, and Scheel made use of the fact in order to promote rapid implementation of the decisions on political cooperation rapidly, to push through the regular notification of the ambassadors of member states in third countries and international organizations about decisions of the foreign ministers, and to institutionalize timely communication with candidates for entry. Right at their first gathering on 19 November 1970, the foreign ministers agreed to work out common positions on the issues of a peace settlement in the Middle East and the planned Conference on Security and Cooperation in Europe (CSCE). With reference to the increasing significance of EPC, Scheel requested an improvement in its structure a year later: more frequent meetings, greater focus on the Community, and the establishment of a permanent secretariat, which had not yet been done.[83]

Pompidou felt that he had been put on the defensive. At a press conference in January of 1971, he found it necessary to express support for the goal of a political Europe and a common foreign policy, with which Europe could once again play an autonomous role in world affairs. In regard to institutional possibilities,

---

[81] Quoted from Charles Zorgbibe, *Histoire de la construction européenne*, Paris: Presses Universitaires de France, 1993, pp. 102ff. Cf. Kramer, *Europäisches oder atlantisches Europa*, pp. 256–267; Dujardin, *Harmel*, pp. 558–574; Hiepel, *Brandt und Pompidou*, pp. 164–171.

[82] Harmel to Schumann, 23 Sept. 1970, quoted in Dujardin, *Harmel*, pp. 571ff.

[83] Hiepel, *Brandt und Pompidou*, pp. 172ff. and 176; on the following, *ibid.*, pp. 231–246; Maria Găinar, *Aux origines de la diplomatie européenne. Les Neuf et la Coopération politique européenne de 1973 à 1980*, Brussels: Peter Lang, 2012, pp. 74–82.

he cited the formation of a "European government." As soon as it was constituted, the Parliamentary Assembly was to be further developed into a genuine European Parliament. All this was in any event clearly a vision for the "distant future," as he admitted to Brandt.[84] For the present, the insistence on the priority of national governments and the necessity of unanimity in their decision-making were more important. In February of 1972, Pompidou conceded the establishment of a "light" secretariat for EPC. With an eye toward traditional Gaullists, however, he insisted that this body must have its seat in Paris. Given that Brandt—supported by the smaller partners and also by Heath—persisted in the view that the seat must be in Brussels so as to promote the integration of political cooperation into the development of the Community, no agreement was reached at that time. In September of 1972, the issue of the EPC secretariat was once again tabled.

Likewise, Pompidou rejected attempts by the Dutch, Belgian, and Italian governments to put the issues of strengthening Community organs and direct election of the European Parliament on the agenda of the upcoming Paris summit. Since November of 1970, Brandt had been pushing for this new summit in order to make substantial advances on the issue of deepening that had been earlier decided in The Hague. When after several delays the French president finally issued the invitations in September of 1972, no wide-ranging decisions on institutional matters were consequently to be expected. Pompidou surprised the summit participants, among them for the first time representatives of the new member states, shortly before the opening on 19 October with a personal draft of a concluding declaration in which the Nine were to proclaim their "intention to transform the totality of their relations into a European Union before the end of this decade." Asked by Luxembourg Foreign Minister Gaston Thorn what that was to be, the French president said that he himself did not know; the concept was however suited to bridge the gap between "my party colleagues" and the advocates of integration.[85]

That was exactly its function. Pompidou had sought to emancipate himself from the traditional Gaullists by means of a referendum on his European policy, but it had failed due to low participation: Only sixty percent of eligible voters had turned out for the 21 April vote. After that, he had only one possibility—to leave the issue of the institutional configuration of the Community open. The summit could thus only decide in general terms "that the decision-making process and the functioning of the organs must be improved in order increase their effectiveness."

---

84 Conversation between Brandt and Pompidou, 25 Jan. 1971, AN 5AG2, 105; Pompidou's vague remarks on "European confederation" of 21 Jan. 1971 in *Europa-Archiv* 26 (1971), pp. D131–D137.
85 Reported by Thorn, 12 Feb. 2001, quoted in Dujardin, *Harmel*, p. 599. On the Paris summit, *ibid.*, pp. 587–603; Kreutzfeldt, *Point of return*, pp. 318–332; Hiepel, *Brandt und Pompidou*, pp. 206–213; Găinar, *Origines*, pp. 82–86.

As to the "how," the organs of the Community were supposed to draft a report by the end of 1975; and a future summit would decide on it. In concrete terms, only the doubling of the number of foreign minister meetings within the framework of EPC was decided on: They were now to occur four times a year rather than two.[86]

Only after French parliamentary elections on 4 and 11 March 1973 did Pompidou find himself ready for clearer engagement on behalf of a political Europe capable of taking action. The elections had inflicted significant losses on the Gaullists while at the same time confirming the government's majority. This enabled Pompidou to dismiss Debré and to fill the government more completely with men in whom he had confidence—among them Jobert, who became foreign minister after Schumann's failure to win re-election. Without having to worry about any more impediments from the traditional Gaullists, he could now yield to pressure from Heath for nuclear cooperation: At a new meeting with the British prime minister on 23 May, it was agreed that there should be expert consultations on the development of the next generation of medium-range missiles; as early as 1975, this initiative was possibly to lead to "something common among Europeans."[87] In a speech to the National Assembly on 19 June, Jobert challenged the partners to consider an autonomous European defense.

The resumption of de Gaulle's plans for a Europe autonomous in defense policy was promoted by an initiative from Henry Kissinger, who was actually aiming at the exact opposite: In a speech before journalists in New York on 23 April, Nixon's national security advisor called for the development of a "new Atlantic Charter" by which 1973 was supposed to become the "Year of Europe"; Kissinger was seeking to firm up again the relations between the US and its European allies and also to put a stop to isolationist tendencies in American society. Given that he called for stronger European participation in common security measures and at the same time very maladroitly distinguished between the global interests of the US and the merely regional interests of Europe, the initiative was widely perceived on the other side of the Atlantic as an attempt to get the Europeans to bear higher costs for the American security guarantee without conceding them greater influence. That promoted understanding for French efforts on behalf of European autonomy, and this new openness to the idea promoted in turn the willingness of Pompidou to pay the necessary price for it.

---

[86] "Erklärung der Konferenz der Staats- bzw. Regierungschefs in Paris 19./20.10.1972" in: *Europa-Archiv* 27 (1972), pp. D502–D508.

[87] AN, 5AG2, 1015. On this and the following, Wilfried Loth, "European Political Co-operation and European Security in the Policies of Willy Brandt and Georges Pompidou," in: van der Harst (ed.), *Beyond the Customs Union*, pp. 21–34.

The understanding on a political Europe also capable of acting in matters of defense came all the easier because Heath—with his assurances to Pompidou about interpreting the Luxembourg Agreements along French lines—had by no means given up this orientation. John Hunt, head of the Europe Department, remembered in July of 1973 that "we joined to give our industry the stimulus and opportunities of a vastly greater market, to secure our security (particularly by anchoring Germany in the West) and to develop the Community into a political entity." For all that, a "qualitative leap" would one day be necessary: "when a sufficient degree of sovereignty is passed over to a central authority to make it a point of no return."[88] Thus, much to Kissinger's surprise, Jobert had Heath to a great extent on his side in his demand that American ambitions be countered.

After an EPC meeting of the foreign ministers on 5 June had not resulted in much, the second report on EPC was passed on 23 July. Beyond a doubling of the foreign minister meetings and an expansion of the gatherings of the Political Committee, this document also contained a pledge not to decide on foreign policy issues touching on the interests of the Community without prior consultation among the partners. Additionally, mechanisms were established for closer coordination of EPC activities with the Commission and the Parliament. The participation of the ambassadors of third countries, already being done in practice, was institutionalized.[89] At the same time, it was agreed that a common European standpoint would be worked out before the conversation with the Nixon administration on a possible joint declaration. Lastly, the Nine also agreed to Heath's proposal to prepare an additional declaration of their own on "European identity."

In preparing the common position, Jobert and Heath worked closely together. Efforts by Brandt to resolve the differences between the Europeans and the Americans by means of dialogue came to naught. At the next meeting (on 10 and 11 September), the foreign ministers approved a draft declaration with which Washington was to acknowledge explicitly the political autonomy of the Europeans: The United States "welcome the intention of the nine that the Community establishes its position in world affairs as a distinct entity."[90] Little was said about contentious issues involving trade or currency policy, on which the US was then demanding concessions; on security issues, a separate declaration was proposed

---

[88] Hunt to Amstrong, 24 July 1973 and 18 June 1973, PREM 15/1520 und 2079, quoted in Kreutzfeldt, *Point of return*, pp. 347 and 17ff. On Heath's efforts toward a common foreign and defense policy, also Ilaria Poggiolini, "How the Heath Government Revised the European Lesson: British Transition to EEC Membership (1972)," in: Varsori (ed.), *Inside the European Community*, pp. 313–346.
[89] *Europa-Archiv* 28 (1973), pp. D515–D522.
[90] Published in the *New York Times*, 24 Sept. 1973.

for passage by the NATO Council. In this way, it was hoped that maintaining the American presence in Europe would not need to be paid for with greater concessions on trade policy and other financial issues.

This was not at all what Kissinger had in mind. He reacted with a counter-proposal stressing the necessity of close cooperation between the Community and the US and calling for intensive consultations on policy toward the East Bloc. Negotiations on the contrasting drafts were carried on between the Political Directors of the Nine and representatives of the US State Department, but the distance between the viewpoints was not reduced. There was only agreement in a formal sense about issuing a declaration on Euro-American relations as well as a NATO declaration. After the Nine had come together on 6 November on a declaration regarding peace in the Middle East, one that differed markedly from the pro-Israeli attitude of the US in the Yom Kippur War, Kissinger largely lost interest in the declarations and in a European visit by Nixon that would have including the signing of the documents. In January of 1974, Kissinger admitted to Douglas-Home that they would not mean much.[91]

While the Nine were wrestling with a redefinition of relations to the US, two other initiatives were aiming at a rapid expansion of their political cooperation: First of all, Brandt took up Jobert's call for talks on an autonomous European defense. In a conversation with Pompidou on 21 June, the chancellor pressed for concrete results as soon as possible in this area. The head of the Political Department of the West German Foreign Office, Günther van Well, published a policy article in which he embraced the goal of an "autonomous role and responsibility for the European Union" in foreign and defense policy as well. In a conversation with Jobert, Scheel explained that this Political Union should also include defense components by 1980. In the longer term, Europe ought to "free itself from this 'indissoluble' dependence" on the US.[92]

In early September, Jean Monnet then urged Pompidou, Heath, and Brandt to accelerate the process of constructing the Political Union by having the heads of state and of government of the Nine constitute a "Provisional European Govern-

---

91 Claudia Hiepel, "Kissinger's Year of Europe – A Challenge for the EC and the Franco-German Relationship," in: van der Harst (ed.), *Beyond the Customs Union*, pp. 277–296; idem., *Brandt und Pompidou*, pp. 304–325; Daniel Möckli, *European Foreign Policy during the Cold War. Heath, Brandt, Pompidou and the Dream of Political Unity*, London and New York: Routledge, 2009, pp. 140–247; idem., "Asserting Europe's Distinct Identity. The EC Nine and Kissinger's Year of Europe," in: Matthias Schulz and Thomas A. Schwartz (eds.), *The Strained Alliance. U.S.-European relations from Nixon to Carter*, Cambridge: Cambridge University Press, 2010, pp. 195–220; Găinar, *Origines*, pp. 109–131; Catherine Hynes, *The Year that Never Was. Heath, the Nixon Administration and the Year of Europe*, Dublin: University College Dublin Press, 2009.
92 AN, 5AG 2, 1012.

ment." Going forward, they would then hold confidential consultations at least three times a year in order to oversee the fulfillment of the program of the Paris summit. "Insofar as it is necessary and after consultation with the president of the Council and the Commission of the European Communities," they should develop "instructions for ministers" that "represent the member states in the Council of the European Communities." This was meant to overcome the logjam in decision-making in the Council's intergovernmental negotiations. Additionally, Monnet immediately prescribed that the heads of state and of government should commit themselves to the creation of a "European government and a European assembly based on general elections."[93]

The two initiatives conducted to different extents. Jobert and Pompidou reacted evasively to Brandt's foray. Jobert wanted to discuss the defense policy problematic primarily within the framework of the WEU, to which obviously neither Denmark nor Ireland belonged. When West German Defense Minister Georg Leber—clearly not having coordinated with Brandt and Scheel in a significant way—encouraged France to join NATO's "Eurogroup," Pompidou decided to shelve the issue for the time being. The idea of a "Provisional European Government" was embraced by Jobert without reservation.[94] Conversely, Pompidou—to whom the broader prospect of establishing a European government with a Parliament had not been presented at all—initially signaled only guardedly his approval for "not all too frequent but regular" consultations on political cooperation "in the circle of those responsible at the highest level."[95] Only after Brandt and Heath had assured him of their support did he officially propose to the partners on 31 October that there be regular summits; at the same time, he urged that the first such meeting be held before year's end.

The Dutch government as well as the European Parliament and the Commission opposed the idea of a "Supreme Council of the Community," as Heath wanted to dub the new institution. They all feared that the Commission would lose its initiative function and that the Council would no longer make any decisions at all. Furthermore, given the form in which Pompidou had made the proposal, it was not clear whether the new entity would not once again steer things in the direction of a strict separation between Political Cooperation and the Community. Thus, at the summit in Copenhagen on 14 and 15 December 1973, it was only decided that the heads of state and of government would in the future "meet more

---

93 Text of the Memorandum in Monnet, *Mémoires*, pp. 591ff.; on the negotiations over this proposal, *ibid.*, pp. 637–644; Marie-Thérèse Bitsch, "Jean Monnet et la création du Conseil européen," in: Bossuat and Wilkens, *Jean Monnet*, pp. 399–410.
94 In conversation with Scheel, 7 Nov. 1973, AN, 5AG2, 1012.
95 Press conference of 27 Sept. 1973, excerpts in *Europa-Archiv* 29 (1974), pp. D26–D28.

often" if the process of European unity or international crisis situations necessitated it; in any event, these meetings were not to hamper the work of the Community organs. More specifics were to be determined in the second half of 1974.[96]

In terms of content, the summit was only able to pass the "Document on the European Identity" that the foreign ministers and the EPC Political Committee had been working on since the summer. This declaration characterized "the principles of representative democracy, of the rule of law, of social justice, and of respect for human rights" as "fundamental elements of the European Identity." It emphasized the necessity "that Europe must unite and speak increasingly with one voice" and affirmed the goal of a European Union "before the end of the present decade." On the volatile issue of a European defense, it stated only that Europe must possess "adequate means of defence"; at the urging of the Federal Republic, the continuation of a "constructive dialogue" with the United States was also included.[97]

In essence, the Copenhagen summit therefore only repeated the vague formulations on which agreement had been reached in Paris more than a year earlier. This result made all the less of an impression given the reaction of the heads of state and of government to the challenge by the OPEC cartel, one that painfully belied the unity that had so recently been proclaimed. Whereas the Federal Republic pushed for short-term measures benefitting the Netherlands above all, which had been affected by the oil embargo especially severely, France and Britain rejected common action and instead negotiated individually with Arab leaders. At the same time, Jobert and Pompidou once again appealed for the development of a Common Market for oil. Considering the newly discovered oil fields in the North Sea, Heath would only agree to that if the planned Regional Fund of the Community were given substantial resources. That was rejected by the Federal Republic at the Council of Ministers meeting following the summit, so both the funding of the Currency Reserve Fund and the project for a common energy policy remained in limbo.

---

[96] "Verlautbarung," *Europa-Archiv* 29 (1974), pp. D54–56. On the prehistory and development of the Copenhagen summit, especially Hiepel, *Brandt und Pompidou*, pp. 254–279.

[97] English version in Christopher Hill and Karen E. Smith (eds.), *European Foreign Policy. Key Documents*, London: Routledge, 2000, pp. 93–97. Cf. Ine Megens, "The December 1973 Declaration on European Identity as the Result of Team Spirit among European Diplomats," in: van der Harst (ed.), *Beyond the Customs Union*, pp. 317–338; Găinar, *Origines*, pp. 134–147.

Crisis and New Beginning

Meanwhile, another initiative by Kissinger led to serious strains in Political Cooperation. In a speech on 12 December 1973, that is, shortly before the Copenhagen summit, the American official had called for the creation of an action group comprised of the most important industrial nations dependent on oil imports. Jobert and Pompidou correctly saw this as an attempt to push American hegemony in the Atlantic world by focusing on then-current worries of Western Europeans about oil supplies. At the same time, this American initiative endangered the French ambition to have Europe become an autonomous actor in this now-urgent field, an actor that could also work against polarization between industrial countries and oil-exporting countries.

In order to avoid the confrontation looming here, Heath urged that the summit examine the issue of cooperation among importing countries within the framework of the OECD. All the EC partners were able to agree on this, and in an attachment to the Copenhagen communiqué, such an action was characterized as "useful." When on 9 January 1974 Nixon nevertheless invited the Western oil importers to a conference, the EC Council of Ministers did in principle agree to participate, but Commission President Ortoli and Council President Scheel were given a restrictive mandate for the gathering: They were not to agree either to the establishment of a permanent organization of importer nations or to any other decisions that could make dialogue with oil-exporting nations more difficult. Additionally, Pompidou made it publicly clear to the US president that France was accepting the invitation only "in order to allow Europe to assert a common position."[98]

When the energy conference convened on 11 February in Washington, the American leadership overtly threatened the Europeans with a break. In a conversation beforehand, Kissinger told Scheel that the US could live without the Europeans but that the Europeans could hardly live without their most powerful ally. At the dinner table after the first day of the conference, Nixon reminded his guests of demands for the withdrawal of American troops that repeatedly came from the US Congress. Given that the West German government was represented by Helmut Schmidt, who regarded the chances for achieving a political Europe much more skeptically than did Brandt and Scheel, these threats sufficed to cause the collapse of the hard-wrought common front of the Nine. It was anyway the case that Heath and Brandt had only half-heartedly agreed to join that front, given their belief that they were dependent on the US for containing the explosion

---

[98] Pompidou to Nixon, 6 Feb. 1974, quoted in Hiepel, *Brandt und Pompidou*, pp. 295ff. On this and the following, cf. *ibid.*, pp. 383–402; Möckli, *European Foreign Policy*, pp. 252–300.

in oil prices and attempting to deal with their consequences. Schmidt warned of a collapse of the balance of power in Europe if US troops were withdrawn; this also convinced the smaller allies to accede to a great extent to the American demand for the establishment of a coordination group as well as for common preparation for a conference with the oil-exporting countries. On 13 February, a communiqué to that effect was signed by eight of the nine EPC representatives. There was nothing left for Jobert to do but withhold his approval of the procedural portions of the document. In a press conference, he complained that Schmidt had opted for the US and thereby against Europe.

Kissinger's triumph was short lived, however. Three weeks later, at an EPC foreign ministers meeting on 4 March, the Eight decided to embrace not only the US plan for establishing a joint front of importing states but also the French concept of an Arab-European dialogue. This envisioned the formation of joint working groups of the Nine and of all nineteen member states of the Arab League, which would aim for a joint foreign ministers conference. Kissinger viewed such a gathering as highly damaging to his own crisis management in the Middle East; in the European plans, he had been taken into account only insofar as the date of the proposed gathering was left open and its occurrence made dependent on productive results from the working groups. This did not prevent Kissinger from asserting that "whatever was achieved in Washington is more than undone by this decision."[99] In a television interview on 15 March, Nixon made a public threat, saying that the Europeans could not have both protection and confrontation at the same time.

In reality, Kissinger was not as far from success as he thought during his initial bout of frustration. True, American threats did not dissuade the Europeans from their project for a Euro-Arab dialogue. Yet, the Europeans were harboring increasing doubts as to whether the goal of an autonomous Europe, which had generated excitement in the second half of 1973, was actually achievable. In a session of his party caucus, Brandt came to the conclusion that he had to "go a bit further with America due to security" than with France; and in a conversation with Kissinger, Scheel explicitly distanced himself from the goal of an "independent European security system."[100] Pompidou, who perceived this at least in the atmosphere, concentrated once again wholly on the national components of his independence policy. In a conversation with Leonid Brezhnev during a state visit to Moscow on 13 March, the Frenchman refused to conceal the tensions among

---

[99] In a conversation with Scheel on 4 March 1974, AAPD 1974 II, pp. 287–289.
[100] SPD caucus session, 12 March 1974; conversation between Scheel and Kissinger, 24 March 1974, quoted in Hiepel, *Brandt und Pompidou*, pp. 311 and 315, respectively.

the Nine with "what only appears to be development of European integration" and declared a common defense with nuclear components to be obsolete.[101]

The project for a political Europe received another blow when Edward Heath was defeated at the polls. Whereas Harold Wilson had been wholly engaged in trying somehow to maintain the balance between a party majority hostile to Europe and British commitments stemming from treaty obligations, Foreign Minister Callaghan roundly rejected the Political Union as well as the economic and currency union due to vague fears of foreign control from "Brussels." After his initial experiences with the pragmatic coordination within EPC, he soon gave his approval to it; yet, regarding its further development into a common foreign policy, he persistently made reference to contrasting national interests and perceptions. A European Union was "unrealistic" and "not desired," as he declared during his first appearance in the EC Council of Ministers on 1 April 1974; and the project of a currency union was "dangerously overambitious."[102]

Without foreign-policy experience and demonstratively turning away from Heath's emphasis on European autonomy, Callaghan moreover believed that he could once again make the "special relationship" with the US the cornerstone of British foreign policy. The West German government sought to establish a consultation mechanism between EPC and Washington, which was intended to defuse the conflict that Kissinger had forced; but Callaghan for his part insisted on absolute freedom of action in British policy toward the US. In a crisis meeting at Schloss Gymnich near Bonn on 20 and 21 April, the foreign ministers were thus only able to approve rules for such a mechanism, ones that opened up possibilities for blocking EPC. Whereas Scheel had proposed that the Council president could consult the American government at a member's request after the Political Committee had already arrived at a common position, the adopted rules allowed member governments to demand a consultation "of an allied or friendly state" at any time.[103] If the partners did not support the demand, then discussion of the issue at hand was in practical terms at an end.

Moreover, Callaghan's aversion to the Political Union offered Kissinger an unexpected opportunity to bring the conflict over the European-American declarations to an end that coincided with his own views after all. Encouraged by Kissinger, the British prime minister had gotten initial agreement from his EC partners at Gymnich for a NATO declaration on the occasion of the twenty-fifth

---

101 AN, 5AG2, 1019; excerpts published in Roussel, *Pompidou*, pp. 617–623.
102 *Bulletin of the European Communities* 3 (1974), pp. 14–19.
103 Only after further negotiations was it written down in a non-paper of the West German Council presidency that was acknowledged by the foreign ministers on 10 June 1974, AAPD 1974 I, p. 717.

anniversary of the alliance, an initiative that was supposed to be independent of the policy statements that had not yet been made. When Callaghan presented the draft of such a declaration in the NATO Council on 15 June, it was so comprehensive that it could *de facto* replace the policy statements. The Eight reacted to the fact that the European Union was not mentioned at all in the document. Finally, Schmidt and Giscard d'Estaing were satisfied with a formulation stating "that further progress towards unity, which the member states of the European Community are determined to make, should in due course have a beneficial effect on the contribution to the common defense of the Alliance." In this form, the "Atlantic Declaration" was passed by the NATO foreign ministers in Ottawa on 19 June, together with a pledge "to strengthen the practice of frank and timely consultations."[104] Nixon attended the signing of the document in Brussels on 26 June.

The Ottawa Declaration did not constitute a pledge by the Europeans to stronger incorporation into the American strategy as Kissinger had envisioned. Still less did it speak of an autonomous role for the Europeans in international politics, as not only Pompidou and Jobert but also Heath and Brandt had sought. As was the case with the new chancellor, the new French president also viewed securing American cooperation in dealing with the acute economic crisis more important than rapid progress on the road to European autonomy. Given that the Ottawa Declaration included a commitment by the US to maintain troop levels high enough so as not to endanger the credibility of allied deterrence, the project for an autonomous European defense became less urgent once again.[105]

Moreover, Callaghan's campaign against any further development of the Community practically brought negotiations on the institutional configuration of the European Union to a halt. Consumed by its own crisis, the EPC Political Committee did not produce any paper at all on this. The Permanent Representatives of the Ministers to the Commission and an *ad hoc* group of high-ranking bureaucrats, to whom the Council of Ministers had in February assigned the task of working out a proposal, delivered nothing more than a nine-page catalogue of questions in the last week of June. Given the impossibility of agreeing on the substance of the European Union, it was nothing less than a stroke of luck that the summit planned for the end of the West German Council presidency had to be postponed due to the death of Pompidou and the resignation of Brandt. In a conversation with Gaston Thorn on 25 June, Wilson remarked that the concept of Union should be dropped and replaced by "some long German word like 'Gemütlichkeit.'"[106]

---

104 *Europa-Archiv* 29 (1974), pp. D339–341.
105 Möckli, *European Foreign Policy*, pp. 301–338.
106 Conversation between Wilson and Thorn, 25 June 1974, PRO PREM 16/11, quoted in Möckli, *European Foreign Policy*, p. 349; cf. *ibid.*, pp. 346–350.

In any event, the efforts by Schmidt and Giscard to ensure good relations with the US did not change the fact that these new leaders of the Franco-German duo were interested in strengthening European identity as well. The two men knew one another from encounters in Monnet's Action Committee, which Schmidt had joined as SPD parliamentary chairman in the era of the Grand Coalition. For both leaders, the awareness of the necessity of economic integration was for the time being at the center of their engagement in European politics; this did not however mean that concern for Europe's ability to take action was foreign to them. In his government declaration of 17 May, Schmidt characterized the "goal of a European Political Union" as "more urgent than ever." At a Franco-German summit on 9 July, Giscard declared his willingness to contribute to "a new stage in the construction of Europe."[107]

Both therefore responded positively when Monnet called for them to take "common action" in order to bring Europe out of the crisis and "inspire hope once again."[108] During a summer vacation, Schmidt worked out "a longish private paper on his conceptions of current Europe policy," as he reported to Italian Prime Minister Mariano Rumor. Schmidt sent the document to Giscard with the request for a conversation and a proposal for "inviting the government leaders of the EC states to a long private dinner—without bureaucrats, only interpreters. If anything positive emerges from the private conversations, the foreign ministers and finance ministers can be asked to pursue those things further. If there is no agreement on this or that point and it remains unknown to the public, then no harm could come of it."[109]

In terms of content, Schmidt wanted increased coordination of EC activities by the Council of Foreign Ministers and their Permanent Representatives, the transition to majority decision-making in the Council, and the incorporation of EPC into the Council of Ministers. In a conversation on the evening of 2 September, he reminded Giscard of the need to develop a common viewpoint on arms control negotiations and strategic questions in general. He also urged the French president to participate in measures that the Eight and the US had embraced in conjunction with the Washington Energy Conference. For his part, Giscard insisted that there first of all must be a common energy-policy program among the Nine. He asked that consideration of the defense problematic be deferred because there

---

[107] Bulletin der Bundesregierung 18.5.1974, pp. 593–604; Soell, *Helmut Schmidt*, p. 364. Cf. Matthias Schulz, "Vom 'Atlantiker' zum 'Europäer'? Helmut Schmidt, deutsche Interessen und die europäische Einigung," in: König and Schulz (eds.), *Bundesrepublik Deutschland*, pp. 185–220.
[108] Monnet to Giscard d'Estaing, 21 June 1974, AMK 29/3/53.
[109] Schmidt to Giscard, 26 Aug. 1974, AN 5AG3 AE 66; conversation between Schmidt and Rumor, 30 Aug. 1974, provided by Soell, *Helmut Schmidt*, p. 371. On the following, *ibid.*, pp. 373–380.

was still a need for clarification about it in Paris. Regarding the incorporation of EPC into the work of the Foreign Ministers Council, he insisted on separate agendas and discussion in the absence of the Commission president. He wanted to concede majority decision-making in the Council of Ministers only for "individual areas to be incrementally expanded." On the other hand, with encouragement from Monnet,[110] Giscard appealed for resumption of the project of regular meetings of the heads of state and of government that had gotten derailed at the Copenhagen summit.

Schmidt and Giscard agreed that if there was a favorable response to the proposals from the other leaders, then the next summit should also be allowed to take place during France's Council presidency; the appropriate decisions were to be dealt with there. During a dinner at the Élysée Palace on 14 September attended by the nine heads of state and of government as well as Commission President Ortoli, Giscard explained that the regular meetings (at least three and as many as four annually) would over time make the new organ the "highest instance" of the Community. As the representatives of the small states' worried that the Commission would be rendered impotent, he offered direct elections and greater authority for Parliament; it was to receive control over the budget as well as initiative rights that were more binding in nature. In the Council of Ministers three days later, Foreign Minister Jean Sauvagnargues officially proposed the creation of the new organ. In so doing, he suggested that it be named "perhaps 'European Council.'"[111]

The concession on the issue of direct elections and parliamentary rights proved sufficient to ease the concerns of the smaller states this time. Wilson—who was clearly on the defensive among the heads of state and of government and who in the meantime had begun wholly concentrating on winning material concessions that could be presented to British voters as an argument for remaining in the Community—raised no fundamental objections. Neither did the Commission voice negative views any longer; by including the Commission in his preparations for the decision, Giscard had taken care to ensure that it would see the new entity as an opportunity rather than a danger to its own place in the decision-making process of the Community.

---

110 Monnet to Sauvagnargues, 1 July 1974, FJME, AMK C/H6.
111 Hattersley to Foreign Office, 17 Sept. 1974, PRO PREM 16/75. On the dinner at the Élysée Palace and above all the notes by Schmidt of 16 Sept. 1974, AAPD 1974 II, pp. 1178–1185; on the following, also Emmanuel Mourlon-Druol, "Filling the EEC Leadership Vacuum? The Creation of the European Council in 1974," in: *Cold War History* 10/3 (2010), pp. 315–339; Găinar, *Origines*, pp. 315–324.

The Paris summit of 9 and 10 December 1974 was thus able to approve the introduction of the European Council, albeit without officially giving it a name. There were to be three summits per year, and more if necessary; a further concession to the smaller states was that one of these meetings was to be held in Brussels or Luxembourg, the other two in the country of the half-yearly Council president. The Commission president was to participate and—something that Giscard had not originally envisioned—so too would the foreign ministers. The issue of a separate secretariat, which France and Britain wanted but the smaller states did not, was left open. The Council was to concern itself with foreign policy and all other questions of common interest; EPC was *de facto* integrated into the work of the Council of Ministers. Likewise, it was decided that the European Parliament would be directly elected starting in 1978; its areas of responsibility were to be expanded; and the practice of unanimous decision-making in the Council was to be dropped.

The British and Danish governments expressed reservations about the introduction of direct elections to Parliament in 1978, and these viewpoints were noted in the common concluding communiqué. Regarding the goal of a European Union, the offer of Belgian Prime Minister Leo Tindemans was accepted: to produce by the end of 1975 a "summary report" based on consultations with all governments, the Commission, the Parliament, as well as important political representatives in all member states. This spared the British government from having to take a position on the further development of the Communities before the completion of renegotiations; at the same time, this also prevented the issues of increased integration and unification from being shoved aside. The communiqué contained a commitment to a "complete conception of the European Union" as well as the strengthening of the goal of economic and currency union. Dates and deadlines earlier agreed upon were not explicitly repeated, however.[112]

Tindemans purposely left plenty of time for the production of the report. He did not visit Britain before the positive outcome of the referendum on 5 June 1975, and his sounding out of Denmark, France, Italy, and the Federal Republic occurred only after he had spoken to the British government as well as representatives of influential parties and organizations in the UK in late June and early July. In mid-November, Helmut Schmidt sought to accelerate the decision-making process by sending his Council colleagues and the Commission president a position paper that stemmed from consultations within the Bonn government. Schmidt hoped that the document could be discussed at the upcoming Council meeting in early December in Rome. After the British government had signaled its

---

112 *Europa-Archiv* 30 (1975), pp. D41–43; on Tindemans' initiative, Kreutzfeldt, *Point of return*, pp. 457–459 and 464ff.

unwillingness to take a position on institutional questions so early, the chancellor gave up the idea of discussing it in Rome. Tindemans then presented his report on 29 December in the form of a confidential letter to his colleagues on the Council. He had initially hoped that discussion of the document could be kept confidential until the next meeting of the Council in the spring of 1976. Then however he opted to present it to the public on 7 January 1976.[113]

Tindemans' report hovered a little above the level that in the meantime was capable of a consensus between Giscard d'Estaing and the West German government. The document spoke out clearly for "strengthening the common institutional apparatus" to the extent necessary, even by means of "adjusting the treaties." Also, the difference between the meetings of the ministers on Political Cooperation and the meetings of the Council ought to be eliminated altogether; the currency snake ought to be transformed into an EC institution that "clearly bears the visible character of the Community." Majority decision-making ought to be "the norm" in Community affairs and also in foreign policy areas in which the members had committed themselves to a common policy. Parliament ought to receive a genuine right of initiative as well as the right to confirm the appointment of the president of the Commission by the European Council. That official ought to be able to choose his own colleagues, though in accordance with the schedule of national distribution; also, the Commission ought to receive more executive authority.[114]

Tindemans may have hoped to be able to get a majority of Council members to commit themselves more or less to this program due to the pressure of public opinion if nothing else. The participation of the Nine at the Conference on Security and Cooperation in Europe had been characterized by unity, solidarity, and deftness and had decisively contributed to its successful conclusion on 1 August 1975.[115] This along with France's return to the currency snake did give encouragement to go beyond consolidation of what had been achieved in the era of Brandt and Pompidou. Regarding possible progress on the way to an economic and currency union—seen by Tindemans as especially urgent—the report embraced the idea of a vanguard made up of a core group of the economically stronger member

---

[113] *Ibid.*, pp. 500–517; the memorandum of the West German government of 3 Nov. 1975 in AAPD 1975, pp. 1587–1595.

[114] "Die Europäische Union. Bericht von Leo Tindemans, Premierminister von Belgien, an den Europäischen Rat," Brussels, 1976; reprinted in, among others, Jürgen Schwarz (ed.), *Der Aufbau Europas. Pläne und Dokumente 1945–80*, Bonn: Osang, 1980, pp. 527–552.

[115] Möckli, *European Foreign Policy*, pp. 99–139; Angela Romano, "The Nine and the Conference of Helsinki: A challenging game with the Soviets," in: van der Harst (ed.), *Beyond the Customs Union*, pp. 83–104.

states, as Brandt had already proposed in November of 1974.[116] It was clearly an open question as to whether the governments supportive of integration would take up this tactical possibility. Just as unclear was the extent to which the British and the Danish governments would be prepared to follow the majority on the way to more efficiency and more democracy in the European construction. In a conversation with Tindemans, Callaghan had indeed spoken as though he were leaning in that direction; however, his conceptions regarding institutional arrangements and the date of their introduction remained rather vague.

Jean Monnet took the establishment of the European Council and the determination that there would be direct elections to the European Parliament in the future as the occasion for dissolving the Action Committee for the United States of Europe on 9 May 1975. His advanced age—he would be celebrating his eighty-seventh birthday in November of 1975—undoubtedly contributed to this decision, but the primary reason was undeniable: Given that the "holders of the highest decision-making power in each state" were watching over the progress of European integration, it seemed to him that the committee "was now less necessary and less in a position to carry out a task that according to all the treaties was entrusted to the organs of the Community, the governments, and the new institutions."[117] He clearly was counting on the abilities of Giscard and Schmidt in the years ahead to fulfill the responsibilities growing out of that.

---

116 "Rede vor der Französischen Sektion der Europäischen Bewegung 19.11.1974," *Europa-Archiv* 30 (1975), p. D36.
117 Monnet, *Mémoires*, p. 606.

5 Consolidation, 1976–1984

The Path to Direct Elections

Helmut Schmidt and his cabinet regarded the Tindemans Report as "realistic and constructive." However, they rejected the proposal to move forward with a monetary union among the economically-stronger states, likewise the proposal for accelerating this move by making short- and medium-term currency assistance automatic and transferring a large portion of foreign currency holdings to the monetary fund. On the other hand, they approved the proposed institutional reforms without exception, even where these went beyond the 3 November program of the West German government—for example, in having the Commission president confirmed by the European Parliament. After a cabinet meeting on 3 March, Schmidt wrote to Council President Gaston Thorn, who was serving in the first half of 1976, that it was very important for the Federal Republic to have the foundations of the European Union laid that year.[1]

In a telephone conversation with Schmidt, however, Valéry Giscard d'Estaing withdrew two concessions that he had made in the autumn of 1974: He now rejected the idea of a right of initiative for the European Parliament and also viewed the transition to majority decision-making in the Council as no longer opportune. Additionally, confirmation of the Commission president by Parliament was completely out of the question for him. Instead, he wanted the jam in decision-making to be resolved through the creation of a "Directorate" of the large member states. It was clear that the harsh criticism coming from traditional Gaullists around Michel Debré to the policy decision for the direct election of Parliament had persuaded the French president to return to de Gaulle's positions regarding the authority of Parliament and the issue of majority decision-making.

Schmidt succeeded in convincing Giscard to abandon the idea of a directorate. It could not have won approval anyway given the justified aversion of the smaller member states to such a plan. Shared positions on institutional issues were no longer sufficient to allow a common initiative on sweeping implementation of the Tindemans Program, however. At the next meeting of the European Council, on 1 and 2 April 1976 in Luxembourg, Schmidt and Giscard concentrated

---

[1] Undated draft letter from Schmidt to Thorn and draft of a declaration by the chancellor, quoted in Matthias Schulz, "The Reluctant European. Helmut Schmidt, the European Community, and Transatlantic Relations," in: Matthias Schulz and Thomas A. Schwartz (eds.), *The Strained Alliance. U.S.-European Relations from Nixon to Carter*, New York: Cambridge University Press, 2009, pp. 279–307, here pp. 284ff. On this and the following, cf. Soell, *Helmut Schmidt*, pp. 437–440.

on having a decision made at least on the issue of organizing direct elections. After a brief though not unfriendly discussion, the Tindemans Report was referred to the foreign ministers for further consultation. The only thing decided was that the review of the report was to be concluded before the end of the year.[2]

Thorn and Tindemans were very displeased that discussion of the report did not advance in the Council of Foreign Ministers either. The document was handed off to the Committee of Permanent Representatives, where the well-known antagonisms collided. New British Prime Minister James Callaghan—replacing Harold Wilson, who had resigned for health reasons on 16 March—did seek to shake off the reputation of being an impediment; he was not prepared however to support substantial reforms that would threaten the unity of the Labour Party, which had been arduously maintained after the positive outcome of the referendum.[3] The Council, meeting again on 29 and 30 November 1976 in The Hague, could thus take only an overall positive position, which required no commitments in the short term at least. The declaration stated that "The European Council indicated its very great interest in the analyses and proposals put forward by Mr. Tindemans. It shared the views expressed by the Belgian Prime Minister on the need to build European Union by strengthening the practical solidarity of the nine Member States and their peoples, both internally and in their relations with the outside world, and gradually to provide the Union with the instruments and institutions necessary for its operation." The Commission was given the task of annually preparing a report on progress toward a European Union.[4]

For the committed proponents of strengthening European institutions, there was great disappointment over the outcome of this process, which in essence had begun seven years earlier with the resolutions of the summit in The Hague. That sentiment, along with the resulting catchword "Eurosclerosis" for describing the second half of the 1970s, should not hide the fact that the positive position on the Tindemans Report did constitute a significant step toward consolidating the European Community: Both the British and the Danish governments, which had demonstratively opposed the extension of economic integration to other policy areas up to that point, had now explicitly acknowledged the goal of a European Union. In general, moreover, the consensus had grown as to what was to be understood by this consciously vague formulation: a coalescence of political and economic integration, the development of a common foreign and defense policy, as well as the strengthening of the institutions necessary for it. Disagreements as to priorities and methods might well continue, even in polemical form; and prog-

---

2 *Bulletin of the European Communities*, 1976/4, p. 83.
3 Kreutzfeldt, *Point of Return*, pp. 528–531.
4 *Bulletin of the European Communities*, 1976/11, p. 93.

ress on the way to this Union might thereby become a protracted, often tortuous and wearisome process. Yet, there was no longer any doubt as to the direction of this progress. The danger that the Community would break apart—undeniable during the economic crisis of 1973–74—no longer existed.

At Rome in early December of 1975, the European Council determined that elections to the European Parliament would take place "at a uniform time between May and June 1978."[5] During discussion of the election law, however, opposition emerged from various directions to the proposal that Parliament had presented only a few weeks after the policy decision at the Paris summit of December 1974. France bridled at differing standards for considering the population totals of the large member states, which would result in a French contingent smaller than that of the British and, above all, of the West Germans. All the large member states found the disproportional consideration of the small states too high. Denmark continued to insist on the principle of indirect elections: This was to ensure that the elections to the European Parliament in the country would be linked to those to the Folketing and that the Danish Parliament would then send deputies from its own ranks to Strasbourg.

An agreement on the distribution of parliamentary mandates was reached only at the Council meeting in Brussels on 12 and 13 July 1976. There were to be 410 seats, just over three times the number sent to Parliament up to that point, and the four "big" ones—West Germany, France, Great Britain, and Italy—would each receive eighty-one. The "small ones" had to content themselves with fewer seats than had been envisioned in Parliament's proposal: the Netherlands with twenty-five, Belgium with twenty-four (half for Flanders and half for Wallonia), Denmark with sixteen, Ireland with fifteen, and Luxembourg with six. They would still however be over-represented: This ensured that in the smaller member states too, various political groupings of any significance would have a chance. Yet, there was no agreement on a uniform electoral procedure, as was required by the Treaties of Rome; nor was a date set for abolishing the provisional system of using the various national election procedures. The Council had to concede to the Danes what was nothing but a concealed deviation from the principle of direct elections for at least a transition period. Only with this condition was it possible for the Council to pass the "Act Concerning the Election of the Representatives of the Assembly by Direct Universal Suffrage" on 20 September 1976.[6]

---

[5] *Europa-Archiv* 31 (1976), pp. D7ff.
[6] See Martin Bangemann and Roland Bieber, *Die Direktwahl – Chance oder Sackgasse für Europa. Analysen und Dokumente*, Baden-Baden: Nomos, 1976; Gerhard Brunn, "Das Europäische Parlament auf dem Weg zur ersten Direktwahl 1979," in: Knipping and Schönwald (eds.), *Aufbruch*, pp. 47–72; Thierry Chopin, "Le Parlement européen," in: Serge Berstein and Jean-François

Before the measure could be implemented, there were further hurdles to be overcome in France and Britain. The Gaullist opposition around Michel Debré attacked the act during its ratification as unconstitutional, a position that notably put them on the same page as the Communists: The argument went that the act amounted to a surrender of national sovereignty not envisioned in the constitution of the Fifth Republic. Giscard d'Estaing responded by presenting the bill to the Constitutional Council for review. In a ruling of 30 December 1976, this body confirmed the constitutionality of the measure but did so on grounds that impeded the envisioned extension of Parliament's authority: Sovereignty could "only be national"; direct elections created "neither a sovereignty nor institutions whose nature" would be "incompatible with observance of national sovereignty."[7] The government then added a stipulation to the ratification law that banned any expansion of the authority of Parliament not assumed to be compatible with the constitution.

In Britain, the ruling Labour Party ran into trouble over the electoral procedure with the Liberals, with whom they were now in coalition after having lost their outright majority. Whereas most Labour MPs wanted to utilize the British majority-vote system for elections to the European Parliament, the Liberals insisted on a proportional system. In February of 1977, Callaghan opted for a bill providing for a proportional electoral system but allowed his party as well as his cabinet, whose members were quite divided on the issue, freedom to vote as they wished. The following November, a majority of the House of Commons approved British participation in the elections but rejected the proportional system. Consequently, a new bill had to be worked out; but it could not be passed in time for the agreed-upon election date of May or June 1978.[8] At a Council meeting on 7 and 8 April 1978 in Copenhagen, it was therefore decided that the elections would be postponed for a year; they were now set for the period of 7 to 10 June 1979.

The prospect of the first direct elections to the European Parliament led the great families of parties in Europe to increase their transnational cooperation. After a "Confederation of the Socialist Parties of the European Community" had been founded in April of 1974, there followed as early as March of 1976 a "Federation of Liberal and Democratic Parties in the European Community" and in April of that year the "European People's Party," an alliance of Christian Democratic parties. They all built upon connections that had already been established in the Parliamentary Assembly of the ECSC. Given the heterogeneity of the participating

---

Sirinelli (eds.), *Les années Giscard. Valéry Giscard d'Estaing et l'Europe 1974–1981*, Paris: Armand Colin, 2006, pp. 153–189.
7 *Ibid.*, p. 173.
8 Young, *Britain and European Unity*, p. 132.

parties and the often very different national contexts in which they operated, the common identity of these alliances remained relatively weak, at least as measured against the coherence of parties on the national level. Thus, for example, the Confederation of the Socialist Parties was unable to agree on a common platform for the European elections and instead had to content itself with a vague "appeal" to the voters. For their part, Christian Democrats were able to adopt such a platform but then began disputing among themselves as to whether they should participate along with the British and other European conservatives in a "European Democrat Union" that had been founded in 1978.[9]

At the same time, the parties made use of the European election campaign for conducting skirmishes on the national level. To an extent, the campaign was exploited as a test vote and for other party-political purposes. For example, by means of a campaign against the alleged enslavement of France by foreign powers and supranational politics, Jacques Chirac positioned his Gaullist party *vis-à-vis* the successful combination of Christian Democrats, Liberals, and Independent Republicans (the party of Giscard). In Britain, the European elections stood wholly in the shadow of recent parliamentary elections, which five weeks earlier had given the Conservatives, now under Margaret Thatcher, a clear majority once again. In Italy, national parliamentary elections took place on 3 June 1979, that is, only a few days before the European vote.

The emergence of a European public was not fostered by this kind of approach to the European election campaign. On the contrary, it served to increase the alienation between European politics and the citizens of the Community, which had grown anyway due to the endless quarrels over expansion and deepening as well as the increasing complexity of regulations on the European level. Under these circumstances, it was the case that voter participation rates were diverging greatly, corresponding to the situation in the national debates on European policy: In Britain, only 31.6 percent of voters saw fit to participate in elections to the European Parliament, and in Denmark, 47.1 percent. With some 57.8 percent, the Netherlands was more or less representative of the whole; likewise France (60.7 percent), Ireland (63.6 percent), and the Federal Republic (65.7 percent). Turnout was significantly over eighty percent in countries with mandatory voting: Italy (85.5 percent), Luxembourg (88.9 percent), and Belgium (91.6 percent). Another factor in these latter two cases was that the seat of European institutions had in the meantime become a significant bond for heterogeneous people groups. Overall, turnout was some 62.4 percent. That was sufficient to legitimize

---

9 Jürgen Mittag (ed.), *Politische Parteien und europäische Integration. Entwicklung und Perspektiven transnationaler Parteienkooperation in Europa*, Essen: Klartext, 2006; Kaiser, *Christian Democracy*, pp. 315–317.

the directly-elected Parliament but did not however contribute significantly to strengthening its position *vis-à-vis* the national governments.[10]

Valéry Giscard d'Estaing made use of the election results to profile his European policy more symbolically once again. After having already demonstratively declined in 1975 to commemorate the anniversary of the German capitulation of 8 May 1945, he now promoted the election of Simone Veil as first president of the directly-elected European Parliament. He had persuaded this liberal minister, a Jew who as an adolescent had survived Auschwitz and Bergen-Belsen, to head the list of candidates for the united "Union pour la Démocratie Française" (UDF). After this list had achieved an impressive victory over the competing Gaullists led by Chirac, Giscard sought to make the election of Veil palatable to Helmut Schmidt in terms of affirming Franco-German reconciliation. Foreign Minister Jean-François Poncet sought to work along the same lines with his counterparts, and Giscard's friend Michel Poniatowski did so among the newly-elected deputies. These efforts were successful: Simone Veil was elected president in the second round of voting on 17 July 1979, even though the liberals were by no means the largest faction in the new Parliament.[11]

Not only did the election of Simon Veil contribute to strengthening Giscard's position *vis-à-vis* his declared rival Chirac and bolstering his image as a "European." Veil was in fact a committed European and with her moral authority contributed greatly to increasing the self-confidence of the European representatives and promoting coherence among them. True, their role remained vague due to their restricted authority, the lack of career prospects, and the large size of their electoral districts, which limited their function as representatives. Yet, by means of a host of inquiries and petitions, they were able to develop a function as perennial admonishers, which went significantly beyond the possibilities available to preceding Parliaments with their indirectly-elected members and their sporadic meetings.[12]

---

10 Cf. Rudolf Hrbek, "Die EG nach den Direktwahlen: Bilanz und Perspektiven," in: *Integration* 2 (1979), pp. 95–109; Birte Wassenberg, "La campagne pour les élections européennes de 1979 en France et en Allemagne: l'image de l'Europe," in: Marie-Thérèse Bitsch, Wilfried Loth, and Charles Barthel (eds.), *Cultures politiques, opinions publiques et intégration européenne*, Brussels: Émile Bruylant, 2007, pp. 264–284.
11 Maurice Szafran, *Simone Veil. Destin*, Paris: Flammarion, 1994, pp. 328–330.
12 Cf. Emil J. Kirchner, *The European Parliament. Performances and Prospects*, Aldershot: Gower, 1984; Richard Corbett, *The European Parliament's Role in Closer EU Integration*, Basingstoke and New York: Palgrave Macmillan, 2001; Aurélie Élisa Gfeller, "Une militante du parlementarisme européen: Simone Veil," in: *Journal of European Integration History* 17 (2011), pp. 61–72.

The greater self-confidence of the directly-elected Parliament also led to greater use of its budgetary instruments. In accordance with an agreement between the Council and the Commission of 22 April 1975, Parliament would from 1977 onward have the right to be heard before the Council passed new legal acts "that have weighty financial impacts and whose issuance is not required on the basis of earlier legal acts." Thanks to a treaty amendment of 22 July 1975, Parliament could also reject the entire budget "for important reasons" by a two-thirds majority of votes cast; additionally, it was given authority to scrutinize the Commission's budgetary policy. In exercising this authority, it was supported by the newly-established European Court of Auditors (ECA).[13] With its very first budget meeting, the new Parliament made use of its right to reject the budget in its entirety, so the Community had to employ an emergency budget until the middle of 1980. Parliament was thereby able to win an increase in expenditures for structural policy and increase the pressure for an expansion of revenue.

From that point onward, Parliament regularly wrestled with the Council over the division of expenditure between the Common Agricultural Policy, which continued to garner the lion's share of the budget, and the promotion of structural improvements through the Regional Fund, Social Fund, industry policy, and the promotion of research—all of which the large majority of MPs regarded as more pressing concerns. Initially, there was only modest progress on this agenda. Over the medium term, however, Parliament succeeded in compelling a debate on the reform of Commission policies, one that took place on the level of both the Council of Ministers and the European Council.

All in all, the European Parliament gained influence over the Commission's proposals and, to a lesser extent, over the decisions of the Council of Ministers as well. This increase in the power of European institutions was partially offset however by the fact that the European Council increasingly took on decision-making on essential issues. True, the Commission participated in these decisions, which still needed to be unanimous, in the role of an advisor and assistant. However, the European Council, as an informal organ not anchored in the treaties, did not need to consult Parliament (unlike the Council of Ministers); nor did it need to offer justifications to Parliament. The decisions of the European Council were *de facto* made without any parliamentary participation. A chasm loomed between the European-policy debate in Parliament and the highest decision-making levels of the Community, something that was detrimental to the legitimization of European policy in the eyes of voters.

The fragility of this construction became manifest in a twofold traveling circus: Whereas the European Council met sequentially in the capital of the

---

13 Text of the agreement and of the treaty amendment in Lipgens, *45 Jahre*, pp. 604–610.

Council president of the first half of the year, then in Brussels or Luxembourg, and then in the capital of the Council president of the second half of the year, the seat of the European Parliament remained in Strasbourg. Parliament was normally in session one week per month. Yet, the meetings of committees and party caucuses between sessions increasingly took place in Brussels due to cooperation with the Council of Ministers and the Commission. The Parliamentary administration continued to have its seat in Luxembourg. The increased burden that resulted from this situation meant that the number of European MPs who also held a seat in a national legislature—still almost one-third in the Parliament of 1979—decreased from election to election. To a corresponding degree, it became an ever-greater problem to connect European politics to the national parliaments.

The European Monetary System

The blocking of substantial Franco-German initiatives by Giscard d'Estaing's Gaullist coalition partners created new space for an initiative by the European Commission. It was thus momentous that as the successor to François-Xavier Ortoli in the role of Commission president, the British government put forth a very politically astute candidate: Roy Jenkins, the spokesman of the Europe advocates in the Labour Party and longtime rival of Wilson and Callaghan in the struggle for party leadership. After Wilson's resignation, Jenkins had lost the leadership contest and now saw a more rewarding task in serving as the head of the Commission. For his part, Callaghan was rid of a troublesome critic within the cabinet and at the same time gained an effective representative of British interests in Brussels.

With the additional political heavyweights Étienne Davignon (as Commissioner for Industry) and Antonio Giolitti (responsible for regional policy), the new Commission regarded its task as first of all the consolidation of economic integration in light of the manifold crises after the end of the era of prolonged growth. It was especially in the crises of the steel industry and the chemical industry that the Commission proved to be the guardian of a policy of competition against strong protectionist impulses. Jenkins repeatedly had occasion to lament the continuing ineffectiveness of the Council of Ministers given that separate meetings with differing compositions were held for dealing with the various areas of responsibility; he was also concerned about the failure to concretize the prospects for development of the Tindemans Plan. After only six months in office, he was so frustrated that he seriously contemplated resigning. In the end, he opted instead to attempt to push forward the European integration process with an initiative of his own.

In searching for an appropriate policy area for such an initiative, Jenkins—like Tindemans two years earlier—hit upon the project of economic and monetary union. It was here that the need for substantive progress was most urgent in light of general inflationary tendencies and the renewed drop of the dollar; at the same time, the political resistance against collectivization in this area seemed to him the most likely to be overcome. He therefore made use of a speech at the recently-opened European University Institute in Florence on 27 October 1977 to call for the reopening of the debate on economic and monetary union. In noticeable contrast to the "Economists" in Germany and the Netherlands, for whom a monetary union was conceivable only as the result of the harmonization of economic power and economic structure, he lauded a Community currency as an instrument of rationalization in the struggle against inflation and currency speculation, an instrument that would enable a return to stable growth and simultaneously reduce dependency on the dollar. Three weeks after the speech, the Commission presented a timetable for completion of the monetary union. It envisioned re-establishing the necessary convergence of European economic policy within a period of five years. The monetary union was to be realized incrementally thereafter.[14]

Jenkins' initiative was aimed first of all at overcoming the skeptical attitude of Helmut Schmidt. Although the chancellor did regard monetary union as fundamentally desirable, it seemed to him impossible to realize in the foreseeable future due to diverging economic development, differing economic-policy courses, and limited West German resources. He also regarded it as less urgent since Richard Nixon's successor Gerald Ford had been pursuing a very successful anti-inflation policy, which had led to an equalization of the balance of payments and a relative stabilization of the dollar's exchange rate. More important now than the assertion of European autonomy in Schmidt's view was agreement on economic policy among the large industrial countries. Therefore, he consented immediately when in July of 1975 Giscard d'Estaing proposed working toward a summit conference of the leading Western industrial countries. Schmidt felt satisfaction that the resulting Rambouillet Meeting of 15 to 17 November 1975 tended toward an understanding between Ford and Giscard regarding the necessity of focusing on stability. The gathering included the US, the Federal Republic, Great Britain, France, and Japan; Italy, which happened to be exercising the presidency of the Council at the time, also joined in after persistent urging.[15]

---

[14] *Europa-Archiv* 33 (1978), pp. D1–19; on the origins of this initiative, Roy Jenkins, *A Life at the Centre*, London: Methuen Publishing, 1994, pp. 461– 470; Andrew Adonis and Keith Thomas (eds.), *Roy Jenkins: A Retrospective*, Oxford: Oxford University Press, 2001.
[15] Soell, *Helmut Schmidt*, pp. 415–433.

As discrepancies in economic performance in early 1976 led once again to pressure first on the Italian lira and then on the French franc too, Schmidt was willing to allow a certain increase in the value of the mark, though not to the extent that Giscard regarded as necessary. In any event, the views of the other members of the currency snake diverged regarding a new setting of internal parities. The parities thus remained unchanged, and France once again left the snake on 15 March 1976 in order to permit a further devaluation against the dollar. The European currency snake was thereby reduced practically to a "mark zone" made up of the Federal Republic, the Netherlands, the Belgium-Luxembourg currency group, and Denmark. Until 1977, Sweden also belonged to it, as did Norway until 1978; Austria and Switzerland were associates.

After France had had to leave the currency snake for a second time, Giscard d'Estaing increased the focus of French economic and budget policy on stability by appointing Raymond Barre prime minister in August of 1976 after the resignation of Jacques Chirac. However, Schmidt was still not prepared to accommodate countries with weaker currencies via more substantial support measures. At the Franco-German summit of 3 and 4 February 1977, Giscard pressed for combining the currency reserves; Schmidt responded by pointing out the disparity of the economic situation within the Community: "In light of [the] difficult economic situation in several EC countries, no far-reaching steps on integration [are] possible, given that they would overtax the power of our partners."[16]

That Schmidt did not stick with this restrictive attitude is attributable primarily to the fact that US President Jimmy Carter abandoned his predecessor's focus on stability and instead sought to improve the American economy with higher government spending and higher levels of oil imports. The consequences were not only a high rate of inflation once again and a return to a balance of trade deficit but also a rapid drop in the dollar, which severely harmed West German exports. At the London world economic summit of 7 May 1977 (dubbed the "G-7 Meeting" because Canada was now participating), Schmidt attempted to convince Carter to alter course; this only resulted in the accusation that Bonn and Tokyo were not doing enough deficit spending. Schmidt was also irritated by the

---

16 Speaking notes, 31 Jan. 1977, quoted in Guido Thiemeyer, "Helmut Schmidt und die Gründung des Europäischen Wirtschaftssystems 1973–1979," in: Knipping and Schönwald (eds.), *Aufbruch*, pp. 245–268, here p. 248; on the following, also Peter Ludlow, *The Making of the European Monetary System. A Case Study of the Politics of the European Community*, London: Butterworth Scientific, 1982; Schulz, *Reluctant European*, pp. 293–305; Soell, *Helmut Schmidt*, pp. 691–708; Harold James, *Making the European Monetary System. The Role of the Committee of Central Bank Governors and the Origins of the European Central Bank*, Cambridge, MA and London: Belknap Press, 2012, pp. 146–180; Emmanuel Mourlon-Druol, *A Europe made of Money. The Emergence of the European Monetary System*, Ithaca and London: Cornell University Press, 2012, pp. 132–260.

strong pressure from Carter to station the neutron bomb in Europe and drew from it the conclusion that reform of the international monetary system—upon which he had placed so much hope—could not be achieved with this US president.

Jenkins must certainly have perceived that Schmidt's confidence in the American leadership was dwindling away even as the recovery in Europe was increasingly being harmed by the fall of the dollar. Nevertheless, the chancellor did not immediately react positively to Jenkins' 27 October appeal in Florence. When the Commission president visited the chancellor in Bonn on 10 November seeking his support for the project, Schmidt only assured him that he would not derail it. At a meeting of the European Council in Brussels on 5 and 6 December, Jenkins received unqualified support only from the leaders of the Benelux states and Italy. Schmidt declared that he was for a European monetary union in principle but also warned that it must not lead to an inflation rate of eight percent. The meeting resulted in giving the Commission the task of working out proposals for improving monetary cooperation; neither concrete measures nor chronological targets were decided on, however.

What exactly had induced Schmidt to become more involved in Jenkins' initiative is in the final instance difficult to determine. If one accepts Raymond Barre's account,[17] it was the impression that the French stability course had born fruit: The reduction of the budget deficit, a halving of the foreign-trade deficit, and a drop in the inflation rate all made France once again seem a reliable partner in constructing a monetary union. More probable, however, is that during February of 1978, Schmidt became convinced that the ongoing weakness of the French economy also threatened its political stability and that Giscard was therefore in urgent need of West German help. In any event, Schmidt confided to Jenkins during the Briton's visit to Bonn on 28 February that "as soon as the French elections are over—assuming the French elections go all right and that there aren't any Communists in the French government—then I shall propose, in response to the dollar problem, a major step towards monetary union; to mobilize and put all our currency reserves into a common pool, [...] and to form a European monetary bloc."[18]

As justification for this step, the chancellor cited not only the dollar crisis, which was growing worse, but also the "confrontation between Europe and Japan, the practical collapse of multinational trade negotiations," and "the great weakness and uncertainty in France." What also came through to Jenkins in this conversation was Schmidt's "deep hostility toward Carter, whose behaviour over

---

17 Conversation with Michèle Weinachter, in: Michèle Weinachter, *Valéry Giscard d'Estaing et l'Allemagne. Le double rêve inachevé*, Paris: Éditions L'Harmattan, 2004, pp. 134ff.
18 Roy Jenkins, *European Diary 1977–1981*, London: Methuen Publishing, 1989, p. 224.

the dollar was intolerable." When negotiations on the "major step" were already in progress, Schmidt justified it in a conversation with Italian Prime Minister Giulio Andreotti by citing the fear of "a collapse of the Common Market" and the potentially dangerous domestic- and foreign-policy consequences that would stem from it. In order to prevent such a collapse, it was necessary to "take risks." The new monetary-policy arrangement was to stabilize the members' currencies, protect them from speculation, and build confidence. If Europe were to succeed in that, it would also help "discipline the balance of payments policy of the United States."[19]

The elections to the French National Assembly on 12 and 19 March did not witness the feared victory of the leftist union of Socialists and Communists; it was rather the case that Giscard's political allies even gained at the expense of the Gaullists. Jenkins then prepared a memorandum for the next meeting of the European Council, set for early April in Copenhagen. He urged that work on the monetary project be intensified such that by the meeting after next (slated for Bremen in July) binding decisions could be made. Like Schmidt, he argued that state support for the economy had only led to higher inflation and that the Europeans had to protect themselves from the irresponsible monetary policy of the US.[20] Parallel to this, Schmidt discussed with Giscard on 2 April at Chateau Rambouillet how the project could be launched at the Council meeting. Both were in agreement that the highest level of confidentiality was called for, not only to avoid speculative withholding of funds by investors but also to circumvent resistance from the French finance ministry and the *Bundesbank*. Technical preparation was assigned to only two men: Bernard Clappier, president of the *Banque de France* and one-time assistant to Robert Schuman in preparation of the Schuman Plan, and Horst Schulmann, head of the economic-policy department in the chancellor's office. The two were to prepare a plan that Schmidt would then present in the confidential round of the Copenhagen meeting. Giscard trusted that the chancellor would be able to persuade the skeptics in the West German financial world.[21]

In Copenhagen, where the heads of state and of government of the Nine met on 7 and 8 April, Jenkins and Giscard first spoke in general terms—as had been agreed—about the necessity of a stable monetary order before Schmidt in a fireside chat after dinner unofficially made a brilliant case for a new monetary-pol-

---

19 Annotation on the conversations between Schmidt and Andreotti, 1 Nov. 1978, quoted in Schulz, *Reluctant European*, p. 305.
20 Memorandum Jenkins, 3 April 1978, PRO FCO 30/4004.
21 In Giscard's recollection of this conversation, the chancellor's earlier skepticism still played a role: Valéry Giscard d'Estaing, *Le Pouvoir et la Vie*, Vol. 1 : *La rencontre*, Paris: Compagnie 12, 1988, pp. 142–14.

icy arrangement through which the dollar would be replaced by a European currency. As for concrete measures, he cited, *firstly*, the creation of a European Monetary Fund, in which the existing institutions and resources of the Community and the currency snake would be integrated; *secondly*, the pooling of fifteen to twenty percent of the member states' currency reserves; *thirdly*, increased use of European currencies in place of the dollar for intervening in currency markets; *fourthly*, increasing use of the European Currency Unit in transactions between the central banks and later also the creation of a new form of reserve asset comparable to the Special Drawing Rights of the International Monetary Fund (IMF). Over time, according to Schmidt, the European Currency Unit—since April of 1975 valued according to the average of the individual currencies weighted for economic strength and foreign-trade percentages—could become a European currency.

The target of the presentation was primarily James Callaghan, whom Schmidt eagerly wanted to have along for this new step in the direction of a monetary union, even if the Labour government up to that point had always decidedly opposed the project. For his part, Callaghan immediately criticized the anti-American orientation of the project; he was still hoping for a restructuring of the international monetary system in concert with the US. Only when Giscard, Schmidt, and Callaghan met privately the next morning and the French leader made it unmistakably plain "that if Callaghan did not come in, he would go along with Schmidt"[22] did the British premier agree to participate in the preparation of draft decisions for the Council meeting in Bremen. The expert group made up of Clappier and Schulmann was augmented by Kenneth Couzens of Her Majesty's Treasury.

In the course of conversations after the Council meeting, Couzens was forced to the conclusion that his French and West German colleagues were indeed serious about mutualizing the currency; and so he withdrew from the talks. In the Treasury, there was even less willingness to give up control over one's own currency than in the *Bundesbank* or the *Directoire du Trésor*. Regarding foreign trade with non-EC states, which was still significant, the British had a preference for an arrangement within the framework of the IMF. Clappier and Schulmann thenceforth worked alone on the concept, and on 23 June, they conferred with Giscard, French Foreign Minister Louis de Guiringaud, and Schmidt at the chancellor's Hamburg home. Schmidt remembered of this meeting that "we worked in the dining room because of the large table. Loki served us coffee. The next day, she told us that every time she had entered the room, we were sitting in a

---

22 Jenkins, *European Diary*, p. 249.

more relaxed posture, initially still in our jackets, then without them and finally without our neckties either."[23]

The result of this summertime round of work was sent by Giscard and Schmidt to their colleagues on the Council shortly before its next meeting on 6 and 7 July; Clappier and Schulmann gave presentations in the various capitals explaining it. The proposal from Schmidt for increased use of the European Unit of Account was made more precise to the effect that it was to constitute the "core" of the improved monetary arrangement, that is, it was not only to serve as a means to simplify payments between the central banks but also serve as the basis for the interventions to preserve the bandwidths. The Franco-German paper, in which the thoughts of Belgian central banker Jacques van Ypersele had been incorporated, therefore spoke of a "European *Currency* Unit" (ECU) and a "European Monetary *System*" (EMS) that went beyond the snake. Regarding the sought-after merging of currency reserves, it was said that "e.g. 20%" of the member states' currency reserves in dollars and gold was to be placed in the European Monetary Cooperation Fund and, additionally, "an amount of comparable order of magnitude" in the currencies of the member states. When purchasing dollars, about twenty percent was likewise to be placed in the common Cooperation Fund; when selling dollars, the central banks would receive about twenty percent in European Currency Units.

Regarding usage of EMS funds made up of deposits of member states' currency assets, it was rather ominously the case that it "will be subject to conditions varying with the amount and the maturity; due account will be given to the need for substantial short term facilities." Clearly, the authors envisioned an expansion and simplification of credits to member states that had come under pressure to devalue. They had not as yet been able to come to agreement as to the exact extent or the conditions; the document only included the reminder that closer monetary-policy cooperation "will only be successful if participating countries will pursue policies conducive to greater stability at home and abroad." Regarding a mechanism for directing exchange rates, there was only mention that the new system would be "at least as strict as the 'snake'"; and "ways to coordinate dollar interventions should be sought."

In essence, the proposed system amounted to having the hard-currency countries (that is, primarily the Federal Republic) accommodate to an extent the weak-currency countries by mutualizing part of the reserves; in return, the latter would subordinate themselves to mechanisms binding them to the goal of stability to a greater extent than heretofore. In order to expand the circle of monetary-union members as far as possible, the paper envisioned that "in the initial stage of its operation and for a limited period of time member countries currently

---

[23] Helmut Schmidt, *Die Deutschen und ihre Nachbarn*, Berlin: Siedler, 1990, p. 228.

not participating in the snake may opt for somewhat wider margins." However, it had not yet been worked out as to how large the concession of the hard-currency countries would be or how strong the obligation of the weak-currency countries. The authors only noted, quite ambitiously, that "two years after the introduction of the system at the latest, the existing agreements and structures would be consolidated in a European Monetary Fund (EMF)."[24]

In Bremen, Schmidt and Giscard first sought to organize another private meeting with Callaghan before the beginning of the actual Council meeting. When the premier declined by citing urgent matters in London, they persisted in seeking a separate meeting after the first afternoon session. Callaghan however stuck to his position of not permitting any decisions based on the Franco-German paper. In the evening session, he was supported by Dutch Prime Minister Andreas van Agt and his Italian colleague Giulio Andreotti in criticizing the preparations for the gathering. Andreotti and Irish Prime Minister Jack Lynch signaled their interest in participating in the new monetary system but at the same time also indicated a need for greater assistance. In order to save this muddled situation, Giscard proposed beginning without Britain. Schmidt was not willing to do so, however. They finally agreed on a declaration for "a closer monetary cooperation leading to a zone of monetary stability in Europe [....] The European Council envisages such a durable and effective scheme," along with a directive for the finance ministers to present a proposal to that effect by the end of October. It was then supposed to be passed by the Council at its December meeting in Brussels. The Franco-German proposal was made public as an "appendix" to this declaration without further qualification.

In discussing the closing communiqué the next morning, Giscard d'Estaing suggested general use of the English-language designation "European Currency Unit" or "ECU." In September of 1974, Ortoli as Commission president had made the same suggestion with the justification that it would please not only the Anglophone members but also the Francophone ones given that the écu had been a popular silver coin in pre-revolutionary France. For his part, Giscard naturally refrained from citing this second reason in the Council and gloated over the fact that Callaghan elatedly agreed with him. That his trick regarding the name had worked made him think that the success of the Bremen meeting was on the whole greater than it actually was.[25]

---

[24] Quoted according to the rendering in the appendix to the "Conclusions" of the European Council in Bremen 7–9 July 1978, in: Ludlow, *Monetary System*, pp. 301ff.
[25] On the course of the Council meeting in Bremen, Jenkins, *European Diary*, pp. 286–290; Giscard d'Estaing, *Le Pouvoir*, Vol. 1, pp. 148–152; and Mourlon-Druol, *A Europe*, pp. 186–189.

In the negotiations of the Council of the Economic and Finance Ministers that had now been made necessary, the haggling continued over the extent of West German concessions and the binding stability commitments for weak-currency countries. In the subcommittee for currency issues, the French representatives argued that having qualified the ECU as the "core" of the new system meant it would be the basis as a reserve currency. Violations of the permitted band width of plus/minus 2.25 percent would then be measured in reference to this reserve currency, and the main burden of intervening would lie with the country that had committed the violation. The British and Italian representatives embraced this interpretation. In contrast, the representatives of the hard-currency countries insisted that the exchange rates should, as before, be measured only bilaterally between two currencies. They drew attention to the fact that the ECU basket of currencies would likewise lose value if individual national currencies lost value. Orienting oneself on it when obliged to intervene would thus mean not only accepting in silence a creeping inflation but even promoting it further due to departure from the focus on stability. This issue engaged the experts for a long while. In the end, a decision along the lines of the interpretation by the hard-currency countries was made at the Franco-German summit in Aachen on 14 and 15 September. This meant that Giscard had *de facto* confirmed his choice for the West German stability model and had thereby won out over the latent opposition in the *Directoire du Trésor*. In light of the position of supplicant in which he found himself *vis-à-vis* the current members of the currency snake, no other decision was possible any longer—at least if one really wanted the monetary union.

In contrast, an ECU basket of currencies was used in measuring the "threshold of divergence" to which governments and central banks were supposed to commit themselves before pre-emptive intervention; this stemmed from a Belgian proposal. There was stubborn resistance from the *Bundesbank* to the pledge to stability-endangering measures resulting from this; the representatives of the banking sector and industry repeatedly made that clear to Schmidt. The French side finally made a concession with the formulation that when a threshold value of seventy-five percent of the maximum deviation range was reached, there would be "a presumption that the authorities concerned will correct this situation by adequate measures." This formally left the *Bundesbank* with its freedom of action but also set it under strong political pressure. As the text ran, "In case such measures on account of special circumstances, are not taken, the reasons for this shall be given [...], especially in the concertation between the central banks." Additionally, consultations at the level of the Council of Ministers were envisioned if individual participants regarded them as necessary. This settlement too was reached at the highest level, during another visit by Schmidt to the Élysée Palace on 2 November.

Another new element that was meant to make it easier for under-performing countries to remain in the currency snake was the establishment of a "Very Short-Term Facility" of an unlimited amount. It could be utilized for forty-five days and then extended for three months. The credit lines for short- and medium-term currency assistance were also significantly expanded to a total of twenty-five billion ecus. Furthermore, short-term credits for a maximum of nine months could be dispersed by the committee of the central bank governors; the Council was responsible for medium-term credits of two to five years, which could be linked to economic-policy requirements. Finally, concessions were made to the weak-currency countries in that the governing exchange rate of individual currencies based on the ECU could be altered by mutual agreement, with the requirement that the European Commission be involved in the decision.

Regarding the size of the currency pool, it was specified that it would consist of twenty percent of dollar and gold reserves; there was no more mention of a comparable contribution of the currencies of the member states. Likewise, under pressure from the *Bundesbank*, the binding nature of the timeline of the goals for further developing the agreed-upon regulations for a European Monetary Fund was reduced: Whereas in the Schmidt-Giscard paper it was specified for a point within two years, it now read only that "we remain firmly resolved to consolidate, not later than two years after the start of the scheme, into a final system the provisions and procedures thus created."[26]

While the technical negotiations were nearing an end, Helmut Schmidt continued hoping that it would be possible to bring the visibly-hesitant Britons onboard. For this purpose, he was now outwardly very friendly toward the US. At the world economic summit in Bonn, he made a concession to Carter by agreeing to contribute to strengthening international demand through tax reductions and investment programs in the range of one percent of GNP. This helped forestall American intervention against the EMS project. Nevertheless, Callaghan could not win approval for British participation. Along with continuing opposition at the Treasury, he was now plagued by worries over vociferous protests from the labor unions as well as a rebellion by anti-Europeans in the cabinet. In light of the necessity of calling elections for the spring of 1979, those were developments he could no longer afford. Shortly before the Council meeting in Brussels on 4 and 5 December 1978, he officially informed Schmidt that Great Britain would not participate in the EMS exchange-rate mechanism. The British government stated only that it was in agreement that the pound sterling be included in the currency basket.

---

[26] Conclusions of the European Council in Brussels 4–5 Dec. 1978, in: Ludlow, *Monetary System*, pp. 303–308.

Callaghan's rejection made Ireland's acceptance all the more noteworthy. To the British premier's consternation, his Irish counterpart had at the Bremen Council meeting already announced that his country would participate in the new monetary system even if Britain did not. Jack Lynch carried through with this, even though it implied giving up the Irish pound's long peg to the British pound and that Ireland would face the risk of significant turbulence in trade with its larger neighbor. Like his Italian colleague Andreotti, he insisted however that in the initial phase, Ireland be allowed greater possibilities for variation—and that there be financial support for the adaptation of the Irish economy to the structure of the hard-currency countries.

In the case of Italy, similar demands were made with still greater force. The Christian Democrat Andreotti was very interested in having his country join in, yet his Socialist coalition partners and the Communists, whose toleration was needed by the government, showed little inclination to participate in the inflation-fighting necessary for this. They raised their demands for concessions higher and higher, and Andreotti felt it necessary to pass them along to his colleagues on the Council. After already insisting in Bremen that Italy be allowed to participate with a range of plus/minus six percent (instead of the level of plus/minus 2.25 percent that was in force for the snake), he came to the Brussels Council meeting with a demand for interest subsidies in the amount of eight hundred million currency units.

In the end, Schmidt and Giscard fully agreed that the newcomers should be given grater maneuvering room. In the Brussels resolution, it was noted only that "these margins should be gradually reduced as soon as economic conditions permit." Nevertheless, both leaders rejected adjustment assistance of the magnitude demanded by Andreotti. Schmidt believed that it might undermine the stability goal. Giscard feared that the Gaullists and the opposition would accuse him of having won too little for France at the bargaining table; he would not consent to more than 300 million units of account each for Italy and Ireland spread out over three years. Schmidt regarded 600 million each over three years as justifiable. In the end, there was agreement on a limit of one billion spread over five years (thus, if France did not make a claim to any of the funds and Britain did not join, that would mean 500 million each for Italy and Ireland).

Andreotti and Lynch did not explicitly accept this. Hence, while the Brussels Council meeting did end in agreement that the European Monetary System would come into force on 1 January 1979, it was not clear that Italy or Ireland would participate.[27] The Italian decision to join—a manifestation of the victory of the mod-

---

[27] On the course of the Brussels meeting, Jenkins, *European Diary*, pp. 349–353; Mourlon-Druol, *A Europe*, pp. 250–255.

ernizers who strove for increased cooperation with European partners—was clear only after a parliamentary vote on 13 December. The Communists answered the defeat they had thereby received by toppling Andreotti four weeks later. Lynch was able to announce Ireland's participation on 15 December, after the representatives of the countries then participating in the snake had on 11 December made concrete commitments to the Irish government regarded financial distributions.

The EMS still could not come into force, however. Chirac made use of the publication of the Brussels decisions in order to announce a dramatic "no" to a "France that abdicates today and dissolves itself tomorrow."[28] Giscard thereupon drew the conclusion that more had to be done than what he had achieved in Brussels regarding demands of French farmers for abolition of the Monetary Compensation Amount (MCA), which they had to pay on exports to the Federal Republic as a consequence of the increase in value of the mark. At the Council meeting, it had only been decided that "The European Council stresses the importance of [...] progressively reducing present MCAs." Agriculture Minister Pierre Méhaignerie made a demand on 18 December that they be completely abolished within a year. When the other governments made no move to agree, the French declared on 29 December that the European Monetary Union could not under those circumstances take effect on 1 January.

Regarding the border-levy problem in the Common Market, there was thus a need for further negotiations, both among the agriculture ministers and at the highest level. An agreement emerged only during a lightening visit by Prime Minister Barre to Schmidt on 23 February 1979. It included the point that the MCAs would in fact be abolished within one year; prices were raised too, however, which eliminated the prospect of a sought-after increase in exports by French farmers. At its next meeting, on 12 and 13 March 1979 in Paris, the European Council could thus implement the European Monetary System immediately. The rough start prevented any feelings of triumph. Added to this was the fact that public attention had in the meantime been almost completely drawn to the fall of the shah of Iran and the resulting second wave of oil price hikes. Because of this, it went unnoticed that with his support of Giscard, Schmidt had accomplished something enormous: Against the opposition of the *Bundesbank*, a majority of public opinion, and the Christian Democratic opposition, he had eliminated the danger of the Common Market's drifting apart in turbulent times for currency policy. Simultaneously, a core of stability had been created through which the European states could reduce their dependence on US monetary policy. The increased engagement of the Federal Republic and the other hard-currency countries as well as the

---

28 "Appel de Cochin," 6 Dec. 1978, printed in Valéry Giscard d'Estaing, *Le Pouvoir et la Vie*, Vol. 3: *Choisir*, Paris: Compagnie 12, 2006, pp. 513–518.

pressure to make consensual changes in exchange rates helped France, Italy, and Ireland stay in the common currency group this time and helped dampen their inflationary tendencies. The strong upward pressure on the mark had simultaneously been removed and more uniformly distributed throughout the Community. Both together prevented the danger of a lasting economic crisis after the end of the big postwar boom. Transformation of the currency snake into the European Monetary System was thereby in keeping with the "material logic" of the integration process, of which Walter Hallstein had spoken in the 1960s. Without the political will and the extraordinary energy of Helmut Schmidt, this logic would not have come to fruition, at least not at this point in time.

The gradual harmonization of economic policies did not begin right away and was not sufficient for substantially reducing the disparities in economic structure and performance. As a consequence, changes in the central rate could not be avoided in 1981–92 following the second oil shock along with a rise in the dollar and in interest rates. By 1983, there had been seven rounds of central rate adjustments; in the process, the value of the mark had been raised four times and that of the French franc reduced three times. Without any spectacular success and with the French presidential elections approaching in the spring of 1981, Giscard d'Estaing did not dare carry through with the creation of a European Monetary Fund as had been agreed upon in Brussels. Giscard's successor François Mitterrand, in office from 10 May 1981, began his term with a program of government support for the economic cycle and employment, a program that went against the stability goal of the EMS. When in September of 1981 the Commission took up the initiative for the "second stage" of the monetary system, in which preventative interventions were to be mandatory when the "deviation threshold" was reached, the *Bundesbank* was successful in arguing that its members were still very far from the stability-oriented convergence.

In the spring of 1983, the European Monetary System was faced with nothing less than the danger of failing. In light of rising unemployment, government debt, and trade deficits, Mitterrand was confronted with the alternative of either returning to a rigorous austerity course or leaving the European Monetary System. Whereas strong forces among the Socialists as well as the Communist coalition partners voted for the second option, Prime Minister Pierre Mauroy and Finance Minister Jacques Delors advocated a change of course in economic policy. It took several weeks for Mitterrand to make a decision for the European solution on 17 March: Another devaluation of the franc within the monetary system was to be accompanied by a whole package of measures for stabilizing the budget. The special socialistic path pursued by the leftist French government was thereby practically at an end, and France's focus on convergence, which Giscard had introduced along with Barre, was thus strengthened.²⁹

Expansion to the South

An additional reason for the efforts to stabilize and expand the currency association was the prospect of another expansion of the Community—the accession of Greece, Portugal, and Spain. One after another in quick succession during the middle of the 1970s, these three southern European countries experienced the end of dictatorial regimes that had always prevented their membership in the European Community. In April of 1974, officers belonging to a "Movement of the Armed Forces" staged a coup against the Salazar-Caetano regime in Portugal; democratic and communist forces then contended over establishing a new order in the country. In Greece in July of the same year, the Regime of the Colonels collapsed seven years after a coup had brought it to power; a provisional government under an earlier conservative prime minister, Constantine Karamanlis, worked to establish a new constitution based on the rule of law. In November of 1975, Spain's long-time dictator Francisco Franco died. In accordance with his plans, Juan Carlos I was proclaimed king; he moderated a process of liberalization and democratization that led to the establishment of a constitutional monarchy by the end of 1978.

These sea changes—which from a long-term perspective were consequences of modernization processes laden with conflict—not only eliminated opposition to these countries' membership in the EC, opposition that stemmed from the EC's self-understanding as a Community of democracies. The European Commission had completed an association agreement with the Greek government of Karamanlis in July of 1961 and had subsequently "frozen" it after the colonels' putsch. An application for association submitted by Spain in February of 1962 had continually been delayed by the governments of the Community. By 1970, this had led only to a trade treaty; negotiations on further tariff reductions had been broken off in October of 1975 after the execution of Basque opponents of Franco. In light of the difficulties in establishing new democratic regimes, the question also came

---

29 Jean-Claude Asselin, "L'expérience sociale face à la contrainte extérieure," in: Serge Berstein, Pierre Milza, and Jean-Louis Bianco (eds.), *François Mitterrand. Les années de changement, 1981–1984*, Paris: Librairie Académique Perrin 2001, pp. 385–430; Pierre Mauroy, *Mémoires. "Vous mettrez du bleu au ciel,"* Paris: Omnibus, 2003, pp. 259–272; Jacques Attali, *C'était François Mitterrand*, Paris: Fayard, 2005, pp. 140–155.

up as to how the countries of the Community could and should assist in the stabilization of new democracies.

The Greek government was the first to answer this question with a bid for EC membership. Immediately after the new republican constitution came into effect in June of 1975, the Karamanlis government submitted the application. Along with hopes for support in economic modernization and access to Western European markets—which had also played a role in the 1959 application for association—there were now other factors too, ones that were closely bound together: interest in assistance for building a modern civil society capable of supporting the parliamentary regime over the long term as well as emancipation from US hegemony. Not completely without justification, the US was held responsible for the longevity of the colonels' regime. Above all, however, the US was blamed for having left the Greeks in the lurch after the Turkish invasion of Cyprus in July of 1974. It had followed an attempted coup by Cypriot supporters of the colonels and had led to the establishment of a Turkish Cypriot regime in the northern part of the island. Following the example of France, Greece had quit the military organization of NATO in August of 1974 and needed membership in the EC as a political counterweight to Turkey, whose policy in the Aegean was still perceived to be revisionist.

The political motives for entry now led Karamanlis to insist on immediate full membership, in contrast to 1959. Only in this way did it seem possible to hold Greece on a fundamentally Western course and to forestall the exploitation of anti-American sentiment by the radical "Pan-Hellenic Socialist Party" (PASOK) of Andreas Papandreou. Karamanlis was supported in this by France, which had promoted his return from French exile as a contribution to democratization of the country and to strengthening French autonomy *vis-à-vis* the dominant power, the US. In December, Karamanlis discussed the entry project with then Prime Minister Jacques Chirac; the following February, Foreign Minister Jean Sauvagnargues conveyed to him official assurance that the French government would support the application. Only thereafter did Karamanlis publically announce his intention, and then on 12 June 1975, one day after the new constitution of Greece had come into effect, he submitted the application in Brussels.

France's enthusiasm for Karamanlis' action was not however shared by all members of the Community. In London, there were reservations about challenging the American role in the eastern Mediterranean. Above all, however, there were concerns about problems arising in relations with Turkey, which was not only an important NATO ally but which since 1963 had also had an association agreement with the prospect of future membership in the EC. In Rome, there were mainly fears of future competition from cheap Greek fruit growers and vintners. In Bonn, there were worries about the general level of development of the Greek economy, which would again make transfer payments necessary to an extent that would be detrimental to the stability goal of West German economic policy. The free movement of Greek workers in the near future was also seen as highly problematic in light of increased unemployment in all the Western industrial countries. When Giscard d'Estaing sought to persuade his friend Schmidt of the necessity of Greek membership in the interest of stabilizing democracy, he was met with "nothing but loud sighs."[30]

The European Commission shared these reservations. In its official position on the application, presented on 28 January 1976, it therefore recommended that Greece be offered only a preliminary membership of indefinite duration. A transition period with full membership rights would follow only when the economic, legal, and administrative reforms deemed necessary for membership had been carried out. In contrast, Karamanlis insisted that the stabilization of Greek democracy was urgent. He also pointed out the necessity of solidarity among democrats in the face of new totalitarian challenges. Moreover, with tactical skill, he made assurances that Greece would not block the development of relations between the EC and Turkey.

The solidarity argument may well have played the key role in the decision that the EC Council of Ministers had to make on 9 February. In the meantime in Portugal, leftist officers of the "Movement of the Armed Forces," with strong support from the Communist Party, had begun attempting to establish a socialist regime; in the Italian communal and regional elections in June of 1975, the Communists had come very close to the level of support of the governing Christian Democrats. It thus seemed imperative to send a clear signal of encouragement to democratic forces in Southern Europe. That made sense to the Ford administration too: It supported Greek engagement with the EC—though along with the desire that it occur in close consultation with the US. Given that support for Greek democracy was also strong in the public opinion of the member states, the partner governments finally put aside their reservations and voted to begin accession negotiations.[31]

These negotiations officially opened on 27 July but actually began in November. The Greek side showed itself willing to subordinate economic interests to

---

[30] Giscard d'Estaing, *Le Pouvoir*, vol. 3, p. 251.
[31] Cf. Antonio Varsori, "L'Occidente e la Grecia: dal colpo di Stato militare alla trasizione alla democrazia (1967–1976)," in: Mario Del Pero *et al.*, *Democrazie. L'Europa meridionale e la fine delle dittature*, Milan: Le Monnier, 2010, pp. 5–94 ; on the negotiations, see Iakovo S. Tsalikoglou, *Negotiating for Entry: The Accession of Greece in the European Community*, Aldershot: Gower, 1995; Kostas Ifantis, "State Interests, External Dependency Trajectories and 'Europe': Greece," in: Wolfram Kaiser and Jürgen Elvert (eds.), *European Union Enlargement. A Comparative History*, London and New York: Routledge, 2004, pp. 70–92.

the goal of rapidly bringing the talks to a conclusion. When chief Greek negotiator Nikolaos Kyriazidis, deputy president of the Greek Central Bank, resigned in protest in January of 1977 due to this negotiating position, he was replaced by Foreign Ministry General Secretary Vyron Theodoropoulos. That the talks dragged into the spring of 1979 was primarily attributable to the member states, which wanted to protect themselves from Greek competition for as long as possible.

The accession agreement signed in Athens on 28 May 1979 thus also included exceptional regulations benefitting countries that were already members. A transition period of five years was agreed upon. However, tomatoes and peaches would be allowed in the Community without tariffs only after seven years, and the free movement of labor was to come into effect only after seven years. As to protecting the Greek development program, the agreement contained only the stipulation that the Greek government could temporarily limit the freedom of capital movement in order to prevent the transfer of excessively large sums. Entry into the European Monetary System would occur only five years after the end of the transition period. Additionally, some assistance was envisioned for modernizing agricultural production, especially that of olive oil. After the agreement had won a majority in the Greek parliament as well as in those of the member states, it came into effect on 1 January 1981.

In Portugal, entry into the EC became an issue only after the decision for a democratic regime had been consolidated with parliamentary elections on 25 April 1976. The governments of the Nine had worked toward this outcome by offering economic support for reorientation after the end of the Portuguese colonial empire, but this support had explicitly been made contingent on the development of a pluralistic democracy. They had supported the democratic forces in the country, had rejected Kissinger's distancing of himself from the Socialists as the largest group of democratic forces, and had successfully pressured Leonid Brezhnev to give up his support for the Portuguese Communists. Furthermore, strong support for the Portuguese Socialists under Mário Soares came from European sister parties; Willy Brandt and the SPD had especially become engaged in terms of financial and moral support.[32]

The Socialists decided to form a government after winning 34.8 percent of the vote and having been confirmed as the largest party. At the same time, this victory also represented a decision for Europe over against the traditional Atlanticist orientation of Portuguese policy and its Third World variant in the policy

---

32 Mario Del Pero, "A European Solution for a European Crisis. The International Implications of Portugal's Revolution," in: *Journal of European Integration History* 15/1 (2009), pp. 15–34; Ana Monica Fonseca, "The Federal Republic of Germany and the Portuguese Transition to Democracy (1974–1976)," *ibid.*, pp. 35–56.

of the leftist officers. This was augmented by the fact that the Christian Democrats also strongly supported rapid entry into the European Community and that the Social Democratic Party, which represented reformist elements of the former Caetano regime, was also inclined in the same direction. Only the Communists categorically rejected membership. As with Karamanlis, membership in the European Community for Soares primarily represented a contribution to stabilizing the young democracy, which according to the constitution of 2 April 1976 still was under the tutelage of the Revolutionary Council. Economic experts' doubts about the problems that would ensue in many branches of the poorly-developed Portuguese economy were dismissed by Soares with reference to the insufficient foundation of democracy.

The first step toward Europe made by the Soares government was entry into the Council of Europe in August of 1976. In doing so, it not only ensured recognition by Western democracies but also demonstratively distanced itself from the self-conception of the old regime, which in the years after the Second World War had not concerned itself at all with joining this fundamental European organization. In September, there followed the signing of a supplementary and financial protocol to the trade treaty of 1972 with the EC (with which the unloved EFTA member Portugal had reacted to the entry of Great Britain, Ireland, and Denmark into the EC). By means of this new addition, transitional assistance was organized, as the Commission had had in mind for Greece with the proposal for a preliminary membership. After a series of bilateral negotiations with the governments of the Nine, the official application for entry was submitted on 28 March 1977.[33]

The Commission needed more than a year—until May of 1978—before it took a positive position on the application. Five more months went by before negotiations began. These talks were endlessly tedious. They lasted far longer than those with Greece and only came to a conclusion in June of 1985. The main reason for this astonishingly long delay, as measured by initial hopes, lay in the fact that the Suárez government in Spain had submitted an application of its own on 27 July 1977, some four months after the Portuguese; and the Commission as well as the Council had by mutual agreement decided to deal with both applications together. Soares wanted to avoid that but was unable to prevail—in contrast to Karamanlis, who succeeded in keeping the Greek negotiations, begun earlier, out of the complex of Iberian issues.

The Spanish application had resulted from constant pressure by the European Community on Franco's successors as well as related efforts to support dem-

---

33 António Costa Pinto and Nuno Severiano Teixeira, "From Atlantic Past to European Destiny: Portugal," in: Kaiser and Elvert (eds.), *European Union Enlargement*, pp. 112–130.

ocratic parties. In May of 1976, Maurice Faure released a report commissioned by the European Parliament; not only did the document explicitly make Spain's entry contingent on democratization, but it also listed in detail the steps necessary for that democratization. Beginning with the appointment of Adolfo Suárez as prime minister in July of 1976, the regime embarked upon this process and thereby made EC accession into the symbolic badge of democratization. After the first free elections on 15 June 1977—by which Suárez's Union of the Democratic Center became the largest party—the new government submitted its application. It was supported by all the parties. Even the Communists threw in their weight; in contrast to the Leninists in Portugal, the Spanish Communists had set a Euro-Communist course under the leadership of Santiago Carrillo.[34]

With the Spanish application, the problem of Southern European competition in the fruit, vegetable, and wine industries presented itself in an entirely new dimension. The producers in the French southwest and Languedoc feared being literally overrun by competition from low-wage countries that also enjoyed climate advantages; both the Communists and the Gaullists became advocates of these concerns. The opposition in Italy was strong too, and Greek voices joined in from 1981 on. The solidarity among democrats demanded by Karamanlis had its limits, just as that of the communists did. Carrillo found himself having to listen to French party chief Georges Marchais arguing that Spanish entry into the Common Market would not contribute to solving the problems of the Spanish working class.

The argument based on urgency, which Karamanlis had effectively employed against opposition within the Community, did not lend itself to the case of Spain and Portugal: *Firstly*, there never was the danger of a "leftist" regime in Spain, something that frightened the conservative governments especially. *Secondly*, fears of radical upheavals or counter-revolutions dwindled to the extent that the processes of democratization advanced; the consolidation of political conditions in Italy after the shock over the murder of Aldo Moro by a terror cell of the Red Brigades in May of 1978 also played a role in this. Under these circumstances, the status of candidate for entry, negotiating with the prospect of success and receiving all manner of transition assistance, sufficed to strengthen the democratic order; entry became less significant in and of itself.

---

[34] Víctor Gavín and Fernando Guirao, "La dimensione internazionale della transizione polica spagnola (1969–1982). Quale ruolo giocarono la Comunità europea e gli Stati Unity?" in Del Pero, *Democrazie*, pp. 173–264; Wolfram Kaiser and Christian Salm, "Transition und Europäisierung in Spanien und Portugal. Sozial- und christdemokratische Netzwerke im Übergang von der Diktatur zur parlamentarischen Demokratie," in: *Archiv für Sozialgeschichte* 49 (2009), pp. 259–282.

Despite the foreseeable implications for the Common Agricultural Policy, the Commission took a positive stance toward Spanish accession as well; this was officially issued on 29 November 1978, shortly after the new Spanish constitution had been ratified. On 19 December, the Council of Ministers gave the green light for the opening of negotiations. After a year and a half, in July of 1980, talks were *de facto* put on ice because Giscard d'Estaing insisted that an understanding on reform of the Common Agricultural Policy and an increase in the Community budget had to be reached first. Neither did talks make much progress after the French presidential elections of May 1981; at the European Council in Brussels in June of 1982, Giscard's successor Mitterrand insisted once again on a comprehensive solution to all questions associated with expansion. Paris regarded expansion of spending on the Common Agricultural Policy to be the solution to the problem of Iberian competition; neither Bonn nor London was prepared to accept that, however. Nor did Spain's entry into NATO on 30 May 1982 suffice to break the opposition.

A way out of the crisis in negotiations first manifested itself when Socialist Prime Minister Felipe González, victor of the Spanish parliamentary elections of 2 December 1982, increased the moral pressure on Paris and Bonn. At the Stuttgart meeting of the Council on 18 and 19 June 1983, a reform of the Common Agricultural Policy was approved that led to the passage of a market for fruit, vegetables, and olive oil. At the same time, Schmidt's successor Helmut Kohl agreed in principle to a hike in the percentage of the value-added tax received by the Community, a source that in the meantime had grown to more than half of its total revenue. One year later, at the Council meeting in Fontainebleau on 25 and 26 June 1984, an increase in the value-added tax percentage from 1.0 to 1.4 percent was agreed upon. In return, Mitterrand gave his approval to a definitive roadmap for entry negotiations. Under the pressure of an ultimatum from Papandreou, who had become head of the Greek government in October of 1981, an "Integrated Mediterranean Program" of the Community was issued that envisioned nearly three billion ecus for promoting modernization in southern France, Italy, and Greece.

With those safeguards in place, negotiations with Portugal and Greece could then be carried to a conclusion at high speed. The treaties signed in Lisbon and Madrid on 12 June 1985 envisioned a seven-year transition period for Spain and ten for Portugal. For the Spanish steel industry, Spanish fruit, and olive oil, transition periods of up to seven additional years were agreed upon. Access by the significant Spanish fishing fleet to territorial waters of other members was even quantitatively limited for a period of seventy years. The escudo and peseta were incorporated into the basket of currencies for calculating the ECU, but participation in the exchange-rate mechanism of the European Monetary Union was deferred until a later date. So, on 1 January 1986, the number of member states in the Community rose from ten to twelve.[35]

Despite the long delay and the difficult compromises, the process of democratization and Europeanization succeeded in all three new member states. It was accelerated during the transition phases along the lines of harmonization with the political structures of Western Europe and catching up on economic development. After taking power in Greece, Papandreou led the originally anti-imperialist oriented PASOK to support EC membership aggressively. Not even the return to the military organization of NATO in October of 1980, which Karamanlis had pushed through due to the lack of European defense structures, was called into question any longer. In Portugal, the prospect of membership made the constitutional reform of 1982 possible, which freed the democratic institutions from the tutelage of the Revolutionary Council and its socialistic program. The conviction that the future of the nation lay in the European Community grew stronger and was henceforth part of the national self-understanding. In Spain, Prime Minister González, supported by a comprehensive national consensus, was able to transition from the battle for entry to the battle for further developing the European Community. The concept of a strong Spain within a strong Europe advanced to a guiding principle of Spanish policy on Europe, contributing to the country's identity.

At the same time, the experience of the stabilization of the southern European democracies strengthened the awareness that the European Community was more than an association devoted to economic benefit. The perception of responsibility for the democratization of the Southern European states underscored that the integration of the Germans after the collapse of the National Socialist regime had not been a one-time task but rather belonged to the core function of creating the prerequisites for the durability of democratic orders. Given that the European Union was largely alone in carrying out this function now—in contrast to the German case—and that it was in the beginning undertaken even in a certain contrast to tendencies in US policy, the EC was strengthening its claim to be an autonomous actor in international politics. This double experience flowed together into the concept of the "civilian power Europe" that now became popular: The perception of the European Community as an international actor that did not wield influence due to military might but rather thanks to the com-

---

35 Lorena Ruano, "The Consolidation of Democracy vs. the Price of Olive Oil: The Story of why the CAP Delayed Spain's Entry to the EC," in: *Journal of European Integration History* 11/2 (2005), pp. 96–118; Ricardo Martín de la Guardia, "In Search of Lost Europe: Spain," in: Kaiser and Elvert (eds.), *European Union Enlargement*, pp. 93–111; Matthieu Trouvé, *L'Espagne et l'Europe. De la dictature de Franco à l'Union européenne*, Brussels et al.: Peter Lang, 2008.

bination of an attractive civilization and targeted employment of its economic means. The report on the significance of the southern expansion, presented by the Commission in 1984, tellingly was prepared by François Duchêne—a political scientist who had in 1973 already interpreted the EC as "a power for the international spread of civil and democratic standards."[36]

The concept of civilian power was not applied to Turkey, however. The Turkish government reacted to the Greek application for entry with a demand for equal participation in European Political Cooperation (EPC). Turkey wanted to ensure that at least the provisions of the supplementary protocol to the association agreement, having taken effect in 1973, would be carried out in accordance with the Turkish interpretation: Only a gradual reduction of protective tariffs for Turkish industrial products over a period of twelve years and for approximately forty-five percent of EC exports over no less than twenty-two years; a gradual reduction of limits on imports of Turkish agricultural products, also over a period of twenty-two years; incremental establishment of free movement for Turkish labor over twelve years; financial assistance, the extent of which was to be re-determined every five years. The Council of Ministers rejected this request as wholly inappropriate, however; in light of the financial burden that the southern expansion already entailed, no political majority could be found in any member state for the idea of compensating for the increased support of Greece by spending more on the development of Turkey. On the contrary: When for once a Turkish product— cotton textiles—enjoyed success in the European market, Great Britain limited imports. The Federal Republic sought to avoid the pledge to accept more guest workers, and in general, the Mediterranean policy of the EC, especially the 1975 free-trade agreement with Israel, devaluated the loosening of import limits and the financial assistance agreed upon in the supplementary protocol. When the Turkish military reacted to the increasing inability to form a stable government in September of 1980 by staging another coup, political contacts were suspended by the European Parliament and the Commission and financial assistance frozen.

This perpetuated a vicious circle that had burdened Turkey's approach to the European Community since the beginning of negotiations on the association treaty: On the one hand, there was a lack of consensus among the governments

---

[36] François Duchêne, "The European Community and the Uncertainties of Interdependence," in: Max Kohnstamm and Wolfgang Hager (eds.), *A Nation Writ Large? Foreign-Policy Problems before the European Community*, London: John Wiley & Sons, 1973, pp. 19–26, here p. 20. Cf. Thomas Derungs, "The Integration of a Different Europe. The European Community's Enlargement to the South and the Evolving Concept of a Civilian Power," in: Michele Affinito, Guiy Migani, and Christian Wenkel (eds.), *Les deux Europes. Actes du IIIe colloque international RICHIE*, Brussels: Peter Lang, 2009, pp. 311–325.

of the Community as to what was the actual goal of the association; while on the other, a coherent and long-term strategy for Europeanization was lacking in Turkey. The conviction that "Turkey is part of Europe,"[37] which to the Adenauer government and the Hallstein Commission, for example, had still been completely obvious, retreated wholly into the background. That this occurred precisely at the time that the European identity of the Community was gaining depth of focus is not without a certain tragic element. The path out of the isolation in which Turkey had fallen in the early 1980s would be extremely arduous.[38]

The Defense of Détente

Whereas the European Community was distinguishing itself as a civilian power, progress on Common foreign and defense policy did not materialize. Regular meetings of EPC and the European Council did ensure that there was an increasing European socialization among the foreign-policy actors as well as the development of common standpoints, not only in regard to southern expansion but also to conflicts in Africa, relations with Latin America, and the crisis in Iran after the fall of the shah in the winter of 1978–79. The European Council of Venice in June of 1980 strengthened the autonomy of European Middle East policy in that it recognized the right of the Palestinians to self-determination and characterized the Palestinian Liberation Organization (PLO) as their legitimate representative.[39] The central question of military autonomy was omitted, however. This was on the one hand the result of the Labour government's rejection of a common foreign policy, a stance that remained unchanged after confirmation of the decision for entry. On the other hand, the defense expert Schmidt, socialized as an Atlanticist, did not regard European autonomy as a high-priority goal; and Giscard d'Estaing was for the time being busy dismantling the anti-American points of French European policy.

---

37 Walter Hallstein at the signing of the association agreement, quoted from Sena Ceylanoglu, "Von der unumstrittenen Beitrittsperspektive zu umstrittenen Beitrittsverhandlungen: Wandlungen des Verhältnisses der Europäischen Union zur Türkei," in: Gabriele Clemens (ed.), *Die Türkei und Europa*, Münster: Lit-Verlag, 2007, pp. 151–169.
38 Elena Calandri, "A Special Relationship under Strain: Turkey and the EEC, 1963–1976," in: *Journal of European Integration History* 15/1 (2009), pp. 57–75; Heinz Kramer and Maurus Reinkowski, *Die Türkei und Europa. Eine wechselhafte Beziehungsgeschichte*, Stuttgart: Kohlhammer, 2008, pp. 154–162.
39 Cf. Daniel Möckli, "Speaking with One Voice? The Evolution of a European Foreign Policy," in: Anne Deighton and Gérard Bossuat (eds.), *The EC/EU: A World Security Actor?* Paris: Soleb, 2007, pp. 132–151; Găinar, *Origines*, pp. 377–476.

However, the problems resulting from the one-sided dependence of Western Europe and especially of the Federal Republic on the US and the inadequacy of a purely nationally-defined defense strategy, which de Gaulle had in the end retreated into, led Schmidt and Giscard to aim for a common European defense strategy. According to Schmidt's testimony—not contradicted by Giscard—it was the French president who made the first step here in the search for a common foreign policy for the Nine, doing so because of discomfort over the status quo in French defense policy, which the self-appointed heirs of the general had elevated to a dogma. Schmidt responded with a series of analyses and proposals, and over the years, a thoroughgoing dialogue developed out of this, which was mostly carried on privately by the two leaders due to its delicate nature.

Schmidt summarized these conversations:

> I presented to my friend primarily three security-policy aspects: *Firstly*, the undesirable, excessive dependence of the Federal Republic on the US, which was unavoidable owing to the refusal of French participation in a common defense organization. [...] Secondly, I emphasized my conviction that French troops and the reserves that could be mobilized, combined with German troops and their reserves, would by themselves almost be sufficient to deter the Soviet Union from any conventional attack on Europe. In doing so, I called Giscard's attention to the neglect of France's conventional armed forces, which has been seen for about fifteen years in terms of weapons and equipment but also in terms of the psychological handling of the army. *Thirdly*, I pointed out the dangerousness of NATO's military plans. How there was a feeling of being severely inferior to the Soviet armed forces in conventional terms, and in the event of a military conflict, there was a desire to answer very early with so-called tactical nuclear weapons; a nuclear detonation on German soil would however immediately shake any further German willingness to resist, regardless of whether it were an American, English, or French nuclear weapon. The French conception of a glacis east of the Rhine that the Germans would defend therefore rested on very dubious theoretical considerations.[40]

Influenced by Schmidt's arguments, Giscard made adjustments to the French defense policy. In May of 1976, General Guy Méry, chief of staff of the French Army, publicly announced the possibility of French participation in a "forward defense" by NATO, that is, a combat mission on German soil and also a phase of conventional warfare before nuclear weapons were employed. Regarding the use of tactical nuclear weapons, top-secret negotiations were carried out with the US that resulted in an agreement in 1979. At the same time, with American support, strategic missiles and cruise missiles were developed that could reach Soviet territory, in contrast to the Pluton missiles that had been ordered by Pompidou and deployed since 1974. In the budget planning for 1977–82, funding for conventional

---

40 Schmidt, *Die Deutschen und ihre Nachbarn*, pp. 170ff.

arms and especially for land forces were increased at the expense of the nuclear component. Lastly, a program for modernizing the French forces stationed in the Federal Republic was begun in 1980. At the Franco-German summit of 4 and 5 February 1980, the construction of a joint Franco-German tank was announced.

Giscard was not prepared to do more, however, such as make a public guarantee of intervention in the event of an attack on the Federal Republic or embark upon a new initiative to develop a European defense structure. The opposition of the Gaullists in the military and in politics was too strong for that. Even Méry's cautious distancing from the concept of a "force de frappe" that was focused solely on protecting national territory ended up generating such a large amount of polemical criticism that Prime Minister Barre felt compelled in a speech on military doctrine a year later to speak only very generally of "neighboring and allied territories" for which "the concept of deterrence was likewise [to be] employed."[41] There was no review of the contradiction between European-oriented praxis and a still nationally-defined doctrine.

As a consequence, in resolving the most urgent security-policy task at hand, Schmidt and Giscard stayed with the traditional division of labor between the autonomy of France and the Atlantic integration of the Federal Republic. This consisted of finding an appropriate response to the modernization of Soviet medium-range missiles targeting Europe. Schmidt feared a decoupling of Europe from the American security guarantee because the new Soviet weapons—designated SS-20 in the West—were to be deployed in the winter of 1976–77 and, in contrast to the previous generation of medium-range missiles (SS-4 and SS-5), would be capable of neutralizing nuclear weapons stationed in Europe with little warning time. In order to banish the danger of decoupling, he demanded—first at the NATO summit in May of 1977—that the next round of arms control talks include weapons systems below the strategic level of the intercontinental weapons with which the Soviet Union and US threatened one another.[42]

Giscard d'Estaing was initially very hesitant about this demand because the negotiations on the so-called "Euro-strategic" weapons threatened the expansion of French medium-range systems to which he had just committed himself. At the Franco-German summit of 14 and 15 September 1978, he recommended to

---

41 Speech of 18 June 1977, quoted from Soutou, *L'alliance incertaine*, p. 364. Cf. *ibid.*, pp. 359–365.
42 On this and the following, Wilfried Loth, *Overcoming the Cold War. A History of Détente, 1950–1991*, Houndsmills and New York: Palgrave, 2002, pp. 150–156; Tim Geiger, "Die Regierung Schmidt-Genscher und der NATO-Doppelbeschluss," in: Philipp Gassert, Tim Geiger, and Hermann Wentker (eds.), *Zweiter Kalter Krieg und Friedensbewegung. Der NATO-Doppelbeschluss in deutsch-deutscher und internationaler Perspektive*, Munich: Oldenbourg, 2011, pp. 95–120.

Schmidt the alternative of stationing American medium-range missiles in Europe that could reach Soviet territory. This did not please Schmidt: In his view, it would be problematic to contribute to the arms spiral; moreover, domestic approval for the proposal would be difficult to gain. Brezhnev paid a state visit to the Federal Republic during the first week of May and showed no openness at all to his host's call to limit the arsenal of medium-range weapons. After this, Schmidt regarded the threat of such an American deployment as an appropriate means by which to compel the Soviet side to concede. He was aware that, depending on circumstances, that threat might actually need to be carried out. He still regarded the deployment as the second-best solution and, furthermore, saw good prospects for the threat to work.

This was the solution that would come to be known as "upgrading" and would go on to be passionately debated in public. It was decided in principle at an intimate meeting of Carter, Callaghan, Giscard, and Schmidt, which the chancellor had requested in early October and which—in order to take French sensitivities into account—took place on the French Caribbean island of Guadeloupe from 4 to 6 January 1979. Here, Carter offered the production and deployment of Pershing II missiles, which could reach the Soviet Union at least from German territory and which could be ready for deployment in four years. Schmidt accepted this offer but, along with Callaghan, emphasized that there first had to be negotiations on limiting medium-range missiles. Giscard highlighted the fact that the West would not have a bargaining chip without the new weapon systems, and so he demanded a limit on the negotiation offer to the four years that would be needed for the Pershings to be ready for deployment. Beyond that, he insisted that the modernization of the French nuclear arsenal not be hindered by the talks.[43]

The emphases of Schmidt and Giscard were thus very divergent: Whereas for the West German chancellor it was primarily a matter of reducing Soviet medium-range missiles, the French president was above all concerned with the expansion of his nation's own medium-range arsenal. Both goals were included in the "double-track decision" passed in Brussels on 12 December 1979 by the foreign ministers and defense ministers of NATO in support of carrying out the basic agreement reached on Guadeloupe: There were to be negotiations to the end of 1983; if no satisfactory results had been achieved by that time, then 108 Pershing II missiles and 464 cruise missiles were to be deployed. Along with the Federal Republic, Italy agreed to accept the weapons; Belgium and the Nether-

---

43 Weinachter, *Giscard d'Estaing*, pp. 207–215; Soell, *Helmut Schmidt*, pp. 728–733; German conversation notes in AAPD 1979 I, pp. 5–20.

lands made their acceptance dependent on the results of negotiations.[44] This was a rather unequal deal insofar as the chances of successful negotiations were lessened not least of all by the fact that French and British nuclear weapons were not to be included. In French public opinion, there predominated a feeling of relief that their country's autonomy had been maintained as well as the Germans' link to the West, whereas in the countries where deployments might occur—and especially in the Federal Republic—fear spread of a new arms race and a lowered threshold for nuclear war.

The divergent priorities in the double-track decision did not prevent Schmidt and Giscard from working closely together in defending détente policy against American overreactions and thereby bringing the Europeans' autonomous role in the East-West conflict into sharper relief. Both had been in agreement in seeking to persuade Carter to give up his bold public denunciation of Soviet human rights violations—Giscard doing so in an attention-getting interview in the American magazine *Newsweek* in September of 1977 and Schmidt with forceful reproaches in private conversation. Along with their partners in EPC, both leaders also sought to prevent the Carter administration from having the follow-up gathering of the Conference on Security and Co-operation in Europe (meeting from October 1977 to March 1978 in Belgrade) devolve into nothing more than a tribunal against Eastern human rights violations. They were not very successful. They did however manage to have the Belgrade meeting end with a declaration proclaiming the desire to continue the dialogue of détente and to hold at least one more follow-up conference. The European governments could link up with that in their bilateral talks with the East Bloc states, and they in fact did so.[45]

When Carter reacted to the entry of Soviet troops into Afghanistan at Christmas time in 1979 by suspending both the détente dialogue and ratification of the SALT II Treaty, Schmidt and Giscard once again made efforts toward moderation. In a joint declaration at the close of the Franco-German summit of 4 and 5 February 1980, they characterized the Soviet intervention as "unacceptable." However, their warning to the Soviet side confined itself to the statement "that détente would not be able to survive another blow of that kind." That was indeed an accurate analysis, but it also carried the message that, unlike the American president, Bonn and Paris did not want to deviate from their détente course. There followed the barely veiled suggestion that under the current circumstances it was the European powers that ought to take on special responsibilities.[46] On French televi-

---

44 *Europa-Archiv* 35 (1980), pp. D35ff. and D99–D110.
45 Loth, *Overcoming the Cold War*, pp. 149ff.; on the following, *ibid.*, pp. 160–164 and 172–174.
46 *Europa-Archiv* 35 (1980), pp. D166.

sion, Giscard characterized this declaration as the "clear date of the reappearance of Europe as a new center of influence and decision-making in world politics."[47]

In fact, the Nine did not participate in the comprehensive trade restrictions that Washington imposed on Moscow as "punishment." Only the Federal Republic responded to Carter's call for a boycott of the Summer Olympics in Moscow, doing so only after strong domestic disputes and out of a concern to avoid damaging the Western alliance any further. At the urging of Polish Prime Minister Edward Gierek, Giscard went to Warsaw on 19 May to meet with Brezhnev in order to warn him of the consequences of a Soviet intervention in Poland. In order to move the USSR to negotiate on limiting medium-range missiles, Schmidt accepted a Soviet invitation to visit Moscow on 30 June. Each leader's mission was discussed with the other in advance,[48] and both proved successful in the end: Moscow shrank back from the idea of military intervention against the Solidarity Movement, and Brezhnev proposed on 21 August that negotiations be started on medium-range missiles. Carter had no easy way of rejecting the offer out of concern for the cohesion of the Western alliance, and so negotiations began on 16 October in Geneva on "Euro-strategic" weapons.

Schmidt and Giscard thus provided one another support in the détente crisis unleashed by the Soviet decision to intervene in Afghanistan. Schmidt's journey to Moscow protected Giscard from Mitterrand's accusation that he was making himself into Brezhnev's "errand boy," and Giscard's journey to Warsaw could be pointed out to those who saw in the chancellor's action only another attempt to curry favor with Moscow for the sake of German reunification. The pressure that Carter exerted on both leaders fizzled absent sufficient resonance in France and the Federal Republic. Schmidt and Giscard had thus secured for Western Europe an influence over containing the "second Cold War," an influence that neither the Federal Republic nor France could have gained by itself. Schmidt confirmed this in retrospect: "Alone, I would without a doubt have been much more circumspect."[49]

In their joint resistance to American pressure, Schmidt and Giscard also found themselves stronger when working together on the issue of European defense. The chancellor was clearly able to convince his friend that preserving the French medium-range arsenal would not spare France the consequences of

---

[47] Declaration of 26 Feb. 1980, quoted in Weinachter, *Giscard d'Estaing*, p. 177.
[48] Valéry Giscard d'Estaing, *Le Pouvoir et la Vie*. Vol. 2: *L'affrontement*, Paris: Compagnie 12, 1991, pp. 417–419; Vol. 3, pp. 217ff. There is no basis for contemporary speculations regarding Giscard's ambition to forestall Schmidt here.
[49] Helmut Schmidt in conversation with Michèle Weinachter: Weinachter, *Giscard d'Estaing*, p. 182.

a nuclear exchange on German soil and that he expected a *quid pro quo* for the exclusion of French and British nuclear weapons from the sought-after negotiations. In any event, the two agreed on a Franco-German defense alliance in July of 1980 that in essence amounted to adding an autonomous European pillar to NATO. According to this agreement, the *Bundeswehr* was to refrain from acquiring tactical nuclear weapons and instead expand its conventional capacities significantly over five years and, along with the French armed forces, become part of a joint high command. In this way, a force was to develop that when mobilized could within one week comprise some eighteen German and twelve French divisions. That would facilitate a reduction of American forces in Europe and offer a promising prospect of "defending the western portion of Central Europe" without resort to nuclear weapons. In return for the expansion of the *Bundeswehr* and the Federal Republic's contribution to the cost of modernizing the French Army, Paris was to expand the mission of its nuclear *force de frappe* "by unilateral declaration to the protection of Germany too." The French president would continue to have sole decision-making power over use of the *force de frappe*; the West German chancellor was to receive a veto right over the use of tactical nuclear weapons, however.[50]

Overall, France was therefore to Europeanize its defense strategy, while the Federal Republic was to free itself from being merely subsumed within the American defense strategy. To what extent this implied a return of France to the military organization of NATO or a modification of the decision-making mechanisms in the Western alliance remained unclear and was not fully negotiated by Schmidt and Giscard. What was primarily important to them was that their approach could raise the nuclear threshold in Europe and that the West Germans would be offered a version of the French nuclear concept that they could back. Both may additionally have helped contain West German anxiety over a nuclear confrontation and thus preempt any tendencies toward neutralization. European autonomy within the Western alliance would thus gain substance, and the extension of this dual alliance to the other members of the Community would accordingly be only a matter of time.

It was the case however that significant opposition had to be overcome in order to push this project through. It did not fit with the dogma of the closest possible interweaving of American and West German security that was accepted

---

[50] As explained by Helmut Schmidt in the Bundestag on 28 June 1984, *Verhandlungen des Deutschen Bundestages*, pp. 5601ff.; the information on a West German veto right in a conversation between Schmidt and Hartmut Soell, reported in Michael Wirth, *Die Deutsch-Französischen Beziehungen während der Kanzlerschaft von Helmut Schmidt (1974–1982)*, Berlin: Wissenschaftlicher Verlag Berlin, 2007, p. 104.

by large segments of the FRG's military establishment and that was also popular with the West German public—and, in the final analysis, with the French public too. It was also not readily compatible with the détente policy approach of Egon Bahr, an approach that promised possibilities for German reunification primarily through reducing conventional forces in Europe and that therefore had placed great hope in the negotiations on Mutual and Balanced Force Reductions (MBFR) in Vienna. Above all, however, the project threatened the illusion of French independence, to which the guardians of Gaullism in the military and politics clung, along with an overwhelming majority of the French populace. If the US administration were to engage in mobilizing the various forces opposing the project, there was thus a good chance of derailing it.

After having successfully warded off an attack by Carter on his détente policy at a meeting of the G-7 in Venice on 22 and 23 June,[51] Schmidt was committed to facing this new challenge too. He speculated that "the waywardness of two American presidents" would certainly contribute "to understanding in European public opinion for the necessary adjustments."[52] For his part, however, Giscard feared that the project of a Franco-German military treaty with such far-reaching implications might reduce his chances of re-election in the coming spring. He therefore asked Schmidt to postpone the working out of the treaty until after the vote and to do nothing beforehand to unsettle French public opinion. The treaty on the formation of a military alliance was then to be signed on the twentieth anniversary of the Élysée Treaty, that is, 22 January 1983. Schmidt perforce agreed to this but warned against waiting too long: "My time in office has its limits."[53]

The only initiative that Giscard d'Estaing wanted to get underway before the French presidential elections in April and May of 1981 was the proposal for a "Conference on Confidence- and Security-Building Measures and Disarmament in Europe." This fit with the new European defense concept in that it was only to involve talks on conventional armaments. In contrast to MBFR, this new initiative was to include Soviet territory up to the Urals. The proposal was strongly supported by Schmidt and was put forward in November of 1980 at the beginning of talks at the Madrid CSCE Conference. It was finally able to win approval there. On 17 January 1984, the negotiations for this new initiative opened in Stockholm.[54]

---

51 Soell, *Helmut Schmidt*, pp. 751–761.
52 Schmidt, *Die Deutschen und ihre Nachbarn*, p. 171.
53 *Ibid.*, p. 284.
54 Veronika Heyde, "Nicht nur Entspannung und Menschenrechte: Die Entdeckung von Abrüstung und Rüstungskontrolle durch die französische KSZE-Politik," in: Matthias Peter and Hermann Wentker (eds.), *Die KSZE im Ost-West-Konflikt. Internationale Politik und gesellschaftliche Transformation 1975–1990*, Munich: Oldenbourg, 2012, pp. 83–98.

After the French presidential elections, the project of a military alliance was put on the back burner. New President François Mitterrand, who had little foreign policy profile, was initially against any privileging of his West German partner above his other allies. In his circle, the priority was especially on an understanding with Britain, in accordance with tradition. In terms of security policy, he reverted to a *"force de frappe"* doctrine that envisioned use of French nuclear forces only in the event of a direct attack on French territory and that limited French engagement in the defense of the Federal Republic to the conventional realm. This was however expanded by the establishment of a "rapid deployment force"; at the same time, links to NATO mission planning were cut back.[55]

At the beginning of 1982, on the occasion of regular Franco-German consultations, Mitterrand conceded to Schmidt "a thorough exchange of ideas between the two governments on security issues." Since then, talks have been conducted between the foreign ministers and defense ministers of the two countries on a regular basis, as had been envisioned in the Franco-German Treaty. Furthermore, a Franco-German Security and Defense Commission was established, made up of the chiefs of the general staffs and the Political Directors of both foreign ministries.[56] In terms of content, however, these talks made hardly any progress. When the foreign ministers and defense ministers gathered for the first time in October of 1982, the social-liberal coalition had just broken apart, with Helmut Kohl having become the new chancellor. The project of a military union now lacked a driving force on the West German side as well: What Kohl primarily conceived of as Franco-German military cooperation was only the return of France to NATO military integration—also a wholly-traditional position. What had made the concretization of plans for a European defense much easier—limiting the dialogue to the smallest circle around both top politicians—proved to be the decisive hindrance in carrying out such plans now that both leaders had lost elections.

In a spectacular way, Mitterrand advocated implementation of the decision for an "upgrading" of intermediate-range missiles in a speech before the Bundestag in January of 1983. In doing so, he was expressing the French interest in the Federal Republic's linkage to American defense strategy as clearly as his own persistence in the ideology of France's independence in security policy.[57] He was clearly unaware that neither the one nor the other could be harmonized with the development of a security-policy identity for Europe. In contrast to Giscard, he was not prepared to pay a price for preventing the feared drift of the Federal

---

55 Cf. Hubert Védrine, *Les mondes de François Mitterrand. À l'Élysée 1981–1995*, Paris: Fayard, 1969, p. 120; Soutou, *L'alliance incertaine*, pp. 373–378.
56 Joint declaration of 25 Feb. 1982, *Europa-Archiv* 37 (1982), p. D194.
57 *Verhandlungen des Deutschen Bundestages*, 30 Jan. 1983, pp. 8978–8992.

Republic into neutrality. When Schmidt presented the bigger picture to him at a private meeting in June of 1983, his reaction was cautiously positive. He could not however bring himself to the decisive concession: a French nuclear guarantee for the Federal Republic.[58]

Not even the decision for jointly building a battle tank was carried out. Mitterrand did indeed push hard for its realization, but the West German arms-industry lobby as well as the budget-policy experts opposed it. In France, a new tank would be necessary by 1990, while that need would not arise in the Federal Republic until 1995. Additionally, there were fears in the Federal Republic of losing the export market for the successful "Leopard" battle tank; from the perspective of competition, there was also opposition to technology transfers to France. Given that the political justification for the project—the military union—had slipped from sight, German opponents of the decision of February 1980 were finally able to win out: The defense committee of the Bundestag halted development of the Franco-German tank in February of 1982.

What remained was the shared will to continue détente policy. Schmidt and Mitterrand were in agreement on putting up a fight against the demand by US President Ronald Reagan to reduce East-West trade in order to discipline the Soviet Union. The two leaders prevailed on the issue of constructing a natural gas pipeline from the USSR and also refused to expand the list of security-sensitive goods that could not be exported to the Eastern Bloc. When a storm of outrage erupted in French public opinion over the allegedly too feeble respond of the West Germans to the imposition of martial law in Poland in December of 1981, Mitterrand publicly emphasized that the views of the two governments were in accord. Both Bonn and Paris rejected the economic sanctions against the Soviet Union that Reagan had imposed in response to the ban on the Solidarity movement. When in June of 1982 the sanctions were extended to technical equipment needed by the Europeans for the construction of the natural gas pipeline, the EC foreign minister condemned the American action as "unacceptable for the Community."[59]

This solidarity continued after Helmut Schmidt had been replaced by Helmut Kohl. Hans-Dietrich Genscher, who remained in the role of foreign minister in the new coalition, had Kohl's support in advocating a declaration by the heads of state and of government of the Community affirming the goal of the "independence of Europe" in world politics. The "proposal for a European Act," for which they were seeking support from the partner governments, aimed "by means of a common foreign policy and common presence and action of the member states in

---

58 Schmidt, *Die Deutschen und ihre Nachbarn*, pp. 286–288.
59 Government declaration by Helmut Schmidt, 25 June 1982, *Europa-Archiv* 37 (1982), pp. D347–D352, quote on p. D350. Cf. Schmidt, *Die Deutschen und ihre Nachbarn*, pp. 260–266.

the world to make it possible for Europe increasingly to take on a global political role in accordance with its economic and political weight."⁶⁰

Thatcher, Genscher, and Colombo

Great Britain kept back from the new discussion over "the idea of a strong Europe that takes on its responsibility to the full extent."⁶¹ It was not only Callaghan who rejected stronger institutionalization and common foreign policy or an autonomous defense. Margaret Thatcher, who in 1975 had replaced Edward Heath as leader of the Conservatives and who had won parliamentary elections in May of 1979, also opted in a wholly-traditional way for national independence and close connections with the US. The "hard" attitude toward the Soviet Union that Carter had taken since the beginning of 1980 fit well with her temperament. Accordingly, she not only reduced diplomatic communication with Moscow but also publicly criticized Giscard's insufficient support for the new American course. She got along famously with Carter's successor Ronald Reagan.⁶²

Instead of developing a common foreign policy, Thatcher concentrated at the beginning of her term on the problem of British net payments to the Community, as it was presented to her by representatives of the British Treasury, which was critical of the EC. Thatcher was not an opponent of British membership. In regard to the European Community and its further development, she behaved like "an agnostic who continues to go to church," as Christopher Soames once remarked.⁶³ On the one hand, this led her to a series of initiatives for reconfiguring the Community according to her views. On the other, she also repeatedly let herself be seduced into sharply anti-European rhetoric, which brought her into conflict with various cabinet colleagues and thwarted her initiatives.

She took up the problem of net payments because, as things turned out at the end of the British transition phase, it had not been resolved by the "self-correcting mechanism" that Wilson had won from his partners: Thanks to North Sea oil reserves that had in the meantime been opened up and the resultant strengthening of the British pound, the UK's gross national product per capita never

---

60 German-Italian draft of 4 Nov. 1981, *Europa-Archiv* 37 (1982), pp. D50–D62.
61 According to Giscard d'Estaing in the French Council of Ministers on 16 July 1980, AN 5AG3 AE 72.
62 Joe Renouard and D. Nathan Vigil, "The Quest for Leadership in a Time of Peace. Jimmy Carter and Western Europe, 1977–1981," in: Schulz and Schwartz (eds.), *The Strained Alliance*, pp. 309–332, here pp. 329ff.
63 Young, *Blessed Plot*, p. 311.

sank below the threshold of eighty-five percent of the average of the member states, which would have triggered limits on the country's contributions to the Community. Because Britain continued to import more food and industrial products from third countries outside the Community and because its agricultural sector received few subsidies due to modernization and production in line with the market, the UK ended up paying approximately twice as much in tariffs and levies to the Community budget as it received from the Community. The Treasury calculated the expected difference as one billion pounds for the year 1980. The UK was thus the largest net payer into the Community, ahead of the Federal Republic, even though Britain's per capita GNP had already fallen behind those of countries such as France, Denmark, and the Netherlands.

Thatcher perceived that as a glaring injustice. With little sense for the economic and political gains that her country could derive from the Community, she demanded nothing less than a balance between payments and benefits. Her mantra became "I want my money back," which made for good publicity and which she repeatedly held against her partners. Schmidt and Giscard were confronted with this during their first encounters with the new prime minister, the other leaders of the Nine having to hear it at the first Council meeting in which she took part. When the Commission responded at the next Council meeting, in November of 1979 in Dublin, by presenting a modified distribution proposal that amounted to a reduction of British contributions by 350 million pounds, she rejected it as completely unsatisfactory. The partners in turn found that highly inappropriate, and so the Dublin Council meeting ended in an argument. Schmidt and Giscard were greatly annoyed by the endless tirades from the "grocer's daughter."[64]

After tempers had once again cooled, the partners made significantly greater concessions to British demands. Schmidt especially regarded those demands as partially justified. Under his influence, the British were offered a deal at the next Council meeting, in Copenhagen in April of 1980: The UK's contribution for the years 1980 and 1981 would be capped at the average amount from 1978 and 1979. That meant a reduction of some 760 million pounds. To the partners, this seemed to be a generous offer. British Foreign Minister Lord Carrington, State Secretary Michael Pallister, as well as Commission President Roy Jenkins urgently advised Thatcher to accept it. She once again refused any compromise, however, and this Council meeting too ended without result. At the end of May, Carrington did agree to this offer at a meeting of the Council of Ministers with the provision that the prospect also be held out of reducing the British contribution for 1982 and that the

---

[64] According to the characterization by a member of Giscard's staff; Jenkins, *European Diary*, pp. 528–531. Cf. *ibid.*, pp. 464–466 und Jenkins, *A Life at the Centre*, pp. 494–500.

Commission be given the task of developing a permanent solution. That was still not acceptable to Thatcher. Only after Carrington and foreign-policy parliamentary speaker Ian Gilmour threatened to resign did she agree to the interim solution.[65]

The Commission, since January of 1981 under the chairmanship of Gaston Thorn, made use of this opportunity to present a comprehensive reform program that overtly combined necessary adjustments to the Common Agricultural Policy with the expansion of intervention into other economic sectors. According to their report of 24 June 1981, agricultural expenditures were to be reduced by capping the subsidies when full supply was reached and then incrementally harmonized with world market prices. At the same time, the Regional Fund and the Social Fund were to be augmented. Thirdly, economic recovery was to be promoted through the expansion of the European Monetary System, increased investment in research and development, common energy-saving programs, and further harmonization of the rules of competition. Taken together, these measures were also to lead to a more uniform distribution of Community financial resources. Until that point had been reached, Great Britain was to receive compensation based on its percentage share of the GDP of the Community. In order to finance all this, the report declared that it was indispensable to increase the Community's share of the value-added tax from the then-current one percent to two percent.[66]

There was no agreement on this program, however. Mitterrand did support the increase in the portion of the value-added tax but rejected the reduction in guaranteed agricultural prices. It was the other way around with Thatcher, who was in agreement with cutting agricultural expenditures but opposed to any expansion of the Community budget. Schmidt joined in: Having in the meantime become the only net payer, he regarded the praxis of subsidy apportionment in the Community with great skepticism. Commission President Thorn was not in a position to break the two-way blockade: As a representative of the smallest member state and as a liberal without backing from any of the large party networks, he had difficulty simply bringing the Commission together on a unified course. He was all the less successful in getting the heads of state and of government to commit themselves to compromises, as Ortoli and Jenkins had previously been able to.

Thorn was forced to look on powerlessly as Thatcher sought to compel decision-making in line with her views by having her agriculture minister, Peter Walker, block the routine raising of agricultural prices for the production period 1982–83 over several months. This British extortion attempt could only be put to an end when France separated the Federal Republic from the bloc of those opposing

---

65 *Ibid.*, pp. 501–508; Jenkins, *European Diary*, pp. 604–607.
66 *Jahrbuch der Europäischen Integration 1981*, pp. 484–495.

increases. On 18 May 1982, the Council of Ministers summarily determined the agricultural increases by majority vote. Claude Cheysson, Mitterrand's foreign minister who had previously served eight years as a commissioner in Brussels, curtly declared that the issue of agricultural prices did not involve vital national interests; and so Great Britain would not be able to cite the Luxembourg Compromise.

As punishment for behavior hostile to the Community, Thatcher had to accept that the reduction of the difference between contributions and subsidies for 1982 ended up somewhat lower than it had for the previous two years. In 1983, she had to fight hard once again in order to emerge triumphantly from the Stuttgart Council meeting of 18 and 19 June with the declaration "I have my check."[67] Yet this too was nothing more than a temporary arrangement for one year. The British contribution question continued to poison the atmosphere and, along with the difficulties in negotiating with Spain and Portugal, contributed once again to the impression that the Community was unable to act or reform itself.

That impression became all the more persistent when, parallel to Thatcher's campaign for repayment, West German Foreign Minister Hans-Dietrich Genscher undertook an initiative to strengthen Community institutions. He was dissatisfied that Schmidt had so quickly accepted Giscard's about-face on the issue of expanding the rights of Parliament and that the decision of the Paris summit of December 1974 on dispensing with unanimity in the Council had more or less been forgotten. The foreign minister also regarded it as necessary to make the European autonomy practiced by Giscard and Schmidt multilateral so as to give it a more stable basis. In general, Genscher was seeking to make the integration process dynamic once again and to work precisely against the impression of a stalemate on Europe policy, which had resulted from Thatcher's campaign for repayment.

To this purpose, a plan for a "Treaty on European Union" was developed in the Europe Department of the West German Foreign Office during the spring of 1980. This was to strengthen the political goal of European unity, better coordinate established activities, and highlight possibilities for further development within a readily comprehensible framework. In other words, it was a matter of now making decisions on those parts of the Tindemans Report that—in contrast to direct elections and the monetary union—had remained in limbo up to that point. Genscher took up this proposal in early 1981 and did so publicly, given that he was chairman of the smaller coalition partner and was eager for the opportunity to have the Free Democrats distinguish themselves in the area of European policy. In a speech at the traditional meeting of the FDP in Stuttgart on Epiphany (6 January 1981), he declared that it was "finally time" for such a treaty. As goals of the European Union, he cited "the development of a common European foreign

---

67 Hans-Dietrich Genscher, *Erinnerungen*, Berlin: Siedler, 1995, p. 366.

policy, expansion of Community policy in accordance with the Treaties of Paris and Rome, coordination in the realm of defense policy, closer cooperation in cultural matters, and the harmonization of lawmaking."[68]

Genscher's initiative was taken up at once by Italian Foreign Minister Emilio Colombo. This Christian Democrat, who had long been an important figure in Italian politics, not only saw a chance to strengthen European institutions, a goal toward which he had already worked as president of the European Parliament from 1977 to 1979. He also welcomed the prospect of breaking up the Franco-German duopoly in formulating European foreign policy so as to have greater influence over shaping it. Two weeks after Genscher's speech in Stuttgart, Colombo joined in the call for a union treaty during a speech in Florence. Thereafter, he met repeatedly with the West German foreign minister in order to exchange ideas about the contents of such a treaty.

Reactions were less enthusiastic in the other capitals. Giscard d'Estaing envisioned attacks on him once again for selling out national sovereignty, attacks that he absolutely did not need before the presidential elections. After those elections, Mitterrand was first of all concerned with preventing his European partners from intervening in the socialistic economic program of the new government. A plan for creating a "great European social space," presented to the public on 13 October by French Europe Minister André Chandernagor, explicitly envisioned "no kind of institutional innovation" and unmistakably distanced itself from an "always somewhat unrealistic over-all concept."[69] Lord Carrington did signal interest in increasing foreign-policy cooperation, but he too was cool toward the notion of further institutional development.

Schmidt viewed these hesitant reactions as confirming his skepticism regarding the chances of achieving this initiative—and thus also his skepticism regarding its utility. When Genscher presented his draft treaty to the West German cabinet on 18 September, he also ran into opposition from Defense Minister Hans Apel, who was not pleased with the proposed expansion of foreign-policy cooperation into the realm of defense policy. After thorough discussion, a majority of the cabinet decided that it would not be possible to win acceptance for a new treaty that would be binding in international law. Genscher was only given permission

---

[68] *Europa-Archiv* 36 (1981), p. D164. Cf. Wilfried Loth, "Deutsche Europapolitik von Helmut Schmidt bis Helmut Kohl," in: Knipping and Schönwald (eds.), *Aufbruch*, pp. 474–488; Hans-Dieter Lucas, "Politik der kleinen Schritte – Genscher und die deutsche Europapolitik 1974–1983," in: *idem.* (eds.), *Genscher, Deutschland und Europa*, Baden-Baden: Nomos, 2002, pp. 85–113; Ulrich Rosengarten, *Die Genscher-Colombo-Initiative. Baustein für die Europäische Union*, Baden-Baden: Nomos, 2008.

[69] *Jahrbuch der Europäischen Integration 1981*, pp. 505–519.

to negotiate on a "political declaration of principle" whereby the heads of state and of government were to implement the pledges of the 1972 Paris summit. There was not to be any mention of establishing a separate council for defense-policy issues, which Genscher had previously advocated.[70]

Nonetheless, in order to give the initiative as much gravity as was still possible, Genscher and Colombo decided to present it as a joint initiative of the governments of the Federal Republic and Italy and to raise the status of the sought-after declaration of principle rhetorically through use of the name "European Act." On 4 November, they presented a joint draft. This reinforced the desire for a common foreign and security policy, completion of the internal market, and further development of the European Monetary System. New realms of cooperation cited in the document were culture, the legal system, and domestic security. In terms of institutions, it envisioned the creation of a secretariat for EPC, semiannual reports by the European Council to Parliament, ratification of international treaties by Parliament, and a commitment to restraint in using the veto right in the Council (those making use of the veto were to justify it in writing). Beyond this, the draft contained a declaration that the agreements would be reviewed after five years. If that review was positive, then a legally-binding treaty would be concluded.[71]

The European Council put off the proposal for the time being. In an *ad hoc* committee created at the Council meeting in London on 27 and 28 November, the various doubts were articulated about institutional augmentation and expanded content. When the Council of Ministers took up the matter on 20 June 1982, Genscher and Colombo did not succeed in dispelling those doubts. Only after Kohl had become chancellor in October of 1982 and had made the "European Act" a core component of *his* European policy did the project gain momentum. As leader of the opposition, he had made intensive efforts to develop the transnational Christian Democratic network of the "European People's Party." Hence, he eagerly made use of the opportunity right at the beginning of his chancellorship to distinguish himself in European politics and so approached Mitterrand with this intention. "I was of the firm conviction," he wrote in retrospect, "that I should dare to take the decisive step on the way to the political unification of Europe in this decade."[72]

---

[70] Werner Link, "Außen- und Sicherheitspolitik in der Ära Schmidt 1974–1982," in: Wolfgang Jäger and Werner Link (eds.), *Republik im Wandel 1974–1982. Die Ära Schmidt*, Stuttgart and Mannheim: Deutsche Verlagsgesellschaft, 1987, pp. 275–432, here p. 35; Genscher, *Erinnerungen*, p. 364.
[71] *Europa-Archiv* 37 (1982), pp. D50–D62.
[72] Helmut Kohl, *Erinnerungen 1982–1990*, Munich: Droemer, 2004, p. 101; on the following, *ibid.*, pp. 108–111, and Hans-Peter Schwarz, *Helmut Kohl. Eine politische Biographie*, Munich: Deutsche Verlags-Anstalt, 2012, pp. 397–407.

He benefited from the fact that in the first half of 1983 it was the turn of the Federal Republic to chair the Council. In the third week of March, he made it easier for Mitterrand to remain in the European Monetary System by pushing through another increase in the value of the mark parallel to the devaluation of the franc and the Italian lira; Kohl did this against the advice of most of the finance ministers and central bank governors. Then, he made use of the trust he had thereby gained in Mitterrand's eyes to convince the French president to commit to a series of weakened formulations along the lines of the Genscher-Colombo program. The result of their agreements was the "Solemn Declaration on European Union," which the European Council passed at its meeting in Stuttgart. At its core, this document was still only a declaration of intent regarding the deepening of existing interrelations and the development of new areas of cooperation. In contrast to the German-Italian proposal, there was mention of agricultural policy, social policy, and promotion of regional development; cooperation in the defense realm was limited to its "political and economic aspects." In institutional terms, there was only the promise of circumspection in exercising the veto right and increased consultation of Parliament. In regard to treaties binding in international law, it was merely the case that official "positions" from Parliament would be necessary.[73]

The value of this weakened form of the "European Act" was further restricted by unilateral declarations. No fewer than five of the ten signatories issued protocols that held to the necessity of unanimity in the Council of Ministers on so-called vital issues: France, Ireland, Greece, Great Britain, and Denmark. The last two of these states did not even want a commitment to justify use of the veto in writing. Additionally, the Greeks declared that their right to shape their foreign policy according to national interests could in no way be encroached upon; for their part, the Danes voiced reservations about six points of the declaration altogether.

Mitterrand's approach to Kohl's policies went beyond the basic commitment to a concerted expansion of the Communities and cooperation among the governments. After he had come to understand that the modernization of France could in the end be ensured only together with the Community and that for this reason, there was no alternative to close partnership with the Federal Republic, he was prepared in the run-up to the Stuttgart Council meeting to agree in principle to limiting the agricultural budget. The French government declared that it was in agreement with a process proposed by Bonn for reforming agricultural policy. This meant that, as already mentioned, a negotiation packet on reform of agricultural policy, the increase in revenue, and the definitive settlement of the British entry issue could be gotten underway at Stuttgart.

---

73 *Europa-Archiv* 37 (1982), pp. D420–D427.

After the Stuttgart meeting, Kohl and Mitterrand intensified their telephone contacts and meetings; informal conversations between the top officials of both governments occurred more frequently too. In the third week of September, staff of the chancellor's office and of the Élysée Palace met for a Franco-German seminar at Konrad Adenauer's one-time vacation spot, Cadenabbia on Lake Como, in order to inform each other about their methods of work and their positions. Here, the unresolved questions of European politics were thoroughly reviewed "in the course of very open discussion."[74] In the process, it seems that Mitterrand's understanding grew regarding the necessity of Europe for securing French independence. "We find ourselves between two empires that treat us like colonies," he said to his advisor Jacques Attali. "What should one do to resist them, if not build Europe?"[75] At the end of the year, Mitterrand replaced Europe Minister Chandernagor with his personal friend Roland Dumas, who quickly succeeded in establishing close contact with Genscher.

In this way, a whole series of points of Franco-German understanding was achieved. Over the winter of 1983–84, Paris and Bonn agreed on the production of a joint attack helicopter, several projects of technical-scientific cooperation within the framework of the Community's ESPRIT research program, as well as a series of technical regulations for the dismantling of protectionism and imbalances in Franco-German trade. In May of 1984, an agreement was concluded that provided for the incremental dismantling of border controls for persons and goods moving between France and the Federal Republic. All these measures were intended to serve as models for extension to other countries of the Community.

Parallel to this, the two parties coordinated their stances on the Stuttgart negotiation packet. The agreement on agricultural policy was concretized to the effect that the price guarantee for milk was to be limited quantitatively; prices for agricultural products were to be generally frozen. In return, Bonn agreed to the incremental dismantling of the so-called currency equalization payments to West German agriculturists who exported to other Community countries. Regarding the portion of the value-added tax that the Community was to receive as revenue, the West German government would not accept a doubling, as the Commission had been seeking, but nevertheless would agree to a hike from 1.0 to 1.4 percent. Regarding British contributions, Mitterrand accepted in the end a reduction of

---

[74] Report from Mitterrand's staffer Pierre Morel, 21 Sept. 1983, AN 5AG5 4, quoted in George Saunier, "Prélude à la relance de l'Europe. Le couple franco-allemand et les projets de relance communautaire vue de l'hexagone 1981–1985," in: Bitsch, *Le couple France-Allemagne*, pp. 463–485, here p. 479.
[75] Notes, 17 Feb. 1984, Jacques Attali, *Verbatim*. Vol. I: *Chronique des années 1981–1986*, Paris: Fayard, 1993, p. 594.

two-thirds of the difference between payments from the value-added tax and subsidies from the Community budget.

On the basis of these agreements, a solution to the budget problems—accumulating since 1979—could have been reached at the Council meeting in Brussels on 19 and 20 March 1984. The breakthrough that had been carefully prepared by Bonn and Paris did not materialize there because Margaret Thatcher was not content with the level of reimbursement of British payments to which Mitterrand had agreed. Given that receipts from tariffs and levies were no longer included in the calculation, the permanent settlement being offered was in fact significantly lower than the one-time payments of previous years. Thatcher found this all the less acceptable given that the portion of the value-added tax going to the Community was to rise by forty percent. Because she persisted in her demands with accustomed stubbornness, Kohl simply refused to negotiate further with her. The heads of state and of government went their separate ways without results.

Up to the time of the next Council meeting, set for 25 and 26 June in Fontainebleau, Mitterrand—who was then serving as Council president—sought out all the governments individually in order to align them with the compromise negotiated between Bonn and Paris. At the same time, he let it be known in several public utterances, most clearly in a speech before the European Parliament in Strasbourg on 24 May, that he was now prepared to have the project for a European Union as advocated by Genscher and Colombo put into the form of a treaty. Bonn and Paris privately agreed on an alternate plan if Mrs. Thatcher were to stick with her noncompliant attitude: In that event, the treaty on the European Union was to be completed without Great Britain and instead only among those countries willing to accept it. For this purpose, the staffs of the Élysée Palace and the chancellery prepared a joint memorandum to be presented at a conference to be called by Mitterrand outside the mechanism of the Council. The French president did not leave the British government in the dark about the fact that Bonn and Paris were seriously contemplating this alternative.[76]

The threat of a core Europe without Great Britain worked. It was the case that at the meeting in Fontainebleau, Thatcher did demonstratively show that she was unimpressed initially. When Mitterrand interrupted the talks on the second day of negotiations with the observation that he saw hardly any prospect of success, however, she suddenly gave in. In a conversation with the French president, she accepted a settlement that was only one percent higher than the position on which Bonn and Paris had agreed. Kohl consented to this under the condition that the Federal Republic, as the largest net payer, would need to shoulder only two-thirds of the British rebate and that the other members take on more on a per-

---

76 Saunier, "Prélude," pp. 481–483.

centage basis. Further, he insisted that the hike in the portion of the value-added tax be linked to the conclusion of negotiations with Spain and Portugal; it was to be in effect from 1 January 1986.[77]

After the budget problems that had been building up since 1979 had finally been solved in this way, the further development of the Community as discussed in the context of the Genscher-Colombo initiative could be taken up concretely. Aware of the alternate plans that Mitterrand and Kohl had prepared, Thatcher came to Fontainebleau with a paper entitled "Europe, the Future," which indicated where Britain saw a need for development: in cooperation on foreign and security policy as well as in liberalizing the Common Market.[78] The partners eagerly took up this signal. In the closing communiqué of the Council meeting, the heads of state and of government announced their intention to provide a new and powerful impetus to economic development in Europe, which was to be accomplished by means of "completing the internal market" as well as developing scientific and technical potential. They then appointed two committees that were to work out measures for the further development of the Community: a "Committee for the Europe of the Citizen," which was to develop proposals for mobility across borders and for citizens' identification with the Community, as well as a Committee for the Further Development of European Institutions and Cooperation.[79]

In the middle of 1984, it was therefore not only the southern expansion that entered the home stretch. It was also the case that the course was set for the further development of the Community, oriented on the needs of the time: the increased necessity of acting autonomously in world politics and the challenge of competition from the up-and-coming economic powers of the Far East, especially Japan. After a moment of crisis stemming from Mitterrand's initial unfamiliarity with the European policy of Giscard d'Estaing, the surprising approach of the Socialist president to Kohl had provided a new ability to take action. It was thus no coincidence that photos of a commemoration at the graves of soldiers in Verdun on 22 September 1984 showing Mitterrand spontaneously taking Kohl's hand became the emblem of a new epoch of Franco-German leadership in European policy.

---

[77] On the course of the Council meeting in Fontainebleau, Genscher, *Erinnerungen*, pp. 369ff.; Jacques Attali, *Verbatim* I, pp. 658–660; Roland Dumas, *Le Fil et la Pelote. Mémoires*, Paris: Omnibus, 1996, pp. 330ff.; Young, *Blessed Plot*, pp. 322–324.
[78] *Europa-Archiv* 39 (1984), pp. D434–D440.
[79] Conclusions of the chair of the European Council, 25 and 26 June 1984, *ibid.*, pp. D440–D443.

6 The Era of Development, 1984–1992

The Single European Act

The *ad hoc* Committee on Further Development of European Institutions and Cooperation, appointed by the European Council in Fontainebleau, took up its work on 28 September 1984. It consisted in equal parts of the state secretaries of the foreign or Europe ministries of the Ten and independent figures holding no governmental office at the time. Given that Ireland had in the meantime assumed the Council presidency, Irish Senator and former Foreign Minister James Dooge was chosen as chairman. In the vaguest of terms, the committee's task was "to put forward proposals for the better functioning of European cooperation in the Community area as well as in the area of Political Cooperation and in other areas." The proposals were to have a function similar to that of the Spaak Report for the development of the Treaties of Rome. In the appointment of this body, there was explicit reference to the Spaak Committee.[1]

In its work, the Dooge Committee could lean upon a draft "Treaty on European Union," which the European Parliament had passed on 14 February 1984. This document traced its origins to Altiero Spinelli, who had given up his attempt to win more political authority for the Commission in May of 1976; now as a member of the European Parliament, elected on the slate of the Italian Communists, he was seeking to convince his colleagues to support a fundamental reform initiative from Parliament. He met with success too, given that members of Parliament were still dissatisfied with the relationship between the amount of effort they put into their positions and their actual influence over Europe policy. In July of 1981, there was a decision to work out a draft treaty that would replace the existing Community treaties. The resulting document, on which the Institutional Committee had labored for over a year, was approved by an overwhelming majority of Parliament: 237 to 31, with 43 abstentions.

There was an awareness of Spinelli's role in developing the draft, and so it later gained the reputation of paying homage to federalist maximal positions. In fact, it differed little from what in the Tindemans Report had already been regarded as capable of achieving a consensus. The draft retained the existing division between the Community realm and intergovernmental cooperation; it only envisioned that, "after consultation with the Commission and with the approval of Parliament," the European Council was to have the right to transfer further political areas into the realm of "common action." Decision-making in the

---

[1] *Jahrbuch der Europäischen Integration 1984*, pp. 436ff.

Council of Ministers was to be by qualified majority; during a transition period of ten years, however, member states were to have the right to demand deferral of a decision by reference to the "vital interest of a state"; such a motion was to be granted if the Commission confirmed such an interest. Parliament was to have equal status with the Council of Ministers in regard to participation in legislative and budgetary proceedings. The draft also gave the Commission president the power to put together the Commission after consultation with the Council. If Parliament passed a motion of no-confidence in the Commission, then the latter would need to resign; in that case, the European Council would then name a new Commission president.

The only really new feature of the draft treaty of the European Parliament was the process envisioned for its implementation: It was not addressed to the European Council or the Council of Ministers but rather directly to the national governments. They were to bring about its ratification after the requisite process in each country. As soon as the treaty had been approved "by a majority of the member states whose populations equal two-thirds of the total population of the Community," a government conference of the involved states was to be called and a process and date of implementation were to be decided—and there was also to be a decision "on relations with the member states that had not yet ratified it." This meant that efforts to block it by countries opposed to reform, such as Britain or Denmark, were ruled out, as was any dilution of the draft by a government conference that was dependent on consensus among all member states.[2]

For their part, the governments were clearly not prepared to give up control over a decision about going forward without Britain or Denmark or probably Greece either. Contrary to what Spinelli had hoped, they were not pressured into doing so by the national parliaments either. Only the Italian Chamber of Deputies—by a large majority—demanded that its government embrace the draft treaty of the European Parliament. In the other parliaments, similar motions either found no majority or were not introduced at all. In a speech before the Strasbourg parliament on 24 May 1984, Mitterrand, who was then serving as Council president, did speak out in principle for a new treaty and let it be known that he was willing to draw inspiration from Parliament's draft. He appointed Maurice Faure as the French non-governmental representative on the Dooge Committee; Faure had played a decisive role in the negotiations on the Treaties of Rome in 1956–57 while serving as state secretary.

---

[2] Text in: Lipgens, *45 Jahre*, pp. 711–736; preliminary drafts, *ibid.*, pp. 654–710. Cf. Daniela Preda, "L'action de Spinelli au Parlement européen et le projet de Traité d'Union européenne (1979–1984)," in: Wilfried Loth (ed.), *La gouvernance supranationale dans la construction européenne*, Brussels: Émile Bruylant, 2005, pp. 185–203.

Given that preparation, the Dooge Committee also came to the conclusion that a new treaty should be made, one that codified the expansion of Community activities and provided "more effective democratic institutions." In doing so, the committee was guided by a report that Faure had introduced into the deliberations. As a means of achieving such a treaty, it was proposed that a government conference be called in accordance with Article 236 of the EEC Treaty. In terms of content, the basis of the negotiations was to be provided by "the *acquis communautaire*, this report, and the Solemn Declaration of Stuttgart"; it was also explicitly stated that "inspiration should come from the spirit and method of the draft treaty passed by the European Parliament." The Dooge Committee made recommendations very similar to those of Parliament regarding the tasks of the European Union, majority voting in the Council of Ministers, co-decision-making by Parliament, and the strengthening of the Commission.[3]

Of course, these were in part the positions of the majority. Representatives of Britain, Denmark, and Greece made clear in annotations at various places that they were of a different opinion. This was especially the case regarding majority-voting by the Council of Ministers and to an extent for the rights of Parliament as well. The minority went on record saying that consultations among the governments should take place before a decision was made to call a government conference. Right at the beginning of the Brussels Council meeting of 29 and 30 March 1985, the heads of state and of government then opted to postpone a decision on the Dooge Report until the next gathering, scheduled for late June in Milan.

The Thatcher government argued that what in its view constituted the heart of the matter—strengthening foreign-policy cooperation and completing the internal market—could be achieved without treaty amendments. At a meeting of the Council of Ministers on 10 June in Stresa, Foreign Secretary Geoffrey Howe presented a plan for committing to a "gentlemen's agreement" as a means of avoiding a logjam on the internal market. In the event of conflict, dissenting members ought simply to abstain. Beyond this, an agreement on Political Cooperation ought to be reached. There was no mention of new institutions in this plan, only talk of closer cooperation under the leadership of the European Council. As Helmut Kohl commented, it was "an agreement not to go very far."[4]

In order to avoid having their initiative for institutional reform get bogged down in this way, Kohl and François Mitterrand had a "Draft Treaty on European Union" prepared in haste a few days before the gathering in Milan. This document focused wholly on the expansion of foreign and defense policy. The

---

[3] *Europa-Archiv* 40 (1985), pp. D240–D253.
[4] Attali, *Verbatim I*, p. 1241. The draft of the Agreement on Political Cooperation was again presented at Milan; text in: *Europa-Archiv* 40 (1985), pp. D 446–D449.

development of a common foreign policy, including the political and economic aspects of defense, was to be promoted by establishing a general secretariat of the European Council. The continued presence of the Commission at the sessions of the Council was to be stipulated in the treaty, likewise regular consultation of Parliament. The draft was announced by Kohl in the Bundestag on 27 June, one day before the beginning of the Milan conference. The text became available to participants only a few hours before the opening of the meeting.[5]

Nowhere in the eleven paragraphs of the draft treaty was there any mention of reforming the decision-making procedures within the existing Community. This gave rise to the suspicion, not only among the representatives of Italy and the Benelux states, that here was another attempt by the Franco-German duo to subordinate the Community to the *diktat* of the governments. Jacques Delors, who had succeeded Gaston Thorn as Commission president at the beginning of the year, met with Kohl and Mitterrand on the sidelines of the Council meeting in Fontainebleau and voiced such misgivings to both leaders. The two quickly realized that tactically they had gotten on the wrong track. Mitterrand suddenly began speaking of nothing more than a "mere work instrument." On the second working day, West German Foreign Minister Hans-Dietrich Genscher presented a new work instrument: a paper that embraced the recommendations of the Dooge Committee on the whole and especially emphasized the necessity of summoning a government conference for reforming the Treaties of Rome. After the foreign ministers' dinner, he did some thinking and dictated his ideas the next morning while shaving.[6]

As expected, Thatcher and her Greek colleague Andreas Papandreou along with Danish Prime Minister Poul Schlüter offered opposition to the new West German proposal. During a pause in the talks, the advocates of a government conference discussed whether it should be called by majority decision. Italian Prime Minister Bettino Craxi and Foreign Minister Giulio Andreotti were immediately in favor of such a move, as were Kohl and Genscher. For his part, Luxembourg Foreign Minister Jacques Poos cautioned against splitting the Community. Then, however, Mitterrand was persuaded by Genscher to support a majority decision. As could already be seen in the run-up to the Council meeting of Fontainebleau,

---

[5] *Europa-Archiv* 40 (1985), pp. D449–D451. Cf. Ulrich Lappenküper, "Die deutsche Europapolitik zwischen der 'Genscher-Colombo-Initiative' und der Verabschiedung der Einheitlichen Europäischen Akte (1981–1986)," in: *Historisch-Politische Mitteilungen* 10 (2003), pp. 275–294; also on the following.

[6] Jacques Delors, *Erinnerungen eines Europäers*, Berlin: Parthas, 2004, pp. 257–261; Genscher, *Erinnerungen*, p. 373.

the French president too believed that, if in doubt, it was more important to make progress on Europe policy than to have Britain come along.[7]

The results of the Milan Council meeting were thereby determined. When the plenary session resumed, Craxi—who was serving as Council president in the first half of 1985—put the German proposal up for a vote, which was a complete surprise to Thatcher. It was adopted by a margin of seven to three. This had been the first use of majority voting in the European Council. When the opponents of a government conference protested, they were told that this was only a vote on a procedural matter; it was thus not possible to resort to claims of vital national interests. By applying a procedural rule of the Council of Ministers, Craxi had in fact made it clear that in the end the European Community itself could decide whether it wanted to take up treaty revision.[8]

Thatcher was absolutely furious about that. With an eye toward her own goals regarding the internal market and foreign policy, however, she could not bring herself to torpedo the government conference that had now been decided upon. Instead, following the counsel of her staff, she quickly concentrated on representing her interests to the Council. By approving the "Conclusions" of the Council, Papandreou and Schlüter also signaled their willingness to participate in the government conference. By the time of the next Council meeting in December in Luxembourg, the conference was to present a draft treaty on common foreign and defense policy as well as proposals for reforming the EEC Treaty and regulations for the new fields of activity.

The Milan Council meeting also approved the report on the "Europe of the Citizens," which had been worked out by the second *ad hoc* committee under the chairmanship of the former Italian MEP Pietro Adonnino. It contained an abundance of proposals for establishing the free movement of people and goods in the Community, simplifying residency and employment in other member states, organizing economic areas that extended beyond borders, recognizing the equivalency of educational degrees and certificates, promoting the establishment of partner cities and student exchanges, simplifying dealings with European authorities, introducing a European passport, and using the European flag. The European Council accepted all the proposals and directed the Commission and the member states "to take the necessary measures for implementation."[9] A decision by the Council of Ministers made the banner with twelve stars on a blue

---

7 Ibid.
8 C. Luuk van Middelaar, *Le passage à l'Europe. Histoire d'un commencement*, Paris: Gallimard, 2012, pp. 171–182.
9 "Schlussfolgerungen des Europäischen Rates von Mailand 28./29.6.1985," *Jahrbuch der Europäischen Integration 1985*, pp. 425–429; the Adonnino Report, *ibid.*, pp. 423–425.

ground, originally used by the Council of Europe, the official flag of the European Communities on 29 May 1986.

Lastly, the Council in Milan also approved a "White Paper for Completing the Internal Market," which had been commissioned from Delors and had been presented on 14 June. This document embraced demands that Étienne Davignon as commissioner for enterprise and industry and especially Karl-Heinz Narjes as commissioner for economic and financial affairs had made but that had always been defeated in the Council of Ministers during Thorn's presidency due to opposition arising from national interests. These demands related not only to the elimination of technical and legal hindrances to trade that had still not been abolished with the completion of the Customs Union in 1968 but also to the many direct and indirect subsidies, administrative rules, and tax advantages that the governments had implemented in order to protect national production in the face of the oil shocks of 1973 and 1979. In the meantime, all this constituted a great danger to economic growth: Entrepreneurs and corporations viewed the Common Market as coming under increasing threat and consequently were hesitating to continue investing in Europe. In the process, competitiveness fell *vis-à-vis* the US and Japan, both of which—in contrast to the Europeans—were again experiencing considerable rates of growth. Year by year, the memoranda in which the Thorn Commission called for measures to complete the internal market had become more urgent; the recommendations by the European Council stemming from these documents remained largely without effect. At the Council meeting in Fontainebleau, a memorandum of 7 June 1984 that listed over one hundred distinct measures necessary for establishing complete market freedom within two years had not even been acknowledged due to the focus on resolving budgetary issues.

After thorough consultations with government heads and having been influenced by demands from industry, Delors now decided to make the internal-market project the central theme of his presidency. He gained Thatcher as an ally: She took seriously the elimination of hindrances to trade in the European Community as a parallel to the liberalization of the British market and was supported by British entrepreneurs as well as the City in her fight for genuine competition in the European market. Delors gave responsibility for economic affairs on the Commission to Lord Francis Arthur Cockfield, a confidant of Thatcher with experience in politics as well as the business world; he directed the operationalization of the internal-market project with great professionalism. Delors then consciously went public with his effort, and beginning with his inaugural address before the European Parliament on 14 January 1985, he promoted a date for completion of the project—by 1992. Lastly, the Commission presented in the white paper a precise timeline for implementing some 282 individual steps and legal acts that in the meantime were regarded as necessary for actually completing the internal market. By not only approving the document in principle but also its timeline, the European Council in Milan gave Delors a means by which to bring pressure on the governments.[10]

Roughly speaking, there were two factions in the government conference that began with the session of the Council of Ministers on 9 and 10 September in Luxembourg: those who sought to implement as much as possible of the institutional reform program of Parliament and of the Dooge Committee—Italy, Ireland, and the Benelux states; and those who wanted to embrace as little as possible of that program—Britain, Denmark, and Greece. That a new logjam did not develop was partly thanks to the close cooperation between Genscher and French Foreign Minister Roland Dumas, who decisively focused the negotiations on what was achievable. After Claude Cheysson had rejoined the Brussels Commission at the beginning of the year, Dumas had returned to the foreign ministry and was now at pains to ensure an even closer coordination between Paris and Bonn. Moreover, the Commission supplied the conference with well-formulated proposed texts on the spot; and Delors was indefatigable in justifying them by reference to the requirements of the internal market. In terms of procedure, he was supported in this by Luxembourg Council President Jacques Santer and his foreign minister, Jacques Poos; the trio quickly became known in the sessions of the Council of Ministers as "the three Jacques."[11]

Regarding the practice of majority voting, Delors succeeded in having it apply for all relevant areas of the internal market, though with the important exceptions of tax policy, free movement of persons, and employee rights. Whereas in accordance with the terms of the EEC Treaty more than two thirds of the measures proposed in the white paper would have required unanimity, it would now be only one quarter. Unanimity was necessary for bringing new policy areas into the Community realm, but as soon as they were introduced, majority voting would apply here as well.

Regarding the rights of Parliament, the maximalists were supported by the Germans and the minimalists by the French. Following a proposal from the Commission, the result was a "Process of Cooperation," which accorded Parliament limited right of participation in those areas in which the Council of Ministers decided by majority vote. Amendments made by Parliament to Council decisions, if approved by the Commission, could now only be rejected by unanimous vote of

---

[10] "Completing the Internal Market. White Paper from the Commission to the European Council," COM (85), 310 final. On Delors' strategy, cf. Helen Drake, *Jacques Delors. Perspectives on a European Leader*, London and New York: Routledge, 2000, pp. 78–112.
[11] Delors, *Erinnerungen*, p. 269.

the Council of Ministers. Nevertheless, there were some areas in which this right of participation would not apply despite majority voting in the Council: in determining foreign-trade tariffs, in granting free movement of services and capital, as well as in transportation and agricultural policy. Additionally, future treaties for the accession of new members and association agreements were to require approval by an absolute majority of Parliament. Also, the status of Parliament was conceptually raised to a certain extent: Whereas up to this point the French government especially had placed emphasis on speaking only of a "Parliamentary Assembly" (in accordance with the formulation in the Treaties of Rome), the new treaty made use of the term "European Parliament," the name that the body had given itself in 1962.

The concern for efficiency in implementing the internal-market project as reflected in these regulations also led to an expansion of the executive responsibilities of the Commission: It was empowered to issue regulations to implement guidelines for harmonizing legal provisions and ensuring competition. Nevertheless, the governments retained the right to take on implementation themselves in "special cases" if the Council of Ministers unanimously decided on this. Beyond that, "regulatory committees" were established by which the governments would oversee implementation. Delors failed in his attempt to have these committees granted merely advisory functions.

In regard to foreign and defense policy, it was essentially the case that the old system was retained. More precisely, the practice up to that point was now put into treaty form. Dumas and Genscher wanted to strengthen it by establishing a general secretariat of the European Council, as had been envisioned in the Franco-German draft of a Union Treaty. However, this did not gain support from the small states, which feared that the Commission would fall under tutelage, or from the British, who—in contrast to the era of Edward Heath—now did not want any new structures for foreign or security policy. The institutional augmentation that the European Council received was limited to a small administrative secretariat in Brussels, to which some officials of the prior, the current, and the next Council president would belong. Furthermore, the Communities and Political Cooperation were now incorporated into a common treaty text, while the European Council was anchored in the treaty as the overarching institution; however, their integration still did not go beyond the presence of the Commission at all gatherings of the Council, of the foreign ministers, and of their directors. Because neither Denmark nor Britain wanted a European Union, the term "Act of the European Union" could not be approved for the new treaty. As a minimal compromise, there remained the qualification of the act as "single," which emphasized the link between the Communities and Cooperation.

The treaty anchored and provided specifications regarding social policy, regional policy, research policy, and environmental policy. The program for a "European Social Space" was not as greatly expanded as Mitterrand had demanded at the beginning of his presidency and as was now also being advocated by the Danish government (which, being a minority government, was dependent on approval from the opposition Social Democrats). Yet, directives for occupational safety and health protection were transferred into the realm of majority decision-making; and the Commission was assigned the task of promoting collective treaties among the social partners on the European level. The Regional Fund was embedded in a program for promoting "economic and social cohesion," which amounted to increased resources for the fund and introduced majority voting on regulations related to implementation. Regarding research and technology policy, the practice of the multi-year Framework Programs for Research that had been implemented by the Commission in 1984 was now institutionalized. At the same time, measures were taken to help these policy areas become more effective by means of majority voting and cooperation with national and international research programs. Lastly, environmental protection was declared to be a goal of the Community. Due to opposition from the less-developed states, this did not go beyond very general stipulations; financing remained the responsibility of individual member states, aside from measures with a Community character.

Despite the program's varied offerings to less-developed and less socially-progressive member states, Delors had to accept some curtailments of his internal-market program. Demands for retention of the veto right had originally extended beyond tax policy, free movement of persons, and employee rights. By this means, Britain and Ireland had wanted to retain oversight of health; Ireland had additionally wanted to retain control over insurance and banking affairs. In general, the free movement of persons ended up being threatened by a situation in which the concept of a "space without internal borders" would be replaced by a market concept. Delors was only able to avoid that by personally requesting help from Mitterrand and Kohl. At the "conclave" of the foreign ministers shortly before the Council meeting in Luxembourg on 2 and 3 December, Dumas and Genscher presented a joint draft that saved the essential provisions of the internal-market program. True, the announcement on realizing the "space without internal boundaries" by 31 December 1992 did not have any legally-binding character. To what extent the resistance of individual states to its achievement could actually be overcome was thus left open.

Delors achieved still less in regard to the completion of the monetary union. In his view, it was a logical counterpart to the free movement of capital and, in the final analysis, also an element of the unified market regulations. He thus wanted to include in the act the stipulation that the European Monetary Fund that was envisioned in the European Monetary System could be created by unanimous decision of the Council. However, the British as well as the Germans and Dutch opposed this. For her part, Thatcher simply could not imagine giving up British sovereignty over the currency; and Kohl heeded warnings from the *Bundesbank* and Finance Minister Gerhard Stoltenberg about renewed adverse effects on the West German stability course. At a meeting in London on 27 November, both leaders agreed that the project of a monetary union should not be mentioned at all in the treaty.

In a bilateral meeting during the Luxembourg Council, Mitterrand threatened Kohl by saying that if the monetary union were not included in the treaty, France would not approve the internal-market program; the chancellor then backed away from the commitment he had made in London. He accepted a formulation from Delors by which the signatories would in regard to economic policy cooperation commit themselves to "take into consideration experiences gained in cooperation in the framework of the European Monetary System (EMS) and the development of the ECU." Acting at the urging of Stoltenberg's State Secretary Hans Tietmeyer, Kohl also insisted that institutional reforms in monetary policy be regarded as treaty amendments and also that before any decision-making, "the Monetary Committee and the Committee of the Central Bank Governors" were to be consulted. This was still far too much for Thatcher. Feeling betrayed once again, she threatened to veto these provisions. Only after her staff had made it clear to her that in essence what was meant was only the continuance of current practice regarding monetary policy cooperation did she back off.

The Single European Act (SEA), as it emerged after more than thirty hours of discussion in the European Council,[12] was thus far from the clear structure that had characterized the draft treaty of the European Parliament. Spinelli, who as reporting secretary of the Institutional Committee had been informed of the course of the negotiations on an ongoing basis, spoke with deep disappointment of the "wretched little mouse" to which the government conference had given birth.[13] It was clearly the case that a more coherent and far-reaching reform was hardly to be expected if one wanted to bring the minimalists further along

---

12 Text in *Europa-Archiv* 41 (1986), pp. D163–D182; on the course of the government conference and the Luxembourg Council meeting, Jean de Ruyt, *L'Acte unique européen. Commentaire*, Brussels: Édition de l'Université de Bruxelles, 1987; Ken Endo, *The Presidency of the European Commission under Jacques Delors. The Politics of Shared Leadership*, London and New York: Palgrave Macmillan, 1999, pp. 140–151; Dietrich Rometsch, *Die Rolle und Funktionsweise der Europäischen Kommission in der Ära Delors*, Frankfurt am Main: Peter Lang, 1999, pp. 112–130.
13 Speech before the Institutional Committee of the European Parliament on 4 Feb. 1986, Altiero Spinelli, *Discorsi al Parlamento europeo 1976–1986*, Bologna: Il Mulino, 1987, p. 370.

toward a European Union. However, a break with them was only a second-best solution in the eyes of Kohl and Mitterrand; and they were happy that Thatcher helped them avoid such an outcome by offering a partial accommodation.[14] In this regard, Delors' internal-market project proved to be functional in a double sense: On the one hand, it evoked memories of the most important challenge that had faced the Community in the middle of the 1980s and thereby made a break with Britain seem particularly inappropriate. On the other hand, it served to make Thatcher somewhat more willing to offer concessions regarding supranational regulations, to an extent far beyond what could be reconciled with her ideological premises. In fact, after years of stagnation, the Single European Act was to make possible a far-reaching attainment of the internal market and thereby also unleash a new dynamic in other areas of integration. Spinelli's harsh judgment was a significant exaggeration.

When on 16 and 17 December the Council of Ministers was in the final debate on the draft treaty, the foreign ministers of Italy and Denmark both withheld their final position—Andreotti doing so because the draft did not go far enough in acceding to the demands of the European Parliament and his Danish colleague doing so because the concessions to Parliament went too far. After the Single European Act had been rejected by the Danish Parliament on 2 January 1986, a referendum had to be organized in the country. This meant that at the signing of the act by the foreign ministers in Luxembourg on 17 February 1986, only nine states were represented, among them the new members Spain and Portugal, which even before their entry had participated in the government conference. The Greek government opted to await the outcome of the referendum in Denmark. One day after the positive outcome of the vote on 27 February (with some 56.2 percent in favor), the foreign ministers of Denmark, Greece, and Italy signed the treaty. After the Supreme Court of Ireland likewise ordered a referendum, the treaty went into force on 1 July 1987.

The Internal-Market Project

Even before regular use of majority voting in the Council of Ministers had significantly accelerated the elimination of non-tariff hindrances to trade, Delors took further steps that were to strengthen the consensus regarding the internal-market

---

14 Andrew Moravscik, "Negotiating the Single European Act: National Interests and Conventional Statecraft in the European Community," in: *International Organization* 45 (1991), pp. 19–56; he presents "all three major states" (*ibid.*, p. 49) schematically as concerned in the same way about the preservation of sovereignty and thereby brushes aside these fundamental facts.

project and in the final analysis thus also promote the cohesion of the Community. Among these were measures that he explained to the Strasbourg parliament on 18 February 1987: a substantial reform of the Common Agricultural Policy, better provisioning of the structural funds and of the new Community policies as well as another expansion of the Community budget, combined with a strengthening of budgetary discipline. This program stemmed from thoughts that the Commission had been developing since the middle of 1986. It gained momentum from another sounding-out that Delors had been able to undertake among all the heads of state and of government in early 1987, and it was presented under the suggestive title "Making a Success of the 'Single European Act.'" It was quickly dubbed the "Delors Package" by the public.

Its passage did not happen as quickly as Delors had hoped. It was the case that the General Council, the Finance Ministers Council, and the Agricultural Ministers Council all approved the major outlines of the project. When the European Council was to make concrete decisions on 4 and 5 December 1987, however, the debate got bogged down in the various details of the program. Margaret Thatcher once again wanted to bring about decisions on reducing the agricultural budget, while rejecting the other aspects of the program. At the next Council meeting on 11 and 12 February 1988 in Brussels, it required the energy and negotiation skill of Kohl—holding the new West German Council presidency—to have a decision reached that was only a little less than what the Commission had been seeking.[15]

In order to contain overproduction and the exorbitant costs of agriculture, it was first of all decided that expenditures over the next few years would not be allowed to increase at more than eighty percent of the growth in gross domestic product. Thus, upper limits were set on annual price adjustments and incentives created to produce in conformity with the market to a greater extent. The quantitative limits on guarantee prices were extended to grains and vegetable oils. At the same time, removal of approximately ten to fifteen percent of total agricultural land from production was promoted; smaller agricultural enterprises were accorded direct income subsidies. Lastly, a currency reserve was amassed that would make agricultural sales on the world market independent of fluctuations in the dollar. At the same time, the Community thereby undertook initial efforts to be able to engage in the upcoming Uruguay Round of the GATT negotiations.

Regarding the Structural Fund, the Council in Brussels agreed to no less than a doubling of its resources—not for the year 1993 as demanded by the Commission but for 1994. In so doing, the goals of the Structural Fund were made more precise: assisting regions that were lagging in development, supporting the struc-

---

[15] Delors, *Erinnerungen*, pp. 285–297; the conclusions of the Brussels Council meeting in *Jahrbuch der Europäischen Integration 1987/88*, pp. 438–458.

tural transformation of industrial regions in decline, battling long-term unemployment, promoting integration of young people into the workforce, modernizing agricultural production, and promoting rural development. Support from the Structural Fund was made contingent on simultaneous allocation of certain percentages of national resources. It was still the case that loans from the European Investment Bank would augment assistance funding, the bank acting in close coordination with the Commission on individual projects. Taken together, these measures were to ensure that the elimination of hindrances to competitiveness would not further exacerbate inequalities but on the contrary open up additional productive potential.

In order to finance the Structural Fund, the research program, and the other Community tasks, the budget for 1988 was raised to 1.15 percent of the cumulative gross national product of the member states; up to 1992, it was to rise incrementally to 1.2 percent. For 1988, this corresponded to an increase of twenty percent—to some forty-five billion ECUs. To the extent that this amount was not taken in from tariffs, levies, and the designated percentage of the value-added tax (1.4 percent), contributions from member states would be added as a fourth source of income, in accordance with each one's share of the cumulative gross domestic product. The Council of Ministers and the Commission were empowered to reach an agreement with Parliament on a five-year "Financial Projection" that structured income and expenditure in advance at the designated levels, thus reducing wearisome and unproductive disagreements over individual budget lines.

In order to increase the pressure on the governments, Delors commissioned a comprehensive scholarly study on "The Cost of Non-Europe" and had the findings made public in late March of 1988. Under the leadership of the Italian economist Paolo Cecchini, the authors expected that completion of the internal market would result in an increase in gross domestic product of approximately five percent. Consumer prices were to drop by an average of six percent, unemployment to be significantly reduced, government budgets to see a gain in income of 2.2 percent of GNP on average, and the foreign-trade balance to improve by approximately one percent of the gross domestic product. The authors emphasized however that these results could only be achieved if systematic elimination of non-tariff barriers to trade were accompanied by targeted economic assistance, strengthened competitiveness policy, and a continuance of the stability course in monetary policy. Beyond that, firms would need to take advantage of the chance offered them to pursue an active investment policy.[16] As with all economic prognoses, this report was of course open to challenge. However, given that the upward

---

[16] Paolo Cecchini, et al., *Europa '92. Der Vorteil des Binnenmarktes*, Baden-Baden: Nomos, 1988.

movement of the world economy in the second half of the 1980s was gradually sweeping over the countries of the European Community, the report enjoyed an overwhelmingly positive reception. Entrepreneurs began making investments in anticipation of the internal market and in turn put pressure on the governments to bring it about.

The spirit of optimism that the Commission generated with its measures and announcements did indeed help overcome the opposition of various lobbies to individual elements of the internal-market project. By the end of 1988, the Council of Ministers had passed 109 of the 279 proposals made in the white paper of 1985. By the deadline of 31 December 1992, some 264 Commission proposals had become directives of the Council of Ministers, which allowed the European Council in Edinburgh on 11 and 12 December 1992 to determine that the goals of the white paper had essentially been achieved or at least initiated. Admittedly, only forty-five percent of the directives had become national law in all member states by that time. The rate of fulfillment was lowest in Greece with 70.4 percent and highest in Denmark with 88.7 percent. With some seventy-seven percent each, France and the Federal Republic had the same rate of non-compliance.[17] Hence, the internal-market project proved to be a long-term endeavor, one that would be a subject of European politics into the twenty-first century.

The Commission achieved the most progress in the elimination of the so-called "technical" hindrances to trade in the form of differing national regulations and technical norms. This was aided by a case-law ruling of the European Court in February of 1979: A ground-breaking decision was handed down in favor of the West German Rewe Trade Group against the ban on importing black-currant liquor of the "Cassis de Dijon" brand. West German officials had justified the ban with reference to the fact that "Cassis de Dijon" was not at least twenty-five percent alcohol by volume, as the FRG's brandy-monopoly law stipulated. The court argued against that position by stating that "every product produced legally in a member state and offered for sale" should also be able to be sold "in the other member states in principle"—insofar as public health and consumer protections as well as the honesty of the trade could be ensured. According to the principle of mutual recognition of national provisions stemming from this decision and additional ones on food products over the following years, the Commission and Council could content themselves with establishing minimal standards for safety, health, and consumer protection. Thus, the replacement of national norms by common European norms in accordance with Article 100 of the EEC Treaty lost

---

[17] Hans-Eckart Scharrer, "Binnenmarktpolitik," in: *Jahrbuch der Europäischen Integration 1988/89*, pp. 132–142; ibid., 1992/93, pp. 139–150.

urgency; it could be left to European committees on norms with which national committees cooperated.[18]

In a similar way, the guidelines for mutual recognition of university diplomas, which the Council had passed in January of 1989, represented significant progress on the free exercise of professions in the common economic area. There followed guidelines for professional qualifications, for eliminating administrative hurdles in the practice of free academic professions, and for opening public service to citizens of other member states. It was the case however that there were delays in incorporating all this into national law, especially in regard to employment in public service. On 1 July 1992, freedom of residency was extended to those citizens of member states who were not employed: students, pensioners, others of independent means, and their relatives. However, approval for residency was contingent on their not being an economic burden on the country. Additionally, the Commission made some efforts to encourage the mobility of scholars and students. It was especially the Erasmus Program for promoting academic exchanges, initiated in 1987, that quickly gained great significance.

Thanks to the transition to majority voting, the Commission was also successful in eliminating hindrances to competition stemming from different forms of national policy on competition and cartels. With the 1989 "Merger Regulation," which the Commission had already proposed in 1973, it finally gained sole right to approve or reject mergers and financial stakes of Community-wide significance. With reference to the need to guarantee competition on the national level, this prohibited bans on capital contributions from other member states; at the same time, mergers that seemed appropriate for strengthening the competiveness of European firms on the world market were made easier. On 1 July 1990, the movement of capital was freed within the Community; however, member states reserved the right to limit it again for a maximum of six months if needed to support their currencies. Likewise, on 1 January 1993, banks gained the right to operate in all member states. In accordance with the principle of mutual recognition, the regulation of banking remained with the land of origin.

Conversely, it proved difficult to grant the same freedom of movement for insurance due to the complexity of the subject matter. From 1990, however, insurance firms were able to offer a portion of their services across the whole Community. Likewise, it proved difficult to open public procurement to competition. Procurement orders above a certain size issued by state agencies did need to be advertised in the *Official Journal* of the Community, and a series of further provisions was made for guaranteeing competition in issuing procurement contracts

---

18 On this and the following, Gerbet, *Construction*, pp. 359–363; Franz Knipping, *Rom, 25. März 1957. Die Einigung Europas*, Munich: Deutscher Taschenbuch-Verlag, 2004, pp. 234–238.

by state agencies. However, the member states retained many exceptional regulations, especially in the field of energy supply. There were also many violations of these stipulations, and it took a long time for an attitudinal change to set in.

Regarding the harmonization of tax rates on goods, services, and investment income, only a certain amount of convergence was possible. In October of 1992, the governments agreed to equalize their value-added tax rates within a period of four years. Fifteen percent was set as the "lowest normal rate," and the normal level for reduced tax rates was to be five percent. Likewise, minimum rates were established for the various special taxes on alcohol, tobacco, mineral oil, and so forth. The Commission was given authority to propose "objective tax rates" in regard to Community goals on health, energy, transportation, and environmental policy; member states were to use them as guidelines in harmonization. It was not at all possible to achieve a harmonization of taxes on investment income that would be necessary to prevent tax avoidance via countries with low taxes or none at all. The Commission proposed a uniform withholding tax of fifteen percent, which corresponded to the average of the taxes on investment income in the member states. Britain and Luxembourg, which profited the most from low tax rates, bridled at this. They claimed that if there were a uniform tax, capital would then flee the European Community altogether.

Free movement of goods within the Community was made easier in 1988 by a standardization of shipping documents, and on 1 January 1993, these were eliminated altogether. The paperwork that arose from differing value-added tax rates was no longer taken care of when borders were crossed but would instead be left to the particular finance office responsible. Likewise, checking of animals and plants at borders was eliminated and replaced by harmonization of national norms under the oversight of the Commission.

In contrast, the checking of persons when crossing borders, the most obvious characteristic of a truly common market, could not be abolished everywhere; nor could progress in this area be very quickly realized. It presupposed uniform regulation of immigration, of crime fighting, and of the art and antiquity trade, which could not be achieved without great effort. Moreover, many countries, especially Britain, did not want it at all. Initially, an agreement was reached only among the Federal Republic, France, and the three Benelux states; it was signed in the Luxembourg border village of Schengen on 14 June 1985. It called for lifting controls on persons in 1990 as an extension of an agreement reached between France and the Federal Republic in 1984. Implementation had to be postponed twice, initially to 1993 and then to 1 July 1995. In the meantime, Spain and Portugal had joined the agreement, so that free movement of persons, along with common entry and asylum regulations as well as cooperation in crime fighting, now encompassed seven states.

With the abolition of national regulations in favor of European framework guidelines and the accompanying development of new political fields, the citizens of the Community got "more Europe." Initially, the Council of Ministers had consisted of only four different specialized formations after the Treaties of Rome came into effect and had grown to twelve distinct formations by 1975. By 1990, however, the total number of Council formations had risen to no less than twenty-two. Almost every ministry in national governments, with the exception of defense, now had a corresponding body at the European level in which ministers from specific fields cooperated and also often made decisions. The number of legal acts issued by the Council of Ministers had already nearly doubled during the 1970s (from 375 in 1970 to 627 in 1980) and grew still further to 724 in 1986. The total number of civil servants working for the Commission rose from approximately five thousand at the end of the 1960s to nearly thirteen thousand in 1990. Likewise, the number of special-interest groups and non-governmental organizations that saw fit to have their own representatives in Brussels grew to over two thousand.[19]

After development toward the internal market had gotten underway, Delors devoted increased efforts to expanding the social dimension of the Community. According to his understanding, the elimination of protectionist regulations at the national level, necessary for the realization of the internal market, should not lead to the unleashing of unhindered capitalistic competition but should be cushioned by the establishment of regulations via partnerships at the European level; this was important to him due to his long connection to the Christian labor movement in France. In light of workers' great fear of the consequences of deregulation, Delors called for "sending a strong political signal in this area" during the Council meeting in Hannover on 27 and 28 June 1988.[20] Shortly thereafter, having just been nominated for a second term as Commission president, he spoke before the European Parliament and called for a further expansion of the Community: In ten years, "80 per cent of the laws affecting the economy and social policy would be passed at a European and not a national level." To achieve this, he let it be known to the deputies—and indirectly to the national governments— that a further strengthening of European institutions would be necessary: "We are not going to manage to take all the decisions needed between now and 1995 unless we see the beginnings of a European government."[21]

---

19 Wolfgang Wessels, *Die Öffnung des Staates. Modelle und Wirklichkeit grenzüberschreitender Verwaltungspraxis 1960–1995*, Opladen: Leske und Budrich, 2000, pp. 195–260.
20 Delors, *Erinnerungen*, pp. 383ff.
21 Speech of 6 July 1988, *Verhandlungen des Europäischen Parlaments*, 2–367/156–157.

This message was understood by the representatives of workers' organizations. The British trade unions, which in light of the simultaneity of British entry into the Community and economic crisis had mostly been in the camp of the EC opponents, now celebrated Delors as nothing less than a savior from the impudence of Thatcherism. When the Commission president spoke at their annual congress in Bournemouth on 7 September 1988 and promised he would advocate for an "internal market beneficial to all" and that "one day Europe-wide conditions secured by treaty" would be achieved, the enthusiastic delegates joined together in singing "Frère Jacques." Chairman Clive Jenkins, who had advocated an exit from the Community during the 1975 referendum, openly admitted that "I got it wrong."[22]

In Margaret Thatcher's eyes, this forcing of regulation at the European level meant that Delors had mutated from an ally in the struggle for the internal market to a megalomaniacal champion of an all-powerful Brussels bureaucracy. She did not realize that with her own engagement for the internal market, she had to a goodly extent contributed to the strengthening of the Community, underestimating the supranational implications of her concessions in the process. She became all the angrier at what she perceived as the creeping transfer to Brussels of responsibilities not covered by treaties. Firmly resolved to halt this tendency, she made use of a speech that she had promised to give to the College of Europe in Bruges in order to present her interpretation of the internal-market program with unmistakable clarity: As she said to the students and professors of this cadre-training school for the European movement, "We have not successfully rolled back the frontiers of the state in Britain only to see them re-imposed at a European level, with a European super-state exercising a new dominance from Brussels." In the heat of the moment, she uttered a general renunciation of the supranational principle—the principle to which British governments, including her own, had committed themselves in the form of treaties. Instead, she conjured up the ideal of "willing and active cooperation between independent sovereign states."[23]

The Foreign Office had seen to it that some particularly provocative passages inserted into the draft of the speech by Thatcher's foreign-policy advisor Charles Powell were stricken—for example, the prideful pronouncement that Britain alone had freed Europe from "Prussian domination" as well as the appeal to "forget" the goal of a United States of Europe. Nevertheless, the long, emotionally-charged speech worked like a beacon. She spoke from the soul to conservatives

---

22 Clive Jenkins, *All against the Collar*, London: Methuen Publishing, 1990, pp. 130, 137–140; Delors, *Erinnerungen*, pp. 368ff.
23 Text in: www.margaretthatcher.org/archive; on the origins and reaction, Young, *Blessed Plot*, pp. 346–351.

plagued by feelings of uncertainty, and she contributed much to popularizing the distorted image of a Brussels "superstate" in Britain. At the same time, however, pragmatic Europeans in the government, such as Foreign Minister Geoffrey Howe and Chancellor of the Exchequer Nigel Lawson, began to turn away from the prime minister. The speech could do nothing against the dynamic that the internal-market project had developed. Instead, Thatcher's words contributed over the long term to her fall in November of 1990.

The Project for an Economic and Monetary Union

The economic upswing and political optimism were furthered by the fact that monetary-policy cooperation was making progress. After the *volte-face* in French economic policy in March of 1983, all member states of the European Monetary System were now without exception prioritizing the fight against inflation. As a consequence, inflation rates edged closer to the low Dutch and West German levels, and monetary re-alignments were more seldom needed. Only Italy and Ireland had to endure significant devaluations: The lira lost six percent of its value in July of 1985, and the Irish pound eight percent in August of 1986. Underperforming countries prevented flight from their currencies by having their central banks purchase marks when their currencies were strong; when their own currencies were threatened with weakening, they then made use of these holdings before the intervention thresholds had been reached. The mark therefore developed more and more into a second reserve currency alongside the dollar and also into the anchor currency of the EMS. Orientation on the mark helped the stabilization efforts of the governments gain vigor and credibility.

With the consolidation of the EMS, its further development into a monetary union came onto the agenda once again. François Mitterrand became a particularly strong advocate of such a move after having decided over the course of 1983 to make the expansion of the European Union into a central theme of his presidency. A memorandum produced by Roland Dumas with support from the Quai d'Orsay and the French Finance Ministry was presented on 1 June 1984. It emphasized the necessity of increased co-ordination of monetary policy and the development of common economic framework planning so as to safeguard stability and growth. Private use of the ECU was still to be promoted. Lastly, the European Monetary Cooperation Fund ought to be expanded into a European Monetary Fund with which the European currencies could be defended against the dollar. In this way, a genuine European and international currency should be developed out of the ECU.[24]

The resumption of plans for a monetary union was justified in the Dumas Memorandum primarily by citing the necessity of overcoming subordination to swings in the dollar exchange rate and American interest-rate policy. With the growing self-commitment to the mark there was a second motive: one-sided subordination to the dollar policy and interest-rate policy of the West German *Bundesbank*. This was all the more difficult to bear because the *Bundesbank* was contributing far less to preserving the parities than the central banks of the weaker countries; this was due to the prevalence of preventative unilateral intervention before the intervention threshold had been reached. The "deviation threshold" on an ECU basis, at which the *Bundesbank* too would be forced to intervene, was seldom reached; and over time, this instrument for balanced promotion of convergence was practically forgotten.[25]

Along with the comfortable position that the *Bundesbank* had attained through this development, there also grew the opposition to mutualizing monetary reserves or monetary policy. Indeed, *Bundesbank* President Karl Otto Pöhl did guard against appearing as the principle opponent of a European Monetary Union. However, by demanding that before any individual reform measures were taken, a definitive institutional design for this union be agreed upon, he did consciously raise the hurdles for realizing such a plan. Kohl was not able to reduce them very easily because Finance Minister Stoltenberg, who worked closely with the *Bundesbank*, was increasingly gaining popularity and soon constituted a potential rival of the chancellor. In principle, Kohl was already in favor of the monetary union; he regarded it as self-evidently belonging to his vision of a unified Europe. He had to be careful however to succeed with it in consensus with West German politics or at least with those of his party, and that led him to hesitate to embrace the French initiatives. The concessions that he found himself willing to make during the formulation of the Single European Act did not go nearly as far as Mitterrand had hoped.

A first breach in the West German defensive front came in the winter of 1986–87, when a dramatic drop in the dollar put the French franc under devaluation pressure and also put pressure on the mark to rise. Jacques Chirac, who had been prime minister under Mitterrand ever since the Gaullists' victory in the parliamentary elections of March 1986, blamed this on the hike in money-market

---

[24] Reported in Kenneth Dyson and Kevin Featherstone, *The Road to Maastricht. Negotiating Economic and Monetary Union*, Oxford: Oxford University Press, 1999, pp. 152ff.

[25] Horst Ungerer, *A concise history of European monetary integration: From EPU to EMU*, Westport: Quorum Books, CT, 1997, p. 163.

interest rates by the *Bundesbank*. Stoltenberg defended the *Bundesbank* against the public criticism from Paris. Internally, however, he had to acknowledge the legitimacy of the criticism and drew the conclusion that the monetary system had to be equipped with better mechanisms to protect against speculative pressure. The *Bundesbank* was in this way to be prompted to take a more flexible approach and at the same time be protected against further attacks. The Franco-German confrontation ended on 12 January 1987 with a decision of the finance ministers to raise the value of the mark and Dutch guilder by a modest three percent and the Belgian-Luxembourg franc by two percent. The demand for devaluing the French franc was dropped.

At the same time, the finance ministers commissioned the Monetary Committee and the Committee of the Central Bank Governors to develop a concept for strengthening the intervention mechanisms of the monetary system. This was passed by the central bank governors on 8 September 1987 in Basel and then confirmed without revision by the finance ministers in Nyborg in Denmark on 12 September. Notably, the Basel-Nyborg Agreement contained two concessions that the *Bundesbank* had rejected in a similar initiative by the European Commission in March of 1982: Very short-term EMS credits could in the future also be used for financing preventative "intra-marginal" interventions, and repayment of intervention credits could in the future be paid entirely in ECUs, not only half in ECUs as had been the case up to that point. Additionally, the central bank governors were to make increased efforts to call attention to cases of inconsistency in national monetary policies and also pursue interest-rate policy with the goal of preserving parities. Pöhl also succeeded in having his colleagues explicitly commit themselves to greater internal and external stability.[26]

Foreign Minister Genscher was obviously not yet satisfied with the increased commitment of the *Bundesbank* to the goal of monetary union as contained in the Basel-Nyborg Agreement. For him, the valuation crisis of late 1986 and early 1987 had made it clear that monetary union needed to be put on Bonn's agenda despite the temporizing opposition of the *Bundesbank*. Not only was he pressured by Dumas, to whom it was abundantly clear that a public initiative needed to come from the German side in order to succeed. Genscher moreover feared that the monetary system could not survive the continuance of the existing asymmetries much longer. The goal of Political Union would also be endangered by such a prospect—and at a point in time when it was needed more than ever, given the reform initiatives of Soviet General Secretary Mikhail Gorbachev.

---

[26] *Ibid.*, p. 180. On this and the following, cf. Dyson and Featherstone, *Road*, pp. 156–180 and 306–342.

The reforms in the Soviet Union and the efforts to overcome the Cold War being undertaken by Gorbachev gave the project of a European Monetary Union a wholly new urgency in Genscher's view: "The East-West rapprochement called for nothing less than an EC more capable of acting, one that worked closely together rather than drifting apart. Moreover, in light of the new developments, the German attitude on this was watched keenly not only in Paris: Would the Germans remain on board the European Union ship or would they again go their own way? As soon as German reunification became an issue, this question would heat up; there could be no uncertainties, no ambiguities, because these would have had devastating consequences."[27] Genscher clearly perceived that behind the growing pressure from the French side there also lay worries about an emancipation of the Germans from the European Community. These worries could only be countered by timely efforts for more strongly integrating the Germans.

The West German foreign minister therefore sought an opportunity for substantially reducing the *Bundesbank*'s influence over Bonn's attitude toward the monetary-union project. He found it when in the national elections of January 1987 his FDP gained significantly and when Stoltenberg lost appreciable influence in the autumn and winter of 1987–88 due to the "Barschel Affair" in his political base of Schleswig-Holstein. After the German success in passing the "Delors Package" at the Brussels Council meeting of 11 and 12 February 1988 had further increased Genscher's esteem in the West German public as well as his European partners, he publicly presented a carefully-worked-out plan for creating a "European monetary area" on 26 February. This was intended to outmaneuver the opposition of the *Bundesbank* and to force the hand of the still-hesitant chancellor.

The memorandum was deliberately not coordinated within the government and therefore functioned as a personal statement by Genscher, not as an official declaration of the foreign minister. It took up the objectives for a monetary union that had been expressed by Pöhl and other representatives of the *Bundesbank* and combined them with a proposed procedure that aimed for realization in short order. The centerpiece of the monetary union was to be the establishment of a European Central Bank, which was to be as autonomous as the *Bundesbank* and likewise committed to the goal of price stability. In order to get this underway, the European Council was to create at its next meeting in June an "expert committee" with "professional and political authority"; within a year's time, this body was to determine the key points for creating a European economic space, to work out the statutes of the European Central Bank, and to develop plans for the transition

---

27 Genscher, *Erinnerungen*, p. 387.

period up to the completion of the monetary union, which were to be guided by the principle of parallelism in economic and monetary integration.[28]

It was now the case that the opponents of the currency union could only raise objections as to the process, and they did so immediately. On 15 March, Stoltenberg sent the State Secretary Committee for European Affairs and monetary committee of the EC Council of Ministers a counter-memorandum that had been developed in close cooperation with the *Bundesbank*. This document listed a whole series of preconditions to be fulfilled before a European Central Bank was established: further "augmentation" of monetary cooperation and orientation on the stability goal, irrevocable freedom of capital movement in the Community, increased convergence of economic development, unrestricted participation of all member states in the monetary system, guaranteed independence of the national central banks, and a substantial transfer of national sovereign rights to the Community level—a transfer that went beyond the field of monetary policy.[29] From this perspective, the monetary union remained a long-term goal that could be realized only if all member states had adjusted to German conditions, thus in keeping with the "crown theory" that was so beloved of German financial experts.

Genscher's arguments made obvious sense to Kohl. However, in light of the now-public conflict within his government, the chancellor continued to lie low, awaiting further reactions to Genscher's initiative. Only after representatives of industry and commerce had expressed themselves overwhelmingly positively and after Mitterrand had been re-elected on 7 May did the chancellor decide take up the proposal for creating a committee of experts. In order to ensure success, he insisted that the membership must include not only a group of independent personages but also the central bank governors. At the Franco-German summit of 2 June in Evian, Kohl proposed that Delors—with whom he was in the meantime working closely—be the chairman of the committee. At the same time, the chancellor asked that Mitterrand fulfill a precondition that was especially important to Stoltenberg: the free movement of capital in the Community.[30] After the French had acceded to this request and after the EC Council of Ministers on 24 June had decided that capital should move freely no later than 1 July 1990, the way was clear for Kohl to emerge at the next Council meeting as the initiator of the monetary union. Stoltenberg's opposition could be neutralized by reference to the success in liberalizing capital movement.

---

28 Henry Krägenau and Wolfgang Wetter, *Europäische Währungsunion. Vom Werner-Plan zum Vertrag von Maastricht. Analysen und Dokumentation*, Baden-Baden: Nomos, 1993, pp. 310–312.
29 *Ibid.*, pp. 337ff.
30 Noted in Jacques Attali, *Verbatim. Tome 3: Chronique des années 1988–1991*, Paris: Fayard, 1995, p. 32.

At the Council meeting in Hannover on 27 and 28 June, Kohl first sought to persuade Thatcher in a private conversation that she had nothing to fear from a committee that consisted essentially of orthodox central bankers. Then, just after the members of the Council had confirmed Delors for another term as Commission president, Kohl made the proposal at dinner that the Frenchman be appointed chairman of the committee. The entity was also to consist of all twelve central bank governors along with Frans Andriessen (as an additional member of the European Commission) as well as Miguel Boyer (president of the Foreign Trade Bank of Spain), Alexandre Lamfalussy (general director of the Bank of International Settlements), and Niels Thygesen (an economics professor in Copenhagen) as independent members. With this constellation, the proposal was accepted by one and all. Thatcher only insisted that the issue of creating a European Central Bank not be explicitly written into the committee's mandate. And Tietmeyer, who once again was part of the delegation as "watchdog" from the finance ministry, succeeded at the last moment in adding a provision that the central bank governors act only in their own names and not for their institutions. In the closing press conference, Kohl—then serving as Council president—stated that he was "ninety percent sure" that the European Central Bank would be realized by the year 2000.[31]

With the creation of a committee to develop a roadmap to monetary union, the transition to a common currency had in fact once again been put on the agenda of the Community; and with the inclusion of the central bank presidents, the opposition of the *Bundesbank* had been neutralized. Pöhl did complain that Delors was an unqualified politician and also sought to shift his committee assignment to another member of the *Bundesbank* directorate. In light of the participation of all the other central bank presidents, however, he could not in the end avoid the assignment. The only possibility remaining to him was to represent the position of the *Bundesbank* as aggressively as possible in the Delors Committee and so keep the hurdles high on the path to monetary union.

The Delors Committee met in Basel, following on the monthly sessions of the committee of the central bank presidents. It quickly became apparent that Pöhl had ended up on the defensive. In his reservations against accelerating the movement toward monetary union, it was true that he was for the most part supported by Danish Central Bank President Erik Hoffmeyer and his Dutch colleague Wim Duisenberg. On the other side, the Italian Carlo Ciampi, the Belgian Jean Godeaux, and the Frenchman Jacques de Larosière were zealous advocates of the monetary union; Boyer and Thygesen, as members of the "Committee for the Monetary Union of Europe" that had been created by Schmidt and Giscard

---

[31] *Europa-Archiv* 43 (1988), pp. D443–D447; on the course of the meeting, also Delors, *Erinnerungen*, pp. 383–385.

in late 1986, were already focused on rapid progress on monetary unification. Yet, Delors concentrated on achieving a common answer among all the members regarding the path to monetary union. Hence, he did not insist further when Pöhl characterized certain demands as non-negotiable; and the chairman also strove for the utmost civility. When an exasperated Pöhl took off his headphones during Delors' French-language remarks, the undaunted chairman continued speaking in his poor English.

Delors' firm purposefulness and the mediation services repeatedly provided by Duisenberg worked to ensure that by 12 April 1989 a report had in fact been produced, one that was supported by all Committee members. It steered the course charted by Genscher but also contained some fuzziness, behind which lay ongoing differences of opinion. It followed the German input in describing the goal of an independent European Central Bank system, led by the directorate of the European Central Bank as well as the presidents of the national banks and committed to the goal of price stability. In this, Mitterrand had given de Larosière his blessing because he knew that the monetary union could not be achieved in any other way. In order to demonstrate the irrevocability of the setting of the exchange rates, there was also nominally to be a Community currency. In contrast, when it came to the parallel development of common economic and fiscal policy, which Delors regarded as necessary if the monetary union were to function over the long term, there was only vague talk of "macro-economic coordination, including binding rules in the budgetary field." The explicit mention of the "transfer of decision power" to the European level contained in an early draft was struck by Delors because he thought it would not be possible to gain approval for it.

Regarding the roadmap, Delors succeeded in winning approval for a process in three stages as well as the recommendation that right at the beginning of this process there be "a clear political commitment to the final stage." Regarding a timetable, as the Schmidt-Giscard Committee had demanded, there remained only the recommendation to let the first stage begin no later than when movement of capital was freed up on 1 July 1990. Aside from that, it was not clearly stated as to which conditions needed to be fulfilled in order to move from the first to the second stage or from the second to the third, nor were any time points specified for these transitions. In the first stage, convergence was to be further promoted by economic development and economic policy; and all member states were to join the exchange-rate mechanism of the EMS. Additionally, a treaty on economic and monetary union was to be worked out. After ratification of the treaty, the second stage was to be entered upon, in which the European Central Bank system was to organize the transition to full monetary union for the third stage.

As to organizing the transition in the second stage, the report of the Delors Commission likewise remained vague. Pöhl successfully fended off de Larosière's demand for the establishment of a European Monetary Fund for this transition phase, likewise the idea of creating a parallel European currency that was to be legal tender alongside the national currencies. The report only retained the provision that the European Central Bank was to have the possibility of accumulating "a certain amount of reserves" and using them for intervening in the foreign-exchange markets. The bandwidths among the national currencies were to be narrowed to the extent allowed by circumstances and by progress toward convergence. Additionally, precise rules were to be agreed upon for the size and financing of budget deficits; these were not yet to be binding, however. "Guidelines" for macro-economic development were to be passed by majority vote; at the same time, "ultimate responsibility" for political decisions in this phase was still to rest at the national level.[32]

It was true that the *Bundesbank*'s fundamental essentials regarding the shape of the future monetary union were thereby retained and that the tempo of its realization remained unclear. Nevertheless, with the recommendation for an immediate launch along with simultaneous commitment to the final goal, a strong impetus had now been given for further developing the monetary system into a monetary union. Immediately after the publication of the report on 17 April, Pöhl began to distance himself from its contents and to warn against a "hasty" realization of the recommended steps. New West German Finance Minister Theo Waigel reacted by publicly affirming the "crown theory"; he clearly rejected acceleration on the path to monetary union. The Academic Advisory Board of the West German Economic Ministry went further by speaking out against binding budgetary rules at the European level. In a letter to Economic Minister Helmut Haussmann, this body warned against beginning treaty negotiations on the basis of the Three-Step-Plan.[33]

Against this, Mitterrand, Delors, and Genscher pushed for approval of the report of the Delors Commission at the next Council meeting in Madrid and also for approval of a government conference to draft the treaty that was necessary for stage two. The fact that it had been possible to get all the central bank presidents to commit themselves to a common program had to be made use of—the iron had to be struck while it was hot. Therefore, Mitterrand spontaneously shoved aside

---

[32] "Bericht zur Wirtschafts- und Währungsunion der EG," in: *Europa-Archiv* 44 (1989), pp. D283–D304; Krägenau and Wetter, *Europäische Währungsunion*, pp. 33–40. On the negotiations in the Delors Committee, Dyson and Featherstone, *Road*, pp. 342–350 and 713–720; Delors, *Erinnerungen*, pp. 385–389; James, *Making the European Monetary Union*, pp. 234–261.

[33] Letter of June 5, 1989, Krägenau/Wetter, *Währungsunion*, pp. 213ff. Cf. Hans Stark, *Kohl, l'Allemagne et l'Europe. La politique d'intégration européenne de la République fédérale 1982–1998*, Paris: Éditions l'Harmattan, 2004, pp. 90ff.; Dyson and Featherstone, *Road*, pp. 348ff.

the reservations of French Finance Minister Pierre Bérégovoy regarding the lack of economic- and fiscal-policy taxing authority for the projected union. During a conversation at the Élysée Palace on 11 May, the president made it clear that the risks entailed by France in allowing the free movement of capital were more than outweighed by the advantages of the monetary union.[34]

With the pressure that the advocates of the monetary union were putting on him, Kohl once again found himself facing a dilemma: On the one hand, he shared their analysis of the situation and the conclusions they drew from it; on the other hand, it was exactly at that time that he needed to act with particular caution in regard to domestic politics. The criticism of his leadership had escalated, and his own general secretary, Heiner Geissler, was about to have him removed. Therefore, he simply could not afford to deceive Finance Minister Waigel, who had succeeded Franz-Josef Strauss as chairman of the Bavarian CSU and who was supporting the chancellor against the criticism within the party. In cabinet discussions, Genscher did succeed in gaining government support the adoption of the Delors Report as well as the start of the first stage on 1 July 1990. However, Waigel and Tietmeyer—whose expertise the new finance minister greatly valued—argued that before a determination had been made on beginning the government conference, there was still a series of "technical issues" that had to be resolved. Kohl did not dare to contradict them.[35]

In Madrid, where the heads of state and of government gathered on 26 and 27 June, it was thus not possible to decide anything more. Kohl made use of Thatcher's opposition to a new treaty to present himself as a mediator and then worked toward a result that would again give him some time: The report of the Delors Commission was hailed as an indispensable basis for the preparations for the monetary union, and the start of the first stage was set for 1 July 1990. The government conference was only to meet after the responsible entities—that is, the General Council, the Finance Ministers Council, the Commission, the Committee of the Central Bank Governors, and the Monetary Committee—had completed the necessary preparations. Under no circumstances was the government conference to begin before the start of the first stage. Additionally, the Council explicitly approved the West German proposal to set unambiguous convergence criteria; it also rejected the French plan for a European Reserve Fund.[36]

Mitterrand then sought to make use of his European Council presidency in the second half of 1989 to give decisive impetus to the preparations for the government conference and to wring from the Germans a binding date for its start. It

---

34 *Ibid.*, p. 188.
35 *Ibid.*, pp. 350–354.
36 *Europa-Archiv* 44 (1989), pp. D406ff.

was at least to begin before the end of 1990. The decisions necessary for it were to be made at the next Council meeting in December in Strasbourg; these were to be prepared by a work group made up of representatives of all foreign and finance ministries under the leadership of Mitterrand's European advisor, Elisabeth Guigou. As Mitterrand said to Thatcher during a lightning visit on 4 September, his intention was "to put the train on its wheels"; and it should not be impeded by "one or two states."[37] In other words, France was prepared to start moving on the monetary union even if Britain would not immediately join in.

In pressing to have a government council summoned, Mitterrand was helped by circumstances: The prospects for overcoming the division of Europe and thereby also the division of Germany—which were becoming more clear over the course of the summer and autumn of 1989—generated wider support for the understanding of strategic necessities that drove Mitterrand and Genscher. In light of the opening of Hungary's border with Austria and the formation of an all-party government in Poland, both Bérégovoy and Waigel began to realize that regardless of their different conceptions as to how it was to be accomplished, the monetary union had to be implemented quickly. At their first encounter within the framework of the Franco-German Economic Commission (at Tegernsee on 24 and 25 August), the two men came to trust one another. Their two agencies no longer worked secretly against the monetary union but now worked constructively toward it. Even Pöhl now became convinced that for political reasons the monetary union had to come.

Added to this was the fact that Kohl was able to prevail in the intraparty power struggle of the CDU at the Bremen party congress during the second week of September. With new self-confidence, he now spoke for the Germans of the GDR too. He also perceived the necessity of making timely gestures so as to counter possible irritation among his allies regarding a new special German path of development away from the Community. On 13 October, European advisor Joachim Bitterlich informed his French colleague Guigou that at the upcoming December Council meeting in Strasbourg, the chancellor would make an appeal for an agreement on the meeting of the government conference. It would open before the end of 1990. Negotiations were to lead to a treaty by the end of 1991, and ratification was then to follow over the course of 1992.[38] Mitterrand understood that these negotiations

---

[37] AN, 5AG4, 88 EG d.1, quoted from Jean-Marie Palayret, "La voie française vers l'Union économique et monétaire durant la négociation du traité de Maastricht (1988–1992)," in: Martial Libera and Birte Wassenberg (eds.), *L'Europe au cœur. Études pour Marie-Thérèse Bitsch*, Brussels: Émile Bruylant, 2009, pp. 197–221, here p. 209.

[38] Guigou to Mitterrand, 13 October 1989, AN, 5AG4, 6874; cf. also Attali, *Verbatim III*, p. 321.

should begin only after the German elections of December 1990 so as to keep the issue of the monetary union out of the election campaign.

Despite the fact that Kohl had backed down, nothing had actually been decided yet, although Mitterrand thought otherwise. Rather, with the upheavals in Hungary and Poland as well as the visible decay of the SED regime in East Germany, the chancellor drew the conclusion that along with economic and monetary integration, the political unification of Europe had to be accelerated. This seemed necessary to him, firstly, in order to create a strong framework for the process of German reunification; secondly, he also saw new tasks for the Community in overcoming the legacies of Communism in Eastern Europe. Eleven days after the message that Bitterlich had communicated, Kohl himself flew to Paris to say this to Mitterrand. As Attali noted during a dinner shared by the two leaders on 24 October, "it would be necessary to take up a political European project after the economic one." The chancellor also made it clear that such an initiative was urgent in his view: "The summit in Strasbourg must send a clear message to the East."

It did not escape Mitterrand that his guest reacted evasively to his question about the date for the government conference: "One can't decide anything before seeing what happens in Strasbourg." That made the French president mistrustful. Attali concluded his notes on this "head-spinning" meeting with the observation that "I feel for the first time that the chancellor is not confiding in us everything that he knows and that he wants."[39] This mistrust grew into great anxiety when Kohl specified his ideas in a letter to Mitterrand on 27 November: In Strasbourg, the finance ministers and central bank presidents should be commissioned to prepare the government conference; and the conference should not only concern itself with the economic and monetary union but also, in a second phase from the end of 1991 onward, deal with the other institutional reforms, especially with the strengthening of the position of the European Parliament. The "political decision for implementing the government conference on the economic and monetary union" should be made only in the middle of December 1990, and the negotiations should first begin in early 1991. Both parts of the negotiations should be wrapped up over the course of 1992, "in December at the latest." As was emphasized in the conclusion of the document, the ratification could then take place promptly before the next elections to the European Parliament in May and June of 1994.[40]

---

39 Attali, *Verbatim III*, pp. 325–327. On this and the following, also Hanns Jürgen Küsters, "La controverse entre le Chancelier Helmut Kohl et le Président François Mitterrand à propos de la réforme institutionnelle de la Communauté européenne (1989/1990)," in: Bitsch, *Le couple France-Allemagne*, pp. 487–516, here pp. 491–496; Dyson and Featherstone, *Road*, pp. 363–366.
40 Kohl to Mitterrand, 27 Nov. 1989, in: *Deutsche Einheit. Sonderedition aus den Akten des Bundeskanzleramtes 1989/90*, Munich: Oldenbourg, 1998, pp. 565–567.

This announcement of postponing the political decision on the monetary union for another year, along with its incorporation into a more comprehensive reform project containing many pitfalls, was perceived in Paris as a covert rejection. "If that really is the position of the chancellor," Attali commented, "then it means that he's been swayed by the British arguments. And that everything is buried. German problems will sweep across the European construction."[41] It was not only the project of the monetary union that threatened to fail at exactly the moment when, in the French view, it was especially urgent but also the incorporation of Germany altogether. This was after all an essential motif of policy on Europe—and not only of French policy.

European Security and German Unity

Fundamentally, Mitterrand could be won over for a project for a political Europe too. Ever since his rapprochement with Kohl in the winter of 1983–84, he had been appealing for a common foreign policy and also a common European defense organization, which was to emerge from cooperation between France and the Federal Republic. In February of 1984, after the resolution of the British contribution question and of the southern expansion, he had told Kohl of his willingness "to go further and speak with you about European defense." In the process, "nothing [was to be] excluded, neither conventional armaments nor, beyond them, nuclear ones." When Kohl immediately raised the possibility of a French commitment to consultation for the use of nuclear weapons on German soil or from it, as had been accepted by President Reagan, Mitterrand only said, "Why not?" Three months later in his keynote speech before the European Parliament, the French president also publicly embraced the necessity of a "common defense by the Europeans."[42]

Behind this lay not only continuing anxiety that neutralization tendencies might achieve a breakthrough in German politics; Mitterrand also appeared increasingly worried about the arbitrary actions and inconsistencies in the policy of Ronald Reagan, especially regarding the SDI program for a space-based missile defense system that wantonly disregarded the security interests of the Europeans. Moreover, the French president was receptive to the vision of his friend Régis Debray, who saw in an autonomous Western Europe the possibility of promoting

---

41 Attali, *Verbatim III*, pp. 349.
42 Conversation between Mitterrand and Kohl, 2 Feb. 1984, Attali, *Verbatim I*, pp. 583ff.; speech of 24 May 1984 in François Mitterrand, *Réflexions sur la politique extérieure de la France. Introduction à vingt-cinq discours (1981–1985)*, Paris: Fayard, 1986, pp. 280–297.

the democratization of Eastern Europe. In any event, Debray's "Thoughts on the Foreign Policy of France," published in early 1986, conjured up the reconciliation of both halves of Europe on the basis of shared values and democratic socialism, which was to become possible after overcoming the excesses of American liberalism as well as those of Communism.[43]

By July of 1985, Mitterrand's Socialist Party had worked out a report on defense policy that had been coordinated with its West German counterpart, the SPD; Egon Bahr had been especially engaged in the project. This document emphasized the strategic solidarity that bound France together with the rest of Western Europe, especially the Federal Republic; it also called for an "internal shifting of weight within the Atlantic Alliance" in light of the erosion of the American security guarantee. This was to be based on "increased and more autonomous cooperation among the Europeans in the area of defense" and an "expansion of French responsibility in this area." The French armed forces, including nuclear components, ought to be explicitly oriented toward the security of Europe.[44]

In concretizing the proposals, however, Mitterrand reduced the French offer. First of all, he emphasized that the Germans and the French should "undertake everything together that isn't forbidden to you [the Germans], that is, space, chemical weapons, and lasers." Especially in regard to an autonomous European missile defense, German support seemed to him both necessary and feasible. As he explained to Kohl in November of 1985, this was to provide the Federal Republic "an actual defense capability" within a period of twenty years. He excluded the idea of an "integration of nuclear weapons": That would hinder the sought-after improvement in relations with the Soviet Union and would rob France of its necessary counterpoise to German economic power. In December, he also spoke out against an extension of the French nuclear guarantee to the Federal Republic, as Schmidt and Giscard had agreed upon; at the same time, he stressed that the discussion in Paris on the participation of French troops in forward defense on German soil had not yet been concluded.[45]

Even the commitment to consultation in the event French nuclear weapons were used on German soil—a commitment Kohl repeatedly urged—was only given by Mitterrand with reservations, due to the opposition of the chief of the French general staff, Jean Saulnier. In a joint declaration issued at the Franco-German summit on 27 and 28 February 1986 in Bonn, the president declared his willingness to make this commitment "on the borders, which necessitates the extraor-

---

[43] Ibid., pp. 12, 68–71, 101; cf. Soutou, *L'alliance incertaine*, pp. 387ff.
[44] *Le Monde*, 4 July 1985; Egon Bahr, *Zu meiner Zeit*, Munich: Blessing, 1996, p. 512.
[45] Conversations between Mitterrand and Kohl, 29 Oct. 1984, 7 Nov. and 17 Dec. 1985, Attali, *Verbatim I*, pp. 513ff., 874ff., 902–905.

dinary haste of such decisions." Moreover, he "reminded" his listeners that "the decision in this area cannot be divided." More satisfactory for the Germans was the assurance made at the same time that the staffs of both sides would work together operationally and that Mitterrand would have French forces march immediately to the inter-German border in the event they were needed for defense.[46]

Disappointment over the meager substance of the French consultation pledge did not prevent Kohl from calling for an expansion of military cooperation on his own. He had reacted positively to the French proposals because, like Mitterrand, he too feared American withdrawal tendencies as well as the German penchant for neutralization. In his view, this latter factor was strengthened by Gorbachev's disarmament initiatives; and so he now pressed for "very close cooperation," as he said to Mitterrand at a meeting at Chateau Chambord on 28 March 1987.[47] Four months later, Kohl's national security advisor, Horst Teltschik, presented his plans on this during a visit by his French counterpart Attali in Bonn: The creation of a Franco-German brigade that could be joined by Luxembourg, the Netherlands, and Italy; more joint maneuvers and expanded joint logistics, the whole thing "within the prospect of a fusion of the EEC and the WEU"; the establishment of a Franco-German defense council and a permanent general staff; and lastly, a more precise definition of the agreed-upon consultation before use of French nuclear weapons.[48]

For Mitterrand, that was again going too far. Yet, he did agree to joint maneuvers; in September of 1987, some twenty thousand soldiers of the First French Army and the Rapid Deployment Force participated in spectacular maneuvers with the Bundeswehr. At the fiftieth Franco-German summit in November of 1987, the creation of the Franco-German brigade was announced; on 22 January 1988, at the twenty-fifth anniversary of the signing of the Franco-German Treaty, the joint Defense and Security Council came into being. Although the joint maneuvers took place outside the framework of NATO and Bundeswehr soldiers in the joint brigade were for the first time acting outside the integrated NATO command structure, Mitterrand was not prepared to extend the commitment to consultation to joint deployment planning or to grant the defense council operative functions. The Franco-German brigade—consisting of some 4,200 soldiers—thus did not go beyond a symbolic function, and the agreement on a joint defense concept still did not come into being.[49]

---

46 *Ibid.*, p. 933. Cf. also Ulrich Lappenküper, *Mitterrand und Deutschland. Die enträtselte Sphinx*, Munich: Oldenbourg, 2011, pp. 224ff.
47 Attali, *Verbatim II*, p. 287.
48 Notes by Attali, 24 July 1987, *ibid.*, pp. 363–365.
49 Soutou, *L'alliance incertaine*, pp. 391–394; Stark, *Kohl*, pp. 130–133; Lappenküper, *Mitterrand*, pp. 237ff.

In dialogue between the two leaders it nevertheless proved possible for their stances on Gorbachev's disarmament initiatives to come closer together so that common European interests could be safeguarded in the then-emerging end of the arms race. At an improvised summit in Reykjavik on 11 and 12 October 1986, Reagan and Gorbachev agreed to eliminate all nuclear weapons within a period of ten years. Kohl and Mitterrand quickly agreed that this would be highly dangerous and that it was therefore in the vital interest of the Federal Republic that the French nuclear deterrent be preserved and further modernized. After quickly conferring with Mitterrand, Thatcher went to Washington to impress upon Reagan that there could be "no second Reykjavik"; Kohl cautioned the American president that before strategic missiles were reduced by more than fifty percent, a conventional balance of power in Europe had to be achieved.[50]

Gorbachev's offer to eliminate all medium-range missiles was viewed positively by Mitterrand, in contrast to the stance of French Defense Minister André Giraud and the officials of the Quai d'Orsay. From the president's perspective, opposing the offer was impossible, not only in light of the expectations of the public in France as well as the Federal Republic: He had in the meantime also come to the conclusion that neither short- nor medium-range missiles contributed to French or American security. As he explained to Kohl, "our nuclear force is the submarines, and added to them, the eighteen British missiles that can reach the USSR."[51] He thus advocated the "double-zero solution" to both the British and West German governments, an option that combined the elimination of all medium-range missiles with the destruction of shorter-range ones. Kohl, under pressure from FRG military experts who wanted to retain at least the old Pershing IA missiles as a counterweight to the conventional superiority of the Warsaw Pact, gave up this position too in August of 1987.[52] Thus, the way was clear for the signing of the Washington Agreement on the elimination of medium-range missiles on 8 December 1987.

According to US strategists, the short-range missiles stationed in the Federal Republic needed to be modernized so as to compensate for the elimination of the medium-range weapons. For his part, Mitterrand advocated negotiations before a decision to modernize. At the same time, he supported Kohl in his demand for talks on reducing the asymmetry in conventional weapons, which might render unnecessary the unpopular deployment of new short-range missiles. At Gen-

---

50 Cf. Mitterrand's memorandum in the French Council of Ministers, 4 March 1987, Attali, *Verbatim II*, pp. 270ff.; on the disarmament talks in general, Loth, *Overcoming the Cold War*, pp. 188–204.
51 Conversation between Mitterrand and Kohl, 28 March 1987, Attali, *Verbatim II*, pp. 287–291.
52 Schwarz, *Kohl*, pp. 446–449.

scher's urging, a speech by Kohl in the Bundestag on 27 April 1989 included a call for the rapid opening of negotiations on short-range weapon systems and also let it be known that the chancellor no longer excluded a third "zero solution" for this area too. Mitterrand worked to calm the Americans and British, who feared a denuclearization of the Federal Republic. He urged Reagan's successor George Bush to concentrate on making progress in the talks on conventional disarmament and to defer the issue of short-range weapons for the time being. In fact, the heads of state and of government of NATO put together a resolution to that effect at a summit in Brussels on 29 and 30 May 1989, allowing the Western alliance to respond to Gorbachev's proposals with great unanimity.[53]

Rapid progress was now made in the talks on conventional forces in Europe that had been going on since 9 March in Vienna. During a state visit by Gorbachev to the Federal Republic from 12 to 15 June, Kohl was able to assure his guest that after those talks had been successfully concluded, the modernization of short-range missiles would no longer be an issue. Mitterrand appealed to Bush to support Gorbachev in his reforms and urged the American president to meet with the Soviet general secretary as soon as possible. The summit in Malta on 2 and 3 December, at which Bush and Gorbachev proclaimed the end of the Cold War, was thus not least of all the result of parallel, though not closely coordinated, action by the West German chancellor and the French president.

As to the danger of a neutralization of the Federal Republic, Mitterrand now regarded it as sufficient, firstly, to support Kohl in the domestic policy dispute and, secondly, to emphasize the necessity of a European framework for reunification. At the conclusion of a state visit by Gorbachev on 5 July, journalists asked the French president about his attitude toward German reunification. He stressed the legitimacy of German desires but hastened to add that naturally the process must "occur peacefully" and must not generate any "new tensions." Three weeks later, he repeated this position in an interview that he gave to five European newspapers at once: Reunification had to occur "peacefully and democratically"; the process needed to involve a dialogue among the Four Powers and agreement between "both German governments."[54]

Conceptually, what lay behind this foray into public discussion of the German question was the idea of a deepening of the European Community as the "hard core of any organization of Europe from the Atlantic to the Urals." Political Director Bertrand Dufourcq of the French Foreign Ministry wrote to the president in

---

[53] Conversation between Mitterrand and Bush, 20 May 1989, Attali, *Verbatim III*, pp. 241–243; Frédéric Bozo, *Mitterrand, la fin de la guerre froide et l'unification allemande. De Yalta à Maastricht*, Paris: Editions Odile Jacob, 2005, pp. 70–79.
[54] *La politique étrangère de la France*, July–August 1989, pp. 21–23 and 78–82.

February of 1989, saying that in light of the loosening of the Soviet imperium, it was necessary to bind the Federal Republic more strongly than ever to the Community and to accelerate the Community's development into a Political Union with a common defense. Requests for entry by EFTA states such as Austria should for the time being be deferred in the interest of deepening the Community. Simultaneously, however, there should be common efforts with these states of the "second circle" to organize cooperation with the East-Bloc states (the "third circle"); this was to include areas such as culture, media, social issues, and technology. The convergence of both halves of Europe and both Germanys should thus happen in sync.[55] In August, Attali expanded this vision to include the dimension of financial support for the reforms of the East-Bloc states: All European countries including the Soviet Union were to discuss the problems involved in the transition at a common forum (Mitterrand spoke of a "confederation"), and a European Development Bank was to assist in dealing with the economic dimension.[56]

In late October, Mitterrand shared the idea of a confederation and a development bank with his European allies. This was not exactly met with great interest, neither from Kohl—who at dinner on 24 October did not respond at all to the president's remarks on the subject—nor from the circle of the twelve heads of state and of government, whom he invited to an informal gathering at the Élysée Palace a few days after the fall of the Berlin Wall. Instead, those dining on 18 November were witness to an intense confrontation between Margaret Thatcher, who could not hide her fear of German reunification, and the chancellor, who did not want to be restricted by his eleven partners in deciding on the steps now necessary in the reunification question. When Kohl quoted a NATO declaration of 1970 that contained support for the German position on reunification, Thatcher interrupted him with the observation that at the time, people "didn't believe it would ever happen." Kohl barked back, "You can't prevent the German people from pursuing its destiny." Thatcher answered this ominous threat with an angry "You see, you see, that's what he wants."[57]

At this point, Mitterrand viewed German-policy developments much more calmly. True, he was worried that an uncontrolled unification movement among the Germans could possibly lead to the fall of Gorbachev and thereby possibly even to a major war between East and West. Yet, at the same time, he—unlike Thatcher—had a conception for a peaceful solution of the German question; and he had strong hopes that Kohl would help him realize this European option. He was therefore all the more alarmed when, on 27 November, the chancellor for all practical pur-

---

55 Memorandum of 20 Feb. 1989, reported in Bozo, *Mitterrand*, pp. 98–101.
56 Attali, *C'était François Mitterrand*, pp. 308ff.
57 Ibid., pp. 311, 315–318.

poses withdrew his approval for the summoning of a government conference on monetary union. The anxiety increased when the very next day Kohl made public a ten-point reunification plan without having informed his partners in advance. Even if the announced path via "confederative structures" left much unclear—not least of all the timeframe of the unification process—it was unmistakably clear that the chancellor had put *political* reunification on the international agenda. This meant for Mitterrand, as he explained to Gorbachev on 6 December at a meeting in Kiev, that Kohl was prioritizing German unification over the deepening of European unity and the creation of a European peace order.[58]

The president now did his utmost to convince the chancellor to offer binding approval for the summoning of a government conference on the monetary union at the upcoming Strasbourg Council meeting. As welcome as an understanding on negotiations for a Political Union would be in principle, it was to be deferred so as not to endanger the breakthrough on the monetary issue. On the afternoon of 28 November, Mitterrand got on the phone to threaten Kohl that France would only approve his reunification plan if Bonn made three distinct commitments beforehand: beginning of negotiations on the monetary union, definitive recognition of the border with Poland, and confirmation of the Federal Republic's renunciation of nuclear weapons. He spoke still more darkly to Genscher, who had sought him out on 30 November in order to smooth the waves that Kohl's solo initiative had generated: "If German unity is achieved before European unity, you'll have the Triple Alliance (France, Great Britain, and the USSR) against you, exactly as in 1913 and 1939. [...] You'll be encircled, and that'll end in a war in which all Europeans will ally themselves against the Germans once again. Is that what you want? Conversely, if German unity is achieved after there's been progress on the unity of Europe, then we'll help you."[59]

No later than when Genscher reported this conversation to Kohl, it must have become clear to the chancellor that his engagement for a Political Union was not sufficient to win France's support for the reunification process. It followed from this that he did after all need to take a bigger domestic-policy risk if he wanted to retain the necessary maneuvering room for the shaping of the reunification process without at the same time endangering the European construct. Nor was it possible to exclude the danger that if the monetary union continued to be blocked, he could lose the initiative to Genscher in the one question as well as the other. Taken together, all those factors led him to give in on the issue of committing to the monetary union. Shortly before the opening of the Council meeting

---

58 Attali, *Verbatim III*, p. 364.
59 Attali, *Mitterrand*, pp. 320–323; on Genscher's visit, also Attali, *Verbatim III*, pp. 353ff. and Genscher, *Erinnerungen*, pp. 390 and 677–680.

on 8 December, the chancellor's office let the Élysée know that Kohl was now willing to set the date for the opening of the government conference in December of 1990.[60]

The Strasbourg Council meeting then began in a relatively relaxed atmosphere. As early as the opening luncheon, Kohl declared that a clear roadmap was necessary "in order to demonstrate our will to achieve progress." As Council president, Mitterrand was able to confirm "that the necessary majority exists for the summoning of a government conference in accordance with Article 236 of the treaty. The government conference will meet before the end of 1990 at the invitation of the Italian government." No decisions were made regarding the Political Union; it was only determined "that the economic and monetary union [was to] take the democratic requirement fully into account." Against the vote of Margaret Thatcher, the "Community Charter on Social Rights of Workers" was adopted, a move for which Mitterrand and Delors had long fought. Lastly, the Twelve also approved the establishment of the "European Bank for Reconstruction and Development." Mitterrand only had to concede to Thatcher that "the other OECD member states"—that is, especially the US—would also be invited to participate in it.[61]

In return for his concession on the monetary issue, Kohl wanted to receive explicit support for his reunification policy. This proved difficult because he was still not prepared to commit himself to the Oder-Neisse border as the future eastern frontier of a reunified Germany; this was out of concern for votes from the conservative camp. In the preparatory group, there was thus no agreement on the exact wording of a declaration; and at dinner on 8 December, Kohl was once against subjected to severe attacks from Thatcher. This time, she was joined by Giulio Andreotti and Ruud Lubbers; only Felipe González supported the chancellor. Mitterrand finally commissioned Dumas and Genscher to find a compromise formulation.

The text, ready the next morning, was closer to Kohl's position than that of his opponents: The Twelve pledged support for the "strengthening of the state of peace in Europe in which the German people in free self-determination achieves its unity." As conditions for this process, however, the document specified only the "preservation of the agreements and treaties as well as all the principles laid down in the Helsinki Final Act" and embedding that process "in the prospect of

---

60 Bozo, *Mitterrand*, p. 152; on the following, *ibid.*, pp. 152–156; Thilo Schabert, *Wie Weltgeschichte gemacht wird. Frankreich und die deutsche Einheit*, Stuttgart: Klett-Cotta, 2002, pp. 425–428; Lappenküper, *Mitterrand*, pp. 269–271.
61 "Schlussfolgerung des Vorsitzes der Straßburger Ratstagung 8./9.12.1989," *Jahrbuch der Europäischen Integration 1989/90*, pp. 421–438.

European integration."⁶² It was rather unclearly formulated regarding the recognition of the western border of Poland, which the Federal Republic had made in the Treaties of Moscow and Warsaw; it was however rather clear on making reunification possible along with the simultaneous strengthening of the European Community. With the definitive commitment to the monetary union, Kohl had been able to secure fundamental support for the process of reunification.

However, this did not mean that giving up the D-mark and the comfortable position in the European Monetary System that the Federal Republic had in the meantime attained was the price that had to be paid for reunification, as the magazine *Der Spiegel* later asserted.⁶³ Kohl had only recognized that, regardless of the reservations of those seeking to protect the currency and the associated domestic political risks, the step to monetary union had to be taken *now* if the growing together of the two German states—in whatever form and at whatever tempo—was not to endanger the continued existence or the deepening of the European Community. On the basis of shared worry over the European project, he could come to agreement with Mitterrand on a formula for German unity within a European perspective.

After he had thus secured the European framework for the reunification of Germany, Kohl could further accelerate the reunification process in response to the decay of the GDR.⁶⁴ In the middle of January 1990, he halted the project for a treaty community that was to be agreed upon with the East German government under Hans Modrow according to the ten-point plan; on 6 February, he offered the East German population participation in the monetary zone of the Federal Republic within six months. Mitterrand viewed that with great unease. As much as he was relieved regarding Kohl's concession on the monetary issue, his apprehension about the possible fate of Gorbachev was growing more intense. "Kohl wants to organize the reunification very quickly," as he assessed the situation after a visit by the chancellor to his country retreat in Latché. "He makes us believe he can't do anything about it, that he's being driven by the crowd. The whole world will cry out—but in vain. Only Gorbachev can stop him. If he doesn't succeed, he'll lose his office. And then we'll have a general in the Kremlin. You'll see that everything will happen very fast. Two or three years at most."⁶⁵

---

62 *Ibid.*, p. 431.
63 "Dunkelste Stunden," in: *Der Spiegel* (18), 27 April 1998, pp. 108–112.
64 On the decision-making process on German policy in 1989–90, see Wilfried Loth, "Michail Gorbatschow, Helmut Kohl und die Lösung der deutschen Frage 1989/1990," in: Gian Enrico Rusconi and Hans Woller (eds.), *Parallele Geschichte? Italien und Deutschland 1945–2000*, Berlin Duncker und Humblot, 2006, pp. 461–477; Andreas Rödder, *Deutschland einig Vaterland. Die Geschichte der Wiedervereinigung*, Munich: C.H. Beck, 2009, pp. 146–225; Schwarz, *Kohl*, pp. 535–580.
65 Attali, *Verbatim III*, p. 390.

The only thing he could do in attempting "to slow down German reunification in order to save the gains of perestroika"[66] was to appeal repeatedly to Kohl's discretion. When on 20 January Thatcher urged him to take joint actions, he told her that ultimately there was not much that could be done, and "nothing would be worse than raising objections that have no effect."[67] During a visit by Kohl on 10 February, Gorbachev recognized in principle the right of the Germans to reunification; this meant that hopes vanished that the Soviet general secretary would block rapid progress toward German unity purely out of his own self-interest. "What's gotten into Gorbachev?" was the question that Mitterrand blurted out after Kohl had informed him via telephone of the results of the conversation in Moscow. "Four days ago, he wrote to me that he would stand firm—and today he concedes every point!"[68]

Deep disappointment over Gorbachev's weakness did not prevent Mitterrand from adjusting to the "new German reality" with remarkable speed. "One must come to terms with it," as he let Kohl know during a dinner at the Élysée on 15 February.[69] He warned his guest to continue to be cautious and to take Gorbachev into consideration. At the same time, the French president made great efforts to have German unity, now unavoidable, formulated in treaty terms acceptable to France and to Europe. Hence, he supported the American proposal to resolve the international aspects of the unification of the two German states at a conference in which the West German government, a democratically-legitimated East German government, and the governments of the four Allied Powers would participate. Mitterrand thought that it should be a "Four-plus-Two" conference rather than a "Two-plus-Four" conference. After it was ascertained that both German states would not only simply present the Four Powers with the results of their internal talks, he accepted the latter formulation. With satisfaction, he noted that Kohl too agreed to this in the end—on 13 February in a telephone conversation with Bush that gave the green light for a decision of the six foreign ministers assembled in Ottawa. In light of the agreement of the Four Powers on this issue, Kohl could no longer fend off the resulting limitations on his freedom of maneuver in decision-making.

---

66 Thusly after the telephone conversation with Gorbachev on 2 February 1990, Attali, *Verbatim III*, p. 411. The material-rich presentation in Bozo, *Mitterrand*, pp. 156–202, edits out this aspect of Mitterrand's policy; in contrast, cf. Lappenküper, *Mitterrand*, pp. 273–302.
67 Conversation between Mitterrand and Thatcher, 20 Jan. 1990, French protocol quoted from Bozo, *Mitterrand*, p. 180.
68 Attali, *Mitterrand*, p. 333.
69 *Ibid*., pp. 333–336; *Deutsche Einheit*, pp. 842–852; Attali, *Verbatim III*, pp. 422–429, the quote on p. 424.

During a dinner on 15 February, Mitterrand then sought to have Kohl stipulate the conditions for German unity that the French president regarded as indispensable: Acceleration of the economic and also the political unification of Europe, a united Germany's continued membership in NATO but without extension of American command authority to the territory of the GDR, confirmation of the renunciation of nuclear weapons, and recognition of the Oder-Neisse border in a treaty. Kohl indicated that he was in complete agreement on the first two points; both were based on the proposal by Irish Council President Charles Haughey to discuss the consequences of German unification for the European Community at a special summit in April. Kohl wanted nothing to do with any determination in advance regarding the issue of nuclear weapons, and he reacted with the greatest indignation to the demand for pre-determination on the border issue. Under the influence of the looming victory of a political movement close to Kohl, the "Alliance for Germany," in the elections to the GDR parliament, the chancellor then began to edge incrementally toward the French positions in early March. In the end, it proved possible to include both the renunciation of nuclear weapons and the renunciation of the former German eastern territories in the "Two-Plus-Four" Treaty. German unification was completed on 3 October 1990 in accordance with the foreign-policy conditions on which Mitterrand had insisted.[70]

The Path to Maastricht

Jacques Delors had been the first to articulate the need for an acceleration of the European integration process to accompany an acceleration of German unification, saying so internally and more or less clearly in public as well. Only three days after the fall of the Berlin Wall, he had declared on German television that according to the provisions of the Treaties of Rome, the way stood open for the citizens of the GDR to enter the European Community. In his inaugural address to the European Parliament at the beginning of his second term, he had argued "that the Community can only retain its attractiveness if it accelerates its integration." In his view, this included the idea "that comprehensive executive authority be transferred to the Commission" and as a consequence, there be an "expansion of the powers of Parliament."[71]

Mitterrand's Europe advisor, Elisabeth Guigou, a one-time staffer of Delors during his time as finance minister, embraced the essentials of this argument in

---

[70] Bozo, *Mitterrand*, pp. 202–241; on Kohl's motives, a telephone conversation with Mitterrand on 5 March 1990, Attali, *Verbatim III*, p. 439.
[71] *Europa-Archiv* 45 (1990), pp. D 269–282; Delors, *Erinnerungen*, pp. 327–329.

a memorandum to the president on 6 February. As she wrote, it is in the interest of "the Community very quickly to invent an institutional structure to make the German situation ordinary" and "to ensure that Germany sets its course within the framework of the Community and not autonomously." She therefore proposed taking up Kohl's initiative for the creation of a Political Union and creating a "European Union" that would overarch existing European institutions. Justifying the urgency of her proposal, she wrote that it would be better "to negotiate a European Union with a Germany that is for the time being still divided into two states and that needs the Community rather than with a reunited German that no longer needs anyone."[72] In the run-up to the dinner on 15 February to which Mitterrand had invited Kohl, Guigou established contact with her West German counterpart Joachim Bitterlich and was able to reinforce her proposal with information on the chancellor's willingness to undertake a joint initiative for the Political Union.

Mitterrand hesitated to agree to the proposal for launching the Political Union, however. He still feared that differing views on the institutional configuration of the final political form of the Community could delay implementation of the monetary union. On 15 February, his only concrete suggestion to Kohl was to bring forward the beginning of the government conference on monetary union, which was swiftly rejected by the chancellor. Mitterrand only gave his approval to a joint Franco-German initiative for the Political Union in late March. This had come only after the Germans had approached the French side with a proposal to that effect and after Kohl had pressured Council President Haughey to make a decision on a government conference for the Political Union at the upcoming special meeting of the heads of state and of government set for 28 April. Meanwhile, Belgian Prime Minister Wilfried Martens had brought more pressure to bear on Mitterrand by means of a memorandum to the partner governments—inspired by Delors—that called for a government conference on institutional reform.

The Franco-German initiative in the form of a joint letter from Mitterrand and Kohl to Council President Haughey on 18 April did not envision making a decision yet on the introduction of a further government conference at the upcoming Council meeting. Because Mitterrand feared a hasty commitment to Bonn's institutional conceptions, it was only possible for the time being to propose that the foreign ministers make preparations for a government conference on the Political Union. Only on the basis of their report was a decision to be made at the next regular Council meeting in late June. Regarding the timeframe for the government conference on Political Union, the joint letter suggested that it occur parallel to the government conference on the monetary union so that "the totality of the

---

[72] Memorandum by Guigou, 6 February 1990, AN, 5AG4, AH 35, quoted from Bozo, *Mitterrand*, pp. 198ff. On the following, *ibid.*, pp. 196–202 and 244–249.

relations among the member states can be transformed into a European Union by 1 January 1993." In terms of content, the proposal was relatively indefinite: The Political Union was to "strengthen the democratic legitimization of the Union" and "flesh out more efficiently" its institutions, but also provide for the "unity and coherence" of its activities "in the areas of economy, currency, and politics" as well as "defining and implementing a common foreign and defense policy."[73]

In Dublin, where the heads of state and of government met on 28 April, the Franco-German initiative ran into opposition from Thatcher, as expected. In the view of the British prime minister, German unification provided no argument for the deepening of the European Community—on the contrary, there was reason to block such a deepening: "The European construct will not bind Germany; it's rather the case that Germany will dominate the European construct," as she had said at a dinner at the French embassy in London in mid-March.[74] As a consequence, it was only possible to decide in Dublin that before the next Council meeting on 25 and 26 June, the foreign ministers were to review the necessity of possible treaty amendments for strengthening democratic legitimacy and for effectively responding to the "challenges of the new situation." It was left open as to whether the summoning of a second parallel government conference would then actually be decided on. The European Council stipulated only that the treaty amendments necessary for the second stage of the monetary union had to be in force by 1 January 1993.[75] For Kohl, that was not the strong signal for progress on political unification that he regarded as necessary in order to secure the monetary union with the German electorate.

With great unanimity, the European Council also approved numerous principles for integrating the GDR into the Community. This was to occur without amendment to the treaties but was to take into consideration transitional provisions for which the Commission was to develop proposals "as soon as possible." At the Council meeting, Delors proposed special integration subsidies, but Kohl rejected these out of consideration for his partners' sensitivities. Instead, it was decided that, like all other Eastern Bloc states, the GDR was initially to participate in the EC Assistance for Economic Reforms, and that the new states of the Federal Republic would then be incorporated into the existing structural program of the Community. Kohl explicitly renounced the idea of an increased presence of the Federal Republic on the Commission as well as stronger weighting of the German voice in the Council of Ministers. Any adjustments that might be necessary should be left to the talks on institutional reform.

---

73 *Europa-Archiv* 45 (1990), p. D 283.
74 Embassy report of 13 March 1990, quoted in Bozo, *Mitterrand*, p. 242.
75 *Europa-Archiv* 45 (1990), pp. D 284–D288.

In accordance with the proposals of the Commission, which were specially put together by the work groups under great time pressure, mutual free access to markets was to be realized as early as the establishment of the German-German monetary union, that is, on 1 July 1990. Transitional regulations were to expire no later than the completion of the internal market on 31 December 1992. Until that time, the trade treaties with the COMECON countries were to remain in effect. Technical regulations relating to law on food, transportation, telecommunications, environmental protection, and workplace safety did not yet come into force. A lump sum was determined for structural assistance. National assistance was permitted for the realignment of agriculture.[76]

Yet, the foreign ministers of the Twelve did succeed in agreeing on numerous principles for the Political Union during a meeting on 19 and 20 May. Kohl and Genscher had reduced their conceptions for the institutional strengthening of the Community to a realistic level so that unity could be more or less achieved on the idea that the European Council would continue to constitute the central institution of the Union; above it, the Community area and the area of political cooperation were to be more strongly interlinked. On the other hand, Dumas accommodated the reservations of various partners regarding a common foreign and defense policy to the effect that these were initially to be developed incrementally. At the regular Council meeting on 25 and 26 June, likewise held in Dublin, it was possible on this basis to reach agreement that parallel to the government conference on the monetary union, a government conference on the Political Union was also to meet. More specifically: The monetary conference was to begin on 13 December 1990 and the "Political" one on 14 December. Both were to complete their work so that the resulting treaties or treaty amendments could be ratified before the end of 1992.[77]

In preparing for the second government conference, Kohl and Mitterrand continued to work closely together. Their motives were to an extent different: For Kohl and the West German government, it was primarily a matter of reducing the democratic deficit of the Community that had emerged after the expansion of Community activities into many new policy areas through the Single European Act; addressing that issue would secure the European orientation of German policy over the long term. The German public's fatigue over Europe, evident in several respects including the lower turnout for elections to the European Parliament in June of 1989, was definitely perceived in Bonn as an alarm signal. For their part, Mitterrand and his advisors were primarily aiming to strengthen common foreign and defense policy. They fully expected that after the end of the

---

76 Cf. Delors, *Erinnerungen*, pp. 346ff.; Stark, *Kohl*, pp. 170–177.
77 *Jahrbuch der Europäischen Integration 1990/91*, pp. 417–420.

Cold War, the American presence in Europe would diminish sooner or later; the French wanted to make use of this opportunity to achieve substantial progress in promoting European autonomy in world politics.

Both governments were however in agreement that the completion of the monetary union had to be accompanied by a strengthening of the political structures of the Community if the integration of the now-sovereign Germans was to succeed over the long term. On the day after German unification had come into effect, Kohl sent a letter to the French president in which he expressed gratitude for Mitterrand's support and pledged to work for the acceleration of European unification. In a conversation with Attali, Mitterrand appeared to have been propitiated and was at the same time resolved to make use of the opportunity for strengthening the European Union that was available to him with Kohl: "The chancellor is sincere. And he will do all that if he has the time. That's a man of very great worth. But after him? One must integrate Germany into the Political Union, dissolve it in it, before Kohl leaves. If not, German arrogance—this time Bavarian rather than Prussian—will once again threaten the peace in Europe."[78] Both statesmen were at pains to demonstrate publicly that their divergences on the question of German unification policy—which had not remained completely hidden from the public—had by no means diminished their resolve to advance European unification together.

Taking up a suggestion that Dumas had made to his German counterpart Hans-Dietrich Genscher at the Franco-German summit of 17 and 18 September in Munich, both sides worked on another joint declaration that was to be presented by Kohl and Mitterrand in the run-up to the opening of both government conferences. In a joint letter of 6 December to the Council president (now Giulio Andreotti), Kohl committed himself more explicitly to the goal of a "common defense" than he had in his efforts for the development of a joint Franco-German defense concept in the summer of 1987. For this purpose, a "clear organic tie" between the Political Union and the WEU was to be created; in the long term, the WEU was to become a component of the Political Union and consequently was also to include those Union members that had not belonged to it up to that time. As areas in which a "genuine common foreign policy" could develop, the document cited relations with the former Eastern Bloc states and the states bordering the Mediterranean, disarmament talks, as well as development policy. Decisions would be made "fundamentally unanimously," but it would also be possible to allow for majority decision-making, especially involving modalities of policy implementation.

Paris acceded to Bonn's demands regarding incorporation of immigration policy and the battle against international crime in the Community. It was in

---

[78] Note, 4 Oct. 1990, Attali, *Verbatim* III, p. 606.

these areas that after the elimination of the "Iron Curtain" and the re-emergence of ethnic conflicts in the former Eastern Bloc states, Bonn was confronted with problems that it did not want to face alone and could not address alone. Therefore, the joint letter also urged the creation of a council of ministers of the interior and justice. Regarding the strengthening of Community organs, Paris and Bonn agreed on "co-decision" by Parliament for legislative acts "in the narrower sense," which ultimately opened up the possibility of a veto right; there was also to be confirmation of the Commission president and the Commission by a majority of Parliament as well as the introduction of majority voting in the Council of Ministers as a rule. Additionally, in order to strengthen the democratic legitimacy of the Community, a "genuine European citizenship" was to be created.[79]

In the Delors' view, however, that was insufficient for actually securing the Community's legitimacy and ability to act. In February of 1991, making use of elaborations by his deputy cabinet chief, François Lamoureux, Delors presented the government conference with a series of draft texts that moved in the direction of more supra-nationality. Actions in the foreign-policy realm were always to be submitted for approval if the Council president, the Commission, or a group of more than six member states required it. The decision to become active in a certain field was still to be made unanimously by the European Council. Regarding the nature of the measures to be taken, it was to be *compulsory* that the Council of Ministers then decide by qualified majority; execution was primarily to be in the hands of the Commission.[80] In general, the Commission was to receive greater freedom of action in issuing provisions for implementation. It was also to assume the representation of the Community in international organizations such as the International Monetary Fund. Lastly, the Commission proposed that the Community be given the right to impose taxes of its own.

This went well beyond any consensus that could have been reached among the twelve governments; it also ran counter to antipathy toward an increase in the Commission's power that had been repeatedly expressed by Mitterrand. Government representatives at the working level showed little inclination to adopt the Commission's proposal. "We simply set aside the Commission's drafts and proceeded with others," as one member of the Council Secretariat remembered.[81] In the middle of April, the

---

[79] *Europa-Archiv* 46 (1991), pp. D25–27. On the course of the government conference on the Political Union, Jim Cloos, Gaston Reinsch, Daniel Vignes, and Joseph Weyland, *Le traité de Maastricht. Genèse, analyse, commentaires*, Brussels: Émile Bruylant, 1994, pp. 73–93; Endo, *Presidency*, pp. 170–190; Rometsch, *Rolle*, pp. 181–195; Stark, *Kohl*, pp. 179–213; Bozo, *Mitterrand*, pp. 303–325; in the view of a participant, Delors, *Erinnerungen*, pp. 403–411.
[80] Commission Proposals on Common External Policy, *Agence Europe, Documents*, Nr. 1697/1698, 7 March 1991.
[81] Interview with Ken Endo, *Presidency*, p. 178.

Luxembourg Council presidency submitted a first draft treaty. This document took up the principle of different "pillars" of the future Union. This had been brought into the discussion by French representative Pierre de Boissieu in order to counter the Commission's claims to power. In accordance with this concept, foreign and defense policy as well as justice and interior policy would each constitute distinct pillars of the Union, ones in which proceedings were to be strictly intergovernmental. In the Community area, the initiative right of the Commission was to lose some of its significance because Parliament would be accorded such a right too. The Council was to be able to alter Commission proposals by simple majority. When there was a difference of opinion between the Council and Parliament, the Commission was no longer to have authority to make amendment proposals or simply withdraw the bill.[82]

Delors attacked this draft as an attempt to reduce the Commission to a kind of secretariat that would be subordinate to the other institutions of the Community. He had some success in this: At an informal Council of Ministers gathering hosted by Genscher in Dresden on 2 and 3 June, Dutch Foreign Minister Hans von den Brock and his Belgian colleague Mark Eyskens severely criticized the proposed pillar structure. Genscher and Italian Foreign Minister Gianni De Michelis, along with their counterparts from Spain, Ireland, and even Greece also voiced criticism. This convinced the Luxembourg Council presidency of the necessity of reworking the draft treaty. In the version presented at the Luxembourg Council meeting on 28 and 29 June, the uniformity of the institutional framework of the Union was more strongly emphasized.[83]

Nevertheless, the pillar structure was retained in the draft, and the Commission would thereby be prevented from having access to the fields of foreign policy and domestic security. The Dutch Council presidency of the second half of 1991 sought to change this once again by advocating its own draft treaty, which bound the three pillars together under Community law and further strengthened the rights of Parliament. Given that the Dutch draft also downplayed the role of common foreign and defense policy, it failed to find support among many advocates of strengthening the Community organs.[84] In late September, Bonn decided—heeding pressure from Paris—to support retention of the Luxembourg draft. At the Council of Ministers session of 30 September, the so-called "Black Monday" of the Dutch presidency, the decision was made.

Delors was only able to eliminate the reductions in Commission authority contained in the Luxembourg draft. During a conclave of government representa-

---

[82] Non-Paper of the Luxembourg Presidency, 15 April 1991, *Agence Europe, Documents*, Nr. 1709/1710, 3 May 1991.
[83] Draft treaty, 18 June 1991, *ibid.*, Nr. 1722/1723, 5 July 1991.
[84] Draft treaty, 23 Sept. 1991, *ibid.*, Nr. 1733/1734, 3 Oct. 1991.

tives at Noordwijk in the Netherlands on 12 and 13 November, it was decided that legislative initiatives of Parliament were first to be presented to the Commission. This meant that the Commission's monopoly on initiatives was preserved, at least in the sense of having a veto right. Also, the Commission was still to be able to withdraw bills if it was not in agreement with the changes made by other organs. The strengthening of Parliament's position was essentially limited to the introduction of a co-decision-making process in individual areas and the expansion of oversight rights; also, the Commission would henceforth need to be confirmed by a parliamentary majority. The terms for Commission members were extended from four to five years. For the Council of Ministers, majority voting was introduced as a rule, but there was to be a group of exceptions, such as when defining research framework programs and industrial policy.

Bonn's decision against the Dutch treaty draft was simultaneously an affirmation of the choice for an autonomous European defense. That had been opposed not only by the Dutch government, but also by the British, Danish, and Portuguese governments, which had argued that one ought not to endanger further the already-threatened cohesion of NATO by emphasizing a European defense identity. The formulation of the Franco-German program, which Dumas and Genscher had presented on 4 February,[85] therefore did not find acceptance everywhere. At the Luxembourg Council Meeting, it was only possible to determine that the decision on it would be postponed until the closing phase of the government conference. In Paris, doubts began to arise as to whether Bonn was actually willing to involve itself in an independent defense; in the main question of the day for common foreign policy—the attitude toward Serbian intervention against the declarations of independence by Slovenia and Croatia in late June—the two partners took opposing positions. Mitterrand was once again worried about the stability of borders in Europe, whereas the German government was under pressure from south German sympathizers of former Habsburg territories.

In order banish the danger that the Franco-German initiative for a common foreign and defense policy would fail, Kohl suggested to Mitterrand that there be another joint foray, he proposed this at a meeting in Lille on 25 June. By the beginning of October, this had resulted in a new joint letter to the Council chair, now Dutch Prime Minister Ruud Lubbers. The document made the goal of foreign and defense policy more specific in three points: *Firstly*, a draft text of treaty terms on these matters was offered, naming the WEU as the organ charged with carrying out common foreign policy but at the same time declaring that the "specifics of the defense policy of individual member states" were "unaffected." A review of

---

85 Der Bundesminister des Auswärtigen informiert. Mitteilung für die Presse vom 6.2.1991 (German Foreign Minister Press Release of 6 Feb. 1991).

these terms was announced for no later than 1996. *Secondly*, Bonn and Paris presented a draft declaration of WEU member states, which was to be appended to the Union treaty; this emphasized the "incremental expansion of the WEU into the defense component of the Union" as well as the goal of "creating a European pillar" of the Atlantic alliance. *Thirdly*, the chancellor and president announced not only an expansion of Franco-German military units, but also declared that these could "constitute the nucleus of a European corps," in which "forces of other members of the WEU" participated.[86]

Thatcher's successor John Major declared to Mitterrand that subordination of the WEU to the guidelines of the Union would be absolutely out of the question. However, after the US government had accepted the "development of a defense identity for Europe" in a declaration of the NATO Council on 8 November, the British prime minister had to content himself with a weakening of the formulations of the Franco-German draft at the conclusion of treaty negotiations at the Council meeting of 9 and 10 December in Maastricht. The treaty text now contained only the statement that the common defense policy "*could* in due course lead to a common defense"; for practical measures following from Council decisions on defense policy, there was an assumption of "accord" between the Council and the organs of the WEU. Additionally, majority decision-making on "questions that have defense-policy characteristics" was explicitly forbidden.[87] Through close cooperation, Mitterrand and Kohl were able to prevent any further watering down of the defense perspectives during the Council meeting in Maastricht.[88]

As to the timetable for the monetary union, Mitterrand and Delors voted in agreement for precise political determinations. The second stage of the monetary union was to begin as soon as possible, that is, when the treaties came into force on 1 January 1993. Conveniently, that was also the date on which the internal market was to be completed. The German finance ministry, now with Theo Waigel and new State Secretary Horst Köhler at the head, were averse to setting a date and instead wanted the fulfillment of objective criteria such as the achievement of price stability and budgetary discipline. Finally, at a Council meeting in Rome on 28 and 29 October 1990, Kohl was ready for a compromise: The second stage was to begin on 1 January 1994, at least if "sufficient" progress in real-economic

---

[86] Letter of 14 Oct. 1991, *Europa-Archiv* 46 (1991), pp. D571–574.
[87] EU Treaty, Art. J.4.
[88] On the course of the meeting, Françoise Carle, *Les Archives du Président. Mitterrand intime*, Paris: Editions du Rocher, 1998, pp. 233–236; Pierre Favier, Michel Martin-Rolland, *La Décennie Mitterrand*, Vol. 4: *Les Déchirements, 1991–1995*, Paris: Éditions du Seuil, 1999, pp. 227ff.; Georges Saunier, "La négociation de Maastricht vue de Paris," in: *Journal of European Integration History* 19 (2013), pp. 45–65.

and monetary convergence had been achieved by then—a vague formulation that no longer left much maneuvering room for the German neo-liberals to delay the actual beginning of the monetary union any further.[89]

Kohl still did not however give in to pressure from Mitterrand to set a date for the transition to the third stage, the introduction of the Community currency. Only when in March of 1991 Genscher publicly pleaded for 1 January 1997 as the transition date did Kohl acknowledge the necessity of a clear timeline. Yet, in order to avoid drawing criticism from those who had a sentimental attachment to the German mark, he still did not want to name a concrete date. It was Andreotti at the Maastricht Council meeting who first brought 1 January 1999 into play as the latest date for the beginning of the currency union, and this was accepted. If before the end of 1996 the Council was to determine by qualified majority that a majority of member states had fulfilled the criteria for joining, the monetary union could then begin on 1 January 1997. Otherwise, there was to be a decision before 1 July 1998 on which states could participate.

Pressure was thus put on the economically-weaker countries to make serious efforts to meet the entry criteria: New debt not over three percent, total debt not over sixty percent of GNP, an inflation rate not over 1.5 percent of the average of the rates in the three most stable states, long-term interest rates not over two percent more than in those states, and no devaluation within the EMS over the previous two years. At the same time, however, there developed a certain amount of maneuvering room for interpreting these criteria generously in case that in 1998 a country such as France still would clearly diverge from the level of the Federal Republic. Waigel and Köhler, who were completely surprised by Kohl's decision to agree to set a firm date for the introduction of the Community currency,[90] had to accept that the chancellor regarded the irreversibility of the decision more highly than an absolute stability guarantee.

Great Britain was granted the possibly, even with a positive assessment of its economic performance, of foregoing participation in the third stage. This was the price that had to be paid in order to avoid having British Prime Minister John Major use his veto to block the necessary treaty amendments. At the same time, this settlement still kept open a path for British participation. Such a decision— fundamentally desired by all partners—could not in fact be excluded from the realm of possibility after the up-coming 1992 parliamentary elections. Earlier, while serving as Chancellor of the Exchequer, Major, along with Foreign Minis-

---

[89] Dyson and Featherstone, *Road*, pp. 395–399; on the following, *ibid.*, pp. 202–255, 370–451, and 726–740; Harold James, "Designing a Central Bank in the Run-Up to Maastricht," in: *Journal of European Integration History* 19 (2013), pp. 105–122.
[90] According to Hans Tietmeyer's account, quoted in Schwarz, *Kohl*, p. 701.

ter Douglas Hurd, had forced through Britain's entry into the EMS on 5 October 1990; then, widespread criticism of Thatcher's aggressively anti-Europe rhetoric had six week later even led to the prime minister's fall. It was not necessarily an intention to participate in the Community currency that lay behind this. Yet, Thatcher's opponents did hope that the problems of the British economy, such as rising inflation and a massive balance of trade deficit, could be better brought under control if the country participated in the European Monetary System. They were also convinced that there would be a better chance of having influence over its construction as a member rather than by standing on the sidelines. Britain should take its place "at the very heart of Europe," Major proclaimed as the new prime minister during his first public appearance in Bonn.[91]

The Dutch government proposed that all member states have the option of quitting the monetary union after the point when the Council had made the decision for the transition to the third stage; this was rejected at an informal meeting of the finance ministers on 1 December 1991 in Scheveningen in the Netherlands. After that, the Danish government demanded a special right to withdraw, citing the provisions of the country's constitution: The Danish government asserted that entry into the monetary union might well require approval in a national referendum, and thus it could not commit itself definitively in a treaty at that juncture. The partners did agree to this demand by providing an additional protocol, knowing that regarding the weight of the Community currency in the world currency structure and the cohesion of the internal market, much less was at stake here than in the British case.

The compromise character of the agreements on the monetary union revealed itself still more clearly in the decisions for the second stage: Köhler, who carried on the negotiations for the German side with backing from Waigel and Kohl, had to accept that the preparations for the third stage were not simply left to the Committee of National Bank Governors but would be taken up by a "European Monetary Institute," which was under the leadership of an external president chosen by the European Council. This monetary institute would not however take over the coordination of national monetary policies at that time, as France—represented by Treasury Director Jean-Claude Trichet—and the Commission were demanding of a European Central Bank to be created at the beginning of the second stage. Likewise, this institute was not to take on responsibility for currency reserves at that time. National central banks would be able to transfer currency reserves to it, but it would then act only under their mandate.

Regarding the already-accepted independence of the European Central Bank system and the commitment to the goal of currency stability, the German side

---

[91] Speech of 11 March 1991, quoted from Young, *Blessed Plot*, p. 374. Cf. *ibid.*, pp. 362–374; Dyson and Featherstone, *Road*, pp. 644–682.

had to accept that the independence of the national central banks would have to be realized before entry into the third stage rather than before entry into the second. On the other hand, French Economy Minister Pierre Bérégovoy's hopes for a comprehensive "economic government" of the Community as a necessary accompaniment to the Community currency were diminished in that instead of binding "guidelines," the Council would only be able to issue a "recommendation"; and financial support for members states that had gotten into difficulties would be dependent on the unanimous vote of the Council. As the *Bundesbank* had demanded, there was an explicit ban on holding the Community liable for the debts of individual member states; for states with an "excessive government deficit," there was the threat of "fines of an appropriate size." At the final ministers meeting in Brussels on 2 and 3 December, Waigel and Köhler were able to have a decision made to the effect that the Council would only be empowered to provide "general orientations" regarding exchange-rate policy, not "guidelines." Additionally, it was determined that these orientations "shall be without prejudice to the primary objective of the ECB to maintain price stability."[92]

Waigel and Köhler were also successful in fending off a Spanish demand for the establishment of a "convergence fund" to assist the weaker member states. Commitment to social and economic cohesion was inserted in a protocol attached to the EU Treaty. This announced the creation of a "Cohesion Fund" with which the weaker member states could be supported on "projects in the areas of environment and trans-European networks." The redistribution to be needed as part of the promotion of convergence was thus kept within narrow boundaries. Likewise, determinations on the authority of the Community in the realm of social policy—securing minimal standards in promoting employment, working conditions, equality between the sexes, and worker participation in management—were relegated to a separate agreement, which Great Britain did not sign. At Maastricht, Kohl was able to push through a decision that a further government conference in 1996 would review the practicability of the agreed-upon stipulations. This preserved the prospect of all participants' having an opportunity to make improvements in line with their views.

The agreement in Maastricht can therefore be regarded in two different lights: On the one hand, Kohl and Mitterrand had succeeded—through significant effort—in saving the European unification process from endangerment by German reunification and had even succeeded in advancing that process further. With a common currency, there was a degree of integration and European state-like structures that made it irreversible. On the other hand, progress in areas

---

[92] Articles 103, 104, and 109 (2) of the EC Treaty. For an overview of the decisions on the monetary union, see Unger, *History*, pp. 229–242.

especially important to either the German chancellor or the French president had remained much more meager than what would have been necessary for lasting success. Contributions to dismantling the deficit of democracy through strengthening the rights of Parliament and expanding majority-voting in the Council of Ministers had to a great extent been offset by the proliferation of procedures. Commitment to the goal of common decision-making structures in the field of defense was relativized by mandating unanimity on the way to their realization.

These shortcomings, which prompted Delors to speak of an "organised schizophrenia,"[93] were to an extent attributable to the fact that cooperation between Delors and Mitterrand had since the turn of the year 1989–90 given way to prickly tension. With an obvious exaggerated self-regard, Delors had neglected to coordinate with Mitterrand on the institutional questions. For his part, the French president had given little thought to how the "economic government" and the common foreign and defense policy were to function. A coherent negotiating strategy for the expansion of the Community could not develop under such circumstances. The network that Delors, Genscher, and Dumas had established (with Guigou as intermediary to Mitterrand), could not completely develop. From the beginning of 1991, Delors was acting largely in isolation. In the end, he had to be content with having preserved the status quo for the Commission.

Several weeks went by before the treaty on the founding of the European Community, which built on the revised EEC Treaty, as well as the Treaty on European Union with all the protocols and declarations could be edited and translated into all official languages. On 7 February 1992, the foreign and finance ministers of the Twelve assembled in Maastricht once again in order to sign the treaties. Three-and-a-half months later, at the conclusion of the Franco-German summit in La Rochelle on 22 May 1992, the two governments announced the formation of the Franco-German corps, which would number approximately 35,000. At the Council meeting in Edinburgh on 11 and 12 December 1992, it was finally possible to make decisions about the seat of important Community organs: The Commission, which in the meantime was employing more than seventeen thousand civil servants, was assigned Brussels as its official seat—shortly after the Berlaymont Building had been vacated due to asbestos contamination. Parliament was to meet once per month in Strasbourg, while further plenary sessions and committee meetings as well as sessions of the Council of Ministers were to take place in Brussels. The multiplicity of the arrangements made in Maastricht was reflected too in the inconsistency of its geographic localization.

---

93 Speech to the European Parliament, 20 Nov. 1991, quoted in Endo, *Presidency*, p. 187.

7 From Maastricht to Nice, 1992–2001

Implementing the Monetary Union

Realizing the Maastricht decisions was not a straightforward affair. Not only was there still the open question as to whether Great Britain and Denmark would participate in the third stage of the monetary union. The completion of the internal market and the introduction of a common currency also brought so many changes to the economic organization and everyday lives of Europeans that it was unknown whether these developments would be readily accepted. Moreover, in achieving the convergence criteria necessary for the transition to the third stage, the member states had to contend with divergent economic developments that they could influence only to a limited extent.

The ratification of the Treaty on European Union and of the revised EEC Treaty (now called the Treaty on Foundation of the European Community) was endangered when on 12 May 1992, the Danish Folketing voted on the ratification bill: Although it did win a majority, it failed to achieve the constitutionally-mandated five-sixths support necessary for immediate adoption. A referendum now had to be organized. In response, those who were against Danish membership in the European Community on principle and those who opposed its further development joined together in a campaign that garnered a surprisingly-high level of support. Against the vote of almost all parties represented in parliament, against the labor unions, and against the major newspapers, some 50.7 percent of the voters opposed the Maastricht Treaties in the referendum of 2 June 1992. The gap between those against and the 49.3 percent who voted in favor amounted to only 46,000 votes altogether.

The surprising Danish "no" caused a considerable shock in the Community. The Council of Ministers immediately decided that the ratification process in the other countries would continue according to the envisaged schedule. Meeting in Lisbon on 26 and 27 June, the heads of state and of government ruled out any renegotiation of the treaties; in other respects, the Danish problem was deferred for the time being. In the public opinion of the other countries, however, those forces opposed to individual aspects of the treaties for various reasons or opposed to the entire direction of the unification process were given a boost. Up to that point, those opponents had not seemed to have much prospect of success; now, they were in a position to spark intense fundamental discussions on the progress of European unification.

In most countries, this changed nothing in terms of the results of the ratification process. In Ireland, supporters of the treaties were successful with 68.7

percent of the vote in a referendum of 18 June. During July, the parliaments of Luxembourg, Belgium, and Greece gave their approval by quite large majorities, likewise the Italian Chamber of Deputies and the Spanish parliament in October, followed by the Portuguese parliament in December. In the Netherlands, the House of Representatives voted in favor on 17 November and the Senate on 15 December. As earlier in the European Parliament, there was much criticism here regarding the democratic deficit, the failure to include foreign and domestic policy in the Community system, and the non-binding character of the European Social Charter. Dissatisfaction with the results of the negotiations did not however lead to any blocking of the progress that had nevertheless been made.

Things transpired differently in France. There, a congress consisting of a joint gathering of the National Assembly and the Senate approved the treaty amendments necessary for the ratification of the Maastricht Treaties on 23 June by a broad majority. Mitterrand however wanted to leave the decision on the treaties themselves to the people; he had decided this in late May in light of the debate in Denmark. On the basis of opinion polls, he figured on winning a majority in his country, one that would at the same time benefit the beleaguered position of the Socialist government. Also, he had convinced himself that a common currency needed the approval of the voters if it were to have success over the long term. Ever since a sudden worsening of his cancer, he had moreover been plagued by a certain weariness of office that served to increase his willingness to take risks. As he said to Jacques Attali, if he were to lose, he would resign, and that would in fact be a fine departure.[1]

Mitterrand announced his decision on 3 June, one day after the rejection of the treaty by a slim majority of the Danes. In the lively debate that ensued, it was not only the Communist Party under Georges Marchais and the "National Front" under Jean-Marie Le Pen that reaffirmed their opposition to European unification. It was also minorities among the Gaullists (Charles Pasqua, Philippe Séguin), the Conservatives (Philippe de Villiers), and the governing Socialists (Jean-Pierre Chevènement), who made names for themselves as the defenders of national identity and sovereignty against "Brussels technocracy" and the hegemony of the Germans. They gained impetus from the Danish "no" as well as from the pressure on the French franc that was unleashed by it and the high interest-rate policy of the *Bundesbank* that threatened the growth of the French economy.

As a majority for the treaty rapidly melted away, Kohl decided to hasten to the aid of the president via an appearance on French television. On 3 September, he

---

[1] Attali, *Mitterrand*, p. 354. On the ratification process overall, Gerbet, *Construction*, pp. 400–409; Finn Laursen and Sophie Vanhoonacker (eds.), *The Ratification of the Maastricht Treaty. Issues, Debates and Future Implications*, Dordrecht: Kluwer Academic Publishers, 1994.

participated in a television marathon in which Mitterrand defended the common currency and celebrated Franco-German friendship. The chancellor vowed to the French people that he would not fail in his support for the great work being undertaken by their president.² It remains difficult to determine whether and to what extent this helped. In any event, a very slim majority of 51.05 percent voted for ratification on 20 September; some 48.95 percent voted against, with a bare third of the voters staying away from the polls. "Maastricht" was thus saved once again. In France as well as the other important member states, the broad support for the European project that Mitterrand had had in mind did not materialize, however.

In the Federal Republic, the tabloid *Bild* and the magazine *Der Spiegel* opposed "the end of the mark"; and some politicians of the CSU—Peter Gauweiler most loudly—stoked fears of "Esperanto money." After the Danish rejection, the *Frankfurter Allgemeine Zeitung* published a "manifesto" of sixty German economists who criticized the convergence criteria stipulated in Maastricht as "too weak" and warned of "severe economic tensions" in the wake of an "overhasty introduction" of the Community currency.³ The *Bundesbank* cautioned once again that a "comprehensive political union" was the prerequisite for the "enduring existence" of the monetary union and pursued its high-interest policy for financing German unity without worrying about endangering a majority for the treaty in France. However, after the decision for ratification was made in the Fifth Republic, Kohl and Waigel succeeded in isolating the opposition voices within the parties. On 2 December, the Bundestag approved the treaties by the overwhelming majority of 543 to seventeen.

In Denmark, meanwhile, the parties in parliament had on 30 October come to agreement on a declaration in which they demanded a special statute for their country in the European Union: no participation in a common defense or the Community currency or Union citizenship or common authority in the areas of justice and police. The European Council however stuck by its position of not negotiating further on exceptional regulations. A the Council meeting in Edinburgh on 11 and 12 December only "acknowledged" that Denmark would not participate in a common defense or the Community currency. In regard to Union citizenship, the Council declared that it would "in no way take the place of national citizenship." In a unilateral declaration, the Danish government added that transfers of authority in the areas of justice and police would have to be approved by referendum.⁴ On the basis of these specifications, some 56.8 percent of Danish voters

---

2 Lappenküper, *Mitterrand*, pp. 324ff.
3 *Frankfurter Allgemeine Zeitung*, 11 June 1992.
4 "Schlussfolgerungen des Europäischen Rates in Edinburgh 11./12.12.1992," in: *Jahrbuch der Europäischen Integration 1992/93*, pp. 439–478, here pp. 457–460.

approved the Maastricht Treaties in a second referendum on 18 May 1993; the government presented the ratification document on 17 June.

In Great Britain, a small but highly-aggressive minority of the governing Conservatives, spearheaded by Margaret Thatcher, along with a minority of the Labour Party fought against the Maastricht Treaties. As a result of the elections of 9 April, the government's majority had dwindled to twenty-one seats; and the Conservative opponents of Maastricht were then able to compel Prime Minister John Major to accept that, after the Danish "no," the process of ratification in the British Parliament would be halted until it could be known what would follow from the rejection of the treaties in Denmark. After the Danish Folketing had issued its demand for a special statute within the framework of the European Union on 30 October, the House of Commons resumed debate. It was only possible to vote after the positive outcome of the second Danish referendum on 18 May 1993 and after serious parliamentary conflict as well as a whole series of amendments. On 20 May 1993, the House of Commons approved the Maastricht Treaties by a vote of 292 to 112. By abstaining, a majority of Labour MPs had helped the treaties succeed.

Even with the submission of the British ratification documents on 2 August, the treaties still could not come into effect. No fewer than twenty-nine opponents of the treaties in Germany submitted complaints to the German Constitutional Court. The court however agreed to hear only one of the complaints, needing until 12 October before announcing its decision. The complaint was rejected, and the German government was then able to submit the ratification document in Brussels the same evening so that the treaties could come into effect on 1 November 1993—some ten months later than anticipated. Nevertheless, the justices linked their approval of the treaties to an interpretation of them that left open further political possibilities for the opponents of Maastricht: They characterized the Union as a "confederacy of states," in which the member states remained masters over the treaties. The transfer of further sovereign rights to the Union was thereby made conditional on the approval of the Constitutional Court, which also certified the right of the Bundestag to reject the transition to the third stage of the monetary union on 1 January 1999 if the stability goals had not been met.[5]

Calling into question a central agreement of the modified Community Treaty was all the more significant as the stability guidelines being followed by the members of the European Monetary System in anticipation of the monetary union became ever more difficult to maintain due to reduced economic growth. Tensions among the participating currencies were heightened by the inflation in the Federal Republic in the wake of the conversion of the GDR's currency at a ratio

---

5 Stark, *Kohl*, pp. 247–253.

of one to one as well as the growing debt from financing German unity, along with a significant drop in the US dollar. The Bundesbank decided to combat this inflation by a drastic hike in the prime rate, with the discount rate rising from 2.0 percent in 1987 to 8.75 percent in July of 1992. This meant that countries with weaker economies faced a dilemma; if they continued to adhere to the rates, sharp economic declines would result.

Then, as the Danish "no" of June 1992 suddenly made the realization of the monetary union uncertain, the markets began to speculate on the devaluation of individual currencies. In late August, the British pound came under severe pressure and shortly thereafter the Italian lira too. John Major and Chancellor of Exchequer Norman Lamont did not initially want to devalue; for its part, the *Bundesbank* showed little inclination to assist its partners by lowering interest rates. Thus, the monetary committee of the central bank governors was only able to decide on devaluing the lira by seven percent during their meeting on 12 and 13 September, along with a negligible reduction of the prime rates of Germany, Belgium, and the Netherlands. This half-hearted decision further increased the pressure on the pound and the lira. On 16 September, "black Wednesday," the pressure reached such intensity that it forced the British government to withdraw from the exchange-rate mechanism of the monetary system—at least "temporarily," as was said. After a hastily-called nighttime meeting of the monetary committee, Italy too had to leave the exchange-rate mechanism; the Spanish peseta was also devalued by five percent. A British demand to suspend the monetary system altogether was rejected by the partners.[6]

After the humiliating defeat of the British, speculation concentrated on the French franc. As Major and Lamont had done earlier, Mitterrand and French Treasury Director Jean-Claude Trichet now requested a reduction in German interest rates. Additionally, they demanded a declaration that nothing would change regarding the parity of the franc and the mark. This was wholly unacceptable to *Bundesbank* President Helmut Schlesinger, who had taken over the post after the resignation of Pöhl in June of 1991. At a meeting between the German and French finance ministers and central bank governors on the fringes of the annual gathering of the International Monetary Fund in Washington on 22 September, he said, "I would not like to expose myself to ridicule by being proven wrong by the facts after twelve or twenty-four or forty-eight hours." For his part, Trichet conjured up the danger of the failure of the common currency project: "The alliance between France and Germany since their reconciliation is the fulcrum of the European

---

6 Ungerer, *History*, pp. 263–265; Dyson and Featherstone, *Road*, pp. 682–685; David Marsh, *Der Euro. Die geheime Geschichte der neuen Weltwährung*, Hamburg: Murmann, 2009, pp. 210–223.

system. What one hears in your words and your tone is the dissolution of the system."⁷

Trichet received support in this critical situation from Helmut Kohl. In a conversation at the Élysée Palace on the same day, Mitterrand made clear to the chancellor the gravity of the situation. Kohl then picked up the phone and told first Horst Köhler and then Hans Tietmeyer, Schlesinger's deputy, that he desired "within the next few hours" a declaration of the governors on the preservation of the parity of the two currencies.⁸ With an eye toward the independence of the *Bundesbank*, he of course added that the bank itself must make the decision in the end. The pressure he exerted was sufficient to change the view of the German delegation in Washington. At the close of an over four-hour session, there emerged a joint communiqué of the central bank governors and the finance ministers in which the parity of the franc and the mark was declared to be inviolable. Moreover, the *Bundesbank* expressed its willingness to increase its loans to the *Banque de France* to thirty-nine billion marks, some four billion more than it had accorded the Bank of England on "black Wednesday."

Together with a minor reduction of German interest rates and a hike in French ones, these measures were in fact sufficient to rein in speculation against the franc. Spain had to accept two more devaluations, as did Portugal; and after the British pound had lost more than ten percent of its worth against the mark by year's end, Ireland too had to devalue despite solid economic data. Finland, Sweden, and Norway dissolved the pegs to the European currency unit that they had established in 1990–91. In contrast, the franc (with an inflation rate of two percent in France) began to replace the mark (with its inflation rate of more than four percent in the Federal Republic) as the anchor currency.

Yet, France had to pay a high price for the policy of the "hard" franc: Unemployment in the country rose to almost twelve percent. During the summer of 1993, this unleashed renewed and now more severe speculation against the franc. When in late July it became clear that parity between the mark and the franc could no longer be maintained, Prime Minister Édouard Balladur asked that Kohl either to bring about a substantial reduction in German interest rates or that the Federal Republic be allowed to leave the exchange-rate mechanism. He hoped that this would reduce the problems of the other countries and at the same time give France the leading role in what would be left of the monetary system. Waigel, Schlesinger, and Tietmeyer sought out the chancellor at his vacation spot on an Austrian lake, the Wolfgangsee; Kohl did not agree to the request.

---

7 Notes by Trichet, 22 Sept. 1992, quoted from Marsh, *Euro*, p. 230. On the following, *ibid.*, pp. 223–235.
8 Meeting between Mitterrand and Kohl, 22 Sept. 1992, French protocol, *ibid.*, p. 227.

In the end, France thus had to be satisfied with an increase in the bandwidths of the exchange-rate mechanism, Kohl accepting that the fluctuations would be expanded from the then-current 2.25 percent to nothing less than fifteen percent. A decision in accordance with this was made by the finance ministers and central bank governors during the night of 1 to 2 August. Only the Netherlands and Germany agreed to retain the limit of 2.25 percent between themselves.[9]

A formal devaluation of the franc was thereby averted once again, and speculation was contained. Speculators witnessed the loss of the profits they had anticipated from a devaluation of the French currency. Henceforth, they had to reckon with much higher risks as to exchange rates, which noticeably reduced their inclination to speculate against individual currencies. At the same time, however, the stability goal of the treaty on monetary union had been loosened. If the countries whose currencies had become the target of speculators were now to lower their interest rates and increase their money supply so as to spur growth and reduce unemployment, the realization of the Maastricht Treaty would recede unreachably far away.

It was of decisive importance for the fate of the project of monetary union that Balladur—whom Mitterrand had named as head of a conservative government after the electoral defeat of the Socialists in late March of 1993—refrained from doing that. The hard-currency countries among the EMS members under attack—Belgium, Denmark, and Ireland—followed his example. As a consequence, the exchange rates of their currencies *vis-à-vis* the mark quickly recovered; and with the exception of the franc, they once again moved mostly within the old, narrow bandwidths. The mark could thus retain its status as anchor currency, and it was ideally protected from speculation on the path toward the community currency.

In order to calm the German public, which was plagued with growing anxiety about inflation, Kohl insisted during a meeting of the European Council on 29 October 1993 that Frankfurt am Main, home to the *Bundesbank*, should be chosen as the seat of the European Monetary Institute. This was to demonstrate to the Germans that the future European Central Bank would be just as independent and just as much focused on stability as the *Bundesbank*.[10] The Monetary Institute took up its work with the transition to the second phase of the monetary union on 1 January 1994, in accordance with the treaty. From late October of 1994, it occupied the former headquarters of the *Bank für Gemeinwirtschaft* in the Frankfurt city center. It initially employed 150 people, coming mostly from the central banks of the member states; the number had grown to six hundred by the

---

9 *Ibid.*, pp. 237–241; Ungerer, *History*, pp. 265–267.
10 Helmut Kohl, *Erinnerungen 1990–1994*, Munich: Droemer 2007, p. 614; "Schlussfolgerungen des Europäischen Rates vom 29.10.1993 in Brüssel," in: *Europa-Archiv* 49 (1994), pp. D2–D9.

time of the actual launch of the Community currency at the end of the decade and had reached some 1,400 by 2008.

After Jacques Chirac had been elected to succeed Mitterrand on 7 May 1995, the German government began pushing for further measures to secure the stability goal. In his election campaign against Balladur, Chirac had called for boosting the French economy and had repeatedly attacked the stability course of the *Banque de France*, which had become independent of the government and had been led by Trichet since September of 1993. In the wake of lower receipts due to recession and increased expenditures for the unemployed, the French budget deficit had risen to five percent. In order to counteract that, Theo Waigel had been calling for the conclusion of a "Stability Pact" since early September of 1995. This agreement was to ensure that budget deficits would have an upper limit of three percent of GNP after completion of the monetary union. Countries going beyond that limit would automatically be subject to punishment in the form of fines.

Waigel's demand found little favor among the advocates of "different" economic policy in France. Nor was there much willingness in the Southern European countries Italy, Spain, Portugal, or Greece to have the Germans keep them from pursuing a policy of economic stimulus. In the end, however, Chirac had to accept that without such security against the threat of inflation, opposition to the actual completion of the monetary union would be too great in Germany. During a meeting with Kohl on 25 October, the chancellor made the concession of promising to speak with *Bundesbank* President Tietmeyer about lowering German interest rates; thereafter, the French president found himself willing to turn away from the course he had been pursuing. In a televised address on 26 October, he took the side of those advocating a strong franc and the Community currency. At the Madrid Council meeting of 15 and 16 December 1995, Kohl was then able to push through a principle commitment to the "Stability Pact." As he assured Chirac in a chummy way, "I see you and me as a common team for Europe. Your success is also my success."[11]

Even in determining the name of the Community currency, the sensitivities of the Germans needed to be taken into account. France wanted to retain the name of the unit of account then in existence, which had been incorporated into the treaty and which was reminiscent of old French silver coins. For Kohl, however, the name "ECU" was completely out of the question—this unit of account had lost almost forty percent of its value *vis-à-vis* the most stable currencies that were part of its composition owing to the many devaluations by individual member states over the sixteen years of its existence. At a Brussels Council meeting there occurred a debate of considerable length. John Major proposed the name

---

[11] Jacques Chirac, *Le temps présidentiel. Mémoires* 2, Paris: Pocket, 2011, pp. 90ff.

"Gulden," which had once been used in English Aquitaine. Helmut Kohl signaled his willingness to accept the name "Franken," which evoked the stable Swiss currency and which also would allow the French to retain the name of their existing currency. That was not acceptable to Filipe González however given that it would conjure up memories of Franco's dictatorship. The Spanish prime minister therefore finally suggested that the new currency simply be named the "Euro." This met with broad agreement. Chirac, who would gladly have stayed with the "ECU," had to accede.

In light of the then-current size of the budget deficits—even the Federal Republic had a deficit of 3.5 percent in 1995 due to the recession—it had in the meantime become clear that there was no prospect of allowing the monetary union to begin on 1 January 1997. In Madrid, the Council therefore definitively set 1 January 1999 as the date; and in accordance with a "Green Book" of the European Commission, it decided on the procedure that would lead to determining which countries would be members of the monetary union. In early 1998, the Commission was to ascertain which member countries in the base year 1997 had met the entry criteria; on this basis, the European Council was to make a decision in the spring of 1998 as to the composition of the monetary union. The European Monetary Institute would accordingly be transformed into the European Central Bank, and the exchange rates of the currencies *vis-à-vis* the Community currency were to be definitively set. The members of the monetary union were to have the possibility of allowing some time to pass before the new banknotes and coins were introduced. No later than 1 January 2002, however, the Euro was to be in circulation; on 1 July 2002, the banknotes and coins of the previous currencies would no longer be legal tender.[12]

As Kohl had foreseen in the negotiations over the Maastricht Treaty, the decisions made at the Madrid Council meeting gave a strong impulse to improving national budgets. Heavily indebted countries such as Italy (with a budget deficit of 6.7 percent in 1996), Spain (6.6 percent in 1995), and Greece (14.1 percent in 1994) also wanted to participate in the introduction of the Euro—in part for reasons of prestige but above all because of the lure of lower interest rates with which they could finance the modernization of their economies. Without participating in the monetary union, there was a danger of languishing in second place indefinitely. Chirac therefore held to his new austerity course despite a wave of strikes in December of 1995 that paralyzed France for four weeks. In Italy and Spain, new heads of government came on the scene with drastic austerity programs (Romano

---

12 "Schlussfolgerungen des Europäischen Rates in Madrid 15./16. Dezember 1995," in: *Internationale Politik* 6/1996, pp. 81–86; on this and the following, Ungerer, *History*, pp. 272–292; Gerbet, *Construction*, pp. 432–445.

Prodi as the candidate of the left and the conservative José Maria Aznar, respectively). After the resignation of Andreas Papandreou in January of 1996 due to health reasons, Kostas Simitis, an economic modernizer, asserted himself as new Prime Minister of the PASOK government in Greece.

The efforts toward budget rehabilitation were assisted by two developments that were not necessarily to be expected: First, the US dollar gained value again from the middle of 1995 onward. This made European and especially German exports less expensive and helped the economies recover. Second, the *Bundesbank* began to understand that continuing devaluations in the Community countries threatened German exports to an extent that was no longer reconcilable with maintaining the current German level of production: Otmar Issing, chief economist of the *Bundesbank*, stated at a conference in November of 2007, "I and others came to the conclusion that the Common Market would not withstand another such monetary crisis [like that of 1992–93]."[13] As a consequence, the guardians of the German currency found themselves willing to accept reductions in interest rates in 1996 to an extent that they had hitherto always rejected. The discount rate was lowered to 2.5 percent, the Lombard rate to 4.5 percent. The cost of borrowing consequently fell not only for German companies but for their European neighbors as well. At the same time, the cost of debt service decreased, and that in turn contributed to the reduction in budget deficits.

In order to satisfy the requirement of two years' membership in the European exchange-rate mechanism, Prodi pushed through the re-entry of Italy at the last minute, on 4 December 1996. The markets thereupon began to adjust to the idea of the country's participation in the monetary union, and interest rates in all of Europe plateaued at the German level. More and more, the financial markets came to assume that the monetary union, despite all difficulties, would begin punctually and with a relatively large membership. Only in Great Britain was there no perceptible willingness to re-enter the exchange-rate mechanism: Free floating and the abandonment of the German interest-rate level had promoted economic growth to such a degree that a return to the discipline of the EMS was no longer seen as a necessity. Tony Blair, who had succeeded John Major after a landslide victory of the Labour Party on 1 May 1997, had new Chancellor of Exchequer Gordon Brown declare that the time for British participation in the monetary union had not yet come.

Despite all the efforts, it nevertheless remained questionable as to whether the Southern European countries along with France and Germany would actually achieve a curtailment of new debt to three percent in the reference year 1997. Consequently, more and more voices also began calling for the recession to be

---

13 Quoted in Marsh, *Euro*, p. 253.

taken into account when budget stability was measured; and the same voices began arguing the case for assessing the "trend" in budget development too. In France, Socialist party leader Lionel Jospin won early parliamentary elections on 25 May and 1 June 1997 with the slogan that the fight against unemployment must take precedence over a pinpoint introduction of the euro. Having been appointed prime minister by Chirac, Jospin refused to sign the Stability Pact in its existing form; signing of the document had been envisioned for the Council meeting in Amsterdam on 16 and 17 June.

For their part, however, the German government and the *Bundesbank* categorically rejected all attempts to weaken the Maastricht criteria or modify the Stability Pact. So often and so doggedly did Waigel repeat his insistence on exact adherence to the upper limit for budget deficits that his forcefully-Bavarian formulated "dreikommanull" ("three point zero") for a time became a German catchphrase in the French press. Passage of the Stability Pact at the Amsterdam Council meeting was only saved when the heads of state and of government—taking up a mediation proposal from Commission President Delors—simultaneously issued a decision by which the coordination of national economic policy in accordance with Articles 102 and 103 of the Maastricht Treaty be extended to social policy, employment policy, and structural reform. Moreover, a special summit for combating unemployment was promised. This took place on 21 and 22 November 1997 in Luxembourg and led to the coordination of national employment strategies with support of the European Investment Bank.

Regarding the Stability Pact itself—now dubbed the "Stability and Growth Pact" following a demand by Chirac—Kohl and Waigel had already had to accept reductions to their vision at a turbulent Council meeting in Dublin on 13 and 14 December 1996. Instead of automatic sanctions, there were to be decisions made by the Council of Ministers on sanctions. Beyond this, the possibility of "extraordinary circumstances" was acknowledged, under which sanctions could be set aside. At a Council of Ministers meeting on 7 July 1997, it was agreed that a recession amounting to two percent of GNP would be regarded as an extraordinary circumstance. In cases of a recession falling between two and .75 percent, the Commission was to provide recommendations regarding sanctions. Violating the upper limit of the budget deficit in the event of a recession amounting to less than .75 percent was to warrant sanctions in every case. For each percentage point by which a country went over the permissible deficit limit, funds equal to .25 percent of GNP were to be deposited with the Commission. The depositing country would lose the sum if the impermissible deficit were not eliminated after two years.

The Amsterdam Council meeting also regulated the relationship between countries that would be included in the introduction of the Community currency and those that could not or would not be: For the latter countries, the European

Monetary System with a bandwidth of plus/minus fifteen percent would continue to be valid. Britain clearly saw no reason in any of this to return to the exchange-rate mechanism. Sweden, which in the meantime had joined the Maastricht Treaty, announced that it wanted to hold off on entry into the monetary union. Denmark however accepted the new regulations and even officially returned to the old fluctuation range of plus/minus 2.25 percent.

The governments interested in participating in the monetary union from the beginning then helped a bit more with short-term stability measures and with more or less creative bookkeeping. Jospin's government followed through with the hike in the value-added tax that had been decided by its conservative predecessor; it also raised the business tax and the increment value tax. The Prodi government undertook sharp cuts in social welfare benefits and decided on a temporary tax hike that two years later was to be refunded at sixty percent. Even the Kohl government incorporated proceeds from privatizations and surpluses in health insurance and old-age pensions into its calculations of the German budget deficit. In the assessment undertaken in the autumn of 1997, the Commission was thus able to determine that all candidates would in fact satisfy the entry criteria. Only Greece, with a current budget deficit of over four percent would need to remain outside the Eurozone. The criterion of total indebtedness of not more than sixty percent—which especially threatened to disqualify Italy and Belgium—was disregarded. Here, the Commission argued with strong political plausibility that progress in debt reduction had been made by all candidates without exception.

The publication of the evaluations by the Commission on 14 October 1997 caused much surprise. A few months earlier, hardly anyone had expected that nearly all members of the monetary system would qualify for the transition to the third stage. Worries about monetary stability and opposition to social welfare cuts after a "summer of uncertainty" thus dwindled, and the implementation of the decisions on the transition could everywhere be carried out in a climate of secure majorities. On 25 March 1998, the Commission and the European Monetary Institute officially announced that eleven countries had met the conditions for entry on 1 January 1999: Germany, France, Belgium, the Netherlands, Luxembourg, Italy, Spain, Portugal, and Ireland as well as new members Austria and Finland. On 2 May 1998, the heads of state and of government issued a decision on the start of the monetary union. In order to forestall speculation at the last minute, it was agreed that the bilateral exchange rates of the currencies to be unified would not be changed up to the end of the transition period.[14]

The decision to create a monetary union with eleven members was overshadowed by wrangling over the appointment to the governorship of the European

---

14 *Agence Europe*, Special issue, 3 May 1998.

Central Bank. The former Dutch Central Bank Governor Wim Duisenberg was in fact envisioned for the post; he had assumed the office of president of the European Monetary Institute on 1 July 1997 only after more or less clear assurances that he would also remain at its head after it had been expanded to become the European Central Bank. The new French government however was of the opinion that the office should be held by a French person, and Chirac concurred. On 4 November 1997, Chirac and Jospin jointly presented Jean-Claude Trichet as their candidate. Tietmeyer and Waigel blocked compromise proposals by which the term would be divided between Duisenberg and Trichet. The struggle over the two candidates stretched into the night of 2–3 May 1998. In the end, it was decided that Duisenberg should receive the appointment but at the same time he was asked not to serve the entire eight-year term due to age; after his resignation, Trichet would succeed him.

This compromise was not at all well received. Duisenberg raised eyebrows in hard-currency countries with his declaration that he had "freely chosen not to serve the whole eight years." When four days later he explained to the European Parliament that he could ultimately remain in office for the whole eight years, the French felt that they had been duped.[15] It was in fact the case that the advocates of a strong Community currency had once again prevailed. In the Federal Republic, however, that was not clearly perceived. Kohl faced criticism for the slightly-absurd Brussels decision. It is difficult to know if this contributed to his electoral defeat on 27 September 1998. What is certain is only that, despite earlier assurances to his wife and to Wolfgang Schäuble (who wanted to succeed him), Kohl once again stood for election not least of all because he feared that the introduction of the euro could fail without him.[16]

That did not happen, however. Kohl's successor Gerhard Schröder had once in an interview with the *Bild-Zeitung* characterized the new currency as a "sickly premature birth" that would increase unemployment in Germany;[17] after his election to the chancellorship, however, he emphasized the opportunities that a weaker Community currency offered to German exports. Duisenberg welded the heterogeneous ECB Council into a collegial body that was wholly committed to the goal of price stability. In October of 1998, the new guardians of the currency agreed to a target of holding the increase in consumer prices to just under two percent over the medium term—exactly as the *Bundesbank* had always practiced. Aided by a continuing economic recovery and historically-low inflation rates, the

---

15 Marsh, *Euro*, p. 273; Schwarz, *Kohl*, pp. 813–815.
16 Heribert Schwan, *Die Frau an seiner Seite. Leben und Leiden der Hannelore Kohl*, Munich: Heyne, 2011, pp. 242ff.
17 *Bild-Zeitung*, 26 March 1998.

transition to the Community currency took place in a relatively-relaxed atmosphere. In December of 2001, the citizens of the Eurozone were able to receive the first common coins and bank notes; and these could then be put to use beginning on 1 January 2002.

Among those citizens were the Greeks. Nothing less than a national trauma had been unleashed by the determination that Greece was the only willing country that had failed—just barely—to meet the entry criteria. The Simitis government had stepped up its reform efforts once again at least in order to be able to join in when Euro cash was introduced. In December of 1999, it announced that the convergence criteria had been achieved; in June of 2000, this finding was confirmed by the Council of Economic and Finance Ministers. Doubts as to the soundness of the Greek figures (which would be confirmed four years later by the conservative successor government) were overshadowed by the concern about fundamentally endangering Simitis' modernization program if the country were to be rejected again. According to the decision of the Ecofin Council, Greek entry into the monetary union could occur on 1 January 2001, that is, still with time enough to prepare for the general introduction of Euro cash.[18]

The Northern Expansion

Parallel to the contention over ratification of the Maastricht Treaties and the implementation of the monetary union, the Council of Ministers and the Commission were negotiating on the accession of countries that up to that point had been hindered from becoming members of the European Union due to their neutral status in the East-West conflict. After the EEC entry of Britain, Ireland, and Denmark in 1972–73, Austria, Switzerland, Liechtenstein, Sweden, and Finland had—along with the remaining EFTA countries Iceland, Portugal, and Norway—completed bilateral tariff and trade treaties with the Community. These amounted to the incremental establishment of free-trade zones for the commercial and industrial sectors but provided for only limited liberalization for the agricultural sector. The Danish government, with its special interest in the dismantling of limitations on trade with its northern neighbors, had in 1982 taken the initiative for a further *rapprochement* between the EC and EFTA. In 1984, this had resulted in an agreement for creating a "unified European Economic Area"

---

[18] Wilfried Loth, "Kreativ, vor allem in Buchführung. Wie Athen in die Eurozone gelangte und Berlin seinen Widerstand aufgab," in: *Frankfurter Allgemeine Sonntagszeitung*, 18 Sept. 2011.

(EEA) that was to be characterized by further dismantling of protectionism and expansion of economic cooperation.[19]

The agreement was signed on 9 April 1984 in Luxembourg, but implementation did not occur. On the EC side, there was too much fear of disrupting the internal-market program, while on the EFTA side there was a too-categorical rejection of supranational elements. In formal negotiations that began in June of 1990, the EC Commission on the one hand demanded complete adoption of all regulations of the internal market, while on the other hand rejecting the creation of common decision-making mechanisms. In the Agreement on the European Economic Area signed on 2 May 1992 in Porto, the EFTA countries had to content themselves with specified transition deadlines for sensitive individual economic areas. Liberalization in the agricultural and fishing sectors was left to future bilateral talks. Beyond that, the EFTA countries had to participate in the Cohesion Fund for structurally-weak EC regions; in the transit agreement, Switzerland and Austria had to concede the passage of increased truck traffic through Alpine passes.

It was not least of all for this reason that the Agreement on the EEA was rejected by a very small majority of 50.3 percent of the Swiss people in a referendum of 6 December 1992. The agreement went into effect on 1 January 1994 after the remaining EFTA countries had committed themselves in an additional adaption protocol to paying some seventy-eight percent of the Swiss portion of the Cohesion Fund.[20]

In the meantime, five of the seven remaining EFTA countries—Portugal of course having joined the Community on 1 January 1986—had already submitted applications for full membership in the EC. The first to do so was Austria on 17 July 1989. Sweden followed suit on 1 July 1991 after Prime Minister Ingvar Carlsson had held conversations with his fellow Socialists Felipe González in Spain and Franz Vranitzky in Austria. The Finnish government submitted its application for membership on 18 March 1992, the Swiss on 26 March 1992, and the Norwegians initiated their second application on 25 November 1992. If they would have to adopt the regulations of the internal market anyway so as not to face discrimination in economic exchanges with their most important trading partners, the governments of all these countries wanted to be able to participate in decision-making on an equal footing. After the Swedish government had submitted

---

[19] Waldemar Hummer, "Annäherung zwischen EG und EFTA-Staaten: Außen-, Neutralitäts- und Wirtschaftspolitische Problemfelder," in: Fritz Schwind (ed.), Österreichs Weg in die EG – Beiträge zur europäischen Rechtsentwicklung, Vienna: OAW Verlag, 1991, pp. 7–52.
[20] Thomas Pedersen, *European Union and the EFTA Countries. Enlargement and Integration*, London, 1994, pp. 33–78; Michael Gehler, *Vom Marshall-Plan bis zur EU. Österreich und die europäische Integration von 1945 bis zur Gegenwart*, Innsbruck: Studienverlag, 2006, pp. 201–203.

its application, the remaining governments additionally became fearful of losing out on the opportunity of increasing their competitiveness.

Among those countries that had been neutral up to this point, there was moreover the necessity of repositioning themselves after the elimination of the East-West division of the European continent. In its application, the Austrian government under Chancellor Franz Vranitzky had emphasized the need to hold fast to the Austrian commitment to neutrality, which raised some eyebrows in Brussels and in Paris too. In the Swedish application that came two years later, there were merely reservations as to participating in Common Foreign and Security Policy (CFSP). The Finnish government even made assurances that it wanted to constructively take part in CFSP, which had in the meantime been secured in the Maastricht Treaty. Now having been freed from the commitments of the Finno-Soviet Treaty, Helsinki was seeking protection against turbulence in neighboring Russia.[21]

It was not only in Copenhagen that the EFTA countries' applications for entry were welcomed. In Bonn and London too, the prospect of opening new markets was appealing. John Major also saw an opportunity to water down the supranational dimension of the Community that had just been strengthened in Maastricht. Conversely, in Paris and Brussels, there were fears for the EU's ability to act if the number of members were to grow so quickly from twelve to seventeen. Delors therefore undertook efforts to revise the decision for the pillar structure of the Treaty on European Union. In a paper that he wanted to present to the European Council in Lisbon in late June of 1992, he advocated for a new institutional model to be developed parallel to the upcoming entry negotiations and for new members to be required to accept it along with the *acquis communautaire*.

The surprising Danish "no" to the Maastricht Treaties in the referendum of 2 June rendered this initiative void. Now, even some of the Commission members no longer saw it as opportune to push the supranational dimension of the treaties. The Commission also issued a warning about assuring the EU's ability to function and reducing the democratic deficit. Nevertheless, as Delors complained, "the members of the European Council dismissed our concerns with a wave of the hand without according them the requisite attention."[22] The Commission was instructed "to accelerate the necessary preparatory work" in order to achieve a "speedy conclusion to negotiations" with the EFTA countries that were seeking admission. Before the opening of accession negotiations, it was the case that only the ratification process of the Maastricht Treaties was to be completed and that

---

21 *Ibid.*, pp. 167–199; Maria Gussarsson, "Combining dependence with distance: Sweden," in: Kaiser and Elvert (eds.), *Enlargement*, pp. 170–188; Hanna Ojanen, "If in 'Europe', then in its 'Core'? Finland," *ibid.*, pp. 150–169.
22 Delors, *Erinnerungen*, p. 431.

the budgetary framework planning of the "Delors II Package" for the years 1993 to 1999 be passed.[23]

The latter was achieved at the Council meeting in Edinburgh on 11 and 12 December 1992. Delors was not able to win the sought-after expansion of the Community's budget volume from 1.20 percent of GNP to 1.37 percent by 1997, but an expansion to 1.27 percent to 1999 was approved. Any increase in the agricultural budget was halted in accordance with a reform decision of 21 May 1992 that foresaw the reduction of guarantee prices as well as quantitative caps along with premiums for shutdowns. Also, a "monetary reserve" was stricken by which a weak dollar's negative effects on the competiveness of agricultural exports were to be compensated. At the same time, the Council was able to raise expenditures for the Regional Fund by seventy-two percent; and with great skill, González was able to push through a proposal whereby the new Cohesion Fund would be accorded a more or less reasonable amount of fifteen billion ECUs. Only on the issue of increasing the research budget did Delors suffer a bitter disappointment.

Mitterrand's second precondition for the opening of accession negotiations—completion of the ratification process—was dropped at this Council meeting. Under pressure from Kohl, the French president now also agreed to the demand that negotiations start right at the beginning of the next year so that entry could take place on 1 January 1995. The German chancellor was convinced that offense would be the best defense in stanching the growing weariness with Europe that had shown itself during the ratification debates. Institutional reforms that Delors had regarded as necessary were put off until negotiations on a revision of the Maastricht Treaty, which were envisioned for 1996.[24]

Talks with Austria, Sweden, and Finland began on 1 February 1993 and with Norway on 5 April. For Switzerland, however, the Commission did not prepare any negotiation package. After the rejection of the EEA Agreement in the referendum of December 1992, the Swiss application was no longer regarded as current, even though it had not officially been withdrawn. Given that large portions of the items for negotiation had already been dealt with as part of the EEA talks, progress was rapidly made. Sweden, like Britain and Denmark, wanted the right to say "no" to the transition to the third stage of the monetary union; this was categorically rejected. The reservations shown by Austria and Sweden regarding Common foreign and security policy were dispelled by assurances that active,

---

23 "Schlussfolgerungen des Vorsitzes des Europäischen Rates vom 26./27.6.1992," *Jahrbuch der Europäischen Integration 1992/93*, pp. 408–433.
24 "Schlussfolgerungen des Vorsitzes des Europäischen Rates vom 11./12.12.1992," *ibid.*, pp. 439–478.

solidarity-focused participation in these policies would be very much compatible with the principles of non-alignment.

Aside from this, the candidates pressed to participate in regional promotion and to receive generous exceptional and transitional regulations for agriculture and fishing. After tough resistance, this was largely conceded at the last minute. With British and German support, Delors succeeded in crafting compromises in February and March of 1994 that accommodated the interests of the applicants. Austria was able to negotiate a certain prolongation of the limits on traffic transiting the country as well as equalization payments for agriculture; Sweden was able to win higher levels of support for its agriculture; Finland got Community assistance for some eighty-five percent of its territory; and Norway obtained the continuation of exclusive fishing rights north of the 62nd parallel for three years. On balance, these exceptional regulations meant that the new members would become net payers into the Community in 1998 for the first time.[25]

There were significant tensions at the close of negotiations on the future weighting of votes in the Council of Ministers. Whereas the issue of representation of the new members in the Commission and in Parliament was resolved simply by expanding the number of seats, the British and Spanish governments refused to accept any increase in the number of votes needed to block a decision by qualified majority in the Council. The British were motivated by a desire to render majority decision-making more difficult, whereas the Spaniards feared a permanent ascendancy of the "northern countries" at the expense of the south. At a meeting of the foreign ministers in the northern Greek city of Ioannina on 24 March 1994, it was agreed that the number needed for a minority block would indeed be raised from twenty-three to twenty-seven. However, when reaching a quorum of at least twenty-three votes, it was to be the case that "everything [would be] attempted" to win over four more votes for a majority solution in "an appropriate timeframe." In vain, the Commission called attention to the fact that this self-commitment had no legal weight given that it was not specified in a treaty. In fact, it became more complicated to reach decisions in the Council due to this "Ioannina Formula."

The European Parliament viewed this all the more critically as its demand that before the Community expanded to accept new members, there be negotiations on improving the functioning of the Union was disregarded, just as the warnings of the Commission had been. When after the initialing of the accession treaties on 30 March 1994 the Council of Ministers submitted the applications to Parliament for approval (as had been foreseen ever since the Single European Act had taken

---

25 Francisco Granelli, "The European Union's Enlargement Negotiations with Austria, Finland, Norway and Sweden," in: *Journal of Common Market Studies* 1/1995, pp. 117–141; Delors, *Erinnerungen*, pp. 463ff.; Gehler, *Vom Marshallplan*, pp. 210–225.

effect), there was thus much unwillingness among the MEPs to take up the matter in the current legislative period. The governments feared however that if a decision had to wait until new parliamentary elections in June, there would not be sufficient time for ratification before the end of the year. The governments therefore put great pressure on the deputies, many of whom had to fear for their re-nomination. In a letter to the chairs of all factions in Parliament, Kohl promised to start a work group to prepare institutional reforms in which Parliament would participate along with representatives of the countries and the Commission. Whole delegations of ministers from the candidate countries implored the deputies not to stir up opposition to the entry applications in their countries via an attitude of refusal.

This multifaceted pressure brought results: On 4 May, a majority of 305 to 150 MEPs (with thirteen abstentions) voted against a bill by Claude Cheysson and others to defer the accession treaties. The treaties themselves were then passed with still greater majorities. On 25 June, they were signed at the meeting of the European Council on the island of Corfu.

In the ratification debates that began immediately thereafter in all four countries, it became clear that entry implied a clear step into globalized modernity. In regions that lived largely from agriculture or fishing, fear of this step predominated, whereas in cities there was often passionate promotion of entry. Those on the left who were conscious of tradition as well as environmentalists often spoke out against it. In Austria, where a referendum occurred at an early date (12 June) there was a clear majority of 66.4 percent in favor. In Finland too, where a referendum was held on 16 October, there was unambiguous approval by a margin of 56.9 percent. Conversely, only a slim majority of 52.2 percent approved Swedish entry on 13 November. In Norway, where a referendum was held on 28 November, a similarly slim majority of 52.2 percent rejected entry; the dynamic coming from the entry decisions of neighboring countries had not been sufficient to overcome the persistent opposition in the north of the country this time either.

On 1 January 1995, it was thus only Austria, Finland, and Sweden that entered the European Union. The Europe of the Twelve had now become the Europe of the Fifteen. Norway remained in a less comfortable European economic sphere, much to the regret of its industry and urban population in the south. So too Iceland, which in order to protect its fishing grounds from the fleets of EU states had not even presented an application for membership. Conversely, Liechtenstein had not applied after the rejection of the EEA Treaty by neighboring Switzerland. The membership numbers of the institutions were once again revised after Norway failed to enter: Now, only three additional votes rather than four were required for a qualified majority according to the Ioannina Formula.[26]

---

26 Gerbet, *Construction*, pp. 413–416.

With the new members, it was possible to continue the course of deepening the EU and making it more substantial overall. Austria experienced a boost in economic internationalization and a rise in productivity, which served to maintain the high approval rating seen in the referendum on entry but which also brought more support to the xenophobic rightwing populism of Jörg Haider. In terms of integration policy, the government was above all engaged in deepening economic integration; it also thereby contributed to the realization of the monetary union on a broad basis. Finland too participated energetically in the establishment of the monetary union. Moreover, Finnish European policy was engaged in the expansion of Common foreign and security policy; it also consistently contributed to the strengthening of European organs. In contrast, Sweden remained aloof from the supranational perspective of the EU and therefore did not participate in the transition to the monetary union. Sweden was however thoroughly engaged In the Common foreign and security policy and also spoke out for eastward expansion of the Union as quickly as possible.

The Way to Amsterdam

The difficulties in which the Maastricht Treaties found themselves after the Danish referendum of 2 June 1992 led the heads of state and of government to extend the mandate of Jacques Delors for two additional years, up to the turn of the year 1994–95. The experience he had in the meantime gained would help not only in steering clear of the rocks that threatened the ratification of the treaties but also in carrying out the upcoming enlargement with the EFTA countries in such a manner that the precarious consensus that underlay the conclusion of the treaties would not be shattered. The European Council in Lisbon on 26 and 27 June 1992 therefore confirmed the extension of Delors' term for two more years.

Delors made use of the additional period in office to initiate a project that had engaged him more and more since the Danish referendum: improving the competitiveness of the European Union in global terms. He saw with concern that the economies of the US and of Far Eastern countries were growing faster than those in Europe and that unemployment in the countries of the Union was at a high level and continuing to increase, whereas it was much lower in the US and the Far East. As he explained to the heads of state and of government at the Copenhagen Council meeting of 21 and 22 June 1993, the unemployment rate in the Community had gone from two percent before the oil crisis of 1973–74 to an average of seventeen percent. Fewer than sixty percent of the working-age population actually held a job. In the US, the figure was approximately seventy percent and more than seventy-five percent in Japan. Not without some justification, Delors saw in this one of the reasons for the growing opposition to deepening the integration process as well as a threat to the stability of the democratic order *per se*.

With support from the Forward Studies Unit ("Cellule de prospective"), which he had established within the Commission in 1989, he therefore developed a plan for securing competitiveness and employment on a European level. He found support for this from Kohl and Mitterrand as well as the Danish Council presidency of the first half of 1993. He was thus able to have the European Council in Copenhagen charge the Commission with drafting a "White Paper on Growth, Competitiveness, and Employment." Presented to the European Council in Brussels on 10 and 11 December 1993, this document emphatically portrayed once again the structural problems in European economies and called for quite varied measures: Firstly, it advocated more flexibility in the job market, part-time work, and division of jobs on the company level, better job-placement services, and continual upgrading of worker qualifications. Secondly, it envisioned massive investment in the expansion of efficient transportation networks, energy supply, and telecommunications across Europe. Thirdly, the introduction and spread of new information technologies were to be promoted; and fourthly, it urged additional efforts in the promotion of research once again.[27]

According to the white paper, the amount of money needed for the necessary infrastructure initiatives totaled some 120 billion ECUs spread over the subsequent six years, that is, twenty billion per year. Five billion of this was to come annually from the Community budget, seven billion from the European Investment Bank, and the remaining eight billion from Community bond issues, the so-called "Union bonds." It was exactly here that the Achilles' heel of the plan was to be found: Although the heads of state and of government approved the white paper in principle, neither John Major nor Helmut Kohl nor Ruud Lubbers would hear of new Community bond issues—the Briton taking this position on principle, the German and the Dutchman doing so with an eye toward the stability goal of the monetary union. At the Brussels Council meeting, there was thus only a decision to create two work groups—on the question of networks and on information technologies—which were to report initially to the Council of the Finance Ministers.

One year later, at the Council meeting of 9 and 10 December 1994 in Essen, it was nonetheless possible to approve a list of priorities for the expansion of transportation infrastructure that encompassed fourteen different major projects. However only three billion Ecus from the Union were available to finance them; thirteen billion was contributed by the member states. In regard to the IT

---

27 "The White Paper on Growth, Competitiveness and Employment. The Challenges and Ways Forward into the 21st century." COM (93) 700 final, Brussels, 1993.

revolution, the heads of state and of government saw their task as primarily one of creating the necessary legal and economic parameters. Beyond this, the white paper essentially aided in initiating and coordinating *national* employment policies, about which there were regular reports at the level of the European Union. Delors' initiative therefore did not bring about a great leap into the leading position in global economic competition as he had envisioned. It did however contribute to having the economic policies of the Union face up to the challenges of globalization, even before the concept became fashionable, and also to having those economic policies become more strongly harmonized.[28]

The launch of the White Paper on Growth, Competitiveness, and Employment also served to increase once again Delors' reputation and political weight at the end of his term in office, both of which had suffered due to his high-handed behavior when the Maastricht Treaties were being worked out. Several heads of government therefore asked that he serve another term. His time in office had already been extended beyond eight years, however; and Delors had stated that this would be his last term. Moreover, Mitterrand had now categorically determined that "It's enough."[29] It is possible that he was thinking that the Commission president, who had in the meantime become quite popular in France too, should be won over as his successor in the French presidency. For his part, Delors certainly did not go in for that proposition. He was now sixty-nine years old and had repeatedly suffered from sciatica; the French presidency seemed to him too grueling and the prospects of winning it too uncertain as well. After maintaining a low profile for several months, he announced in early December of 1984 that he was not willing to be a candidate for the office.

Dutch Prime Minister Ruud Lubbers was initially suggested as Delors' successor in the office of Commission president. However, neither Kohl nor Mitterrand was willing to accept that—the chancellor because the Christian Democrat Lubbers had all too clearly sided with those wanting to slow down the process of German unification and the French president because he was convinced that Lubbers had steered the Maastricht Summit all too much to the benefit of the British. Consequently, the two presented a competing candidate at the Council meeting on Corfu on 24 and 25 June: Belgian Prime Minister Jean-Luc Dehaene, likewise a Christian Democrat. With both candidates having their foreign ministers represent them, the Council gave eight votes to Dehaene and four to Lubbers. As president of the Council, Papandreou then wanted to push through the candidacy of Dehaene. However, he ran into fierce opposition from Major, whose slogan was that there should be no second Delors and who rejected Dehaene as

---

28 Endo, *Delors*, pp. 191–206; Drake, *Delors*, pp. 113–143; Delors, *Erinnerungen*, pp. 465–479.
29 *Ibid.*, p. 454.

"too federalist." In the end, the decision on the nomination of the next Commission president had to be deferred—to a special meeting of the European Council set for 15 July in Brussels.[30]

After returning from Corfu, Kohl reached an agreement with Major, Mitterrand, and new Italian Prime Minister Silvio Berlusconi that Luxembourg Prime Minister Jacques Santer be the common candidate. Santer too was a Christian Democrat and from his whole political socialization no less federalist in orientation than Dehaene. Since 1987, he had been chairman of the European Peoples Party and had been in close contact with Kohl. This may have been unknown to Major, or perhaps he felt it sufficient to have demonstrated his toughness to the British public at least once. Santer hesitated somewhat to take up the post given that Luxembourg's voters had just confirmed him for a second term as prime minister. Only after Kohl explained to him that he was the only candidate who could find all-round acceptance did he agree. On 15 July, he was unanimously nominated by the Council. The office of prime minister of Luxembourg was assumed by Foreign Minister Jean-Claude Juncker.

As a compromise candidate, it was difficult for Santer to garner authority. The newly-elected European Parliament confirmed him on 21 July by a margin of only 260 to 238, with twenty-three abstentions. The mistrust that was expressed in those results stemmed less from the person of Santer than from the process by which he had come to office. Santer however understood how to apportion responsibility in the new Commission such that effective cooperation among the now-twenty commissioners was assured. Parliament honored this in that it approved the Commission as a whole on 18 January 1995 by a margin of 416 to 103, with fifty-nine abstentions. In regard to further implementation of the Internal Market, the transition to the monetary union, as well as engagement for growth and employment, the Santer Commission continued the course charted by Delors.

Conversely, in regard to the strengthening of European institutions, the new Commission did not evince the strong profile that had characterized Delors. Santer initially had to concern himself with building consensus in the heterogeneous Commission. This did not allow him any opportunity to make a mark personally as an advocate of effective government in the Union. He left the representation of the Commission within the Reflection Group, which was to prepare the revision of the Maastricht Treaty, to former Spanish Foreign Minister and General Secretary of the European Council Marcelino Oreja.

---

30 *Ibid.*, p. 480; Michael Gehler, "Jacques Santer (1995–1999): President of the Commission in times of transition," in: Jan van der Harst and Gerrit Voerman (eds.), *An Impossible Job? - The Presidents of the European Commission, 1958–2014*, London: John Harper Publishing, 2015, pp. 197–222.

The Reflection Group was established by the European Council in Corfu in accordance with Kohl's promise to the faction leaders in the European Parliament. Mitterrand's former European advisor Élisabeth Guigou and the German Christian Democrat Elmar Brok represented Parliament in the body. Together with the representative of the Commission president, they saw to it that the report the group presented on 5 December 1995 under the chairmanship of former Spanish Foreign Office State Secretary Carlos Westendorp actually did list the problems of the Maastricht construct: The inadequacy and lack of coherence of the second and third pillars as well as the extraordinary complexity of the decision-making process. The report offered a three-part objective for treaty revision: To bring Europe closer to the citizens, to strengthen the Union's ability to act in the wider world, and to organize the institutions of the Union so as to be more democratic and more effective—especially with an eye toward the next (and larger) expansion to the east that was coming up.[31]

Discussion of the pending reform was enlivened by a position paper published by the CDU/CSU faction of the German Bundestag on 1 September 1994 under the names of its chairman, Wolfgang Schäuble, and his foreign-policy spokesman, Karl Lamers. In the document, these two German specialists in European policy voiced support for accelerated integration of the Eastern-European countries into the Union as well as development of a common foreign policy and creation of a European defense. Secondly, they called for a stronger focus of the Union on "the model of a federative state structure": The reform should orient itself on conceptions "according to which the European Parliament incrementally develops into a law-making organ on an equal footing alongside the Council [...] and the Commission takes on characteristics of a European government." Thirdly, these two German Christian Democrats demanded that the "hard core of countries focused on integration and willing to cooperate" be institutionalized and further solidified. The countries belonging to this core—in the view of the CDU/CSU faction there were only France, Germany, and the Benelux states at that time—should be involved in all projects of increasing integration or cooperation, the other countries only insofar as they were interested and insofar as it was possible for them.[32]

---

[31] Bericht der Reflexionsgruppe, Messina 2. Juni 1995 / Brüssel 5. Dezember 1995. Dokument des Generalsekretariats des Rates, Nr. SN 520/1/95/REV 1 (REFLEX 21); excerpts in: Mathias Jopp and Otto Schmuck (eds.), *Die Reform der Europäischen Union. Analysen – Positionen – Dokumente zur Regierungskonferenz 1996/97*, Bonn: Bundeszentrale für politische Bildung, 1996, pp. 107–114.

[32] CDU/CSU Fraktion des Deutschen Bundestages, "Überlegungen zur europäischen Politik, 1.9.1994;" published in: *Blätter für deutsche und internationale Politik* 10/1994, pp. 1271–1280.

The Schäuble-Lamers Paper generated manifold criticism. Some rejected the focus on federalism, some bridled at the creation of a hard core, whereas others rejected both. Berlusconi immediately complained to Kohl about the attempt to shove Italy—a founding member—into the ranks of a second-class of less-integrated states. Mitterrand appeared "troubled." Major polemicized against the attempt to accord individual states a "privileged status." The intense and sometimes rather muddled debate[33] nevertheless led in the run-up to the government conference on reform of the Maastricht Treaties to agreement between Chirac and Kohl to anchor the principle of selective integration in the Union Treaty; this principle was already being practiced in regard to the Franco-German corps, the abolition of border controls, and the monetary union. On 6 December 1995, they wrote a joint letter to the chairman of the Council, stating that "While preserving the unitary institutional framework of the Union, states that desire it and are in a situation" to do so should have "the opportunity opened to them of developing increased cooperation."[34]

The government conference opened with a meeting of the Council of Ministers on 29 March 1996 in Turin. The main work lay with a committee consisting of representatives from among the foreign ministers and the Commission. The representatives of Parliament who had participated in the work of the Reflection Group were not part of this committee; they were however regularly informed as to the progress of the negotiations and could express their opinions on them. Moreover, the president of Parliament could present positions at the monthly meetings of the Council of Ministers and the gatherings of the European Council. Up to the end of 1996, this office was held by German Social Democrat Klaus Hänsch; in accordance with an internally-coordinated agreement of the two largest parliamentary factions, he was succeeded by the Spanish Conservative José-Maria Gil-Robles. With this setup, there was greater openness in the negotiations, though with more contingency in the results.

The draft treaty was ready by 12 June 1997 and was then once again modified and made more precise in some important points at the Amsterdam Council meeting of 16 and 17 June.[35] Regarding the introduction of "increased coopera-

---

33 Cf. Stefan Honecker, "Die Debatte um das 'Kerneuropa'-Papier der CDU/CSU-Fraktion," in: Roland Erne, et al. (eds.), *Transnationale Demokratie. Impulse für ein demokratisch verfasstes Europa*, Zurich: Realotopia Verlag, 1995, pp. 330–341; Valérie Guérin-Sendelbach, *Frankreich und das vereinigte Deutschland*, Opladen: Leske und Budrich, 1999, pp. 205–220.
34 Jopp and Schmuck, *Reform*, pp. 115–117.
35 On the course of the government conference and the results, Mathias Jopp, Andreas Maurer, and Otto Schmuck (eds.), *Die Europäische Union nach Amsterdam. Analysen und Stellungnahmen zum neuen EU-Vertrag*, Bonn: Europa Union, 1998; Werner Weidenfeld (ed.), *Amsterdam in der Analyse*, Gütersloh: Bertelsmann Stiftung, 1998.

tion," it was above all the British government that voiced opposition. This resulted in a significant limitation on the possibilities for applying it. In principle, it was only to be possible when more than half of the member states wanted to participate. Only in regard to the third pillar of justice and police cooperation could there be a decision by qualified majority. Its use was not foreseen at all in the realms of foreign and security policy, and in the Community area, a veto right was enshrined against its introduction by majority decision. Furthermore, motions could only be proposed after the Commission had given its approval to them; and they were not allowed to involve areas that lay solely within the responsibility of the Community. This meant that a systematic strengthening of the core of the Union, as the authors of the Schäuble-Lamers Paper had envisioned, was as good as eliminated.

Of immediate practical significance in this context was only that the abolition of border controls within the EU area was a concrete case of increased cooperation that was taken up in the treaty; this had been agreed upon by Kohl and Mitterrand in May of 1984 and had in the meantime been gotten underway via the Schengen Agreement of 14 July 1985 and an implementation agreement of 19 June 1990. The original agreement among France, Germany, Belgium, the Netherlands, and Luxembourg had in the meantime been joined by Italy (1990), Spain (1991), as well as Portugal and Greece (both 1992). Austria joined in 1995, and at the end of 1996 so too did Denmark, Sweden, and Finland. This meant that only the island nations of Britain and Ireland remained outside the Schengen Agreement. Border crossing without checkpoints had been achieved for the core group of Schengen states in March of 1995. It also applied to Austria from 1997 and to the Scandinavian states from 2000.[36] Owing to the designation of the Schengen agreements as "increased cooperation," Community organs became responsible for carrying them out.

In general, a substantial portion of cooperation in the area of "internal affairs and justice" (the so-called third pillar of the Maastricht Treaty) was taken into the Community sphere with the Amsterdam Treaty. It was not only in regard to the lifting of internal borders and common regulation of external borders but also in common regulation of visa issuance, asylum and immigration policy, punishment of organized crime, terrorism, and drug trafficking as well as cooperation in civil law areas that a "space of freedom, security, and law" was to emerge within five years. At the urging of some German states and Austria, all of which

---

36 Hans-Claudius Taschner, *Schengen. Die Übereinkommen zum Abbau der Personenkontrollen an den Binnengrenzen von EU-Staaten*, Baden-Baden: Nomos, 1997; Andreas Pudlat, "Der lange Weg zum Schengen-Raum: Ein Prozess im Vier-Phasen-Modell," in: *Journal of European Integration History* 17 (2011), pp. 303–325.

saw themselves confronted to an especially great degree by the flood of immigrants from Eastern Europe, the countries reserved the right of retaining unanimous decision-making on visa issuance even after the expiration of the five-year period.[37] In the area of police and judicial cooperation in criminal affairs, which remained in the third pillar, procedures were simplified and agreement was reached on increased participation by the common police authority Europol in criminal investigations within five years.[38]

Also contributing to the strengthening of the common legal area was the fact that the Council in its constellation of heads of state and of government was given a guardian role in the preservation of the "basic principles of freedom, democracy, and respect for human rights and fundamental freedoms as well as the rule of law." If it were unanimously determined that a country was impinging on these basic principles (and here the vote of the country in question would not be included), the Council could then by qualified majority decide to suspend "certain rights" of said country indefinitely; the country's responsibilities would however remain. Respect for the basic principles was also explicitly declared to be a criterion for accepting further candidates for membership. Lastly, the European Court was given authority to monitor adherence to the European Convention on Human Rights in the activities of Community organs. Out of this came a higher level of protection of fundamental rights of EU citizens by the Union.

The desired increase in the Union's closeness to the citizenry would also serve to strengthen the social responsibilities of the Community. Right after the election victory of the Labour Party on 1 May 1997, new British Prime Minister Tony Blair declared that Great Britain would join the social policy protocol of the Maastricht Treaty. This meant that the agreement on introducing minimum standards in occupational safety, equality between men and women, social security, and collective exercise of workers' interests—which during the treaty negotiations of 1991 had met with the stubborn opposition of John Major—could be included in the new Community treaty at the last minute. Moreover, a section on employment could be included and was additionally fostered by the victory of leftist parties in the French parliamentary elections of 1 June 1997. It declared the promotion of a "higher level of employment" to be a goal of the Union and sought to further it via regular required reporting by member states, recommendations, exchange of information, and pilot projects. Farther-reaching conceptions for promoting employment-policy measures financially were derailed by opposition from the German government. At base, the conservative-liberal government in Bonn did

---

37 Amsterdam Treaty, Articles 61–69.
38 Amsterdam Treaty, Articles 30–32.

not think much of such measures; furthermore, it did not want its voters to incur any further financial burden via the Community.

The change of government in London also made possible an expansion of the rights of Parliament: The process of equal co-decision-making by Parliament was extended to almost every area of Community policy in which the Council decided by qualified majority with the exception of the monetary union. This involved approximately seventy percent of all legislative acts of the Community; beforehand, it had been only roughly thirty percent. Beyond that, the process of co-decision-making was significantly simplified: Legal acts could from now on be passed at their first reading (as long as Parliament made no changes to the Council proposal or in cases when the Council accepted all such changes). A third reading, which put the blame for the failure of a mediation process one-sidedly on Parliament, was completely eliminated. It continued to be the case that the Council would need to consult Parliament before passing binding legal acts in the area of criminal law and police cooperation. In regard to the naming of the Commission president, it would in the future be the case that a hearing in advance would no longer suffice—Parliament would now be explicitly required to approve the mutual proposal of the governments.

The latter was all the more significant because in naming the other Commission members, it would no longer suffice to consult the designated president. Rather, mutual agreement would need to be reached with him or her. Beyond this, the president was given the "political leadership" of the Commission. In a declaration passed by the government conference, it was additionally specified "that he will enjoy broad discretion in the allocation of tasks within the Commission, as well as in any reshuffling of those tasks during a Commission's term of office."[39] This amounted to a kind of power to direct in the areas of strategies and division of tasks. Taken together, Parliament's required approval along with the strengthening of the position of the Commission president opened up the chance for the European party alliances to name alternative candidates for the office of president, thus having the voters participate in the decision on the next president and his or her program.

For the European Parliament, the expansion of its rights and the strengthening of the position of the Commission president constituted "a breakthrough," as President of the European Parliament Klaus Hänsch commented in retrospect: "In Maastricht the door from advisory to decision-making parliament had been opened a crack; it now stood open."[40] This success was due not least of all to its two representatives, Guigou and Brok, who had largely concentrated on these

---

39 Erklärung zur Organisation und zur Arbeitsweise der Kommission.
40 Klaus Hänsch, *Kontinent der Hoffnungen. Mein europäisches Leben*, Bonn: Dietz, 2011, p. 113.

points in the negotiations and were thereby able to exercise significantly more influence over the results of those negotiations than had been formally accorded them. Important too was that Kohl had been able to win over his new partner Chirac—who had been hesitant at first—for the generalization of the co-decision-making process.

Parliament's success was nevertheless significantly limited given that the number of policy fields in which the Council decided by qualified majority was hardly expanded at all. It was only Belgium and Luxembourg that were prepared to accept thoroughgoing application of the majority principle. France, Spain, and Britain rejected the introduction of majority voting in institutional questions; the German delegation opposed majority voting in sensitive individual areas such as cultural policy, industrial policy, and environmental policy due to pressure from individual ministries and German states. In general, there was little willingness to allow majority voting for legal acts that would directly affect the budget of the Community. In the end, of some fifty-six policy areas in which unanimous decision-making had been in effect, only four were transferred into the category of majority decision-making, mainly in the realm of research and technology policy. It was not only the case that the Council and Commission alone would continue to decide on policies regarding agriculture, industry, competitiveness, and taxes, but also that Parliament would have no co-decision-making authority on basic questions of the monetary union or on policy regarding water, regional planning, energy, or the introduction of increased cooperation.

The French government would have been willing to offer greater concessions on the issue of majority decision-making if there had simultaneously been a recalculation of vote strength in the Council to the benefit of the larger member states. In fact, the already-completed inclusion of new states and the accession of additional members implied a loss of voting weight by those states that in terms of population and economy were the largest; at the same time, this situation offered Parliament greater opportunities for finding allies in the Council for a blocking minority. However, the smaller states rejected a reweighting of the votes to the benefit of larger states either completely (as was the case with Greece, Ireland, Finland, and Sweden), or appealed for a system of double majorities (that is, majority of the weighted votes plus majority of the population) along with simultaneously raising the minimum number of votes needed for majority decisions. Likewise, they opposed reducing the number of Commission members to the number of distinct task areas (approximately ten) and instead insisted that each country be represented by a member on the Commission. Mediation attempts by the German delegation, which advocated a system of double majorities without an increase in the minimum number of votes required, failed due to the resistance of the French representatives. They did not want to accept the loss of equal status with Germany that such a system threatened to bring about. In the event that the number of Commission members was reduced, the French were also unwilling to forgo a French Commission member occasionally, as the smaller states were demanding.

The government conference almost threatened to collapse over the issues of the distribution of weight within the Council and the Commission's ability to act. In light of the sluggish pace of negotiations, Kohl had already signaled in the autumn of 1996 that "Maastricht II" might well need to be followed by a "Maastricht III"; he therefore suggested to his colleagues on the Council in Amsterdam on the night of 17–18 June 1997 that the disputed issues be deferred to a subsequent government conference.[41] They decided to do that. In the treaty, the status quo as to the weight of votes and the number of Commission members was confirmed. A protocol was then passed in which an agreement in two stages was envisioned: If the weighting of votes in the Council had been "changed in a way that was acceptable to all member states" by the time the next enlargement of member states had come into effect, then from that point onward, each member state would be able to appoint only one commissioner. "No later than one year from the date on which the number of member states exceeds twenty," a further government conference was to be called "in order to review comprehensively the terms of the treaties regarding the composition and operating principles of the organs."[42]

In the final analysis, adjusting the weight of votes in the Council and the composition of the Commission to the demands of expansion had failed due to the refusal of French policy to give up the central role that France had up to that point always played at the European level.[43] Conversely, the continuing Franco-German harmony regarding Common Foreign and Security Policy led to some progress compared to the terms of the Maastricht Union Treaty. The foreign and Europe ministers of the two countries agreed on common guidelines, which they passed on 27 February 1996. These called for improving the decision-making ability in foreign and security policy by introducing the principle of constructive abstention, the creation of a planning and analysis unit for developing common strategies, and the establishment of a "new function, which will contribute to better visibility and coherence of CFSP."[44]

---

41 Weidenfeld, *Amsterdam*, p. 32.
42 Protokoll über die Organe im Hinblick auf die Erweiterung der Europäischen Union.
43 In the contemporary French literature, a supposed backing away by Kohl from the goal of deepening the integration is often made responsible for the failure of the reform proposals regarding representation on the Council and in the Commission; see, for example, Stark, *Kohl*, p. 387. However, this ignores the French attitude toward mediation proposals.
44 Jopp and Schmuck, *Reform*, pp. 118–120.

It proved possible to have these goals approved in the government conference in their essentials, though also with nuances. The instrument of constructive abstention was defined to the effect that a country declaring itself not bound to participate in implementation would still be bound to participate in financing. In the future, majority voting was to be possible not only in the implementation of common actions but also in all measures within the framework of a commonly-defined strategy. Nevertheless, dissenting Council members were accorded the right, as in the case of setting up "increased cooperation," to prevent application of majority voting. Such a decision could only occur if the heads of state and of government in the European Council had decided differently than their foreign ministers had done previously in the Council of Ministers. Additionally, majority rule was not to be in effect for the sending of troops on a foreign military mission. On this point, German Foreign Minister Klaus Kinkel and Defense Minister Volker Rühe differed from French conceptions.

Further, a declaration of the government conference created a "policy planning and early-warning unit," which was to be recruited from the ranks of the General Secretariat of the European Council, the ministries of the member states, the Commission, and the WEU. Its leadership lay with the general secretary of the European Council, who now additionally took on the task of a "High Representative for Common Foreign and Security Policy." French conceptions of shaping the CFSP representation as a political office with great foreign impact could not be approved given opposition from the British and the neutral states. Also, the German proposal to entrust the High Representative with the chairmanship of the Political Committee—the weekly gathering of the political directors of the foreign ministries of all member states—was rejected as too far-reaching.

Neither did the French and Germans succeed in anchoring in the treaty a roadmap for transferring the WEU into the EU. However, there was a decision regarding "closer institutional links to the WEU with a view to the possibility of the integration of the WEU into the Union"; these were to be worked out within a year after the treaty came into effect. It was to be possible for the European Council to decide on further steps as to common defense policy and the integration of the WEU in the EU. Aside from that, the European Council's responsibility for guidelines was already to be extended to the WEU at that time. In regard to "humanitarian tasks and rescue efforts, peacekeeping tasks, as well as combat deployments for overcoming crises," as defined in June of 1992 to be tasks of WEU military deployments (the "Petersberg Declaration" of the WEU Council of Ministers), those EU member states that were not also members of the WEU gained the right of equal participation.[45]

---

45 Amsterdam Treaty, Article 17 and Protocol to Article 17.

The instrument of "increased cooperation" was not extended to the provisions on foreign and security policy. It was indeed the case that the German government had been willing to do so in October of 1996. However, after the representatives of Britain, Sweden, and Denmark had insisted on being able to prevent the introduction of increased cooperation by means of a veto, it was only the French delegation that continued to advocate the possibility of a group of states acting in the name of the Union. German Foreign Minister Klaus Kinkel no longer felt himself bound by the proposal that he had made together with his French colleague Hervé de Charrette. Increased defense policy cooperation by a core along the lines of the Franco-German model was thus left out of the treaty's regulations.[46]

The strengthening of Common Foreign and Security Policy thus did not end up being exactly as clear as Kohl and Chirac had called for in their joint letter of December 1995. Nothing else was to be expected given a situation in which the British and Dutch resistance from the time of the Maastricht negotiations had been augmented by the reticence of the new neutral and non-aligned members.

Together with the glaring failure of French leadership on the issues of the weighting of votes in the Council and the number of future Commission members, the impression arose that the government conference on reform of the Maastricht Treaties had contributed little to overcoming the problems facing the EU. "Muted jubilation," was the headline of the *Frankfurter Allgemeine Zeitung* over its report on the results of the Amsterdam Council meeting.[47] It was the case that the rights of the European Parliament had been considerably expanded and that the Commission president had seen a significant strengthening of his position, but those results ended up somewhat in the background. Little discussed by the public, the Amsterdam Treaty was signed on 2 October 1997. After conclusion of the ratification process, it came into effect on 1 May 1999.

Inspired by its success in the reform negotiations, the European Parliament exercised its oversight rights extensively even before the treaty had come into force. In so doing, it encountered all sorts of inconsistencies in the Commission's budget management for the year 1996. The approval envisioned for March of 1998 had to be postponed, and then more and more irregularities began coming to light. The criticism applied especially to Commissioner for Research, Innovation, and Science Édith Cresson, who had briefly served as a French prime minister under Mitterrand and who had clearly engaged in cronyism, as well as the Commissioner for External Relations with the Southern Mediterranean, Latin America, and the Middle East Manuel Marín, a Spaniard, in whose area of responsibility there was fraud in the handling of humanitarian aid. After demands for the resig-

---

46 Stark, *Kohl*, pp. 352–358 and 376ff.
47 *Frankfurter Allgemeine Zeitung*, 19 June 1997.

nation of Cresson and Marín had brought no result, Parliament for the first time in its history refused to give the Commission its approval on 17 December 1998.

When this step did not lead to the voluntary resignation of the tainted commissioners, the MEPs pursued a vote of no confidence against the entire Commission, although a motion to that effect did not garner the required two-thirds majority on 14 January 1999. An investigatory commission was instead created and served to bring the Commission into still greater difficulties. In this body's report, presented on 15 March, the accusations against Cresson were expanded still further; and the Commission in general was accused of having lost control over the activities in its administration. There was no willingness, either individual or collective, to assume responsibility; and it was "difficult to find someone who exhibits the least sense of responsibility in this regard."[48]

After the disastrous impression that the report of the independent investigatory commission had produced, the Santer Commission could no longer hold. On the evening after the report's release, those deputies of the Socialist faction who had backed the Commission up to that point informed the president that they too would support a vote of no confidence. Santer, who up till then had been counting on the national governments to withdraw the controversial commissioners, was only able to avoid having the entire Commission removed from office by pushing through a decision for the collective resignation of all the commissioners on the evening of 15 March. The resignation was declared on the 16th. Santer and his colleagues remained in office as caretakers until a new Commission could be appointed.

Chancellor Gerhard Schröder, who held the Council presidency in the first half of 1999, now busied himself as a crisis manager. Already at the Council meeting of 24 and 25 March 1999 in Berlin, he succeeded in having Romano Prodi named the new president of the Commission; while serving as prime minister of Italy, Prodi had been able to bring his country into the Eurozone. The European Parliament confirmed Prodi in his new post on 5 May, and the appointment of the remaining Commission members then followed according to the co-decision-making process of the Amsterdam Treaty. Only a few people from the Santer Commission were named to the new Commission: Neil Kinnock as representative for the upcoming administrative reform, the Austrian Franz Fischler as commissioner for agriculture and fisheries, and the Italian Mario Monti as commissioner for competition. Among the newcomers who would have a significant impact were the Frenchman Pascal Lamy, former cabinet chief under Delors, as commissioner for trade; as commissioner for enlargement, the German Günter Verheugen, who up to that point had been Social Democratic minister of state in the Foreign Office;

---

[48] Quoted from Hänsch, *Kontinent*, p. 109. Cf. *ibid.*, pp. 105–109 and Dietrich Rometsch, "Die Europäische Kommission," in: *Jahrbuch der Europäischen Integration 1998/99*, pp. 71–78.

and as commissioner for external relations, the Briton Chris Patten. After all the nominees had individually gone through hearings, Parliament voted to appoint the new Commission on 15 September 1999 by a very large majority. The new Commission then took up its work on 18 September.

Overall, the European Parliament emerged further strengthened from the confrontation with several members of the Santer Commission. The European Council also gained prominence, and the authority of the Commission was again increased over the medium term. The forced change in the membership of the Commission did not however suffice to arrest the loss of confidence in European politics by citizens. In the fifth direct election of the European Parliament, which took place between 10 and 13 June 1999, the percentage of nonvoters, which in 1994 had already been 43.2 percent, rose to 50.6 percent. It was also the case that the pressure to concentrate on necessary administrative reforms hindered the Prodi Commission, at least in its beginnings, from aggressively fulfilling its role of providing impetus to the integration process.

Security and Eastern Policy

Implementing decisions for developing a common foreign and defense policy remained arduous. On the level of the Council of Ministers, it was indeed the case that a whole series of common positions was worked out, for example, in regard to pacification policy after the disintegration of Yugoslavia, the civil wars in Central Africa, and the prolonged conflict between Israel and the Palestinians. Incrementally, the Western European Union oriented itself toward its role as an instrument of common defense policy: with the transfer of its Permanent Representatives Council and its general secretariat from London to Brussels; the establishment of a satellite center, a logistics center, a planning unit, and a crisis-monitoring center; as well as the acceptance of new member Greece along with the NATO countries Turkey, Iceland, and Norway as associate members and the neutral EU countries Ireland, Austria, Sweden, and Finland as observers. Several multinational military units developed: for example, the Eurocorps consisting of fifty thousand French, German, Belgian, Spanish, and Luxembourger soldiers that was ready for deployment at the end of 1995; a Multinational Division made up of Belgian, British, Dutch, and German units; and the multinational Mediterranean forces Eurofor and Euromarfor.

However, common actions remained largely confined to the posting of Union representatives to crisis regions, support for democratization and rebuilding programs, and the sending of election observers. The armed forces of the WEU were hardly made use of. It was only the case that from 1992 to 1996, the WEU together with NATO and the UN secured an arms embargo against the countries of the former Yugoslavia and a trade embargo against Serbia-Montenegro. Beyond that, the EU administration of Mostar was supported by a military police force numbering about 180. Participation in the UN peace mission for Bosnia-Herzegovina was primarily by France, along with Belgium, the Netherlands, Spain, and lastly Great Britain; Italy provided air logistics. The weakness of the Europeans became clear when in May of 1995 some four hundred Blue Helmets were taken hostage by Bosnian Serbs and two months later when Dutch Blue Helmets had to stand by helplessly as soldiers of the Bosnian-Serbian Army murdered approximately eight thousand Muslims during the capture of the Protected Zone of Srebrenica. Only after American NATO warplanes had bombed Serbian positions in August was it possible to force a cessation of hostilities. The Dayton Peace Accords of 14 December 1995 were mediated by the US and overseen by an international peacekeeping force under the leadership of NATO.

The Europeans' glaring weakness in the conflict in Bosnia-Herzegovina could be attributed not least of all to the hesitancy of the Germans to engage militarily in an area outside the boundaries of NATO. This contributed to a situation in which the advantage gradually shifted in favor of NATO in the struggle over the autonomy of European defense. At the beginning of the 1990s Mitterrand had expected that after the end of the Cold War NATO would be dissolved and that an autonomous European armed force could take its place; it was now the case however that the Germans were gradually losing interest in a French nuclear umbrella and that NATO could acquire new tasks in the absence of available European alternatives. After a debate on the resumption of French nuclear testing by President Chirac in June of 1995 had once again made clear the difficulties that stood in the way of an Europeanization of nuclear strategy, Chirac decided in November to seek an European pillar *within* NATO. On 5 December, he announced that the French defense minister and chief of the general staff would in the future participate in the operations of the alliance. Six months later, Paris and Washington signed an agreement on the exchange of nuclear development data that was to make further test explosions unnecessary.

With this, French efforts for European autonomy were *de facto* reduced to the conventional sphere. Specifically, the Europeans would have the opportunity to receive material and logistical support from NATO for carrying out their own operations if and insofar as the US abstained from having American ground troops participate. At the NATO Council meeting in Berlin on 3 June 1996, a principle decision to that effect was formulated: The WEU was supposed to be able to operate in the future with support from NATO, though only if the particular operation had been unanimously approved by the NATO Council in advance. France pledged to return to the command structure of NATO at the implementation of this decision and to give up its special role within the Western alliance.⁴⁹

Implementation of this decision did not come about however. France sought the permanent transfer of regional command authority in Europe to European generals. The Clinton administration in Washington was not willing to do that, however; it did not want to go beyond conceding individual, carefully defined missions that would be carried out autonomously by the Europeans. In February of 1997, Chirac then declared to US Secretary of State Madeleine Albright during her visit to Paris that the conditions for France's return to the command structure of NATO had not yet been fulfilled. Hubert Védrine, foreign minister in the Socialist government formed by Jospin in June of 1997, reinforced him in this decision. For him, the rapprochement of France with NATO undertaken by Chirac in December of 1995 constituted a strategic blunder that needed correcting.⁵⁰ At the Madrid meeting of the NATO Council on 8 and 9 July 1997, the continuing antagonism between France and the US became public; for its part, the German government, which was still not prepared to undertake military action outside allied territory, did nothing to support the French position. As a consequence, the exact structure of the "European pillar" of NATO remained unresolved.⁵¹

At the same time, NATO took a major step toward lastingly establishing itself as the decisive security organization on the European continent: Poland, Hungary, and the Czech Republic were invited to negotiate on entry into the Atlantic Alliance in 1999. It was less a clear strategy that lay behind this than Bill Clinton's desire to make a name for himself in foreign policy, along with his receptiveness to Polish and Czech desires. NATO got more problems than solutions with this eastward expansion but was from that point onward always present in the countries of Eastern-Central Europe; it was also to be expected that the expansion would go still further. Slovenia and Romania, which had likewise submitted applications, were not yet admitted despite support from a majority of European members of the alliance; in the closing communiqué of the Madrid NATO Council meeting, they were however named as possible candidates for the next round of expansion.⁵²

New dynamism came into European security policy only in the autumn of 1998 with the threatened escalation of the conflict between Serbian military forces and Kosovo-Albanians, who were fighting to gain independence from Serbia. Blair, who a year earlier had not yet had the courage to advocate British

---

49 Soutou, *L'Alliance incertaine*, pp. 414–426.
50 Chirac, *Le temps présidentiel*, pp. 220ff.
51 Stark, *Kohl*, pp. 339–348.
52 Vojtech Mastny, *Reassuring NATO. Eastern Europe, Russia, and the Western Alliance* (*Forsvarsstudier* 5/1997), Oslo: IFS, 1997.

participation in the Community currency, now saw a chance to profile himself in the sphere of European politics in which a leadership role for Britain was most likely to be had. With the Europeans' fear of a repetition of the traumatic experience of Bosnia-Herzegovina in mind, he advocated "fresh thinking" in security policy at an informal gathering of the European Council on 25 and 26 October in the Austrian town of Pörtschach: the assembly of credible European crisis reaction forces capable of deployment and that could engage autonomously if the US was not willing to get involved; this initiative could potentially be combined with the full integration of the WEU into the EU.[53]

Chirac immediately made use of this British change of course in security policy to get Blair to commit himself to the greatest extent possible to accelerated implementation of the Amsterdam decisions on security policy. At a meeting in St. Malo on 3 and 4 December, he gained Blair's agreement to a joint declaration in which the French president and the British prime minister announced that they wanted to work together because "the European Union needs to be in a position to play its full role on the international stage. [...] To this end, the Union must have the capacity for autonomous action, backed up by credible military forces, the means to decide to use them, and a readiness to do so, in order to respond to international crises." As to the transfer of the WEU into the EU, there was still rather vague mention of "taking account of the existing assets of the WEU and the evolution of its relations with the EU."[54]

Military intervention in Kosovo was once again left to NATO. After the Serbian Army had begun a broad offensive against the Kosovo Albanians on 20 March 1999, NATO reacted on 24 March with air attacks on military and economic targets in Serbia, Kosovo, and Montenegro. After more than two months of bombardment, Serbian President Slobodan Milošević agreed to a withdrawal from Kosovo on 3 June; the UN decided on an international peacekeeping force, organized by NATO, with a temporary occupation of the province seeking independence.

The renewed experience of powerlessness in determining the targets of air strikes strengthened the will of the Europeans to achieve the ability to act autonomously. Still more important was the fact that because of the dispute in Kosovo, new German Foreign Minister Joschka Fischer had been compelled to push through in his "Green" Party—which traditionally had tendencies toward pacifism—fundamental approval of Bundeswehr deployments outside of NATO territory and have such deployments become capable of winning majority support in Germany overall. In order to avoid the isolation of Germany or the collapse of the Red-Green coalition even before its assumption of power, Fischer had to agree to participation of the

---

53 *Agence Europe*, 26–27 Oct. 1998, pp. 4ff.
54 www.fco.gov.uk/en/newsroom/latest-news/?view=News&id=2244063.

Bundeswehr in a possible NATO intervention against the Greater-Serbian Army in the middle of October 1998. In mid-March, Milošević refused to sign a "temporary agreement" for the partial autonomy of Kosovo, an agreement that had come about not least of all due to pressure from the German government. He then began his offensive, and the government of Schröder-Fischer honored its commitment. Fischer justified his actions with the argument that he had drawn the lesson from recent German history not only of "never again war" but also of "never again Auschwitz."[55]

At the same time, Fischer made use of the German Council presidency during the first half of 1999 in order to develop more substance in European security policy at the European level, which had become possible due to the British change of course. At an informal gathering of the Council of Ministers on 13 and 14 March 1999 in the town of Reinhartshausen, he presented a discussion paper that made concrete proposals for implementing the St. Malo program. On that basis, the Cologne Council meeting of 3 and 4 June 1999 decided to improve the structures for a "European Security and Defense Policy" (ESDP): At the Council meetings of the foreign ministers, the defense ministers would now also participate as needed. The Political Committee of CFSP was to be expanded into a standing "Political and Security Committee" made up of high officials or ambassadors. Further, an EU Military Committee was to be created consisting of the national chiefs of general staffs as well as an EU Military Staff, which along with strategic planning was also to be responsible for implementing operations. The tasks of the WEU were to be "integrated" into the EU by the end of 2000.[56]

Beyond this, the German government ensured that with the very first strategy decided on after the Amsterdam Treaty came into effect—it involved the future relationship with Russia—the enforcement of unanimity for implementation measures would be dispensed with, and the treaty stipulations on it receded into the background. Likewise, the German government participated decisively in efforts to have none other than NATO Secretary General and former Spanish Foreign Minister Javier Solana named as first "High Representative" for CFSP. This gave the office political weight that went significantly beyond what had been decided in Amsterdam. Taking up his new post on 1 November 1999 and also assuming the office of WEU general secretary in a personal union, he gave the foreign policy line of the EU a face that was noticed by the public too.

---

[55] Joschka Fischer, *Die rot-grünen Jahre. Deutsche Außenpolitik – vom Kosovo bis zum 11. September*, Cologne: Kiepenheuer & Witsch, 2007, p. 185. Cf. *ibid.*, pp. 110–147, 156–251.

[56] Europäischer Rat in Köln 3./4.6.1999, Schlussfolgerungen des Vorsitzes, Ziffer 17 und Anhang III. Cf. Uwe Schmalz, "Aufbruch zu neuer Handlungsfähigkeit. Die Gemeinsame Außen-, Sicherheits- und Verteidigungspolitik unter deutscher Ratspräsidentschaft," in: *Integration* 3/1999, pp. 191–204.

Taking into account the qualms of NATO-oriented EU states as well as those of non-aligned ones, there were efforts up to the Council meeting in Helsinki on 10 and 11 December 1999 to specify that the EU military structure would actually only deal with crises outside the territory of the alliance. One result—contrary to what the German government had sought—was that the WEU was retained as an organization with a collective obligation of its members, even if its instruments and missions were taken over by the EU. Additionally, the heads of state and of government in Helsinki, following a British suggestion, committed themselves to organizing their militaries by the year 2003 so that a rapid deployment force of fifty to sixty thousand troops could be mobilized and its deployment be maintained for at least a year. At an "input conference" of the foreign and defense ministers on 20 November 2000, this decision was concretized to the effect that the sixty thousand ground troops were to be augmented by thirty thousand marines and air force personnel; some four hundred military aircraft and one hundred ships would be needed for this. Including the reserves necessary to maintain a deployment for more than a year, a total of approximately 150,000 personnel would be needed altogether.

In March of 2000, work began on setting up new institutions, regulating their relationships to NATO and the non-aligned EU states, as well as determining their modes of operation. In June, a Council committee on civil crisis management was added. Additionally, in the Portuguese city of Feira on 19 and 20 June, the European Council decided to keep five thousand police personnel available for civil crisis management. One thousand were to be deployable within thirty days. At the Council meeting in Nice from 7 to 10 December 2000, the responsibilities, mode of operation, and forms of cooperation were definitively regulated. The chiefs of the general staffs were to meet in the Military Committee two to four times a year, and the military representatives accredited in Brussels were to meet once a week. For those countries participating in NATO integration, these representatives were to be the same ones who were part of the NATO Military Committee. The Political and Security Committee was to meet twice per week at the level of ambassadors in Brussels; it could also however come together in the then-current form of a conference of the Political Directors of the Foreign Offices. An attempt by Germany and France to establish the High Representative of CFSP as chairman of the Political Committee was not successful; in the Nice reform treaty, it was only the case that there would be the possibility of entrusting him or her with the chairmanship in times of crisis.[57]

---

57 Mathias Jopp, "Gemeinsame Europäische Sicherheits- und Verteidigungspolitik," in: *Jahrbuch der Europäischen Integration* 1999/2000, pp. 243–250; idem., "Europäische Sicherheits- und Verteidigungspolitik," in: *Jahrbuch der Europäischen Integration* 2000/2001, pp. 233–242.

With such results, France was no nearer to the goal of autonomous defense planning for Europe. It had received the option of doing such planning, however, at least in the conventional sphere. At the same time, the EU had created the military capability to act autonomously as crisis manager outside the territory of the alliance. It thereby had reacted in a basically appropriate way to Europe's changed security situation and so prevented further damage to European self-confidence.

This was all the more important given that the way had in the meantime been opened for enlargement of the European Union toward the east. Many countries and interest groups had hoped that the date of such expansion could be put off still further—the membership of numerous formerly communist states constituted a threat owing to competition from cheaper products and labor, transfer of production to countries with lower wage levels, as well as massive increases in expenditure for agricultural policy and structural improvements or the reduction of such expenditures or their transfer to the countries of Eastern and Southeastern Europe. In June of 1991, Mitterrand had said that it would take "decades" until membership in the Community would be possible for these countries.[58] The association agreements that the EU had completed with Poland, Hungary, and Czechoslovakia in December of 1991 after difficult negotiations—with similar agreements following in 1993 with Romania and Bulgaria, in 1995 with the Baltic States and Slovenia—explicitly included the proviso that these agreements would not predetermine later entry into the Union.[59]

The governments of the associated countries had however quickly declared that they could not be satisfied with mere association over the long term. They were supported in this by the German government, which had an active interest in the establishment of stable and prosperous democracies to the east of Germany. The British and Danish governments pushed even more strongly for the quickest possible accession of the associated countries, not least of all because they saw in eastward expansion a possibility of slowing down the supranational deepening of the Union. The hesitant governments of Western and Southern Europe ultimately could not close their minds to the demands for stabilizing the Eastern-European region. Thus, after repeated forays by the Commission, the European Council in Copenhagen on 21 and 22 June 1993 agreed to a declaration that "future cooperation with the associated countries is to be coordinated with the now-established

---

[58] Radio interview, 12 June 1991, quoted from Bozo, *Mitterrand*, p. 357.
[59] On this and the following, cf. Graham Avery and Fraser Cameron, *The Enlargement of the European Union*, Sheffield: Sheffield Academic Press, 1998; Barbara Lippert (ed.), *Osterweiterung der Europäischen Union – die doppelte Reifeprüfung*, Bonn: Europa Union, 2000; Stark, *Kohl*, pp. 397–417; Peter Becker, *Die deutsche Europapolitik und die Osterweiterung der Europäischen Union*, Baden-Baden: Nomos, 2011, pp. 27–63 and 143–202.

goal of membership." At the same time, criteria were set down that would have to be met if the desire for entry were to be granted: Stable democratic order and rule of law, a functioning market economy, economic competitiveness, willingness to accept the *acquis communautaire* and the political objectives of the Union in full, as well as the existing Union's capacity to accept such countries.[60]

In order accelerate the fulfillment of these criteria, the European Council in Essen on 9 and 10 December 1994—after input from the Commission and the German Council presidency—established a "Structured Dialogue" between the governments of the member states, the European Parliament, and the governments of the associated countries. Already in the run-up to the Essen Council meeting, ministers with expertise from the candidate countries were brought into the process of working out a pre-accession strategy; it was essentially a matter of getting to know the Union's methods of operation. With his sense for symbolism, Kohl invited the heads of state and of government of the associated countries a few days before the Essen meeting for a first encounter with the members of the European Council on the fringes of the Council meeting; in the candidate countries themselves, this was regarded as a clear sign of the actual willingness of the Union to accept them.

However, the material preparation strategy could only be partially implemented through further measures to facilitate trade and promote investment as agreed to in Essen. In light of manifold opposition to unwelcome competition from the candidate countries, it took until November of 1995 before there was a majority in the Council of Ministers for a mere five percent increase in the tariff quota for Central- and Eastern-European countries. The German agricultural minister was among those opposing a greater increase or more flexibility in the quota. Intensive pressure from the German chancellor was once again needed for the European Council of 15 and 16 December 1995 in Madrid to hold out a concrete date for the beginning of entry negotiations: six months after conclusion of the government conference on reform of the Maastricht Treaties, that is, at the beginning of the year 1998. The only countries that received a firm commitment to the opening of negotiations at that time were the Mediterranean states Cyprus and Malta, which had submitted applications in 1990. For the Central- and Eastern-European countries, it was only the case that the Council was "anxious to reach" the beginning of negotiations at the same point in time. The European Commission was given the task of taking a position on the entry requests and producing a report on all the issues involved.[61]

---

60 "Europäischer Rat in Kopenhagen 21./22.6.1993, Schlussfolgerungen des Vorsitzes." in: *Europa-Archiv* 48 (1993), pp. D258–D276, the quote on p. D264.
61 "Europäischer Rat von Madrid 15./16.12.1995, Schlussfolgerungen des Vorsitzes, Teil A, Abschnitt III," in: *Bulletin der Europäischen Union* 12/1995, pp. 9–85, the quote on p. 20.

In accordance with the prevailing trend among the governments, the Commission decided to seek entry dates that varied according to the developmental level of the applicants and to organize the entry process so that the Union would not be faced with any additional financial requirements. After evaluating the application materials submitted by the candidates, Commission President Santer came to the conclusion that along with Cyprus (Malta had withdrawn its candidacy), entry negotiations should initially begin only with Poland, Hungary, and the Czech Republic. However, the German, British, and Dutch commissioners called for including at least one Baltic State and one country from the former Yugoslavia for political reasons. Thus, in the Report "Agenda 2000" that was presented by the Commission on 16 July 1997, the start of negotiations with Estonia and Slovenia was also recommended; different views could be taken on their ability to compete in five years. It was emphasized however that the beginning of negotiations did not in any way predetermine that they could be concluded at the same time.[62]

At the Luxembourg Council meeting of 12 and 13 December 1997, the European Council agreed to the recommendation to start accession talks with the six nominated countries. A Greek proposal to include Romania and Bulgaria in the first round of negotiations was disregarded, as was an appeal made by Denmark and Sweden for the participation of Latvia and Lithuania. At the same time, "accession partnerships" were agreed on between the Union and all ten Eastern-European candidate countries; under the auspices of these partnerships, financial and other assistance for restructuring was linked to annual progress reports. Also, following the recommendation of the Commission, a "European Conference" was established in which all European countries with a possibility of entry (that is, going beyond the circle of Eastern-European reform states) could confer about issues of cooperation beyond the pillars of the Community. In this way, a differentiated expansion was to be secured without holding back those countries in the second rank from intensifying their reform efforts.

In contrast, it was not possible for the heads of state and of government to come to agreement on the reform of cost-intensive Community policies as the Commission had also proposed: a further reorientation of agricultural policy away from guarantee prices to direct assistance or a geographical and thematic concentration of regional structural promotion. Speaking on behalf of all net-recipient countries, the conservative Spanish Prime Minister José Maria Aznar opposed any reduction or reapportionment of the current transfer payments, while Kohl once again made it clear that Germany was not prepared to see its position as a net payer expanded but would much rather even have it reduced in the future.

---

[62] Europäische Kommission, "Agenda 2000. Eine stärkere und erweiterte Union," KOM (97) 2000 endg., 15 July 1997.

However, with an eye toward parliamentary elections in Germany in the autumn of 1998, Kohl was also unwilling to hear of reductions in guarantee prices for agricultural products. Negotiations with the first six candidates for entry thus began on 31 March 1998 without the financing of the expansion having been settled.

No agreement on the difficult financial issues came about at the Council meetings in Cardiff in June or in Vienna in December either. Only at the Berlin Council meeting of 24 and 25 March 1999 was there agreement on the financial framework for the years 2000 to 2006—after a dramatic nighttime session and at the price of lasting resentment between Schröder and Chirac. The German government had had to give up its demand for national co-financing of agricultural subsidies. In return, the guarantee prices for agricultural products were reduced (though not as much or as quickly as the Commission had proposed, on average by about fifteen percent); expenditures for structural policy were also reduced by a small amount (from 230 to 213 billion euros). Another forty billion euros was to be available for the first new countries. The Commission had calculated that a hike of approximately twenty-five percent by 2006 ought to be made in total expenditures based on assumed annual rates of growth, but this was not undertaken.[63]

In any event, the German government had achieved a result by which eastern expansion would not include with any further increase in its financial burden. Those countries receiving subsides in the Union had to accept only small reductions; for Greece, Ireland, Spain, and Portugal, there was even an increase in the Cohesion Funds. No major breakthrough in agricultural reform occurred. At the same time, there did remain questions as to the financing of eastward expansion. Lengthy transitional deadlines for incorporating entering countries into Community programs as well as further disputes about reform of the budget had been built in.

The experience of the Kosovo War then led to a shift of emphasis in the expansion strategy: It was especially Fischer and Schröder who envisaged more clearly the dimension of security and stability in expansion. This led them to see expansion in the area of the former Yugoslavia as more urgent, and they also developed new arguments for the inclusion of Turkey. In the autumn of 1998 in its first progress report on developments in the candidate countries, the Commission found that there had been significant progress on the political criteria for entry among the candidates of the second rank; it was anyway the case that the Danish and Swedish governments had already been demanding (in vain up to that point) the beginning of entry negotiations with Latvia and Lithuania. This resulted in an orientation toward negotiations with all the other candidates.

---

63 Winfried von Urff, "Agrar- und Fischereipolitik," in: *Jahrbuch der Europäischen Integration 1998/99*, pp. 125–134; from the viewpoint of the German government, also Fischer, *Die rot-grünen Jahre*, pp. 287–297.

Encouraged by the German government, new Commission President Romano Prodi decided to make the upcoming eastward expansion the focal point of his Commission; and so he set up a separate general directorate for expansion with horizontal responsibility. He entrusted that function in the Commission to Fischer's deputy Verheugen. After a further review of the situation in the candidate countries and assessment of political conditions, he made the recommendation that negotiations now be started with all the candidates of the second rank, that is, Latvia, Lithuania, Slovakia, Romania, and Bulgaria—as well as Malta, which after an electoral victory by the pro-European Nationalist Party had renewed its application for membership. A decision to this effect was made at the Council meeting in Helsinki on 10 and 11 December 1999. At the same time, it was agreed that the preparations for accepting further members should be completed by the year 2003.[64]

That decision did not imply giving up on the strategy of differentiation then in effect. The conclusion of negotiations and the actual completion of accession remained dependent on reform measures and the performance of the land in question. This decision made the expansion process more dynamic only to the extent that, for political-strategic reasons, there was more willingness to take greater risks in evaluating economic problems. Furthermore, it was now the case that significantly greater personnel capacity of the Commission was invested in simultaneous negotiations with no fewer than twelve candidates.

Additionally, the heads of state and of government in Helsinki granted Turkey the status of a candidate for accession. This was a noteworthy step insofar as the EU had always rejected the Turkish desire to enter, even after the country's return to a parliamentary system in 1983. Freedom of movement for workers, pledged for 1986, had been rejected due to German efforts; the official entry request of 14 April 1987 had been put on the back burner by the Community. In March of 1995, agreement was successfully reached that the completion of the customs union between Turkey and the Community was the "end phase" of association. Then, however, Greece had blocked the release of financial assets frozen since 1981; in the decision on expansion issued in Luxembourg in December of 1997, Turkey was not taken into account this time either.

In Turkey, the bitterness over the new postponement of the entry decision was all the greater given that the new round of enlargement was characterized as the "reunification of Europe." It was not possible to miss the message that the governments of the member states and the candidates for entry no longer

---

[64] Europäischer Rat. Tagung vom 10. und 11. Dezember 1999 in Helsinki, Schlussfolgerungen des Vorsitzes, excerpts in: *Internationale Politik* 2/2000, pp. 80–85. Cf. Günter Verheugen, *Europa in der Krise. Für eine Neubegründung der europäischen Idee*, Cologne: Kiepenheuer & Witsch, 2005, pp. 78–85.

regarded Turkey as part of Europe or no longer unambiguously did so. Additional pain resulted from the fact that Cyprus was invited to the entry negotiations even though the Turkish regime in the north of the island did not want it. The government of Turkish Prime Minister Mesut Yilmaz therefore rejected an invitation to participate in the "European Conference" of potential candidates for entry and froze all links to the EU with the exception of the customs union.

The bestowal of candidate status and the financial assistance connected with it were attempts to prevent the looming isolation of Turkey. Involved in bringing this about was the government of Yilmaz's successor Bülent Ecevit, which correctly regarded defiance as none too productive, as well as the Clinton administration, which admonished the Europeans not to close themselves to EU entry by the NATO member Turkey. The American admonitions had an effect not only on the government of Schröder-Fischer but also on Greece's Simitis government. In the summer of 1999, Greek Foreign Minister Georgios Papandreou succeeded in initiating a *rapprochement* with Ankara. This was accelerated by the unexpected wave of mutual willingness to provide assistance after the severe earthquakes in Turkey in August and in Greece in September. The conferring of candidate status did not however mean that any actual breakthrough had been achieved on accession negotiations: Given that Turkish entry appeared to be looming, a debate about the "European" character of Turkey now took place in the member states; for its part, the Turkish government showed little inclination to make necessary reforms within the meaning of the Copenhagen criteria.[65]

The Nice Complex

After the decision to broaden the entry negotiations, the European governments felt it necessary to tackle the last hurdle before carrying out eastern expansion: the adjustment of European institutions. This was indispensable according to a declaration made by the heads of state and of government of France, Belgium, and Italy at the close of negotiations on the Amsterdam Treaty. The ambition of the German government was therefore to have a decision made on calling a further government conference—necessary before the membership expanded beyond twenty—under the auspices of the German Council presidency. This effort

---

65 Oya Susanne Abali, "Türkei," in: *Jahrbuch der europäischen Integration 1999/2000*, pp. 437–442; Jürgen Reuter, "Werden Athen und Ankara ihren historischen Konflikt beilegen? Griechisch-türkische Beziehungen im Lichte der türkischen EU-Beitrittskandidatur," in: Wilfried Loth (ed.), *Das europäische Projekt zu Beginn des 21. Jahrhunderts*, Opladen: Leske und Budrich, 2001, pp. 295–323; Kramer and Reinkowski, *Die Türkei und Europa*, pp. 161–166.

succeeded in that at the Cologne Council meeting of June 1999 it was decided that over the course of the year 2000, there would be negotiations on the future composition of the Commission and the weighting of votes in the Council of Ministers.

Fischer clearly did not want to content himself with a mere adjustment of Community organs to an appreciably larger number of member states. He interpreted the commitment of the Council members to "comprehensive" review of the organs' composition and methods of work in such a way that there was now an opportunity with the elimination of deficits to make a major leap forward in political integration at last. With strong emphasis on the "historical challenges" that he saw the Union facing, he sought out his French counterpart Hubert Védrine so as to win his support for a common initiative to strengthen European institutions. The Frenchman put him off, however: As the servant of two masters, a Socialist prime minister and a conservative president, he was not in a position to make his own mark on French European policy. However, after the Commission had also spoken out for a "far-reaching reform of European institutions in its position on the government conference,"[66] Fischer decided to go it alone: With a personal programmatic speech, he sought—in a way similar to Genscher in 1981 and 1987—to give European unification policy an impetus that would steer negotiations among the governments in the direction he desired.

In his speech at Berlin's Humboldt University on 12 May 2000, to whose preparation Jacques Delors and others had contributed, Fischer spoke dramatically of "probably the greatest challenge ever faced by the Union since its founding," and then called for nothing less than "the transition from the Union's grouping of states to full parliamentarization in a European federation." This was to be achieved by passage of a "European Constitutional Treaty," as Wolfgang Schäuble and Karl Lamers had proposed one year earlier.[67] Fischer termed this "a conscious political refounding act for Europe" to be accomplished "within the next decade" either by "a majority of member states" or by a "smaller group" that, as the "center of gravity," was ready "to advance" with political integration. As to which countries should belong to this group, Fischer—unlike Schäuble and Lamers—purposely did not name names; he also left open the issue of the relationship of the current government conference to the proposed act of foundation.[68]

---

66 KOM (2000) 34, 26 Jan. 2000.
67 Wolfgang Schäuble and Karl Lamers, "Europa braucht einen Verfassungsvertrag," in: *Frankfurter Allgemeine Zeitung*, 4 May 1999.
68 Joschka Fischer, "Vom Staatenbund zur Föderation – Gedanken über die Finalität der europäischen Integration," in: *Bulletin der Bundesregierung*, 24 May 2000, reprinted in among others: Wilfried Loth, *Entwürfe einer europäischen Verfassung. Eine historische Bilanz*, Bonn: Europa Union, 2002, pp. 241–252; on the origins, Fischer, *Die rot-grünen Jahre*, pp. 298–304.

Chirac actually responded very positively to Fischer's foray. In a speech to the German Bundestag on 27 June 2000 (now meeting in the Reichstag Building in Berlin), the French president committed himself to the principle of "common sovereignty" (a remarkably courageous step for a Gaullist) as well as to increased democratization and the expansion of majority decision-making. He then agreed to the creation of a "pioneer group," if only in the form of increased cooperation. Lastly, he also embraced the idea of a constitutional treaty. Here, he was more concrete than Fischer: This treaty was not to be worked out under the auspices of a government conference but instead soon thereafter with the inclusion of the people's representatives in the European Parliament and in the national parliaments.[69] Adjustments necessary for the expansion should not be delayed by lengthy disputes as to fundamental reform of the Union.

In the wake of this, some improvements in the Union's ability to act could be achieved at the government conference that had been meeting since 14 February 2000. According to the treaty completed in Nice in early December, the Commission president and the commissioners would in the future be elected by qualified-majority vote, likewise the High Representatives for Foreign Affairs and Security Policy as well as special representatives in the area of CFSP. The Commission president was to be able to decide on the division of responsibilities and be able to dismiss commissioners. In the future, majority decision-making was to be the practice in foreign economic policy as well as foreign and security policy, this latter area to feature the development of "common standpoints and actions" in cases of "increased cooperation." In the areas of the Structural and Cohesion Funds as well as the issuance of visas, immigration, and freedom of movement, majority decision-making was likewise to be introduced, though with the reservation that agreement be reached on the adoption of the next financial projection as well as regulations for entry and for immigration.

The rights of the European Parliament were also increased. Its right to participate within the framework of co-decision-making was extended to six new cases; in three new areas, its approval was now necessary. Yet, the extension of Parliament's rights did not keep pace with the expansion of majority decision-making. To the disappointment of MEPs, majority decision-making in areas relevant to finance was not linked to co-decision-making by Parliament. The instrument of "increased cooperation" was indeed extended to the area of foreign and security policy and its use was made easier (by reducing the minimum number of participating states to eight and by the possibly of deciding by qualified majority in the area of police and justice cooperation), but it could not be used for opening up new political areas or for altering the procedural rules in a particular polit-

---

69 The text in among others Bossuat, *Faire l'Europe*, pp. 513–520.

ical field. It was still not very appropriate for forming an avant-garde group. A "Charter of Fundamental Rights of the European Union," commissioned by the European Council in Cologne, was approved; but taking the opposition of the British government into account, it was not integrated into the treaty.[70]

It certainly would have been possible to achieve more clear progress and less of a confusing overall picture if Germany and France had been in agreement as to conference strategy. That was not the case, however. Instead, Schröder and Chirac engaged in a fierce battle over the weighting of votes in the Council of Ministers, hindering productive decisions until the final phase of the Council Meeting in Nice. With brutal openness, Schröder let Chirac know that the Federal Republic's population increase stemming from reunification must finally result in a higher vote weight in the Council; Chirac answered engagingly but also with determination that forsaking the principle of equal ranking for France and Germany was out of the question. The result, completed on the night of 10–11 December in an "abominable climate" (Chirac) consisted of preserving equal ranking but simultaneously granting the Federal Republic (and every other member state) the possibility of insisting on a majority of sixty-two percent of the total population of the Union. The "large" states (including Spain and Poland) were accorded a bare fifty percent higher weight than before; for the "smaller" states, there was a success via the introduction of the additional criterion of the "majority of the member states."[71]

Thus, a difficult-to-calculate threefold majority had been introduced without thoroughly rectifying the problem of deficiency in representation. The remaining disproportions between population and share of the vote created dissatisfaction among the disadvantaged members. Only Aznar and Poland (which was not even represented in Nice) could regard themselves as victors. Moreover, the lack of agreement among the "big ones" meant that there was no resolution to the problem of the Commission's ability to act: Germany, Britain, France, and Italy did dispense with having a second commissioner; but the other countries did not give up the principle that each nation be represented with one seat on the Commission. Only after the signing of the accession treaty of the twenty-seventh country (that is, after the successful conclusion of all ongoing entry negotiations) was the rotation principle for the composition of the Commission to be

---

[70] On the analysis of the Treaty of Nice, cf. Wilfried Loth, "Nach Nizza. Die Aufgaben der Europapolitik nach den Ergebnissen des Europäischen Rates in Nizza," in: *idem., Das europäische Projekt*, pp. 383–389; Mathias Jopp, Barbara Lippert, and Heinrich Schneider (eds.), *Das Vertragswerk von Nizza und die Zukunft der Europäischen Union*, Bonn: Europa Union, 2001; Werner Weidenfeld (ed.), *Nizza in der Analyse. Strategien für Europa*, Gütersloh: Bertelsmann Stiftung, 2001.

[71] With opposing assessments, cf. Fischer, *Die rot-grünen Jahre*, pp. 342–356 and Chirac, *Le temps présidentiel*, pp. 301–311, the quote on p. 310.

introduced. It remained open as to how many countries would then have to forego a seat on the Commission for a term.[72]

With the devastating impression that this conclusion of the government conference in Nice had made not only among many participants but also among the public and in the European Parliament, the progress that had been achieved on the Union's ability to act and its democratic oversight was largely missed. The "Declaration on the Future of the Union," with which the heads of state and of government announced a "more thorough and broader discussion about the future development of the European Union" as well as a further government conference for 2004,[73] appeared to be an admission of failure in the negotiations at Nice. In fact, it only put on the agenda of European politics that which Fischer had urged and Chirac had embraced.

The heads of state and of government additionally declared that the new treaty was to come into effect by the end of 2002, and they expressed the hope that the first new member states would be able to participate in elections to the European Parliament in June of 2004. For the candidate countries, a potential timeline had thereby been given for the first time. The Treaty of Nice was signed by the foreign ministers on 26 February 2001. Surprisingly, its ratification failed initially in Ireland, where the government had done little in the way of bringing together a majority for the referendum of 7 June 2001. A second referendum on 19 October, this time with massive support of the government, rectified that vote. On 1 February 2003, the Treaty of Nice was able to come into force.

In the decade after the signing of the Treaty of Maastricht, the EU had by and large succeeded with the essential steps of enlargement and deepening that were necessary after the collapse of the Soviet imperium. Once again, Helmut Kohl had played a large part in this success. Even with occasional Franco-German discord after the end of the Mitterrand era, one must not overlook the importance of Jacques Chirac's repeated success in going beyond the ideological shadow of the Gaullist tradition. Additionally, for the creation of a security-policy crisis instrument, the turns made by Tony Blair and Joschka Fischer were decisive. It was the case however that the plethora of differing individual regulations that the heads of state and of government accepted did to an extent void the progress in reducing the democratic deficit. As a consequence, the development of the European consciousness also lagged behind the Europeanization of ever more political fields.

---

72 Protocol 10 to Treaty of Nice, Article 4.
73 Vertrag von Nizza (Amtsblatt der Europäischen Gemeinschaften 2001/C 80/ 01), pp. 85–86.

8 Constitutional Struggle and Euro Crisis, 2001–2012

The Eastward Enlargement

No expansion of the designated financial resources was linked to the extension of accession negotiations to six further candidate countries that had been approved by the European Council in December of 1999 in Helsinki. As a result, countries of the first negotiation group, set up in December of 1997 in Luxembourg, reacted to the increased competition with something less than enthusiasm. At the same time, however, a "race to Brussels" also developed among the candidates: Each country now wanted to attain the status of readiness for entry as early as possible and thus secure the best conditions for that entry. The pace of reform in the countries of the first group, which had slackened after the success of Luxembourg, once again accelerated; and the countries of the Helsinki group made intensive efforts to catch up with the Luxembourg group.

Clearly, there was a danger of problematic setbacks in the modernization and democratization process in those countries relegated to the last place in the system of successive entries based on the principle of competition. It was especially in Poland and the Czech Republic, both of which were noticeably not at the forefront of reform measures, that opposition to entry under the conditions set by Brussels threatened to become insurmountable. Doubtful too was that there would be political majorities in all the existing member states for an expansion round without Polish or Czech participation. Hence, Enlargement Commissioner Günter Verheugen ventured a major effort: In a newspaper interview in October of 2000, he hinted at the possibility that ten countries could enter at the same time in the year 2004. He then presented to the European Council in Nice a roadmap for further accession negotiations that divided the various negotiation chapters among the next three Council presidencies and envisioned a conclusion of talks at the end of 2002.[1]

Many of the heads of state and of government regarded the entry of ten new members in 2004 as utopian. They did however accept the Commission road map

---

[1] Europäische Kommission: Strategiepapier zur Erweiterung. Bericht über die Fortschritte jedes Bewerberlandes auf dem Weg zum Beitritt 2000, KOM (2000) 700, 8 Nov. 2000. On this and the following, Graham Avery, "The Enlargement Negotiations," in: Fraser Cameron (ed.), *The future of Europe. Integration and Enlargement*, London and New York: Routledge, 2004, pp. 35–62; Verheugen, *Europa in der Krise*, pp. 83–103; Becker, *Die deutsche Europapolitik*, pp. 63–77 and 202–260.

and thereby sparked a competition among the Council presidents, firing their ambitions to complete the negotiation chapters assigned to them within their terms of office. And to a great extent, it did succeed. During the Swedish presidency in the first half of 2001, the chapters on freedom of movement, social policy, and environment (among other things) were negotiated. During the Belgian presidency in the second half of 2001, far-reaching agreement was achieved in the areas of agriculture, energy, as well as justice and domestic affairs.

In regard to the free movement of workers, which the bordering countries Germany, Austria, and Italy viewed with great concern, it proved possible to work out a complex compromise: For a transition period of initially two years, individual member states could limit access. If necessary, this could be extended for three years and for a final time for another two years. In the area of agriculture, there was broad agreement on production quotas and the promotion of rural development; in the case of seven countries, there was also the commitment to standards for protecting animals and plants. A multi-stage plan was agreed with Lithuania for shutting down the gigantic and highly-dangerous Soviet-era nuclear power plant Ignalina. With Verheugen acting as intermediary, the Czech Republic and Austria reached an agreement allowing the new nuclear power plant in Temelin—close to the Austrian border—to enter service but also requiring that it be subject to an environmental review one more time as well as a system of communication and cooperation across borders.

In its next progress report in November of 2001, the Commission projected—after a thoroughly-critical review of developments in the candidate countries—that if the then-current reform tempo were maintained, all the candidates except Romania and Bulgaria would be ready for accession by the end of 2002. Then, in a gathering at the Brussels Royal Palace of Laeken on 14 and 15 December 2001, the European Commission declared that Estonia, Poland, Slovenia, the Czech Republic, Hungary, and Cyprus as well as Lithuania, Latvia, Slovakia, and Malta should comprise the group for which negotiations were to be completed by the end of 2002. For Romania and Bulgaria, entry in 2007 was envisaged.

In order to achieve this negotiation goal, it was necessary to deal with some areas that were sensitive (because they were financially related): direct payments for the Common Agricultural Policy, promotion of structurally-weak regions, and participation of the new member states in the financing of the Community. It proved possible to neutralize struggles over inevitable apportionment thanks to the fact that the Council presidency in the first half year of 2002 had to be held by Spain. This meant that the Spanish government could no longer serve as the spokesman for those in the South who were protective of the status quo. Moreover, the governments of all the member and candidate countries were now condemned to success: After a common timetable for no fewer than ten accession candidates had become binding, no one could any longer risk taking the blame for the failure of the great accession project.

In late January of 2002, the Commission presented an apportionment proposal with 40.16 billion euros of additional resources for the years 2004 to 2006. This was admittedly somewhat below the financial framework agreed in Berlin in 1999, but with incremental incorporation of the new members into the system of direct subsidies of the Common Agricultural Policy, it opened the way for significant additional burdens in the future. In the first year of membership, farmers in the new member states were to receive twenty-five percent of that which was paid in older member states, thirty percent in the second year, and so on until one hundred percent was reached in 2013. As to regional structural promotion, the existing assessment ceilings for recognition of areas to be promoted were to be retained. Accordingly, all the countries entering (except Cyprus) would fall into the highest category ("Target 1"). Only the capital regions of Prague, Bratislava, and Budapest would fall within the limits of "Target 2" in terms of eligibility for assistance. A sum of 25.6 billion euros was earmarked for the first three years of assistance.

In the eyes of the net-payers Germany, Great Britain, Sweden, and the Netherlands, it was especially the inclusion of the new countries in the system of direct subsidies that went too far. Instead, they called for a reduction in direct subsidies for the old members as well, so as to free up additional resources for assistance to the new members. France opposed this, and so over the course of the first half of 2002, a severe Franco-German dispute developed over agricultural reform. It was resolved only via a meeting between Schröder and Chirac in the run-up to the Brussels Council of 24 and 25 October 2002: Germany now accepted the direct payments to the new members. However, the total expenditure for direct payments and for the organization of markets was frozen until 2013 at the (high) level of 2006. The incremental incorporation of the new member states thereby implied an incremental reduction of the payments in the old states from 2007 onward. Furthermore, Chirac finally conceded in the struggle over greater weighting of German votes in the Council of Ministers.[2] On the basis of this compromise, the Council was able to make the policy decision for acceptance of the ten applicant countries on 25 October. In the process, the maximum contribution for the Structural and Cohesion Fund was reduced from 25.6 to 23 billion euros. The annual inflation adjustment of 1.5 percent that Schröder had conceded to Chirac for the assessment of the agricultural budget from 2007 onward was reduced to one percent in the face of stubborn insistence from Dutch Prime Minister Jan-Pieter Balkenende.

---

2 Chirac, *Le temps présidentiel*, pp. 526.

The accession candidates were visibly disappointed by the outcome of the struggle over the apportionment of the resources for assistance. It was especially Polish Prime Minister Leszek Miller, being pushed by his coalition partner the Farmer's Party, who fought back strongly against a situation in which (due to the complex regulations for requesting structural resources) his country was threatened with becoming a net payer right from the beginning of its membership in the Community. The governments of the Fifteen initially accommodated the concerns of the Ten by postponing the envisioned accession date from 1 January to 1 May 2004; by this means, four months' contributions could be saved during the first year of membership. At the concluding Council meeting on 12 and 13 December 2002 in Copenhagen, Poland and the Czech Republic were accorded special cash-flow facilities for a transition period, which would be financed from the budget for structural assistance; this arrangement stemmed from a mediation proposal made by Schröder. The structural policy budget was reduced still further to 21.7 billion euros. Likewise, the new member countries were allowed the possibility of increasing the annual direct-payment quotas through the year 2006, though at the cost of resources earmarked for rural structural assistance. Poland was additionally granted higher milk-production quotas.[3]

Due to the increase in agricultural production quotas and the allocation of additional funds for the complete incorporation of the new countries into the Schengen area as well as securing the new external border of the Union, the total cost of obligations and payments for the new countries rose to 40.85 billion euros. Nonetheless, that figure was 10 billion lower than the highest contribution level agreed upon in Berlin. To that extent, the calculus of the Commission had been successful, having created maneuvering room for negotiation solutions by means of a lower proposal. The shifting of structural assistance into consumption—further increased by the concessions made in Copenhagen—was problematic in regard to the success of the integration process of the former planned economies. That represented the price to be paid politically for avoiding a situation in which entry into the Common Market was allowed to fail due to modernization anxieties stirred up at the last minute.

On 9 April 2003, the European Parliament approved the entry of each individual country with over ninety percent of the vote in each case. Then, the accession treaty was signed by twenty-five heads of state and of government along with their foreign ministers in a solemn ceremony in the Stoa of Attalos, the ancient marketplace at the foot of the Acropolis in Athens. Owing to the many transition

---

3 Cf. Barbara Lippert, "Erweiterungspolitik der Europäischen Union," in: *Jahrbuch der Europäischen Integration 2002/2003*, pp. 417–430; Peter Ludlow, *The Making of the New Europe. The European Councils in Brussels and Copenhagen 2002*, Brussels: EuroComment, 2004.

regulations, unilateral declarations, and exchanges of correspondence, the treaty comprised almost five thousand pages bound in two thick folios. In part, these additions concerned basics such as restrictions on the free movement of labor for up to seven years and restrictions on purchasing agricultural and forest land in the new countries for seven years (in Poland for no less than twelve years). There were also declarations regarding very specific interests such as the possibility of the continued hunting of brown bears in Estonia and the protection of the domestic honey bee breed in Slovenia. The entry of the new countries into the Schengen Area was made dependent on a later vote of the European Council; envisaged for October of 2007, it would actually take place only a year later. As to entry into the euro area, the same criteria and procedures used for the founding members were to apply to the new countries. The first new member to join the monetary union was Slovenia on 1 January 2007. One year later, there followed Cyprus and Malta; a year after that, Slovakia; and Estonia on 1 January 2011.

Overall, the many transition regulations ensured that opposition to the great expansion was meager in the existing EU member countries and remained below the critical threshold in the applicant countries as well. In the parliaments of the old members, only a few deputies voted against the accession of the new members. In the referenda held in all entering countries except Cyprus, the approval rate varied between fifty-four percent in Malta, which was divided as to European politics, and ninety-two percent in Slovakia. In Poland and the Czech Republic, more than seventy-seven percent of voters gave their approval, whereas in Hungary it was eighty-four percent.

Memories of the energy-sapping struggle over the terms for Eastward expansion faded into the background at the special summit of the twenty-five heads of state and of government held on 1 May 2004 at Phoenix Castle some twenty miles from Dublin. "I saw many a teary eye this afternoon in Ireland," reported Verheugen, "No one at this moment was thinking of milk quotas, internal-market regulations, or convergence programs." What prevailed was satisfaction over the Community achievement, in which outstanding politicians of the old as well as the new member countries, such as Danish Prime Minister Anders Fogh Rasmussen as Council president during the last negotiation period and Polish President Alexander Kwasniewski, had had their share, just as Prodi and Verheugen did too. And there was a sense for the symbolic meaning of the day: "This is Europe's triumph over the twentieth century," was how Latvian Foreign Minister Sandra Kalniete formulated it; she was to become one of the first members of the EU Commission from the former Soviet imperium.[4]

---

4 Verheugen, *Europa in der Krise*, pp. 63, 68.

The self-confidence and solidarity of the network of expansion strategies that had developed here rubbed off on the European institutions. After representatives of the new member states had already been participating in the work of Parliament and the Council of Ministers as "active observers" since the signing of the accession treaty, the Commission was expanded by ten new members on 1 May 2004. As in the case of Latvia, it was predominantly experienced European politicians of the rank of minister or top-level civil servant who transferred to the Commission. The new countries had been represented in a normal manner in the European Parliament since the elections of 10 to 13 May 2004. It was the case however that the euphoria over the successful expansion did not go far enough to have Borislaw Geremek elected president of the European Parliament. This prominent Polish historian, longtime advisor to the Solidarity Movement and foreign minister from 1997 to 2000, had been put up by the liberal faction but lost in the first round of voting on 20 July owing to the now-traditional arrangement between the two largest factions, the European People's Party and the Socialists. Spanish Socialist Josep Borrell was elected president for the first two and a half years of the new legislative period and was to be followed by the Christian Democrat Hans-Gert Pöttering in 2007.

Only to a very limited extent did the population in the old as well as the new member countries join in the euphoria over the clear success of the reunification of Europe. It was too seldom recognized that the path into the European Community contributed significantly to stabilizing an order based on democracy and rule of law and to promoting prosperity in the post-Communist countries. Instead, there lingered diffuse anxieties in the older member countries over low-wage competition in the employment market, unforeseeable funding commitments, and a Union of twenty-five or even twenty-seven members being ungovernable. In the new member countries, conflicts continued between winners and losers of the transformation; and the tendency to revert to buried nationalist conceptions also remained strong. There was little understanding of the mechanisms of the Union and thus also of the implications of accession, which large majorities had approved.

Hence, the tension between European and Europeanizing elites on the one hand and large segments of the population of the member states on the other continued with a changed emphasis. Gains in European élan on the one side were offset by increasing nationalist reflexes on the other. In the elections to the European Parliament in May of 2004, the participation rate in the old member countries rose to 52.6 percent *vis-à-vis* the 1999 level of 49.4 percent. In the new member countries, however, the average turnout was 31.2 percent of those eligible. This was in part due to unfamiliarity with the new institutions, together with the tendency to punish those parties that had successfully managed the accession negotiations.

What the architects of the great enlargement could not do was overcome the division of Cyprus. Initially, the leader of the Turkish ethnic group in the north, Rauf Denktaş, had opposed giving back land to Greeks who had fled to the south during the war of 1974. Then, when a majority of Turkish Cypriots became convinced that their economic problems could only be resolved by membership in the EU, the view became dominant among Greek Cypriots that the plan for the unification of both halves of the island in a federation—as presented by UN General Secretary Kofi Annan—granted too many special rights to the Turkish minority. In the referendum of 24 April 2004, the Annan Plan was approved by 64.9 percent of Turkish Cypriots and rejected by 75.8 percent of Greek Cypriots. This was much to the disappointment of the Commission, which had hoped to be able to use the accession application by the Greek Cypriot government as a means of promoting reunification of the island. Accordingly, the residents of the northern part were regarded as citizens of the EU; but the *acquis communautaire* could only be applied in the southern part for the time being. Exports from the northern part of the island to other EU countries remained dependent upon approval from Greek-Cypriot authorities, so that pledges of support from the EU Council of Ministers for accession of the north to the south could only be partially obtained.[5]

In the negotiations with Bulgaria and Romania, the same criteria were used that had already been in effect for the "Ten." In the process, it became apparent that Bulgaria was making more progress than its northern neighbor in terms of ability to participate in the market, rule of law, and administrative organization. The bitter poverty of Romania, the destruction of its civil society by the Ceauşescu regime, as well as the high level of criminality and corruption resulting from it presented challenges that would not be easily overcome. In February of 2004, the reporter of the European Parliament therefore called for the Commission to suspend talks with Romania for the time being. Whereas all negotiation chapters for Bulgaria could be provisionally concluded in June of 2004, the accession of Romania was threatened with postponement until 2008.

The especially difficult negotiation chapters on competitiveness as well as justice and domestic affairs could be finalized with Romania only on 8 December 2004. The Commission thereupon took a positive position on the Romanian application as well on 22 February 2005, and the Council approved the accession treaty with both Bulgaria and Romania on 25 April 2005. Immediately thereafter,

---

5 Cf. Heinz-Jürgen Axt, "Zypern: Mitglied der Europäischen Union, aber weiterhin geteilt," in: Rudolf Hrbek (ed.), *Die zehn neuen EU-Mitgliedsländer. Spezifika und Profile*, Baden-Baden: Berliner Wissenschaftsverlag, 2006, pp. 115–130; Verheugen, *Europa in der Krise*, pp. 83ff. and 93ff.

the document was signed by all twenty-seven contracting parties in Luxembourg. In order to take into account reservations as to Romania's readiness for entry, a protective clause was added whereby a postponement of the treaty's effective date from 1 January 2007 to 1 January 2008 was stipulated in the event the Council determined that severe deficiencies in the areas of competitiveness or justice and domestic affairs had not yet been eliminated; the decision was to be based on the Commission's Monitoring Reports. In the case of Bulgaria, a unanimous vote of the Council would be necessary for postponement, whereas for Romania a qualified majority would suffice.[6]

In its Monitoring Report of 26 September 2006, the Commission chided Bulgaria for lagging in the passage of laws and revision of its constitution. The lack of sweeping successes in combating corruption and organized crime was attested in both countries. However, the Commission could not bring itself to recommend postponing accession. Instead, it proposed continued oversight for three years after entry and mandated semi-annual progress reports from the countries. If they did not meet their commitments, they would be threatened with having their judgments and judicial decisions go unrecognized. Additionally, a mechanism was to be created for punishing deficiencies in the administration of EU agricultural funds. The Council approved these recommendations on 17 October 2006, such that the accession of Bulgaria and Romania could in fact take place on 1 January 2007. The package for financing their entry in the years 2007 to 2009, which the Council had already agreed upon in March of 2004, amounted to an additional 15.4 billion euros.[7]

Both of these new members certainly remained the problem children of the Eastward enlargement. In 2009, the monitoring system was extended indefinitely. In Romania, the fight against corruption and criminality was hindered by ongoing power struggles between President Traian Băsescu, elected in November of 2004, and changing prime ministers. In July of 2011, the Commission confirmed "significant steps" by the Romanian government in the reform of justice and the investigation of cases of corruption, even at the highest level.[8] Then in May of 2012, when incoming Social Democratic head of government Victor Ponta sought to rule by decree and remove Băsescu from office, the implementation of reforms was once again called into question. "Among us, there are cliques carry-

---

[6] Barbara Lippert, "Erweiterungspolitik der Europäischen Union," in: *Jahrbuch der Europäischen Integration 2005*, pp. 425–434; Anneli Ute Gabanyi, "Rumänien," *ibid.*, pp. 441–444.
[7] Barbara Lippert, "Die Erweiterungspolitik der Europäischen Union," in: *Jahrbuch der Europäischen Integration 2007*, pp. 423–434.
[8] Europäische Kommission: Bericht über den Fortschritt Rumäniens im Rahmen des Kooperations- und Kontrollverfahrens, KOM (2011) 460 endgültig.

ing on a battle of life and death to conquer the state and plunder it," commented EU anti-corruption advisor Alina Mungiu-Pippidi.[9]

The experience with Bulgaria and Romania, along with some minor difficulties in the new European work apportionment and with the new competitors contributed to skepticism regarding further applications for entry. This was especially the case with the western Balkan states, to which the European Council in Thessaloniki in June of 2003 had conceded a "European prospect." Croatia had submitted an application as early as February of 2003. It was followed by Macedonia's in March of 2004, Montenegro's in December of 2008, Albania's in April of 2009, and Serbia's in December of that year. In April of 2004, the Commission certified that Croatia was fundamentally capable of accession; after a delay due to insufficient cooperation on the part of Croatian authorities with the International Criminal Court for the former Yugoslavia, negotiations began in October of 2005. The Commission—now under the presidency of José Manuel Barroso of Portugal and with Olli Rehn of Finland as enlargement commissioner—developed an incremental process that made the beginning of accession negotiations explicitly dependent on the fulfillment of preconditions: Initially, there was to be a review to determine if the preconditions for the conclusion of a Stability and Association Agreement (SAA) existed; then, if the commitments of the SAA were adhered to, the status of candidate for accession would be awarded. Entry negotiations were to begin only after there had been significant progress on economic and *acquis* criteria.[10]

Macedonia was accorded candidate status in December of 2005, and in October of 2009, the Commission recommended that accession talks be started. In the Council, however, this recommendation was blocked by Greece: The Athens government insisted that the Republic of Macedonia change its name such that any claim to Macedonian areas of Greece would be excluded: Up to that point, a formulation acceptable to both sides had not been found. Montenegro received candidate status in December of 2010, and entry negotiations began in June of 2012. Serbia had been declared a candidate in March of that year, and entry negotiations started in January 2014. Albania has up to this point not yet gone beyond the status of an associated state, however. Bosnia-Herzegovina and Kosovo, which have not yet submitted applications for accession, are still in the run-up to a Stability and Association Agreement. Impulses for negotiation in the

---

9 Quoted from the *Westfälische Nachrichten*, 22 Aug. 2012.
10 Europäische Kommission: Strategiepapier zur Erweiterung, KOM (2005) 561 endgültig, 9 Nov. 2005. Cf. Barbara Lippert, "Die Erweiterungspolitik der Europäischen Union," in: *Jahrbuch der Europäischen Integration 2006*, pp. 429–440.

neighboring states Austria and Greece have proven too weak to unleash a stronger integration dynamic in the Balkan States.

The Commission sought to respond to the languishing integration dynamic in the Western Balkans by seeking a breakthrough in negotiations with Croatia in 2009. This plan was however thwarted when Slovenia blocked the opening of the last twelve negotiation chapters with reference to the conflict between Slovenia and Croatia over the course of the border in the Adriatic. Only after the Slovenian government in September of 2009 had—under pressure from the Swedish Council presidency—declared its willingness to leave the final settlement of the border to an international court of arbitration could negotiations then enter the final phase. Here, it was especially the governments of the Netherlands, Denmark, and Great Britain that once again stepped on the brakes because they still perceived significant deficits in justice, the fight against corruption and criminality, as well as cooperation with the tribunal in The Hague. On 11 June 2011, however, Commission President Barroso was able to declare the negotiations completed. The accession took place on 1 July 2013.[11]

While the expansion in the Balkans suffered due to the painful aftereffects of inherited ethnic conflicts and significant lack of a democratic tradition, it was the case with Turkey that concerns increasingly arose over the cultural compatibility of a state shaped by Islam and over the Community's capacity to absorb it. Critics of the country's entry repeatedly pointed out that in 2013 Turkey's population of seventy-nine million was about as large as all ten of the countries that had entered in 2004; but it was expected to have only half the combined economy of those ten members.[12] The accession of Turkey would mean "the end of the European Union," as former French President Giscard d'Estaing warned in *Le Monde* in November of 2002.[13]

The reforms that the Turkish political system had brought itself to undertake in the period from 2002 to 2004 thus did not have the hoped-for success. In August of 2002, the Turkish National Assembly voted for the permanent abolition of the death penalty (which notably meant not executing PKK leader Abdullah Öcalan), approval of the Kurdish language in radio and television programming and also in private educational institutions, the right of religious minorities to purchase land, as well as the admission of liaison offices of foreign non-governmental organizations. After the electoral victory of the conservative-religious Justice Party (AKP) in November of 2002, new Prime Minister Recep Tayyip Erdoğan achieved

---

11 *Ibid.*, 2011, pp. 503–516; Sisina Kusic, "Kroatien," *ibid.*, pp. 513–516.
12 Cf. for example Wolfgang Quaisser and Alexandra Reppegather, *EU-Beitrittsreife der Türkei und Konsequenzen einer EU-Mitgliedschaft*, Munich: Working Papers, 2004.
13 *Le Monde*, 9 Nov. 2002.

a fundamental liberalization of Turkish criminal law and the "civilianizing" of the National Security Council, which up to that point had been dominated by the military. Moreover, he brought about a transformation in Turkey's policy on Cyprus: From the winter of 2003–2004 onward, the reunification of the island on the basis of the Annan Plan was supported by Turkey.

After contentious internal discussion, the Commission found in its progress report of 6 October 2004 "that Turkey fulfills the political criteria to a satisfactory extent" and recommended the opening of negotiations on accession. No concrete date for this was specified, however. Instead, the Commission announced stepped-up oversight of the reform process, made mention of the possibility of the suspension of negotiations, and emphasized "that this is an open-ended process whose outcome cannot be guaranteed in advance." It declared that a conclusion could only come after decision-making on the financial preview for the period from 2014 onward. Additionally, the accession treaty was to have long transition regulations and perhaps even indefinite protective clauses in regard to the free movement of labor, for example.[14] After further contentious discussion, the European Council in a Brussels meeting of 16 and 17 December 2004 opted for beginning negotiations on 3 October 2005. It insisted however that the measures on the reform of criminal law be implemented beforehand and that a supplementary agreement for harmonizing the Customs Union between Turkey and the Community with the ten new members be signed as well. Indirectly, the Council thereby made the recognition of the new EU member Cyprus by Turkey a precondition for the actual start of negotiations.[15]

Of necessity, the Erdoğan government agreed to sign the additional protocol to the Treaty of Ankara. Under domestic pressure over the prospect of becoming a second-class member, however, the Turkish government declared at the signing on 29 July 2005 that this action was not be regarded as recognition of the Republic of Cyprus. It therefore did not apply the protocol to Cyprus; that is, Turkish ports and airports remained closed to ships and aircraft from the Republic of Cyprus. This did indeed allow the opening of talks on 3 October 2005 as planned. An attempt by the Austrian government to write into the negotiation framework a mere "partnership" as an alternative goal was derailed at the last moment. Yet, after the Turkish government stood firm in its position of not applying the addi-

---

14 Europäische Kommission: Empfehlung der Europäischen Kommission zu den Fortschritten der Türkei auf dem Weg zum Beitritt, KOM (2004) 656 endgültig, 6 Oct. 2004.
15 European Council: Presidency Conclusions, Brussels, 16-17 Dec. 2004. Cf. Peter Ludlow, *Dealing with Turkey. The European Council of 16–17 December 2004*, Brussels: EuroComment, 2005; Barbara Lippert, "Die Türkei als Sonderfall und Wendepunkt der klassischen EU-Erweiterungspolitik," in: *Integration* 28 (2005), pp. 119–135.

tional protocol even after the "screening" phase of negotiations, the EU Council of Ministers decided on 11 December 2006 to suspend talks on all chapters directly linked to the Customs Union and therefore affecting the economic core of the Community.

A spectacular failure of negotiations was thereby avoided. The reform dynamic in Turkey nevertheless waned, and the date of possible entry into the EU retreated ever further into the future. German Chancellor Angela Merkel, in office since September of 2005, assessed the strategic necessity of Turkish EU membership significantly lower than had her predecessor. Chirac's successor Nikolas Sarkozy, elected in May of 2007, even spoke out explicitly against Turkish membership as a goal of negotiations. He vetoed the opening of five further negotiation chapters (economic and monetary union, Common Agricultural Policy, regional policy, institutions, and budget) that he viewed as favorable to membership. Additionally, Cyprus blocked the opening of the chapters on energy as well as education and culture. Up to 2012, only thirteen of thirty-five chapters were able to be opened; only one chapter (science and research) could be provisionally concluded.[16]

After Erdoğan's major victory in parliamentary elections in June of 2011, Turkish politicians began to search for alternatives to EU membership due to the stagnation in negotiations. Trade relations with the growing economies of the Middle East, Central Asia, and North Africa were expanded, the ambition grew for creating a regional power that could act autonomously, and legal harmonization with EU norms was postponed indefinitely due to the high costs involved. When in the second half of 2012 the Cypriot government took its turn chairing the EU Council, Ankara even implemented a temporary freeze in relations with the EU. This history of Turkey's approach to Europe is not thereby at an end, but its progress is however highly uncertain.

Whereas the issue of Turkish membership remained open, a consensus gradually emerged in the EU that for the foreseeable future no prospect of membership should be offered to any other countries undergoing transformation. Instead, economic development and democratic structures should be promoted by means of financial and technical assistance along with granting market access, as the Commission had envisioned since 2004 within the framework of the "European Neighborhood Policy." Relations with the sixteen countries for which this program was conceived have up to now developed in very different ways; agreement on a coherent strategy has not yet been reached. In 2008, at Sarkozy's urging, a "Union for the Mediterranean" was created with the goal of

---

16 *Jahrbuch der Europäischen Integration 2006*, pp. 431–435; *ibid.*, 2007, pp. 425–429; *ibid.*, 2008, pp. 454–458; *ibid.*, 2009, pp. 448–450; *ibid.*, 2010, pp. 468–471; *ibid.*, 2011, p. 507ff.

promoting regional cooperation among Mediterranean neighbors. In 2009, at the initiative of Sweden and Poland, there followed an "Eastern Partnership" that included Belarus, Ukraine, Moldavia, Armenia, Georgia, and Azerbaijan. The possibilities of neighborhood policies have been used to the greatest extent by Ukraine, Moldova, and Georgia. Up to this point, however, these countries have hoped in vain for any prospect of accession.[17]

In contrast, the institutions of the EU and the governments of the member states had no problem in positively receiving the accession application of Iceland, submitted to the chair of the European Council on 16 July 2009. The small island nation in the North Atlantic had decided on this step after the financial collapse of 2008 brought its government to the verge of bankruptcy. A majority of Icelanders believed that the financial turbulence could only be overcome via membership in the Eurozone. To accomplish this, they were prepared to accept reductions in the exclusive use of their fishing grounds. Given that Iceland had already been integrated into the European Economic Area since 1994 and had additionally joined the Schengen Agreement in 2001, the complete adoption of the *acquis communautaire* seemed relatively unproblematic to arrange. Entry negotiations began on 27 July 2010 and made rapid progress.[18] After the massive devaluation of the Icelandic króna had helped the fishing and tourism industries get back on their feet, however, the attitude of the descendants of the Vikings changed over the course of 2012. Following the victory of the conservative Independence Party in parliamentary elections in May 2013 the new government suspended the negotiations for an indefinite time.

With the conclusion of the expansion project of 1999, the signs thus predominantly pointed toward consolidation of the EU 28. This was and will be rightfully seen as the prerequisite for having the Union remain capable of acting and for having its interests on the European and international stages to be appropriately represented.

The Constitutional Treaty

There had been fears, primarily in France, that the Union would become incapable of acting after the great expansion; yet it did not turn out that way. This was above all attributable to the talks over further treaty reform, approved by

---

[17] Karin Böttger, *Die Entstehung und Entwicklung der europäischen Nachbarschaftspolitik. Akteure und Koalitionen*, Baden-Baden: Nomos, 2010.
[18] Burkhard Steppacher, "Island," in: *Jahrbuch der Europäischen Integration* 2010, pp. 479ff. and *ibid.*, 2011, pp 511ff.

the European Council in Nice in 2000, and running parallel to negotiations on accession.

In preparing for the government conference of 2004, France and Germany once again worked closely together. Given the hangover from the disastrous impression that their confrontation during the Nice summit had left, Chirac and Schröder very quickly came to agreement that they would in future meet every six to eight weeks on very intimate terms, accompanied only by their foreign ministers, to discuss ongoing problems of European politics over dinner. At the first of these meetings, held at Chirac's initiative on 31 January 2001 in the Alsatian town of Blaesheim near Strasbourg, the two leaders agreed to work out a joint position in preparing for the government conference. This did not come about as quickly as anticipated however because Foreign Minister Herbert Védrine was anxious not to give up control over the reform process. On 31 May, the European Parliament voiced its support for organizing the preparations for the government conference in the form of a convention following the model and the division of mandates of the Convention on Fundamental Rights. Chirac and Schröder then pushed through the vote for a convention and for the development of a constitution as a joint position. In a joint resolution issued at the seventy-eighth Franco-German summit on 23 November in Nantes, they proclaimed their resolve "to seek agreement consistently and persistently on all issues that will arise from the activity of the convention."[19]

Belgian Prime Minister Guy Verhofstadt could thus be sure of support from Chirac and Schröder when as Council president in the second half of 2001 he sought suggestions from the governments for institutional reform of the Union. These were to be discussed at a convention made up of representatives of the governments, the national parliaments, the European Parliament, and the Commission. He also advocated giving the reform the character of a constitutionalization. In order to structure the talks, he presented to the European Council in the Laeken district of Brussels on 14 and 15 December 2001 a catalogue of no fewer than sixty-seven questions on which the convention was to take a position. The convention's talks were to begin on 1 March 2002 and be completed within a year. It was to meet publicly and to be open to input from civil society.

Verhofstadt's proposal to charge the convention with the development of a single draft constitution that would then be binding to a great degree on the subsequent government conference could not win acceptance at Laeken. After contentious discussion, it remained an open question in the "Laeken Declaration" as to whether several alternative drafts could be available at the end of the

---

[19] *Internationale Politik* 67 (2002), p. 101. On the initiation of the Blaesheim process, also Chirac, *Le temps présidentiel*, p. 311.

talks. In other respects, however, the heads of state and of government accepted the Belgian proposal, including the composition of the convention (one representative per government, two per national parliament, sixteen members of the European Parliament, two representatives of the Commission, along with representatives of the governments and of the parliaments of the candidate countries in an advisory capacity). They also accepted the strong position of the convention president, who was to produce an initial working basis for the convention and "evaluate" the public debate in the plenum for each successive session.[20]

Valéry Giscard d'Estaing became the president of the convention. The former president of France had since late September insistently put his name in play for this office, and Chirac supported him—firstly, because Chirac wanted to see a French person hold the position and, secondly, because he hoped to be able to neutralize a potential opponent in his own re-election bid. When Schröder immediately concurred with Chirac's choice, no other candidate had a chance— neither Jacques Delors, who had hesitated all too long, nor Dutch Prime Minister Wim Kok, nor his former Italian college Giuliano Amato, whom the leaders of the smaller member countries, among them Verhofstadt, would have preferred. In the end, the nomination of Giscard was unanimous after Verhofstadt had proposed adding two vice presidencies and had also put forward Amato and former Belgian Prime Minister Jean-Luc Dehaene for those posts. Amato and Dehaene, a Socialist and a Christian Democrat respectively, were also nominated unanimously.[21]

The convention took up its work on 28 February 2002. Rather than being led by its president, it was *de facto* under the leadership of a twelve-person presidium that consisted of representatives of all member groups. Giscard certainly had his own ideas as to how the convention was to be run and to what results it should come; in the nonpublic debates of the presidium however he occasionally had to defer to the better argument. Klaus Hänsch, one of the two representatives of the European Parliament on the presidium, confirmed that the seventy-six-year-old president exhibited an "astounding combination of leadership ability and willingness to learn."[22] The presidium succeeded with its proposal that the conven-

---

[20] Erklärung von Laeken zur Zukunft der Europäischen Union, among others in: Daniel Göler, *Die neue europäische Verfassungsdebatte. Entwicklungsstand und Optionen für den Konvent*, Bonn: Europa Union, 2002, pp. 112–122. Cf. *idem.*, "Der Gipfel von Laeken. Erste Etappe auf dem Weg zu einer europäischen Verfassung?" in: *Integration* 25 (2002), pp. 99–110; Peter Ludlow, *The Laeken Council*, Brussels: EuroComment, 2002; Fischer, *Die rot-grünen Jahre*, pp. 357–360.
[21] Didier Pavy, "Giscard: retour par l'extérieur," in: *Le Nouvel Observateur*, 20 Dec. 2001.
[22] Hänsch, *Kontinent*, p. 166. On the work of the convention, *ibid.*, pp. 161–205; Alain Lamassoure, *Histoire secrète de la Convention européenne*, Paris: Albin Michel, 2003; Andrew Duff, *The Struggle for Europe's Constitution*, London: Federal Trust for Education and Research, 2007; Peter Norman, *The Accidental Constitution. The Story of the European Convention*, Brussels:

tion commit itself to seeking consensus. This meant that instead of having the plenum vote on differing proposals, the president would in the end determine where the consensus on an issue lay. Consensus was to be determined by that which had not met with "considerable opposition" in any member group. What exactly constituted "considerable opposition" was left to the discretion of the president.

In fact, opposition needed to be watched especially when it came from of the ranks of the governments. The convention was programmed to reach a compromise that could not be called into question by the subsequent government conference. The process ensured that at the end there would not be several drafts but rather only one—a draft behind which there stood something more than a slim majority. Such a draft could not be sidestepped by the governments. Foreseeable opposition by individual governments to individual points would thereby be isolated; the veto power of each government, which had made previous government conferences so arduous, thus tended to be devalued. Compromise no longer amounted to the least common denominator but rather constituted that which was genuinely achievable with common sense in light of actual power relations.

In order to have time enough to find consensus, the presidium approved an additional three months' work time for the convention right at the beginning. The results were however to be available for the European Council in June of 2003. Nevertheless, the exchange among working committees, led by a member of the presidium, in meetings with member groups and with families of political parties had progressed so far in the plenum and in the presidium that Giscard d'Estaing could present the presidium with a first skeleton of the draft treaty by October of 2002.

This outline foresaw the dissolution of previous treaties on the European Union and the European Community as well as the replacement of the three-pillar structure of Maastricht with a unified treaty. A first section would describe the principles, the organs, and the processes. The Charter of Fundamental Rights approved in Nice would follow as a second section. A third would consist of the previous treaty contents regarding the three pillars, including process modifications. The treaty was to be termed a "constitution" regardless of the fact that it would be approved by the states involved and would not rest upon the vote of the European people. For the first time, there would also be provision for the possibility of an exit from the Union.[23] Some individual participants such as Hänsch

---

EuroComment, 2003; Mathias Jopp and Saskia Matl, "Perspektiven der deutsch-französischen Konventsvorschläge für die institutionelle Architektur der Europäischen Union," in: *Integration* 26 (2003), pp. 99–110; as well as the contributions in *Integration* 26 (2003), vol. 4, pp. 283–575.
23 Preliminary draft Constitutional Treaty, 28 Oct. 2002, CONV 369/02.

had concerns about employing the constitution concept, thinking that it might give impetus to criticism of a presumed "superstate"; but Giscard knew how to push such concerns aside.

With the presentation of the outlines of a constitutional treaty on 28 October, the character of the convention's work changed. Whereas up to that point skepticism had predominated as to whether the convention would bring forth anything more than nonbinding declarations of intent, now it seemed that it actually would be in a position to predetermine the future character of the Union to a great extent. Hence, the governments now increasingly sought to influence the results of the talks. Foreign minister Joschka Fischer took over the representation of the German government in the convention himself; SPD General Secretary Peter Glotz had earlier held that position. Chirac's new Foreign Minister Dominique de Villepin replaced Europe Minister Pierre Moscovici, who had been appointed by the Socialist government of Lionel Jospin. The French and German governments then submitted a series of joint positions to the convention.

The compromises that they had to accept in so doing primarily affected the configuration of the executive of the Union. Whereas Chirac had initially joined Giscard in supporting the appointment of a fulltime president of the European Council, who could access the executive powers of the Commission, the German government along with those of most of the smaller states advocated the election of the Commission president by the European Parliament and his assignment as chairman in the European Council. The compromise consisted essentially in that the German government now also backed the introduction of a fulltime president; however, he was to be elected for only two-and-a-half years (with the possibility of one re-election). Also, he would not be able to encroach upon the purview of the Commission. The convention revised the election process of the Commission president by Parliament (which was now acceptable to France) by stipulating that it take place at the recommendation of the European Council. However, the Council was to make its recommendation while "taking into account the elections to the European Parliament."[24]

The German proposal to assign the Commissioner for External Relations the chairmanship of the Council for External Relations and Defense and so to become the "foreign minister" of the Union was modified: The foreign minister named by the European Council with the approval of the Commission president would at the same time be a member of the Commission. He would be solely responsible for initiatives in the areas of foreign policy; the Commission would no longer hold that authority collectively. As a vice president of the Commission, however, he would also be intimately involved into the work of the Commission. The Direc-

---

24 Article I-26 of the draft Constitution.

torate-General for External Relations and the foreign-policy areas of the Council Secretariat were to be combined in one European Diplomatic Service. The Franco-German demand for majority decision-making in foreign policy (but not for military or defense-policy aspects) failed once again in the face of British opposition. The advocates of a more effective foreign policy only won the possibility of increased cooperation among a core group of states extending to all areas of CFSP and ESDP, along with the establishment of higher hurdles for blocking it by individual members.

The role of the European Parliament as a legislature was further strengthened—above all by abolishing the distinction between obligatory and nonobligatory expenditures, a proposal made by the Benelux states. This meant that the agricultural budget, the largest item in the budget, was now in the area of co-equal legislation. In the future, Parliament was to collaborate in ninety-two political areas rather than only thirty; in some seventy of those areas, it was now to be on an equal footing with the Council of Ministers, rather than only thirty as heretofore. The scope of the budget was still to be determined by the Council of Ministers on a unanimous basis. Its apportionment was however to be made by majority decision and a parliamentary majority would also be needed.

Following upon a Franco-German proposal, meetings of the Council of Ministers were to be public insofar as the body acted in a legislative capacity; and "as a rule" it was to decide by qualified majority. However, fearing that otherwise the whole treaty would be blocked by some governments, majority rule would be breached not only in regard to foreign policy. Other areas that would continue to require unanimity were decisions on the system and upper limit of financial resources, important measures in the realms of domestic affairs and justice policy (harmonization of penal law, creation of a European attorney general, police cooperation) and sensitive areas of trade policy (services in the realms of culture, radio and television, social policy, education, and health). At Germany's behest, the choice of various sources of energy was still to remain at the national level.

After Chirac had given up his resistance to more strongly taking into account the demographic factor in the weighting of votes in the Council, the principle of double majority (that is, majority of the member states plus majority of the population) could be put through. It was indeed the case that the representative of Spain in the presidium sought to defend the settlement made in Nice, which was significantly more favorable to both Spain and Poland; in so doing, however, he ended up more and more isolated. At the end of a stormy session of the presidium in late May of 2003, Giscard d'Estaing determined shortly before midnight that there was consensus on the formulation "majority of the member states, which represented at least three fifths of the population of the Union."[25] There was no further attempt in the plenum to call this result into question.

Still more intense was the controversy over the issue of the size of the Commission. Whereas Giscard and most of the representatives of the larger countries spoke in favor of a significant reduction in the number of seats on the Commission, the representatives of the smaller countries persisted in their position that each member state must appoint one commissioner, especially in light of the decision for a fulltime president. In the end, Giscard voted for a compromise that left hard feelings on both sides: A Commission consisting of fifteen members (president, foreign minister, and thirteen commissioners) along with non-voting Commission members from those countries not represented among the fifteen (with twenty-seven member countries, there would thus be another twelve members). In contrast, there was general agreement on the further strengthening of the position of the Commission president: He was in the future to be able to choose his Commission members from among three proposed candidates from the respective countries. He was also to be able to determine the structure of his Commission and exercise policy-making power for its work.

In the compilation of individual treaty elements into a complete draft, Giscard presented to the presidium and to the public in late April the idea of setting up a congress of national and European deputies, an idea originally shared by the French government as well. It was to gather once a year to pronounce upon the condition of the Union and later also to elect the president of the Union. Because this construction threatened to disrupt the arduously-achieved balance between Council and Parliament, it was rejected in the very next session of the presidium. The body then accepted some deviations from the majority principle and sent Giscard in advance to sell the result to individual member groups in separate sessions. This proved successful: "With a brilliant mixture of argument and appeal, the president won over the national and the European parliamentarians for the final compromise and pacified the grumbling representatives of the governments."[26] He followed up by announcing at a press conference that consensus had been reached. It only remained for the convention members to confirm this in the plenary session of 13 June.

The draft treaty was thereby ready in time for the European Council in Thessaloniki on 19 and 20 June. There was not however enough time for a thoroughgoing discussion by the heads of state and of government. Also, the old treaty texts still needed to be revised and incorporated into the operative third part on the political areas of the Union. The members of the convention made use of the time

---

25 Article I–24 of the draft Constitution; see Hänsch, *Kontinent*, p. 195.
26 *Ibid.*, pp. 201ff.

required for these technical adjustments in order to make a few more additions to the basic section of the document. For example, a paragraph on symbols of the Union was added. This specified the circle of twelve golden stars on a blue field as its flag, Beethoven's "Ode to Joy" as its anthem, "United in diversity" as its motto, and the 9th of May as Europe Day. At the suggestion of German Social Democrat Jürgen Mayer, a European Citizens' Initiative was made possible. The Austrian Green Party member Johannes Voggenhuber succeeded in his effort to keep the Euratom Treaty out of the Constitutional Treaty; opponents of nuclear energy were not to be given a reason to decide against the document.

After final quarrels over the French demand for unanimity in decision-making on trade treaties that "could infringe upon the cultural and linguistic diversity in the Union," all members of the convention signed the revised draft on 10 July. Many did so only with grumbling and internal reservations, but the overwhelming majority was convinced that an acceptable compromise had been found, one that for the sake of needed success ought not to be reopened. On 18 July, President Giscard d'Estaing submitted the convention document in Rome to new Council President Silvio Berlusconi.[27]

When the government conference came together on 4 October, the foreign ministers of Spain and Poland demanded that the convention's draft not be considered at all but that instead the Treaty of Nice be taken as the starting point of negotiations. The Austrian and Finnish representatives joined with them. Passionate appeals by Fischer and Villepin were needed before the body brought itself to accept the Constitutional Treaty as the basis of negotiations. There were still demands for retaining the weighting of votes as decided in Nice (Spain and Poland) as well as for having one commissioner for each member state (Austria and Finland). Disputes over these issues were not resolved at the Council meeting in Brussels on 12 and 13 December. Berlusconi, who would gladly have signed the convention document as a new "Treaty of Rome," failed miserably in his efforts to mediate between the opposing sides.

A breakthrough in the talks first began to emerge when the Socialist José Luis Zapatero replaced the Conservative José María Aznar in elections to the Spanish Congress of Deputies on 14 March 2004. The new prime minister immediately signaled his willingness to compromise on the constitution issue, and so his Polish colleague Leszek Miller found himself isolated. With new efforts to sound out views, the Irish Council president worked out a compromise proposal, which was adopted with some modifications after a long struggle at the Brussels Council meeting of 17 and 18 June 2004. It retained the principle of the double majority

---

27 Draft Constitutional Treaty, Official Journal of the European Union, Information and Notices series, C 169 of 18 July 2003.

but with the quorum of member states raised from fifty to fifty-five percent and from sixty to sixty-five percent of the population. Additionally, a majority would require the affirmative votes of fifteen states or rejection by fewer than four. For the areas of justice and domestic affairs, foreign policy, as well as economy and finance, a majority of seventy-two percent was required if the proposal in question did not stem from the Commission or from the European foreign ministers, respectively.

In the putting together of the Commission, the distinction between voting and non-voting members was given up. For the first Commission formed after the Constitutional Treaty had been implemented, the Nice regulations would continue to be in force. Thereafter (that is, from 2014 onward), only two thirds of the members states would be represented in the Commission. In regard to the multi-year financial framework, the heads of state and of government insisted on unanimity in the Council; the transition to qualified-majority voting was only incorporated into the treaty text as a possibility. In the annual passage of the budget, Parliament's power to make the final decision was taken away; instead, in the event there was a lack of unity between the Council and Parliament, the Commission would have to produce a new draft.[28]

With these alterations, the treaty lost some of the coherence of the original draft from the presidium; and the Union lost some of its ability to act, along with some of its democratic legitimation as well. Substantial progress in collectivization, as many had wanted in regard to foreign and security policy as well as finance and budget policy, were not by and large achieved. Yet, compared to the Treaty of Nice, all the organs of the Union had been substantially strengthened structures and procedures harmonized and at least partially tightened up as well. Above all, however, there was success in getting closer to the principle of the equivalence of majority decision-making and equal co-decision-making by Parliament. This prevented the danger that with the expansion of the Union's ability to act, its democratic legitimation would be reduced.[29] This was made possible, firstly, by Chirac's willingness to give up Gaullist dogmas and the resulting convergence of the French and German governments on institutional questions. Secondly, however, an essential role was played by the strategic abilities of Giscard d'Estaing and his colleagues on the presidium. The representatives of the governments were torn out of their national program schemata and were confronted

---

[28] Treaty establishing a Constitution for Europe. 29 Oct. 2004, Luxembourg: Office for Official Publications of the European Communities, 2005.

[29] On the significance of this principle, see Wilfried Loth, "Die Verfassung für Europa in historischer Perspektive," in: *idem.* (ed.), *Europäische Gesellschaft. Grundlagen und Perspektiven*, Wiesbaden: Verlag für Sozialwissenschaften, 2005, pp. 245–264.

with the majority opinions of elected representatives of the people, which they could not well defy.

The "Treaty establishing a Constitution for Europe" was signed on 29 October 2004 by a total of now twenty-five heads of state and of government of the Union. The ceremony took place in the same Hall of the Horatii and Curiatii in the Palazzo dei Conservatori on the Capitoline Hill in Rome in which the Treaties of Rome had been signed in 1957. It was probably without conscious intent that the signatories thereby signaled that they stood in continuity with European treaty creation up to that point. The European Union had thus far exhibited a constitutional quality insofar as it possessed an autonomous sovereign authority. Nevertheless, it did not become a state via the new treaty—the member states and their parliaments remained the masters of the treaty and its potential further development. Despite what the first-time use of the term "constitution" in the title of the treaty suggested, the heads of state and of government had in actuality approved a constitutional improvement, not the issuance of a constitution.[30]

From Prodi to Barroso

Hopes for strengthening the international profile of the European Union, which Tony Blair, Joschka Fischer, and others had linked to the Eastward expansion and the project for a constitutional treaty, were only partially fulfilled, however. Yet, it was certainly the case that the formation of a European rapid-deployment force, a permanent military committee, and a military staff (decided on in 1999) were proceeding as planned. Common standpoints among the EU countries on foreign-policy issues became more frequent occurrences, thanks not least of all to the energetic and suave engagement of High Representative Javier Solana. When voting in the United Nations, the representatives of the EU countries succeeded in taking common positions approximately seventy-five percent of the time; and the High Representative received the right to speak in the Security Council. In January of 2003, the EU took over the international police mission in Bosnia-Herzegovina from the UN. Three months later, the EU assumed the military mission in Macedonia from NATO. From June to September 2003, the EU undertook a quickly-arranged peacekeeping action in the civil war in the province Ituri in eastern Congo. Altogether, some nineteen police or military missions in crisis regions had been

---

[30] Cf. Franz C. Mayer, "Verfassungsstruktur und Verfassungskohärenz – Merkmale europäischen Verfassungsrechts?" in: *Integration* 26 (2003), pp. 398–413; in general, Werner Weidenfeld (ed.), *Die Europäische Verfassung in der Analyse*, Gütersloh: Bertelsmann Stiftung, 2005.

initiated up to the summer of 2007, and some had also been completed by that point.[31]

These missions received little attention from the public, however. They remained modest in scope and at least in the beginning still suffered from difficulties in coordination and conflicts over financing. After the attacks of 11 September 2001, the EU did succeed in developing a coherent strategy for combating international terrorism; this was accomplished under the aegis of Council President Guy Verhofstadt. Due to deficient military preparation and differing viewpoints, however, it was not in a position to offer a common strategy for waging war and so counter the American option for a "coalition of the willing" to fight the Taliban in Afghanistan. After the defeat of the Taliban regime, thirteen EU members and four accession candidates took part in forming an international protective force at the beginning of 2002, coordinated by the British, that was to safeguard the construction of a liberal-democratic state. A special representative of the EU made efforts—not always successful—to coordinate the national activities on site.

The European position in world politics was further weakened when Blair, Chirac, and Schröder fell out in the second half of 2002 over the issue of military action against the Iraqi dictator Saddam Hussein. In the autumn of 2001, the "Big Three" of the EU were still repeatedly coordinating with each other in the struggle against terrorism and thereby provoking dissatisfaction among the smaller EU partners. Now, however, Blair decided to embrace the American option for energetic action against the Iraqi program for producing weapons of mass destruction—even if as a consequence there would be a war that toppled the Saddam regime. For the British leader, Saddam was a "monster" who threatened the peace in the Middle East and who unhesitatingly supported the terrorism of Al Qaida. Moreover, Blair regarded it as fatal to part the company with his American ally on an issue that for the latter had become existential after the shock of 11 September 2001.[32]

In contrast, Chirac and Schröder were convinced that Saddam posed no immediate danger and that military action to remove him from power would only make the struggle against terrorism and the efforts to achieve peace in the Middle East more difficult. At the same time, they saw in the insistence on collective action by the United Nations an opportunity to cut down to size the high-handed unilateralism of President George W. Bush's administration and to give new

---

[31] Cf. the compilation in Mittag, *Kleine Geschichte*, pp. 301–303; in general, Christopher Hill, "Renationalizing or Regrouping? EU Foreign Policy since 11 September 2001," in: *Journal of Common Market Studies* 42 (2004), pp. 143–63; Mathias Jopp and Peter Schlotter (eds.), *Kollektive Außenpolitik – Die Europäische Union als internationaler Akteur*, Baden-Baden: Nomos, 2007.
[32] Tony Blair, *A Journey*, London: Hutchinson, 2010, p. 423; see also pp. 395–476.

impetus to the vision of an independent Europe in world politics. After a meeting in Schröder's private apartment in Hanover on 7 September, the French president and German chancellor declared that there could be no deviation from the decision of the Security Council to have inspectors once again search for weapons of mass destruction in Iraq. With an eye to the ongoing parliamentary election campaign in Germany, Schröder added that the Federal Republic would under no circumstances participate in a military action against Iraq. Chirac avoided such a categorical commitment for the time being, likewise with an eye to the uncertain outcome of the German elections.[33]

In light of the hostility of broad segments of the European public to the unilateral action of the Bush administration against the "axis of evil," Paris and Berlin regarded it as opportune to propose to the European Convention "the continued development of the ESDP into a European Security and Defense Union." In a joint paper of 22 November, French Foreign Minister Villepin and his counterpart Fischer sketched out a union that would not only take on crisis missions if NATO as a whole was not involved but also would guarantee "the security of its territory and its people" and contribute to "the stability of its strategic environment." In order to become fully capable of acting, the Europeans not only ought to increase their efforts to modernize their armaments; but the Union ought also to develop its own command structures parallel to NATO.[34]

At the same time, Commission President Romano Prodi began to make public criticism of the British alignment with American unilateralism and to advocate a Europe "with a single voice on all aspects of external relations." In a speech to the European Convention on 5 December, he called on the heads of government to "act on their commitment to make Europe a superpower," to "build the first true supranational democracy in the world." As he continued, "speaking with one voice is essential to defend Europe's social model in a globalised world and protect our values." Particularly targeting the British government, he warned against hopes of having influence via nurturing the "special relationship" with Washington. The British ought to join in the efforts of the other Europeans in creating Europe because "Britain's full participation in Europe was required if the two continents were ever to develop into a partnership of equals."[35]

---

[33] Chirac, *Le temps présidentiel*, pp. 372ff. Cf. *idem*. pp. 361–401; Joschka Fischer, *"I am not convinced." Der Irak-Krieg und die rot-grünen Jahre*, Cologne: Kiepenheuer & Wisch, 2011, pp. 151–153.
[34] Europäischer Konvent: Gemeinsame deutsch-französische Vorschläge für den Europäischen Konvent zum Bereich Europäische Sicherheits- und Verteidigungspolitik, CONV 422/02, 22 Nov. 2002.
[35] "Prodi Seeks Strong Power for Brussels," 5 Dec. 2002, at http://news.bbc.co.uk/2/hi/europe/2545331.stm.

In the meantime, Tony Blair was working to escape from the threat of isolation by seeking support for his position on the Iraq issue among his European allies. He was relatively successful in this. He published a declaration in *The Times* of London on 30 January 2003 in which he warned of "the continuing threat to world security by the Iraqi regime" and the breakdown of trans-Atlantic relations, calling for the "disarmament" of Saddam's regime. This declaration drew support not only from conservative Spanish Prime Minister José María Aznar along with his Atlanticist-oriented Portuguese colleague José Manuel Barroso, Danish Prime Minister Anders Fogh Rasmussen, and Italian Prime Minister Silvio Berlusconi. It was also the case that the heads of state or of government of the three largest accession candidates lent their support to Blair's appeal: Leszek Miller of Poland, Václav Havel of the Czech Republic, and Péter Medgyessy of Hungary.[36] Concerned about France and Germany affiliating with Russia, these leaders made use of the opportunity to demonstrate autonomy in the face of a feared Franco-German dominance. A few days later, the other candidate countries in the East voiced similar views in the framework of a declaration of the "Vilnius Group."[37]

For the advocates of an autonomous Europe, that was a nasty surprise and a bitter setback. Bush's Secretary of Defense Donald Rumsfeld poured salt in the wound by deriding France and Germany as representative of the "old Europe," which time had passed by: "If you look at all of the European NATO members, the center of gravity has shifted to the east. And there are many new members there."[38] With a veto in the UN Security Council on 10 March, Chirac was able to prevent the legitimization of an attack on Iraq through a resolution of the United Nations. Nevertheless, the "old" Europeans were powerless in the face of the opening of the war on 20 March, and they came under heavy attack from the "Atlanticists." US Secretary of State Colin Powell declared that Russia was to be "forgiven," France "punished," and Germany "ignored" in the future.[39]

A lack of support from the governments of the Eight did not prevent Chirac and Schröder from further advancing the project of an independent defense. At Belgian initiative, they met on 29 April with Belgian Prime Minister Guy Verhofstadt and his Luxembourgish colleague Jean-Claude Juncker in Brussels to discuss details of the path toward a defense union. In anticipation of the union, the four agreed "to get

---

[36] German translation in: *Internationale Politik* 58/3 (2003), p. 79.
[37] Declaration of 5 Feb. 2003. On this and the following, cf. Mathias Jopp and Sammi Sandawi, "Europäische Sicherheits- und Verteidigungspolitik," in: *Jahrbuch der Europäischen Integration 2002/2003*, pp. 241–250.
[38] Press conference of 22 Jan. 2003, U.S. Department of Defense. Presscenter: News Transcript, 22 Jan. 2003.
[39] *Frankfurter Allgemeine Zeitung*, 24 April 2003.

going with various concrete initiatives": a "rapid response capability," a strategic air command, a common ABC defensive capability, a system of emergency relief aid, and European training centers. By the summer of 2004, there was above all, however, to be the creation of the "nucleus of a collective capability for planning and conducting deployments." In concrete terms, it was planned that this central command would be based in the Belgian town of Tervuren.[40]

Atlanticist-oriented observers attempted to make the meeting in Brussels laughable by dubbing it a "praline summit." Yet, the governments of the Eight increasingly came under pressure in their own countries; also, the vision of a common European foreign and security policy gained more plausibility when the victorious troops had found no weapons of mass destruction in Iraq and when a difficult-to-comprehend civil war among Sunnis, Shia, and Kurds broke out after the dictator's fall. In October of 2003, even Blair showed tendencies toward agreeing to the creation of an autonomous command center.[41]

It did not come to that however because Bush was able to make it clear to the British premier that he would regard such a step as a splitting of NATO. In the end, Fischer and Villepin were nevertheless still able to put through in the constitutional convention the expansion of increased cooperation in security and defense policy. At the European Council in Thessaloniki on 19 and 20 June 2003, the heads of state and of government authorized the creation of a European armaments agency. At the Brussels Council meeting of 12 and 13 December, there was approval for a "European Security Strategy" prepared by Solana and his staff. Here, the EU committed itself explicitly to a world order "which rests on an effective multilateralism" and called for improving Europe's ability to act through better coordination among the members, increasing the allocation of civil resources, and improving the building of "more flexible mobile deployment forces."[42] None of this brought the defense *union* any closer, but security *policy* was given substance.

Blair's ambition of having his British compatriots, even if they did not participate in the monetary union, lead the development of a powerful common foreign and security policy at the center of the Union fell by the wayside. After he had so decidedly taken the side of Bush in the dispute over the Iraq War, his appeals for

---

[40] Gemeinsame Erklärung Deutschlands, Frankreichs, Luxemburgs und Belgiens zur Europäischen Sicherheits- und Verteidigungspolitik, Brussels, 29 April 2003.
[41] Stephen Wall, *A Stranger in Europe: Britain and the EU from Thatcher to Blair*, Oxford: Oxford University Press, 2008, pp. 172–175; Hans Stark, *La politique internationale de l'Allemagne. Une puissance malgré elle*, Villeneuve d'Ascq: Presses universitaires du Septentrion, 2011, p. 139.
[42] Europäischer Rat: Europäische Sicherheitsstrategie. Ein sicheres Europa in einer besseren Welt, Doc. 1088/03, Brussels, 12 Dec. 2003.

a united Europe that would play a strong role in world politics no longer had credibility. The Conservatives let themselves be seduced by their American political counterparts into placing their hopes wholly in a close alliance of Great Britain with the US. In the public sphere the reigning Euro-skepticism mutated into nothing less than hysterical hostility to Europe. "Newspapers with a combined circulation of eight million," as Blair recalled, "were absolutely, totally, and hopelessly hostile and reported completely subjectively about it. For them, it was very simple: Everything that Brussels favored was bad for the British. The Murdoch press was especially malicious." Given that the British, as Blair felt, "had stopped loving me," he was no longer in a position to fight against it.[43]

The disputes between Blair on the one hand and Schröder and Chirac on the other continued to have an effect when in June of 2004 it came to selecting a new Commission president. Extending Romano Prodi's term was out of the question because the president now also needed confirmation from Parliament—and the new conservative majority there was not of a mind to express support for a representative of the left. It was also held against Prodi that the fundamental administrative reform that Neil Kinnock had gotten underway led to a loss of effectiveness and creativity among EU bureaucrats in a climate of general suspicion. Prodi had understood neither how to create significant authority for himself within the administration nor how to attract attention to himself in the public or hold his own against the governments. The Commission had not played a meaningful role in the development of the Treaty of Nice or in the subsequent negotiations of the European Convention. Blair and other "Atlanticists" resented the fact that Prodi had taken the opposing side in the Iraq War; for his part, Berlusconi did not want to give a rival in domestic politics a platform any longer.

At the Council meeting of 17 and 18 June 2004, Blair and Berlusconi initially supported the candidacy of Commissioner for External Relations Chris Patten, a member of the British Conservative Party; his candidacy was promoted by the European People's Party faction. For fundamental reasons, however, Chirac rejected a candidate from a country that belonged neither to the Eurozone nor to the Schengen Area. The French president thus underscored the fringe position in which the British had in the meantime ended up. Together with Schröder, he proposed Guy Verhofstadt. This candidate was however "too federalistic" and too anti-American for Blair. Together with Berlusconi, the British prime minister formed a defensive front, which all the "Atlanticists" joined. A resolution to this standoff could have been found in the person of Jean-Claude Juncker, but he rejected the idea of leaving his post in Luxembourg for Brussels. The Council meeting ended without having nominated a candidate.

---

43 Blair, *A Journey*, p. 533.

After further consultations, Irish Council President Bertie Ahern presented José Manuel Barroso as a compromise candidate. The Portuguese prime minister had indeed made a name for himself as an "Atlanticist" but had also won confidence for his consistent efforts to rehabilitate the Portuguese government budget. From his beginnings as a Maoist in his youth to his successes as a liberal-conservative prime minister, he had had a brilliant career. With his perfect command of French, English, and Spanish, he offered a refreshing contrast to Prodi, who could only express himself in his native Italian. Chirac and Schröder accepted him perforce, and so he was nominated at a special summit on 29 June. The German chancellor clearly had not forgiven Blair for having impeded Verhofstadt: "During the dinner at which Verhofstadt's appointment was blocked, he attacked me in a very personal way. I attempted to explain to him that I was not in agreement with Verhofstadt's conception of Europe. It was nothing personal. But Schröder made it clear to me that it was personal for him. Period."[44]

A portion of the Socialists in the European Parliament continued to reject Barroso. Hence, he was unable to win the necessary majority and was compelled to make a deal: In order to gain the decisive votes of the liberals, he would refrain from giving the commissioner for industrial policy a coordinating function for all portfolios related to economic policy, a move that Schröder had demanded. With this precondition, he was elected on 22 July. Verheugen, who after the successful conclusion of the great Eastward expansion had been proposed by Schröder for this key task of the Commission, had to content himself with the title of vice president and with a normal share of the industry portfolio.

In the process of appointing members, Parliament put through further changes in the composition of the new Commission: Rocco Buttiglione, who was intended for the justice portfolio, was rejected due to discriminatory remarks about women and homosexuals; Foreign Minister Franco Frattini was given the post instead. The Hungarian candidate László Kovács had to switch from the energy portfolio to the tax portfolio, and the Latvian candidate Ingrida Udre was replaced by Andris Piebalgs, who took over the energy portfolio. Aside from that, Barroso sought to ensure the necessary coherence of the Commission, now expanded to twenty-five members, by assigning the portfolios himself and not shying away from conflicts with governments in the process. Convinced of the necessity of making promotion of economic growth, competitiveness, and employment the centerpiece of the new Commission, he saw to it that the portfolios important for those issues went to people who shared his liberal viewpoint. Thus, the Dutchwoman Neelie Kroes, who came from the private sector, held the portfolio for competitiveness;

---

44 Tony Blair, *Mein Weg*, Munich: Bertelsmann, 2010, p. 590. This passage is not found in the English original. On the dispute, Gerbet, *Construction*, pp. 506–508.

the internal market was entrusted to the Irishman Charlie McGreevy; and trade went to Peter Mandelson, who had provided ideas to Blair.[45]

The decision to make economic growth the focus of the new Commission was proceeded by intense criticism of the results to date of the "Lisbon strategy" that had been approved by the European Council in 2000. At that time, the heads of state and of government had set the ambitious goal of making the EU "the most competitive and most dynamic knowledge-based economic sphere in the world" by the end of the decade; they had done so at the urging of Portuguese Council Chairman Antonio Guterres, who was advised by the dynamic economist Maria João Rodrigues. The weakness in growth that Europe had been experiencing since the 1990s compared to the US was to be overcome through "open coordination" (read: agreement on targets and measures and regular review of them). Additionally, it was declared important to create an "information society for all" and a "European area of research and integration," a "favorable environment for the founding and development of innovative enterprises," as well as "efficient and integrated financial markets." The "modernization of the European societal model" was to be advanced by means of investments in education and an active welfare state.[46]

In the following two years, the targets had been made more precise. In 2001, ecological sustainability had been added to the catalogue of goals; in 2002, there was agreement to increase expenditures on research and development by 2010 to nearly three percent of GNP. In actuality, however, achievements in nearly all areas remained significantly below the objectives, such that the gap between American and European growth widened still further. The Commission appointed a group of experts under the chairmanship of former Dutch Prime Minister Wim Kok, which presented a provisional appraisal in November of 2004 that came to the sobering conclusion that it would not be possible to overtake or even catch up with the US by 2010.[47]

Barroso also saw stronger economic growth, more and better jobs and a rise in the quality of life as the key to increased acceptance of the EU and greater confidence in its institutions on the part of the population. At the beginning of his term, he therefore announced nothing less than a "renewal of Europe" to be

---

45 *Jahrbuch der Europäischen Integration 2003/2004*, pp. 85–87; *ibid.*, 2005, pp. 91ff.
46 Rat der Europäischen Union: Schlussfolgerungen des Vorsitzes, Europäischer Rat (Lissabon), 23–24 March 2000, SN 100/00. Cf. Daniel Göler, "Die Lissabon-Strategie: Ein europäischer Gestaltungsversuch?" in: Christoph Linzbach, et al. (eds.), *Globalisierung und europäisches Sozialmodell*, Baden-Baden: Nomos, 2007, pp. 147–166; Maria João Rodrigues (ed.), *Europe, Globalization and the Lisbon Agenda*, Cheltenham and Northampton, MA: Edward Elgar Publishing, 2009.
47 Bericht der Hochrangigen Sachverständigengruppe unter Vorsitz von Wim Kok, Nov. 2004, Luxemburg 2004.

achieved via a "revived and newly-oriented Lisbon agenda."[48] It was especially the case that he wanted to make labor markets more flexible, modernize social welfare systems, improve the qualifications and adaptability of workers, and also employ the Structure and Cohesion Fund in a more targeted manner. "Open coordination" was to be more strongly structured via the introduction of a three-year cycle: firstly, the provision of "integrated guidelines" by the Commission, then development of national reform programs and a Community program oriented on them, and, lastly, annual reports on implementation in the member countries and at Community level.[49]

The commitment to national programs and annual reporting, which the European Council was willing to embrace in its Brussels session of 22 and 23 March 2005, led to increased opening of protected areas that had thus far eluded the competition of the internal market, for example, telecommunications and the realm of local government services. The level of educational attainment and the flexibility of the workforce rose. At the same time, however, the number of precarious and temporary employment situations also grew; and the ranks of the unemployed fell only marginally—the EU average dropping from 9.2 percent in 2004 to 7.0 percent in 2008, with great variations from country to country.[50] The economy grew at a rate of .7 percent per year—sufficient to prevent the gap with the US from increasing but too little to reduce it either. The requirements for economic growth proved too complex to be promoted with equal effectiveness via one unified strategy everywhere. At the same time, deregulation and the market focus of educational efforts associated with it posed threats that were not easy to ward off: new societal polarizations and a loss of creativity.

The efforts of the Barroso Commission within the framework of the Lisbon strategy thus did not contribute to overcoming the loss of confidence in the European project. On the contrary, they fostered the strengthening of an oppositional movement that perceived the EU and its institutions as nothing other than agents of a globalization aimed at dismantling the European social model and maximizing capital gains. It was especially within the milieu of militant globalization critics of the ATTAC organization along with neo-socialist parties and party wings

---

48 Kommission der Europäischen Gemeinschaften: Strategische Ziele 2005–2009, Europa 2010: Eine Partnerschaft für die Erneuerung Europas, Wohlstand, Solidarität und Sicherheit, KOM (2005) 12 endgültig, Brussels, 26 Jan. 2005.
49 Europäische Kommission: Mitteilung für die Frühjahrstagung des Europäischen Rates. Zusammenarbeit für Wachstum und Arbeitsplätze – Ein Neubeginn für die Strategie von Lissabon, KOM (2005) 24 endgültig, Brussels, 2 Feb. 2005; Für Wachstum sorgen und Arbeitsplätze schaffen: Ein neuer und integrierter Koordinierungszyklus für Wirtschaft und Beschäftigung in der EU, SEK (2005) 193, Brussels, 3 Feb. 2005.
50 Eurostat: File Unemployment Rate, National Level, 2004–2009.

that such views gained popularity. Such critics deliberately overlooked the fact that the Commission also had a concern measures to secure the social cohesion of society and, for example, called for "bringing flexibility and employment security into a balanced relationship" in the spring of 2005.[51]

A clear gap loomed between the grandiloquent pronouncements and actual successes of the new Commission. Furthermore, Barroso was unable to attain much of a profile in other areas of Union policy. Forging coalitions and putting through majority decisions were not his forte. It was rather the case that he withdrew proposals when there was a threat of too intense a disagreement with individual governments. "It doesn't make sense to publish plans if the member-states will not do anything with them," as he said, which dampened the zeal of his Commission colleagues on many occasions.[52]

On the other hand, Barroso succeeded in consolidating the Commission, with inclusion of the members from the many newly-entering countries. Communication between the different departments of the administration was significantly improved, and the decision-making processes within the Commission were tightened up. Many decisions were now reached during informal rounds with the president before being confirmed in weekly sessions of the commissioners. Barroso "loves to be the center of attention, and he communicates extremely well," wrote the co-author of a study that examined decision-making practices in the Commission in the autumn of 2007.[53] Meetings of the twenty-seven commissioners took less time than had the sessions of the fifteen under Prodi. Over 22,000 public officials of the Commission—even then fewer than the number needed to administer a large European city such as Cologne—could once again be credited with efficiency.

The overcoming of internal crises within the Commission, ones that ultimately stretched back to the Delors era, found their symbolic expression in the return to the Berlaymont Building on the Schuman Roundabout in Brussels in the autumn of 2004—more than twelve years after the structure's closure due to asbestos, after the failure of plans to demolish it, and after a costly renovation. Across from it now stood the building of the Council of Ministers, named for the early-modern antiquary Justus Lipsius and completed in 1996. Since 2001, Parliament had been convening a few hundred meters away in an ostentatious glass palace on the Place Léopold; due

---

51 Europäische Kommission: Mitteilung der Kommission für die Frühjahrstagung des Europäischen Rates. Zusammenarbeit für Wachstum und Beschäftigung. Integrierte Leitlinien für Wachstum und Beschäftigung (2005–2008), Brussels, 2005, p. 6.
52 Quoted from Anjo G. Harryvan and Jan van der Harst, "José Manuel Barroso 2004–2014: The cautious reformer in troubled times," in: van der Harst and Voerman, *Presidents*, pp.249–276.
53 *Ibid.* The study was published in February of 2008: S. Kurpas, C. Gron, and P.M. Kaczynski, *The European Commission after Enlargement: Does More Add up to Less?* Brussels, 2008.

to its half-round middle section reminiscent of a well-known brand of camembert, the edifice was soon dubbed "Caprice des Dieux." Numerous other administrative offices and representations had settled in the vicinity. Hence, a well-manicured, exclusive residential district dating from the time of rapid industrial expansion in the 19th century had gradually been transformed into a government district for the Union and was also perceived as such.

The Barroso Commission had a thoroughly-constructive effect on the development of the financial framework of the Union for the years 2007 to 2013, which the Council, Commission, and Parliament approved on 17 May 2006 in an inter-institutional agreement. In the run-up to this agreement, the usual tough controversies between net-payers and net-receivers as well as beneficiaries and opponents of the Common Agricultural Policy were dealt with; the original draft, having been worked out by the Prodi Commission, was severely scaled back. The net-payers had pushed through a dwindling of the "state ratio," that is, the claim of resources by the EU budget—from a maximum of 1.09 percent of GNP in the year 2006 to a maximum of .95 percent in 2013. The Commission was successful however in preserving the tendency toward shifting resources into the new policy areas they had sought. Thus, the "Lisbon" spending rose by seventy-one percent and expenditures for Union citizenship by seventy-eight percent, whereas moneys designated for agriculture and the development of rural areas dropped by eight percent.

Under pressure from the new member states, Tony Blair had to accept at the Brussels Council meeting of 15 and 16 December 2005 that the "British rebate" from 2009 onward could only be partially applied to the costs of expansion since 2004 and not at all from 2011. That was equivalent to a reduction in the rebate of approximately twenty percent. Other member states now also received accession discounts, though with time limits. Farther-reaching reforms were put off, though they did remain on the agenda: Under public pressure from Chancellor Gordon Brown, Blair agreed to the reduction of the "British rebate" only under the condition that the Commission be given the task of undertaking a comprehensive review of all aspects of EU expenditure and income by 2008–9. Through skillful mediation, Barroso was able to win on a series of individual items that were especially close to his heart, such as a globalization fund for re-incorporating into working life those who had been laid-off. In subsequent negotiations with Parliament, he was willing to find savings in the administrative budget that made it possible to increase expenditures for research, life-long learning, and Trans-European Networks.[54]

---

[54] *Jahrbuch der Europäischen Integration 2003/2004*, pp. 163–167; *2005*, pp. 95ff., 171–176; ibid., *2006*, pp. 92ff., 176–183; Peter Becker, "Die Fortschreibung des Status Quo. Die EU und ihr neuer Finanzrahmen Agenda 2007," in: *Integration* 29 (2006), pp. 106–121; on the course of the Brussels Council meeting, also Blair, *Mein Weg*, pp. 591–594.

The Constitutional Crisis

The ratification of the new Treaty of Rome occurred quickly and largely without difficulty in many countries, winning approval from broad to very broad majorities. The parliament of Lithuania was the first to approve the treaty, doing so on 11 November 2004. Hungary followed on 20 December, Slovenia on 1 February 2005, Italy on 6 April, Greece on 19 April, Estonia (in the first reading) on 9 May, Slovakia on 11 May, Austria on 23 May, and Germany on 27 May. In Spain, a referendum on the treaty was held on 20 February, with some 76.7 percent of the voters approving it; the parliament confirmed the decision on 11 May.

Blair and Chirac had likewise decided to have the Constitutional Treaty approved by referendum. The British prime minister had done so not completely of his own free will. The Conservative opposition had demanded such a referendum, and Rupert Murdoch had apparently also informed him that if the prime minister did not put the treaty up for a vote by the people, then Murdoch would withdraw the support of his mass-circulation newspapers for the prime minister. It was a surprise to all observers when on 20 April 2004 Blair announced that the voters "will be asked for their opinion"; he made this move without any prior consultation with other heads of government. He feared that without a referendum, the treaty would not pass the House of Lords. Even in the House of Commons, he was not completely sure of a majority. Additionally, it could be seen that in the next year's parliamentary elections, the Conservatives would profit from a refusal to hold a referendum. What remained was a vague hope that a turnaround in public opinion regarding EU membership could at last come about through advocacy of the treaty. If that did not succeed, Blair would probably have to resign in favor of Gordon Brown.[55]

Blair's decision put pressure on Chirac. Unlike the situation with the Maastricht Treaties, if France dispensed with a referendum on this treaty while Great Britain held one, it would have been difficult to explain to the French public. The decision for a referendum, announced during the traditional television interview on 14 July 2004, was all the easier for Chirac to make because practically all the leaders of French political parties had publicly called for one and because surveys indicated a high level of support for the constitution project. An impressive vote

---

[55] *The Guardian*, 21 April 2004; Blair, *Mein Weg*, pp. 547ff., 582; David Gowland, Arthur Tuner, and Alex Wright, *Britain and European Integration since 1945. On the Sidelines*, London and New York: Routledge, 2010, pp. 176ff.

for the treaty might even help halt the decline in popularity of the president and his party in the face of a continuing recession.[56]

In the process, Chirac overlooked the fact that the recession gave fertile soil to the critics of globalization—who held the EU and its neo-liberal orientation responsible for growing unemployment and cuts in social services—and that this criticism could without any great effort be directed against a reform treaty, one which even with all the efforts toward coherence had still ended up being quite complex. The referendum had hardly been announced when strong polemics developed against the alleged attempt to carve in stone the ultra-liberal orientation of Europe. Laurent Fabius, onetime prime minister under Mitterrand, could not resist putting himself at the head of this criticism so as to win the battle to be Jospin's successor as leader of the Socialist Party and have the presidential candidacy for 2007 decided in his favor. Traditional conservative opponents of Europe such as Philippe de Villiers as well as opponents of Chirac in his own party even linked the Constitutional Treaty to a possible entry by Turkey into the European Union and frightened voters with the specter of the impending islamization of Europe.

In March of 2005, the opponents of ratification began to outstrip the advocates. Nor was it helpful that Chirac strictly forbade Barroso, the poster child of forced liberalization, to show his colors in the French debate. European Parliament deputy Daniel Cohn-Bendit of the Greens averred that the opponents of the constitution within the alternative milieu were "complètement meschugge" (Yiddish for "crazy").[57] Yet such appeals to reason could no longer prevent the campaign to strengthen the European Union from becoming a campaign against unpopular Prime Minister Jean-Pierre Raffarin and Chirac too. Nicolas Sarkozy, the leader of the UMP who was impatiently speculating as to the possibility succeeding Chirac, took cover by differentiating between fatuous EU fundamentalists and more levelheaded EU realists of his own cut. On 29 May, some 54.7 percent of French voters opposed the Constitutional Treaty.

The setback for the reform plans was all the more bitter when three days later, on 1 June, the Dutch also rejected the treaty. With some 61.6 percent of the vote, the naysayers in the Netherlands had even achieved a significantly larger victory. Here too, populist criticism from the right and the left combined with general dissatisfaction with a government that had had to make painful budget cuts and that had in other respects also drawn much criticism. The rightwing populist party of Geert Wilders, which at the beginning of the year had split from the

---

56 Chirac, *Le temps présidentiel*, pp. 527–529. The criticism from the German side that Chirac had "unnecessarily called for a referendum only so as to split the socialist opposition" (according to Fischer, *"I am not convinced,"* p. 246; Hänsch, *Kontinent*, p. 211), is unfounded.
57 Quoted from *Die Zeit*, 14 April 2005.

right-liberal VVD, found great resonance with its warnings against cheap competition from Eastern Europe and against islamization; the radical leftwing Socialist Party around Jan Marijnissen scored points by raising the specter of a "dissolution of the Netherlands" and its social-welfare model. Although all the parties in the government as well as the opposition Social Democrats and Greens had voiced support for the Constitutional Treaty, a majority of voters—additionally mobilized by the French "no" at the last minute—came out against it, though the turnout was low (62.8 percent). The rifts in Dutch consensus democracy, which had become all the more apparent since the murder of the rightwing extremist Pim Fortuyn in May of 2002, grew still deeper.

As soon as the results of the referendum in France had been announced, Council President Jean-Claude Juncker, Commission President Barroso, and European Parliament President Borrell issued a joint declaration in which they called for the continuation of the ratification process in those countries that had not yet decided on the treaty, despite the negative vote of the French. All EU countries were to have the opportunity to ratify the Constitutional Treaty. After the vote in the Netherlands, they repeated this declaration; Chirac and Schröder added their voices too. French and Dutch voters were to be put under pressure to revise their decision, following the model of the handling of the Danish "no" to the Maastricht Treaties. It was to be made clear to them that there would be no renegotiations on a "more social" Europe, which was a prospect that the pro-European maximalists among the opponents of the treaty had been holding out.

In fact, the parliament of Latvia did not let the dramatic events in France and the Netherlands keep it from ratifying the treaty on 2 June. For Blair, however, the rejection of the Constitutional Treaty by a majority of French and Dutch voters was a welcome opportunity to escape the very real danger of a personal defeat. "Great news," as Jack Straw commented on the reports from Paris and The Hague.[58] While the British opponents of Europe were crowing over this, the cabinet decided on 6 June to suspend the ratification process for the time being. In light of the vote in two core countries of the Union, the path that had been embarked upon with the Constitutional Treaty had to be reconsidered—that was Blair's argument at the European Council in Brussels on 16 and 17 June.

Given the suspension of the ratification process in Great Britain, no clear message could any longer be directed to the French or Dutch. True, the Council did declare that continuation of the ratification process was not to be called into question. At the same time, however, it appealed to all the affected parties to think over the situation together. The Council also postponed the anticipated date of the treaty's coming into effect by one year, from 1 November 2006 to 1 November

---

58 Blair, *A Journey*, p. 531.

2007. In some countries, majorities for the treaty then began to crumble, and their governments decided to postpone projected referenda or parliamentary votes, respectively—this was the case in Denmark, Sweden, Poland, the Czech Republic, Portugal, and Ireland. In Luxembourg, Juncker demonstratively persisted in holding a referendum planned for 10 July, threatening to resign if there were a rejection; the treaty ended up achieving a positive vote of 56.5 percent. That alone however would not compel a revision of the decisions in France and the Netherlands nor would the support that came from the parliament of Cyprus (on 30 June) and Malta (16 July). Neither did conclusion of the ratification process in Belgium on 8 February 2006 or in Estonia on 9 May or in Finland on 18 May lead to any *volte face* in public opinion.

As Council president in the second half of 2005, Blair studiously avoided any initiative for overcoming the crisis in the ratification process. The "pause to think" that he had forced through thus became a "pause in thinking," in which the consensus that had been laboriously achieved in the development of the Constitutional Treaty now faded away. With an eye toward the next parliamentary elections in the Netherlands, set for November of 2006, the government around Jan-Pieter Balkenende declared the treaty "dead." Chirac, likewise keeping in mind the next electoral hurdle (in this case the presidential elections in May of 2007), developed the idea of starting from the Nice Treaty in making reforms and, furthermore, separating the institutional and content reforms. Sarkozy advocated reform in three steps: Initially, near-term reforms as soon as possible to eliminate the current grinding of the gears in the Europe of the Twenty-Five, then substantive reforms via the path of increased cooperation and, lastly, the summoning of a major new convention after the parliamentary elections of 2009.[59]

As had been agreed a year earlier, the European Council was to assess reflections on 15 and 16 June 2006, but it was only possible to decide on extending the reflection phase another year. German Chancellor Angela Merkel—Schröder's successor at the head of a grand coalition of Christian Democrats and Social Democrats since September of 2005—was given the task of presenting the Commission with a report on the status of deliberations and possible future developments in the constitutional project; this report was to be submitted at the conclusion of the German Council presidency in the first half of 2007 and was to serve as the basis for further decisions. This move made it clear that there was to be no decision on the issue of further dealings with the Constitutional Treaty until after the elections in the Netherlands and France.[60]

---

[59] Jacques Chirac, Declaration at the European Council 15-16 Dec. 2005, www.elysee.fr; Nicolas Sarkozy, Speech in Berlin 16 Feb. 2006, www.botschaft-frankreich.de.
[60] European Council: Presidency Conclusions, 15-16 June 2006.

On the other hand, postponing the decision meant that it had essentially already been decided how it would turn out: not in favor of new negotiations on the basis of the Nice Treaty, as Blair and Chirac ultimately wanted, but rather in favor of a minor modification of the reform treaty that would enable the electorate in France and the Netherlands to revise the votes of May and June 2005. From the beginning, Angela Merkel had left no doubt as to the fact that to her the substance of the treaty was not open to negotiation and that she did not regard a division into individual parts for negotiation as a promising strategy. As she argued to the representatives of the other fifteen states that had already ratified the treaty, one should not so easily brush aside the votes of nearly two-thirds of the member states. The European Parliament was threatening to block the expansion process if the reforms were not carried out as decided upon.

On 17 January 2007, Angela Merkel made clear to the European Parliament her aspiration to bring about a solution on the basis of the Constitutional Treaty and to hammer out its decisive contours during the June summit at the end of her presidency. The details were then to be worked out in a brief government conference under the Portuguese presidency in the second half of 2007 so that the modified treaty could then still be passed before the end of the year and could come into force before new elections to the European Parliament in June of 2009. She found support for this ambitious goal among a gathering of representatives of the eighteen countries that had already ratified the treaty (in the meantime, the new members Romania and Bulgaria were among them) along with two other countries that were at base positively disposed toward the treaty (Ireland and Portugal); this gathering took place on 26 January in Madrid at the initiative of Zapatero and Juncker. The "Friends of the Constitutional Treaty," as they dubbed themselves in a common declaration, proclaimed their resolve to adhere to the substance of the treaty, thereby putting the opponents of the treaty on the defensive.[61]

Council President Merkel joined together with the presidents of the Commission and Parliament on 25 March 2007 to issue the "Berlin Declaration" on the occasion of the fiftieth anniversary of the signing of the Treaties of Rome. With the votes of the twenty supporters of the treaty on their side, Merkel's emissaries were able to move the opponents of the treaty to include in the document a passage in which the organs of the Union declared their intention "to put the EU on a renewed, common foundation by the elections to the European Parliament in 2009."[62] The chancellor's roadmap was thereby *de facto* accepted. Czech Pres-

---

[61] Ministertreffen der Freunde des Verfassungsvertrags: Für ein besseres Europa, Madrid, 26 Jan. 2007.
[62] Text in, among others, Michel Gehler, Österreichs Weg in die Europäische Union, Innsbruck, 2009, pp. 325–327. Cf. Timo Goosmann, "Die 'Berliner Erklärung' – Dokument europäischer

ident Václav Klaus, a longtime declared opponent of the Constitutional Treaty, distanced himself from this declaration after the fact. In Poland, the Kaczyński brothers (Lech Kaczyński as president and his twin Jarosław Kaczyński, initially chairman of the new government party "Right and Justice" and from July of 2006 also prime minister) were critics of Europe and continued to oppose the lack of a reference to Europe's Christian inheritance. That could not however hinder Merkel from resolving the issue of what a compromise would look like between the "Friends of the Constitutional Treaty" and its opponents from tactical and substantive perspectives; she did so in bilateral talks at the highest level.[63]

The decisive line of compromise was found as early as the run-up to these bilateral conversations: After the German government had given up on incorporating the "constitution" concept into the Berlin Declaration, Nicolas Sarkozy as a presidential candidate—with clear recognition of the altered power relations—backed away without protest from his demand that the treaty package be broken into distinct reforms. From the first step of a "mini-treaty" that would do without a referendum, the rhetoric of the French election campaign shifted to the "simplified treaty" that dispensed with the constitution concept as well as the inclusion of symbols. On the very day he assumed the French presidency, 16 May 2007, Sarkozy sought out Angela Merkel in order to make clear that he would support her in the upcoming negotiations. And he did so too: Not without a sidelong glance at his own public, to whom he wanted to present himself as the person who really had overcome the constitutional crisis, he traveled to London, Brussels, Rome, Lisbon, and Warsaw in order to persuade the heads of government there to align themselves with the position on which he and Merkel had agreed.[64]

With this return of Franco-German cooperation, the way to overcoming the constitutional crisis was practically clear. A treaty that did not include an emphasis on a constitutional character and therefore did not require ratification via referendum was in principle also acceptable to Dutch Prime Minister Balkenende. The Dutch government that emerged from elections in November of 2006 was a coalition of Christian Democrats, Social Democrats, and Christian Union; it only called for a kind of veto right for national parliaments over the transfer of new tasks to the EU. This meant that the advocates of at least temporary retention of

---

Identität oder pragmatischer Zwischenschritt zum Reformvertrag?" in: *Integration* 30 (2007), pp. 251–263.
63 On the organization of the negotiation process, Andreas Maurer, "Die Verhandlungen zum Reformvertrag unter deutschem Vorsitz," in: *Aus Politik und Zeitgeschichte* 43/2007, pp. 3–8.
64 Joachim Schild, "Sarkozys Europapolitik: Das zunehmende Gewicht der Innenpolitik," in: *Integration* 30 (2007), pp. 238–250; Paul Legoll, *Nicolas Sarkozy. Un Européen en action*, Paris: l'Harmattan, 2012, p. 97.

the Nice Treaty—especially Blair and the brothers Kaczyński—ended up in isolation. It was now only possible for them to seek to separate out from the treaty complex some elements that for them clearly went too far. Thus, the British government demanded that the character of a legal personality be taken away from the Union and that the Charter of Fundamental Rights be struck out. Beyond that, the veto right was not to be so severely limited; and the European foreign minister was to be called "High Representative for Foreign Affairs and Security Policy" as heretofore. The Polish government additionally demanded—accompanied by a heated campaign under the motto "Nice or death"—that the weighting of votes in the Council as decided in Nice be retained.

Little of that could be passed at the Council meeting in Brussels on 21 and 22 June. It was the case though that the Charter of Fundamental Rights as Part II of the treaty was taken out. The new document took on the character of an amendment treaty to the Treaty on European Union (corresponding to part I of the Constitutional Treaty) and to the Treaty on the Founding of the European Communities (corresponding to part III of the Constitutional Treaty). The legally-binding nature of the Charter of Fundamental Rights did remain however, even if in a footnote to the mandate for the government conference it was maintained that there could be no appeal to the charter in British courts. Other than that, only the title of the European foreign minister fell by the wayside. Nothing of the position or its competencies was changed, and in other respects the substance of parts I and III was preserved. Lech Kaczyński stubbornly resisted the introduction of the principle of the double majority but under pressure from Sarkozy and Juncker assented to having it come into force in 2017. When his brother Jarosław declared in a television speech from Warsaw that he rejected this compromise, Merkel announced that the mandate for the government conference could then be decided without Poland. That sufficed to have the Polish prime minister back down.

It was then possible to complete the mandate for the new government conference by the early morning hours of 23 June. The Netherlands was assured that there would be notification given to the national parliaments by the European Council six months before the expansion of majority voting or of the regular legislative procedure.[65] The mandate had been formulated in such detail that the government conference that met on 23 July under Portuguese chairmanship practically had only editorial work to do. The British government was nevertheless able to push through some exceptional regulations in the realm of domestic affairs and justice, and Poland joined the British declaration stating that no appeals to the Charter of Fundamental Rights would be permitted in national

---

[65] European Council: Presidency Conclusions, Brussels, 21-22 June 2007, document number 11177/07, 23 June 2007: draft IGC mandate.

courts. The Portuguese presidency energetically opposed all other amendment attempts. At an informal gathering of the European Council on 18 and 19 October in Lisbon, the final treaty text was passed after eight more hours of negotiation. On 13 December, the heads of state and of government along with the foreign ministers signed the "Treaty of Lisbon" in a solemn ceremony within the historic walls of the Hieronymite Monastery in the Portuguese capital.

For the advocates of strengthening the European Union, the reform treaty of Lisbon[66] was a belated triumph. Governance of the Union became more democratic. Its efficiency in some areas was increased; in other areas, the terms of the reform ensured that, despite the great expansion, efficiency did not fall below the level of Maastricht. Angela Merkel, who with resolute exercise of her leadership role had played the decisive part in overcoming the constitutional crisis, received general recognition; on 1 May 2008, she was awarded the prestigious Charlemagne Prize of the city of Aachen. The jubilation was admittedly subdued: It was less possible to achieve additional transparency and greater closeness to the citizenry in a treaty that had to avoid explicit constitutional rhetoric and the symbols of European statehood than would have been the case in the treaty of 2004, which had already been ratified by a majority of the countries involved.

Nevertheless, the new treaty served to help not only the governments in Paris and The Hague out of a tight spot but also Blair's successor Gordon Brown: He could now assert that the Lisbon Treaty was not a Constitutional Treaty and therefore did not require approval in a referendum. That was indeed contested by the Conservatives as well as Euro-skeptics within the ranks of Labour, but the campaign for a new referendum did not find any great support in the populace. In the House of Commons on 5 March 2008, a motion by the Conservative opposition calling for a referendum was rejected by a vote of 311 to 248. Six days later, the MPs approved the reform treaty by a vote of 346 to 206. Brown remained in office, and Great Britain remained in the EU, which was growing stronger. With its numerous "opt outs," however, the UK clearly remained both mentally and politically on the fringes of the Union. It was no longer conceivable that Britain could take on a leadership role as had been envisioned by Blair. That Brown arrived late for the signing of the treaty and thus is absent from the official photo would prove telling.[67]

---

[66] Text in, among others, Klemens H. Fischer, *Der Vertrag von Lissabon. Text und Kommentar zum Europäischen Reformvertrag*, Baden-Baden: Nomos, 2008. For interpretation, Werner Weidenfeld (ed.), *Lissabon in der Analyse – Der Reformvertrag der Europäischen Union*, Baden-Baden: Nomos, 2008.

[67] David Allen, "Vereinigtes Königreich," in: *Jahrbuch der Europäischen Integration* 2009, pp. 437–442.

The ratification of the Lisbon Treaty occurred with large majorities in most of the other member states. Only in Ireland did troubles arise: According to a ruling by the country's Supreme Court, a referendum on the amendment treaty was mandatory. Opponents of the treaty falsely claimed that the Lisbon Treaty endangered tax sovereignty as well as the ban on abortion and euthanasia, along with the neutrality of the country. There were also polemics against the alleged dwindling influence of Ireland (loss of a seat in the European Parliament, rotation in the occupancy of the Commission). In a climate of general distrust of the government, the result of the referendum on 13 June was a negative majority of 53.4 percent with a turnout of 53.1 percent, which was higher than originally anticipated.

The repeated "no" in a referendum gave rise to despair and perplexity for a short while. The old fronts once again emerged: Czech President Klaus declared the treaty "dead"; his Polish counterpart Kaczyński announced that he would for the time being not sign the treaty given that the Irish voted had made it "irrelevant."[68] On the other side, such figures as Jürgen Habermas called upon the states that were ready for deepening the Union to embark at last upon the path to a "European core" and to put up a consistently democratic European constitution for a Europe-wide referendum.[69]

In contrast to the situation after the French and Dutch "no," the heads of state and of government this time insisted that the ratification process must continue to move forward. The Irish government was only called upon to provide its opinion by the next Council meeting. At that gathering in Brussels on 11 and 12 December, the heads of state and of government then agreed on what seemed appropriate—easing Irish approval in a second referendum: "legal guarantees" that the treaty would not place limitations on Ireland in its tax policy or its position on the abortion issue or in its security and defense policy. Furthermore, the treaty was to be revised to the effect that every member state was always to be represented by a seat on the Commission.[70] The guarantees were given at the Council meeting of 18 and 19 June 2009; as to amending the treaty, the leaders continued in their position that it would occur on the occasion of the next accession treaty.

These assurances and concessions were meant to suffice for turning around the sentiment in Ireland. Together with a fundamental information campaign as to the actual content of the treaty, it was primarily the fear that Ireland could be

---

[68] Traktat jest martwy. Nie podpiszę go, in: *Dziennik* 1 July 2008.
[69] Jürgen Habermas, "Ein Lob den Iren," in: *Süddeutsche Zeitung*, 17 June 2008.
[70] European Council: Presidency Conclusions, Brussels, 11-12 December 2008, document 17271/1/08, Annex I.

isolated in the financial crisis that in the meantime had developed that made the referendum of 2 October 2009 come out very differently than the previous one: With a turnout of fifty-eight percent, some 67.1 percent now voted for the Lisbon Treaty. After that, Polish President Lech Kaczyński finally acceded to the demand of Prime Minister Donald Tusk (in office since 2007) to sign the treaty, which had long before been ratified by parliament. In early November, the Czech Constitutional Court rejected a complaint filed by Czech opponents of the treaty. This meant that it could come into force on 1 December 2009—eleven months after the date that the heads of state and of government had agreed on in June of 2007 and some three years after the original deadline for the Constitutional Treaty to take effect.

Consequently, the elections to the European Parliament of June 2009 took place within the framework of the Nice Treaty. Once again, turnout fell slightly, from 45.5 to 43 percent. Decisive for that was again the extremely low mobilization in many Central and Eastern European states; in those areas, only an average of 32.2 percent of the electorate went to the polls. In countries that had already been members before the EU expansion of 2004, turnout was an average of 52.4 percent, only just below the numbers in 1999 and 2004. Overall, the parties had not understood how to make use of the opportunities for mobilization already contained in the Nice Treaty. The European People's Party did indeed voice its support for a second term for Barroso but did not make it a theme in the campaign. The Social Democrats discussed a possible candidacy by their party chief Poul Nyrup Rasmussen but could not come to agreement in the end. The deputies of the Labour Party as well as the Spanish and Portuguese Socialists openly advocated a second term for Barroso. As ever, national themes predominated in the campaign; in terms of European politics, only unsophisticated slogans flew back and forth.

Both the EPP and the PES lost votes in the election. Among the winners were smaller parties from the spectrum of those amicably disposed to integration as well as parties skeptical of and hostile to Europe. The results indicated that a grand coalition was still possible in the European Parliament, but the weight between Christian Democrats and Social Democrats had shifted significantly: The Christian Democrats could now form an alternative majority with the Liberals and the new Conservative faction (consisting predominately of conservatives from Britain, Poland, and the Czech Republic). On the other hand, the Social Democrats would require not only the Liberals and the Greens but also the Communists and representatives of both Euro-skeptic factions. Following a proven model, Polish EPP deputy Jerzy Buzek was elected president of Parliament for the first half of the legislative period. For the time being, assumption of the office by someone from the ranks of the Social Democrats remained open. In fact, the

German Martin Schulz, up to that point chairman of the Socialist faction, took office in January of 2012.[71]

The campaign of the majority of the Social Democrats and Greens against a second term for Barroso as the allegedly "weakest Commission president in the history of the EU" (in the words of Martin Schulz)[72] failed in light of the election results. At a "Blaesheim" meeting on 11 June 2009 in Berlin, Merkel and Sarkozy agreed to recommend Barroso for a second term; the European Council added its voice without any nays on 18 June. This Commission president was a bit too much consensus oriented for the tastes of the German chancellor and the French president, but in their eyes that was no reason to prevent him from continuing to serve.[73] Guy Verhofstadt, now chairman of the Liberal faction in the European Parliament, signaled the need for clarification regarding the future program of the Commission president and hence prevented a vote before the summer recess.

Barroso understood that it was no longer sufficient to offer his services to the governments. He promised the deputies that he would in the future exert more effort on the social dimension of the integration process, fight for an expansion of the budget, and work more closely with Parliament. Beyond that, he announced the installation of new Commission members for three tailored areas of responsibility: for Justice, Fundamental Rights, and Citizenship; for Internal Affairs and Migration; and for Climate Action. That was sufficient for him to gain the support of the European Peoples Party, the Conservatives, and the Liberals in the vote of 16 September. Most of the Social Democrats and Greens along with the European United Left voted against him or abstained. Thereafter, Barroso fended off downright sovereign claims of individual governments over certain areas of responsibility. Michel Barnier, the French Commission member, received responsibility for the Internal Market; the German Günther Oettinger had to content himself with responsibility for energy.[74]

Differing conceptions collided when it came to filling the top positions that had been added by the Lisbon Treaty. Under no circumstances did Merkel want Tony Blair for the office of Permanent President of the European Council, as Sarkozy had proposed. For his part, Sarkozy vetoed Jean-Claude Juncker, who would have gladly accepted the office—in contrast to his unwillingness to take on the Commission presidency five years earlier. The Frenchman had taken offense

---

71 Andreas Maurer, "Europäisches Parlament," in: *Jahrbuch der Europäischen Integration 2009*, pp. 47–54.
72 Quoted from the *Financial Times*, 17 Sept. 2009.
73 Legoll, *Sarkozy*, pp.169ff.
74 Udo Diederichs, "Europäische Kommission," in: *Jahrbuch der europäischen Integration 2009*, pp. 73–82; *ibid.*, 2010, pp. 75–84.

at the Luxembourg prime minister above all because as chairman of the Economic and Financial Affairs Council (Ecofin) in the summer of 2007, Juncker had stifled Sarkozy's nascent plans for turning away from the stability course. The twofold "no" led to unity on a compromise candidate: In the run-up to the informal Brussels summit of 19 November 2009, Merkel and Sarkozy came to agreement on Herman Van Rompuy, a Christian Democrat, who had been serving as Belgian prime minister for just over a year.[75]

Barroso played the key role in filling the office of the High Representative for Foreign Affairs and Security Policy: By nominating Catherine Ashton, who a year earlier had replaced Peter Mandelson as trade commissioner, he accommodated both the Social Democrats and Sarkozy. Barroso offered the French president this colleague of Blair's as compensation for the fact that Sarkozy had been unable to put through his preferred candidate for the Council presidency.

The year before, Sarkozy had made use of the French Council presidency to give new impetus to Common Foreign and Security Policy: In the conflict between Georgia and Russia, which in early August 2008 had escalated into a military confrontation, Sarkozy—in discreet agreement with his most important European partners—mediated first an armistice (12 August) and then a withdrawal of Russian troops from the core Georgian area (8 September). The recognition of the rebellious provinces South Ossetia and Abkhazia by Russia would thereby not be called into question by sanctions; the EU only sent observers who were to monitor the armistice. In the understanding among the heads of state and of government on this course, the High Representative for Foreign and Security Policy, at that time still Solana, had played no role, however.[76] With the decision to appoint Trade Commissioner Ashton, who had hardly any foreign-policy experience, Sarkozy could be assured that despite the institutional strengthening of the Foreign Office, not much would change in regard to the pre-eminence of the governments in the foreign-policy profile of the Union.

This foreign policy profile remained half-hearted in that Sarkozy also failed in his effort to have a permanent headquarters of European NATO generals created. Under pressure from the military establishment, he and Chirac too had originally made that demand as a prerequisite for completing the announced return of France into the integrated command of NATO. However, Sarkozy had to content himself with less prestigious *quid pro quos* after Gordon Brown, fearing that he would appear too pro-European in the eyes of British voters, had backed away from such a step and after Angela Merkel had also refrained from campaign-

---

75 Legoll, *Sarkozy*, pp. 173–175; on the confrontation between Sarkozy and Juncker, also Petra Pinzler, "Sarkozys Zähmung," in: *Die Zeit*, 12 July 2007.
76 Legoll, *Sarkozy*, pp. 136–142.

ing for the move. In October of 2008, the Pentagon conceded that France would receive command over the planning headquarters in Norfolk in the US state of Virginia as well as the headquarters of the NATO Response Force in Lisbon.[77] On 11 March 2009, Sarkozy announced the return of France under these terms; at the celebratory summit of NATO on 3 and 4 April, which Merkel's instigation took place in the cities of Strasbourg and Kehl together, he let himself be honored for this.

The boundaries of Common Foreign and Security Policy became clear once again when in the spring of 2011 Sarkozy urged military intervention on behalf of the rebels who had begun fighting against Libya's dictator Muammar Gaddafi. Guido Westerwelle, as foreign minister of the coalition of Christian Democrats and Liberals that had succeeded Merkel's first government in November of 2009, made it clear to Sarkozy that the risk of becoming entangled in a protracted ground war could not be discounted. He stood by this position with the tacit approval of Merkel even when both the government of Barack Obama in Washington and that of David Cameron in London came out in support of Sarkozy. When on 11 March 2011 the UN Security Council voted to support the rebels with air strikes on Gaddafi's forces and on Libyan infrastructure, Westerwelle abstained along with the representatives of Russia and China. The strikes were coordinated by NATO and carried out primarily by French and British units.[78]

In order to defend itself against accusations from its allies regarding deficient solidarity, the German government in late March decided to send an additional three hundred soldiers to Afghanistan to assist in radar surveillance by AWACS aircraft. This could not however undo the fact that both sides had once again ignored the commitment, contained in the Franco-German Treaty that agreement would be reached on a common position before making fundamental foreign-policy decisions. The EU had to be satisfied with activities of second rank: It organized the evacuation of EU citizens from the combat areas and engaged in humanitarian aid to the Libyan population.

Given the fact that the Germans and other EU members had remained on the sidelines, the British drew the conclusion that a further strengthening of European security structures was neither sensible nor necessary: As the success of the Libyan rebels had demonstrated, bilateral cooperation between Britain and France had worked very well and also seemed to suffice to compensate for the clear reduction of American engagement in Europe and the surrounding areas. After Gaddafi's fall in the summer of 2011, Cameron and Sarkozy visited Tripoli

---

[77] Vincent Jauvert, "Otan: Histoire secrète d'un retour," in: *Le Nouvel Observateur*, 2 April 2009.
[78] Mathias Jopp and Daniel Göler, "L'Allemagne, la Libye et l'Union européenne," in: *Politique étrangère* 2/2011, pp. 417–428.

together for a demonstrative celebration of their victory. The Germans found themselves subject to intense criticism regarding their alleged lack of solidarity within the alliance, and the dialogue on the development of a common European strategy completely collapsed. Catherine Ashton was not in a position to get such a dialogue going once again, nor did she apparently see it as her task to do so. Joschka Fischer, who had once dreamed of becoming the first European foreign minister, observed with a touch of despair: "One can become frightened for Europe."[79]

The Euro Crisis

After the belated completion of institutional reform, the European project was not only burdened by irritations regarding the Common Foreign and Security Policy. Over the long term, the problems arising from the completion of the monetary union would prove more dangerous.

Initially, it seemed as if the monetary union could absolutely fulfill the expectations that people had placed on it. Under the sometimes brusque leadership of Wim Duisenberg, who in 2003 succeeded the suave Jean-Claude Trichet, the European Central Bank knew how to hold the inflation rate below two percent. Only at the time of the unrest in the financial markets in 2007–08 did it rise somewhat above that level, so that the average for the years 1999 to 2010 was 2.2 percent. Even if selective price hikes during the changeover gave the impression to many consumers that they had been subjected to a pricey new currency, this rate was significantly lower than those during the same period in the US (2.7 percent) and during the fifty years of the D-mark in Germany (2.8 percent).[80]

Price stability in connection with the emergence of large and liquid financial markets and the disappearance of the interest rate premium for defending the exchange rate *vis-à-vis* the D-mark led to low interest rates. This unleashed a burst of growth, especially in the member states of the monetary union that had earlier been plagued by inflationary tendencies. The average annual growth in the first decade of the monetary union was 3.6 percent in Spain, four percent in Greece, and even eight percent in Ireland. France witnessed annual growth of 2.1 percent. In regard to the whole Eurozone, the growth rate at an average of 2.2 percent per year still lay below that of the US with 2.6 percent—but that was essentially attrib-

---

[79] Joschka Fischer, "Deutsche Außenpolitik – eine Farce," in: *Süddeutsche Zeitung*, 22 March 2011. On Fischer's ambitions, Fischer, *I am not convinced*, pp. 242, 244.
[80] Werner Becker, "Zwölf Jahre Euro. Aus ruhigen Gewässern in stürmische See," in: *Vierteljahrshefte für Zeitgeschichte* 59 (2011), pp. 445–466; also on the following.

utable to the higher population growth of the US. Per capita growth in the Eurozone was 1.8 percent, whereas it was only 1.6 percent in the US.[81]

The monetary union also led to greater integration among the participating economies. For example, the share of trade of the euro countries within the Eurozone went from approximately 26 percent of GDP in 1998 to approximately 33 percent in 2008. It was the case that with most of the member states, intra-EMU trade reached a share of fifty percent of imports and exports. Cross-border investment increased significantly thanks to the expansion of the financial markets and the falling away of currency risk. "For example, German investors have increased their foreign security investment in euros to just over 600 billion from 1999 to September 2007. This was approximately three and a half times more than the level of 1999."[82] Without the monetary union, Germany would once again have come under strong pressure to raise the value of its currency, with corresponding negative consequences for its exports and thus for growth.

The advantages of the euro were so clear that a group of new EU members joined the monetary union when the convergence criteria had been met in accordance with the treaty: Slovenia in 2007, Malta and Cyprus in 2008, Slovakia in 2009, Estonia in 2011, Latvia in 2014, and Lithuania in 2015. Denmark linked the exchange rate of the krone with the euro, which meant that it *de facto* participated in the monetary union; yet the price that Denmark paid for its fear of a negative vote by a majority of its citizens was the inability to have any influence over the bodies governing the monetary union. Furthermore, the euro advanced to become the anchor currency for about thirty-five countries closely intertwined with the EU. Its share of the currency reserves of national banks rose from eighteen to twenty-six percent over ten years; its share in the circulation of international bonds went from nineteen to 31.4 percent. Trade in euros also expanded. As the second most important currency in the world after the dollar, the euro thereby grew significantly beyond the importance of the D-mark, while the Japanese yen lost considerable weight. In global cash circulation, the euro even surpassed the dollar.

However, the weaker member states of the EMU did not make use of the lower interest rates for energetic continuation of structural reforms and investments in modernization. Instead, they let themselves be led astray into raising wages beyond the level of productivity increases and into assuming new debt as well. Given the low interest rates, private debt levels also increased significantly. This led to growing imbalances in the current accounts of those economies, and as soon as these became visible, it led to a considerable spread in interest rates for government securities. Whereas Germany's current account grew by nine percent

---

[81] Marsh, *Euro*, pp. 311 and 401.
[82] Becker, "Zwölf Jahre Euro," p. 451.

of GDP in the first ten years of the monetary union, Austria's by six percent, and the Netherlands' by three percent, it fell in Finland by three percent, in Belgium and Italy by four percent, in France and Portugal by five percent, in Ireland by six percent, in Spain by nine percent, and in Greece by no less than thirteen percent. Germany not only remained the top export country in the world but also took the leading position in the increase in exports within the euro area.[83]

Efforts to put a check on growing indebtedness remained half-hearted. When in 2002 Germany found itself in a growth crisis, the Schröder government, as advised by economists from all over the world, reacted by increasing government expenditures so as to revive the economy. The consequence was that in Germany too new indebtedness grew beyond the three-percent level permitted by the Growth and Stability Pact. After this three-percent threshold was crossed for a second time and another violation was looming for 2004, the European Commission on 18 November 2003 dutifully demanded a reduction of the structural deficit for the budget year 2004 under threat of monetary penalties. Against this, Finance Minister Hans Eichel mobilized resistance among the other indebted countries: along with France (against which procedures were already underway), also Italy, the Netherlands, Portugal, and Greece. On 25 November, the Ecofin Council agreed to suspend the proceedings against Germany and France. Eichel and his French counterpart Francis Mer only made voluntary commitments that the deficit for 2004 would be reduced in part and would be completely eliminated in 2005.[84]

In material terms, the voluntary commitments were just a bit below the demands of the Commission. In political terms, however, the Stability Pact was severely damaged by the suspension of the two proceedings. This was all the more the case after the European Court had ruled against that Council decision, and then the Council had gone on to pass a reform of the stability pact that considerably expanded the scope for assessing budget policy in March of 2005. True, the new version specified that members were committed to reducing their budget deficits during times of strong economic conditions by 0.5 percent of GDP per year, yet no sanctions were passed for cases in which this commitment was not sufficiently kept. At the same time, there was an expansion of the list of special circumstances that allowed for disregarding penal procedures when the stability goal was not being met: It now included factual findings of periods of longer weakness in growth; also, there was now a possibility of extending the period of adjustment in cases of excessive deficits beyond the previously-stipulated one-year deadline for a second year. That may well have been thoroughly sensible in economic terms. However, together

---

[83] Marsh, *Euro*, p. 312.
[84] Barbara Bötticher, "Währungspolitik," in: *Jahrbuch der Europäischen Integration 2003/2004*, pp. 197–202.

with the determination that in general all factors that "in the view of the affected member state are of significance" were to be taken into account, the upshot was that there would be many possibilities for dragging out or even completely blocking deficit proceedings that were in fact warranted.[85]

France actually did succeed in reducing its deficit in 2005 to 3.0 percent as promised. In contrast, Germany failed to reach the stability goal in 2005 with its 3.3 percent deficit and only in 2006 was able to bring it below the three-percent-threshold. Thanks to favorable economic conditions, it was possible to suspend the proceedings against the other budget violators over the course of 2007. When the European economies suffered a considerable downturn in the wake of the worldwide financial crisis in the winter of 2008–09, however, deficits in almost all Eurozone countries quickly rose well above the three-percent-threshold once again. On the one hand, government receipts fell, while considerable sums had to be invested in stabilizing the banking system and in promoting economic growth. In Germany, the deficit climbed to 3.3 percent again in 2009, in Austria to 4.1 percent, in Italy to 5.4 percent, in France to 7.5 percent, in Portugal to 10.1 percent, in Ireland to no less than 14.2 percent, and in Greece to 15.8 percent.[86]

This dramatic new debt was not a problem specific to the monetary union. On average, the budget deficits of the euro countries were 6.4 percent of GDP in 2009, whereas Britain's deficit amounted to 11.5 percent, somewhat higher than Spain's 11.2 percent. Problematic however was that the structurally-weaker countries of the Eurozone had greater difficulties getting out of the economic lows, and as a result, there was great doubt in the financial markets as to whether they would be in a position to repay their debts. Thus, the interest rates demanded for the government bonds of these countries rose dramatically even while the rates for German bonds, for example, were tending toward zero. It was out of the financial and economic crisis in Europe that a government debt crisis developed.

The first country threatened with government bankruptcy stemming from these developments was Greece. Here, the loss of credit worthiness had been intensified by reckless domestic political maneuvers: The oppositional PASOK under the leadership of Georgios Papandreou (son of the legendary prime minister of the accession period) denied the conservative government of Kostas Karamanlis support for initial measures to cut the deficit. Then, when PASOK won the sped-up elections in October of 2009 and came into power, it vigorously demanded new expenditures in order to follow through on its election promises.

---

85 European Council: Presidency Conclusions, Brussels, 22-23 March 2005, Annex II.
86 Compilation from the AMECO Database in Tobias Kunstein and Wolfgang Wessels, "Die Europäische Union in der Währungskrise: Eckdaten und Schlüsselentscheidungen," in: *Integration* 34 (2011), pp. 308–322, here, p. 312.

It then visibly expanded the deficit still further by including the debts of publically-owned firms in the reckoning and also accused the previous government of having knowingly falsified statistics. The Karamanlis government had envisioned a budget deficit of some 6 to 8 percent for 2009, but with these developments it reached 12.7 percent by year's end. As it later turned out, even that number was too low. The great deviation from previous estimates was sufficient to cause severe alarm in the finance markets.[87] Banks, insurance companies, and pension funds either refused to issue any more loans to the Greek government or demanded significantly-higher risk premiums and insured themselves against loan defaults. The speculators who sold such default insurance made it still more expensive for the Greeks to borrow new money.

The threatened bankruptcy of Greece quickly brought demands for assistance measures onto the agenda of the monetary union. Numerous financial firms, not least of all German and especially French ones, had invested in Greek government paper and had earned much in the process; such a bankruptcy threatened to affect them severely. Above all, however, other weakening member states faced the threat of being discredited and hence end up insolvent if speculation on a Greek bankruptcy were to prove true. In contrast, defenders of European monetary stability—among them former chief economist of the ECB Otmar Issing—argued that the EMU Treaty explicitly precluded mutual liability among the member states.[88] The Germans generally felt little inclination to pour their money into a bottomless pit, and their chancellor was so dismissive of demands for support that the European public dubbed her the new "Iron Lady."

After Merkel had again rejected any kind of assistance measures during an informal gathering of the heads of state and of government on 11 February 2010, she had to concede at the Council meeting of 25 and 26 March that coordinated bilateral loans to Greece would be possible in the event that refinancing via the financial markets were no longer sufficient. However, the decision for that had to be unanimous; moreover, the International Monetary Fund (IMF) had to be a participant in the rescue action. Sarkozy and the ECB had initially rejected that, but Merkel insisted on it so that the violation of the "no-bailout" clause of the EMU Treaty would not become any too obvious. On the other hand, the chancellor gave in a bit to the persistent pressure of Sarkozy to set up a "European Economic Government": Council President Herman Van Rompuy was given the task of pre-

---

87 "So, What Is the Real Truth about the Greek Catastrophe?" in: *New Europe*, 22–28 Jan. 2012.
88 Otmar Issing, "Die Europäische Währungsunion am Scheideweg," in: *Frankfurter Allgemeine Zeitung*, 29 Jan. 2010.

senting proposals for improving the "economic-policy governance" of the Union; these were to be due by the end of the year.[89]

By 2 May, after further dramatic negotiations, the European finance ministers, in consultation with the IMF and the ECB and the Commission, had come to agreement on the exact nature of the aid to Greece: Up to eighty billion euros in loans could be made by the countries of the Eurozone and up to thirty billion by the IMF, at an interest rate of five percent in each case. The amount of the guarantee by individual countries was based on their proportion of the capital of the ECB. Germany therefore had to guarantee 22.4 billion, of that some 8.4 billion in the current year and 14 billion in each of the two following years. In return, Greece committed itself to a rigorous program of austerity and reform through which competitiveness and the ability to service loans were to be achieved once again. A troika made up of the Commission, the ECB, and the IMF was to supervise adherence to the consolidation commitment.[90]

At the instigation of ECB President Trichet, the heads of state and of government of the Eurozone in a session during the night of 7 to 8 May decided not only on this rescue package for Greece. After Sarkozy had threatened to break off the negotiations,[91] Merkel also agreed to the creation of a "rescue fund" for the entire Eurozone for the next three years so that countries such as Ireland, Portugal, and Spain would not be infected by the Greek crisis. The details of this rescue fund were agreed upon by the finance ministers in the wee hours of the morning of 10 May: On the one hand, credits of up to 60 billion euros were to be given by the Commission within the framework of a "European Financial Stabilization Mechanism" (EFSM); on the other, credit guarantees by the euro states of up to 440 billion euros for a three-year "European Financial Stability Facility" (EFSF) with its seat in Luxembourg would be able to take out loans on the market with favorable terms and pass them on to crisis states. A little later, the IMF pledged a further 250 billion euros, so that there would now be up to 750 billion euros available to defend against speculation targeting euro countries susceptible to crises.

At the same time, the ECB began buying government and private debt of the weakening euro countries on the secondary market. This was intended not only to help reduce the refinancing costs of Greece, Ireland, Portugal, and Spain but also limit the threat to German and French banks that held substantial amounts of these countries' bonds. The decision was made in the face of opposition from

---

89 European Council: European Council meetings of 25 and 26 March 2010 in Brussels. Presidency Conclusions, EUCO 7/10.
90 On this and the following, Kunstein and Wessels, "Währungskrise."
91 Report in Franz-Olivier Giesbert, *M. le Président. Scènes de la vie politique 2005–2011*, Paris: Flammarion, 2011, pp. 193.

German ECB council members Axel Weber and Jürgen Stark, who perceived it as a threat to the focus on stability. However, it served as a kind of first-aid measure to calm the markets, promoting confidence in the implementation of government decisions, a process that was per force somewhat protracted.[92]

After the danger of a financial wildfire within the euro area had been eliminated for the time being, a discussion began as to how the stability of the Eurozone could be secured over the long term. There would be intense wrangling over two ideas during the following months: Firstly, the idea of continuing the rescue fund and, secondly, that of increased access at the European level into governments and countries that wantonly disregarded the focus on stability. Merkel initially opposed both ideas with an eye toward monetary-policy orthodoxy and the mood in Germany. Realizing the catastrophic consequences of a severe reduction of the Eurozone—upward valuation that would put a damper on exports, the collapse of financial institutions that had long since been operating across Europe, enormous write-downs, along with lasting damage to the European idea—she was here following the urgings of Wolfgang Schäuble, who as finance minister of the Christian Democrat-Liberal coalition (since November 2009) was aiming at a consistent expansion of the monetary and economic union.

At a meeting with Sarkozy in the resort of Deauville on the coast of Normandy on 18 October, Merkel agreed to continue the rescue fund, with the additional provision that private creditors must also be included in the costs of any government bankruptcy in the future. At the same time, the two leaders reached agreement on sharper and quicker sanctions against governments that endangered the Community currency due to excessive debt levels. These were not however to be imposed automatically, as the chancellor and the European Commission had earlier demanded. The Commission was to have the right to require deposit payments from governments that were dragging their feet on reform; the decision to impose fines was to be retained by the Ecofin Council. Member states that were in ongoing violation of the stability pact could possibly have their voting rights in the Council taken away.[93]

The agreement between Sarkozy and Merkel ran into manifold criticism. Some argued that the communitization of risk went much too far, while others asserted that intervention into national budget sovereignty did not go far enough. Nevertheless, the European Council at its Brussels meeting of 28 and 29 October agreed in principle to a limited expansion of the Lisbon Treaty to create "a permanent crisis mechanism to safeguard the financial stability of the euro area

---

92 See Martin Sedlmayr, "Europäische Zentralbank," in: *Jahrbuch der europäischen Integration 2010*, pp. 95–106.
93 Franco-German Declaration. Statement for the Franco-German-Russian Summit, Deauville, 18 Oct. 2010.

as a whole."[94] In configuring it, however, Merkel had to make deletions in two respects: Firstly the idea of taking away voting rights was refused as being discriminatory; secondly, the participation of private creditors in financial assistance or debt reductions was left to individual cases. On 16 and 17 December, the European Council passed the draft of a corresponding amendment to the Lisbon Treaty. From July of 2013, a permanent "European Stability Mechanism" (ESM) would take action; and within its framework financial assistance could be given with "stringent requirements."

Three months later, on 24 and 25 March 2011, there followed decisions on the financial configuration of the permanent rescue fund: It was to have 80 billion euros in basic capital that the euro countries would pay beginning in 2013, along with credit guarantees at a level of 620 billion and funds from the IMF of up to 250 billion. There were not however to be any common securities of the euro countries, the so-called "euro bonds" that Jean-Claude Juncker had been demanding as chairman of the Eurogroup of finance ministers as a means of lowering interest rates for and promoting growth in the crisis countries. Merkel argued that such common bonds could weaken the willingness of the crisis countries to implement reforms and cut spending; at a meeting in Freiburg on 10 December 2010, she found support from Sarkozy on this. In fact, the introduction of euro bonds would have meant a rise in interest rates not only in Germany but also in France, the Netherlands, and Finland.[95]

In regard to strengthening the Stability Pact, the heads of state and of government accepted a compromise at their meeting of 16 and 17 December, one that the members of the "task force" under Herman Van Rompuy had agreed upon back on 21 October: There were now to be automatic sanctions but only after a period of six months during which countries in violation could implement the necessary corrective measures, and sanctions would only follow if a majority of the Council did not vote against them. Also, the supervisory and sanction mechanism would in future be applied not only for preserving the threshold for new debt but also the upper limit for total indebtedness. Lastly, governments were to present their budget plans to the Commission and the Council, respectively, in the first half of the year so that their recommendations could be taken into account in the decision-making process in the parliaments.[96] Augmented with an expansion of the system of fines and supervision of macro-economic imbalances, this reform of

---

[94] European Council: meeting of the European Council of 28 and 29 October 2010 in Brussels, conclusions, EUCO 25/1/10.
[95] Legoll, *Sarkozy*, p. 195; Stark, *Politique internationale*, pp. 270–274.
[96] Rat der Europäischen Union: Abschlussbericht der Arbeitsgruppe, Brussel, 21 Oct. 2010 (25.10).

the Growth and Stability Pact was passed by Parliament and by the Council of Ministers on 16 November 2011.[97]

Going beyond that, Merkel demanded in return for continuing the financial guarantees that there be a stronger obligation on the part of the member states to pursue economic-policy solidarity and to focus on competitiveness. At the Council meeting of 4 February 2011, she and Sarkozy together proposed a "Pact for Competitiveness" that called for incorporating a brake on debt in national constitutions, along with a ban on automatic wage adjustments based on the inflation rate, a harmonization of the retirement age, and an equalization of business taxes. These demands also met with manifold criticism; Juncker, for example, accused the chancellor of wanting to impose the German austerity model on the other member states. Merkel and Sarkozy, who had been somewhat contemptuously dubbed "Merkozy" due to their partnership, had to accept that the European Council on 24 and 25 March approved only a "Euro Plus Pact" that included the obligation "to implement in national law the budget provisions of the EU contained in the Stability and Growth Pact." Decision-making on concrete measures for increasing competitiveness and convergence was to be reserved for annual meetings of the Council. Not all EU member states voted for the pact: Aside the seventeen euro states, only Bulgaria, Denmark, Latvia, Lithuania, Poland, and Romania made these commitments.[98]

Under the pressure of circumstances in the summer of 2011, Merkel acceded to Sarkozy's demand for stronger economic governance of the Eurozone. After a meeting in Paris on 16 August, both leaders repeated their call for including a brake on indebtedness in national constitutions—this time limited to the seventeen euro countries, however; those national regulations were to follow within one year, that is, by the summer of 2012. At the same time, the two advocated establishment of "genuine economic governance" of the Eurozone in the form of a European Council of the Seventeen. At least twice per year, the heads of state and of government of the euro countries would assess measures for adhering to the Stability Pact and for averting crises.[99] Several weeks later, in light of the further need of financial resources for the rescue fund, Sarkozy gave up his opposition to automatic imposition of sanctions and thereby also his opposition to strengthening the supranational level of crisis management.

---

[97] In the form of five regulations and a guideline (the so-called "Sixpack"), printed in *Amtsblatt der EU*, Nr. L 306, 23 Nov. 2011, pp. 1–47.
[98] European Council: European Council meetings of 24 and 25 March 2011 in Brussels. Presidency Conclusions, EUCO 10/1/11.
[99] See the joint Franco-German letter to EU President Herman Van Rompuy, 16 Aug. 2011, published in *Presse- und Informationsamt der Bundesregierung*, 17 Aug. 2011.

The joint threat by Merkel and Sarkozy to seek treaty amendments with only the seventeen euro states[100] led to a willingness on the part of all EU states to accept a stronger commitment to stability in the end—all states except Great Britain, as it turned out at the Council meeting of 8 and 9 December 2011. After the electoral defeat of Gordon Brown in May of 2010, David Cameron had formed a coalition government of Conservatives and Liberal Democrats. With an eye toward the growing Euro-skepticism in his party, Cameron insisted that in return for strengthening the Stability Pact there also be a loosening of the commitments in social and employment policy. After failing to push this through, he rejected further amendment of the Lisbon Treaty.

The other twenty-six heads of state and of government thereupon agreed to an intergovernmental "fiscal contract." This contained, firstly, the stipulation that sanctions automatically be imposed on states with excessive deficits as soon as the Commission had determined that permissible levels had been breached; deviation from this automatic imposition of sanctions would only be possible if a qualified majority of the Council opposed sanctions. Secondly, participants in the fiscal contract would pledge to hold their annual structural budget deficit below .5 percent of GDP (countries with a total indebtedness of significantly less than sixty percent of GDP would pledge to keep the level under one percent). This was "preferably" to be anchored in national law but there was no compulsion for it to be at the constitutional level. If a state did not adhere to the commitment to introduce this brake on debt and if charges were filed, it could be punished with fines of up to .1 percent of GDP by the European Court. This fiscal contract was passed on 2 March 2012 and came into effect on 1 January 2013. Along with Britain, the Czech Republic opted not to participate at the last minute.[101]

Meanwhile, Merkel's repeated hesitation as well as all-too-draconian austerity measures, and the unclear signals coming from the half-hearted decisions of the heads of state and of government had led to a situation in which the Greek crisis worsened and other countries also ended up in refinancing difficulties. In the autumn of 2010, the threatened collapse of three of the four national banks in Ireland compelled the Irish government to be the first to seek assistance from the temporary euro rescue fund. On 28 November, loans of altogether 85 billion euros for Ireland were approved. In the spring of 2011, Portugal had to appeal for help after the failure of a consolidation package in parliament had led to a vola-

---

[100] *Frankfurter Allgemeine Zeitung*, 6 Dec. 2011.
[101] Cf. Friedrich Heineman, Marc-Daniel Moessinger, and Steffen Osterloh, "Feigenblatt oder fiskalische Zeitenwende? Zur potenziellen Wirksamkeit des Fiskalvertrags," in: *Integration* 35 (2012), pp. 167–182.

tile climb in interest rates for government loans. On 17 May, up to seventy-eight billion euros were granted in support.

Further assistance payments were necessary for Greece after consolidation measures had led to a severe increase in unemployment along with a drop in consumption and tax receipts. The Germans (together with the Dutch and the Finns) initially refused to grant the aid. Only when in the early summer of 2011 the bankruptcy of the Greek government once again became more likely and speculators were already eyeing Spain, Italy, and Belgium did Merkel find herself willing to support new assistance. In consideration of the pressure of public opinion in Germany and the opposition of her own government coalition, she did however insist once again that private creditors participate in the assistance action. She was able to push this through in this individual concrete case: After the banks had agreed to give up twenty-one percent of the amount they were owed and had granted longer repayment terms for Greece (which amounted to a loss of some fifty billion euros) the heads of state and of government of the Eurozone on 21 July approved—after six hours of tough negotiations—a package of longer repayment terms, lower interest rates, purchases of debt, as well as guarantees for the remaining claims of private investors amounting to a total of 109 billion euros. Beyond this, the term of the EFSF guarantees for Greek loans was extended (from 7.5 to thirty years) and the interest rate on EFSF loans was lowered (from 4.5 to approximately 3.5 percent). The EFSF itself was accorded the possibility of buying the government paper of ailing euro countries and taking preventative action to ward off an emergency in a euro country.[102]

Three months later, it became clear that this package of measures would not be sufficient to give Greece a prospect of bringing its debt under control. Merkel now insisted on an expansion of the sacrifice by private investors from twenty-one to fifty percent. At the same time, the guarantees for the remaining private debt were raised to 30 billion euros. The volume of the second government assistance package thereby rose from 109 to 130 billion euros. It was enjoined upon the banks to raise their core capital ratio by the middle of 2012 to nine percent so that they could deal with the losses from this debt reduction. However, there was not to be a doubling or even tripling of the EFSF credit guarantees, as Sarkozy had called for, with the critical situation in Italy and Spain in mind. Nevertheless, EFSF guarantees could from now on be employed to collateralize government bonds in crisis countries preferentially at twenty or twenty-five percent.[103]

---

[102] European Council: Statement by the heads of state or government of the euro area and EU institutions, Brussels, 21 July 2001.
[103] Euro Summit statement, 26 Oct. 2011.

Among the measures approved at a meeting of the heads of state and of government of the euro countries during the night of 26–27 October was also the expansion of the supervision of Greek reform measures by the "Troika" consisting of the EU Commission, the EFSF, and the IMF; the commitment to further reform efforts; and a call for the Greek opposition to support this commitment. When opposition leader Antonis Samaras rejected that and when similar views manifested themselves within the ruling PASOK, Prime Minister Papandreou on 31 October announced a referendum on the decisions by the summit—to the dismay of all the euro partners. Under pressure from them, he had to retract that announcement on 4 November and yield to a transition government under former ECB Vice President Loukas Papademos. This government accepted the reform package, whose details were finalized in negotiations by the spring of 2012. It took another six months full of nervous tension (until the formation of a government after the elections of 17 June 2012) before a parliamentary majority emerged that was serious about implementing the package.

The government made up of conservatives, PASOK, and the Democratic Left with Samaras as the new prime minister did however demand two additional years for the agreed-upon debt reduction: Less-drastic cuts were to increase the chances for a return to economic growth. The finance ministers of the Eurozone could not easily reject that even if it would of necessity lead to higher burdens for creditors. IMF head Christine Lagarde therefore demanded that after the private debt write-off there also be a partial write-off of government debt. The German finance minister opposed this, once again keeping in mind the voters and the critics of assistance for Greece in the government coalition. After long wrangling, the euro finance ministers agreed on 26 November 2012 to finance a modified assistance package by means of interest-rate reductions, forbearances, sacrifice of profits from interest on bonds that the ECB had issued, and use of credits for buying back bonds from private creditors at thirty-five percent of face value. Further, the prospect of a debt reduction for 2014 was *de facto* held out—under the condition that Greece shows a clear budget surplus (not including debt service) up to that time and that consequently no further loans would be necessary.[104]

The modification of the assistance to Greece did not however mean that the danger of infection in other weak euro countries had been eliminated. Investors were less and less willing to make long-term investments in Portugal, Spain, or Italy. As a consequence, it was not only interest rates for government loans that rose (exacerbated by the private debt cuts in Greece) but also rates for private loans. Reform measures aimed at reducing structural deficits in these countries also slowed growth and further increased the need for interim financing. The call

---

104 Eurogroup statement on Greece, 27 Nov. 2012.

for communitizing the debts consequently became all the louder, and Merkel countered with the demand that European access to national budgets must also become even stronger. Views collided at an informal working lunch in Brussels on 23 May 2012 to which Van Rompuy had invited all twenty-seven heads of state and of government. The Council president, along with Commission President Barroso, Eurogroup head Juncker, and new ECB President Mario Draghi were given the task of presenting practicable proposals for the long-term stabilization of the euro and the EU, to be submitted by the next Council meeting in late June.

In its report of 26 June, this group of four first of all proposed the creation of a European bank union, which would include European supervision of banks with right of access to national banks along with a common deposit guarantee system and a liquidation fund for ailing banks. The report also advocated "a qualitative move towards a fiscal union": Right of access to national budgets was to open a pathway to a collectivization of debts. Nothing was said as to how any of this was to look; the four only noted that it would be possible to consider various forms of fiscal solidarity and that a fully-developed fiscal union, which would perhaps exist in ten years, would presuppose the creation of a kind of European finance ministry to administer a European budget. The European Parliament and the national parliaments would naturally have to be wholly included in the process of deciding on this budget.[105]

In their meeting of 28 and 29 June, the heads of state and of government accepted Merkel's call to "consider as a matter of urgency at the end of 2012" the setting up of European bank supervision. In return, the chancellor declared that she was in agreement that the ESM (which according to a Council decision of December 2011 was to come into effect in the current year) be given the authority to recapitalize ailing banks directly "when an effective supervisory mechanism is established."[106] There was once again contentious discussion of further steps toward a bank and fiscal union. The heads of state and of government were able to commit themselves to the principle "of taking the necessary measures in order to secure financial stability, competitiveness, and prosperity in Europe." Van Rompuy was commissioned, in collaboration with the three other presidents and in close consultation with the governments, to develop a "specific timetable with

---

[105] European Council. The President: Towards a Genuine Economic and Monetary Union. Report by the President of the European Council Herman Van Rompuy, Brussels, 26 June 2012, EUCO 120/12.
[106] Euro Area Summit Statement, 29 June 2012.

specification of dates" for the necessary decisions and treaty amendments by the end of the year.[107]

The progress toward deepening the monetary union that was contained in these decisions was however somewhat obscured: Italy's Prime Minister Mario Monti, who after Berlusconi's fall in November of 2011 undertook a serious program to improve his country's budget situation, employed an adroit maneuver to get the chancellor to agree to the issuing of bank loans and the purchase of ailing government bonds by the ESM even without negotiating additional requirements: He made his agreement to a new growth pact, which the oppositional German SPD wanted as the prerequisite for ratification of the fiscal package and the ESM, dependent on Merkel's acceptance of this easing of access to ESM financial assistance. Suddenly, the chancellor stood as the loser *vis-à-vis* Monti and new French President François Hollande, who had advocated the growth pact: To his own public, Monti could present himself as the victor—the person who had at last wrestled from the iron chancellor an escape from the austerity trap.

The ECB Council decided on 6 September to buy up the government bonds of ailing euro countries on the secondary market once again. This was because the then-current ESM financial framework was not sufficient to supply funds to Ireland, Portugal, and Greece along with Spain and Italy, and because a majority in the Bundestag for providing more funds was harder to find than ever after the humiliation of Merkel. In presenting this decision, ECB President Draghi declared that "there are no ex-ante limits on the amount" of such purchases. However, they were only to occur under the provision that the affected country submit itself to an ESM regime and that it adhere to agreed-upon reform restrictions stemming from it. This commitment did not seem secure enough to *Bundesbank* President Jens Weidmann and so, like his predecessor Axel Weber at the time of the first purchase action in May of 2010, he voted against the decision.[108]

It was in fact the case that the ECB decision, in connection with the ESM's coming into force after a ruling by the German Constitutional Court on 12 September, did allow interest rates to drop in the crisis countries; the first investors then began putting new money back into them. This removed much of the pressure to act that had been on the leaders at the European level during the spring, and as a result, the differing priorities once again emerged more clearly. In Berlin, The Hague, and Helsinki, the agreement at the June summit was now interpreted to mean that ESM assistance for ailing banks would only apply to future crisis cases. Conversely, there was the assumption in Paris and the southern capitals that the

---

[107] European Council: meeting of the European Council of 13 and 14 December 2012, conclusions, EUCO 205/12.
[108] ECB: Press conference and press release, Frankfurt am Main 6 Sept. 2012.

current crises would of course be included, especially the Spanish banking crisis; and there was thus a desire that the bank union be realized on 1 January 2013. On the other hand, Merkel and Schäuble urged that there be quick decisions to strengthen the right of access to national budgets—in the best case, the summoning of a constitutional convention with a precise mandate and narrow timeframe as early as December; François Hollande, for his part, saw no need of that.

The antagonisms became evident in the run-up to the Council meeting of 18 and 19 October. Seconded by Merkel, Schäuble went public with a proposal that the EU monetary commissioners be empowered to reject national budgets that violated the agreements on stability policy. Over against that, Hollande maintained that the priority was to decide on the banking union, not the fiscal union. At the meeting, it was thus only possible to reach an understanding that the decision for the creation of European bank oversight would be made before the end of the year. During the night of 12 to 13 December, the finance ministers of the Eurogroup agreed on the details of this "Single Supervisory Mechanism" (SSM): It was to begin on 1 March 2014, be located at the ECB, and be responsible only for the large, systemically-relevant banks (thus not for other banks of various kinds that had rejected a collectivization of their liability risks). The ECB was to have authority to examine in advance those banks that were to be refinanced by the ESM. This Single Supervisory Mechanism started on 1 November 2014. As agreed by the finance ministers and the European Parliament in March 2014 a "Bank Recovery and Resolution Mechanism" (BRRM) was to start in January 2015 and be completed eight years later on.

The introduction of "an increasing degree of common decision-making on national budgets" and a European budget for managing crises were announced for the period "after 2014" in the concluding report that the group of four around Van Rompuy presented on 5 December 2012. This meant that decisions would likely be made only after the European elections of 2014.[109] After the Council meeting of 13 and 14 December 2012, it remained open however as to whether any of it would actually come about. The heads of state and of government had only agreed that the definition of "old burdens," the creation of regulations on liquidating ailing banks, and the organization of the deposit security system would occur by the middle of 2013. Van Rompuy was given the task, in cooperation with Barroso, of determining by that time to what extent it would be possible to implement the chancellor's proposal to conclude treaties for rehabilitation with indi-

---

[109] Herman Van Rompuy in close collaboration with José Manuel Barroso, Jean-Claude Juncker, and Mario Draghi, *Towards a Genuine Economic and Monetary Union*, 5 Dec. 2012.

vidual member states for which the common rehabilitation funds would then be available.[110]

The danger that the European Union would break apart, a danger that had arisen from the mutual rejection of solidarity—rejection of painful structural reforms in the crisis countries and rejection of support for those reforms by the economic draft horses, especially the Germans, who without intending it had risen to be the leading economic power—was a danger that thus seemed to have been warded off at the end of 2012. During a difficult period of adjustment, the Union had equipped itself with instruments by which it essentially seemed possible to overcome the government debt crisis. No later than the ruling of the German Constitutional Court that allowed German participation in the fiscal pact and the ESM, the opponents of a common strategy to deal with the crisis had everywhere ended up on the defensive. It admittedly remained an open question as to how much strengthening of the European level would be achievable in the process of resolving the crisis. And it also remained an open question as to how high a price each individual citizen of the Union and each member country would have to pay for overcoming the crisis.

---

[110] European Council: meeting of the European Council of 13 and 14 December 2012, conclusions, EUCO 205/12.

Conclusion: The Future of the Union

On 12 October 2012, the chairman of the Norwegian Nobel Committee, Thorbjörn Jagland, surprised the world with the announcement that the European Union was the recipient of the Nobel Peace Prize for the year 2012. The Nobel Committee justified its decision with the observation that this Union had contributed decisively to peaceful development in Europe over the previous six decades. Specifically, it cited the *rapprochement* and close bond between the two large Continental powers France and Germany; the promotion of democratic development in Southern Europe after the end of dictatorships in Greece, Spain, and Portugal; the integration of the states of East-Central Europe after the end of the Communist East Bloc; the promotion of pacification in the Balkan region after the wars of the 1990s; as well as the advancement of democracy and human rights in Turkey, a state seeking accession to the Union.[1] In the middle of an acute crisis in the European integration process, the Nobel Committee had thus offered a reminder that—despite all the crises—the history of European integration has ultimately been a success story. At the same time, the committee appealed to Europeans not to give up this success frivolously in the face of impositions stemming from the desire to preserve the Community currency.

In truth, crises have been a constant accompaniment to the emergence and development of the European Union. It has required and still requires a "daily plebiscite," as Ernest Renan once formulated it in reference to the nation[2]—and this plebiscite is by no means taken for granted. This stems from the multidimensional nature of the driving forces at the root of the integration process: The desire for securing the peace, the efforts toward a solution to the German question, the quest for larger markets, and the concern for self-assertion in the world have not always been equally strong and have not always worked in the same direction. For example, the need for self-assertion as well as the unresolved German question made a union of Western Europe seem wholly appropriate; in terms of securing the peace, however, *this* form of union—perforce limited to Western Europe—became problematic. The common necessity of unification stood against the very different sensitivities and needs of the states to be unified; the overarching interest in a common market stood against the very diverse economic needs of the individual states and the differing interests of individual production sectors. Accordingly, Europe policy could not be a unitary policy; it has been and remains

---

1 The Norwegian Nobel Committee, Announcement of 12 Oct. 2012.
2 Ernest Renan, "Qu'est-ce qu'une nation?" in: Œuvres Complètes, vol. 1, Paris: Pierre Bordas et fils, 1947, pp. 887–906.

the continuation of disputes among different conceptions of order and different interests at the European level.

Nevertheless, it was a certain combination of these four impulses that led in the 1950s to the emergence of the first European institutions: the interest in incorporating the new West German state, which had become an indispensable partner in Western European security policy, combined with the Dutch interest in a rapid opening of markets, as well as the French and ultimately also German interest in self-assertion *vis-à-vis* the United States. After the decision for the European Economic Community as a modernization project cushioned by the social-welfare state, the economic motives steadily gained weight. At the same time, the development of the system of bipolar nuclear deterrence meant for a greater impulse to achieve European autonomy. The two projects did not necessarily correspond: This explains the sluggish pace of political integration even as progress has been made in realizing the internal market of an enlarged Community. With the end of the Cold War, the goal of a European nuclear force quickly lost significance; conversely, the European Community was now needed more than ever to incorporate the central power Germany. In place of the ambivalence of the European project in the peace question, there now arose new responsibilities on the European and the global level. In the meantime, economic productivity, social consensus, and democratic stability are now no longer conceivable without the bases of the Common Market; the common interest in securing the peace tremendously outweighs potential national rivalries, and the ability to act on the global level is more dependent than ever on a common front among Europeans.

The European Union thereby constitutes an attempt to preserve and further develop the civilizational achievements of the democratic nation-state under conditions of increasing globalization. It rests on the awareness of the common and complementary interests of the European nations and a knowledge of common values and traditions, which suggests that there are good prospects for taking up the common exercise of these interests.[3] As a societal project, "Europe" thus exhibits characteristics corresponding to the nation-state projects of earlier periods in history.

This project has undoubtedly been promoted by the growing harmonization of economic, social, and societal structures that began in the wake of the enduring economic boom of the 1950s and 1960s; this is a harmonization with which the post-Communist states of the eastern half of Europe must now catch up via a

---

3 Cf. Wilfried Loth, "European Identity: Traditions, Constructions, and Beliefs," in: *Du Luxembourg à l'Europe. Hommages à Gilbert Trausch à l'occasion de son 80ᵉ anniversaire*, Luxembourg, 2011, pp. 549–555.

difficult process of adjustment.[4] Likewise, the multifaceted interconnections in Europe tend to contribute to its implementation: market integration, professional and private mobility, transnational encounters and contacts, transnationally-operating enterprises, increasingly transnationally-active academic communities, and, finally, the internationalization of attitudes, fashions, and cultural production facilitated by the media. Yet, these linking processes do not encompass all parts of European societies to an equal extent; and Western civilization, which spreads along with them, extends far beyond Europe. Consequently, there is no direct path leading to the emergence of a genuinely European public sphere as a medium of self-reference for a European society.

Accordingly, the institutional development of the European Union up to now has primarily occurred in a technocratic manner without wide societal discussion or deep identification of the citizens of the European Union with its institutions. In light of the various possibilities for conceiving a united Europe, there were always majorities for affirming Europe *in principle* in the countries that had decided to join the European Community; at the same time, however, there was also always a lack of unequivocal support for the *form* of European unification that was feasible. The discrepancy between the Europe that was desired and the Europe that was achievable explains, *firstly*, the outstanding significance of individual figures in the decision-making process on Europe policy from Robert Schuman and Konrad Adenauer to Jacques Delors, Helmut Kohl, and Angela Merkel: Given the ambivalences in public opinion, strong leader personalities could clear the way via direct contact with their partners, circumventing the routine of the bureaucracies and pledging majorities for their projects. *Secondly*, the discrepancy between the Europe that was desired and the Europe that was feasible explains why a form of integration as seen in the European Coal and Steel Union as well as the Treaties of Rome could come to be, a form that placed little value on citizen participation and that withdrew the integrated political areas from public discussion: Only when one left the implications vague was it possible to prevent negative coalitions from blocking the continually-contested steps toward integration.

Thirdly, with this background, it becomes clear how the so-called deficit of democracy has in the meantime become the most pressing problem of the European Union: Given the expansion of the Community's responsibilities and the increasing regulation that is concomitant with it as well as the majority deci-

---

4 Cf. Hartmut Kaelble, *Auf dem Weg zu einer europäischen Gesellschaft. Eine Sozialgeschichte Westeuropas 1880–1980*, Munich: C.H. Beck, 1987; idem., *Sozialgeschichte Europas seit 1945*, Munich: C.H. Beck, 2007; Günther Heydemann and Karel Vodička (eds.), *Vom Ostblock zur EU. Systemtransformationen 1990–2012 im Vergleich*, Göttingen: Vandenhoeck & Ruprecht, 2013.

sions made in the twilight of the various minister formations, the negotiations in COREPER and the European Council along with the low democratic legitimation of the Commission—all this is no longer acceptable to the citizen, independent of what is said by constitutional scholars who orient themselves on the category of the nation-state as a model. The technocratic roundabout route to Europe initiated by Jean Monnet in 1950 and successful over many years—most recently once again with the launch of the Maastricht program—has now reached an end. This was clearly seen in the intense public debates over the Maastricht Treaty and the difficulties in winning its ratification. Since the rejection of the Constitutional Treaty by a majority of the French and the Dutch, it is wholly apparent. The future of the European Union is thus to a very decisive degree dependent on the extent to which there is success in making the decisions in the European Union transparent, subject to oversight, and open to correction.

The referenda in France and the Netherlands have also demonstrated that this is not simple to achieve. Essentially, here was an attempt to provide more transparency and democracy that failed in its beginnings exactly because of a lack of transparency and democracy—a process that exhibits all the hallmarks of a Greek tragedy. The societies of the Eurozone quickly reacted to the threat posed by the European debt crisis with a revival of nation-state reflexes, and illusionists oriented on the nation-state along with unprincipled populists did not hesitate to make use of those developments for their own purposes. It is uncertain as to whether the coalition of Europe-policy realists in the net-payer and net-receiver countries will be strong enough and enduring enough to win approval for the combination of Community bonds and democratically-regulated access to national budgets that is necessary for overcoming the debt crisis.

Yet, the chances are good that in the course of the upcoming reform debate, the European dimension of identity will become more prominent in the European consciousness and that European society will become more articulate. Evidence for that is provided not only by the experience of ratifying the Lisbon Treaty, the European Stability Mechanism, the Fiscal Compact, and the bank union—instruments that even with all the delays and all the half-measures actually do help deal with the acute problems of the Union. It may also be of great importance that the current extent of economic and financial links in the Union as well as the realities of globalization permit of no plausible alternative to the further development of the Community, at least no alternative with a lower cost. Moreover, there is the fact that the common European tradition has at the ready wholly sufficient stimuli for the creation of a European collective.

Since the middle of the 1980s, the European Community has more and more come to be understood as a community of values committed to pluralism and democratic freedoms, the rule of law, human rights, and the protection of minorities. To that extent, a common constitutional inheritance has evolved in the discussions of the previous decades, one that could lead to a constitutional patriotism on the European level. This European patriotism, which expresses an affirmation of a system of values rather than an emotional affiliation, is compatible with national patriotism. In times of dynamic transformation, it even contributes to stabilizing national patriotism, which is shaped by different historical experiences as well as different languages and cultures. In this respect, one can definitely speak of a European identity in the singular. It is not however a matter of an exclusionary conception of identity but rather a universal one that respects national identities and the achievements of nations.[5]

Hence, the "Europe Project" will not lead to the dying off of nation-states, at least for the foreseeable future. Instead, it constitutes the precondition for their survival, which can only be survival in a changed form and with restricted function, however. European identity will therefore not simply replace national identity in the foreseeable future. Instead, what seems to be emerging is that people in Europe are living with a multilayered identity, an identity in which regional, national, and European aspects are united. This is regularly apparent in *Eurobarometer* surveys when Union citizens are asked about their self-understanding. In May of 2012, thirty-eight percent of the citizens of the EU Twenty-Seven characterized themselves exclusively as members of their nation. Some forty-nine percent however saw themselves primarily as members of a European nation and at the same time in a wider dimension as Europeans too. Six percent even saw themselves primarily as Europeans and only secondarily as members of a nation too. Three percent regarded themselves exclusively as Europeans.[6]

Behind these aggregated numbers there are of course different levels of awareness in the different member states of the Union and also within each population. In examining the results more closely, it becomes clear that the orientation on Europe is correlated with a person's age, level of education, and amount of societal responsibility. The younger, the more educated, and the higher in societal position, the stronger is the European dimension of identity. Accordingly, "Europe" is still a rather elite project; at the same time, however, the "pro-European" faction can reckon with further growth over the long term. With the increasing density of relationships within the Union, the strengthening of European institutions, the foreseeable increase in mobility beyond national boundaries, and the increasing

---

[5] Cf. Wilfried Loth, "Regionale, nationale und europäische Identität. Überlegungen zum Wandel europäischer Staatlichkeit," in: Wilfried Loth and Jürgen Osterhammel (eds.), *Internationale Geschichte. Themen – Ergebnisse – Aussichten*, Munich: Oldenbourg, 2000, pp. 357–369.
[6] Standard Eurobarometer 77, Spring 2012: European Citizenship.

significance of professional qualifications, the European dimension of personal and collective identity will come to loom larger.

Whether and how long national identity can exercise stronger binding effects than European identity must remain an essentially open question. There is no plausible evidence for the claim made by Ralf Dahrendorf in 1994 that the nation-state alone is able to create deep-rooted bonds among societal forces.[7] As the priority of European values and the increasingly transnational nature of life styles demonstrate, empirical evidence is already pointing in a different direction. It takes neither special courage nor excessive optimism to predict that the commonalities among Europeans will more strongly emerge with the expansion of social tasks and with the democratization of European politics, despite all the reactive flaring up of nationalism.

That which results on the level of constitutional law is what might be termed a "federation of nation-states," in the words of Jacques Delors.[8] It is true that in terms of constitutional law, this concept is not very exact; yet, it expresses quite well the ongoing tension between the nation-state and supranationality. This federation, which does actually exist now (even if hardly anyone dares to characterize it as such) will not dissolve or mutate into a mere free-trade zone, as many fear: That is because the benefit all participants receive from the current construction is much too great, which becomes clear again and again in cases of conflict. On the other hand, we cannot expect any qualitative leap to a Europe capable of acting on the world stage anytime soon in the way Europe enthusiasts such as Daniel Cohn-Bendit and Guy Verhofstadt have increasingly been calling for recently:[9] This is because the nation-state remains too important for the overwhelming majority of Europeans and because the level of suffering occasionally caused by the unilateralism of the United States as a world power is overall too meager.

It was the case that the large European party associations and their contingents in the European Parliament succeeded in significantly strengthening the supranational level of the Union in 2014. As the Lisbon Treaty had increased Parliament's right of participation in the appointment of the European Commission, the parties made use of that by putting up candidates in the European elections on 25 May 2014 who were willing and able to assume the office of the next president of the Commission. First of all, this meant that they had succeeded in politicizing the European election campaign. Whereas the average turnout of 40.09

---

7 Ralf Dahrendorf, "Die Zukunft des Nationalstaates," in: *Merkur* 48 (1994), pp. 751–761.
8 Delors, *Erinnerungen*, p. 506.
9 Daniel Cohn-Bendit and Guy Verhofstadt, *For Europe! A Manifesto for a Postnational Revolution*, Munich: Carl Hanser, 2012.

percent was hardly higher than five years earlier, it did prove possible for the first time to debate on the first front questions of European policy – thanks to the Europe-wide campaign made by top candidates such as Jean-Claude Juncker for the European People's Party, Martin Schulz for the Socialists, and Guy Verhofstadt for the Liberals. On election night, Schulz and Juncker agreed that the candidate of the largest faction—that was, Juncker—would be put forward by Parliament to head the Commission.

Parliament's proposal brought British Prime Minister David Cameron onto the scene: For him, the appointment of the pro-integration former Luxembourg premier was exactly the wrong signal for an already anti-European British public. In order to keep Britain for the Union, the German chancellor Angela Merkel initially maintained a low profile on the issue of the Commission president. Her voters were angered by that, however, and so she finally had to give in, speaking out in favor of Juncker on 30 May. She also consented to dispensing with unanimity when the European Council decided on the proposed candidate. At the Council meeting of 25 and 26 June, Juncker was put forward by twenty-six heads of state and of government—against the votes of Cameron and Hungarian Premier Victor Orbán. Thus strengthened and with a broad majority in the European Parliament, Juncker was able to assume his new office on 1 November 2014. With a Commission firmly led by seven vice presidents, he was hoping to be able to break through numerous roadblocks to reform in the coming years.

Europe policy has always been the art of the possible, and top-level European politicians will in the future too be judged by the extent to which they master this art. It is possible that the introduction of Eurobonds will be added to the instruments for overcoming the current debt crisis after all and that as a *quid pro quo* a European-level authority legitimized by parliamentary means will receive the right to intervene when national budget discipline is violated. Yet, the prerequisite for such a step to a fiscal union would be agreement between France and Germany, the duo without whose cooperation progress in European integration is unachievable. That, in turn, presupposes that François Hollande can dispel the delusion of the French electorate that the French economy can be rehabilitated without painful cuts and without further without further collectivization of national sovereignty. It is also conceivable that the aggressive course taken by Russian President Vladimir Putin against Ukraine since February of 2014 will lead to a strengthening of the Common Foreign and Security Policy. In any event, the governments in Paris and Berlin developed a high level of unity in crisis management after the annexation of the Crimea and the support of pro-Russian separatists in Eastern Ukraine by the Russian Federation. The government in Warsaw was also included in this coordination. With the appointment of Donald Tusk—up to that point the Polish prime minister—as the new president of the European

Council on 1 December 2014, the heads of state and of government provided an example of the assertion of European principles in the face of revived Russian great-power ambitions.

It is very unlikely that Great Britain would participate in a fiscal union. It is instead possible that David Cameron's announcement of 23 January 2013 about holding a referendum in the year 2017 on Britain's continued membership in the Union will lead to the country's complete withdrawal. In contrast to the situation on the Continent, the number of British citizens who regard themselves as exclusively members of their nation has always been higher than the number who also perceive of themselves as Europeans (the figure was sixty to forty-two percent in May of 2012). After Tony Blair failed to summon the courage to go on the offensive against this, continental Europeans have been showing little inclination to help Cameron in overcoming the problems with EU opponents in his own ranks. In any event, continental Europeans will not be prepared to give up Community areas of responsibility merely to keep Britain in the Union. However, it could also be the case that Britons will begin to rethink the situation as soon as it becomes apparent where the priorities of the continental Europeans lie.

The more convincingly the members of the Eurozone succeed in reducing excesses of debt and in generating new growth, the more likely that may become. Nothing makes the European Union as attractive as success. To that extent, one can expect that success in overcoming the euro debt crisis will not only strengthen Community consciousness further. One would do well to keep the successes of the past more clearly in mind than is usually the case when fixating on current frustrations.

Afterword

A history of European unification that begins in the 1940s and extends to the present perforce rests on very diverse sources. In regard to the foundational years that led to the emergence of the first European institutions, there has been much progress in the exploration of government archives and private papers. Here, I was able to draw on a great wealth of relevant studies, starting with the work of my mentor Walter Lipgens on the inception of the European unification movement as well as my own dissertation on the French Socialists and the postwar European order. The first two decades after the signing of the Treaties of Rome in March of 1957 have increasingly become the focus of historical research in recent years. Here, I was especially able to profit from numerous studies produced in connection with my chair at the University of Duisburg-Essen: the dissertations of Carine Germond, Philip Bajon, and Henning Türk as well as the habilitations of Wolfram Kaiser, Kiran Klaus Patel, and Claudia Hiepel. For this middle period, additional research was only necessary in some areas. In contrast, for the period since the mid-1970s, the archives and private papers have only been very selectively explored at this point. Here, there was much pioneer work to be done, sometimes using archival collections and private information, more often by recourse to memoirs and contemporary political commentary, which is quite rich in detail.

Altogether, it is thus a historiographical hybrid that has emerged: a synthesis that increasingly transitions into a pioneering study. The closer it approaches the present, the more original the information and the assessments and the more provisional the character of the presentation as well. The imbalance in the source base is the price that had to be paid for a work providing more in the way of comprehensive perspectives and orientation for the present.

Divergences from previous views and positions on research controversies have only been very briefly noted in the citations. Those wanting to become more familiar with the progress of research on European integration history can turn to the balance provided by the contributions in a collection that I published on the occasion of the fiftieth anniversary of the signing of the Treaties of Rome in 2007.[1] A systematic overview is offered in a stimulating essay by Kiran Klaus Patel in a newly-published collection entitled *Dimensionen internationaler Geschichte*.[2] My own position in the research landscape is spelled out in an essay that seeks to situate the work of Alan Milward in the development of historical writing on Euro-

---

[1] Wilfried Loth (ed.), *Experiencing Europe. 50 Years of European Construction 1957–2007*, Baden-Baden: Nomos, 2009.
[2] Kiran Klaus Patel, "Europäische Integration," in: Jost Dülffer and Wilfried Loth (eds.), *Dimensionen internationaler Geschichte*, Munich: Oldenbourg, 2012, pp. 353–372.

pean integration.³ More detailed information on individual problematics can be found in the specialized studies cited in the footnotes. Essays and book reviews in the *Journal of European Integration History* regularly report on the further development of research, as does the website of the European Union Liaison Committee of Historians at the European Commission (www.eu-historians.eu).

I am grateful for the many suggestions that have come from my colleagues on the Liaison Committee, to which I have belonged for over thirty years. The continuous exchanges as well as the common work toward the development of an international community of integration historians have helped me avoid the narrowness of a national perspective—something that for a theme such as European integration would prove especially fatal. All this has aided me in developing what I hope at least is a European view of the history of European integration. My thanks go to the earlier members of the Liaison Committee as well as the more recent members, especially to companions of long standing: Marie-Thérèse Bitsch, Gérard Bossuat, Anne Deighton, Klaus Schwabe, and Antonio Varsori.

Additionally, I am thankful for important insights and information from exchanges with political scientists, jurists, and economists studying the novel phenomenon of European integration. Collaboration in different interdisciplinary and often international work groups and project groups has, insofar as I can gain an overview, led to mutual stimuli along with the beginnings of a common scholarship of integration. Special thanks in this context goes to my friend and colleague in Cologne, Wolfgang Wessels, who knows better than anyone how to bring together colleagues of the most diverse origin and bent for joint work. Those wanting to gain a more detailed perspective on the operation of European institutions than is possible to provide in a presentation of their development would be well served by turning to the great overview of the institutional structure from the pen of Wolfgang Wessels.⁴

I would also like to express my thanks to the members of my staff in Essen. Sümeyra Kaya and André Postert have at different times provided important research support. André Postert has also been of assistance in getting the book to press and contributing judicious observations for the organization of the text. Raluca Frincu and Stephanie Hück have helped with the arrangement of the text; with disarming charm, Stephanie Hück has also seen to it that I was not exces-

---

3 Wilfried Loth, "Integrating Paradigms. Walter Lipgens and Alan Milward as Pioneers of European Integration History," in: Fernando Guirao, Frances M. B. Lynch, and Sigfrido M. Ramírez Pérez (eds.), *Alan S. Milward and a Century of European Change*, London and New York: Routledge, 2012, pp. 255–267.
4 Wolfgang Wessels, *Das politische System der Europäischen Union*, Wiesbaden: VS Verlag für Sozialwissenschaften, 2008.

sively burdened by demands of all sorts while focusing on the completion of the manuscript. The team spirit during my last years as holding a chair in Essen will never be forgotten.

The present book was firstly published in German language in February 2014.[5] In order to being up-to-date this English edition is in addition covering the developments of the year 2014. For this edition, very special thanks go to my translator Robert F. Hogg. His intuition, diligence, and continual engagement have significantly contributed to making a politically- and technically-complex history comprehensible. Finally, I would also like to thank my editors at de Gruyter Oldenbourg, Martin Rethmeier and Elise Wintz. I very much appreciate their engagement for this book.

The story told in this book goes on. As one can well imagine, that fact has presented a special challenge in the writing but has also imbued the project with a special appeal. Whether the finished product can itself exercise any influence over the further unfolding of the story is of course highly uncertain and presumably rather improbable. I ask however that the reader please allow me to regard such a development as an especially appealing prospect.

Münster, January 2015
Wilfried Loth

---

[5] Wilfried Loth, *Europas Einigung. Eine unvollendete Geschichte*, Frankfurt/New York: Campus, 2014.

The European Parliament 1979–2014: Party memberships

Parliamentary party	1979	1984	1989	1994	1999	2004	2009	2014
European People's Party	108	110	121	157	233	268	265	221
European Democrats	64	50	34					
European Progressive Democrats	22	29	20	26				
				27[1]				
Social Democratic Party	112	130	180	198	180	200	184	191
Communists / Party of the European Left	44	41	28[2]	28	42	41	35	52
			13[3]					
Liberal and Democratic Party	40	31	49	43	50	88	84	67
Independent / The Greens	11	20	13[4]	19	16[6]	33	32[7]	48[7]
			30[5]	23	48	42	55	50
Union for Europe of the Nations				19	30	27		
Group of the European Right		16	17					
Conservatives and Reformists							55	70
Independent	9	7	12	27	27	33	26	52
Mandates	410	434	518	567	626	732	736	751

Sources: Der Aufbau eines Parlaments: 50 Jahre Geschichte des Europäischen Parlaments 1958-2008, Luxemburg 2008, pp. 79-91; Jahrbuch der Europäischen Integration 2009, p. 49; www.ergebnisse-wahlen2014.eu.

1 Sforza Europa
2 European United Left
3 Left Union
4 Rainbow Group
5 The Greens
6 Group for a Europe of Democracies and Diversities
7 Europe of Freedom and Democracy

The European Parliament 1979–2014: Presidents

Elections	Term	President/woman president	Party	Country of origin
7–10 June **1979**	1979–1982	Simone Veil	Liberal and Democratic Party	France
	1982–1984	Pieter Dankert	Social Democratic Party	Netherlands
14–17 June **1984**	1984–1987	Pierre Pflimlin	European People's Party	France
	1987–1989	Lord Henry Plumb	European People's Party	Great Britain
15–18 June **1989**	1989–1992	Enrique Barón Crespo	Social Democratic Party	Spain
	1992–1994	Egon Klepsch	European People's Party	Germany
9–12 June **1994**	1994–1997	Klaus Hänsch	Social Democratic Party	Germany
	1997–1999	José María Gil-Robles Gil-Delgado	European People's Party	Spain
9–13 June **1999**	1999–2002	Nicole Fontaine	European People's Party	France
	2002–2004	Pat Cox	Liberal and Democratic Party	Ireland
10–13 June **2004**	2004–2007	Josep Borrell	Social Democratic Party	Spain
	2007–2009	Hans-Gert Pöttering	European People's Party	Germany
4–7 June **2009**	2009–2012	Jerzy Buzek	European People's Party	Poland
	2012–2014	Martin Schulz	Social Democratic Party	Germany
25 April **2014**	2014–2016	Martin Schulz	Social Democratic Party	Germany

The Presidents of the High Authority and the Commissions

The Presidents of the High Authority ECSC

1952–1955	Jean Monnet (1899–1979), France
1955–1957	René Mayer (1895–1972), France
1958–1959	Paul Findet (1897–1965), Belgium
1959–1963	Piero Malvestiti (1899–1964), Italy
1963–1967	Dino Del Bo (1916–1991), Italy
1967	Albert Coppé (1911–1999), Belgium

The Presidents of the EURATOM-Commission

1958–1959	Louis Armand (1905–1971), France
1959–1962	Etienne Hirsch (1901–1994), France
1962–1967	Pierre Chatenet (1917–1997), France

The President of the EEC-Commission

1958–1967	Walter Hallstein (1901–1982), Germany

The President of the EC-/EU-Commission

1967–1970	Jean Rey (1902–1983), Belgium
1970–1972	Franco Maria Malfatti (1927–1991), Italy
1972–1973	Sicco Mansholt (1908–1995), Netherlands
1973–1977	François-Xavier Ortoli (1925–2007), France
1977–1981	Roy Jenkins (1920–2003), Great Britain
1981–1985	Gaston Thorn (1928–2007), Luxembourg
1985–1995	Jacques Delors (*1925), France
1995–1999	Jacques Santer (*1937), Luxembourg
1999–2004	Romano Prodi (*1939), Italy
2004–2014	José Manuel Barroso (*1956), Portugal

Sources

Archival Sources

Archives Diplomatiques du Ministère des Affaires Étrangères, La Courneuve (MAE)

Coopération économique 1961–66 (CE-DE)
Archives Historiques de la Commission Européenne, Bruxelles (AHCE)
European Commission (COM)
Procès-verbaux des réunions du collège de la Commission (PV Commission)
    Secrétariat Exécutif (SEC)

Bundesarchiv Koblenz (BA)

Bestand Bundeskanzleramt (B136)
Nachlass Walter Hallstein (WH)

Centre Historique des Archives Nationales, Paris (AN)

Archives de la présidence de la République : La Ve République :
    Charles de Gaulle 1958–1969 (5AG1)
    Georges Pompidou 1969–1974 (5AG2)
    Valéry Giscard d'Estaing 1974–1981 (5AG3)
    François Mitterrand 1981–1995 (5AG4)

Documents of the European Convention (CONV)

Documents of the European Council (EUCO)

Fondation Jean Monnet pour l'Europe, Lausanne (FJME)

Fonds « Comité d'Action pour les États-Unis d'Europe » (AKM)
Fonds Robert Marjolin (ARM)

Historical Archives of the European Union, Florenz (HAEU)

Émile Noël papers (EN)

The National Archives / Public Record Office, Kew (PRO)

Prime Minister's Office (PRO)
Foreign and Commonwealth Office (FCO)

Politisches Archiv des Auswärtigen Amts, Berlin (PAAA)

Bestand Referat 1A2 "Europäische Gemeinschaften" (B20-200)

Bestand "Akten zur Auswärtigen Politik der Bundesrepublik Deutschland" (B150)

Interviews

Interview with Fernand Braun, 8.12.2003
Interview with Hans von der Groeben, 16.12.2003
Interview with Karl-Heinz Narjes, 24.5.2004

Monographs, Memoirs, Editions

Adenauer, Konrad: *Erinnerungen 1945–1953*, Stuttgart: Deutsche Verlags-Anstalt, 1965.
Adenauer, Konrad: *Briefe 1955–1957*, Berlin: Siedler, 1998.
Akten zur Auswärtigen Politik der Bundesrepublik Deutschland (AAPD).
Attlee, Clement R.: *Labour's Peace Aims*, London: Peace Book Co., 1940.
Attali, Jacques : *Verbatim, 3 vols.*, Paris: Fayard, 1993–1995.
Attali, Jacques : *C'était François Mitterrand*, Paris: Fayard, 2005.
Bahr, Egon: *Zu meiner Zeit*, Munich: Blessing, 1996.
Blair, Tony: *A Journey*, London: Hutchinson, 2010.
Blair, Tony: *Mein Weg*, Munich: Bertelsmann, 2010.
Blum, Léon: *For All Mankind*, London and New York: Gollancz, 1946.
Bonnefous, Edouard: *L'idée européenne et sa réalisation*, Paris: Éditions du Grand siècle, 1950.
Bossuat, Gérard (eds.) : *Faire l'Europe sans défaire la France. 60 ans de politique d'unité européenne des gouvernements et présidents de la République Française (1943–2003)*, Paris: Peter Lang, 2005.
Brandt, Willy: *Begegnungen und Einsichten. Die Jahre 1960–1975*, Hamburg: Hoffmann und Campe, 1976.
Brandt, Willy: *Erinnerungen*, Zürich: Ullstein, 1989.
Brown, George: *In My Way. The Political Memoirs of Lord George-Brown*, London: Gollancz, 1971.
Bussière, Éric / Émilie Willaert (eds.), *Un projet pour l'Europe. Georges Pompidou et la construction européenne*, Brussels u.a.: Peter Lang, 2010.

Carstens, Karl: "Das Eingreifen Adenauers in den Europa-Verhandlungen im November 1956," in: *Dieter Blumenwitz et a. (eds.), Konrad Adenauer und seine Zeit. Politik und Persönlichkeit des ersten Bundeskanzlers. Beiträge von Weg- und Zeitgenossen*, Stuttgart: Deutsche Verlags-Anstalt, 1976, pp. 591–602.

Cecchini, Paolo et a.: *Europa '92. Der Vorteil des Binnenmarktes*, Baden-Baden: Nomos, 1988.

Chirac, Jacques : *Le temps présidentiel. Mémoires 2*, Paris: Pocket, 2011.

Debré, Michel: *Mémoires, Vol. IV: Gouverner autrement 1962–1970*, Paris: Editions Albin Michel, 1993.

De Gaulle, Charles: *Lettres, Notes et Carnets, Mai 1945 – Juin 1950*, Paris: Plon, 1984.

De Gaulle, Charles: *Lettres, Notes et Carnets, 1958 – 1960*, Paris: Plon, 1985.

De Gaulle, Charles: *Lettres, Notes et Cahiers, 1961 –1963*, Paris: Plon, 1986.

De Gaulle, Charles: *Lettres , Notes et Cahiers 1964–1966*, Paris: Plon, 1987.

De Gaulle, Charles: *Discours et messages*, vols. 1–5, Paris: Plon, 1970.

Delors, Jacques: *Erinnerungen eines Europäers*, Berlin: Parthas Verlag, 2004.

Deniau, Jean-François : *Mémoire de 7 vies. Vol. II : Croire et oser*, Paris: Omnibus, 1997.

Documents Diplomatiques Français (DDF).

Documents on British Policy Overseas, Series II, Vol. I: *The Schuman Plan, the Council of Europe and Western European Integration, May 1950 – December 1952*, London 1986.

Dumas, Roland: *Le Fil et la Pelote. Mémoires*, Paris: Omnibus, 1996.

Duff, Andrew: *The Struggle for Europe's Constitution*, London: Federal Trust for Education and Research, 2007.

Europa. Dokumente zur Frage der *europäischen* Einigung, 2 vols., Munich: Oldenbourg, 1962.

Erhard, Ludwig: *Deutsche Wirtschaftspolitik. Der Weg der Sozialen Marktwirtschaft*, Düsseldorf: Econ, 1962.

Genscher, Hans-Dietrich: *Erinnerungen*, Berlin: Siedler, 1995.

Giscard d'Estaing, Valéry: *Macht und Leben. Erinnerungen*, Frankfurt am Main: Ullstein, 1988.

Giscard d'Estaing, Valéry: *Le Pouvoir et la Vie*, Vol. 2: L'affrontement, Paris: Compagnie 12, 1991.

Giscard d'Estaing, Valéry: *Le Pouvoir et la Vie*, Vol. 3: Choisir, Paris: Compagnie 12, 2006.

Europe Unites. The story of the campaign for European Unity, including a full report of the Congress of Europe, held at The Hague, London 1949.

Faure, Edgar: *Mémoires*. Vol. II, Paris: Plon, 1984.

Fischer, Joschka: *Die rot-grünen Jahre. Deutsche Außenpolitik – vom Kosovo bis zum 11. September*, Köln: Kiepenheuer & Witsch, 2007.

Fischer, Joschka: *"I am not convinced". Der Irak-Krieg und die rot-grünen Jahre*, Köln: Kiepenheuer & Witsch, 2011.

Fischer, Klemens H.: *Der Vertrag von Lissabon. Text und Kommentar zum Europäischen Reformvertrag*, Baden-Baden: Nomos Verlag, 2008.

Foreign Relations of the United States (FRUS).

Groeben, Hans von der: *Aufbaujahre der Europäischen Gemeinschaft. Das Ringen um den Gemeinsamen Markt und die Politische Union (1958–1966)*, Baden-Baden: Nomos, 1982.

Hallstein, Walter: *United Europe. Challenge and Opportunity*, Cambridge, Mass.: Cambridge University Press, 1962.

Hallstein, Walter: *Der unvollendete Bundesstaat. Europäische Erfahrungen und Erkenntnisse*, Düsseldorf/Wien: Econ, 1969.

Hänsch, Klaus: *Kontinent der Hoffnungen. Mein europäisches Leben*, Bonn: Dietz 2011.

Happrecht, Klaus: *Im Kanzleramt. Tagebuch der Jahre mit Willy Brandt*, Reinbek: Rowohlt, 2001.

Hill, Christopher / Karen E. Smith (eds.); *European Foreign Policy. Key Documents*, London: Routledge, 2000.
James, Robert Rhodes (ed.), *Winston S. Churchill. His complete speeches 1897–1963*, vol. VII: 1943–1949, New York: Chelsea House, 1974.
Jenkins, Clive: *All against the Collar*, London: Methuen Publishing, 1990.
Jenkins, Roy: *European Diary 1977–1981*, London: Methuen Publishing, 1989.
Jenkins, Roy: *A Life at the Centre*, London: Methuen Publishing, 1994.
Die Kabinettsprotokolle der Bundesregierung 1956, Bd. 9, Munich: Oldenbourg, 1998.
Kogon, Eugen: "Der Haager Europäische Kongreß," in: *Frankfurter Hefte* 3 (1948), pp. 481–483.
Kohl, Helmut: *Erinnerungen 1982–1990*, Munich: Droemer, 2004.
Kohl, Helmut: Erinnerungen 1990-1994, Munich: Droemer, 2007.
Küsters, Hans Jürgen (ed.): *Deutsche Einheit. Sonderedition aus den Akten des Bundeskanzleramtes 1989/90*, Munich: Oldenbourg, 1998.
Lamassoure, Alain: *Histoire secrète de la Convention européenne*, Paris: Albin Michel, 2003.
Lapie, Pierre-Olivier : *De Léon Blum à de Gaulle. Le caractère et le pouvoir*, Paris: Fayard, 1971.
Lemaignen, Robert: *L'Europe au Berceau. Souvenirs d'un technocrate*, Paris: Plon, 1964.
Lipgens, Walter (ed.): , *45 Jahre Ringen um die Europäische Verfassung. Dokumente 1939–1984*, Bonn: Europa Union, 1986.
Lipgens, Walter (ed.): *Documents on the History of European Integration.* Vol. I: *Continental Plans for European Union 1939–1945*, Berlin / New York: De Gruyter, 1985; Vol. II: *Plans for European Union in Great Britain and in Exile 1939–1945*, Berlin / New York: De Gruyter, 1986.
Lipgens, Walter / Wilfried Loth (eds.): *Documents on the History of European Integration.* Vol. III: *The Struggle for European Union by Political Parties and Pressure Groups in Western European Countries, 1945–1950*, Berlin / New York: De Gruyter, 1988; Vol. IV: *Transnational Organizations of Political Parties and Pressure Groups in the Struggle for European Union, 1945–1950*, Berlin / New York: De Gruyter, 1990.
Labour Party (ed.): *Let us work together – Labour's way out of the crisis*, London 1974.
Marjolin, Robert: *Le travail d´une vie. Mémoires 1911–1986*, Paris: Robert Laffont, 1986.
Massigli, René: *Une comédie des erreurs 1943–1956*, Paris: Plon, 1978.
Mauroy, Pierre: *Mémoires.* "Vous mettrez du bleu au ciel", Paris: Omnibus, 2003.
Mitterrand, François : *Réflexions sur la politique extérieure de la France. Introduction à vingt-cinq discours (1981–1985)*, Paris: Fayard, 1986.
Monnet, Jean: *Mémoires*, Paris: Fayard, 1976.
Osterheld, Horst: *Adenauers letzte Kanzlerjahre – ein dokumentarischer Bericht*, Mainz: M. Grünewald, 1986.
Osterheld, Horst: *Außenpolitik unter Ludwig Erhard 1963–1966. Ein dokumentarischer Bericht*, Düsseldorf: Droste, 1992.
Peyrefitte, Alain: *C'était de Gaulle*, 3 vols., Paris: Gallimard, 1994–2000.
Pineau, Christian / Rimbaud, Christiane: *Le Grand Pari. L'ouverture du traité de Rome*, Paris: Fayard, 1991.
Pisani, Edgard: *Le Général indivis*, Paris: Albin Michel, 1974.
Rougement, Denis de: "The Campaign of the European Congresses," in: *Government and Opposition*, Vol. 2, No 3 April–July 1967, pp. 329–349.
Schmidt, Helmut: *Die Deutschen und ihre Nachbarn*, Berlin: Siedler, 1990.
Schwarz, Jürgen (ed.): *Der Aufbau Europas. Pläne und Dokumente 1945–80*, Bonn: Osang, 1980.

Siegler, Heinrich (ed.): Europäische *politische Einigung. Dokumentation von Vorschlägen und Stellungnahmen 1949–1968*, Bonn /Vienna / Zürich: Siegler, 1968.
Spaak, Paul-Henri: *Combats inachevés*. Bd. 2 : *De l'espoir à la déception*, Paris: Fayard, 1969.
Spaak, Paul-Henri: *Memoiren eines Europäers*, Hamburg: Hoffmann und Campe, 1969.
Spinelli, Altiero: *Discorsi al Parlamento europeo 1976–1986*, Bologna: Il Mulino, 1987.
Strang, William: *Home and Abroad*, London: André Deutsch, 1956.
Strauß, Franz Josef: *Die Erinnerungen*, Berlin: Siedler, 1989.
Védrine, Hubert : *Les mondes de François Mitterrand. À l'Élysée 1981–1995*, Paris: Fayard, 1996.
Verhofstadt, Guy / Daniel Cohn-Bendit: *For Europe! A Manifesto for a postnational revolution*. Munich: Carl Hanser, 2012.
Verheugen, Günter: *Europa in der Krise. Für eine Neubegründung der europäischen Idee*, Köln: Kiepenheuer & Witsch, 2005.
Die Vertragswerke von Bonn und Paris. Frankfurt/Main: Verlag für Geschichte und Politik, 1952.
Wilson, Harold: *The Labour Government, 1964–70: a personal record*, London: Weidenfeld and Nicolson, 1971.

Periodicals

Agence Europe
Amtsblatt der EU
L'Année politique
Archiv der Gegenwart
Blätter für deutsche und internationale Politik
Bulletin der Europäischen Wirtschaftsgemeinschaft
Bulletin der Europäischen Gemeinschaften
Bulletin der Europäischen Union
Bulletin des Presse- und Informationsamtes der Bundesregierung
Europa-Archiv
Europäischer Gerichtshof, Amtliche Sammlung
Hansard Parliamentary Debates, House of Commons
Internationale Politik
Jahrbuch der Europäischen Integration
Journal Officiel de la République française, Assemblée nationale, Débats parlementaires
Verhandlungen des Deutschen Bundestages, Stenographische Berichte
Verhandlungen des Europäischen Parlaments

Newspapers and Magazins

Bild-Zeitung / Dziennik / Financial Times / Frankfurter Allgemeine Zeitung / The Guardian / Le Monde / New Europe / Le Nouvel Observateur / Der Spiegel / Süddeutsche Zeitung / Westfälische Nachrichten / Die Zeit

Bibliography

Adonis, Andrew / Thomas, Keith (eds.): *Roy Jenkins. A Retrospective*, Oxford: Oxford University Press, 2001.
Allen, Hillary: *Norway and Europe in the 1970s*, Oslo: Universitetsforlaget, 1979.
Allers, Robin M.: *Besondere Beziehungen. Deutschland, Norwegen und Europa in der Ära Brandt (1966–1974)*, Bonn: Dietz, 2009.
Allers, Robin M.: "Attacking the Sacred Cow. The Norwegian Challenge to the EC's Acquis Communautaire in the Enlargement Negotiations of 1970–72," in: *Journal of European Integration History* 16/2 (2010), pp. 59–82.
Ambrose, Stephen F.: "Die Eisenhower-Administration und die europäische Sicherheit 1953–1956," in: Bruno Thoß / Hans-Erich Volkmann (ed.), *Zwischen Kaltem Krieg und Entspannung. Sicherheits- und Deutschlandpolitik der Bundesrepublik im Mächtesystem der Jahre 1953–1956*, Boppard am Rhein: Boldt, 1988, pp. 25–34.
Asselin, Jean-Claude: "L'expérience sociale face à la contrainte extérieure," in: Serge Berstein / Pierre Milza / Jean-Louis Bianco (ed.), *François Mitterrand. Les années de changement, 1981–1984*, Paris: Librairie Académique Perrin, 2001, pp. 385–430.
Avery, Graham / Cameron, Fraser: *The Enlargement of the European Union*, Sheffield: Sheffield Academic Press, 1998.
Avery, Graham: "The enlargement negotiations," in: Fraser Cameron (ed.), *The future of Europe. Integration and enlargement,* London / New York: Routledge, 2004, pp. 35–62.
Axt, Heinz-Jürgen: "Zypern. Mitglied der Europäischen Union, aber weiterhin geteilt," in: Rudolf Hrbek (ed.), *Die zehn neuen EU-Mitgliedsländer. Spezifika und Profile*, Baden-Baden: Berliner Wissenschaftsverlag, 2006, pp. 115–130.
Badel, Laurence / Éric Bussière: *François-Xavier Ortoli. L'Europe, quel numéro de téléphone ?*, Paris: Descartes & Cie, 2011.
Bajon, Philip: "De Gaulle finds his 'Master'. Gerhard Schröder's 'Fairly Audacious Politics' in the European Crisis of 1965–66," in: *Journal of European Integration History* 17/2 (2011), pp. 253–269.
Bajon, Philip: *Europapolitik "am Abgrund". Die Krise des"leeren Stuhls" 1965–66*, Stuttgart: Franz Steiner, 2012.
Bangemann, Martin / Bieber, Roland: *Die Direktwahl – Chance oder Sackgasse für Europa. Analysen und Dokumente*, Baden-Baden: Nomos, 1976.
Becker, Peter: *Die deutsche Europapolitik und die Osterweiterung der Europäischen Union*, Baden-Baden: Nomos, 2011.
Becker, Peter: "Die Fortschreibung des Status Quo. Die EU und ihr neuer Finanzrahmen Agenda 2007," in: *Integration* 29 (2006), pp. 106–121.
Becker, Werner: "Zwölf Jahre Euro. Aus ruhigen Gewässern in stürmische See," in: *Vierteljahrshefte für Zeitgeschichte* 59 (2011), pp. 445–466.
Birkner, Thomas: *Comrades for Europe? Die "Europarede" Helmut Schmidts 1974*, Bremen: Edition Temmen, 2005.
Bitsch, Marie-Thérèse : *Histoire de la construction européenne de 1945 à nos jours*, Brussels: Editions Complexe, 1996, 4th. edition 2004.
Bitsch, Marie-Thérèse : "Le rôle de la France dans la naissance du Conseil de l'Europe," in: Poidevin, *Débuts*, pp. 165–198.

Bitsch, Marie-Thérèse / Wilfried Loth / Raymond Poidevin (eds.): *Institutions européennes et identités européennes*, Brussels: Émile Bruylant, 1998.
Bitsch, Marie-Thérèse: "La création de la Commission unique : réforme technique ou affirmation d'une identité européenne ?" in: Bitsch / Loth / Poidevin, *Institutions*, pp. 327–347.
Bitsch, Marie-Thérèse : "Le sommet de la Haye. La mise en route de la relance de 1969," in: Loth, *Crises*, pp. 539–565.
Bitsch, Marie-Thérèse (ed.) : *Le couple France-Allemagne et les institutions européennes*, Brussels: Émile Bruylant, 2001.
Bitsch, Marie-Thérèse : "Le sommet de la Haye. L'initiative française, ses finalités et ses limites," in: *Journal of European Integration History 9/2* (2003), pp. 83–99.
Bitsch, Marie-Thérèse/ Wilfried Loth: "The Hallstein Commission 1958–67," in: *The European Commission 1958–72*, pp. 51–78.
Bitsch, Marie-Thérèse: "The development of the Single Commission (1967–72)," in: *The European Commission 1958–72*, pp. 125–151.
Bitsch, Marie-Thérèse (ed.): *Cinquante ans de traité de Rome 1957–2007. Regards sur la construction européenne*, Stuttgart: Franz Steiner, 2009.
Bjøl, Erling: *La France devant l'Europe. La politique européenne de la IVe République*, Copenhagen: Munksgaard ,1966.
Bossuat, Gérard: "La vraie nature de la politique européenne de la France (1950–1957)," in: Trausch (ed.), *Die Europäische Integration vom Schuman-Plan bis zu den Verträgen von Rom*, pp. 191–230.
Bossuat, Gérard.: "De Gaulle et la seconde candidature britannique aux Communautés européennes (1966–1969)," in: Loth, *Crises, pp.* 511–538.
Bossuat, Gérard: "Le président Georges Pompidou et les tentatives d'Union économique et monétaire," in: Association Georges Pompidou (ed.), *Georges Pompidou et l'Europe. Colloque 25 et 26 novembre 1993*, Brussels: Émile Bruylant, 1995, pp. 405–447.
Bossuat, Gérard: "Drei Wege nach dem Gipfel von Den Haag. Monnet, Brandt, Pompidou und das Europa der 70er Jahre," in: Wilkens, *Interessen verbinden*, pp. 353–386.
Bossuat, Gérard / Andreas Wilkens (eds.): *Jean Monnet, l'Europe et les chemins de la Paix*, Paris: Publications de la Sorbonne, 1999.
Bossuat, Gérard: "Jean Monnet et l'identité monétaire européenne," in: Bossuat / Wilkens, *Jean Monnet*, pp. 369–398.
Bossuat, Gérard: "Emile Noël dans la tourmente de la crise communautaire de 1965," in: Loth, *Gouvernance*, pp. 89–113.
Bossuat, Gérard: "Face à l'histoire ! Les décideurs politiques français et la naissance des traités de Rome," in: Gehler, *Vom gemeinsamen Markt zur Europäischen Unionsbildung*, pp. 147–168.
Bossuat, Gérard : Émile Noël, *premier secrétaire général de la Commission européenne*, Brussels: Émile Bruylant, 2011.
Bossuat, Gérard : *La France et la construction de l'union européenne : De 1919 à nos jours*, Paris: Armand Colin, 2012.
Bozo, Frédéric: *Mitterrand, la fin de la guerre froide et l'unification allemande. De Yalta à Maastricht*, Paris: Editions Odile Jacob, 2005.
Böttger, Katrin: *Die Entstehung und Entwicklung der europäischen Nachbarschaftspolitik. Akteure und Koalitionen*, Baden-Baden: Nomos, 2010.

Böttcher, Barbara: "Währungspolitik," in: *Jahrbuch der Europäischen Integration 2003/2004*, pp. 197–202.

Brenke, Gabriele: "Europakonzeptionen im Widerstreit: Die Freihandelszonen-Verhandlungen 1956–1958," in: *Vierteljahreshefte für Zeitgeschichte* 42 (1994), pp. 595–633.

Broad, Roger: *Labour's European Dilemmas – From Bevin to Blair*, Basingstoke: Palgrave, 2001.

Brugmans, Henri: *L'idée européenne 1920–1970*, Bruges: De Tempel, 1970.

Brunn, Gerhard: "Das Europäische Parlament auf dem Weg zur ersten Direktwahl 1979," in: Knipping / Schönwald, *Aufbruch, pp.* 47–72.

Brunn, Gerhard: *Die Europäische Einigung*. 3rd. edition, Stuttgart: Reclam, 2009.

Bullen, Roger: "The British Government and the Schuman Plan, May 1950 – March 1951," in: Schwabe (ed.), *Die Anfänge des Schuman-Plans 1950/51*, pp. 199–210.

Burgess, Jim / Edwards, Geoffrey: "The Six plus One: British policy making and the question of European economic integration, 1955," in: *International Affairs* 64 (1988), pp. 393–413.

Burgess, Michael, Federalism and European Union: *The Building of Europe*, 1950–2000, London / New York: Routledge, 2000.

Bussière, Éric: "Not quite a common market yet," in *The European Commission 1958–72*, pp. 289–301.

Bussière, Éric: "Competition," in: *The European Commission 1958–72*, pp. 303–316.

Bussière, Éric: "Moves towards an economic and monetary policy," in: *The European Commission 1958–72*, pp. 391–410.

Bussière, Éric / Migani, Guia: *Les années Barroso, 2004–2014. Europe : crises et relance*, Paris: Tallandier, 2014.

Butler, David / Kitzinger, Uwe (eds.): *The 1975 Referendum*, London: Macmillan, 1976.

Calandri, Elena: "A special relationship under strain: Turkey and the EEC, 1963–1976," in: *Journal of European Integration History* 15/1 (2009), pp. 57–75.

Carle, Françoise: *Les Archives du Président. Mitterrand intime*, Paris: Editions du Rocher, 1998.

Chopin, Thierry: "Le Parlement européen," in: Serge Berstein / Jean-François Sirinelli (eds.), *Les années Giscard. Valéry Giscard d'Estaing et l'Europe 1974–1981*, Paris: Armand Colin, 2006, pp. 153–189.

Ceylanoglu, Sena: *Europäische Wirtschaftsgemeinschaft, Griechenland und die Türkei. Die Assoziationsabkommen im Vergleich (1959–1963)*, Baden-Baden: Nomos, 2004.

Ceylanoglu, Sena: "Von der unumstrittenen Beitrittsperspektive zu umstrittenen Beitrittsverhandlungen: Wandlungen des Verhältnisses der Europäischen Union zur Türkei," in: Gabriele Clemens (ed.), *Die Türkei und Europa*, Münster: Lit-Verlag, 2007, pp. 151–169.

Clemens, Gabriele: "'Zwischen allen Stühlen'. Ludwig Erhards Europa-Initiative vom November 1964," in: idem (ed.), *Nation und Europa. Studien zum internationalen Staatensystem im 19. und 20. Jahrhundert*, Stuttgart: Franz Steiner, 2001, pp. 171–193.

Clemens, Gabriele: "Der Beitritt Großbritanniens zu den Europäischen Gemeinschaften," in: Knipping / Schönwald, *Aufbruch*, pp. 306–328.

Clemens, Gabriele / Alexander Reinfeldt / Gerhard Wille: *Geschichte der europäischen Integration*, Paderborn: Schöningh, 2008.

Cloos, Jim / Gaston Reinsch /Daniel Vignes / Joseph Weyland : *Le traité de Maastricht. Genèse, analyse, commentaires*, Brussels: Émile Bruylant, 1994.

Cohen, William B.: "De Gaulle et l'Europe d'avant 1958," in: *De Gaulle en son siècle*, vol. 5, Paris: Édition Plon, 1992, pp. 53–65.

Conrad, Yves : "Évolution de l'organisation administrative de la Commission et de la question du siège. Un long chemin vers la fusion des exécutifs (1960–1967)," in: Varsori, *Inside the European Community*, pp. 79–94.

Conrad, Yves: "Jean Rey, moderate optimist and instinctive European," in: *The European Commission 1958–72*, pp. 109–123.

Conze, Eckart: *Die gaullistische Herausforderung. Die deutsch-französischen Beziehungen in der amerikanischen Europapolitik 1958–1963*, Munich: Oldenbourg, 1995.

Coppolaro, Lucia: "The European Economic Commission in the GATT negotiations of the Kennedy Round (1961–1967): global and regional trade," in: Varsori, *Inside the European Community*, pp. 347–366.

Corbett, Richard: *The European Parliament's Role in Closer EU Integration*, Basingstoke / New York: Palgrave Macmillan, 2001.

Cousté, Pierre-Bernard / Visine, François: *Pompidou et l'Europe*, Paris: Libraries techniques, 1974.

Coutrot, Aline: "La politique atomique sous le gouvernement de Mendès France," in: François Bédarida / Jean-Pierre Rioux (eds.), *Pierre Mendès France et le Mendésisme*, Paris: Fayard 1985, pp. 309–316.

Daddow, Oliver (ed.): *Harold Wilson and European Integration: Britain's Second Application to Join the EEC*, London: Institute of Contemporary British History, 2003.

Daddow, Oliver: *Britain and Europe since 1945: Historiographical Perspectives on Integration*, Manchester / New York: Manchester University Press, 2004.

Daddow, Oliver: *New Labour and the European Union. Blair and Brown's Logic of History*, Manchester / New York: Manchester University Press, 2011.

Dahrendorf, Ralf: "Die Zukunft des Nationalstaates," in: *Merkur* 48 (1994), pp. 751–761.

Defrance, Corine / Ulrich Pfeil (eds.), *La France, l'Allemagne et le traité de l'Élysée 1963–2013*, Paris: CNRS, 2012.

De Gaulle en son siècle, Vol. 4: *La sécurité et l'indépendance de la France*; Vol. 5: *L'Europe*, Paris: Plon, 1992.

Deighton, Anne / Alan S. Milward (eds.): *Widening, Deepening and Acceleration: The European Economic Community 1957–1963*, Baden-Baden: Nomos, 1999.

Deighton, Anne: "The Second British Application for Membership of the EEC," in: Loth, *Crises*, pp. 391–405.

Del Pero, Mario e.a., *Democrazie. L'Europa meridionale e la fine delle dittature*, Milano: Le Monnier, 2010.

Derungs, Thomas: "The Integration of a Different Europe. The European Community's Enlargement to the South and the Evolving Concept of a Civilian Power," in: Michele Affinito / Guia Migani / Christian Wenkel (eds.), *Les deux Europes. Actes du IIIe colloque international RICHIE*, Brussels: Peter Lang, 2009, pp. 311–325.

Dilks, David: "Britain and Europe, 1948–1950: The Prime Minister, the Foreign Secretary and the Cabinet," in: Poidevin, *Débuts*, pp. 391–418.

Dinan, Desmond: *Europe Recast. A History of European Union,* Basingstoke: Palgrave Macmillan, 2004, 2th. Edition 2014.

Dinan, Desmond (ed.): *Origins and Evolution of the European Union*, Oxford / New York: Oxford University Press, 2006.

Drake, Helen: Jacques Delors. *Perspectives on a European leader*, London / New York: Routledge, 2000.

Duchêne, François: "The European Community and the Uncertainties of Interdependence," in: Max Kohnstamm / Wolfgang Hager (eds.), *A Nation Writ Large? Foreign-Policy Problems before the European Community*, London: John Wiley & Sons, 1973, pp. 19–26.

Dujardin, Vincent: *Pierre Harmel*, Brussels: Éditions Le Cri, 2004.

Dumoulin, Michel (ed.): *Plans des temps de guerre pour l'Europe d'après-guerre 1940–1947*, Brussels: Émile Bruylant, 1995.

Dumoulin, Michel : *Spaak*, Brussels: Édition Racine, 1999.

Dumoulin, Michel: "The Interim Committee (April 1957 to January 1958)," in: *The European Commission 1958–72*, pp. 37–49.

Dyson, Kenneth / Featherstone, Kevin: *The Road to Maastricht. Negotiating Economic and Monetary Union*, Oxford: Oxford University Press, 1999.

Elvert, Jürgen: "Weichenstellungen für die Römischen Verträge – Akteure und Überlegungen der Bundesregierung 1955," in: *Integration* 30 (2007), pp. 301–312.

Endo, Ken: *The Presidency of the European Commission under Jacques Delors. The Politics of Shared Leadership*, London / New York: Palgrave Macmillan, 1999.

The European Commission, 1958–72. History and Memories, Luxemburg: Office for Official Publications of the European Communities, 2007.

The European Commission, 1973–86. History and Memories, Luxemburg: Office for Official Publications of the European Communities, 2014.

Favier, Pierre / Martin-Rolland, Michel: *La Décennie Mitterrand. Vol.4: Les Déchirements, 1991–1995*, Paris: Éditions du Seuil, 1999.

Fonseca, Ana Monica: "The Federal Republic of Germany and the Portuguese Transition to Democracy (1974–1976)," in: *Journal of European Integration History* 15/1 (2009), pp. 35–56.

Frøland, Hans-Otto: "The Second Norwegian EEC-Application, 1967: Was There a Policy at all?" in: Loth, *Crises*, pp. 437–458.

Găinar, Maria: *Aux origins de la diplomatie européenne. Les Neuf et la Coopération politique européenne de 1973 à 1980*, Brussels: Peter Lang, 2012.

Gammelin, Cerstin / Löw, Raimund : *Europas Strippenzieher. Wer in Europa wirklich regiert*, Berlin: Econ, 2014.

Gassert, Philipp: "'Wir müssen bewahren, was wir geschaffen haben, auch über eine kritische Zeit hinweg' – Kurt Georg Kiesinger, Frankreich und das europäische Projekt," in: König / Schulz, *Bundesrepublik*, Stuttgart: Franz Steiner, 2004, pp. 147–166.

Gavín, Víctor / Guirao, Fernando: "La dimensione internazionale della transizione politica spagnola (1969–1982). Quale ruolo giocarono la Comunità europea e gli Stati Unity ?" in: idem / Mario del Pero / Antonio Vasori (eds.), *Democrazie. L'Europa meridionale e la fine delle dittature*, Milano: Le Monnier, 2010, pp. 173–264.

Geary, Michael J.: "Enlargement and the European Commission: An Assessment of the British and Irish Applications for Membership in the EEC, 1958–73," Diss. EUI Florence: European University Institute, 2009.

Geary, Michael J.: *An Inconvenient Wait. Ireland's Quest for Membership of the EEC 1957–73*, Dublin: Institute of Public Administration, 2009.

Geddes, Andrew: *The European Union and British Politics*, Basingstoke: Palgrave Macmillan, 2004.

Gehler, Michael / Kaiser, Wolfram (eds.), *Transnationale Parteienkooperation der europäischen Christdemokraten. Dokumente 1945–1965*, Munich: K. G. Saur, 2004.

Gehler, Michael: *Vom Marshall-Plan bis zur EU. Österreich und die europäische Integration von 1945 bis zur Gegenwart*, Innsbruck: Studienverlag, 2006.
Gehler, Michael: Österreichs Weg in die Europäische Union, Innsbruck: Studienverlag, 2009.
Gehler, Michael (ed.): *Vom gemeinsamen Markt zur europäischen Unionsbildung. 50 Jahre Römische Verträge 1957–2007*, Vienna / Cologne / Weimar: Böhlau, 2009.
Gehler, Michael / Wolfram Kaiser / Brigitte Leucht (eds.), *Netzwerke im europäischen Mehrebenensystem. Von 1945 bis zur Gegenwart*, Vienna / Cologne / Weimar: Böhlau, 2009.
Gehler, Michael: *Europa. Ideen, Institutionen, Vereinigung*, Munich: Olzog, 2010.
Gehler, Michael: "Jacques Santer (1995–1999): President of the Commission in times of transition," in: van der Harst / Voerman, *The Presidents*, pp. 197–222.
Geiger, Tim: *Atlantiker gegen Gaullisten. Außenpolitischer Konflikt und innerparteilicher Machtkampf in der CDU/CSU 1958–1969*, Munich: Oldenbourg, 2008.
Geiger, Tim: "Die Regierung Schmidt-Genscher und der NATO-Doppelbeschluss," in: Philipp Gassert / Tim Geiger / Hermann Wentker (eds.), *Zweiter Kalter Krieg und Friedensbewegung. Der NATO-Doppelbeschluss in deutsch-deutscher und internationaler Perspektive*, Munich: Oldenbourg, 2011, pp. 95–120.
Gerbet, Pierre : "La 'relance' européenne jusqu'à la conférence de Messine," in: Serra, *Rilancio*, pp. 61–91.
Gerbet, Pierre : "La naissance du Plan Schuman," in: Wilkens, *Plan Schuman*, pp. 13–51.
Gerbet, Pierre: *La construction de l'Europe*, 4th. edition, Paris: Armand Colin, 2007.
Germond, Carine : "Partenaires de raison? Le couple France-Allemagne et l'unification de l'Europe (1963–1969)," Thèse Strasbourg 2009.
Germond, Carine: "Les projets d'Union politique de l'année 1964," in: Loth, *Crises*, pp. 109–130.
Gfeller, Aurélie Élisa : "Une militante du parlementarisme européen: Simone Veil," in: *Journal of European Integration History* 17/1 (2011), pp. 61–72.
Gilbert, Marc: *Surpassing Realism. The Politics of European Integration since 1945*, Lanham, Md.: Rowman & Littlefield Publishers, 2003.
Gillingham, John: *European Integration 1950–2003. Superstate or New Market Economy?*, Cambridge, Mass.: Cambridge University Press, 2003.
Girvin, Brian: "The Treaty of Rome and Ireland's Developmental Dilemma," in: Gehler, *Vom gemeinsamen Markt zur europäischen Unionsbildung*, pp. 573–595.
Giesbert, Franz-Olivier: *M. le Président. Scènes de la vie politique 2005–2011*, Paris: Flammarion, 2011.
Girault, René: "La France entre l' Europe et l' Afrique," in: Serra, *Rilancio*, pp. 351–378.
Golub, Jonathan: "Did the Luxembourg Compromise Have Any Consequences?" in: Palayret / Wallace / Winand, *Visions, Votes and Vetoes*, pp. 279–299.
Goosmann, Timo: "Die 'Berliner Erklärung' – Dokument europäischer Identität oder pragmatischer Zwischenschritt zum Reformvertrag?" in: *Integration* 30 (2007), pp. 251–263.
Göler, Daniel: *Die neue europäische Verfassungsdebatte. Entwicklungsstand und Optionen für den Konvent*, Bonn: Europa Union, 2002.
Göler, Daniel: *Europapolitik im Wandel. Deutsche Integrationsmotive und Integrationsziele nach der Wiedervereinigung*, Münster: Monsenstein und Vannerdat, 2004.
Göler, Daniel: "Die Lissabon-Strategie: Ein europäischer Gestaltungsversuch?" in: Christoph Linzbach et a. (eds.), *Globalisierung und europäisches Sozialmodell*, Baden-Baden: Nomos, 2007, pp. 147–166.

Göler, Daniel: "Der Gipfel von Laeken. Erste Etappe auf dem Weg zu einer europäischen Verfassung?", in: *Integration* 25 (2002), pp. 99–110.

Gowland, David/ Tuner, Arthur / Wright, Alex: *Britain and European Integration since 1945. On the Sidelines*, London / New York: Routledge, 2010.

Granelli, Francisco: "The European Union's Enlargement Negotiations with Austria, Finland, Norway and Sweden," in: *Journal of Common Market Studies* 1/1995, pp. 117–141.

Greenwood, Sean: Ernest Bevin, "France and 'Western Union': August 1945 – February 1946," in: *European History Quarterly* 14 (1984), pp. 319–338.

Griffith, Richard T. / Lynch, Frances M. B. : "L'échec de la 'Petite Europe': les négociations Fritalux/Finebel, 1949–1950," in: *Revue historique* 109 (1985), pp. 159–193.

Griffith, Richard T. / Milward, Alan S.: "The Beyen Plan and the European Political Community," in: Werner Maihofer (ed.), *Noi si mura*, Florence: European University Institute, 1986, pp. 596–621.

Griffith, Richard T. / Brusse, Wendy A.: "The Dutch Cabinet and the Rome Treaties," in Serra, *Rilancio*, pp. 461–493.

Griffith, Richard T.: *Europe's First Constitution. The European Political Community (1952–1954)*, London: Federal Trust, 2000.

Guardia, Ricardo Martín de la: "In search of lost Europe: Spain," in: Kaiser / Elvert. *Enlargement*, pp. 93–111.

Gussarsson, Maria: "Combining dependence with distance: Sweden," in: Kaiser / Elvert, *Enlargement*, pp. 170–188.

Guasconi, Maria Eleonora: "Italy and the Hague Conference of December 1969," in: *Journal of European Integration History* 9/2 (2003), pp. 101–116

Guérin-Sendelbach, Valérie: *Frankreich und das vereinigte Deutschland*, Opladen: Leske und Budrich, 1999.

Guieu, Jean-Michel / Le Dréau, Christophe (eds.): *Le "Congrès de l'Europe" à la Haye (1948–2008)*, Brussels: Peter Lang, 2009.

Guillen, Pierre: "Le projet d'union économique entre la France, l'Italie et le Benelux," in: Poidevin, *Débuts*, S. 143–157.

Guillen, Pierre: "Die französische Generalität, die Aufrüstung der Bundesrepublik und die EVG 1950–1954," in: Volkmann/ Schwengler, *Europäische Verteidigungsgemeinschaft*, pp. 125–157.

Guillen, Pierre: "La France et la négociation du Traité d´Euratom," in: *Relations internationales* 44, 1985, pp. 391–412.

Guillen, Pierre: "L'Europe remède à l'impuissance française? Le gouvernement Guy Mollet et la négociation des traités de Rome (1955–1957)," in: *Revue d'histoire diplomatique* 102 (1988), pp. 319–335.

Guillen, Pierre: "La France et la négociation des traités de Rome : L' Euratom," in: Serra, *Rilancio*, pp. 513–524.

Haftendorn, Helga: "The Adaption of the NATO Alliance to a Period of Détente: The 1967 Harmel Report," in: Loth, *Crises*, pp. 285–322.

Hambloch, Sibylle: "Die Entstehung der Verordnung 17 von 1962 im Rahmen der EWG-Wettbewerbsordnung," in: *Europarecht* 17/6 (2002), pp. 877–897.

Harryvan, Anjo G. / Kersten, Albert E.: "The Netherlands, Benelux and the relance européenne 1954–1955," in: Serra, *Rilancio*, pp. 125–157.

Harryvan, Anjo G.: "In Pursuit of Influence. Aspects of the Netherlands' European Policy during the Formative Years of the European Economic Community, 1952–1973," Diss. EUI Florence, 2007.

Harryvan, Anjo G. / Jan van der Harst: *Max Kohnstamm. A European's Life and Work*, Baden-Baden: Nomos, 2011.

Anjo G. Harryvan and Jan van der Harst, "José Manuel Barroso 2004–2014: The cautious reformer in troubled times," in: van der Harst / Voerman, *Presidents*, pp.249–276.

Heinemann, Friedrich / Moessinger, Marc-Daniel / Osterloh, Steffen: "Feigenblatt oder fiskalische Zeitenwende? Zur potenziellen Wirksamkeit des Fiskalvertrags," in: *Integration* 35 (2012), pp. 167–182.

Heyde, Veronika: "Nicht nur Entspannung und Menschenrechte: Die Entdeckung von Abrüstung und Rüstungskontrolle durch die französische KSZE-Politik," in: Matthias Peter / Hermann Wentker (eds.), *Die KSZE im Ost-West-Konflikt. Internationale Politik und gesellschaftliche Transformation 1975–1990*, Munich: Oldenbourg, 2012, pp. 83–98.

Heydemann, Günther / Karel Vodička (eds.): *Vom Ostblock zur EU. Systemtransformationen 1990–2012 im Vergleich*, Göttingen: Vandenhoeck & Ruprecht, 2013.

Hiepel, Claudia: "In Search of the Greatest Common Denominator. Germany and the Hague Summit Conference 1969," in: *Journal of European Integration History* 9/2 (2003), pp. 63–81.

Hiepel, Claudia: "Willy Brandt, Georges Pompidou und Europa. Das deutsch-französische Tandem in den Jahren 1969–1974," in: Knipping / Schönwald, *Aufbruch*, pp. 28–46.

Hiepel, Claudia: "Willy Brandt – Georges Pompidou et la gouvernance européenne," in: Loth, *Gouvernance*, pp. 163–183.

Hiepel, Claudia: "Kissinger's Year of Europe – A challenge for the EC and the Franco- German relationship," in: Van der Harst, *Beyond the Customs Union*, pp. 277–296.

Hiepel, Claudia: "Willy Brandt, Frankreich und Europa zur Zeit der Großen Koalition 1966–1969," in: Wilkens, *Wir sind auf dem richtigen Weg*, pp. 209–225.

Hiepel, Claudia: *Willy Brandt und Georges Pompidou. Deutsch-französische Europapolitik zwischen Aufbruch und Krise*, Munich: Oldenbourg, 2012.

Hiepel, Claudia: "Europakonzeptionen und Europapolitik," in: Bernd Rother (ed.), *Willy Brandts Außenpolitik*, Wiesbaden: Springer VS 2014, pp. 21–91.

Hiepel, Claudia (ed.): *Europe in a Globalising World. Global Challenges and European Responses in the "long" 1970s*, Baden-Baden: Nomos 2014.

Hill, Christopher: "Renationalizing or Regrouping? EU Foreign Policy since 11 September 2001," in: *Journal of Common Market Studies* 42 (2004), pp. 143–163.

Hitchcock, William I.: *France Restored. Cold War Diplomacy and the Quest for Leadership in Europe, 1944–1954*, Chapel Hill / London: University of North Carolina Press, 1998.

Hogan, Michael J.: *America, Britain and the Reconstruction of Western Europe, 1947–1952*, Cambridge: Cambridge University Press, 1987.

Honecker, Stefan: "Die Debatte um das 'Kerneuropa'-Papier der CDU/CSU-Fraktion," in: Roland Erne et a. (eds.), *Transnationale Demokratie. Impulse für ein demokratisch verfasstes Europa*, Zurich: Realotopia Verlag 1995, pp. 330–341.

Hubert, Laurence: "La politique nucléaire de la Communauté européenne (1956–1968)," in: *Journal of European Integration History* 6/1 (2000), pp. 129–153.

Hudemann, Rainer / Hartmut Kaelble / Klaus Schwabe (eds.): *Europa im Blick der Historiker. Europäische Integration im 20. Jahrhundert: Bewußtsein und Institutionen*, Munich: Oldenbourg, 1995.

Hummer, Waldemar: "Annäherung zwischen EG und EFTA-Staaten: Außen-, Neutralitäts- und wirtschaftspolitische Problemfelder," in: Fritz Schwind (ed.), Österreichs Weg in die EG – Beiträge zur europäischen Rechtsentwicklung, Vienna: OAW Verlag, 1991, pp. 7–52.

Hynes, Catherine: *The Year that Never Was. Heath, the Nixon Administration and the Year of Europe*, Dublin: University College Dublin Press, 2009.

Ifantis, Kostas: "State interests, external dependency trajectories and 'Europe': Greece," in: Kaiser / Elvert, *Enlargement*, pp. 70–92.

James, Harold: *Rambouillet, 15. November 1975. Die Globalisierung der Wirtschaft*, Munich: Deutscher Taschenbuch-Verlag, 1997.

James, Harold: *Making the European Monetary Union*, Cambridge, Mass.: Belknap Press, 2012.

James, Harold: "Designing a Central Bank in the Run-Up to Maastricht," in: *Journal of European Integration History* 19/1 (2013), pp. 105–122.

Jopp, Mathias / Schmuck, Otto (eds.): *Die Reform der Europäischen Union. Analysen – Positionen – Dokumente zur Regierungskonferenz 1996/97*, Bonn: Bundeszentrale für politische Bildung, 1996.

Jopp, Mathias / Andreas Maurer / Otto Schmuck (eds.): *Die Europäische Union nach Amsterdam. Analysen und Stellungnahmen zum neuen EU-Vertrag*, Bonn: Europa Union, 1998.

Jopp, Mathias / Barbara Lippert / Heinrich Schneider (eds.), *Das Vertragswerk von Nizza und die Zukunft der Europäischen Union*, Bonn: Europa Union, 2001.

Jopp, Mathias / Matl, Saskia: "Perspektiven der deutsch-französischen Konventsvorschläge für die institutionelle Architektur der Europäischen Union," in: *Integration* 26 (2003), pp. 99–110.

Jopp, Mathias / Schlotter, Peter (eds.): *Kollektive Außenpolitik – Die Europäische Union als internationaler Akteur*, Baden-Baden: Nomos, 2007.

Jopp, Mathias / Göler, Daniel: "L'Allemagne, la Libye et l'Union européenne," in: *Politique étrangère* 2/2011, pp. 417–428.

Jouve, Edmond: *Le Général de Gaulle et la construction de l'Europe (1940–1966)*, Paris: Librairie Générale de Droit et de Jurisprudence, 1967.

Judt, Tony: *Postwar: A History of Europe since 1945*, London: Heinemann, 2005.

Kaelble, Hartmut: *Auf dem Weg zu einer europäischen Gesellschaft. Eine Sozialgeschichte Westeuropas 1880–1980*, Munich: C.H. Beck, 1987.

Kaelble, Hartmut: *Sozialgeschichte Europas. 1945 bis zur Gegenwart*, Munich: C.H. Beck, 2007.

Kaelble, Hartmut: *Kalter Krieg und Wohlfahrtsstaat. Europa 1945–1989*, Munich: C.H. Beck, 2011.

Kaiser, Wolfram: "The Bomb and Europe. Britain, France, and the EEC Entry Negotiations, 1961–63," in: *Journal of European Integration History* 1/1 (1995), pp. 65–85.

Kaiser, Wolfram: *Großbritannien und die Europäische Wirtschaftsgemeinschaft 1955–1961. Von Messina nach Canossa*, Berlin: Akademie-Verlag, 1996.

Kaiser, Wolfram: "Challenge to the Community: The Creation, Crisis and Consolidation of the European Free Trade Association, 1958–72," in: *Journal of European Integration History* 3/1 (1997), pp. 7–33.

Kaiser, Wolfram / Jürgen Elvert (eds.): *European Union Enlargement. A comparative history*, London: Routledge, 2004.

Kaiser, Wolfram: *Christian Democracy and the Origins of European Union*, Cambridge / New York: Cambridge University Press, 2007.

Kaiser, Wolfram / Salm, Christian: "Transition und Europäisierung in Spanien und Portugal. Sozial- und christdemokratische Netzwerke im Übergang von der Diktatur zur parlamentarischen Demokratie," in: *Archiv für Sozialgeschichte* 49 (2009), pp. 259–282.
Kaiser, Wolfram: "Not present at the creation. Großbritannien und die Gründung der EWG," in: Gehler, *Vom gemeinsamen Markt zur europäischen Unionsbildung*, pp. 225–242.
Kaiser, Wolfram / Brigitte Leucht / Morten Rasmussen (eds.): *The History of the European Union. Origins of a trans- and supranational polity 1950–72*, New York / London: Routledge, 2009.
Kaiser, Wolfram / Antonio Varsori (eds.): *European Union History: Themes and Debates*, Basingstoke / New York: Palgrave Macmillan, 2010.
Kaiser, Wolfram / Jan-Henrik Meyer (eds.): *Societal Actors in European Integration. Polity-Building and Policy-Making 1958–1992*, Basingstoke / New York: Palgrave Macmillan, 2013.
Kerkhoff, Martin: *Großbritannien, die Vereinigten Staaten und die Saarfrage 1945 bis 1954*, Stuttgart, Franz Steiner, 1996.
Kiersch, Gerhard: "Parlament und Parlamentarier in der Außenpolitik der IV. Republik," Diss. Berlin 1971.
Kim, Seung-Ryeol: *Der Fehlschlag des ersten Versuchs zu einer politischen Integration Westeuropas von 1951 bis 1954*, Frankfurt am Main: Peter Lang, 2000.
Kirchner, Emil J.: *The European Parliament. Performances and Prospects*, Aldershot: Gower, 1984.
Kluge, Ulrich: "Du Pool noir au Pool vert," in: Serra, *Rilancio*, pp. 239–280.
Knipping, Franz: *Rom, 25. März 1957. Die Einigung Europas*, Munich: Deutscher Taschenbuch-Verlag, 2004.
Knipping, Franz / Matthias Schönwald (eds.): *Aufbruch zum Europa der zweiten Generation. Die europäische Einigung 1969–1984*, Trier: Wissenschaftlicher Verlag Trier, 2004.
Knudsen, Ann-Christina L.: "Politische Unternehmer in transnationalen Politiknetzwerken. Die Ursprünge der Gemeinsamen Agrarpolitik," in: Gehler / Kaiser / Leucht, *Netzwerke*, pp. 105–120.
Knudsen, Ann-Christina L.: *Farmers on Welfare. The Making of Europe's Common Agricultural Policy*, Ithaca: Cornell University Press, 2009.
König, Mareike / Matthias Schulz (eds.): Die *Bundesrepublik Deutschland und die europäische Einigung 1949–2000*, Stuttgart: Franz Steiner, 2004.
Kopeinig, Margaretha: *Jean-Claude Juncker. Der Europäer*, Vienna: Czernin, 2014.
Koerfer, Daniel: *Kampf ums Kanzleramt. Erhard und Adenauer*, Stuttgart: Deutsche Verlags-Anstalt, 1987.
Kramer, Esther: *Europäisches oder atlantisches Europa? Kontinuität und Wandel in den Verhandlungen über eine politische Union 1958–1970*, Baden-Baden: Nomos, 2003.
Kramer, Heinz / Reinkowski, Maurus: *Die Türkei und Europa. Eine wechselhafte Beziehungsgeschichte*, Stuttgart: Kohlhammer, 2008.
Krägenau, Henry / Wetter, Wolfgang: *Europäische Währungsunion. Vom Werner-Plan zum Vertrag von Maastricht. Analysen und Dokumentation*, Baden-Baden: Nomos, 1993.
Krämer, Hans R.: *Die Europäische Wirtschaftsgemeinschaft*, Frankfurt am Main / Berlin: Metzner, 1965.
Kreutzfeldt, Jens: *"Point of return," Großbritannien und die Politische Union Europas 1969–1975*, Stuttgart: Franz Steiner, 2010.

Krieger, Eugen: *Die Europakandidatur der Türkei. Der Entscheidungsprozess der Europäischen Wirtschaftsgemeinschaft während der Assoziierungsverhandlungen mit der Türkei 1959–1963*, Zürich: Chronos, 2006.

Kristoffersen, Dag Axel: "Norway's Policy towards the EEC. The European Dilemma of the Centre Right Coalition (1965–1971)," in: Katrin Rücker / Laurent Warlouzet (eds.), *Quelle(s) Europe(s)? Nouvelles approches en histoire de l'intégration européenne*, Brussels: Peter Lang, 2006, pp. 209–224.

Krotz, Ulrich / Joachim Schild: *Shaping Europe. France, Germany, and Embedded Bilateralism from the Elysée Treaty to Twenty-First Century Politics*, Oxford: Oxford University Press, 2013.

Krüger, Dieter: *Sicherheit durch Integration? Die wirtschaftliche und politische Zusammenarbeit Westeuropas 1947 bis 1957/58*, Munich: Oldenbourg, 2003.

Kunstein, Tobias / Wessels, Wolfgang: "Die Europäische Union in der Währungskrise: Eckdaten und Schlüsselentscheidungen," in: *Integration* 34 (2011), pp. 308–322.

Küsters, Hanns Jürgen: *Die Gründung der Europäischen Wirtschaftsgemeinschaft*, Baden-Baden: Nomos, 1982.

Küsters, Hanns Jürgen: "Adenauers Europapolitik in der Gründungsphase der Europäischen Wirtschaftsgemeinschaft," in: *Vierteljahrshefte für Zeitgeschichte 31* (1983), pp. 646–673.

Küsters, Hanns Jürgen: "La controverse entre le Chancelier Helmut Kohl et le Président François Mitterrand à propos de la réforme institutionnelle de la Communauté européenne (1989/1990)," in: Bitsch, *Le couple France-Allemagne*, pp. 487–516.

Lacouture, Jean: *De Gaulle, Bd. II: Le politique 1944–1959*, Paris 1985 ; Bd. III.: Le souverain 1959–1970, Paris: Éditions du Seuil, 1986.

Lafon, François: *Guy Mollet. Itinéraire d'un socialiste controversé (1905–1975)*, Paris: Fayard, 2006.

Lappenküper, Ulrich: "'Ich bin wirklich ein guter Europäer'. Ludwig Erhards Europapolitik 1949–1966," in: *Francia* 18/3 (1991), pp. 85–121.

Lappenküper, Ulrich: "Der Schuman-Plan. Mühsamer Durchbruch zur deutsch-französischen Verständigung," in: *Vierteljahrshefte für Zeitgeschichte* 42 (1994), pp. 403–445.

Lappenküper, Ulrich: *Die deutsch-französischen Beziehungen 1949–1963. Von der "Erbfeindschaft" zur "Entente élémentaire"*, 2 vols., Munich: Oldenbourg, 2001.

Lappenküper, Ulrich: "Die deutsche Europapolitik zwischen der 'Genscher-Colombo-Initiative' und der Verabschiedung der Einheitlichen Europäischen Akte (1981–1986)," in: *Historisch-Politische Mitteilungen* 10 (2003), pp. 275–294.

Lappenküper, Ulrich: *Mitterrand und Deutschland. Die enträtselte Sphinx*, Munich: Oldenbourg, 2011.

Lamatsch, Dorothea: *Deutsche Europapolitik der Regierung Schröder 1998–2002. Von den strategischen Hügeln zur Mühsal der Ebene*, Hamburg: Verlag Dr. Kovac, 2004.

Laursen, Finn/ Vanhoonacker, Sophie (eds.): *The Ratification of the Maastricht Treaty. Issues, Debates and Future Implications*, Dordrecht: Kluwer Academic Publishers, 1994.

Laursen, Johnny: "Next in line: Denmark and the EEC Challenge," in: Richard Griffith / Stuart Ward (eds.), *Courting the Common Market: The first attempt to enlarge the European Community 1961–1963*, London: Lothian Foundation Press 1996, pp. 211–227.

Laursen, Johnny: "Denmark, Scandinavia and the Second Attempt to Enlarge the EEC, 1966–67," in: Loth, *Crises*, pp. 407–436.

Laursen, Johnny: "'Europa aus der Lethargie herausreißen': Ludwig Erhards Europapolitik 1949–1966," in: König / Schulz, *Bundesrepublik*, pp. 106–127.

Laursen, Johnny (ed.), *The Institutions and Dynamics of the European Community 1973–83*, Baden-Baden: Nomos, 2014.
Legoll, Paul: *Nicolas Sarkozy. Un Européen en action*, Paris: L'Harmattan, 2012.
Libera, Martial: "Jean Monnet et les personnalités allemandes du Comité d'action pour les États-Unis d'Europe (1995–1975)," in: *Une dynamique européenne. Le Comité d'action pour les États-Unis d'Europe*, Paris: Economica 2011, pp. 37–56.
Link, Werner: "Außen- und Sicherheitspolitik in der Ära Schmidt 1974–1982," in: Wolfgang Jäger / Werner Link, *Republik im Wandel 1974–1982. Die Ära Schmidt*, Stuttgart / Mannheim: Deutsche Verlagsanstalt, 1987, pp. 275–432.
Lipgens, Walter: *A History of European Integration 1945–1947. The Formation of the European Unity Movement*, Oxford: Clarendon Press, 1982.
Lipgens, Walter: "EVG und politische Föderation. Protokolle der Konferenz der Außenminister der an den Verhandlungen über eine europäische Verteidigungsgemeinschaft beteiligten Länder am 11. Dezember 1951," in: *Vierteljahrshefte für Zeitgeschichte* 32 (1984), pp. 637–688.
Lipgens, Walter: "Die Bedeutung des EVG-Projekts für die politische Einigungsbewegung," in: Volkmann/Schwengler, *Europäische Verteidigungsgemeinschaft*, pp. 9–30.
Lippert, Barbara (ed.): *Osterweiterung der Europäischen Union – die doppelte Reifeprüfung*, Bonn: Europa Union, 2000.
Lippert, Barbara: "Die Türkei als Sonderfall und Wendepunkt der klassischen EU-Erweiterungspolitik," in: *Integration* 28 (2005), pp. 119–135.
Loth, Wilfried: *Sozialismus und Internationalismus. Die französischen Sozialisten und die Nachkriegsordnung Europas 1940–1950*, Stuttgart: Deutsche Verlags-Anstalt, 1977.
Loth, Wilfried: "Die Saarfrage und die deutsch-französische Verständigung. Versuch einer Bilanz," in: *Zeitschrift für die Geschichte der Saargegend* 34/35 (1986/87), pp. 276–291.
Loth, Wilfried: "Deutsche Europa-Konzeptionen in der Gründungsphase der EWG," in: Serra, *Rilancio*, pp. 585–602.
Loth, Wilfried: *Der Weg nach Europa. Geschichte der europäischen Integration 1939–1957*, Göttingen: Vandenhoeck & Ruprecht, 1990, 3rd edition 1996.
Loth, Wilfried: "De Gaulle und Europa. Eine Revision," in: *Historische Zeitschrift* 253 (1991), pp. 629–660.
Loth, Wilfried / Robert Picht (eds.): *De Gaulle, Deutschland und Europa*, Opladen: Leske und Budrich, 1991.
Loth, Wilfried: "Der Abschied vom Europarat. Europapolitische Entscheidungen im Kontext des Schuman-Plans," in: Schwabe, *Anfänge des Schuman-Plans*, pp. 183–195.
Loth, Wilfried: "Die EVG und das Projekt der Europäischen Politischen Gemeinschaft," in: Hudemann / Kaelble / Schwabe, *Europa im Blick der Historiker*, pp. 191–201.
Loth, Wilfried: "Deutsche und französische Interessen auf dem Weg zu EWG und Euratom," in: Andreas Wilkens (ed.), *deutsch-französische Wirtschaftsbeziehungen 1945–1960*, Sigmaringen: Jan Thorbecke, 1997, pp. 171–187.
Loth, Wilfried: "Franco-German relations and European security, 1957–1963," in: Deighton / Milward, *Widening*, pp. 41–53.
Loth, Wilfried: "Jean Monnet, Charles de Gaulle und das Projekt der Politischen Union (1958–1963)," in: Wilkens, *Interessen verbinden*, pp. 253–267.
Loth, Wilfried: "Der Prozess der europäischen Integration. Antriebskräfte, Entscheidungen und Perspektiven," in: *Jahrbuch für Europäische Geschichte* 1 (2000), pp. 17–30.

Loth, Wilfried: "Regionale, nationale und europäische Identität. Überlegungen zum Wandel europäischer Staatlichkeit," in: Wilfried Loth / Jürgen Osterhammel (eds.), *Internationale Geschichte. Themen – Ergebnisse – Aussichten*, Munich: Oldenbourg, 2000, pp. 357–369.

Loth, Wilfried (ed.): *Crises and compromises. The European project 1963–1969*, Baden-Baden: Nomos, 2001.

Loth, Wilfried: "Français et Allemands dans la crise de la chaise vide," in: Bitsch, *Le couple France-Allemagne*, pp. 229–243.

Loth, Wilfried (ed.): *Das europäische Projekt zu Beginn des 21. Jahrhunderts*, Opladen: Leske und Budrich, 2001.

Loth, Wilfried: "Nach Nizza. Die Aufgaben der Europapolitik nach den Ergebnissen des Europäischen Rates in Nizza," in: idem., *Das europäische Projekt*, pp. 383–389.

Loth, Wilfried: "Beiträge der Geschichtswissenschaft zur Deutung der Europäischen Integration," in: Wilfried Loth / Wolfgang Wessels (eds.), *Theorien europäischer Integration*, Opladen: Leske und Budrich, 2001, pp. 87–106.

Loth, Wilfried: *Overcoming the Cold War. A History of Détente, 1950–1991*, Basingstoke and New York: Palgrave, 2002.

Loth, Wilfried: *Entwürfe einer europäischen Verfassung. Eine historische Bilanz*, Bonn: Europa Union, 2002.

Loth, Wilfried: "Deutsche Europapolitik von Helmut Schmidt bis Helmut Kohl," in: Knipping / Schönwald, *Aufbruch*, pp. 474–488.

Loth, Wilfried: "Konrad Adenauer und die europäische Einigung," in: König / Schulz, *Bundesrepublik*, pp. 81–105.

Loth, Wilfried (ed.): *La gouvernance supranationale dans la construction européenne*, Brussels: Émile Bruylant, 2005.

Loth, Wilfried: "Die Verfassung für Europa in historischer Perspektive," in: idem. (ed.), *Europäische Gesellschaft. Grundlagen und Perspektiven*, Wiesbaden: Verlag für Sozialwissenschaften, 2005, pp. 245–264.

Loth, Wilfried: "Michail Gorbatschow, Helmut Kohl und die Lösung der deutschen Frage 1989/1990," in: Gian Enrico Rusconi / Hans Woller (eds.), *Parallele Geschichte? Italien und Deutschland 1945–2000*, Berlin: Duncker und Humblot, 2006, pp. 461–477.

Loth, Wilfried: "European Political Co-operation and European security in the policies of Willy Brandt and Georges Pompidou," in: van der Harst, *Beyond the Customs Union*, pp. 21–34.

Loth, Wilfried: "Guy Mollet und die Entstehung der Römischen Verträge 1956/57," in: *Integration* 30 (2007), pp. 313–319.

Loth, Wilfried: "Walter Hallstein, a committed European," in: *The European Commission 1958–72*, pp. 79–90.

Loth, Wilfried: "The ‚empty chair'crisis," in: *The European Commission 1958–72*, pp. 91–108.

Loth, Wilfried: "Vor 60 Jahren. Der Haager Europa-Kongress," in: *Integration* 31 (2008), pp. 179–190.

Loth, Wilfried (ed.): *Experiencing Europe. 50 Years of European Construction 1957–2007*, Baden-Baden: Nomos, 2009.

Loth, Wilfried: "Abschied vom Nationalstaat? Willy Brandt und die europäische Einigung," in: Bernd Rother (ed.), *Willy Brandt: neue Fragen, neue Erkenntnisse*, Bonn: Dietz 2011, pp. 114–134.

Loth, Wilfried: "Kreativ, vor allem in Buchführung. Wie Athen in die Eurozone gelangte und Berlin seinen Widerstand aufgab," in: *Frankfurter Allgemeine Sonntagszeitung* 18.9.2011.

Loth, Wilfried: "European identity: traditions, constructions, and beliefs," in: *Du Luxembourg à l'Europe. Hommages à Gilbert Trausch à l'occasion de son 80ᵉ anniversaire*, Luxembourg: Éditions Saint Paul, 2011, pp. 549–555.

Loth, Wilfried: "Integrating Paradigms. Walter Lipgens and Alan Milward as Pionniers of European Integration History," in: Fernando Guirao / Frances M. B. Lynch / Sigfrido M. Ramírez Pérez (eds.), *Alan S. Milward and a Century of European Change*, London / New York: Routledge, 2012, pp. 255–267.

Loth, Wilfried: "Negotiating the Maastricht Treaty," in: *Journal of European Integration History* 19/1 (2013), pp. 67–83.

Loth, Wilfried: "Helmut Kohl und die Währungsunion," in: *Vierteljahrshefte für Zeitgeschichte* 61/4 (2013), pp. 321–346.

Loth, Wilfried / Nicolae Paŭn (eds.), *Disintegration and Integration in East-Central Europe, 1919 – post-1989*, Baden-Baden: Nomos, 2014.

Lucas, Hans-Dieter: "Politik der kleinen Schritte – Genscher und die deutsche Europapolitik 1974–1983," in: idem. (ed.), *Genscher, Deutschland und Europa*, Baden-Baden: Nomos, 2002, pp. 85–113.

Ludlow, N. Piers: *Dealing with Britain. The Six and the First UK Application to the EEC*, Cambridge: Cambridge University Press, 1997.

Ludlow, N. Piers: *The European Community and the Crises of the 1960s. Negotiating the Gaullist challenge*, London / New York: Routledge, 2006.

Ludlow, N. Piers (ed.): European *Integration and the Cold War. Ostpolitik – Westpolitik, 1965–1973*, London / New York: Routledge, 2007.

Ludlow, Peter: *The Making of the European Monetary System. A case study of the politics of the European Community*, London: Butterworth Scientific, 1982.

Ludlow, Peter: *The Laeken Council*, Brussels: EuroComment, 2002.

Ludlow, Peter: *The Making of the new Europe. The European Councils in Brussels and Copenhagen 2002*, Brussels: EuroComment, 2004.

Ludlow, Peter: *Dealing with Turkey. The European Council of 16-17 December 2004*, Brussels: EuroComment, 2005.

Lynch, Frances: "De Gaulle's First Veto. Fance, The Rueff Plan and the Free Trade Area," in: *Contemporary European History* 9 (2000), pp. 111–135.

Magagnoli, Ralf: *Italien und die Europäische Verteidigungsgemeinschaft. Zwischen europäischem Credo und nationaler Machtpolitik*, Frankfurt am Main: Peter Lang, 1999.

Maier, Klaus A.: "Die internationalen Auseinandersetzungen um die Westintegration der Bundesrepublik Deutschland und um ihre Bewaffnung im Rahmen der Europäischen Verteidigungsgemeinschaft," in: *Anfänge westeuropäischer Sicherheitspolitik 1945–1956*, Bd. 2: Die EVG-Phase, Munich: Oldenbourg, 1990, pp. 1–234.

Malmborg, Mikael af / Laursen, Johnny: "The Creation of EFTA," in: Torsten B. Olesen (ed.), *Interdependence versus Integration. Denmark, Scandinavia and Western Europe, 1945–1960*, Odense: University Press of Southern Denmark, 1995, pp. 197–212.

Malmborg, Mikael af: *Den ståndaktiga nationalstaten. Sverige och den västeruopeiska integrationen 1945–1959*, Lund: Lund University Press, 1994.

Malmborg, Mikael af: "Divergent Scandinavian responses to the proposed first enlargement of the EEC,"in: Deighton / Milward, *Widening*, pp. 299–315.

Mangenot, Michel / Sylvain Schirmann (eds.): *Les institutions européennes font leur histoire. Regards croisés soixante ans après de traité de Paris*, Brussels: Peter Lang, 2012.

Marsh, David: *Der Euro. Die geheime Geschichte der neuen Weltwährung*, Hamburg: Murmann, 2009.
Mastny, Vojtech: *Reassuring NATO. Eastern Europe, Russia, and the Western Alliance (= Forsvarsstudier 5/1997)*, Oslo: IFS, 1997.
Maurer, Andreas: "Die Verhandlungen zum Reformvertrag unter deutschem Vorsitz," in: *Aus Politik und Zeitgeschichte* 43/2007, pp. 3–8.
Mayer, Franz C.: "Verfassungsstruktur und Verfassungskohärenz – Merkmale europäischen Verfassungsrechts?" in: *Integration* 26 (2003), pp. 398–413.
Meier-Dörnberg, Wilhelm: "Die Planung des Verteidigungsbeitrags der Bundesrepublik Deutschland im Rahmen der EVG," in: *Anfänge westeuropäischer Sicherheitspolitik 1945–1956, Bd. 2: Die EVG-Phase*, Munich: Oldenbourg, 1990, pp. 605–756.
Melchionni, Maria Grazia /Roberto Ducci : *La Genèse des traités de Rome*, Paris: Economica, 2007.
Meyer, Jan-Henrik: "Transnational communication in the European public sphere. The summit of the Hague 1969," in: Kaiser / Leucht / Rasmussen, *History*, pp. 110–128.
Milward, Alan S., *The Reconstruction of Western Europe, 1954–51*, London: Routledge, 1984.
Milward, Alan S. / George Brennan / Frederico Romero: *The European Rescue of the Nation State*, London: Routledge 1992, 3rd edition 2000.
Milward, Alan S.: *The United Kingdom and the European Community, Vol. 1: The Rise and Fall of a National Strategy 1945–1963*, London: Whitehall History: Frank Cass cop., 2002.
Milward, Alan S.: "The Hague Conference of 1969 and the United Kingdom's Accession to the European Economic Community," in: *Journal of European Integration History* 9/2 (2003), pp. 117–126.
Mittag, Jürgen (ed.): *Politische Parteien und europäische Integration. Entwicklung und Perspektiven transnationaler Parteienkooperation in Europa*, Essen: Klartext, 2006.
Mittag, Jürgen: *Kleine Geschichte der Europäischen Union. Von der Europaidee bis zur Gegenwart*, Münster: Aschendorff, 2008.
Molènes, Charles Melchior de: *L'Europe de Strasbourg. Une première expérience de parlementarisme européen*, Paris: Édition Roudil, 1971.
Möckli, Daniel: "Speaking with one voice? The evolution of a European Foreign Policy," in: Anne Deighton / Gérard Bossuat (ed.), *The EC/EU: A World Security Actor?*, Paris: Soleb, 2007, pp. 132–151.
Möckli, Daniel: *European Foreign Policy during the Cold War. Heath, Brandt, Pompidou and the Dream of Political Unity*, London / New York: Routledge, 2009.
Moravscik, Andrew: "Negotiating the Single European Act: national interests and conventional statecraft in the European Community," in: *International Organization* 45 (1991), pp. 19–56.
Moravscik, Andrew: *The Choice for Europe: Social Purpose and State Power from Messina to Maastricht*, Ithaca / New York: Cornell University Press, 1998.
Mourlon-Druol, Emmanuel: "Filling the EEC leadership vacuum? The creation of the European Council in 1974," in: *Cold War History* 10/3 (2010), pp. 315–339.
Mourlon-Druol, Emmanuel: *A Europe Made of Money. The Emergence of the European Monetary System*, Ithaca / London: Cornell University Press, 2012.
Niess, Frank: *Die europäische Idee aus dem Geist des Widerstands*, Frankfurt am Main: Suhrkamp, 2001.
Noack, Paul: *Das Scheitern der Europäischen Verteidigungsgemeinschaft. Entscheidungsprozesse vor und nach dem 30. August 1954*, Düsseldorf: Droste, 1977.

Noël, Gilbert: *Du Pool vert à la politique agricole commune. Les tentatives de Communauté agricole européenne entre 1945 et 1955*, Paris: Economica, 1989.
Norman, Peter: *The Accidental Constitution. The Story of the European Convention*, Brussels: EuroComment, 2003.
Ojanen, Hanna: "If in 'Europe', then in its 'core'? Finland, Sweden," in: Kaiser / Elvert, *Enlargement*, pp. 150–169.
Olivi, Bino: *L'Europe difficile. Histoire politique de la Communauté européenne*, Paris: Gallimard, 1998.
Olivi, Bino / Alessandro Giacone : *L'Europe difficile. Histoire politique de la construction européenne*, Paris: Folio, 2007.
O'Neill, Con: *Britain's Entry into the European Community*, London: Routledge, 2000.
Palayret, Jean-Marie : "Les décideurs français et allemands face aux questions institutionnelles dans la négociation des traités de Rome," in: Bitsch, *Le couple France-Allemagne*, pp. 105–150.
Palayret, Jean-Marie / Helen Wallace / Pascaline Winand (eds.): *Visions, Votes and Vetoes: The Empty Chair Crisis and the Luxembourg Compromise Forty Years On*, Brussels: Peter Lang, 2006.
Palayret, Jean-Marie: "La voie française vers l'Union économique et monétaire durant la négociation du traité de Maastricht (1988–1992)," in: Martial Libera / Birte Wassenberg (eds.), *L'Europe au cœur. Études pour Marie-Thérèse Bitsch*, Brussels: Émile Bruylant, 2009, pp. 197–221.
Parr, Helen: *Harold Wilson and Britain's World Role: British Policy towards the European Community, 1964–1967*, London: Routledge, 2005.
Parr, Helen: "Anglo-French nuclear collaboration and Britain's policy towards Europe, 1970–1973," in: van der Harst, *Beyond the Customs Union*, pp. 35–59.
Patel, Kiran Klaus: *Europäisierung wider Willen. Die Bundesrepublik in der Agrarintegration der EWG 1955–1973*, Munich: Oldenbourg, 2009.
Patel, Kiran Klaus (ed.): *Fertile Ground for Europe? The History of European Integration and the Common Agricultural Policy since 1945*, Baden-Baden: Nomos, 2009.
Patel, Kiran Klaus, "Europäische Integration," in: Jost Düllfer / Wilfried Loth (eds.), *Dimensionen internationaler Geschichte*, Munich: Oldenbourg, 2012, pp. 353–372.
Pedersen, Thomas: *European Union and the EFTA Countries. Enlargement and Integration*, London: Pinter, 1994.
Perron, Régine: "Le discret projet de l'intégration monétaire européenne (1963–1969)," in: Loth, *Crises*, pp. 345–367.
Pero, Mario Del: "A European Solution for a European Crisis. The International implications of Portugal's Revolution," in: *Journal of European Integration History* 15/1 (2009), pp. 15–34.
Philippe, Hartmut: "'The Germans hold the key': Britain's Second Application to the European Economic Community and the Hope for German Help, 1966–67," in: Christian Haase (ed.), *Debating Foreign Affairs. The Public and British Foreign Policy since 1867*, Berlin / Vienna: Philo Fine Arts, 2003, pp. 153–182.
Pine, Melissa: "Perseverance in the Face of Rejection: Towards British Membership of the European Communities, November 1967 – June 1970," in: Knipping / Schönwald, *Aufbruch*, pp. 287–305.
Pine, Melissa: *Harold Wilson and Europe: Pursuing Britain's Membership of the European Community*, London: I.B. Tauris, 2008.

Pinto, António Costa/ Teixeira, Nuno Severiano: "From Atlantic past to European destiny: Portugal," in: Kaiser / Elvert, *European Union Enlargement*, pp. 112–130.
Pistone, Sergio: *The Union of European Federalists*, Milano: Giuffrè, 2008.
Poidevin, Raymond: "Frankreich und das Problem der EVG: Nationale und internationale Einflüsse (Sommer 1951 bis Sommer 1953)," in: Volkmann / Schwengler, *Europäische Verteidigungsgemeinschaft*, pp. 101–124.
Poidevin, Raymond: *Robert Schuman – homme d'Etat 1886–1963*, Paris: Imprimerie nationale, 1986.
Poidevin, Raymond (ed.) : *Histoire des débuts de la construction européenne (mars 1948 – printemps 1950)*, Brussels: Émile Bruylant, 1986.
Poidevin, Raymond: "Le facteur Europe dans la politique allemande de Robert Schuman (été 1948 – printemps 1949)," in: Poidevin, *Débuts*, pp. 311–326.
Poidevin, Raymond: "De Gaulle et l'Europe en 1958," in: *De Gaulle en son siècle*, vol. 5, pp. 79–87.
Posselt, Martin: "Richard Coudenhove-Kalergi und die Europäische Parlamentarier-Union," Diss. Graz 1987.
Preda, Daniela: *Alcide De Gasperi federalista europeo*, Bologna: Il Mulino, 2004.
Preda, Daniela: "L'action de Spinelli au Parlement européen et le projet de Traité d'Union européenne (1979–1984)," in: Loth, *Gouvernance*, pp.185–203.
Preda, Daniela (ed.) : *Altiero Spinelli e i Movimenti per l'Unità Europea*, Padova: Cedam, 2010.
Pudlat, Andreas: "Der lange Weg zum Schengen-Raum: Ein Prozess im Vier-Phasen-Modell," in: *Journal of European Integration History* 17/2 (2011), pp. 303–325.
Quaisser, Wolfgang / Reppegather, Alexandra: *EU-Beitrittsreife der Türkei und Konsequenzen einer EU-Mitgliedschaft*, Munich: Working Papers, 2004.
Ranieri, Ruggero: "The origins and achievements of the EEC Customs Union (1958–1968)," in: Varsori, *Inside the European Community*, pp. 257–281.
Rasmussen, Morten: "The Hesitant European. History of Denmark's Accession to the European Communities 1970-73," in: *Journal of European Integration History* 11/2 (2005), pp. 47–74.
Rasmussen, Morten, "Joining the European Communities. Denmark's Road to EC-Membership, 1961–1973," Diss. EUI Florence, 2006.
Rasmussen, Morten: "The Origins of a Legal Revolution – The Early History of the European Court of Justice," in: *Journal of European Integration History* 14/1 (2008), pp. 77–98.
Renouard, Joe / Vigil, D. Nathan: "The Quest for Leadership in a Time of Peace. Jimmy Carter and Western Europe, 1977–1981," in: Schulz / Schwartz, *Strained Alliance*, pp. 309–332.
Reuter, Jürgen: "Werden Athen und Ankara ihren historischen Konflikt beilegen? Griechisch-türkische Beziehungen im Lichte der türkischen EU-Beitrittskandidatur," in: Loth, *Das europäische Projekt*, pp. 295–323.
Reyels, Lili: *Die Entstehung des ersten Vertrags von Lomé im deutsch-französischen Spannungsfeld 1973–1975*, Baden-Baden: Nomos, 2008.
Riondel, Bruno: "Itinéraire d'un fédéraliste. Maurice Faure," in: *Journal of European Integration History* 2/1 (1997), pp. 69–82.
Rioux, Jean-Pierre: "Französische öffentliche Meinung und EVG: Parteienstreit oder Schlacht der Erinnerungen?" in: Volkmann / Schwengler, *Europäische Verteidigungsgemeinschaft*, pp. 159–176.
Rodrigues, Maria João (ed.): *Europe, Globalization and the Lisbon Agenda*, Cheltenham / Northampton/Mass.: Edward Elgar Publishing, 2009.

Romano, Angela: "The Nine and the Conference of Helsinki: A challenging game with the Soviets," in: van der Harst, *Beyond the Customs Union*, pp. 83–104.

Romano, Angela: *From Détente in Europe to European Détente. How the West Shaped the Helsinki CSCE*, Brussels: Peter Lang, 2009.

Rometsch, Dietrich: *Die Rolle und Funktionsweise der Europäischen Kommission in der Ära Delors*, Frankfurt am Main: Peter Lang, 1999.

Rosengarten, Ulrich: *Die Genscher-Colombo-Initiative. Baustein für die Europäische Union*, Baden-Baden: Nomos, 2008.

Roussel, Éric: *Jean Monnet 1888–1979*, Paris: Fayard, 1996.

Roussel, Éric: *Georges Pompidou 1911–1974*, enlarged edition Paris: Fayard, 2004.

Ruano, Lorena: "The Consolidation of Democracy vs. the Price of Olive Oil: The Story of why the CAP Delayed Spain's Entry to the EC," in: *Journal of European Integration History* 11/2 (2005), pp. 96–118.

Rücker, Kathrin: "Le triangle Paris-Bonn-Londres et le processus d'adhésion britannique au marché commun 1969–1973," Thèse Paris 2009.

Ruyt, Jean de: *L'Acte unique européen. Commentaire*, Brussels: Édition de l'Université de Bruxelles, 1987.

Saunier, George: "Prélude à la relance de l'Europe. Le couple franco-allemand et les projets de relance communautaire vue de l'hexagone 1981–1985," in: Bitsch, *Le couple France-Allemagne*, pp. 463–485.

Saunier, Georges: "La négociation de Maastricht vue de Paris," in: *Journal of European Integration History* 19/1 (2013), pp. 45–65.

Schabert, Thilo: *Wie Weltgeschichte gemacht wird. Frankreich und die deutsche Einheit*, Stuttgart: Klett-Cotta, 2002.

Schild, Joachim: "arkozys Europapolitik: Das zunehmende Gewicht der Innenpolitik," in: *Integration* 30 (2007), pp. 238–250.

Schmalz, Uwe: "Aufbruch zu neuer Handlungsfähigkeit. Die Gemeinsame Außen-, Sicherheits- und Verteidigungspolitik unter deutscher Ratspräsidentschaft," in: *Integration* 3/1999, pp. 191–204.

Schoenborn, Benedikt: *La mésentente apprivoisée. De Gaulle et les Allemands, 1963–1969*, Paris: Presses Universitaires de France, 2007.

Schulz, Matthias: "Die politische Freundschaft Jean Monnet – Kurt Birrenbach, die Einheit des Westens und die ‚Präambel' zum Elysée-Vertrag von 1963," in: Wilkens, *Interessen verbinden*, pp. 299–327.

Schulz, Matthias / Thomas A. Schwartz (eds.): *The Strained Alliance. U.S.-European Relations from Nixon to Carter*, New York: Cambridge University Press, 2009.

Schulz, Matthias: "The Reluctant European. Helmut Schmidt, the European Community, and Transatlantic Relations," in: Schulz / Schwartz, *Strained Alliance*, pp. 279–307.

Schwaag, Sylvie M.: "Currency Convertibility and European Integration. France, Germany and Britain," in: Deighton / Milward, *Widening*, pp. 89–106.

Schwabe, Klaus: "Der Marshall-Plan und Europa," in: Poidevin, *Débuts*, pp. 47–69.

Schwabe, Klaus (ed.): *Die Anfänge des Schuman-Plans 1950/51*, Baden-Baden: Nomos, 1988.

Schwan, Heribert: *Die Frau an seiner Seite. Leben und Leiden der Hannelore Kohl*, Munich: Heyne, 2011.

Schwarz, Hans-Peter: *Adenauer. Der Aufstieg: 1876–1952*, Stuttgart: Deutsche Verlags-Anstalt, 1986.

Schwarz, Hans-Peter: Adenauer: *Der Staatsmann 1952–1967*, Stuttgart: Deutsche Verlags-Anstalt, 1991.
Schwarz, Hans-Peter: "Präsident de Gaulle, Bundeskanzler Adenauer und die Entstehung des Elysée-Vertrages," in: Wilfried Loth / Robert Picht , *De Gaulle, Deutschland und Europa*, pp. 169–179.
Schwarz, Hans-Peter: *Helmut Kohl. Eine politische Biographie*, Munich: Deutsche Verlags-Anstalt, 2012.
Seidel, Katja: "Taking Farmers off Welfare. The EEC Commission's Memorandum 'Agriculture 1980' of 1968," in: *Journal of European Integration History* 16/2 (2010), pp. 83–101.
Segers, Mathieu L. L.: *Deutschlands Ringen mit der Relance. Die Europapolitik der BRD während der Beratungen und Verhandlungen über die Römischen Verträge*, Frankfurt am Main: Peter Lang, 2008.
Seidel, Katja: "DG IV and the origins of a supranational competition polcy. Establishing an economic constitution for Europe," in: Kaiser / Leucht / Rasmussen, *History*, pp. 129–147.
Serra, Enrico: (ed.), *Il rilancio dell'Europa e i Trattati di Roma*, Milano: Émile Bruylant, 1989.
Soell, Hartmut: *Helmut Schmidt. Macht und Verantwortung*, Munich: Deutsche Verlags-Anstalt, 2008.
Soutou, Georges-Henri : "La France, l'Allemagne et les accords de Paris," in: *Relations internationales,* No. 52, 1987, pp. 451–470.
Soutou, Georges-Henri : "Le général de Gaulle et le plan Fouchet," in: *De Gaulle en son siècle*, vol. 5, pp. 126–143.
Soutou, Georges-Henri : *L'alliance incertaine. Les rapports politico-stratégiques franco-allemands, 1954–1996*, Paris: Fayard, 1996.
Spierenburg, Dirk / Poidevin, Raymond: *Histoire de la Haute Autorité de la Communauté Européenne du Charbon et de l'Acier. Une expérience supranationale*, Brussels: Émile Bruylant, 1993.
Stark, Hans: *Kohl, l'Allemagne et l'Europe. La politique d'intégration européenne de la République fédérale 1982–1998*, Paris: L'Harmattan, 2004.
Stark, Hans: *La politique internationale de l'Allemagne. Une puissance malgré elle*, Villeneuve d'Ascq: Presses universitaires du Septentrion, 2011.
Steininger, Rolf: *Wiederbewaffnung. Die Entscheidung für einen westdeutschen Verteidigungsbeitrag: Adenauer und die Westmächte 1950*, Erlangen/Bonn/Vienna: Straube, 1989.
Steininger, Rolf: "Das Scheitern der EVG und der Beitritt der Bundesrepublik zur NATO," in: *Aus Politik und Zeitgeschichte* B 17, 1985, pp. 3–18.
Stelandre, Yves: "Les Pays du Benelux, l'Europe politique et les négociations Fouchet," in: Deighton / Milward, *Widening*, pp. 73–88.
Sutton, Michael: *France and the Construction of Europe, 1944–2007. The Geopolitical Imperative*, Oxford / New York: Berghahn Books, 2007.
Szafran, Maurice: *Simone Veil. Destin*, Paris: Flammarion, 1994.
Taschner, Hans-Claudius: *Schengen. Die Übereinkommen zum Abbau der Personenkontrollen an den Binnengrenzen von EU-Staaten*, Baden-Baden: Nomos, 1997.
Thiemeyer, Guido: *Vom "Pool Vert" zur Europäischen Wirtschaftsgemeinschaft. Europäische Integration, Kalter Krieg und die Anfänge der Gemeinsamen Europäischen Agrarpolitik 1950–1957*, Munich: Oldenbourg, 1999.
Thiemeyer, Guido: "Die Ursachen des 'Demokratiedefizits' der Europäischen Union aus geschichtswissenschaftlicher Perspektive," in: Loth, *Das europäische Projekt*, pp. 27–47.

Thiemeyer, Guido: "Helmut Schmidt und die Gründung des Europäischen Wirtschaftssystems 1973–1979," in: Knipping / Schönwald, *Aufbruch*, pp. 245–268.
Thiemeyer, Guido: "Sicco Mansholt and European Supranationalism," in: Loth, *Gouvernance*, pp. 39–53.
Thiemeyer, Guido: "The Mansholt Plan, the definite financing of the Common Agricultural Policy and the enlargement of the Community, 1969–1973," in: Van der Harst, *Beyond the Customs Union*, pp. 197–222.
Thiemeyer, Guido: "From Convertibility to the Werner-Plan. European Monetary Integration 1958–1959," in: Régine Perron (ed.), *The Stability of Europe. The Common Market: Towards European Integration of Industrial and Financial Markets? (1958–1969)*, Paris: Presses de l'Université de Paris-Sorbonne 2004, pp. 161–178.
Thiemeyer, Guido: *Europäische Integration. Motive – Prozesse – Strukturen*, Cologne / Weimar / Vienna: Böhlau, 2010.
Thomas, Brigitta: *Die Europa-Politik Italiens. Der Beitrag Italiens zur europäischen Einigung zwischen EVG und EG*, Baden-Baden: Nomos, 2005.
Tracy, Michael: "The Spirit of Stresa," in: *European Review of Agricultural Economics* 21 (1994), pp. 357–374
Trausch, Gilbert: "Robert Schuman, le Luxembourg et l'Europe," in: *Robert Schuman. Les racines et l'œuvre d'un grand Européen*, Luxembourg 1986.
Trausch, Gilbert (ed.): *Die Europäische Integration vom Schuman-Plan bis zu den Verträgen von Rom. Pläne und Initiativen, Enttäuschungen und Mißerfolge*, Baden-Baden: Nomos, 1993.
Trausch, Gilbert: "Der Schuman-Plan zwischen Mythos und Realität. Der Stellenwert des Schuman-Plans," in: Hudemann / Kaelble / Schwabe, *Europa im Blick der Historiker*, pp. 105–128.
Trouvé, Matthieu: *L'Espagne et l'Europe. De la dictature de Franco à l'Union européenne*, Brussels: Peter Lang, 2008.
Tsalikoglou, Iakovos S.: *Negotiating for Entry: The Accession of Greece in the European Community*, Aldershot: Gower, 1995.
Türk, Henning: "'To Face de Gaulle as a Community': The Role of the Federal Republic of Germany during the Empty Chair Crisis," in: Palayret / Wallace / Winand, *Visions*, pp. 113–127.
Türk, Henning: *Die Europapolitik der Großen Koalition 1966–1969*, Munich: Oldenbourg, 2006.
Ungerer, Horst: *A concise history of European monetary integration: From EPU to EMU*, Westport/Connecticut: Quorum Books, 1997.
Vaïsse, Maurice : "De Gaulle, l'Italie et le projet d'union politique européenne 1958–1963," in: *Revue d'histoire moderne et contemporaine 1995*, pp. 658–669.
Vaïsse, Maurice : *La grandeur. Politique étrangère du général de Gaulle 1958–1969*, Paris: Fayard, 1998.
Vaïsse, Maurice : "La politique européenne de la France en 1965: pourquoi 'la chaise vide'?" in: Loth, *Crises*, pp. 193–214.
Van der Harst, Jan: "The common agricultural policy: a leading field of action," in: *The European Commission 1958–72*, pp. 317–337.
Van der Harst, Jan: "Sicco Mansholt: courage and conviction," in: *The European Commission 1958–72*, pp. 165–180.
Van der Harst, Jan (ed.): *Beyond the Customs Union: The European Community's Quest for Deepening, Widening and Completion, 1969–1975*, Brussels: Émile Bruylant, 2007.

Van der Harst, Jan / Voerman, Gerrit (eds.), *An Impossible Job? - The Presidents of the European Commission, 1958–2014*, London: John Harper Publishing, 2015.

Van Middelaar, Luuk : *Le passage à l'Europe. Histoire d'un commencement*, Paris: Gallimard, 2012.

Vanke, Jeffrey : *Europeanism and European Union. Interests, Emotions, and Systemic Integration in the Early European Economic Community*, Palo Alto, Ca.: Academica Press, 2010.

Varsori, Antonio: *Il Patto di Bruxelles (1948) : tra integrazione europea e alleanza atlantica*, Rome: Bonacci, 1988.

Varsori, Antonio: "Jean Monnet e il Comitato d'Azione per gli Stati Uniti d'Europa fra MEC ed Euratom (1955–1957)," in: Sergio Pistone (ed.), *I movimenti per l'unità europea 1954–1969*, Pavia 1996, pp. 349–371.

Varsori, Antonio: "Italy and the 'Empty Chair' Crisis (1965–66)," in: Loth, *Crises*, pp. 215–255.

Varsori, Antonio (ed.): *Inside the European Community. Actors and Policies in the European Integration 1957–1962*, Baden-Baden: Nomos, 2006.

Varsori, Antonio: "Franco Maria Malfatti: a presidency cut short," in: *The European Commission 1958–72*, pp. 153–163.

Varsori, Antonio: "L'Occidente e la Grecia: dal colpo di Stato militare alla trasizione alla democrazia (1967–1976)," in: Mario Del Pero et a., *Democrazie. L'Europa meridionale e la fine delle dittature*, Milan: Le Monnier, 2010, pp. 5–94.

Varsori, Antonio: *La Cenerentola d'Europa? L'Italia e l'integrazione Europea dal 1947 a oggi*, Soveria Manelli: Rubbettino, 2010.

Volkmann, Hans-Erich / Walter Schwengler (ed.): *Die Europäische Verteidigungsgemeinschaft. Stand und Probleme der Forschung*, Boppard: Boldt, 1985.

Waechter, Matthias: *Helmut Schmidt und Valéry Giscard d'Estaing. Auf der Suche nach Stabilität in der Krise der 70er Jahre*, Bremen: Edition Temmen, 2011.

Wall, Stephen: *A Stranger in Europe: Britain and the EU from Thatcher to Blair*, Oxford: Oxford University Press, 2008.

Wanninger, Susanne: *New Labour und die EU. Die Europapolitik der Regierung Blair*, Baden-Baden: Nomos, 2007.

Warlouzet, Laurent: "La France et la mise en place de la politique de la concurrence communautaire (1957–64)," in: Éric Bussière / Michel Dumoulin / Sylvain Schirmann (eds.), *Europe organisée, Europe du libre-échange. Fin XIXe siècle – Années 1960*, Brussels: Peter Lang, 2006, pp. 175–201.

Warlouzet, Laurent: *Le choix de la CEE par la France. L'Europe économique en débat de Mendès-France à de Gaulle (1955–1969)*, Paris: Comité pour l'Histoire économique et financière, 2011.

Warner, Geoffrey : "Die britische Labour-Party und die Einheit Westeuropas 1949–1952," in: *Vierteljahrshefte für Zeitgeschichte* 28 (1980), pp. 310–330.

Wassenberg, Birte : "La campagne pour les élections européennes de 1979 en France et en Allemagne: l'image de l'Europe," in: Marie-Thérèse Bitsch / Wilfried Loth / Charles Barthel (eds.), *Cultures politiques, opinions publiques et intégration européenne*, Brussels: Émile Bruylant, 2007, pp. 264–284.

Weidenfeld, Werner (ed.): *Amsterdam in der Analyse*, Gütersloh: Bertelsmann Stiftung, 1998.

Weidenfeld, Werner (ed.): *Nizza in der Analyse. Strategien für Europa*, Gütersloh: Bertelsmann Stiftung, 2001.

Weidenfeld, Werner (ed.): *Die Europäische Verfassung in der Analyse*, Gütersloh: Bertelsmann Stiftung, 2005.

Weidenfeld, Werner (ed.): *Lissabon in der Analyse – Der Reformvertrag der Europäischen Union*, Baden-Baden: Nomos, 2008.

Weilemann, Peter: *Die Anfänge der Europäischen Atomgemeinschaft. Zur Gründungsgeschichte von Euratom 1955–1957*, Baden-Baden: Nomos, 1983.

Weinachter, Michèle: *Valéry Giscard d'Estaing et l'Allemagne. Le double rêve inachevé*, Paris: L'Harmattan, 2004.

Wessels, Wolfgang: *Die Öffnung des Staates. Modelle und Wirklichkeit grenzüberschreitender Verwaltungspraxis 1960–1995*, Opladen: Leske und Budrich, 2000.

Wiggershaus, Norbert: "Zur Frage einer militärischen Integration Westdeutschlands (bis Mai 1950)," in: Poidevin, *Débuts*, pp. 343–366.

Wiggershaus, Norbert: "Die Entscheidung für einen westdeutschen Verteidigungsbeitrag 1950," in: *Anfänge westdeutscher Sicherheitspolitik 1945–1956, Bd. 1: Von der Kapitulation bis zum Pleven-Plan*, Munich: Oldenbourg, 1982, pp. 325–402.

Wilkens, Andreas (ed.): *Interessen verbinden. Jean Monnet und die europäische Integration der Bundesrepublik Deutschland*, Bonn: Bouvier, 1999.

Wilkens, Andreas: "Der Werner-Plan. Währung, Politik und Europa 1968–1971," in: Knipping / Schönwald, *Aufbruch*, pp. 217–244.

Wilkens, Andreas (ed.): *Le Plan Schuman dans l'Histoire. Intérêts nationaux et projet européen*, Brussels: Émile Bruylant, 2004.

Wilkens, Andreas (ed.): *Wir sind auf dem richtigen Weg. Willy Brandt und die europäische Einigung*, Bonn: Dietz, 2010.

Wilkens, Andreas: "In der 'Logik der Geschichte'. Willy Brandt und die europäische Zäsur 1969/1970," in: idem., *Wir sind auf dem richtigen Weg*, pp 241–275.

Wille, Gerhard: "'Which Europe? Quelle Europe? Welches Europa?'. British, French and German Conceptions of Europe and Britain's Second Attempt to Join the EEC," in: Rücker / Warlouzet, *Quelle(s) Europe(s)*, pp. 225–237.

Winand, Pascaline: *Eisenhower, Kennedy and the United States of Europe*, New York: Palgrave Macmillan, 1993.

Wirsching, Andreas: *Der Preis der Freiheit. Geschichte Europas in unserer Zeit*, Munich: C.H. Beck, 2012.

Wirth, Michael: *Die Deutsch-Französischen Beziehungen während der Kanzlerschaft von Helmut Schmidt (1974–1982)*, Berlin: Wissenschaftlicher Verlag Berlin, 2007.

Wünsche, Horst: "Wirtschaftliche Interessen und Prioritäten. Die Europavorstellungen von Ludwig Erhard," in: Rudolf Hrbek / Volker Schwarz (eds.), *40 Jahre Römische Verträge: Der deutsche Beitrag*, Baden-Baden: Nomos, 1998, pp. 36–49.

Young, Hugo: *This Blessed Plot. Britain and Europe from Churchill to Blair*, London: Macmillan, 1998.

Young, John W.: *Britain and European Unity, 1945–1992*, London: Palgrave Macmillan, 1993.

Ziebura, Gilbert: *Die deutsch-französischen Beziehungen seit 1945. Mythen und Realitäten*, Pfullingen: Neske 1970; überarbeitete Neuauflage Stuttgart: Klett-Cotta, 1997.

Zorgbibe, Charles : *Histoire de la construction européenne*, Paris: Presses Universitaires de France, 1993.

Index

Acheson, Dean 27, 30, 31, 36, 38
Action Committee for the United States of
    Europe 72, 104, 119, 162, 170, 217, 221
Adenauer, Konrad 11, 13, 14, 30, 31, 39, 40,
    45, 46, 50-52, 54, 55, 58, 60, 64-73,
    78, 88, 89, 99, 100,102-105, 107, 108,
    113-117, 123, 126, 127, 161, 251, 268, 435
Adonnino Committee 275
Adonnino, Pietro 275
Afghanistan 255, 256, 394, 416
Agenda 2000 364
agricultural policy 71, 75, 76, 78, 85, 96-101,
    112, 113, 129, 130, 137, 139, 150-152, 161,
    171, 173-175, 179-181, 184, 185, 193, 228,
    248, 262, 278, 282, 363, 364, 373, 374,
    383, 403
Agt, Andreas van 236
Ahern, Bertie 399
Ailleret, Charles 149, 150
Albania 359, 360, 380
Albright, Madeleine 358
Amato, Giuliano 386
Amsterdam Treaty 342, 347-354, 359, 360,
    367
Andreotti, Giulio 201, 233, 236, 239, 240,
    274, 281, 307, 314, 319
Andriessen, Frans 294
Annan, Kofi 378
Apel, Hans 265
Armand, Louis 54, 60, 73, 120
Arnold, Karl 11
Aron, Raymond 7
Ashton, Catherine 415, 417
atomic weapons, atomic armament 31, 47, 48,
    103, 110, 111, 115, 122, 123, 131, 253-255,
    257, 258, 300-304, 310, 357
Attlee, Clement 3
Attali, Jacques 268, 299, 300, 302, 304, 314,
    324
Auriol, Vincent 37
Austria, Austrian government 105, 109, 231,
    298, 305, 334, 336-339, 341, 342, 348,
    356, 359, 373, 380-382, 391, 404, 419,
    420

Aznar, José Maria 332, 364, 370, 391, 396

Bahr, Egon 205, 258, 301
Balkan, Balkan states 355, 356, 358-360, 380,
    433
Balkenende, Jan-Pieter 374, 407, 409
Balladur, Édouard 328, 329
banks (national) 10, 92, 196, 197, 199, 200,
    233, 234, 237, 238, 241, 280, 285,
    290-296, 319-321, 325, 327-330, 332,
    333, 335, 418, 420, 422, 427, 429-431
Barber, Anthony 185
Barnier, Michel 414
Barre Plan 195
Barre, Raymond 155, 182, 186, 195, 196, 231,
    240, 242, 253
Barroso, José Manuel 380, 381, 396, 399-403,
    405, 406, 413, 414, 429
Băsescu, Traian 379
Bastid, Paul 7
Baunsgaard, Hilmar 189
Bech, Joseph 35
Belgium, Belgian government 5, 7, 10, 11, 21,
    22, 25, 29, 33, 34, 39, 41, 50, 54, 57, 58,
    73, 78, 95, 102, 103, 107, 108, 120, 121,
    161, 172, 181, 204, 206, 223, 224, 226,
    254, 255, 324, 327, 329, 334, 348, 351,
    356, 373, 407, 419, 427
Benelux states 29, 33, 41, 57, 75, 77, 82, 90,
    91, 95, 102, 121, 160, 201, 231, 274, 277
Bérégovoy, Pierre 297, 298, 321
Berlin Declaration 408, 409
Berlusconi, Silvio 345, 347, 391, 398, 430
Bernard, Jean-René 188, 199, 202
Bevin, Ernest 12, 21-28, 31, 33
Beyen, Johan Willem 43, 44, 54-58
Bidault, Georges 21, 22, 29, 31, 44
Bitterlich, Joachim 298, 299, 311
Blaesheim meeting 385, 414
Blair, Tony 332, 349, 359, 371, 393, 394,
    396-400, 403, 404, 406-408, 410, 411,
    414, 415, 440
Blankenhorn, Herbert 157
Blum, Léon 2, 11, 12, 18, 22, 28

Index — 475

Bohlen, Charles 27
Boissieu, Pierre de 316
Bömke, Eberhard 142
Bonnefous, Édouard 7, 13
Boothby, Robert 4
Borrel, Joseph 377, 406
Borschette, Albert 147
Borten, Per 158
Bosnia-Herzegovina 357, 359, 380, 393
Boyer, Miguel 294
Brandt, Willy 153-155, 157, 158, 160, 162, 164, 171-177, 179, 180, 187, 193, 196, 197, 199-201, 203, 205, 207, 210, 211, 213, 214, 216, 220, 245
Bratelli, Trygve 190, 191
Brauer, Max 11, 12
Brentano, Heinrich von 11, 60, 66, 115
Breshnev, Leonid 214, 245, 254, 256
Briand, Aristide 2
Brok, Elmar 346, 350
Brown, George 156-158
Brown, Gordon 332, 403, 404, 411, 415, 426
Brugmans, Hendrik 8-10, 14, 18
Brussels Pact 21-23, 27, 41, 52
Bulgaria, Bulgarian government 13, 362, 364, 366, 373, 378, 379, 408
Bush, George 304, 309
Bush, George W. 394, 395, 397
Butler, Harold 5
Buttiglione, Rocco 399
Buzek, Jerzy 413

Caetano, Marcelo 242, 246
Callaghan, James 192, 193, 215, 216, 221, 223, 225, 229, 234, 236, 238, 239, 254, 261
Cameron, David 416, 426, 439, 440
Carlson, Ingvar 337
Carrillo, Santiago 247
Carrington, Peter 262, 263
Carstens, Karl 67, 115, 127, 129
Carter, Jimmy 231, 232, 238, 254-256, 258, 261
Cattani, Attilio 131
Cecchini, Paolo 283
Chaban-Delmas, Jacques 61, 170, 183
Chalfont, Alun 166
Chandernagor, André 265, 268

Charrette, Hervé de 354
Charter of Fundamental Rights 370, 387, 410
Chatenet, Pierre 120
Chevènement, Jean-Pierre 324
Cheysson, Claude 264, 277, 341
Chirac, Jacques 226, 227, 231, 240, 243, 290, 330, 331, 333, 335, 347, 351, 354, 357, 359, 364, 369-371, 374, 383, 385, 386, 388-390, 392, 394-396, 398, 399, 404-408, 415
Churchill, Winston 1, 4-14, 18, 19, 21, 25, 31, 40, 45, 47, 50, 165
Ciampi, Carlo 294
Clappier, Bernard 31, 233-235
Clay, Lucius 115
Claudel, Paul 7
Clinton, Bill 358, 367
Cockfield, Francis Arthur 264
Cohn-Bendit, Daniel 405, 438
Cold War 3-7, 36, 48, 255, 256, 260, 292, 300-306, 336, 434
College of Europe 288
Colombo, Emilio 144, 145, 265-267, 269, 270
Committee for the Monetary Union of Europe 294
Committee of Permanent Representatives (COREPER) 82, 83, 138, 142, 146, 147, 155, 216, 217, 223, 436
Common Agricultural Policy (CAP) 68, 69, 81, 96-101, 129, 130, 132-143, 150, 151, 165, 170, 171, 174-181, 198, 240, 263, 365, 373-376
Common Foreign and Security Policy (CFSP) 317, 318, 338, 339, 342, 353, 354, 359-362, 369, 389, 397, 415-417, 439, 440
Conference on Confidence- and Security-Building Measures and Disarmament in Europe 258
Conference on Security and Cooperation in Europe (CSCE) 206, 220, 255, 258
consumer protection 284
Convention on the Future of Europe 385-391, 395, 397, 398, 431
convergence criteria 297, 318, 323, 325, 334, 336, 418-420
Copenhagen criteria 362, 363, 367

Coppé, Alfred 181
Coste-Floret, Paul 7
Coty, René 60
Coudenhove-Kalergi, Richard 2, 5-7, 11, 12, 14, 86, 165
Council of Economic and Finance Ministers (Ecofin) 336, 415, 419, 423, 424, 429
Council of Europe 1, 20-26, 28, 29, 36, 58, 246
Courtin, René 6, 7
Couve de Murville, Maurice 88, 100, 106, 108, 112-114, 126, 129, 130, 134-138, 140-144, 154
Couzens, Kenneth 234
Craxi, Bettino 274, 275
Cresson, Édith 354
crime fighting 286, 315, 316, 348, 378, 379, 381
Cripps, Stafford 11, 24
Croatia, Croatian government 317, 380, 381
cultural policy 266, 351
currencies (national) 16, 27, 28, 87, 90, 161, 186, 189, 195, 197-201, 203, 203, 231-240, 245, 289, 290, 308, 313, 320, 323, 325, 327-329, 334, 335, 417, 418, 420, 423
Currency snake 199-203, 220, 231, 234, 237, 241
customs union, customs policy 5, 26, 29, 43-45, 54, 55, 59, 65, 75, 78, 84, 90, 91, 95, 111, 132, 136, 140, 150, 152, 153, 195, 276, 366, 367, 383
Cyprus 243, 363, 367, 373, 374, 376, 378, 382, 383, 407, 418
Cyrankiewicz, Jósef 139
Czechoslovakia 13, 362
Czech Republic, Czech government 364, 372, 408, 409, 412, 413, 426

Dahrendorf, Ralf 181, 438
Daladier, Édouard 13
Dalton, Hugh 12, 23
Davignon, Étienne 205, 229, 276
Debray, Régis 300, 301
Debré, Michel 7, 86, 160, 164, 165, 178, 197, 208, 222, 225
Defferre, Gaston 62

De Gasperi, Alcide 11, 13, 18, 36, 40, 42, 43
Dehaene, Jean-Luc 344, 345, 386
Dehler, Thomas 11
Del Bo, Dino 121
Delors Committee 294-297
Delors, Jacques 241, 274, 276-283, 287, 288, 293-297, 307, 310-312, 315, 316, 318, 322, 333, 338-340, 342, 345, 355, 368, 435, 438
Delors Package 281, 282, 292
defense and security policy 101-103, 106-108, 114, 115, 125-127, 130, 131, 176, 186, 204, 205, 211, 223, 251-255, 265, 274, 278, 300-304, 312-318, 322, 338, 339, 342, 346, 353, 354, 356-362, 389, 393, 410, 412, 415-417, 439
De Michelis, Gianni 316
Deniau, Jean-François 187
Denktaş, Rauf 378
Denmark, Danish government 105, 109, 113, 158, 168, 182, 189, 194, 195, 201, 211, 219, 221, 223, 224, 226, 231, 246, 262, 267, 272, 273, 277-279, 281, 284, 317, 320, 323-326, 329, 334, 336, 339, 348, 354, 364, 365, 381, 407, 418, 425
Dooge Committee 271, 273, 274, 277
Dooge, James 271-273
Douglas-Home, Alec 186
Draghi, Mario 429, 430
Drees, Willem 55
Duchêne, François 250
Dufourcq, Bertrand 304
Duisenberg, Wim 294, 335, 417
Duhamel, Jacques 170
Dulles, John Foster 46-52
Dumas, Roland 268, 277-279, 289-291, 307, 314, 322

eastward enlargement 342, 362-366, 372-381, 399
Ecevit, Bülent 367
Economic and Monetary Union (EMU) 20, 175, 189, 195-198, 202, 215, 219-221, 230, 289-300, 306-308, 318-321, 333-336, 347, 383, 417-432
Eden, Anthony 13, 47, 52, 60, 67
education policy 183, 389, 400, 401

Egypt 66
Eichel, Hans 419
Eisenhower, Dwight D. 39, 46-48, 103
elections (European Parliament) 105, 133, 176, 183, 211, 219, 221, 224-227, 299, 313, 341, 356, 371, 377, 388, 407, 408, 413, 431, 439
elections (national) 13, 40, 43, 72, 99, 130, 142, 144, 155, 185, 192, 201, 226, 238, 241, 244, 245, 247, 248, 258, 261, 265, 290, 292, 298, 310, 319, 332, 349, 365, 383, 384, 391, 404, 407, 409, 420, 428
employment policy 333, 344, 349, 426
energy policy 153, 161, 212-214, 217, 351
Ennals, David 194
environmental and climate policy 279, 286, 313, 351
Erdoğan, Recep Tayyip 381-383
Erhard, Ludwig 55, 62-65, 84, 89, 95, 100, 116, 123-131, 135, 137, 138, 140, 148-150, 152
Estonia, Estonian government 364, 373, 376, 407, 418
Etzel, Franz 53, 64
Eurocorps 356
Euro crisis, monetary crisis 164, 202, 203, 326-329, 372, 373, 375, 418-432, 440
European Atomic Energy Community (EAEC, Euratom) 54-56, 59-61, 63, 64, 69, 70, 79, 119, 120, 122, 144, 145, 391
European Central Bank (ECB) 292-296, 320, 329-331, 334, 335, 417, 421, 422, 428-431
European Coal and Steel Community (ECSC) 31-36, 43, 44, 53, 54, 57-59, 63, 72, 79-81, 84, 86, 87, 105, 119, 121, 145, 155, 182, 226, 435
European Commission 75-83, 91-94, 97-100, 110, 125, 129, 130, 132-135, 137, 138, 140, 141, 145, 146, 151-155, 162, 172, 181-183, 186, 195, 196, 218, 229, 236, 244, 263, 272, 274, 276, 277, 281-288, 294, 310, 313, 315-317, 322, 331, 333, 334, 338-340, 342-345, 352, 354-356, 364-366, 372-383, 385, 388-390, 392, 395, 398-403, 406, 414, 415, 419, 426, 429, 431, 438, 439

European Community, European Communities (EC) 155, 156, 161-163, 165-167, 170-172, 176, 188, 191, 194, 198, 213, 217, 219, 220, 242-244, 247, 249-251, 260, 261, 284, 286, 288, 292, 293, 310, 312, 316, 322, 336, 337, 387, 410, 434, 437
European Council 15, 217-223, 228, 233, 234, 236-240, 248, 251, 266, 267, 269, 270, 273-277, 280, 282, 284, 287, 294, 297, 307-309, 312, 315, 321, 330, 339, 342-345, 359, 363, 372, 376, 385, 386, 391, 397, 406, 410, 423, 424, 426, 429-431, 436, 439, 440
European Court of Auditors 228
European Court of Justice 34, 76, 93, 118, 119, 284, 285, 349, 419, 426
European Defense Community (EDC) 34-52, 68, 72, 74, 86
European Economic Area (EEA) 26, 336, 337, 339, 383, 384
European Economic Community (EEC) 72, 77-79, 84-102, 104-107, 109, 115, 117-119, 121-124, 129, 132, 133, 137, 138, 142, 143, 145-147, 150, 151, 155, 156, 273, 275, 277
European Financial Stability Facility (EFSF) 422, 427, 428
European Free Trade Association (EFTA) 105, 106, 109, 125, 150, 155, 167, 192, 246, 305, 336-338, 342
European Monetary Fund (EMF) 234-236, 238, 289, 296
European Monetary System (EMS) 233-242, 245, 248, 249, 263, 267, 289, 295, 319, 320, 327-329, 332, 334
European Movement 1, 8, 18-21, 24, 25, 43, 176, 288
European Parliament 34, 42, 43, 70, 104, 105, 107, 132, 133, 135-137, 141, 176, 178, 179, 205, 211, 218, 219, 222, 224-229, 271, 272, 278, 316, 317, 340, 345, 350, 354, 355, 375, 385, 388, 408, 413, 414, 429, 438, 439
European Parliamentary Union (EPU) 7, 11, 12, 25
European Payments Union (EPU) 35, 90
European People's Party (EPP) 225, 226, 266, 377, 398, 413, 414, 439

European Political Cooperation (EPC) 182, 205-211, 214-218, 250, 251, 255, 266, 273, 274, 278
European Political Community (EPC) 42-46
European Security and Defense Policy (ESDF) 360, 389, 393-395
European Stability Mechanism (ESM) 424, 429-432, 436
eurosclerosis 223
Eyskens, Mark 316

Fabius, Laurent 405
Fanfani, Amintore 102, 105, 114, 131, 137
fatigue over Europe 313, 323-326, 377, 378, 404-407, 440
Faure, Edgar 13, 54-60, 66
Faure, Maurice 61, 63, 66, 68, 72, 247, 272, 273
Federation of Liberal and Democratic Parties in the European Community (ELD) 225, 226, 377, 413, 414
finance and budget policy 195, 196, 202, 231, 392, 419, 423-426, 439
Finet, Paul 121
Finland, Finish government 105, 328, 334, 336-342, 348, 351, 356, 380, 407, 419, 427
Fischer, Joschka 359, 360, 365-371, 388, 391, 393, 397, 417
Fischler, Franz 355
Focke, Katharina 173
Ford, Gerald 230, 244
foreign policy (European) 102, 103, 106, 114, 115, 124-129, 131, 163, 204-207, 214-216, 218, 219, 252, 260, 261, 264, 265, 274, 300, 301, 314, 317, 318, 346, 352-354, 356-362, 388, 389, 393-398, 415-417, 439, 440
foreign trade 35, 55, 60, 64, 65, 83-89, 91, 92, 95, 105, 106, 118, 123, 124, 151, 152, 159, 187, 256, 278, 283, 355
Fortuyn, Pim 406
Fouchet, Christian 104-107
Fouchet Plans 106, 107, 128, 206
France, French government 4-7, 9, 10, 13, 16, 20, 21, 24, 26-29, 31-34, 37-41, 44-55, 57, 59, 60-73, 77, 82, 86-94, 96, 97, 99-108, 110-115, 118-121, 124-129, 134-142, 144-179, 183-188, 193, 196-203, 205-212, 214, 215, 217, 218, 222, 224-243, 248, 252-260, 262, 263, 267-270, 272-274, 278, 280, 284, 286, 289-291, 293, 295-311, 313-315, 317-322, 324-335, 344, 346-348, 351-354, 356-359, 362, 365, 367, 369, 370, 374, 381, 383, 385, 388, 389, 391, 394-396, 404-409, 415, 416, 419-421, 424-426, 430, 431, 433, 436, 439
François-Poncet, André 13
Franco, Francisco 242, 246, 331
Franco-German brigade 302
Franco-German corps 322, 347
Franco-German relations 31, 32, 65, 66, 73, 88, 89, 103, 108, 113-117, 125-129, 140, 148-150, 152, 153, 173, 174, 197, 198, 200, 203, 217, 218, 267-270, 297-303, 305-314, 322, 324, 325, 374, 385, 395, 416
Franco-German Treaty 103, 113-117, 126, 129, 302, 416
Frattini, Franco 399
Frenay, Henri 11

Gaddafi, Muammar al- 416
Gafencu, Gregor 11
Gaillard, Félix 59
Gaulle, Charles de 4, 28, 45, 79, 86-90, 95, 96, 99-108, 110-115, 117, 119, 120, 124-129, 133-150, 152-162, 164-170, 182, 195, 208, 222, 252
Gaullists 7, 42, 44-46, 61, 86, 116, 125, 127, 142, 168, 170, 175, 179, 203, 207, 208, 222, 225-227, 229, 233, 239, 240, 247, 253, 290, 324, 369, 371
Gauweiler, Peter 325
Geißler, Heiner 297
General Agreement on Tariffs and Trade (GATT) 81, 88, 91, 95, 96, 124, 126, 130, 145, 147, 150-152, 155, 178, 282
Genscher-Colombo initiative 264-267, 269, 270
Genscher, Hans-Dietrich 260, 264-267, 270, 274, 277-279, 291-293, 295, 296, 298,

303, 304, 306, 307, 314, 316, 319, 322, 368
Geremek, Borislaw 377
German Democratic Republic (GDR) 113, 151, 298, 299, 307-310, 312, 326, 327
German question, German unity 2, 300, 304-310, 433
German rearmament 36-40, 48, 50
Germany, German government (Federal Republic) 2, 4, 6, 11, 20, 21, 24, 26-30, 34, 36, 37, 39, 40, 42, 45, 46, 50-53, 55-67, 69-73, 77, 78, 85, 86, 88, 89, 103-105, 107, 108, 113-118, 120, 121, 124-130, 134-137, 140, 143, 145, 146, 148-154, 157, 159-162, 164, 165, 172-176, 179, 180, 193, 197-203, 205-207, 209-211, 213-219, 222, 226, 230-240, 243-245, 248, 252-260, 262, 264-270, 273, 274, 278, 280, 282, 287, 290-294, 296-299, 302-308, 310-314, 316-321, 324-326, 328-330, 333-336, 341, 343-348, 352-356, 359-363, 367, 370, 374, 383, 385, 386, 388, 394-399, 407-409, 411, 414-427, 429-431, 434, 439
Gibson, George 4
Gierek, Edward 256
Gilmour, Ian 263
Gil-Robles, José-Maria 347
Gilson, Étienne 17
Giolitti, Antonio 229
Giraud, André 303
Giscard d'Estaing, Edmond 13
Giscard d'Estaing, Valéry 170, 193, 196, 197, 200, 203, 216-222, 225-227, 229-242, 244, 248, 251-259, 261, 262, 264, 265, 270, 294, 295, 301, 381, 386-392
Glotz, Peter 388
Godeaux, Jean 294
Gollancz, Victor 4
González, Felipe 248, 249, 307, 331, 337, 339
Gorbachev, Mikhail 291, 292, 302-304, 306, 308, 309
Greece, Greek government 7, 242-244, 247-250, 267, 272, 273, 277, 281, 284, 324, 330, 331, 334, 336, 348, 351, 356, 365, 367, 380, 404, 417-422, 426-430

Groeben, Hans von der 59, 60, 68, 75, 79, 81, 92-94, 97, 181
Guigou, Elisabeth 298, 310, 311, 322, 346, 350
Guiringaud, Louis de 234
Guterres, Antonio 400

Habermas, Jürgen 412
Hague Summit 172, 174-177, 196, 197, 207, 223
Haider, Jörg 342
Hallstein, Walter 11, 14, 58, 59, 64, 66, 73, 75, 78-83, 88, 100, 126, 129, 132-137, 139-143, 145-147, 152-155, 178, 182, 195, 241, 251
Hancock, Patrick 167
Hänsch, Klaus 347, 350, 386
Harmel, Pierre 149, 161, 162, 172, 204, 206
Haughey, Charles 310, 311
Haussmann, Helmut 296
Havel, Václav 396
Healey, Denis 12
health policy 279, 284-286, 389
Heath, Edward 110, 112, 162, 184-188, 192, 194, 201, 207-213, 215, 216, 261, 278
heavy industry 2, 24, 30-32, 34, 53, 120-122, 248
Heinemann, Gustav 11
Herriot, Édouard 7, 11, 22
Hirsch, Étienne 120
Hoem, Knut 191
Hoffmeyer, Erik 294
Hollande, François 430, 431, 439
Howe, Geoffrey 273, 289
human rights 6, 17, 26, 212, 255, 348, 349, 433, 437
Hungary, Hungarian government 13, 298, 358, 362, 373, 376, 396, 399, 404, 439
Hunt, John 209
Hurd, Douglas 320
Hussein, Saddam 394

Independent League of European Co-operation (ILEC) 5, 8, 9, 16
Indochina War 48, 49
internal market 81, 91, 93, 94, 100, 266, 270, 273, 276, 278-286, 313, 323, 337, 400

International Monetary Fund (IMF) 233, 327, 421-424, 428
Iraq War 394-396
Ireland, Irish government 23, 108, 109, 113, 158, 168, 189, 190, 193, 211, 224, 226, 239-241, 271, 277, 279, 281, 289, 323, 324, 329, 334, 336, 348, 351, 356, 365, 407, 412, 413, 417, 420, 422, 426, 430
Issing, Otmar 332, 421
Italy, Italian government 7, 11, 13, 23, 29, 33, 39, 42, 43, 52, 70, 77, 86, 91, 102, 119-121, 131, 135, 160, 161, 163, 166, 171, 177, 180, 182, 201, 202, 204, 207, 219, 224, 226, 230, 231, 236, 239-241, 243, 247, 254, 265, 274, 277, 281, 289, 302, 307, 316, 327, 330-332, 334, 347, 348, 357, 367, 370, 373, 404, 419, 420, 427, 430

Jagland, Thorbjörn 433
Jenkins, Clive 288
Jenkins, Roy 156, 229, 230, 232, 233, 262, 263
Jobert, Michel 187, 209-212, 214-216
Johnson, Lyndon B. 126, 131, 149
Josephy, Frances L. 12
Jospin, Lionel 333-335, 358, 388, 405
Juncker, Jean-Claude 345, 396, 398, 407, 408, 410, 414, 415, 424, 425, 429, 439
justice 266, 315, 325, 348, 373, 379, 410, 414

Kaczyński, Lech 409, 410, 412
Kaczyński, Jarosław 409, 410
Kaisen, Wilhelm 11, 12
Kalniete, Sandra 376
Karamanlis, Constantine 242-244, 246, 247
Karamanlis, Kostas 420, 421
Kennan, George F. 32, 33
Kennedy, John F. 95, 96, 110, 113, 115-117, 124
Kerstens, Pieter 9, 10
Khrushchev, Nikita 103
Kiesinger, Kurt-Georg 152-155, 157-162, 167, 168, 176
Kinkel, Klaus 353, 354
Kinnock, Neil 355, 398
Kissinger, Henry 208, 210, 213-216, 245
Klaus, Václav 409, 412

Kogon, Eugen 14, 15
Köhler, Horst 318-321, 328
Kohl, Helmut 248, 259, 260, 266-270, 273, 274, 279-282, 290, 293, 294, 297-314, 317-321, 324, 325, 328-331, 333-335, 339, 343-348, 351, 352, 354, 363, 364, 371, 435
Kok, Wim 386, 400
Korean War 34, 36
Korvald, Lars 192
Kosovo War 359, 365
Kovács, László 399
Krag, Jens Otto 113, 158
Kroes, Neelie 399
Kwasniewski, Alexander 376
Kyriazidis, Nikolaos 245

labor market, labor market policy 81, 92, 321, 343, 377, 400
Lacoste, Robert 7
Laeken Declaration 385, 386
Lagarde, Christine 428
Lahr, Rolf 136, 153
Laloy, Jean 20
Lamers, Karl 346-348, 368
Lamfalussy, Alexandre 294
Lamont, Norman 327
Lamoureux, François 315
Lamy, Pascal 355
Land, Gordon 5
Laniel, Joseph 45, 49
Lapie, Pierre-Olivier 13
Larosière, Jacques de 294, 295
Latvia, Latvian government 364, 366, 373, 377, 406, 418
Lawson, Nigel 289
Lecourt, Robert 119
Leenhardt, Francis 7, 29
Lemaignen, Robert 75, 81
Lemnitzer, Lyman 150
Le Pen, Jean-Marie 324
Le Trocquer, André 7
Liechtenstein 336, 341
Lipkowski, Jean de 162, 165, 166
Lipsius, Justus 387
Lisbon Treaty 411, 412, 414, 423, 424, 426, 436, 438

Lithuania, Lithuanian government 364, 366, 373, 404, 418
Lubbers, Ruud 307, 317, 343, 344
Luns, Joseph 102-108, 137, 145, 146, 148, 163, 171, 174, 206
Luxembourg, Luxembourg government 5, 21, 33, 35, 38, 39, 66, 73, 75, 77, 79, 82, 95, 102, 104, 106, 135, 146, 147, 155, 219, 226, 229, 274, 277, 286, 302, 324, 334, 345, 348, 351, 372, 396, 398, 407, 422, 439
Luxembourg agreement 146, 176, 188, 209, 264
Lynch, Jack 236, 239, 240

Maastricht Treaties 318, 319, 321-326, 338, 342, 344-346, 348, 352, 363, 371, 387, 404, 406, 411, 436
Macedonia 380, 393
Mackay, Ronald W. G. 12, 15, 16, 25
Macmillan, Harold 5, 15, 84, 85, 88-90, 103, 105, 106, 108-113, 155, 185
Madariaga, Salvador de 13-17
Major, John 318-320, 326, 327, 330, 332, 338, 343-345, 347, 349
Malfatti, Franco Maria 181, 182
Malta 304, 363, 364, 366, 373, 376, 407, 418
Malvestiti, Piero 75, 81
Mandelson, Peter 400, 415
Mansholt, Sicco 70, 73, 75, 78, 81, 96-98, 100, 101, 112, 130, 134, 139, 141, 155, 180-183
Marc, Alexandre 8, 9, 18
Marchais, Georges 247, 324
Marín, Manuel 354
Marijnissen, Jan 406
Marshall Plan 6, 12
Martens, Wilfried 311
Marjolin, Robert 67, 71, 75, 78, 79, 81, 88, 98, 139, 141, 155
Martino, Gaetano 54
Maudling Committee 87-89
Maudling, Reginald 83, 87-89
Mauroy, Pierre 241
Mayer, Jürgen 391
Mayer, René 7, 31, 45
McGreevy, Charlie 400

Medgyessy, Péter 396
Méhaignerie, Pierre 240
Mendès France, Pierre 49-52, 54
Menthon, François de 7, 13, 22
Mer, Francis 419
Merkel, Angela 383, 407-411, 413-416, 421-427, 429-431, 435, 439
Méry, Guy 252
Messina Conference 58, 60, 66
Messmer, Pierre 183
Meyer, Klaus 126
Miller, Leszek 375, 391, 396
Milošević, Slobodan 359, 360
Mitterrand, François 13, 144, 241, 248, 256, 259, 260, 263-270, 272-274, 279-281, 289, 293, 295-311, 313-315, 317-319, 321, 322, 324, 325, 327-330, 339, 343-348, 354, 355, 357, 362, 371, 405
Moch, Jules 37
Modrow, Hans 308
Mollet, Guy 23, 50, 60-73, 82, 87
Monnet, Jean 20, 24, 31-38, 53-56, 64, 69, 72, 73, 103, 104, 115, 116, 119, 162, 170, 174, 196, 202, 210, 211, 217, 218, 221, 436
Monick, Emmanuel 7
Monti, Mario 355, 430
Morgan, Charles 17
Moro, Aldo 131, 171, 174, 181, 204, 247
Moscovici, Pierre 388
Müller-Armack, Alfred 89
Mungiu-Pippidi, Alina 380
Murdoch, Rupert 398, 404
Müller-Armack, Alfred 89

Narjes, Karl-Heinz 134, 276
Nasser, Gamal Abdel 66, 68
Nenni, Pietro 163
Netherlands, Netherlands government 1, 9, 10, 13, 21, 29, 30, 32, 39, 43, 44, 50, 54, 55, 69, 70, 73, 75, 77, 78, 96, 97, 102, 105, 108, 118, 120, 130, 133, 135, 143, 148, 151, 154, 160, 161, 163, 171, 177, 199, 211, 212, 224, 226, 231, 254, 255, 262, 280, 302, 316, 317, 324, 327, 329, 334, 343, 348, 356, 374, 381, 399, 405-408, 410, 419, 424, 427, 436

Nice Treaty 361, 369-371, 385, 387, 389, 391, 392, 398, 407-410, 413
Niemöller, Martin 11
Nixon, Richard M. 198, 199, 208-210, 213, 214, 230
Noël, Émile 82, 183
Norstad, Lauris 103
North Atlantic Treaty, North Atlantic Treaty Organization (NATO) 26, 36-42, 48-53, 88, 103-105, 112, 115, 116, 128, 131, 148-150, 167, 168, 209-211, 215, 216, 243, 248, 249, 252-254, 257, 259, 304, 305, 310, 317, 318, 356-361, 367, 393, 395-397, 415, 416
Norway, Norwegian government 105, 109, 113, 150, 158, 168, 182, 190-192, 231, 328, 336, 337, 339-341, 356, 433

Obama, Barack 416
Öcalan, Abdullah 381
Oettinger, Günther 414
Ollenhauer, Erich 72
Ophüls, Carl Friedrich 56
Orbán, Victor 439
Oreja, Marcelino 345
Organization of European Economic Cooperation (OEEC) 22, 27, 35, 43, 58, 63, 68, 78, 83-85, 87, 89, 90, 95, 97, 105
Ortoli, François-Xavier 182, 213, 218, 229, 236, 263

Pan-European Movement 2, 5, 165
Pallister, Michael 262
Papademos, Loukas 428
Papandreou, Andreas 243, 249, 274, 275, 332, 344
Papandreou, Georgios 367, 420, 428
Party of European Socialists (PES) 225, 226, 377, 399, 413, 414, 439
Pasqua, Charles 324
Patten, Chris 355, 398
Pella, Guiseppe 36
Petersberg Declaration 354
Petrilli, Guiseppe 75, 81
Petsch, Maurice 36
Peyrefitte, Alain 111, 117, 126, 129, 134, 138, 139

Pflimlin, Pierre 68
Phillips, Morgan 12
Piebalgs, Andris 359
Pinay, Antoine 42, 54, 58
Pineau, Christian 61, 62, 64-66
Pleven Plan 37-39
Pleven, René 31, 37-39
Plowden, Edwin 24
Poher, Alain 170
Pöhl, Karl Otto 290, 291, 294-296, 327
Poland, Polish government 5, 13, 125, 139, 256, 260, 298, 299, 306, 308, 358, 362, 364, 370, 372-377, 384, 391, 396, 409, 410, 412, 413, 425, 439, 440
Pompidou, Georges 170-177, 179, 180, 182-188, 196-203, 205-208, 210-214, 216, 220, 252
Poncet, Jean-François 227
Poniatowski, Michel 227
Ponta, Victor 379
Poos, Jacques 274, 277
Portugal, Portuguese government 13, 105, 109, 168, 242, 245-249, 264, 270, 281, 286, 317, 324, 328, 330, 334, 336, 337, 348, 361, 365, 396, 399, 407, 408, 410, 413, 419, 420, 422, 426, 427, 430, 433
Pöttering, Hans-Gerd 377
Poullain, Ludwig 199
Powell, Colin 396
Powell, Charles 288
Prodi, Romano 331, 332, 334, 355, 356, 366, 376, 395, 398, 399, 402
protectionism 62, 63, 68, 69, 84, 86, 95, 98, 99, 151, 229, 268, 287, 336
Putin, Vladimir 439

Rabot, Louis 98
Raffarin, Jean-Pierre 405
Ramadier, Paul 7, 11-14, 20, 22
Rasquin, Michel 75, 81
Rasmussen, Anders Fogh 376, 396
Rasmussen, Poul Nyrup 413
ratification 35, 42, 45, 46, 48-51, 72, 73, 114, 116, 117, 248, 255, 266, 272, 295, 299, 323-326, 336, 338, 341, 371, 376, 404-408, 411, 412, 436
Reagan, Ronald 260, 261, 300, 303

referendum 103, 114, 169, 194, 207, 281, 323-326, 337, 339, 341, 342, 404-407, 409, 411, 412, 439
Rehn, Olli 380
Rehwinkel, Edmund 130
Renan, Ernest 433
Retinger, Joseph 5, 9, 10, 17, 22
Rey, Jean 73, 75, 78, 81, 95, 154, 155, 162, 172, 181, 182
Reynaud, Paul 7, 13, 16, 22
Rippon, Geoffrey 185
Robinson, John 167
Rodrigues, João 400
Romania, Romanian government 11, 13, 358, 362, 364, 366, 379, 380, 408, 424
Rome Treaties 72, 73, 75-82, 84, 86, 88, 92, 103, 106, 107, 123, 137, 139, 141, 142, 145, 153, 155, 167, 177, 224, 265, 271, 272, 274, 278, 287, 310, 404, 408
Rougement, Denis de 14, 17
Ruhr District, Ruhr industry 2, 4, 17, 26, 30, 32, 34, 121
Rueff, Jacques 87, 90
Rühe, Volker 353
Rumor, Mariano 217
Rumsfeld, Donald 396
Russell, Bertrand 4, 18
Russia, Russian government 439, 440

Saar District, Saarland 30, 46, 52, 65, 66, 68
Salazar, António 13, 242
Samaras, Antonis 428
Sandys, Duncan 4-15, 18, 22
Santer, Jacques 277, 345, 355, 356, 364
Saragat, Giuseppe 149
Sarkozy, Nicolas 383, 405, 409, 410, 413-416, 421-427
Saulnier, Jean 301
Sauvagnargues, Jean 218, 243
Scandinavia 7, 23, 72, 348
Schäuble, Wolfgang 335, 346-348, 368, 423, 431
Scheel, Walter 173, 180, 206, 210, 211, 213, 215
Schengen Agreement, Schengen Area 286, 348, 376, 384, 398
Schiller, Karl 13, 164, 197-200

Schlesinger, Helmut 327, 328
Schlüter, Poul 274, 275
Schmid, Carlo 12, 173
Schmidt, Helmut 72, 193, 200, 213, 214, 216-219, 221, 222, 227, 230-241, 244, 248, 251-260, 262-265, 294, 295, 301
Schmidt, Loki 234
Schröder, Gerhard (Foreign Minister, CDU) 114, 115, 123, 124, 128, 135-137, 140-146, 149-153, 155
Schröder, Gerhard (Chancellor, SPD) 335, 355, 360, 365, 367, 370, 374, 375, 385, 386, 398, 399, 406, 407
Schulmann, Horst 233-235
Schulz, Martin 414, 439
Schuman Plan 31, 32, 37, 233
Schuman, Robert 20, 22, 23, 30-33, 37-40, 43, 44, 50, 51, 54, 233, 435
Schumann, Maurice 170, 171, 175, 178, 197
Schwarz, Werner 99, 125
Segni, Antonio 107
Séguin, Philippe 324
Serbia 317, 357, 359, 360, 380
Sergent, René 64
Sforza, Carlo 11
Shinwell, Emanuel 38
Siegfried, André 7
Sikorski, Władysław 5
Silone, Ignazio 17
Simitis, Kostas 332, 336, 367
Single European Act 278, 280, 281
Slovakia 366, 273, 376, 404, 418
Slovenia 317, 358, 362, 364, 373, 376, 381, 404, 418
Soames, Christopher 165-168, 187, 261
Soares, Mário 245, 246
Socialist Europe Movement (EUSE, MSEUE) 11, 24, 25, 36
social policy 67, 71, 81, 85, 87, 175, 279, 321, 333, 373
Solana, Javier 360, 393, 396, 415
Soustelle, Jacques 89
Soviet Union, Soviet leadership 3, 6, 10, 20, 30, 45, 50, 67, 115, 121, 252-256, 260, 261, 291, 292, 303-306, 308, 309
Spaak Committee 58-61, 64, 271

Spaak, Paul Henri 11, 12, 18, 22, 25, 49, 50, 54-68, 105-108, 112, 113, 128, 142
Spain, Spanish government 13, 168, 242, 247-250, 264, 281, 294, 316, 321, 324, 328, 330, 331, 334, 337, 345-348, 351, 354, 357, 360, 364, 370, 373, 377, 391, 396, 399, 404, 413, 417, 420, 427-431
Spinelli, Altiero 9, 28, 43, 181, 183, 271, 280
Stability and Association Agreement (SAA) 380
Stability and Growth Pact 330, 333, 419, 420, 425
Stalin, Josef 3, 45
Stark, Jürgen 423
Stewart, Michael 156, 163, 166-168
Stikker, Dirk 35, 43
Stoltenberg, Gerhard 280, 290-292
Strauß, Franz Josef 50, 55, 62, 65, 125, 127, 164, 285
Straw, Jack 406
Suárez, Adolfo 246, 247
Suez Crisis 66, 67
supra-nationality 25, 31-33, 41, 44, 47, 50, 51, 70, 71, 78, 143, 315, 392, 393, 438
Sweden, Swedish government 105, 109, 168, 192, 231, 334, 336-342, 348, 354, 356, 364, 365, 373, 374, 381, 384, 407
Switzerland 105, 109, 231, 331, 336, 337, 339, 341

Teitgen, Pierre-Henri 7, 22
Teltschik, Horst 302
terrorism 348, 394
Theodoropoulos, Vyron 245
Thatcher, Margaret 226, 261-264, 269, 273-276, 280-282, 288, 289, 294, 297, 298, 303-305, 307, 312, 318, 320, 326
Third Force 6, 24, 27, 48
Thorn, Gaston 207, 216, 222, 223, 263, 274, 276
Thornton, Peter 188
Thygesen, Niels 294
Tietmeyer, Hans 280, 294, 297, 328, 330, 335
Tindemans, Leo 219-223, 230
Tindemans Report 319-223, 229, 264, 271
Trabucci, Alberto 119

trade unions 1, 5, 7, 16, 17, 21, 121, 238, 288, 323
Trichet, Jean-Claude 320, 327-329, 335, 417, 422
Triffin, Robert 195, 197, 202
Troika 428
Turkey, Turkish government 13, 243, 244, 250, 251, 356, 366, 367, 378, 381-383, 405, 433
Tusk, Donald 413, 439

Udre, Ingrida 399
Ukraine Crisis 439, 440
Ulrich, Maurice 142
Union Européenne des Fédéralistes (UEF) 6, 8, 9, 14, 18, 28, 36
Union for the Mediterranean 383, 384
Union pour la Démocratie française (UDF) 227
United Europe Movement (UEM) 5-7, 9, 18, 19
United Kingdom, British government 4-11, 13, 21-33, 35, 38, 42, 50, 52, 59, 60, 65-67, 83-85, 90, 105-113, 121, 155-159, 162-169, 174, 175, 182-189, 192-194, 201, 202, 209, 212, 213, 215, 216, 219, 224-226, 236-239, 261-264, 269, 270, 272-278, 280, 286, 288, 289, 297, 298, 305, 307, 309, 319-321, 323, 326, 327, 332, 339, 348-350, 354, 357-359, 370, 374, 381, 395-399, 404, 406, 407, 410, 411, 416, 420, 426, 439, 440
United Nations (UN) 357, 359, 378
United States, US government 3, 6, 26, 27, 30, 36, 37, 40, 46-50, 67, 83, 95, 96, 105, 106, 115, 116, 120, 121, 124, 126-129, 131, 149, 151, 152, 164, 167, 196, 198, 200, 204, 206, 209, 210, 213-217, 230, 234, 241, 243, 244, 252-256, 276, 307, 318, 357, 358, 394-397, 400, 401, 417, 434
Uri, Pierre 56-60, 68

Van Rompuy, Herman 415, 421, 424, 429, 431
Van Ypersele, Jacques 235
Van Zeeland, Paul 5, 11, 14, 18, 34
Védrine, Hubert 358, 368, 385
Veil, Simone 227
Verheugen, Günter 355, 366, 372, 373, 376, 399

Verhofstadt, Guy 385, 386, 394, 396, 398, 414, 438, 439
Vermeil, Edmond 7
Vietnam War 126
Villepin, Dominique de 388, 391, 395, 397
Villiers, Philippe de 324, 405
Voggenhuber, Johannes 391
Von den Brock, Hans 316
Vranitzky, Franz 337, 338

Waigel, Theo 296-298, 318-321, 325, 328, 330, 333, 335
Walker, Peter 263
Warsaw Pact 303
Weber, Axel 423, 430
Wehner, Herbert 72
Weidmann, Jens 430
Well, Günther van 210

Werner, Pierre 146, 197
Werner Plan 197, 198
Western European Union (WEU) 52, 66, 128, 161, 162, 166, 211, 302, 314, 317, 318, 353, 356-360
Western integration 30, 40, 52, 73
Wigny, Pierre 102
Wilders, Geert 405
Wilson, Harold 149, 155-159, 162, 163, 184, 185, 192-194, 215-218, 223, 229
Withaker, Kenneth 109
Wormser, Olivier 136
Westerwelle, Guido 416
Westendorp, Carlos 346

Yilmaz, Mesut 367

Zapatero, José Luis 391, 408

www.ingramcontent.com/pod-product-compliance
Lightning Source LLC
Chambersburg PA
CBHW071808230426
43670CB00013B/2389